CONSTITUTIONAL PROTECTION OF HUMAN RIGHTS IN LATIN AMERICA

Together with the expansive process of human rights constitutional decla-rations, in addition to the writ of habeas corpus and of habeas data, Latin American constitutions created a specific judicial remedy for the protection of constitutional rights, known as the suit, action, recourse, or writ of am-paro. It originated in Mexico in 1857 and developed into the amparo suit or judgement (*juicio de amparo*), still to be found only in Mexico. In slightly different forms, it spread throughout Latin America and was incorporated in the American Convention of Human Rights. It is similar to the "injunctions" and the other equitable remedies of the United States legal system.

This book examines, with a comparative constitutional law approach, the most recent trends in the constitutional and legal regulations in all Latin American countries regarding the amparo proceeding. It is an up-to-date abridged version of the course of lectures the author gave at the Columbia Law School of Columbia University in the city of New York, analyzing the regulations of the seventeen amparo statutes in force in Latin America, as well as the regulation on the amparo guarantee established in Article 25 of the American Convention of Human Rights.

Since 1963 Allan R. Brewer-Carías has been Professor at the Central Uni-versity of Venezuela, where he served as Director of the Public Law Institute (1978–1989). He has been professor of post-graduate courses at the Law Faculties of the University of Cambridge U.K. (LLM Course, 1985–1986), where he was Fellow of Trinity College, of the University of Paris II (1990), and of the University of Rosario and the University Externado of Colombia in Bogotá (since 2000). In 2006 and 2007, he was Adjunct Professor of Law at the Columbia Law School, Columbia University in New York. He is Vice-President of the International Academy of Comparative Law (The Hague); Member of the Board of Directors of the Inter-American Institute of Human Rights; and Member of the Venezuelan National Academy of Political and Social Sciences, where he served as President in 1997–1999. Since 1980, he has been the Director of the *Public Law Journal (Revista de Derecho Público)*, Editorial Jurídica Venezolana, Caracas.

CONSTITUTIONAL PROTECTION OF HUMAN RIGHTS IN LATIN AMERICA

A Comparative Study of Amparo Proceedings

Allan R. Brewer-Carías

Central University of Venezuela
International Academy of Comparative Law

CAMBRIDGE
UNIVERSITY PRESS

CAMBRIDGE UNIVERSITY PRESS
Cambridge, New York, Melbourne, Madrid, Cape Town, Singapore, São Paulo, Delhi

Cambridge University Press
32 Avenue of the Americas, New York, NY 10013-2473, USA

www.cambridge.org
Information on this title: www.cambridge.org/9780521492027

First published 2009

Printed in the United States of America

A catalog record for this publication is available from the British Library.

Library of Congress Cataloging in Publication Data

Brewer-Carías, Allan Randolph.
Constitutional protection of human rights in Latin America : a comparative study of amparo
proceedings / Allan R. Brewer-Carías.
   p. cm.
Includes bibliographical references and index.
ISBN 978-0-521-49202-7 (hardback)
1. Human rights – Latin America.   2. Civil rights – Latin America.   3. Amparo (Writ) –
Latin America.   I. Title.
KG574.B745   2008
342.808′5 – dc22   2008014579

ISBN   978-0-521-49202-7 hardback

Additional resources for this publication at www.allanbrewercarias.com

CONTENTS

INTRODUCTION

The amparo proceeding is a Latin American extraordinary judicial remedy specifically conceived for the protection of constitutional rights against harms or threats inflicted by authorities or individuals. Although indistinctly called as action, recourse or suit of amparo, it has been configured as a whole judicial proceeding that normally concludes with a judicial order or writ of protection (*amparo, protección* or *tutela*).[1]

This remedy was introduced in the American Continent during the nineteenth century, and although similar remedies were established in the twentieth century in some European countries, like Austria, Germany, Spain and Switzerland, it has been adopted by all Latin American countries, being considered as one of the most distinguishable features of Latin American constitutional law. As such, it has influenced the introduction of a similar remedy in the Philippines, the writ of amparo, which was created by the Supreme Court in 2007.

This amparo proceeding is one of the most important pieces of a comprehensive constitutional system the Latin American countries have been establishing for the protection of constitutional rights, taking statutory shape in parallel to a long and unfortunate history of their violations and disdain. This system can be identified through a few basic and important trends, the first being the long-standing tradition the countries have had of inserting in their constitutions very extensive declarations of human rights, comprising not only civil and political rights, but also social, cul-

---

[1] See Héctor Fix-Zamudio and Eduardo Ferrer Mac-Gregor (Coord.), *El derecho de amparo en el mundo*, Edit. Porrúa, México, 2006; Allan R. Brewer-Carías, *El amparo a los derechos y libertades constitucionales. Una aproximación comparativa*, Cuadernos de la Cátedra de Derecho Público, n° 1, Universidad Católica del Táchira, San Cristóbal, 1993, 138 pp.; also published by the Inter-American Institute on Human Rights, (Interdisciplinary Course), San José, 1993 (mimeo), 120 pp. and in *La protección jurídica del ciudadano. Estudios en Homenaje al Profesor Jesús González Pérez*, Tomo 3, Editorial Civitas, Madrid, 1993, pp. 2.695–2.740; and Allan R. Brewer-Carías, *Mecanismos nacionales de protección de los derechos humanos (Garantías judiciales de los derechos humanos en el derecho constitucional comparado latinoamericano)*, Instituto Interamericano de Derechos Humanos, San José, 2005.

1

tural, economic and environmental rights. This trend contrasts with the relatively reduced content of the U. S. Bill of Rights or inclusive with the content of the 1987 Philippines Constitution, which in Article 3, when referring to the Bill of Rights, basically enumerates only the civil rights.

This Latin American declarative trend began two hundred years ago with the adoption in 1811 of the "Declaration of Rights of the People" by the Supreme Congress of Venezuela, four days before the declaration of the Venezuelan Independence from Spain. That is why, in spite of being Spanish colonies for three centuries, no Spanish constitutional influence can be found at the beginning of the Latin American modern state, which was conceived following the American and the French eighteenth century constitutional revolutionary principles, later followed in Spain after the 1812 Cádiz Constitution was sanctioned.

Yet in parallel to this declarative tradition, the second trend of the Latin American constitutional system in the matter of human rights, has been the unfortunate process of their violations, which even today and in a more sophisticated way, continue to occur in some countries where authoritarian governments have been installed in defraudation of democracy and of the constitution.

The third trend of this Latin American system of constitutional protections of human rights is the continuous effort the countries have made to assure its constitutional guaranty, by progressively enlarging the declarations, adding economic, social, cultural, environmental and indigenous People's rights to the classical list of civil and political rights and liberties. In this sense, another important characteristic has been the progressive and continuous incorporation in the constitutions, of "open clauses" of rights, in the same sense of the Ninth Amendment (1791) to the U. S. Constitution that refers to the existence of other rights "retained by the people" that are not enumerated in the constitutional text. The fact is that a similar clause can be found in all Latin American constitutions, except in Cuba, Chile, Mexico and Panama, but referring in a wider sense to other rights inherent to the human person or to human dignity, or derived from the nature of the human person.

The fourth trend of the human rights constitutional regime in Latin America also related to the progressive expansion of the content of the constitutional declarations of rights is the express incorporation in the constitutions of the rights listed in international treaties and conventions. For such purpose, international treaties and covenants only have been given statutory rank, similar to the United States' constitutional solution on the matter, but in many cases, supralegal rank, constitutional rank and even supraconstitutional rank. In the latter case, inclusive, some constitutions grant preemptive status to international treaties on human rights regarding the constitution itself, whenever they provide for more favorable rules for the exercise. This is the case, for example, of the Venezuelan Constitution (Article 23).

However, regarding the hierarchy of international treaties on human rights, even in the absence of express constitutional regulations in some Latin American countries, through constitutional interpretation such treaties have also acquired constitutional value and rank, in particular when the constitutions themselves establish, for example, that on the matter of constitutional rights their interpretation must always be made according to what is set forth in international treaties on human rights. This is the case, for instance, of the Colombian Constitution (Article 93) and of the Peruvian Constitutional Procedural Code (Article V).

Within this process of internationalization of human rights, a particular international treaty on the matter, the 1969 American Convention on Human Rights, has had an exceptional importance in the continent, not only regarding the content of the declaration of rights, but also in relation to the development of the judicial protection of human rights, inclusive at the international level by the creation of the Inter-American Court of Human Rights whose jurisdiction has been recognized by the Member States. This Convention was signed in 1969 and was ratified by all Latin American countries except Cuba. The only American country that did not sign the Convention was Canada, and even though the United States of America signed the Convention in 1977, it has not yet ratified it. This has also been the case of many Caribbean states, in particular, Antigua and Barbuda, Bahamas, Belize, St. Kitts and Nevis, St. Lucia, St. Vincent and the Grenadines. Trinidad and Tobago ratified the Convention but in 1998 denounced it. Regarding Latin American countries, the American Convention has been a very effective instrument for the consolidation of a very rich minimal standard of regulation on civil and political rights, common to all countries.

In addition to all these trends that characterize the Latin American constitutional system of protection of human rights, as aforementioned, the other main feature of such a system is the express provision in the constitutions of the judicial guaranty of the rights, by regulating the specific judicial remedy for their protection called the amparo action, recourse, suit or proceeding, to which different procedural rules regarding those provided in the general procedural codes for the protection of personal or property rights, are applied.

This means that judicial protection of human rights can be achieved in two ways: First, by means of the general established ordinary or extraordinary suits, actions, recourses or writs prescribed in the general procedural codes; and second, in addition to those adjective means, through specific and separate judicial suits, actions or recourses particularly established for the protection of the constitutional rights and freedoms. As aforementioned, this last solution is the one adopted in Latin American countries, being considered one of their most important constitutional features regarding the protection of human rights. The provision of this remedy contrasts, for example, with the constitutional system of the United States, where the effective protection of human rights is effectively assured through the general judicial actions and equitable remedies, which are also used to protect any other kind of personal or property rights or interests. In Latin America, on the contrary, and in part due to the traditional deficiencies of the general judicial means for granting effective protection to constitutional rights, the amparo proceeding has been developed to assure such protection.

This remedy was first introduced in Mexico in 1857 as the *juicio de amparo*, which according to the unanimous opinion of all the Mexican scholars, had its origins in the American judicial review of constitutionality of statutes system, as was described by Alexis de Tocqueville (*Democracy in America*) a few years after *Malbury v. Madison* U.S. (1 Cranch), 137; 2 L. Ed. 60 (1803). Nonetheless, the fact is that contrary to that model, the amparo suit evolved into a unique and very complex institution, exclusively found in Mexico, which in addition to the protection of human rights (*amparo libertad*), also comprises a wide range of other protective judicial actions that can be filed against the state, which in all the other countries are always separate actions or recourses. It includes, the actions for judicial review of the constitutionality and legality of statutes (*amparo contra leyes*), the actions for judicial review of administrative actions (*amparo administrativo*), the actions for judicial review of judicial decisions (*amparo casación*), and the actions for protection of peasant's rights (*amparo agrario*). Even with this comprehensive and unique character, the Mexican amparo is the most commonly quoted "amparo" outside Latin America.

After its introduction in Mexico, and during the same nineteenth century, the amparo proceeding subsequently spread across all Latin America, giving rise in all the other countries to a very different specific judicial remedy established with the exclusive purpose of protecting human rights and freedoms, becoming in many cases more protective than the original Mexican institution.[2] In addition to the habeas corpus recourse, the amparo was introduced in the second half of the nineteenth century in the Constitutions of Guatemala (1879), El Salvador (1886) and Honduras (1894); and during the twentieth century, in the Constitutions of Nicaragua (1911), Brazil (*mandado de securança*, 1934), Panama (1941), Costa Rica (1946), Venezuela (1961), Bolivia, Paraguay, Ecuador (1967), Peru (1976), Chile (*recurso de protección*, 1976) and Colombia (*acción de tutela*, 1991). Since 1957, and through court decisions, the amparo action was admitted in Argentina, being regulated in a special statute in 1966, and subsequently included in the 1994 Constitution. In the Dominican Republic, since 2000, the Supreme Court also admitted the amparo action, which in 2006 was regulated in a special statute.

The consequence of this constitutional process is that in all the Latin American countries, with the exception of Cuba, the habeas corpus and amparo actions are regulated as specific judicial means exclusively designed for the protection of constitutional rights. In all the countries, except the Dominican Republic, the provisions for the action are expressly set forth in the constitutions[3]; and in all of them, except in Chile, the proceeding has been the object of statutory regulation.[4] These statutes

---

[2]See Joaquín Brague Camazano, *La Jurisdicción constitucional de la libertad. Teoría general, Argentina, México, Corte Interamericana de Derechos Humanos*, Editorial Porrúa, México, 2005, pp. 156 ff.

[3]Argentina. Constitución Nacional de la República Argentina, 1994; Bolivia. Constitución Política de la República de Bolivia, 1967 (Last reform, 2005); Brazil. Constitução da República Federativa do Brasil, 1988 (Last reform, 2005); Colombia. Constitución Política de la República de Colombia, 1991 (Last reform 2005); Costa Rica. Constitución Política de la República de Costa Rica, 1949 (Last reform 2003); Cuba. Constitución Política de la República de Cuba, 1976 (Last reform, 2002); Chile. Constitución Política de la República de Chile, 1980 (Last reform, 2005); Dominican Republic. Constitución Política de la República Dominicana, 2002; Ecuador. Constitución Política de la República de Ecuador, 1998; El Salvador. Constitución Política de la República de El Salvador, 1983 (Last reform, 2003); Guatemala. Constitución Política de la República de Guatemala, 1989 (Last reform 1993); Honduras. Constitución Política de la República de Honduras, 1982 (Last reform, 2005); Mexico. Constitución Política de los Estados Unidos Mexicanos, 1917 (Last reform, 2004); Nicaragua. Constitución Política de la República de Nicaragua, 1987 (Last reform 2005); Panama. Constitución Política de la República de Panamá, 1972 (Last Reform, 1994); Paraguay. Constitución Política de la República de Paraguay, 1992; Peuú. Constitución Política del Peru, 1993 (Last reform, 2005); Uruguay. Constitución Política de la República Oriental del Uruguay, 1967 (Last reform, 2004); Venezuela. Constitución de la República Bolivariana de Venezuela, 1999.

[4]Argentina. Ley N° 16.986. Acción de Amparo, 1966; Bolivia. Ley N° 1836. Ley del Tribunal Constitucional, 1998; Brazil. Lei N° 1.533. Mandado de Segurança, 1951; Colombia. Decretos Ley N° 2591, 306 y 1382. Acción de Tutela, 2000; Costa Rica. Ley N°

---

are, in general, special ones passed for the specific purpose of providing for the amparo proceedings. In some countries this special legislation also contains regulations regarding the other judicial means for the protection of the Constitution like the judicial review methods, and the petitions for habeas corpus and habeas data, as is the case in Bolivia, Guatemala, Peru, Costa Rica, Ecuador, El Salvador and Honduras. Only in Panama and Paraguay the amparo proceeding is regulated in a specific Chapter of the General Procedural Judicial Code.

In some constitutions, like the Guatemalan, Mexican and Venezuelan ones, the amparo action is conceived to protect all constitutional rights and freedoms, including the protection of personal liberty, in which case, the habeas corpus is considered as a type of amparo, named for instance, recourse for personal exhibition (Guatemala) or amparo for the protection of personal freedom (Venezuela). However, in general, in all the other Latin American countries (Argentina, Bolivia, Brazil, Colombia, Costa Rica, Chile, the Dominican Republic, Ecuador, El Salvador, Honduras, Nicaragua, Panama, Paraguay, Peru and Uruguay), in addition to the amparo action, a different recourse of habeas corpus has always been expressly established in the constitutions for the specific protection of personal freedom and integrity. In recent times, in some countries (Argentina, Ecuador, Paraguay, Peru and Venezuela), in addition to the amparo and habeas corpus recourses, the constitutions have also provided for a separate recourse called habeas data, by which any person can file a suit in order to ask for information regarding the content of the data referred to himself, contained in public or private registries or data banks, and in case of false, inaccurate or discriminatory information, to seek for its suppression, rectification, confidentiality and updating.

As a result of this human rights protective process, currently, the constitutional regulations regarding the protection of constitutional rights in Latin America are established in three different ways: First, by providing

---

7135. Ley de la Jurisdicción Constitucional, 1989; Dominican Republic. Ley N° 437-06 que establece el Recurso de Amparo, 2006; Ecuador. Ley N° 000. RO/99. Ley de Control Constitucional, 1997; El Salvador. Ley de Procedimientos Constitucionales, 1960; Guatemala. Decreto N° 1-86. Ley de Amparo. Exhibición personal y Constitucionalidad, 1986; Honduras. Ley sobre Justicia Constitucional, 2004; Mexico. Ley de Amparo, reglamentaria de los artículos 103 y 107 de la Constitución Política, 1936; Nicaragua. Ley N° 49. Amparo, 1988; Panama. Código Judicial, Libro Cuarto: Instituciones de Garantía, 1999; Paraguay. Ley N° 1.337/88. Código Procesal Civil, Título II. El Juicio de Amparo, 1988; Peru. Ley N° 28.237. Código Procesal Constitucional, 2005; Uruguay. Ley N° 16.011. Acción de Amparo, 1988; Venezuela. Ley Orgánica de Amparo sobre Derechos y Garantías Constitucionales, 1988.

for three different remedies: the amparo, the habeas corpus and habeas data, as is the case in Argentina, Brazil, Ecuador, Paraguay and Peru; second, by establishing two remedies: the amparo and the habeas corpus, as is the case in Bolivia, Colombia, Costa Rica, Chile, Dominican Republic, El Salvador, Honduras, Nicaragua, Panama and Uruguay, or the amparo and the habeas data as is the case in Venezuela; and third, by just establishing one general amparo action comprising the protection of personal freedom as is the case in Guatemala and Mexico.

In general terms, the rights to be protected by means of the amparo proceedings are all those declared in the Constitution or those considered as having constitutional rank. Some exceptions exist when constitutions reduce the protective scope of the amparo protection to only some constitutional guaranties or fundamental rights as is the case in Colombia, Chile and Mexico. This is the trend that was also followed in Germany and Spain with the individual recourse for the protection or the amparo recourse, and more recently in Philippines, with the writ of amparo only directed to protect the right to life, liberty and security.

Yet as aforementioned, the amparo action in Latin America is not only a national constitutional law remedy, but also an international law institution, which has been incorporated in the provisions of the American Convention on Human Rights (1969) as a "right to judicial protection," that is, the right of everyone to have "a simple and prompt recourse, or any other effective recourse, before a competent court or tribunal for protection (*que la ampare*) against acts that violate his fundamental rights recognized by the Constitution or laws of the State or by this Convention" (Article 25). In order to guaranty such right, the Convention imposes on the Member States the duty "to ensure that any person claiming such remedy shall have his rights determined by the competent authority provided for by the legal system of the state"; to develop "the possibilities of judicial remedy"; and "to ensure that the competent authorities shall enforce such remedies when granted."

In the words of the Inter-American Court on Human Rights, this Article of the American Convention is a "general provision that gives expression to the procedural institution known as amparo, which is a simple and prompt remedy designated for the protection of all of the rights recognized in the Constitution and laws of the Member States and by the Convention."[5] The American Convention also provides for the recourse of

---

[5]See *Advisory Opinion OC-8/87, of January 30, 1987, Habeas corpus in emergency situations*, Paragraph 32. See in Sergio García Ramírez (Coord.), *La Jurisprudencia de la*

habeas corpus for the protection of the right to personal freedom and security, established in favor of anyone deprived of his liberty in cases of lawful arrests or detentions (Article 7). Examining both the habeas corpus and the amparo recourses, the Inter-American Court on Human Rights has declared that the "'amparo' comprises a whole series of remedies and that habeas corpus is but one of its components," so that in some instances "habeas corpus is viewed either as the 'amparo' of freedom or as an integral part of 'amparo.'" [6]

All these provisions of the American Convention can also be considered as the conclusion of the process of internationalization of the protection of human rights, in particular regarding the provision for the specific judicial mean for their protection, considered by the Inter-American Court of Human Rights as "one of the basic pillars not only of the American Convention, but of the rule of Law in a democratic society." [7]

Through a comparative constitutional law approach, this book is intended to highlight the most recent trends in the constitutional and legal regulations on this amparo proceeding in all Latin American countries, and in the Philippines, identifying the character of this extraordinary judicial remedy, also established in some cases as a constitutional right (*derecho de amparo*); the competent courts to grant the protection; the general rules of procedural to file the action for protection; the constitutional rights that can be protected; the individuals or legal entities that are entitled to the extraordinary protection (the aggrieved, affected or injured party; the standing requirements to file the action; the defendant parties' perpetrator of the nuisance, whether a State body, a public officer, individuals or private entities; the particular types of public or private actions or omissions violating constitutional rights that can be challenged through the amparo action; and finally, the sort of judicial adjudication that can be awarded and the means for its enforcement.

Even considering that in general terms the most important duty of any judicial branch of government is to decide and resolve in specific cases,

---

Corte Interamericana de Derechos Humanos, Universidad Nacional Autónoma de México, Corte Interamericana de Derechos Humanos, México, 2001, pp. 1.008 ff.

[6] *Idem*, Paragraph 34.

[7] See *Castillo Páez* case, (Peru) 1997, Paragraph 83; *Suárez Roseo* case (Ecuador) 1997, Paragraph 65 and *Blake* case (Guatemala) 1998, Paragraph 102, *Idem*. pp. 273 ff., 406 ff. and 372 ff. See also the *Advisory Opinion OC-8/87 of January 30, 1987, Habeas Corpus in Emergency Situation*, Paragraph 42; and the *Advisory Opinion OC-9/87 of October 6, 1987, Judicial Guaranties in Status of Emergency*, Paragraph 33, *Idem*, pp. 1.008 ff. and pp. 1.019 ff.

questions or controversies regarding individual rights and interests, this comparative law study tries to explain why Latin American countries have established this special and extraordinary judicial mean for the protection of human rights; that is, why the common and general judicial means established in the civil codes and civil procedure codes are not the only ones devoted to guarantying their effective protection.

For this comparative constitutional law approach, we have divided the book into the following five parts and twenty-two chapters:

Part One refers to *the constitutional and international declaration of rights and its judicial guaranties*, analyzing the constitutional declaration of human rights in Latin America and its internationalization (**One**), and the *judicial guaranties of the declarations of human rights* (**Two**).

Part Two refers to *the amparo proceeding as a constitutional and international Latin American institution*, analyzing the amparo within the judicial review systems (**Three**), the constitutional amparo in countries with only the diffuse system of judicial review legislation (**Four**) or with the concentrated systems of judicial review legislation (**Five**); as a constitutional right (**Six**) and as a constitutional guaranty in countries with mixed systems of judicial review of legislation (**Seven**); and the amparo within the American Convention on Human Rights (**Eight**).

Part Three refers to *the injured party and the constitutional protected rights through the amparo proceeding*, by analyzing the injured party and the general standing conditions (**Nine**), the justiciable constitutional rights by the amparo and habeas corpus actions (**Ten**); and in particular, the question of the justiciability of social constitutional rights (**Eleven**).

Part Four refers to *the injury, the injuring party and the injuring acts in the amparo proceeding*, studying the general conditions of the harms and threats (**Twelve**), the reparable character of the harms (**Thirteen**); the imminent character of the threats (**Fourteen**); the injuring party (**Fifteen**); and the injuring acts or omissions of public authorities causing the harm or the threats to constitutional rights (**Sixteen**).

Part Five refers to *the extraordinary character of the amparo proceeding*, studying the relation between the amparo proceeding and the ordinary judicial means (**Seventeen**); the main principles of the procedure in the amparo proceeding (**Eighteen**); its specific procedural phases (**Nineteen**); the adjudications in the amparo proceeding and the preliminary amparo decisions (**Twenty**); the definitive rulings: preventive and restorative decisions and their effects (**Twenty-One**); and the revision of the amparo decisions by the Constitutional Courts or the Supreme Courts (**Twenty-Two**).

PART ONE

THE CONSTITUTIONAL AND INTERNATIONAL DECLARATION OF HUMAN RIGHTS AND ITS JUDICIAL GUARANTIES

Among the rights attributed to a person, there are those declared or recognized in the constitutions, as "constitutional rights," and among them there are the "human rights," referred to those attributed only to human beings. Within the latter it is also possible to distinguish the civil rights or civil liberties, that is, the individual rights of personal liberty or freedom guaranteed in the Constitution, such as freedom of speech, press, assembly, movement or religion. However, "civil rights" do not exhaust the list of constitutional rights, nor of human rights, which today also comprises social, economic, cultural and environmental rights. "Civil rights" were those first declared in the constitutions, what is called the first generation of rights, but at present time they are accompanied by a long list of other rights belonging to what has been called second and third "generations" of rights.

Another expression that must be kept in mind and mainly used in Europe, particularly in Germany and Spain, is that of "fundamental rights,"[8] used for the purpose of identifying certain constitutional rights that can be protected by a special judicial mean for protection also called amparo in Spain, which in general terms is equivalent to individual or civil rights.[9] This expression of "fundamental rights" is also used in the

---

[8] Article 93.1.4 a) German Constitution (1949); Article 53,2 Spanish Constitution. See Fernando Garrido Falla *et al*, *Comentarios a la Constitución*, Ed. Civitas, Madrid, 1980, p. 578.

[9] According to these provisions, it is possible to distinguish among the constitutional rights those that can be considered as "justiciable rights" particularly by means of the specific judicial action or recourse of amparo, and constitutional rights not considered "fundamental rights." The latter group is left to be protected by means of the general or common judicial means. Constitutional rights can always be considered essentially justiciables, but their "justiciability" as the quality or state of being appropriate or suitable for

Colombian Constitution (Articles 11-41), to identify a category of constitutional rights, mainly individual rights, which are of immediate application and can be protected by the *acción de tutela* (Article 86). In the United States, the expression "fundamental rights" is also used when referring to civil rights that are protected in the Constitution, as "fundamental civil rights." As has been ruled by the Supreme Court in *United States v. Wong Kim Ark*, 169 U.S. 649; 18 S. Ct. 456; 42 L. Ed. 890 (1898), when referring to "fundamental civil rights for the security of which organized society was instituted, and which remain, with certain exceptions mentioned in the Federal Constitution..."

This expression "fundamental rights" has also been commonly used in Latin America with various meanings: First, from a formal point of view, they can be considered as the rights declared or numerated in the constitutions; second, from a substantive point of view, fundamental rights can also be considered as the most important rights that according to their own principles and value are recognized in each society[10]; and third, from a judicial point of view, as in Colombia, they are rights that can be judicially protected by special means such as the amparo.

The main concern regarding constitutional or fundamental rights[11] in modern Constitutional States, is referred to their protection, which has been assured by declaring them in the text of the Constitution and in international treaties, thus out of the reach of the legislator, and by establishing the indispensable judicial guaranties in order to assure their exercise.

---

reviewing by a court, will vary depending on the judicial means available in the legal system for such purpose. In some countries, all constitutional rights are justiciables by means of the general judicial means of protection, such as in the United States; in other countries all constitutional rights are justiciables by means of a specific judicial mean of protection like the habeas corpus or amparo action or recourse, such as in the case of Venezuela; and in other countries, the constitutional rights are protected by a special mean of protection if they are "fundamental rights," being the other constitutional rights justiciables through the common judicial means.

[10] See Alfonso Gairaud Brenes, "Los Mecanismos de interpretación de los derechos humanos: especial referencia a la jurisprudencia Peruana," in José F. Palomino Manchego, *El derecho procesal constitucional Peruano. Estudios en Homenaje a Domingo García Belaunde,* Editorial Jurídica Grijley, Lima, 2005, Tomo I, p. 124.

[11] The expression "constitutional rights" in this book is used as equivalent to "fundamental rights," among which are "human rights." In general terms, all of them are declared in the constitutions and can be protected by means of the amparo action.

CHAPTER ONE

THE CONSTITUTIONAL DECLARATION OF HUMAN RIGHTS IN LATIN AMERICA AND ITS INTERNATIONALIZATION

I. THE SCOPE OF THE CONSTITUTIONAL DECLARATION

The practice of declaring rights in the text of the constitutions began with constitutionalism itself, and with the very notion of constitution as a superior law,[12] with the first Declaration of Rights in constitutional history adopted by the Convention of Virginia in 1776, at the beginning of the independence process of the American colonies; a practice that was subsequently followed by the other colonies.[13] Those rights declared in the Bill of Rights of those colonies were "natural rights" in the sense of being "inherent rights" to all men, who by nature were declared "equally free and independent."[14]

---

[12]See in general Allan R. Brewer-Carías, *Reflexiones sobre la Revolución Americana (1776) y la Revolución Francesa (1789) y sus aportes al constitucionalismo moderno,* Editorial Jurídica Venezolana, Caracas, 1992; and *Reflexiones sobre la Revolución Americana (1776), la Revolución Francesa (1789) y la Revolución Hispanoamericana (1811-1830) y sus aportes al constitucionalismo moderno,* Universidad Externado de Colombia, Bogotá, 2008.

[13]See George Ticknor Curtis and Joseph Culbertson Clayton, *Constitutional History of the United States from their Declaration of Independence to the Close of the Civil War,* New York: Harper & Brothers, 1889, 1896, Two volumes, Reprinted 2002 by The Lawbook Exchange, Ltd; Francis Newton Thorpe, *Constitutional History of the United States 1765–1895,* Da Capo Press Reprints in American Constitutional and Legal History, 1896 edition, June 1974; Homer Carey Hockett, *The Constitutional History of the United States, 1776–1826,* MacMillan & Co., 1961.

[14]In the brief preamble to that Declaration (which precedes the text of the *Constitution or Form of Government of Virginia* of June 29, 1776), the relation between natural rights and government was clearly established. Also evident is the direct influence of Locke's theories in the sense that political society forms itself upon those rights as the basis and foundation of government. See J. Locke, *Two Treatises of Government* (ed. Peter Laslett), Cambridge

The first ten amendments to the 1789 U. S. Constitution, in force since 1791, also enumerated a few essential rights but the express statement that enumeration, "shall not be construed to deny or disparage other [rights] retained by the people" (IX), reinforcing the "declarative" character of the constitutional declaration of rights.

On August 26, 1789, one month before the approval of the first ten amendments to the U.S. Constitution, the French National Assembly at the beginning of the French Revolution also adopted the Declaration of the Rights of Man and of the Citizen, which was subsequently incorporated in the first French Constitution of 1791,[15] recognizing and proclaiming all the fundamental rights of man, and particularly that "men are born and remain free and equal in rights," "having natural and inalienable rights" that were not granted by political society, but rights inherent to the nature of human beings.

The main objectives in both the American and the French declarations were the same: to protect the citizen against arbitrary power and to establish the rule of law.

All the principles deriving from the French and the American Revolutions had an immediate impact in Latin American constitutionalism, influencing the drafting of the constitutions of the newly independent states.[16]

1967; quoted in W. Laquer and B. Rubin (Ed)., *The Human Rights Reader*, New York, 1979, p. 64.

[15]See in general Michael P. Fitzsimmons, *The Remaking of France: The National Assembly and the Constitution of 1791*, Cambridge University Press, 2002; Allan R. Brewer-Carías, *Reflexiones sobre la Revolución Americana (1776) y la Revolución Francesa (1789) y sus aportes al constitucionalismo moderno*, Editorial Jurídica Venezolana, Caracas, 1992.

[16]It must be understood that the process of independence of the Spanish Colonies in Latin America started in 1810, only twenty-three years after the sanctioning of the American Constitution, and seven years after *Marbury v. Madison* U.S. (1 Cranch), 137; 2 L. Ed. 60 (1803) judicial review case. This happens in a moment in which Spain was occupied by French troops after Napoleon had imposed the Bayonne Constitution of 1808 to the invaded realm. Spain was fighting for independence from France, and the American colonies, repudiating the French invasion, began to seek independence from Spain. So the principles of modern constitutionalism were first adopted in Latin America, from 1811 on, before being adopted in Spain. In Spain these principles were embodied with a monarchical framework a few months later, in the Cadiz 1812 Constitution, which remained in force only for two years, until the monarchy was restored in 1814. See Allan R. Brewer-Carías, "El paralelismo entre el constitucionalismo venezolano y el constitucionalismo de Cádiz (o cómo el de Cádiz no influyó en el venezolano)," in *La Constitución de Cádiz. Hacia los orígenes del Constitucionalismo Iberoamericano y Latino*, Unión Latina-UCAB, Caracas,

That is why, for instance no Spanish constitutional influence can be found at the beginning of Latin American modern constitutionalism, which basically followed the United States and French trend.[17]

So after the American and French Declarations, the third formal declaration of rights by an independent state in constitutional history was the "Declaration of Rights of the People" adopted by the Supreme Congress of Venezuela in 1811,[18] four days before the formal Venezuelan Independence Act of July 5 was approved. This Declaration mainly followed the trends of the French Declaration, but had a much more detailed enumeration of rights, including new ones such as the right to industrial and commercial freedom, and the freedom to work (20). It also had a reference to a social right when it states that "instruction is necessary for all. The society must favor with all its power the progress of public reason to put instruction at the reach of all" (Ch. 4, 4). The Declaration was also incorporated as a final chapter in the Venezuelan Constitution of December 21, 1811. With the adoption in 1811 of these two Venezuelan Declarations of Rights, a very long tradition of almost two hundred years began of continuous, extensive and always enlarging Latin American Declarations of Rights; a tradition very different from the European one.

2004, pp. 223–331; and in *Libro Homenaje a Tomás Polanco Alcántara, Estudios de Derecho Público*, Universidad Central de Venezuela, Caracas, 2005, pp. 101-189.

[17]It can be said that, in general, the American − North American and Latin American − constitutional revolution process and its declarations of rights were very different from the French and even the Spanish ones. In the French Revolution and Declaration, it was not a case of establishing a new state but of the continuation of a national state already in existence, within the monarchical principle. The same occurred in Spain. On the contrary, in the American Revolution and Declarations, new states were being built upon a new basis. The purpose of the French Declaration, as stated in its introduction, was to solemnly remind all members of the community of their natural rights and duties. Hence the new principle of individual liberty appeared only as an important modification within the context of a political unity already in existence. On the other hand, in the North American and Latin American declarations, the enforcement of rights was an important factor in the independence process, and thus, in the building of the new states upon a new basis. Particularly relevant was the principle of the sovereignty of people with all its democratic content. Therefore, on the American continent, the solemn Declaration of Fundamental Rights meant the establishment of principles on which the political unity of the nations was based, and the validity of which was recognized as the most important assumption in the emergence and formation of that unity. See Allan R. Brewer-Carías, *Reflexiones sobre la Revolución Americana (1776), la Revolución Francesa (1789) y la Revolucion Hispanoamericana (1811-1830) y sus aportes al constitucionalismo moderno*, Universidad Externado de Colombia, Bogotá, 2008.

[18]See the text in Allan R. Brewer-Carías, *Las Constituciones de Venezuela*, Academia de Ciencias Políticas y Sociales, Caracas, 1997, pp. 279 ff.

1. *The expansion of the constitutional declarations of rights*

The "first generation" of human rights were the individual and civil rights set forth in the constitutions, as was the case of the 1789 United States Bill of Rights or of the French Declaration of Rights of Citizens and Man, and of the nineteenth century Latin American constitutional declarations, containing those rights essential to human nature, or essential to the quality of the human being, or common to all human persons.

At the beginning of constitutionalism in the eighteenth century, as mentioned before, those rights were reduced to personal liberty or freedom, equality before the law, personal safety and safety of property, to which the American Bill of Rights added the freedom of religion and cult, freedom of speech and of the press, the right to peaceably assemble, the right to petition, the due process of law guaranties, the right to movement and the right to vote.

During the twentieth century the list of political rights was also enlarged, adding to the right to vote the right to public demonstration, the right to participate in political parties, the right to seek asylum and in general terms, the right to participate in political life.

All those rights have configured what has been called the "first generation" of human rights,[19] as civil or individual rights essential to all human beings, which were regulated in all of the nineteenth and twentieth centuries' constitutions.

These rights have been extensively regulated in the more recent Latin American constitutions like the Colombian (1991) and Venezuelan (1999) ones, and were all incorporated in the United Nations International Covenant on Civil and Political Rights of 1966, which all Latin American countries have ratified.

The "second generation" of human rights refers to the social, economic and cultural rights that began to be incorporated in the constitutional Declarations of Rights with the Mexican Constitution of 1917 and with the Weimar Constitution of Germany of 1919. All those rights were also the object of another United Nations Covenant, the International Covenant on Social, Economic and Cultural Rights of 1966, also ratified by all Latin American countries.

---

[19]The classification of human rights in "generations" only serves to more or less appreciate the chronological trends of the evolution process of their constitutionalization. See the comments rejecting the classification in Antonio A. Cancado Trindade, "Derechos de solidaridad," in *Estudios Básicos de Derechos Humanos*, Vol I, Instituto Interamericano de Derechos Humanos, San José, 1994, pp. 64 ff.

However, well before the adoption of the UN Covenant and after World War II, almost all Latin American constitutions started to incorporate in their Declarations of rights, in addition to the civil and political rights, these social, economic and cultural rights. For instance, the right to education and the right to health care were constitutionalized, as well as the labor rights such as the right to work, the right to membership of labor unions, the right to strike, the right to social security; and additionally, the right to equal treatment at work and the right to a salary. Also, the rights to social benefits and to have stability at work were incorporated in the constitutions, as well as the right to bargain collectively for labor benefits.

Other rights that were progressively constitutionalized were the right to cultural heritage; as well as all the rights to social protection or welfare, such as the right to have a family, to get married, and to grant protection to pregnancy, childhood, elderly and disabled persons.

Many of these social rights were incorporated in the constitutions in order to set forth a constitutional duty or obligation for the state to provide social protection to the people or to render certain public services as public utilities, particularly regarding health care and protection, social security and education.

Economic rights were also constitutionalized in addition to the property rights and the right not to be expropriated without compensation. These "second generation" of rights, particularly the economic freedom, implied the freedom of industry and trade and the freedom to work. Some constitutions like the Brazilian, the Colombian and the Venezuelan ones are examples of extensive regulations referring to these social and economic rights.

More recently, a "third generation" of rights has been developed related to collective rights, considered as humankind rights or solidarity rights, like the right to have a healthy environment; the right to development; the right to free competition; the consumer's right to have products and services of quality; the right to have a certain standard of living; the right to humankind heritage, the rights of the indigenous communities and even the right to peace; the latter is set forth in the Colombian Constitution of 1991 (Article 22).

Some of these rights have also been the object of international regulations, as is the case for instance of the right to development incorporated in Article 1 of the United Nations Declarations on the Right of Development (1986).

Finally, besides these collective rights, in the contemporary world a "fourth generation" of human rights is beginning to appear and is in the process of being constructed, such as the human right to the protection of the human genome and the genetic identity, and also the rights that could derive from progress communications technology.[20]

2. *The changes in the obliged party regarding constitutional rights and freedoms*

According to the initial concept behind the way the declaration of civil rights were conceived, the responsible party in the relation right/duty was always the State. This means that the rights were originally formulated in relation to the State, in order to be protected from State actions or intrusions, so the active subject was always a human being, or the citizen, and the passive subject, the obligated party, was always the State.

This initial concept of the formulation of constitutional rights, particularly regarding civil or individual rights, led to the original conception of the amparo action as a protective mechanism basically against the State. So in its origin, the amparo action was not conceived to protect individuals from other individuals' offenses, but only to sue the State.

This, of course, has changed with the alteration of the way of conceiving the relationship between rights and duties, in the sense that regarding the violations of human rights the passive subject in the contemporary world is not exclusively the State. Now the scope of rights and the field of the passive subject have been progressively universalized, creating obligations that correspond, naturally, to individuals, to groups, to communities, and even to the international community. This is the case of the "third generation" of rights, like the right to the environment or the right to development, rights that, moreover, are not only held by man as an individual but by peoples and communities and also by the international community.

On the other hand, as mentioned before, the situations of duty that exist regarding constitutional rights are not always of the same nature.

Often the situations of duty are configured as situations of being obliged to provide or give or render something, accomplishing a positive obligation. This is the common situation regarding social rights, such as the right to education or right to health care, in relation to which the State is obliged to carry out a positive activity or render a public service or

---

[20] See Florentín Meléndez, *Instrumentos internacionales sobre derechos humanos aplicables a la administración de justicia.Estudio constitucional comparado,* Cámara de Diputados, México, 2004, p. 19.

utility that citizens have the right to receive or enjoy as the active subjects in the juridical relationship.

In other cases of constitutional rights, instead of being rights to receive something as a service, they are "freedoms" because the situation of the passive subject, for example of the State itself, does not correspond to any obligation to do or to give; but to abstain from acting, to not disturb, to not harm, to not stop, to not deprive. Therefore, from the strictly legal viewpoint, these are more freedoms or liberties than rights. For example, the freedom of movement implies a more correlative situation of duty consisting in the obligation of the State not to restrict the free movement of people. Regarding the rights to free expression of thoughts, to free speech or to free press, they imply the State's duty not to bother, not to censor, not to prevent or impede the exercise of such rights.

From this point of view, regarding the rights in the strictest sense, it can be said that the obliged party is the State, which is the party with the duty to provide health care or education to the people. Instead, regarding freedoms, not only is the State obliged not to restrict or impede its exercise, but also other individuals have the duty to abstain or to refrain. That is why, in contemporary constitutional law, the action of amparo in many countries can also be exercised against individuals and not only against the State, as was the intent of the initial constitutional trend.

3. *The declarative nature of the constitutional declarations of rights and the open constitutional clauses*

Referring to the nature of the constitutional declarations of rights, they are not "constitutive" of such rights, in the sense that they do not create such rights, but rather, they are of a declaratory nature, in the sense that they only recognize the existence of rights, or they admit them as being inherent to the human person, as natural rights.

So one of the most important aspects of the extensive process of the constitutional declarations of human rights in Latin America has been the progressive and continuous incorporation in the constitutions of the "open clauses" of rights, which was initiated with the U.S. Ninth Amendment (1791) in which it was stated that "the enumeration in the Constitution, of certain rights, shall not be constructed to deny or disparage others retained by the people."

According to these clauses, the list of constitutional rights does not end with those that are expressly listed in the constitutional declaration, but include all other rights that are inherent to the individual. As was argued in the case *Griswold v. Connecticut* decided on June 7, 1965 (381 U.S.

479; 85 S. Ct. 1678; 14 L. Ed. 2d 510; 1965) by Justice Goldberg, delivering the opinion of the Court, holding the unconstitutionality of Connecticut's birth-control law because it intruded upon the right of marital privacy:

> The Ninth Amendment shows a belief of the Constitution's authors that fundamental rights exist that are not expressly enumerated in the first eight amendments and an intent that the list of rights included there not be deemed exhaustive...
>
> The entire fabric of the constitution and the purposes that clearly underlie its specific guarantees demonstrate that the rights to marital privacy and to marry and raise a family are of similar order and magnitude as the fundamental rights specifically protected. Although the Constitution does not speak in so many words of the right of privacy in marriage, I cannot believe that it offers these fundamental rights no protection. The fact that no particular provision of the Constitution explicitly forbids the State from disrupting the traditional relation of the family –a relation as old and as fundamental as our entire civilization–, surely does not show that the Government was meant to have the power to do so. Rather, as the Ninth Amendment expressly recognizes, there are fundamental personal rights such as this one, which are protected from abridgment by the Government though not specifically mentioned in the Constitution.[21]

---

[21]The Supreme Court also ruled: "As any student of this Court's opinions knows, this Court has held, often unanimously, that the Fifth and Fourteenth Amendments protect certain fundamental personal liberties from abridgment by the Federal Government or the States." See, e.g., *Bolling v. Sharpe*, 347 U.S. 497; *Aptheker v. Secretary of State,* 378 U.S. 500; *Kent v. Dulles*, 357 U.S. 116; *Cantwell v. Connecticut*, 310 U.S. 296; *NAACP v. Alabama*, 357 U.S. 449; *Gideon v. Wainwright*, 372 U.S. 335; *New York Times Co. v. Sullivan*, 376, U.S. 254. The Ninth Amendment simply shows the intent of the Constitution's authors that other fundamental personal rights should not be denied such protection or disparaged in any other way simply because they are not specifically listed in the first eight constitutional amendments... In sum, the Ninth Amendment simply lends strong support to the view that the "liberty" protected by the Fifth and Fourteenth Amendments from infringement by the Federal Government or the States is not restricted to rights specifically mentioned in the first eight amendments. *Cf. United Public Workers v. Mitchell*, 330 U.S. 75, 94-95. In determining which rights are fundamental, judges are not left at large to decide cases in light of their personal and private notions. Rather, they must look to the "traditions and [collective] conscience of our people" to determine whether a principle is "so rooted [there]... as to be ranked as fundamental." *Snyder v. Massachusetts*, 291 U.S. 97, 105. The inquiry is whether a right involved "is of such a character that it cannot be denied without violating those 'fundamental principles of liberty and justice which lie at the base of all our civil and political institutions' ..." *Powell v. Alabama*, 287 U.S. 45, 67. "Liberty" also "gains content from the emanations of ... specific [constitutional] guaran-

Almost all Latin American constitutions, with the exception of Cuba, Chile, Mexico and Panama, contain open clauses of this kind, emphasizing that the declaration or enunciation of rights made in the constitution shall not be understood to be a denial of others not listed therein that are inherent to the individual or to human dignity. Clauses of this type are found in the constitutions of Argentina (Article 33), Bolivia (Article 33), Colombia (Article 94), Costa Rica (Article 74), Ecuador (Article 19), Guatemala (Article 44), Honduras (Article 63), Nicaragua (Article 46), Paraguay (Article 45), Peru (Article 3), Uruguay (Article 72) and Venezuela (Article 22).

The Dominican Republic Constitution is less expressive, only indicating that the constitutional list (Articles 8 and 9) "is not limitative, and therefore does not exclude other rights and duties of a similar nature" (Article 10).

These rights inherent to the individual, for instance, have been defined by the former Supreme Court of Justice of Venezuela (decision of January 31, 1991, *Anselmo Natale* case), as:

[...] natural, universal rights which find their origin and are direct consequence of the relationships of solidarity among men, of the need for the individual development of mankind and for the protection of the environment.

The same Court concluded by stating that:

[...] such rights are commonly enshrined in Universal declarations and in national and supranational texts, and their nature and content as human rights shall leave no room for doubt, since they are the very essence of a human person and shall therefore be necessarily respected and protected.[22]

---

ties" and "from experience with the requirements of a free society." *Poe v. Ullman*, 367 U.S. 497, 517.

[22] See the reference in Carlos Ayala Corao, "La jerarquía de los instrumentos internacionales sobre derechos humanos," in *El nuevo derecho constitucional latinoamericano, IV Congreso Venezolano de Derecho constitucional*, Vol. II, Caracas, 1996, and in *La jerarquía constitucional de los tratados sobre derechos humanos y sus consecuencias*, México, 2003. Accordingly, Article 22 of the Constitution of Venezuela, following the tradition of previous constitutions, expressly establishes that "the enunciation of the rights and guaranties contained in this constitution and in the international instruments on human rights shall not be understood to be a denial of others that being inherent to the human person, are not expressly set forth in those texts"; adding that "the absence of the regulating statute of such rights do not impede its exercise" (Article 22). This article, like Article 94 of the 1991 Colombian Constitution and Article 44 of the Guatemalan Constitution, refers to the "in-

However, in some cases like Colombia and Venezuela, the open clause allows for the identification of rights inherent to human persons, not only regarding those not listed in the constitution, but also not listed in international human rights instruments, thus considerably broadening their scope.

According to this open clause, for instance, the former Supreme Court of Justice of Venezuela, annulled statutes basing its rulings in the violation of rights set forth in the American Convention on Human Rights considering it as rights inherent to human beings.

It was the case in 1996, in a decision issued deciding a judicial review action that was brought before the Court against a statute sanctioned in the State of *Amazonas*, a Member State of the Venezuelan Federation mainly populated by indigenous people, establishing its territorial internal division.

The Court considered that the sanctioning of such legislation without hearing the opinion of the indigenous communities violated their constitutional right to political participation. Such right was not expressly regulated in the 1961 Constitution, so the Court founded its ruling in the open clause (Article 50), considering the right to political participation as inherent to human beings, and as a "general principle of constitutional rank in a democratic society," adding, regarding the case, that "because of being a minorities rights (indigenous peoples in the case), they must be judicially protected."[23]

---

herent rights of a human person," thus incorporating notions of a natural right, in the sense that human rights precede the state and the constitutions themselves. The Constitution of Paraguay, in the same sense, refers to "rights inherent to human personality" (Article 45).

[23]In the December 5, 1996, ruling it was provided: "In the case, there was no evidence of the accomplishment of the provisions regarding citizens participation, lacking the statute of its original legitimacy derived from the popular hearing. The defendants argued that the advice of public bodies such as the Ministry of the Environment and the Environment Autonomous Services of the Amazon States were asked, as well as the advice of some indigenous organization. The Court deems that such procedures only constitute a timid and insignificant expression of the constitutional right to political participation in the process of elaborating statutes, which must be guarantied before and pending the legislative activity and not only when the legislation is promulgated... Regarding a statute referred to the political-territorial division of a State like the *Amazonas* State (mainly populated by indigenous communities), it is a statute that changes and modifies the economic and social conditions of the region, the vital environment of individuals, the municipal boundaries, the land ownership regime and the daily life of indigenous peoples. Thus their participation must be considered with special attention, due to the fact that indigenous peoples are one of the most exposed groups to human rights violations, due to their socioeconomic and

In another case, in 1997, the same former Supreme Court of Justice of Venezuela, annulled a national (federal) statute referring to wicked and crooked persons (*Ley de vagos y maleantes*), which was considered unconstitutional because it allowed executive detentions without due process guaranties. The decision was issued considering that the challenged statute was unconstitutional because it omitted the guaranties for a fair trial set forth in Articles 7 and 8 of the American Convention on Human Rights and Articles 9 and 14 of the International Covenant on Civil and Political Rights, and because it was discriminatory, violating Article 24 of the same American Convention.[24]

More recently, in 1999 and regarding the challenge of the proposed call for a consultative referendum for the convening of a National Constituent Assembly that was not regulated in the Venezuelan 1961 Constitution, the former Supreme Court also issued two rulings deciding interpretative recourses, allowing the convening of the referendum for such Constituent Assembly based on the right of the people to political participation, also basing its decisions in the open clause on human rights, considering it as an implicit, constitutionally nonenumerated right inherent in the human person.[25]

---

cultural conditions, in whose habitat various interest intervenes, sometimes contrary to the legitimate rights of autochthonous populations... It is in this context that the rights of indigenous peoples acquire more force, as it is expressly recognized by this Court." See *Antonio Guzmán, Lucas Omashi et al.* case, in *Revista de Derecho Público*, n° 67-68, Editorial Jurídica Venezolana, Caracas, 1996, pp. 176 ff. According to the aforementioned, the Court's decision referred to the violation of constitutional rights of minorities set forth in the Constitution and in the international treaties and conventions on human rights, particularly the right to citizenship participation in the statute elaborating process, particularly because no public consultation was made in the case to the minority indigenous communities, as a consequence of which, the Court decided to annul the challenged statute.

[24]See in *Revista de Derecho Público* n° 71-72, Editorial Jurídica Venezolana, Caracas, 1997, pp. 177 ff.

[25]Considering the referendum as a right inherent to the human person, the Court specifically indicated that: "This is applicable, not only from a methodological point of view, but ontologically as well, since if the right to a constitutional referendum were considered to depend on a reform of the current Constitution, it would be subordinate to the will of the constituted power, which in turn would be placed above the sovereign power. The absence of such a right in the Fundamental Charter must be interpreted as a gap in the Constitution, since it could not be sustained that the sovereign power had renounced, *ab initio*, the exercise of a power that is the work of its own political decision." See in *Revista de Derecho Público*, n° 77-80, Editorial Jurídica Venezolana, Caracas, 1999, p. 67. The conclusion of the Court's decision was that it was not necessary to previously reform the Constitution in order to recognize the referendum or popular consultation on whether to convene a Con-

As mentioned, open clauses of human rights of the same nature are found in almost all Latin American constitutions, even with different contents. The Constitution of Ecuador, for instance, refers to the rights "derived from the nature of the human person which are necessary for his or her full moral and material development" (Article 19).[26]

In other cases, such as the Constitution of Brazil, the open clause, without referring to the inherent rights of human persons, indicates that the listing in the Constitution of rights and guaranties, does not exclude others "derived from the regime and principles adopted by the Constitution or by international treaties to which the Federative Republic of Brazil is a party" (Article 5.2).

The Constitution of Costa Rica refers to those rights "which derive from the Christian principle of social justice" (Article 74), an expression that can be interpreted in the sense of human dignity and social justice.

In other constitutions, instead of referring to the rights inherent to human beings, the open clauses refer to the sovereignty of the people and to the republican form of government and, therefore, more emphasis is made regarding political rights than on the inherent rights of human persons. This is the case of Argentina, where Article 33 of the Constitution states that:

> The declarations, rights and guaranties enumerated in the Constitution, can not be understood as to deny others rights and guaranties not enumerated, but

---

stituent Assembly as being a constitutional right. See the comments in Allan R. Brewer-Carías, "La configuración judicial del proceso constituyente o de cómo el guardián de la Constitución abrió el camino para su violación y para su propia extinction," in *Revista de Derecho Público,* n° 77-80, Editorial Jurídica Venezolana, Caracas, 1999, pp. 453 ff.

[26] This provision is complemented by Article 18 in which it is stated that the rights and guaranties enshrined in the Constitution and in the international instruments are directly and immediately applicable by and before any court or authority; and that the absence of regulatory statutes cannot be alleged in order to justify the violation or the ignorance of the rights set forth in the Constitution, or to reject the action for its protection, or to deny the recognizance of such rights. In Nicaragua the constitution is more detailed regarding the listing of international instruments and, as such, more limitative, when its Article 46 provides as follows: "Article 46. Every person in the land shall enjoy State protection and the recognition of the rights inherent to the human person, of the unrestricted respect, promotion and protection of human rights, and of the full enforcement of the rights consigned in the Universal Declaration of Human Rights; in the American Declaration of the Rights and Duties of Man; in the International Covenant on Economic, Social and Cultural Rights; in the United Nations' International Covenant on Civil and Political Rights; and in the American Convention on Human Rights of the Organization of American States."

that rose from the principle of the people's sovereignty and from the republican form of government.

Similar regulations are contained in the constitutions of Bolivia (Article 55) and of Uruguay (Article 72). In Peru (Article 3) and Honduras (Article 63) the constitutions refer to other rights of an analogous nature or that are based on the "dignity of man, or on the sovereignty of the people, of the democratic rule of law and of the republican form of government."

In all these cases, the incorporation of open clauses in the constitution regarding human rights implies that the absence of statutory regulation of such rights cannot be invoked to deny or undermine its exercise by the people, as it is expressed in many constitutions (Argentina, Bolivia, Paraguay, Venezuela and Ecuador).

This, of course, responds to the principle of the direct applicability of the constitution in human rights matters, which excludes the traditional concept of the so-called "programmatic clauses," which were constructed under the constitutionalism of some decades ago, particularly regarding social rights, which impeded their being fully exercised and judicially protected until legally regulated.

4. *The absolute or limitative character of the declarations*

One final remark must be made regarding the human rights regime in Latin America, referred in particular to the absolute or limitative character of the declarations on human rights.

It is true that there are absolute rights, as are all the rights considered and declared as inviolable and not limitable, such as the right to life, the right not to be tortured, and the right not to receive shameful sentences or the right to self-defense.

Yet beyond these, there exists the principle of the limitability of rights and freedoms, whose borderline in a democratic society is always marked by both the rights of other persons and the public and social order, because, unquestionably, rights are exercised in society and they have many titleholders.[27] This requires, therefore, the need to conciliate the exercising of rights by everyone, in order to avoid the violation of other people's rights and, in general, of public and social general order.

---

[27]Article XXVIII, American Declaration of Rights and Duties of Man; Article 29,2, Universal Declaration on Human Rights. See Florentín Meléndez, *Instrumentos internacionales sobre derechos humanos aplicables a la administración de justicia. Estudio constitucional comparado*, Cámara de Diputados, México, 2004, pp. 100 ff.

Of course, this principle of the limitative character of rights can lead to extreme, dangerous situations such as the one that unfortunately still remains in the Constitution of Cuba, which leaves open an "unlimited" possibility of limitations to human rights, founded on the preservation of principles that can only be determined by the established power, thus rendering the rights futile. In this regard, Article 62 of the Cuban Constitution provides that:

> None of the citizens' recognized freedoms may be exercised against the provisions of the Constitution and the laws, or against the existence and purposes of the socialist State, or against the Cuban people's decision to construct socialism and communism. Offenses against such principle are punishable.

Leaving aside this isolated case, the limitations to rights allowed by the constitutions are only linked to the demands for public and social general order or to the exercise of the same rights by others.

Additionally, these limitations can only be imposed by means of statutory regulations or formal laws sanctioned by the elected legislative body; and not by means of executive or administrative regulations. It is what is called in Spanish the guaranty of the "*reserva legal,*" or of the limitations only to be established by statutes. This principle has also been included in Article 30 of the American Convention on Human Rights, which has been interpreted by the Inter-American Court for Human Rights in its *Advisory Opinion OC-6/86* on the expression "laws" in Article 30 of the American Convention on Human Rights.[28]

Finally, because the exercise of rights is limited by the exercise of the same rights by others, a balance must always be established between the different rights in order to avoid the infringement of other's rights. This, of course, can only be achieved through the progressive application of constitutional texts by an effective and efficient autonomous and independent judiciary, which is the only branch of government that can clarify when the exercise of one right shall outweigh that of another.

In this regard, there have been many legal cases, for example in relation to freedom of speech, that have determined how far freedom of speech can go, for instance, regarding the infringement of the individual rights to honor, reputation or privacy, or of the child's rights. A similar exercise has to be done, for instance, regarding the extent of the freedom of the

---

[28] *Idem*, p. 102.

press in relation to national security interest, which has been traditionally discussed in the United States.

In all these cases the judge is the one who has to decide which right shall prevail in a specific moment, or under what circumstances precedence shall be given to the rights of a child, for instance, in regard to the right to free expression of thought.[29]

In this task of interpretation, the principles of progressiveness, interdependence, reasonableness, *favor libertatis* and the concept of the essential nucleus of rights, among others, are essential for guaranteeing their exercise and enforceability.

II. THE INTERNATIONALIZATION OF HUMAN RIGHTS AND ITS CONSTITUTIONALIZATION

The process of the "constitutionalization of human rights," which until the Second World War characterized the protection of human rights by means of the expansion of the declarations of rights, freedoms and guaranties incorporated in the constitutions, was a stage in the protection of human rights only concerned with constitutional law and constitutional regulations. This process was followed by a second one that has developed during the second half of last century, in which human rights also became a main and essential matter, not only of constitutional law, but of international law. That is why we can then talk of a process of "internationalization of the constitutionalization" of human rights in which both branches of law have mutual feedback in setting forth new and universal declarations and regulations regarding human rights.

This second stage began in 1948 with the approval of two general declarations on human rights, one in the United Nations and the other in the Organization of American States, when the wounds caused by the war and those discovered after 1945, showed that the sole national constitutional provisions were not enough for the effective protection and enforcement of human rights.

These international declarations, which referred basically to civil, social and political rights, were the American Declaration of the Rights and Duties of Man approved by the Organization of American States, and the Universal Declaration of Human Rights approved by the United Nations Organization.

---

[29]See for example, Allan R. Brewer-Carías *et al.*, *Los derechos del niño vs. los abusos parlamentarios de la libertad de expresión*, Editorial Jurídica Venezolana, Caracas, 1994.

A few years later, in 1950, the European Convention on Human Rights was signed, and became the first multilateral treaty on the matter (entered in force in 1953).

This process of internationalization of human rights was later consolidated in 1966, with the adoption of two United Nations International Covenants that referred to Civil and Political Rights, and to Economic, Social and Cultural Rights, both in effect since 1976.

The International Covenant on Civil and Political Rights, after enumerating a complete list of them, imposed upon the Member States the duty to adopt the necessary constitutional reform, new laws and all other measures deemed necessary to give effect to the rights recognized in the Covenant.

In particular, regarding the guaranties for the protection of those rights, it declared (Article 2,3) that each Member State was due:

(a) To ensure that any person whose rights or freedoms as herein recognized are violated shall have an effective remedy, even if the violation has been committed by persons acting in an official capacity;

(b) To ensure that any person claiming such a remedy shall have his right thereto determined by competent judicial, administrative or legislative authorities, or by any other competent authority provided for by the legal system of the State, and to develop the possibilities of a judicial remedy;

(c) To ensure that when granted, the competent authorities shall enforce such remedies.

Accordingly, the Covenant also established a general right of any person to have access to an effective remedy to seek protection of their rights, even though not necessarily of judicial nature.

1.   *The American internationalization of human rights*

The process of internationalization of the constitutionalization of human rights continued in the American continent, with the adoption, in 1969, of the American Convention on Human Rights (*Pacto de San José*), that has been ratified by all Latin American countries except Cuba. Those countries, as well as other Caribbean Anglo-speaking countries[30] that ratified

---

[30]The Convention has also been ratified by Barbados, Dominica, Grenada, Haiti, Jamaica, and Suriname.

the Convention, have recognized the jurisdiction of the Inter-American Court on Human Rights created by the Convention.

The only American country that did not sign the Convention was Canada, and even though the United States of America signed the Convention in 1977, it has not yet ratified it.[31] This American Convention has consolidated a very rich minimal standard regulation on civil and political rights, which are enumerated and extensively defined in the text of the declaration. In this case also, in addition to all the substantive rights declared in the Convention, and in a more complete way to what was established in the International Covenant on Civil and Political Rights, the American Convention also provides for the right of everyone to be judicially protected on their rights, in particular by means of the amparo action, regulated in Article 25 of the Convention as the "right to judicial protection," as follows:

> 1. Everyone has the right to a simple and prompt recourse, or any other effective recourse, before a competent court or tribunal for protection (*que la ampare*) against acts that violate his fundamental rights recognized by the constitution or laws of the concerned state or by this Convention, even though such violation may have been committed by persons acting in the course of their official duties.

The Convention also provides, in similar terms as the International Covenant, that the Member States must take measures to ensure that any person claiming such remedy shall have his rights determined by the competent authority provided for by the legal system of the state; to develop the possibilities of judicial remedy; and to ensure that the competent authorities shall enforce such remedies when granted.

This Convention has been extremely important for the Latin American countries, not only because of its contents showing regulations in many cases written as reaction against so many violations of human rights the countries suffered during military dictatorships in the sixties and seventies, but because it created the Inter-American Commission on Human Rights, and the Inter-American Court of Human Rights (Article 33), which have played a very important role condemning States' violations on human rights.

---

[31]The following Member States of the Organization of American States did not ratify the American Convention: Antigua and Barbuda, Bahamas, Belize, Canada, Cuba, the United States of America, St. Kitts and Nevis, St. Lucia, St. Vincent and the Grenadines. Trinidad and Tobago ratified the Convention but in 1998 denounced it.

The Convention recognized the right of any person or group of persons to file petitions before the Commission denouncing violation of the Convention by a State Party (Article 44), which gave the Commission the monopoly to act on behalf of individuals, bringing cases before the Inter-American Court on Human Rights.[32] Notwithstanding this limitation, it has produced a very rich and important international protective jurisprudence and doctrine in the matter of human rights.[33]

In the European system the protective doctrine has been even richer, because individuals can bring direct petitions against Member States before the European Tribunal on Human Rights regarding the protection of their rights.[34]

However, in spite of this restriction in the American Convention, since the beginning of its activities in 1979, the Commission and the Court have been very active in the exercise of their functions, and have decided

---

[32] The following Member States have recognized the jurisdiction of the Inter-American Court: Argentina, Barbados, Bolivia, Brazil, Colombia, Costa Rica, Chile, Ecuador, El Salvador, Guatemala, Haiti, Honduras, México, Nicaragua, Panama, Paraguay, Perú, Dominican Republic, Suriname, Uruguay and Venezuela.

[33] Following a very extensive regulated procedure, the Commission can bring before the Inter-American Court on Human Rights cases of violation of the Member States obligations and if the Court, following the procedure set forth in the Convention, finds that there has been a violation of a right or freedom protected by the Convention, the Court shall rule that the injured party be ensured the enjoyment of his right or freedom that was violated, and if appropriate, can also rule that the consequences of the measure or situation that constituted the breach of such right or freedom be remedied and that fair compensation be paid to the injured party (Article 63). The general rule of admissibility of the petition is that "the remedies under domestic law have been pursued and exhausted in accordance with generally recognized principles of international law"(Article 46,1,a); rule that has the following exceptions: when in the internal law of the State the due process for the protection for the violated rights is non-existent; when the affected party has been impeded in his rights to access to the internal jurisdictional recourses, or when he has been impeded of exhausting them; or when an unjustified delay has occurred regarding such recourses (Article 77,2 of the Internal regulation of the Commission).

[34] In some Latin American constitutions, as is the case of the 1999 Venezuelan Constitution, the right to petition for the protection of human rights before international organizations has been regulated as an individual constitutional right. In this regard, Article 31 sets forth: "According to what is set forth in the treaties, covenants and conventions on human rights ratified by the Republic, everybody has the right to file petitions or complaints before the international organizations created for such purposes, in order to seek for the protection (amparo) of his human rights. The Constitution also imposes on the State the obligation, according to the procedures provided in the Constitution and the statutes, to adopt the necessary measures in order to comply with the decisions of the above-mentioned international organizations."

in numerous cases condemning Member States for violations of human rights. Also by means of Advisory Opinions, the Court has produced a very important doctrine on human rights in Latin America.[35]

From all these international regulations on human rights, it is then possible to appreciate that following the initial process of constitutionalization of human rights by means of the progressive extension of national constitutional declarations, a second stage was developed, marked by the internationalization of such constitutionalization process, by means of the international declarations of rights and treaties on the matter.

2. The constitutionalization of the internationalization of human rights

In recent times, a third stage in this process of protecting human rights can also be identified, once again, as "a process of constitutionalization," but with an emphasis on the "internationalization of human rights," developed by means of the incorporation of the international systems of protection within the constitutional internal regulations.

According to this process, the national constitutions have now expressly determined the value given to the international instruments on human rights,[36] regarding the same constitution as well as regarding statutes, even determining in some cases which shall prevail if there is a conflict among them.

This process has resulted in the incorporation in some constitutions, of provisions giving four different ranks to international instruments on human rights regarding internal law: a supraconstitutional rank, a constitutional rank, a supralegal rank or a statutory rank.[37]

---

[35]See Sergio García Ramírez (Coord.), *La Jurisprudencia de la Corte Interamericana de Derechos Humanos*, Universidad Nacional Autónoma de México, Corte Interamericana de Derechos Humanos, México, 2001, 1.200 pp.

[36]See Ariel Dulitzky, "Los tratados de derechos humanos en el constitucionalismo iberoamericano," in Thomas Burgental *et al.*, *Estudios especializados de derechos humanos*, Vol I, Instituto Interamericano de Derechos Humanos, San José, 1996, pp. 158 ff.; Humberto Nogueira Alcalá, "Los derechos fundamentales y los derechos humanos contenidos en los tratados internacionales y su ubicación en las fuentes del derecho: doctrina y jurisprudencia," in *Revista Peruana de Derecho Público*, n° 12, Lima, 2006, pp. 67 ff.

[37]For a general comment regarding this classification, see Rodolfo E. Piza R., *Derecho internacional de los derechos humanos: La Convención Americana*, San José 1989; Carlos Ayala Corao, "La jerarquía de los instrumentos internacionales sobre derechos humanos," in *El nuevo derecho constitucional latinoamericano, IV Congreso venezolano de Derecho constitucional*, Vol. II, Caracas, 1996 and *La jerarquía constitucional de los tratados*

A. The supraconstitutional rank of international instruments of human rights

In the first case of supraconstitutional rank, some constitutions have expressly given the international treaties on human rights a superior rank regarding the constitution itself, therefore in some cases prevailing over their own provisions, as is the case of the Constitutions of Colombia (Article 93), Guatemala (Article 46), Honduras (Article 16) and Venezuela (Article 23).[38] This supraconstitutional rank given to international treaties, for instance, has allowed the Supreme Courts or the Constitutional Court to decide cases by directly applying the American Convention.

It was the case, for instance, of a decision of the Constitutional Court of Guatemala issued on May 27, 1997, regarding the freedom of expression and the rectification rights. Even though the right to seek for rectification in cases of press information affecting the honor, reputation and privacy of a person was not expressly declared in the constitution, the Constitutional Court applied Articles 11, 13 and 14 of the American Convention that guaranty to any person affected by information published in newspa-

sobre derechos humanos y sus consecuencias, México, 2003; Florentín Meléndez, Instrumentos internacionales sobre derechos humanos aplicables a la administración de justicia. Estudio constitucional comparado, Cámara de Diputados, México, 2004, pp. 26 ff.; and Humberto Henderson, "Los tratados internacionales de derechos humanos en el orden interno: la importancia del principio pro homine," in Revista IIDH, Instituto Interamericano de Derechos Humanos, n° 39, San José, 2004, pp. 71 ff. See also, Allan R. Brewer-Carías, Mecanismos nacionales de protección de los derechos humanos, Instituto Internacional de Derechos Humanos, San José, 2004, pp. 62 ff.

[38]The Constitution of Guatemala, set forth in Article 46 the general principle of pre-eminence of international law, by stating that in declaring that "in human rights matters, the treaties and conventions accepted and ratified by Guatemala shall have preeminence over internal law," in which it must be included other than the statutes, the Constitution itself." In Honduras, Article 16 of the constitution sets forth that all treaties subscribed with other States (not only related to human rights), are part of internal law; and Article 18 establishes the preeminence of treaties over statutes in case of conflict between them. In addition, the Honduran Constitution admits the possibility of ratification of treaties contrary to what is set forth in the Constitution, in which case they must be approved according to the procedure set forth for constitutional revision (Article 17). A similar regulation is established in Article 53 of the Perúvian Constitution. In Colombia, the constitution has also established a similar provision, with Article 93 providing that: "international treaties and conventions ratified by Congress, which recognize human rights and forbid their limitation in states of emergency, shall prevail over internal law." In this case, also, internal law must be understood to comprise not only statutes but the constitution itself.

pers, to seek for "rectification and answer (response) that must be published in the same newspaper," considering such provisions as forming part of the constitutional order of Guatemala.[39]

In Colombia (Article 93), based on the preeminence of treaties over statutes, the Constitutional Court in a decision nº T-447/95 of October 23, 1995, has recognized the right of everybody to have an identity as a right inherent to human beings, even though not expressly declared in the constitution. The Court based its ruling on what is established in the international treaties and covenants, particularly the International Covenant on Civil and Political Rights and the American Convention on Human Rights, effectively recognizing their supraconstitutional rank.

The Court ruled that those covenants ratified by Colombia prevail in the internal order (Article 93 Constitution) and imposes on the State the duty to adopt "legislative or other measures in order to make human rights effective" (Article 2, American Convention; Article 2,2, International Covenant on Civil and Political Rights). Among these "measures," the judicial rulings, particularly those issued by the Constitutional Court, were considered to count for the enforcement of rights, the Court said, because "it is for legitimate courts and in particular, for the Constitutional Court, when deciding cases, to consider within the legal order the rights recognized in the Constitution and in the Covenants."[40]

---

[39] See in *Iudicum et Vita, Jurisprudencia nacional de América Latina en Derechos Humanos*, nº 5, Instituto Interamericano de Derechos Humanos, San José, Costa Rica, Diciembre 1997, pp. 45 ff. Nonetheless, in other decisions, the Constitutional Court of Guatemala has considered that "the international treaties on human rights are incorporated in the internal legal order with the character of constitutional norm but without reformatory of derogatory powers." See the reference to decision of October 10, 1990, in Ariel Dulitzky "Los tratados de derechos humanos en el constitucionalismo iberoamericano," in Thomas Burgenthal *et al*, *Estudios especializados de derechos humanos*, Vol I, Instituto Interamericano de Derechos Humanos, San José, 1996, p. 158; and in Humberto Nogueira Alcalá, "Los derechos fundamentales y los derechos humanos contenidos en los tratados internacionales y su ubicación en las fuentes del derecho: doctrina y jurisprudencia," in *Revista Peruana de Derecho Público*, nº 12, Lima, 2006, p. 89.

[40] The Court began by referring to the previous ruling of the former Supreme Court of Justice that had determined their supralegal value, by arguing: "Since 1928 the Supreme Court of Justice has given prevalent value to international treaties regarding legislative internal order; due to the fact that such international norms, by will of the Colombian state, enter to form part of the legal order with supralegal rank, setting forth the coactive force of provisions the signing State has the obligation to enforce. The supralegal value has been expressly established in Article 93 of the Constitution of Colombia, as has been recognized by the Supreme Court of Justice, arguing that it must be added that such superiority has

Based on these arguments, the Court concluded that being "the right to have an identity implicitly set forth in all the international covenants and conventions, and thus, legally protected," it is possible to affirm such right "as being inherent to human person fully guaranteed due to the obligatory force of the international covenant."[41]

The 1999 Constitution of Venezuela can also be considered within this first system of supraconstitutional hierarchy of human rights contained in treaties. Article 23 of this Constitution provides that:

> Treaties, covenants and conventions referring to human rights, signed and ratified by Venezuela, shall have constitutional hierarchy and will prevail over internal legal order, when they contain regulations regarding their enjoyment and exercise, more favorable than those established in this Constitution and the statutes of the Republic.
>
> Those treaties and conventions shall be immediately and directly applicable by the courts and all other official authorities.

Undoubtedly, this is one of the most important articles on matters of human rights[42] in all the Latin American system, not only because it establishes the supraconstitutional rank of human rights treaties, but also because it prescribes the direct and immediate applicability of such treaties by all courts and authorities of the country.

Based on this constitutional provision, for instance, the Constitutional Chamber of the Supreme Tribunal of Justice in 2000 gave prevalence to the American Convention regulations regarding the "the right to appeal

---

been sustained as an invariable doctrine that "is a public law principle, that the Constitution and the international treaties are the superior law of the land and their dispositions prevail over the legal norms contrary to their provisions even if they are posterior laws." See the text in *Derechos Fundamentales e interpretación Constitucional, (Ensayos-Jurisprudencia)*, Comisión Andina de Juristas, Lima, 1997; and in Carlos Ayala Corao, "Recepción de la jurisprudencia internacional sobre derechos humanos por la jurisprudencia constitucional," in *Revista del Tribunal Constitucional*, n° 6, Sucre, Bolivia, Nov. 2004, pp. 275 ff. See also, Decision C-225/95 of the Constitucional Court in which the Court considered that international treaties had preemptive status, forming part of the "constitutional block," in Humberto Nogueira Alcalá, "Los derechos fundamentales y los derechos humanos contenidos en los tratados internacionales y su ubicación en las fuentes del derecho: doctrina y jurisprudencia," in *Revista Peruana de Derecho Público*, n° 12, Lima, 2006, p. 87.

[41]Idem.

[42]See the proposal of the draft of this article to the National Constituent Assembly, in Allan R. Brewer-Carías, *Debate Constituyente, (Aportes a la Asamblea Nacional Constituyente)*, Fundación de Derecho Público, Caracas, 1999, pp. 88 ff. and 111 ff.

judgments before a higher court" (Article 8,2,h), considered as forming part of internal constitutional law of the country. In a decision n° 87 of March 13, 2000, interpreting in an extensive way what is provided in the Convention, the Chamber compared the provision of its Article 8,2,h with Article 49,1 of the Constitution where the right to appeal was only granted to those who have been declared guilty in criminal cases. Consequently, the Supreme Tribunal concluded by saying that "the norm of the Convention is more favorable to the exercise of such right, due to the fact that it guaranties the right of everybody to be heard not only regarding criminal procedures, but also regarding rights and obligations in civil, labor, taxation or any other procedure, in which the right to appeal without any exception is established." Based on these arguments, the Court then compared the international provision of the American Convention with one article (185) of a statute regulating the Administrative Jurisdiction procedure (Supreme Court of Justice 1976 Statute), which excluded the appeal in certain cases on Administrative Jurisdiction courts' decisions, interpreting "that the latter is incompatible with the former, because it denies in absolute terms, the right that the Convention guaranties."[43]

Based on the aforementioned, the Constitutional Chamber concluded its ruling by stating that the right to appeal recognized in Article 8,1 and 2,h of the American Convention on Human Rights, which is "part of the Venezuelan constitutional order," is more favorable regarding the exercise of such right in relation to what is set forth in Article 49,1 of the Constitution; and that such provisions were of direct and immediate application by courts and authorities."[44]

Nonetheless, three years later, after a few decisions and protective preliminary orders were issued by the Inter-American Commissions on Human Rights against the Venezuelan State, in cases where the right to free expression of thoughts were denounced as violated, the same Constitutional Chamber of the Supreme Tribunal interpreted the article in a very different way, as a reaction against the effects of the constitutionalization of the internationalization of human rights contained in this very clear constitutional provision of Article 23. In a ruling n° 1942 of July 7, 2003, it denied the powers of all courts to directly apply international conven-

---

[43] *C.A. Electricidad del Centro (Elecentro) y otra vs. Superintendencia para la Promoción y Protección de la Libre Competencia. (Procompetencia)* case, in *Revista de Derecho Público*, n° 81, Editorial Jurídica Venezolana, Caracas, 2000, pp. 157 ff.

[44] *Idem.*

tions, and declared that the Chamber itself was the only court with powers to "determine which norms on human rights contained in treaties, covenants and conventions, prevail in the internal legal order."[45] By doing this, the Tribunal also assumed the monopoly to determine which human rights not incorporated in such international instruments but considered inherent to human beings, have effects in Venezuela. With this ruling,[46] the effects of the supraconstitutional rank of treaties when estab-

---

[45]The Chamber ruled: "Once the human rights substantive norms contained in Conventions, covenants and treaties have been incorporated to the constitutional hierarchy, the maximum and last interpreter of them, vis-à-vis internal law, is the Constitutional Chamber, which determines the content and scope of the constitutional norms and principles (Article 335), among them are the treaties, covenants and conventions on human rights, duly subscribed and ratified by Venezuela"; adding: "This power of the Constitutional Chamber on the matter, derived from the Constitution, cannot be diminished by adjective norms contained in the treaties or in other international texts on human rights subscribed by the country, allowing the Member States to ask international institutions for the interpretation of rights referred to in the Convention or covenant, as established in Article 64 of the Approbatory statute of the American Convention of Human Rights, San José Covenant, because otherwise, the situation would be of a constitutional amendment, without following the constitutional procedures, diminishing the powers of the Constitutional Chamber, transferring it to international or transnational bodies, with the power to dictate obligatory interpretations." See in *Revista de Derecho Público*, n° 93-96, Editorial Jurídica Venezolana, Caracas, 2003, pp. 136 ff.

[46]This restrictive interpretation was really issued in a ruling devoted to deny any constitutional value and rank to the recommendations of the Inter-American Commission on Human Rights, thus refusing to consider unconstitutional some articles of the Penal Code regarding restrictions to the freedom of expression when referring to public officials that were contrary to the recommendations of the Commission that was argued were obligatory for the country. The Constitutional Chamber argued that according to the American Convention, the Commission may formulate "recommendations" to the governments in order for them to adopt progressive measures in favor of human rights within their internal laws and constitutional prescriptions, as well as provisions to promote the respect of such rights (Article 41.b), adding: "If what is recommended by the Commission must be adapted to the Constitution and statutes of the States it means they do not have obligatory force, because the internal laws or the Constitution could be contrary to the recommendations. Thus, the articles of the Convention do not refer to the obligatory character of the recommendations; in contrast, they refer to the powers assigned to the other organ: the Court, which according to Article 62 of the Convention, can give obligatory interpretations of the Convention when requested by the States, which means that they accept the opinion. If the Court has such power, and the Commission does not, it is compulsory to conclude that the recommendations of the latter do not have the character of the opinions of the former, and consequently, the Chamber declares that the recommendations of the Inter-American Commission of Human Rights are nonobligatory regarding internal law. The Chamber considers that the recommendations must be weighed by the Member States. They must adapt their legislation to the recommendations if they do not collide with the constitutional

lishing more favorable regulations regarding human rights that can be applied by any court, was suddenly eliminated by the Constitutional Chamber. By assuming the absolute monopoly of constitution interpretation, the Tribunal limited the general powers of all the other courts to resolve by means of judicial review on the matter and to directly apply

provisions, but for such adaptation there is no timing set, and until it is done, the statutes in effect that do not collide with the Constitution, or according to the Venezuelan courts with the human rights enshrined in the international conventions, will remain in force until declared unconstitutional or repealed by other states." The restrictive approach of the Venezuelan Constitutional Chamber regarding the importance on internal law of the Inter-American Commission on Human Rights recommendations was previously stated in a decision dated May 5, 2000. In this decision the Constitutional Chamber objected to the quasi-jurisdictional powers of the Inter-American Commission on Human Rights. The case was as follows: After a magazine (*Revista Exceso*) filed an amparo action before the national jurisdictions seeking constitutional protection of its right to free expression and information, the plaintiff went before the Inter-American Commission on Human Rights denouncing the malfunctioning of internal jurisdiction regarding the amparo action filed, and seeking international protection against the Venezuelan State for violation of its rights to freedom of expression and due process and against judicial harassment practices against one of its journalists and the director of the magazine. In the case, the Inter-American Commission issued provisional protective measures. When the time arrived to decide the amparo action, the Constitutional Chamber considered that in the case, the plaintiff's due process rights had been effectively violated (independently of its right to freedom of expression), but regarding the provisional measures adopted by the Inter-American Commission, qualifying it as "unacceptable," the Chamber stated that the Constitutional Chamber "also considers unacceptable the instance of the Inter-American Commission on Human Rights of the Organization of American States in the sense that asking for the adoption of measures that imply a gross intrusion in the country's judicial organs, like the suspension of the judicial proceeding against the plaintiff, are measures that can only be adopted by the judges exercising their judicial attributions and independence, according to what is stated in the Constitution and the statutes of the Republic. Additionally, Article 46,b of the American Convention on Human Rights sets forth that the petition on denunciations or complaint for the violations of the Convention by a State requires the presentation and exhaustion of the internal jurisdiction remedies according to the generally accepted principles of international law, which was allowed in this case, due to the fact that the judicial delay was not attributable to the Chamber," *Faitha M. Nahmens L. y Ben Ami Fihman Z., Revista Exceso* case, Exp. n° 00-0216, decision n° 386 de 17-5-2000. See in Carlos Ayala Corao, "Recepción de la jurisprudencia internacional sobre derechos humanos por la jurisprudencia constitucional," in *Revista del Tribunal Constitucional*, n° 6, Sucre, Bolivia, Nov. 2004, pp. 275 ff. This unfortunate ruling can also be considered contrary to Article 31 of the Venezuelan Constitution, which sets forth the individual rights of anybody to bring before the international organizations on human rights, as it is the Inter-American Commission on Human Rights, petitions or complaints to seek protection (amparo) of their violated rights.

and give prevalence to the American Convention regarding constitutional provisions.[47]

B. The constitutional rank of international instruments of human rights

In other Latin American countries a second system regarding the rank of international instruments of human rights can also be distinguished by granting in their constitutions a constitutional rank to international treaties on human rights. Consequently, the Supreme Courts and Constitutional Courts in many cases have applied the international instruments on human rights in order to control the constitutionality of internal legislation.

This is the case of Argentina, where the constitutions grant such constitutional hierarchy to a group of instruments that are expressly listed in Article 75.22, namely: the American Declaration of the Rights and Duties of Man; the Universal Declaration of Human Rights; the American Convention on Human Rights; the International Covenant on Economic, So-

---

[47]Contrary, for instance, to what was resolved in Argentina, once the Inter-American Commission determined that the amnesty statutes (*Punto Final* and *Obediencia Debida*) and the pardon measures adopted regarding the crimes committed by the military dictatorship were contrary to the American Convention, some courts began to consider such statutes as unconstitutional because they were in violation of international law. See Decision de 4-03-2001, Juzgado Federal n° 4, *Pobrete Hlaczik* case, in por Kathryn Sikkink, "The transnational dimension of judicialization of politics in Latin America," in Rachel Sieder *et al.* (ed), *The Judicialization of Politics in Latin America,* Palgrave Macmillan, New York, 2005, pp. 274, 290. The Venezuelan Constitutional Chamber, in any case, concluded its restrictive interpretation by stating that: "A different interpretation means giving the Commission a supranational character which weakened the Member State's sovereignty, something that is prohibited by the Constitution.." Decision n° 1942 of July 15, 2003, in *Revista de Derecho Público,* n° 93-96, Editorial Jurídica Venezolana, Caracas, 2003, pp. 136 ff. Anyway, after the Constitutional Chamber's ruling, the Penal Code was reformed but not in the relevant parts regarding the crimes referred to as "*leyes de desacato.*" This decision was contrary to what was decided in 1995 by the Argentinean Congress regarding the same matters, by repealing the articles related to the same crimes in compliance with the Inter-American Commission recommendation on the matter. *Verbistky* case*, Report of the Comisión* n° 22/94 of September 20, 1994, *11.012* case (Argentina). See the comments by Antonio Cançado Trindade, "Libertad de expresión y derecho a la información en los planos internacional y nacional," in *Iudicum et Vita, Jurisprudencia nacional de América Latina en Derechos Humanos,* n° 5, Instituto Interamericano de Derechos Humanos, San José, Costa Rica, Diciembre 1997, pp.194–195. See the "Informe sobre la compatibilidad entre las leyes de desacato y la Convención Americana sobre Derechos Humanos de 17 de febrero de 1995," in *Estudios Básicos de derechos Humanos*, Vol. X, Instituto Interamericano de Derechos Humanos, San José, 2000.

cial and Cultural Rights; the International Covenant on Civil and Political Rights and its Optional Protocol; the Convention on the Prevention and Punishment of the Crime of Genocide; the International Convention on the Elimination of All Forms of Racial Discrimination; the Convention on the Elimination of All Forms of Discrimination against Women; the Convention against Torture and Other Cruel, Inhuman or Degrading Treatment or Punishment; the Convention on the Rights of the Child.

According to these constitutional provisions, the Supreme Court of the Nation of Argentina has also applied the American Convention on Human Rights, giving prevalence to its provisions regarding internal statutes, as was the case of the same right to appeal declared in the American Convention, which the Criminal Procedural Code excluded in some judicial decisions depending upon the duration or gravity of the punishment. The Supreme Court of the Nation declared the invalidity of the said Code's provisions on the grounds of its unconstitutionality, applying the American Convention.[48]

Additionally, in Argentina, and in contrast to the aforementioned Venezuelan Supreme Tribunal reaction, the courts have also considered that not only the decisions of the Inter-American Court but also those of the Inter-American Commission as obligatory,[49] considering "as a guide for the interpretation of constitutional provisions"[50]; and for instance, repealing lower court decisions when considering that their interpretation was

---

[48]Decision of April, 4, 1995, *Giroldi, H.D. et al.* case, in Aida Kemelmajer de Carlucci and Maria Gabriela Abalos de Mosso, "Grandes líneas directrices de la jurisprudencia argentina sobre material constitucional durante el año 1995," in *Anuario de Derecho Constitucional Latinoamericano 1996*, Fundación Konrad Adenauer, Bogotá, 1996, pp. 517 ff.; in Carlos Ayala Corao, "Recepción de la jurisprudencia internacional sobre derechos humanos por la jurisprudencia constitucional," in *Revista del Tribunal Constitucional*, n° 6, Sucre, Bolivia, Nov. 2004, pp. 275 ff.; and in Humberto Nogueira Alcalá, "Los derechos fundamentales y los derechos humanos contenidos en los tratados internacionales y su ubicación en las fuentes del derecho: doctrina y jurisprudencia," in *Revista Peruana de Derecho Público*, n° 12, Lima, 2006, pp. 67 ff.

[49]Decision of July 7, 1992, *Miguel A. Ekmkdjiam, Gerardo Sofivic et al,* case, in Ariel E. Dulitzky, "La aplicación de los tratados sobre derechos humanos por los tribunales locales: un studio comparado," in *La aplicación de los tratados sobre derechos Humanos por los tribunales locales*, Centro de Estudios Legales y Sociales, Buenos Aires, 1997. See Carlos Ayala Corao, "Recepción de la jurisprudencia internacional sobre derechos humanos por la jurisprudencia constitucional," in *Revista del Tribunal Constitucional*, n° 6, Sucre, Bolivia, Nov. 2004, pp. 275 ff.

[50]*H Giroldi/Cassation Recourse* case, April 7, 1995 in *Jurisprudencia Argentina*, Vol. 1995-III, p. 571. See Carlos Ayala Corao, *Idem,* 275 ff.

made in an incompatible way regarding the decision's doctrine of the Inter-American Commission on Human Rights.[51]

In Panama, even though the Constitution has no express provision regarding the normative rank of treaties, the Supreme Court has deduced such rank by considering that any violation of an international treaty must be considered as a violation of Article 4 of the constitution, which establishes that "The Republic of Panama respects the norms of international law."

Such norm has allowed the Supreme Court of Justice to consider as unconstitutional any violation of norms of international treaties. For instance, this was the case in a decision of March 12, 1990, where the Supreme Court declared the unconstitutionality of an Executive Decree that established general arbitrary conditions for the exercise of the rights to free expression and press (censorship), ruling that "such act violates Article 4 of the Constitution that obliges the national authorities to respect the international law norms" considering that in the case there was a "violation of the International Covenant on Human Rights and of the American Convention on Human Rights," which "rejects any prior censorship regarding the exercise of the freedoms of expression and press, as fundamental human rights."[52]

One of the consequences of giving constitutional rank to international treaties, such as to the American Convention, is that the rights declared in it are out of the reach of the legislative body, which cannot legislate diminishing in any way the enforcement or scope of such rights.

An example of this is the due process of law rights enshrined in the American Convention on Human Rights, like the right to a fair trial "with due guaranties and within a reasonable time, by a competent, independent, and impartial tribunal, previously established by law" (Article 8,1). And regarding the right to personal liberty, Article 7,2 and 7,5 set forth the right of every person not to "be deprived of his physical liberty ex-

---

[51]*Bramajo* case, September 12, 1996, in *Jurisprudencia Argentina*, Nov. 20, 1996. See Carlos Ayala Corao, "Recepción de la jurisprudencia internacional sobre derechos humanos por la jurisprudencia constitucional," in *Revista del Tribunal Constitucional*, n° 6, Sucre, Bolivia, Nov. 2004, pp. 275 ff. On the contrary, the Constitutional Chamber of the Supreme Tribunal of Justice in Venezuela has expressly ruled that: "It is a matter of prevalence of norms that is of treaties, covenants or agreements referred to human rights, but not to reports or opinions of international bodies which pretend to interpret the scope of international instruments." See decision n° 1942, July 7, 2003, in *Revista de Derecho Público*, n° 93-96, Editorial Jurídica Venezolana, Caracas, 2003, pp. 136 ff.

[52]See in *Iudicum et Vita, Jurisprudencia nacional de América Latina en Derechos Humanos,* n° 5, Instituto Interamericano de Derechos Humanos, San José, Costa Rica, Diciembre 1997 pp. 80–82.

cept for the reasons and under the conditions established beforehand by the constitution of the State Party concerned or by a law established pursuant thereto"; and the right of "any person detained shall be brought promptly before a judge or other officer authorized by law to exercise judicial power and shall be entitled to trial within a reasonable time or to be released without prejudice to the continuation of the proceedings."

These rights are also enshrined in the national constitutions and due to their declaration in the Convention, have constitutional rank, prohibiting in Latin America any possibility for the creation of special commissions to try any kind of offenses; and also prohibits for civilians to be tried by ordinary military courts and of course by military commissions. It also prohibits the creation of special courts to hear some criminal procedures after the offenses have been committed, in the sense that every person has the right to be heard only before courts existing prior to the offenses. In this regard, the Inter-American Court on Human Rights has issued important rulings against Member States of the Convention, for its violations.

For instance, in the *Cantoral Benavides* case (Peru) (2000), the Inter-American Court on Human Rights decided that Peru violated Article 8,1 of the Convention because Mr. Cantoral-Benavides was prosecuted by a military judge, which was not the "competent independent and impartial judge" provided for in that provision. Consequently the Court considered that Peru had also violated Article 7,5 of the Convention because the victim had been brought before a criminal military court.[53] By ruling this way it can even be considered that the Court has ruled that not any judiciary body can examine the legality and reasonability of a detention, but only those that do not violate the principle of "natural judge."[54]

---

[53] *Cantoral Benavides* case, Augst 18, 2000. Paragraph 75: "Also, the Court considers that the trial of Mr. Luis Alberto Cantoral Benavides in the military criminal court violated Article 8(1) of the American Convention, which refers to the right to a fair trial before a competent, independent and impartial judge (infra para. 115). Consequently, the fact that Cantoral-Benavides was brought before a military criminal judge does not meet the requirements of Article 7(5) of the Convention. Also, the continuation of his detention by order of the military judges constituted arbitrary arrest, in violation of Article 7(3) of the Convention." Paragraph 76: "The legal principle set forth in Article 7(5) of the Convention was not respected in this case until the accused was brought before a judge in the regular jurisdiction. In the file, there is no evidence of the date on which this occurred, but it can be reasonably concluded that it took place in early October 1993, since on October 8, 1993, the 43rd Criminal Court of Lima ordered that the investigation stage of a trial be opened against Cantoral Benavides." See in Sergio García Ramírez (Coord.), *Jurisprudencia de la Corte Intermericana de Derechos Humanos*, Universidad Nacional Autónoma de México, Corte Interamericana de Derechos Humanos, México, 2001, pp. 452 ff.

[54] See Cecilia Medina Quiroga, *La Convención Americana: Teoría y Jurisprudencia*, Universidad de Chile, Santiago, 2003, p. 231

And this is in fact one of the cores of the due process of law rights according to the Convention, the right to be heard by a competent court set forth not only by statute but by a statute that must be sanctioned previously to the offense. This is a provision tending to proscribe ad hoc courts or commissions.

The Inter-American Court has also referred to this due process of law right in the *Ivcher Bronstein* case (Peru) (2001). In this case, the Peruvian Executive Commission of the Judiciary, weeks before a resolution depriving Mr. Bronstein of his Peruvian citizenship was issued, altered the composition of a Chamber of the Supreme Court and empowered such Chamber to create, in a transitory way, specialized Superior chambers and Public Law specialized courts. The Supreme Court Chamber created one of such courts and appointed its judges, who heard the recourses filed by Mr. Bronstein. The Inter-American Court ruled as follows:

> 114.   The Court considers that by creating temporary public law chambers and courts and appointing judges to them at the time that the facts of the case *sub judice* occurred, the State did not guarantee to Mr. Ivcher Bronstein the right to be heard by judges or courts "previously established by law," as stipulated in Article 8 (1) of the American Convention.[55]

The Inter-American Court also ruled on these matters in the *Castillo Petruzzi et al.* case (Peru) (1999), where it decided that:

> 129.   A basic principle of the independence of the judiciary is that every person has the right to be heard by regular courts, following procedures previously established by law. States are not to create "tribunals that do not use the duly established procedures of the legal process [...] to displace the jurisdiction belonging to the ordinary courts or judicial tribunals.[56]

---

[55]*Ivcher Bronstein* case, February 6, 2001. Paragraphs 113–114. See in Sergio García Ramírez (Coord.), *Jurisprudencia de la Corte Intermericana de Derechos Humanos*, Universidad Nacional Autónoma de México, Corte Interamericana de Derechos Humanos, México, 2001, pp. 768 ff.

[56]*Castillo Petruzzi et al.* case, May 30, 1999, Paragraph 129. See in Sergio García Ramírez (Coord.), *Idem*, pp. 589 ff. The quotation corresponds to Basic Principles on the Independence of the Judiciary, adopted by the Seventh United Nations Conference on the Prevention of Crime and Treatment of Offenders, held in Milan August 26–September 6, 1985, and confirmed by the General Assembly in its resolutions 40/32 of November 29, 1985 and 40/146 of December 13, 1985.

Particularly regarding the need of a competent court, and referring to the military courts, the Inter-American Commission on Human Rights has considered that "to prosecute ordinary crimes as though they were military crimes simply because they had been committed by members of the military breached the guaranty of an independent and impartial tribunal;"[57] and the Inter-American Court ruled in the *Castillo Petruzzi et al.* case that due process of law rights were violated when ordinary common offenses are transferred to the military jurisdiction; that judging civilians for treason in such courts imply to exclude them from their "natural judge" to hear those proceedings; and that because military jurisdiction is set forth for the purpose of maintaining order and discipline within the armed forces, civilians cannot engage in behavior contrary to such military duties. The Court ruled as follows:

128.   The Court notes that several pieces of legislation give the military courts jurisdiction for the purpose of maintaining order and discipline within the ranks of the armed forces. Application of this functional jurisdiction is confined to military personnel who have committed some crime or were derelict in performing their duties, and then, only under certain circumstances. This was the definition in Peru's own law (Article 282 of the 1979 Constitution). Transferring jurisdiction from civilian courts to military courts, thus allowing military courts to try civilians accused of treason, mean that the competent, independent and impartial tribunal previously established by law is precluded from hearing these cases. In effect, military tribunals are not the tribunals previously established by law for civilians. Having no military functions or duties, civilians cannot engage in behaviors that violate military duties. When a military court takes jurisdiction over a matter that regular courts should hear, the individual's right to a hearing by a competent, independent and impartial tribunal previously established by law and, a fortiori, his right to due process is violated. That right to due process, in turn, is intimately linked to the very right of access to the courts.[58]

Finally, in the *Durand and Ugarte* case (1999) (Peru) the Inter-American Court ruled that:

117.   In a democratic Government of Laws, the penal military jurisdiction shall have a restrictive and exceptional scope and shall lead to the protection of special juridical interests, related to the functions assigned

[57] *Genie Lacayo* case, January 29, 1997, Paragraph 53. (Nicaragua). See in Sergio García Ramírez (Coord.), *idem,* pp. 181 ff.

[58] *Castillo Petruzzi et al.* case, May 30, 1999, Paragraph 128 and 132, in Sergio García Ramírez (Coord.), *idem,* pp. 589 ff.

by law to the military forces. Consequently, civilians must be excluded from the military jurisdiction scope and only the military shall be judged by commission of crime or offenses that by its own nature attempt against legally protected interests of military order.[59]

This excludes not only the processing of civilians by military courts, but additionally the possibility to assign to military courts cases of common felonies committed by military, even in the exercise of its functions. As was ruled by the same Inter-American Court:

118.   In this case, the military in charge of subduing the riots that took place in El Frontón prison resorted to a disproportionate use of force, which surpassed the limits of their functions thus also causing a high number of inmate deaths. Thus, the actions which brought about this situation cannot be considered as military felonies, but common crimes, so investigation and punishment must be placed on the ordinary justice, apart from the fact that the alleged active parties had been military or not.[60]

In contrast with the aforementioned, the absence of similar constitutional provisions in the United States, for instance, allowed endless legal discussions regarding the validity or invalidity of military commissions to try non-citizens for "acts of international terrorism" after the September 11 terrorist attacks;[61] the exclusion by statute for the federal court's jurisdiction to hear habeas corpus cases brought by detainees at the United States naval base at Guantanamo Bay, in Cuba;[62] and the denial for de-

---

[59] *Durand and Ugarte* case, August 16, 2000, Paragraph 117, in Sergio García Ramírez (Coord.), *idem,* pp. 484 ff.

[60] *Idem,* Paragraph 118.

[61] Like those set up by a military order of November 13, 2001, after the September 11 terrorist attacks. Nonetheless, the Supreme Court decided in June 29, 2006, in *Hamdan v. Rumsfeld* (Case n° 05-184) 126 S. Ct. 2749; 165 L. Ed. 2d 723, that "the military commission at issue lacks the power to proceed because its structure and procedure violate" both the Uniform Code of Military Justice and the Geneva Convention. See also *In re Hamdan* (Case n° 05-790), June 30, 2006, 126 S. Ct. 2981; 165 L. Ed. 2d 990, in which the petition for a writ of habeas corpus was denied.

[62] In *Hamdan v. Rumsfeld* case n° 05-184, on June 29, 2006, the Supreme Court ruled that such exclusion cannot apply to pending cases, 126 S. Ct. 2749; 165 L. Ed. 2d 723. On the same matter, Congress in September 2006, passed a *Military Commission Act,* preventing the Guantanamo detainees of the habeas corpus right to challenge their detention in court. The Supreme Court in *Boumediene v. Bush,* case n° 06-1195 and in *Al Odah v. United States* case n° 06-1196, after denying in previous decisions (127 S. Ct. 1478; 167 L. Ed. 2d 578) writs of certiorari filed by foreign citizens imprisoned at Guantanamo Bay, based on rules requiring the exhaustion of administrative remedies as a precondition to accepting

tainees to have access to a lawyer and to keep them in an open-ended detention.[63]

The references to the Inter-American Court cases are made in order to highlight what can happen in situations where there are no express constitutional rank given to some of these judicial guaranties and particularly to the right to be tried by judicially competent, independent and impartial courts established before the offenses were committed, as set forth in the American Convention on Human Rights. With those regulations, the matter cannot legally be discussed. Conversely, in the absence of such regulations, the discussions evidencing the struggle on the supremacy between the courts and the government, with the intervention of Congress, can finish by excluding the needed injunctive protection of constitutional rights in such cases.

In Latin America, after so many cases, experiences and stories of ad hoc commissions or special courts to try people with no due process of law rights, the provisions of the American Convention and those set forth in the constitutions do not allow even the discussion to be sustained. The violations of the constitution unfortunately can occur in a *de facto* way, as has happened many times, but without legal support, because the due process of law, with all its content, is a right declared in the constitutions out of the reach of Congress, so no legislation can be passed to restrict the courts' jurisdiction. And being a constitutional right, the amparo and habeas corpus protection can always be sought by the affected party, and eventually reach the American Court on Human Rights for the protection, as shown in the aforementioned cases.

jurisdiction over habeas applications; on June 12, 2008, on certiorari, accepted that alien detainees were entitled to seek a writ of habeas corpus to challenge their detention at Guantanamo Bay, Cuba, considering that 28 U.S.C.S. § 2241(e) violated art. I, § 9, cl. 2, of the U.S. Constitution, as the procedures of the Detainee Treatment Act, 109 Pub. L. No. 148, 119 Stat. 2680 (2006), were not an adequate and effective substitute for habeas corpus.

[63] In *Rumsfeld v. Hamft*, decided on April 3, 2006, 547 U.S. 1062; 126 S. Ct. 1649; 164 L. Ed. 2d 409, the Supreme Court denied the request of Mr. Padilla to hear his case, which left standing a decision of September 9, 2005 by the United States Court of Appeals for the Fourth Circuit, 423 F.3d 386, 2005 U.S. App., that endorsed the government's power to seize a citizen on United States soil declared as "enemy combatant" and keep him in indefinite detention, even though remaining in civilian custody.

C. The supra-statutory rank of international treaties on human rights

The third system regarding the rank of international treaties on human rights in internal law is characterized by granting to the treaties a supra-legal rank, in which cases, the treaties are subject to the constitution, but prevail over the statutes.

This is the solution followed in some European constitutions like the German (Article 25), Italian (Article 10) and French (Article 55) ones, and in Latin America, it is the solution expressly followed in the constitutions of Costa Rica (Article 7), El Salvador (Article 144) and Paraguay, which has allowed the Supreme Courts to exercise their powers of judicial review regarding internal legislation.

For instance, Article 7 of the Costa Rican Constitution provides that:

> Public treaties, international agreements and covenants duly approved by the Legislative Assembly shall... have superior authority to that of the laws.

Accordingly, the Constitutional Chamber of the Supreme Court, in a decision n° 2313-95, annulled the provision (Article 22) of the law regulating the profession of Journalism that imposed the obligatory membership or affiliation to the journalist board or association (*Colegio de Periodistas*) in order to exercise the profession, basing the annulment of the Statute provision on what the Inter-American Court on Human Rights previously had declared in an *Advisory Opinion n° OC-5 of 1985*. In that opinion, the Inter-American Court considered that "the compulsory affiliation of journalists is incompatible with Article 13 of the American Convention, because it impedes any other person to the full use of the media as a mean to express or transmit his information."[64]

---

[64]Consequently, the Chamber concluded the case by arguing that because Costa Rica was the Member State that requested from the Inter-American Court its Advisory Opinion: "When the Inter-American Court on Human Rights, in its *OC-05-85* unanimously decided that the obligatory affiliation of journalists set forth in Statute n° 4420 is incompatible with Article 13 of the American Convention on Human Rights because it impedes persons the access to the Media, [such Opinion] cannot but oblige the country that started the complex and costly procedure of the Inter-American system of protection of human rights..." The Chamber added "Being international instruments in force in the country, Article 7 of the Constitution does not apply, due to the fact that Article 48 of the same Constitution contains a special provision regarding treaties on human rights, giving them a normative force of constitutional level. To the point, as has been recognized by this Chamber's jurisprudence, the international instruments on human rights in force in Costa Rica, have not only a similar value to the Political Constitution, but they prevail over the Constitution when

The Constitutional Chamber considered that the Inter-American Court on Human Rights was the natural body for the interpretation of the American Convention, giving those interpretations "the value of an interpreted norm"[65]; thus annulling the article of the statute that "impedes certain persons to be affiliated to the Board of Journalists" considering as "incompatible, because it impedes the full use of the media as a vehicle to express and transmit information."[66]

The Court then exercising its powers on judicial review, decided not to "duplicate rulings," and based "on the same arguments of that Advisory Opinion" considered "that it is clear to Costa Rica that the provision of Statute n° 40... are illegitimate and contrary to the right to information in the wide sense which is developed in Article 13 of the San José of Costa Rica Convention, as well as in Articles 28 and 29 of the Political Constitution."[67]

It was also the case regarding the same aforementioned right to appeal, established in the American Convention. In a decision n° 719-90, the same Constitutional Chamber of Costa Rica, considering that Article 8.2 of the American Convention "recognizes as a fundamental right of everybody who has been criminally indicted, to appeal the judicial decision" declared the unconstitutionality of Article 474 of the Criminal Procedure Code which limited the filing of the cassation recourse in criminal matters.[68]

---

giving to persons more rights or guaranties (*vid.* decisions n° 3435-92 and n° 5759-93)." See Decision n° 2313-95 of May 9, 1995, in Rodolfo Piza Escalante, *La justicia constitucional en Costa Rica,* San José 1995; and in Carlos Ayala Corao, "Recepción de la jurisprudencia internacional sobre derechos humanos por la jurisprudencia constitucional," in *Revista del Tribunal Constitucional,* n° 6, Sucre, Bolivia, Nov. 2004, pp. 275 ff.

[65]Decision n° 2313-95 of May 9, 1995, in Rodolfo Piza Escalante, *idem,* and in Carlos Ayala Corao, *idem,* pp. 275 ff.

[66]*Advisory Opinion OC-5/85 of November 13, 1985.* La colegiación obligatoria de periodistas (arts. 13 y 29 Convención Americana sobre Derechos Humanos). See in Sergio García Ramírez (Coord.), *Jurisprudencia de la Corte Intermericana de Derechos Humanos,* Universidad Nacional Autónoma de México, Corte Interamericana de Derechos Humanos, México, 2001, pp. 963 ff.

[67]See also the text of the decision in Alfonso Gairaud Brenes, "Los Mecanismos de interpretación de los derechos humanos: especial referencia a la jurisprudencia Perúana," in José F. Palomino Manchego (ed), *El derecho procesal constitucional Perúano. Estudios en Homenaje a Domingo García Belaunde,* Editorial Jurídica Grijley, Lima, 2005, Tomo I, p. 133, note 21.

[68]Case of violation of Article 8.2 of the American Convention on Human Rights by the repealed Article 472 of the Criminal Procedures Code.

It must also be mentioned that through interpretation, the Constitutional Chamber of Costa Rica, in some decisions, has also given the international instruments on human rights supraconstitutional rank. Basing its ruling on Article 48 of the Constitution that refers to the action for amparo,[69] the Chamber has considered first, that "all the international instruments on human rights have been given a constitutional rank, and therefore, they must be incorporated in the interpretation of the Constitution particularly on this matter"[70]; and second, that they have "not only similar value as of the Constitution, but when they grant better rights or guaranties to people, they have prevalence regarding the Constitution."[71]

In a similar sense, the Constitutional Chamber of the Supreme Court of Justice of El Salvador has also applied international treaties on human rights when deciding cases on which the international regulations are considered to prevail, particularly in matters referring to the presumption of innocence and regarding the exceptional character of preventive detentions in criminal procedures. In a decision of November 17, 1994, the Court based its ruling in Article 11,1 of the Universal Declaration on Human Rights, Article 9,3 of the International Covenant on Civil and Political Rights, Article XXVI of the American Declarations of Human Rights and Articles 7,2 and 8,2 of the American Convention on Human Rights, concluding by stating that "it is within this constitutional and international context where the analysis of the provisional detention must be framed, because such provisions, due to their superior place in the normative hierarchy, are obligatory."[72]

---

[69]Established for the protection "of the rights set forth in the Constitution as well as those of fundamental character established in international instruments on human rights, applicables in the republic" (Article 48).

[70]See decision 10963-02 dated November 7, 2002, in Gilbert Armijo, "La tutela supraconstitucional de los derechos humanos en Costa Rica," in *Revista Ius et Praxis*, año 9, n° 1, Lima, p. 61; and in Humberto Nogueira Alcalá, "Los derechos fundamentales y los derechos humanos contenidos en los tratados internacionales y su ubicación en las fuentes del derecho: doctrina y jurisprudencia," in *Revista Peruana de Derecho Público*, n° 12, Lima, 2006, p. 87.

[71]Decision n° 3435-95 dated May 19, 1995, in Humberto Nogueira Alcalá, *Idem*, p. 87.

[72]In accordance with these provisions, the Constitutional Chamber of the Supreme Court of Justice of El Salvador has also applied international treaties on human rights in deciding cases on which the international regulations are considered to prevail. It was the case of a November 17, 1994, decision issued regarding a provisional detention of a former commander of the irregular armed forces, ordered in a defamatory criminal trial brought against him. The Chamber stated: "For the adequate comprehension of the provisional detention institution in our system, we must additionally bear in mind, according to Article 144 of the Constitution, what is set forth in the international treaties ratified by El Salvador." See in *Iudicum et Vita, Jurisprudencia nacional de América Latina en Derechos*

In another decision of the same Constitutional Chamber of the Supreme Court of El Salvador issued on June 13, 1995, the Chamber declared the unconstitutionality of a local government regulation (*Ordenanza municipal*), which established restrictions to the exercise of the political rights to assembly and to demonstration, basing its decision on Article 15 of the American Convention on Human Rights and in Article 21 of the International Covenant on Civil and Political Rights, according to which limitations to such rights can only be regulated by means of statutes.[73]

Humanos, n° 5, Instituto Interamericano de Derechos Humanos, San José, Costa Rica, Diciembre 1997, p. 157. So the Court analyzed Articles 11,1 of the Universal Declaration on Human Rights, and Article 9,3 of the International Covenant on Civil and Political Rights, which refers to the presumption of innocence and to the exceptional character of the preventive detention, which must not be considered as a general rule. The Court also analyzed Article XXVI of the American Declaration of Human Rights, which refers as well to the presumption of innocence; and Articles 7,2 and 8,2 of the American Convention on Human Rights, which refer to the rights of persons regarding detentions, particularly the principle *nulla pena sine lege*. From the aforementioned the Court concluded by stating that "It is within this constitutional and international context where the analysis of the provisional detention must be framed, because such provisions, due to their superior place in the normative hierarchy, are obligatory," *Idem*, p. 157. Consequently and based on the international regulations, regarding the preventive detention, the Chamber concluded that "It must never be considered as a general rule in criminal proceedings —as expressly forbidden in Article 9,3 of the International Covenant on Civil and Political Rights—, so that it cannot be automatically decided," because it cannot be understood as an anticipated sanction. On the contrary, in order to be decided, there needs to be in each case the judge's evaluation of the circumstances regarding its need and convenience for the protection of fundamental public interest. Based in the aforementioned, the Chamber concluded regarding the case, that "when the provisional detention was decided, the judge did not base its decision in any justification at all, thus being unconstitutional," *Idem*, p. 158.

[73] The Chamber argued as follows: "The international treaties in force in our country, having supremacy regarding secondary regulations, and among them, the Municipal Code, recognized the freedom of meeting and public demonstration and established that such rights can only be subjected to limitations or restrictions as are necessary in a democratic society and are provided in statutes," which "must be sanctions by the Legislative Assembly following the formalities set forth in the Constitution." The Chamber also ruled that such statute, according to Article XXVIII of the American Declaration on Human Rights, can only set forth limitations subjected to the "principle of reasonability," which means that they must be "intrinsically just, that is to say, that they must be in accordance to certain rules of enough value in order to give the sense to the substantive notion of justice enshrined in the Constitution." In this regard, the Chamber concluded its decision regarding the case, declaring the unconstitutionality of the challenged municipal regulation, stating: "None of these elements are found in the challenged instrument on grounds of unconstitutionality, that is to say, it is a typical case of authority abuse, not only because without any authorization it regulated a constitutional right, but because it usurped a function reserved to the legislative body." See in *Iudicum et Vita, Jurisprudencia nacional de*

In Paraguay the Constitution (Articles 137, 141), establishes the order of preference to be given to legal regulations; the treaties being located under the constitution but above the statutes. This has led the courts to apply with pre-emptive effects the American Convention, as was the case in a Court of Appeal's decision in criminal cases dated June 10, 1996, revoking a judicial decision of an inferior court that had sentenced a person for a defamation offense regarding a public political person, invoking for the revocation not only constitutional articles, but also Article 13 of the American Convention on Human Rights.[74]

D. The statutory rank of international treaties on human rights

Finally, regarding the legal hierarchy of international instruments of human rights, the fourth system on the matter attributes international treaties the same hierarchy as statutes. This system is the one most widespread in contemporary constitutional law, following the orientation that began with the Supremacy clause of the Constitution of the United States of America (Article VI. 2).

In such systems, therefore, "international law is part of the law of the land," the treaties having the same legal rank as the statutes as for instance is the case expressly regulated in Mexico, Uruguay and the Dominican Republic.

The Constitution of Mexico is perhaps the one among the Latin American countries that more closely resembles the U.S. Constitution in the wording of the Supremacy clause, giving the treaties the same rank as statutes (Article 133). Based on this provision, the Supreme Court of the Nation in a ruling C/92, June 30, 1992, decided that because the statutes have the same rank as treaties, they are "immediately below the Constitution in the hierarchy of norms of the Mexican legal order," consequently considering in the case that:

> [...] international treaties cannot be the criteria in order to determine the unconstitutionality of a statute, nor vice versa. Thus [-in the case-], the Commerce and Industrial Associations Statute cannot be considered un-

América Latina en Derechos Humanos, n° 5, Instituto Interamericano de Derechos Humanos, San José, Costa Rica, Diciembre 1997, pp. 47–53.

[74]See in *Iudicum et Vita, Jurisprudencia nacional de América Latina en Derechos Humanos*, n° 5, Instituto Interamericano de Derechos Humanos, San José, Costa Rica, Diciembre 1997, pp. 82–86.

constitutional because it is contrary to what is regulated in an international treaty.[75]

Nonetheless, this criteria was abandoned in 1998 by the same Supreme Court in a ruling n° 1475/98, in which the Court, interpreting Article 133 of the Constitution according to the 1969 Vienna Convention on Treaties determined that because "the international compromises are assumed by the Mexican State as a whole and all its authorities regarding the international community," the international treaties are located in a second level immediately under the Constitution and above the federal and local statutes.[76]

In Uruguay, based on Article 6 of the constitution, the Supreme Court of Justice in a decision of October 23, 1996, has also directly applied international treaties, by rejecting the question of unconstitutionality raised in a case regarding the Statute of the Press sanction system, which contained regulations guarantying the right of the defendant in cases of press offenses to be prosecuted while free. In the case, the Supreme Court carefully analyzed the human right of freedom of expression as regulated in Article 19 of the International Covenant of Civil and Political Rights and in Article 13.1 of the American Convention on Human Rights, referred to the *Advisory Opinion OC-O5* of the Inter-American Court on Human Rights on the incompatibility of the freedom of expression with the obligatory affiliation of journalists to the Journalist's Board in Costa Rica, and also referred to the presumption of innocence right "expressly set forth in the international Declarations and Conventions"; considering that all of them allowed the defendant to be tried in freedom.[77]

The Dominican Republic constitutional system can also be classified in this group of countries with a constitution that gives treaties the same legal rank as statutes. This system must be highlighted, particularly because of its importance regarding the amparo action, due to the fact that

---

[75] *Tesis* P. C/92, in *Gaceta del Semanario Judicial de la Federación*, n° 60, diciembre de 1992, México, p. 27.

[76] See Guadalupe Barrena y Carlos Montemayor "Incorporación del derecho internacional en la Constitución mexicana," *Derechos Humanos. Memoria del IV Congreso Nacional de Derecho Constitucional,* Vol. III, Instituto de Investigaciones Jurídicas, Universidad Nacional Autónoma de México, México, 2001, *cit.,* by Humberto Henderson, "Los tratados internacionales de derechos humanos en el orden interno: la importancia del principio *pro homine,*" in *Revista IIDH,* Instituto Interamericano de Derechos Humanos, n° 39, San José, 2004, p. 82, note 15.

[77] See in *Iudicum et Vita, Jurisprudencia nacional de América Latina en Derechos Humanos,* n° 5, Instituto Interamericano de Derechos Humanos, San José, Costa Rica, Diciembre 1997, pp. 72–79.

apart from Cuba, the Dominican Republic is the only other Latin American country that does not have in its constitution an express regulation regarding the amparo action. And it was precisely because of this lack of regulation that the Supreme Court applied the American Convention of Human Rights in order to admit and create the amparo recourse.[78]

It happened with a Supreme Court decision of February 24, 1999, in which the amparo action was admitted (*Productos Avon S.A.* case), considering it as a "public law institution" of the country, and in which the Court determined the basic rules of procedure for such actions. The Supreme Court, in order to decide, considered that Articles 8 and 25,1 of the American Convention on Human Rights, were part of internal Dominican law, admitting the amparo action as a guaranty for the judicial protection of fundamental rights recognized in the Constitution.[79]

---

[78]Article 3 of the Dominican Republic Constitution states that "The Dominican Republic recognizes and applies international law regulations, general and American ones, when they have been approved by the State organs," and accordingly, in 1977 the Congress approved the American Convention on Human Rights, whose Articles 8 and 25,1 as aforementioned, regulate the general due process of law rules and the amparo action or recourse for the judicial protections of human rights. Thus, according to these regulations, if it is true that the Constitution does not set forth the amparo action, it is regulated in the American Convention and then it can be exercised by anybody seeking protection of his human rights. But the problem was the absence of procedural rules, comprising the absence of formal attribution to specific courts of the power to decide upon amparo suits. That explains why actions or recourses of amparo were never brought before courts, until 1999, when a private company, the Avon enterprise, did so before the Supreme Court of Justice, against a judicial decision on labor matters, alleging violations of constitutional rights.

[79]See the text *Iudicum et Vita, Jurisprudencia nacional de América Latina en Derechos Humanos*, n° 7, Tomo I, Instituto Interamericano de Derechos Humanos, San José, Costa Rica, Diciembre 2000, p. 329 ff. The case developed as follows: 1. The plaintiff company claimed that a judicial decision on labor matters, issued by a lower court, violated its rights to be judged by the competent court of justice, asking the Supreme Court: First: To declare in its ruling that the amparo recourse be considered as a Dominican public law institution; and second, that the Supreme Court, according to the provisions of the Organic Judicial statute that attributed to the Supreme Court the power to resolve on adjective matters when a specific procedure does not have a statutory regulation, to set forth the procedure to be followed regarding the amparo recourses. Additionally, the plaintiff asked the Court to issue a preliminary order suspending the effects of the challenged judicial labor decisions, pending the course of the trial. 2. The Supreme Court, in order to decide, fixed the criteria that the international treaties invoked by the plaintiff, particularly Articles 8 and 25,1 of the American Convention on Human Rights, as internal Dominican law, have the purpose to guaranty the judicial protection of fundamental rights recognized in the Constitution, the law and the said Convention, against acts that violate such rights, committed by any person acting or not in their public functions thus also against individuals' actions. In this regard,

A few years later, in 2006, an amparo law was sanctioned in the Dominican Republic, based on the fact that by ratifying the American Convention, the Dominican Republic incorporated the amparo action into its internal law, as one of the procedural means or guaranties for the protection of constitutional rights, that the legislator was due to regulate following the simple and prompt character of such action as was set forth in the Convention.

the Supreme Court decided that: "Contrary to what has been decided in the sense that the offending acts must be issued by judicial officials or persons acting in such functions, the amparo recourse, it is considered that as a protection mechanism of individual freedom in its various aspects, the amparo must not be excluded as a judicial remedy in order to resolve situations originated by persons accomplishing judicial functions. Article 25,1 of the Convention, provides that the amparo recourse is open in favor of anybody against acts which violate his fundamental rights even when the violation is committed by individuals that are not acting accomplishing public functions; evidently including the judicial functions; ... as well as against any action or omission from individuals or public administration officials, including omissions or non- jurisdictional administrative acts from the courts, if they affect a constitutional protected right" (*Idem*. p. 332). 3. Regarding the Dominican Republic Supreme Court decision, it additionally decided that even in the absence of procedural rules for the amparo recourse, contrary to what happens regarding habeas corpus recourses (where there is a statute establishing the competent court and the procedure); and because the amparo recourse is a simple, speedy and effective judicial mean for the protection of all constitutional rights other than those protected by means of habeas corpus, no judge can refuse to admit it adducing the absence of statutory regulation. For that purpose, the Supreme Court invoked its power according to Article 29,2 of the Judicial Organization Statute, to establish the procedural rules in order to avoid the confusion that can cause the absence of such rules. Consequently, the Supreme Court decided "to declare that the recourse set forth in Article 25,1 of the November 22, 1969 San José, Costa Rica American Convention on Human Rights, is an institution of Dominican positive law, due to its approval by the National Congress through resolution n° 739 of December 1977, according to Article 3 of the Constitution." On the other hand, the Supreme Court resolved the practical problems derived from the acceptance of the amparo suit, by setting forth the procedural rules, as follows: First, by determining that the competent courts to decide on the matter are the courts of first instance in the place in which the challenged act or omission has been produced; and second, by stating adjective rules of procedure, similar to those established in Articles 101 and following the Statute n° 834 of 1978, adding references to the delay to bring the action before the court, to the hearing that has to take place, the delay for the decision and the delay for the appeal. The Supreme Court finally remembered, in order to avoid abuses in the use of the action, that the amparo recourse must not be understood as the introduction of a third instance in the judicial process. See the comments in Allan R. Brewer-Carías, "La admisión jurisprudencial de la acción de amparo en ausencia de regulación constitucional o legal en la República Dominicana" (*Idem*, pp. 334).

3. *The interpretative constitutional rules regarding the international instruments on human rights*

Regardless of the absence of express constitutional regulations regarding the hierarchy of international treaties on human rights in the internal legal system, whether supraconstitutional, constitutional, supra-statutory or statutory rank, in some Latin American countries such instruments are also considered as having constitutional value and rank by means of different constitutional interpretation rules established in the same constitutions.

This is the case, for instance, when they refer to the interpretation of constitutional rights prescribing that it must always be done according to what is set forth in the international treaties; and also, when the preambles or general declarations of the constitutions make references to the universal declarations on human rights.

A. The interpretation of the constitution according to the provisions of international instruments

In the first cases, some constitutions expressly set forth a guiding rule for interpreting human rights declared in their text, requiring that such interpretation be made in accordance to what is set forth in the international treaties on human rights. This technique was initiated with the Spanish (Article 10,2) and Portuguese (Article 16,2) Constitutions, which influenced the drafting of the 1991 Colombian Constitution, in which Article 93 establishes that:

> The rights and duties provided in this Charter shall be interpreted pursuant to the international treaties on human rights ratified by Colombia.

Following this constitutional provision –in addition to the recognition of supraconstitutional rank to treaties–, all State bodies have to interpret the constitutional regulations regarding human rights pursuant to the provisions of the international treaties on the matter, which has resulted in the recognition by the Supreme Courts or Constitutional Courts of constitutional value for those rights declared in international treaties, which are the ones that must guide the interpretation of the rights declared in the constitution.

In this sense, the Constitutional Court in Colombia has frequently used this technique when interpreting the extent of constitutional rights, as it was the case in a decision of February 22, 1996, issued in a judicial review process filed on the grounds of unconstitutionality against the statute that regulates television networks, considered by the plaintiff as being contrary to the constitutional right to inform.

The Constitutional Court considered that "the internal validity of a statute is not only subjected to the conformity of its regulations to what is set forth in the Constitution, but also to what is prescribed in the international treaties approved by Congress and ratified by the President of the Republic."[80] In order to decide the case, the Constitutional Chamber referred to the constitutional freedom of expression of thoughts and of information, established in Article 19,3 of the International Covenant on Human Rights and in Article 13,2 of the American Convention on Human Rights, particularly regarding the universality of the exercise of such rights "without any considerations of frontiers"; and concluded by ruling that:

> To forbid in the national territory the installation or functioning of land stations devoted to receive and later to diffuse, transmit or distribute television signals coming from satellites, whether national or international, is a flagrant violation of the right to be informed which everybody has pursuant to Article 20 of the Constitution.[81]

This interpretative technique of human rights according to what is established in international instruments on the matter has also been established, for instance, in the Peruvian Constitutional Procedure Code, that sets forth:

> *Article V. Interpretation of constitutional rights.* The content and the scope of constitutional rights protected by means of the constitutional process established in this Code must be interpreted according to the Universal Declaration on Human Rights, the treaties on human rights, as well as to the decisions issued by the international courts on human rights established according to treaties in which Peru is a Party.

B.   The constitutional general references to the universal declarations on human rights

In other cases, the interpretative technique through which international declarations on human rights can also acquire constitutional rank and value, results from the general declarations contained in the preambles or in the constitutional text precisely referring to those international declara-

---

[80]See in *Iudicum et Vita, Jurisprudencia nacional de América Latina en Derechos Humanos,* n° 5, Instituto Interamericano de Derechos Humanos, San José, Costa Rica, December 1997, pp. 34–35.

[81]*Idem,* p. 37.

tions on human rights.[82] This is the case of Guatemala, Chile, Ecuador, Nicaragua and Brazil.

Following these provisions in which the general purpose of the countries' constitution to guaranty, to promote and to encourage the full enjoyment and enforcement of human rights referred to their universal context, the rights contained in the international declarations and treaties have been considered or interpreted as having the same value and rank to those expressly declared in the Constitution's texts themselves.

In Chile, for instance, the constitution has a declaration limiting the exercise of sovereignty by the "respect for the essential rights to be found in human nature;" also prescribing as a "duty of State bodies to respect and promote the rights guaranteed by this Constitution, as well as by international treaties ratified by Chile and currently in force" (Article 5,II). Hence, if it is the State's duty to respect and promote human rights that are guaranteed by international treaties, such rights acquire the same rank and value as the constitutional rights expressly listed in the constitutional text itself.

The Constitution of Ecuador also prescribes the State's obligation "... to respect and to assure for the respect of human rights guaranteed by this Constitution" (Article 16); assuring to "all its citizens, with no discrimination whatsoever, the free and effective exercise and enjoyment of the human rights established in this Constitution and in the declarations, covenants, agreements and other current international instruments in force," which therefore have been considered as acquiring the same rank and value of constitutional rights.

Also in Nicaragua, the constitution guarantees the protection of the State for the "full enforcement of the rights enshrined in the Universal Declaration of Human Rights; in the American Declaration of the Rights

---

[82]Regarding the preambles of the constitution, many of the post-war constitutions contain general declarations regarding human rights, with particular reference to universal declarations. The classic example is the 1958 French Constitution in which, without containing in its text a Bill of Rights, the following general declaration is contained in its Preamble: "The French people hereby solemnly proclaim their dedication to the Rights of Man and the principle of national sovereignty as defined by the Declaration of 1789, reaffirmed and complemented by the Preamble to the 1946 Constitution." By means of this general declaration the Constitutional Council has enlarged the constitutionality block, attributing constitutional value and rank to all the fundamental rights contained in the 1789 Declaration of Rights of Citizens and Man. See J. Rivero, "Rapport de Synthèse," in L. Favoreu, (ed.), *Cours constitutionnelles europeenes et droit fondamentaux*, Aix-en-Provence, 1982, p. 520.

and Duties of Man; in the United Nations' International Covenant on Civil and Political Rights; and in the American Convention on Human Rights of the Organization of American States" (Article 46). Based on this article, statutes have been challenged before the Supreme Court on the grounds of unconstitutionality because they violate the rights declared in international treaties.

It was for instance the case of a 1989 judicial review process against the General statute on Media (*Ley General sobre los medios de la Comunicación Social, Ley n° 57*), in which the Supreme Court, in a decision of August 22, 1989, even if it rejected the "amparo of unconstitutionality" recourse filed against the statute, in order to decide, extensively considered the denounced violations not only regarding Article 46 of the Constitution but also through it, considered the corresponding articles of the Human Rights Declaration, the International Covenant on Civil and Political Rights and the American Convention on Human Rights.[83]

The Constitution of Brazil can also be mentioned when it proclaims that the State in its international relations, is governed by the principle of the prevalence of human rights (Article 4,III; Article 5,2), which has been interpreted as a mean for inserting the constitution in the general trend of Latin American constitutionalism that gives a special treatment in internal law to the rights internationally guaranteed.

C. The enforcement of rights regardless of their statutory regulation

Other constitutions have also accepted the application of international treaties on human rights in internal law, by inserting in their texts clauses prescribing the principle of the enforcement of constitutional rights regardless of the existence of statutory regulations; a very important provision, particularly in matters of social rights that for instance can be found in Ecuador and Venezuela.

In Ecuador, the constitution states that: "The absence of statute cannot be alleged in order to justify or ignore rights set forth in this Constitution,

---

[83] See the text in *Iudicum et Vita, Jurisprudencia nacional de América Latina en Derechos Humanos*, n° 5, Instituto Interamericano de Derechos Humanos, San José, Costa Rica, December 1997, pp. 128–140. See the comments of Antonio Cancado Trindade, "Libertad de expresión y derecho a la información en los planos internacional y nacional," *Idem*, p. 194.

or to deny the admission of actions for their protections, or to deny the acknowledgment of such rights" (Article 18).

A similar clause exists in Venezuela that was incorporated in the 1961 constitution, and it was precisely based on that clause, that the amparo action was initially admitted in Venezuela even in the absence of statutory regulation.

The 1961 constitution provision regarding the amparo action (Article 49) provided in general terms that "the courts shall protect (*"ampararán"*) all inhabitants of the Republic in the exercise of their rights and guaranties set forth in the Constitution, according to the law" (statute). The wording of this article, particularly the phrase "according to what is established in the law," was initially interpreted by the courts in the sense that the admissibility of the amparo suit needed the previous enactment of a statute regulating the matter; an interpretation that was reinforced by the fact that the constitution in a transitory provision established in an exceptional way for the immediate admissibility of the amparo action only when seeking for the protection of personal freedom, called the habeas corpus action.[84]

Because of this, the Supreme Court of Justice in a decision dated December 14, 1970, considered Article 49 of the Constitution to be what it called a "programmatic" clause, thus not directly applicable, and in order to bring before a court an action of amparo, the previous enactment of the statute on the matter would be necessary.[85]

This constitutional judicial approach began to change precisely after the approval by the Venezuelan Congress in 1977 and 1978, of the American Convention on Human Rights and the International Covenant on Civil and Political Rights; which regulated the need for a simple and prompt judicial mean for the protection of human rights.

Consequently, contrary to the Supreme Court initial interpretation, since 1982 the lower courts began to admit amparo actions, precisely basing their rulings on the American Convention.[86] This situation finally led the Supreme Court in a decision of October 20, 1983, to change its

---

[84]See Allan R. Brewer-Carías, *Instituciones Políticas y Constitucionales, Tomo V, Derecho y Acción de Amparo*, Caracas, 1998, pp. 111 ff.

[85]See in *Gaceta Forense*, n° 70, Caracas, 1970, pp. 179 ff.; and in Allan R. Brewer-Carías, *Instituciones Políticas y Constitucionales, Tomo V, El derecho y la acción de amparo*, Universidad Católica del Táchira, Editorial Jurídica Venezolana, Caracas, 1998, pp. 113 ff.

[86]See the references in Allan R. Brewer-Carías, "La reciente evolución jurisprudencial en relación con la admisibilidad del recurso de amparo," in *Revista de Derecho Público*, n° 19, Editorial Jurídica Venezolana, Caracas, 1984, pp. 211 ff.

own criteria, admitting the amparo action by applying the open clause on human rights inherent to persons, and particularly the provision that states that the absence of a regulatory statute regarding human rights cannot affect the exercise of the rights declared in the constitution.[87] Later, in 1988 the Amparo Statute was sanctioned by Congress.

D. The principle of progressive interpretation of constitutional rights

In spite of the absence of express constitutional provisions for the interpretation of human rights, the international instruments have also been applied in internal law, by means of the principle of progressiveness in the interpretation of human rights,[88] in the sense that as a matter of principle, no interpretation of statutes related to human rights can be admitted if the result is to diminish the effective enjoyment, exercise or guaranty of constitutional rights; and also that in cases involving various provisions, the one that should prevail is the one that contains the more favorable regulation.[89]

The principle of progressiveness in some cases has been expressly regulated in the constitutions, as is the case, for example, in the 1999 Constitution of Venezuela, where Article 19 provides that the enjoyment and exercise of human rights shall be guaranteed to everybody by the State, "pursuant to the principle of progressiveness and without any discrimination." Other constitutions also expressly establish the principle, as is the case of the Ecuadorian Constitution, providing that "in matters of constitutional rights and guaranties, the interpretation that most favors its effective enforcement shall be the one upheld" (Article 18).

This principle of the progressiveness has also been called as the *pro homine* principle of interpretation, which implies that in resolving a case, the courts must always prefer the provisions that are in favor of man (*pro homine*),"[90] which is also incorporated in the Ecuatorian Constitution (Article 18).[91]

[87]See in *Revista de Derecho Público*, n° 11, Editorial Jurídica Venezolana, Caracas, 1983, pp. 167–170.

[88]See Pedro Nikken, *La protección internacional de los derechos humanos: su desarrollo progresivo*, Instituto Interamericano de Derechos Humanos, Ed. Civitas, Madrid, 1987.

[89]See the former Supreme Court of Venezuela Decision of July 30, 1996, in *Revista de Derecho Público*, n° 67-68, Editorial Jurídica Venezolana, Caracas, 1996, p. 170.

[90]See Mónica Pinto, "El principio *pro homine*. Criterio hermenéutico y pautas para la regulación de los derechos humanos," in *La aplicación de los tratados sobre derechos Humanos por los tribunales locales,* Centro de Estudios Legales y Sociales, Buenos Aires, 1997, p. 163. Also see, Humberto Henderson, "Los tratados internacionales de derechos

It also has been deduced as incorporated in other constitutions, as is the case of the Constitution of Chile (Article 5) and of Peru (Article 1), when they provide as one of the essential purposes of the State, the protection of human rights.[92]

This has led, for instance, the Constitutional Tribunal in Peru to define "the *pro homine* principle as the one according to which a rule referred to human rights must be interpreted 'in the most favorable way for the person, that is, for the beneficiary of the interpretation."[93]

humanos en el orden interno: la importancia del principio *pro homine,*" in *Revista IIDH,* Instituto Interamericano de Derechos Humanos, n° 39, San José, 2004, p. 92; and Florentín Meléndez, *Instrumentos internacionales sobre derechos humanos aplicables a la administración de justicia. Estudio constitucional comparado,* Cámara de Diputados, México, 2004, pp. 118 ff.

[91]See Hernán Salgado Pesantes, *Manual de Justicia Constitucional Ecuatoriana,* Corporación Editora Nacional, Quito, 2004, p. 92.

[92]See Iván Bazán Chacón, "Aplicación del derecho internacional en la judicialización de violaciones de derechos humanos," in *Para hacer justicia. Reflexiones en torno a la judicialización de casos de violaciones de derechos humanos,* Coordinadora Nacional de Derechos Humanos, Lima, 2004, p. 27; Humberto Henderson, "Los tratados internacionales de derechos humanos en el orden interno: la importancia del principio *pro homine,*" in *Revista IIDH,* Instituto Interamericano de Derechos Humanos, n° 39, San José, 2004, p. 89, footnote 27. As it has been indicated by Henderson, the *pro homine* principle has various application forms: first, when various provisions on human rights can be applied in the case, the one to be chosen is the one with the best and must favorable provisions regarding the individual; second, in case rulings succession, it must be understood that the last provision does not repeal the previous one if this has better and more favorable provisions that must be preserved; and third, when it is a matter of application of just one legal provision on human rights, the same must be interpreted in the way resulting more favorable to the protection of the person. *Idem,* pp. 92–96.

[93]See decision 1049-2003-AA/TC of January 30, 2004, in Alfonso Gairaud Brenes, "Los Mecanismos de interpretación de los derechos humanos: especial referencia a la jurisprudencia Perúana," in José F. Palomino Manchego, *El derecho procesal constitucional Perúano. Estudios en Homenaje a Domingo García Belaunde,* Editorial Jurídica Grijley, Lima 2005, Tomo I, p.138; and in Humberto Henderson, "Los tratados internacionales de derechos humanos en el orden interno: la importancia del principio *pro homine,*" in *Revista IIDH,* Instituto Interamericano de Derechos Humanos, n° 39, San José, 2004, pp. 92–96.

This principle of progressivism,[94] regarding the interpretation of constitutional rights, has also been incorporated in the American Convention on Human Rights by providing rules (Article 29) in order to guaranty that "no provision of this Convention shall be interpreted" as permitting any State Member, group, or person to suppress the enjoyment or exercise of the rights and freedoms recognized in the Convention or to restrict them to a greater extent than is provided in it; or to preclude other rights or guaranties that are inherent in the human personality or derived from representative democracy as a form of government.[95]

The principle also implies that if a constitutional right is regulated with different contexts in the constitution and in international treaties, then the most favorable provision must prevail and be applicable to the interested party."[96]

[94]In a certain way this *pro homine* interpretation was the one that guided Chief Justice Warren of the United States Supreme Court in its 1954 opinion in *Brown v. Board of Education of Topeka, Kansas*, 347 U.S. 483 (1954). in which, when referring to the fourteenth Amendment, he said that: "In approaching this problem, we cannot turn the clock back to 1868 when the Amendment was adopted, or even to 1896 when *Plessy v. Fersugon* was written. We must consider public education in the light of its full development and its present place in American life throughout the Nation. Only in this way can it be determined if segregation in public schools deprives these plaintiffs of the equal protection of the laws." From this he concluded saying: "We conclude that in the field of public education the doctrine of "separate but equal" has no place. Separate educational facilities are inherently unequal. Therefore, we hold that the plaintiffs and others similarly situated for whom the actions have been brought are, by reason of the segregation complained of, deprived of the equal protection of the laws guaranteed by the Fourteenth Amendment. This disposition makes unnecessary any discussion whether such segregation also violates the Due Process Clause of the Fourteenth Amendment."

[95]See Florentín Meléndez, *Instrumentos internacionales sobre derechos humanos aplicables a la administración de justicia. Estudio constitucional comparado*, Cámara de Diputados, México, 2004, pp. 124 ff.

[96]It was the case, for instance of an amparo decision issued by the former Supreme Court of Justice of Venezuela on December 3, 1990, in which the Court applied the principle regarding the rights of a pregnant public employee not to be unjustifiably dismissed of her job during pregnancy. The matter was not regulated at that time in the Statute on Labor, and it was only set forth in the Covenant n° 103 of the Labor International Organization and in the Convention eliminating all forms of discrimination against women. Notwithstanding the Supreme Court, after analyzing the protection asked for by the employee whose dismissal impeded her from enjoying the maternity leave, admitted the amparo and declared the requested protection, considering such right as inherent to human beings. See in *Revista de Derecho Público*, n° 45, Editorial Jurídica Venezolana, Caracas, 1991, pp. 84–85; and in *Revista de Derecho Público*, n° 97-98, Editorial Jurídica Venezolana, Caracas, 1996, p. 170.

CHAPTER TWO

JUDICIAL GUARANTIES OF THE DECLARATION OF HUMAN RIGHTS

Constitutional declarations of rights, in the constitutions or in international treaties and covenants, would be of no use at all if those rights were not supported by a set of constitutional guaranties for their protection.

So, if the first of all constitutional guaranties is the guaranty of the supremacy of the constitution and its content; the second is the judicial guaranty, that is to say, the set of judicial means established in benefit of persons in order to assure not only the supremacy of the constitution but the effective exercise and protection of the rights therein contained.

Regarding the supremacy of the constitution and the role of the judiciary, one important feature of the Latin American contemporary constitutionalism is that they are not just a deduction constructed from constitutional clauses, as was formulated by Alexander Hamilton in his writings in *The Federalist*[97] (1788), where he referred to the constitution as a fun-

---

[97] The idea of Rule of Law is indissolubly bound to the idea of the constitution as an essential and supreme rule that shall prevail over any state rule or action. This was the great and principal contribution of the American Revolution to modern constitutionalism, and its progressive development has provided the basis for the constitutional systems of justice in the modern world, particularly those aimed at protecting and defending the rights and freedoms enshrined in the constitutions. It can be said that this idea of constitutional supremacy, that is, of the constitution as a fundamental and supreme law, was first developed in America in 1788 by Alexander Hamilton in *The Federalist*, when referring to the role of judges as interpreters of the law, stating: "A constitution is, in fact, and must be regarded by the judges, as a fundamental law. Therefore, it belongs to them to ascertain its meaning, as well as the meaning of any particular act proceeding from the legislative body. If there should happen to be an irreconcilable variance between the two, that which has the superior obligation and validity ought, of course, to be preferred; or, in other words, the constitution ought to be preferred to the Statute, the intention of the people to the intention of their agents." He added in response to the assertion that "the rights of the courts to pronounce legislative acts void, because contrary to the constitution" would "imply a superior-

damental and superior law; to the role of judges as the interpreters of the constitution, being obliged to prefer it to the statutes, and to their power to pronounce legislative acts void, when contrary to the constitution. This was the doctrine later developed by the courts, and in particular, by the Supreme Court after *Marbury v. Madison* U.S. (1 Cranch), 137; 2 L. Ed. 60 (1803).[98]

Instead, in Latin America, the principles have been explicitly set forth in the text of many constitutions. For instance, as declared in the Constitution of Colombia (1991):

> *Article 4.* The Constitution is the law of laws. Whenever a case of incompatibility between the Constitution and a statute or other legal norms arises, the constitutional provisions shall be applied.

The 1999 Constitution of Venezuela similarly establishes that "the Constitution is the supreme rule and basis of the legal system" (Article 7) and that "in case of incompatibility between this Constitution and a statute or other legal norm, the constitutional provisions shall be applied,

---

ity of the judiciary to the legislative powers," the following: "Nor does this conclusion – that the Courts must prefer the constitution over statutes– by any means supposes a superiority of the judicial to the legislative body. It only supposes that the power of the people is superior to both; and that where the will of the legislature, declared in its Statutes stands in opposition to that of the people declared in the constitution, the judges ought to be governed by the latter rather than the former. They ought to regulate their decisions by the fundamental laws, rather than by those which are not fundamental." Thus, his conclusive assertion that: "No legislative act, therefore, contrary to the constitution, can be valid. To deny this, would be to affirm, that the deputy is greater than his principal; that the servant is above his master; that the representative of the people are superior to the peoples themselves; that men acting by virtue of powers, may do not only what their powers do not authorize, but what they forbid." Thus, in *The Federalist*, Hamilton not only developed the doctrine of the supremacy of the constitution, but most importantly the doctrine of "the judges as guardians of the constitution," as the title of letter n° 78 reads where Hamilton said, considering the constitution as a limit to state powers and particularly to the legislative authority, that "Limitations of this kind can be preserved in practice no other way than through the medium of courts of justice, whose duty it must be to declare all acts contrary to the manifest tenor of the constitution, void. Without this, all the reservations of particular rights or privileges would amount to nothing." See *The Federalist* (ed. by B. F. Wright), Cambridge, Mass., 1961, p. 491–493.

[98]See for instance the references to the *Vanhorne's Lessee v. Dorrance* case, 1776, in Allan R. Brewer-Carías, *Judicial Review in Comparative Law*, Cambridge University Press, Cambridge, 1989. On *Marbury v. Madison* see in general, Mark A. Graber and Michael Perchac, *Marbury versus Madison: Documents and Commentary*, CQ Press, Washington, 2002.

being the courts empowered to decide on the matter, even *ex officio*" (Article 334).

So, after the U. S. principles and experience and after the judicial evolution and creation of judicial review of constitutionality of legislation, judicial review was expressly enshrined in Latin American constitutional provisions, empowering the courts, not only to declare the unconstitutionality of statutes in a particular case, but also, through constitutional courts and tribunals to annul such statutes with general, *erga omnes* effects; and in addition, by means of the amparo action, to assure the protection of constitutional rights.[99]

Another guaranty of the constitution that can be found in Latin America regarding constitutional rights is the so-called "objective guaranty" of the constitutional text, explained by Hans Kelsen[100] almost one century ago, according to which, any act contrary to the constitution shall be considered null and void; a principle that is also established in an express way in some constitutions, like the Venezuelan (Article 25) and the Peruvian (Article 31) ones. In the former, it is established that:

> *Article 25:* Any State act that violates or harms the rights guaranteed in this Constitution and the law is null; and the public officials who orders or execute them shall be criminally, civilly and administratively liable, without any possible excuses based on superior orders.

However, among all these guaranties, the fundamental and basic one referred to constitutional rights is of course the possibility of bringing claims before the courts in order to assure that such rights are protected, preventing their violation or restoring the affected party in its exercise.

---

[99]Therefore, modern constitutionalism is founded not only on the principle of constitutional supremacy, but also on the principle that the *citizens have a constitutional right to such supremacy*, that in fact, pursuant to the principle of separation of powers, becomes *a fundamental right to the judicial protection of such constitutional supremacy*, both regarding the organic part of the constitution (separation of powers, territorial distribution of powers), as well as regarding the dogmatic part of the constitution (human rights), for the preservation of which a set of guaranties are established.

[100]See Hans Kelsen, "La garantie jurisdictionnelle de la Constitution (La justice constitutionnelle)," in *Revue du droit public et de la science politique en France et à l'étranger*, Paris, 1928, p. 250.

I. THE JUDICIAL GUARANTIES OF CONSTITUTIONAL RIGHTS

Regarding constitutional rights and freedoms (those embodied in the constitutional declarations of rights), their judicial protection and guaranty in general terms can only be achieved when an independent and autonomous judiciary exists, in two ways:

First, by means of the general established (ordinary or extraordinary) suits, actions, recourses or writs regulated in procedural law; and

Second, in addition to those general means, through specific judicial suits, actions or recourses seeking remedies specifically and particularly established in order to protect and enforce constitutional rights and freedoms and to prevent and redress wrongs regarding those rights.

That is, the judicial guaranty of constitutional rights can be achieved through the general procedural regulations that are established in order to enforce any kind of personal or proprietary rights and interest, as for instance is the case in the United States and in Europe; or it can also be achieved by means of a specific judicial proceeding established only and particularly for the protection of the rights declared in the constitution. This last solution can be considered as the general trend in Latin America, mainly because the traditional insufficiencies of the general judicial means for granting effective protection to constitutional rights.

In the United States, in effect, following the British procedural law tradition, the protection of civil, constitutional and human rights has always been achieved through the general ordinary or extraordinary judicial means, and particularly, by means of the remedies established in Law or in Equity.

This distinction between Law and Equity in order to construct two judicial systems of courts, traditionally inherent to the Anglo-American legal system,[101] is the consequence of the distinction between causes at

---

[101] The concept of equity has also penetrated the civil law countries, where the judges can also decide cases based on *"equidad,"* a term also used in procedural law. For example, in the Venezuelan Civil Code, Article 12 imposes upon the judges the duty to decide cases in conformity with the rules of law (*normas de derecho*), unless a statute authorizes them to decide accordingly to *"equidad"*; and Article 13 indicates that the courts will decide the merits of the case based on *"equidad"* only when asked to do so by the agreed consent of the parties and the rights involved in the controversy are rights that can be renounced or transferred, such as property rights. The code also distinguishes between "law arbiters" (*árbitros de derecho*) and arbitrators. The former must always decide according to the legal procedure and to the law; the latter will proceed with complete liberty, according to their most convenient view in the parties' interest, particularly according to *"equidad"* (Article

law and actions in equity, and between the legal remedies as opposed to equitable ones.

The most common legal remedies are the damage remedies, the restitution remedies and the declaratory remedies[102]; and regarding the equita-

618). The Venezuelan Constitution, when referring to the State as rule of law and justice, also uses the expression "*justicia equitativa*" (equitable justice), which has led the Supreme Court to consider the possibility of the existence of two sorts of jurisdictions: law and equity jurisdiction, identifying within the latter, the "peace judges" (*jueces de paz*), which in the local neighborhoods must try to decide controversies by means of conciliation and when the result is impossible, according to equity except when a law solution is imposed by a statute (Article 3, Peace Justice Statute). Peace judges must also decide according to equity when expressly asked by the parties. Regarding this concept of "*equidad,*" the Constitutional Chamber of the Supreme Court has indicated that the concept: "Of difficult comprehension, refers to a value judgment, related to the idea of justice when applied to a particular case, a view that is not based on the law, but in the conscience, the moral, the natural reason and other values. Due to the personal and subjective character of these values, the treatment of decisions based upon them ought to be different to the decisions issued based on legal norms." Decision n° 1139 of October 10, 2000, *Héctor L. Quiroga* case, in *Revista de Derecho Público*, n° 84, Editorial Jurídica Venezolana, Caracas, 2000, p. 351. But with exceptions (such as the "peace judges" jurisdictions), in general, it can be said that in civil law countries the law jurisdiction prevails, and no general distinction can be found between law and equity courts.

[102]See in William Tabb and Elaine W. Shoben, *Remedies,* Thomson West, 2005, p. 13; and James M. Fischer, *Understanding Remedies,* LexisNexis 2006. The damage or compensatory remedies allow the injured party or the plaintiffs to seek compensation for losses sustained in violations of his rights. It is the main instrument to resolve disputes in contract law and regarding tort cases. These compensatory remedies find their equivalent in the actions for damages and prejudices in civil law countries. On the other hand, restitution remedies are intended to restore property to its rightful owner or to obtain from the defendant any illegal profits or unjust enrichment he obtained as a consequence of the wrong made to the plaintiff property. The judicial ordinary writ or order commanding the offender party to do or to refrain from doing something that can be issued in these cases of restitution remedies, are the writ of detinue, issued to recover personal property; the writ of ejectment, for the recovery of land; the writ of entry, which allows a person wrongfully dispossessed of real property to enter and retake the property; and the writ of possession, issued to recover the possession of a land. In civil law countries, the equivalent remedies are the property restitution action ("*acción reivindicatoria*") or the action for enrichment without cause. It can also be identified as an equivalent the actions to restore possession of land or to prevent its invasions ("*interdictos*"). The declaratory remedies are intended to obtain from a court a declaration of the rights or legal relations between parties, being commonly used in cases or controversy, to determine the constitutionality of a statute. It is also used to construct a private instrument between parties so that the interested party may obtain a resolution of the dispute. The latter is equivalent to the declaratory actions on civil law countries, and the former, to the petition to declare in a case or controversy, the nonapplicability of a statute on the grounds of its unconstitutionality, requesting the prevalent application of the constitution.

ble remedies they are the ones, particularly the injunctions, in which the judicial resolution "does not come from established principles but simply derives from common sense and socially acceptable notions of fair play."[103] By means of these equitable remedies, a court of equity can adjudicate extraordinary relief to an aggrieved party, consisting of an order by the court commanding the defendant or the injuring party to do something or to refrain from doing something. They are called coercive remedies because they are backed by the contempt power, that is to say, the power of the court to directly sanction the disobedient defendant.

Both legal and equitable remedies are used for the protection of rights, so that there are no specific remedies conceived for the protection of constitutional rights. They are all remedies that can and are also commonly used for the protection of all constitutional rights and legal rights in the sense of being based on statutes or contracts or that are derived from common law.[104]

Regarding the protection of civil or constitutional rights, the extraordinary coercive equitable remedies, particularly the writ of injunction, can be classified in the following four types:[105]

First, the preventive injunctions, in the sense of avoiding harm, as a court order designed to avoid future harm to a party by prohibiting or mandating certain behavior by another party, that is, to prevent the defendant from inflicting future injury to the plaintiff.[106] Within these pre-

---

[103]See William Tabb and Elaine W. Shoben, *Remedies,* Thomson West, 2005, p. 13.

[104]The most important procedural rule regarding remedies is that equitable remedies are always subordinated to the legal ones, in the sense that they proceed when the remedy at law is inadequate; in other words, the legal remedies are preferred in any individual case if they are adequate. As it was stated in *In re Debs case,* 158 U.S. 564, 15 S.Ct 900, 39 L Ed. 1092 (1895): "As a rule, injunctions are denied to those who have adequate remedy at law. Where the choice is between the ordinary and the extraordinary process of law, and the former are sufficient, the rule will not permit the use of the latter." See in Owen M. Fiss, *Injunctions,* The Foundation Press, 1984, p. 8.

[105]See William Tabb and Elaine W. Shoben, *Remedies,* Thomson West, 2005, pp. 13 ff. and 86 ff.

[106]Regarding the preventive injunctions, they are "preventive" in the sense that they tend to avoid harm, so they are not equivalent to the preliminary injunctions. This is important to be stressed in order to avoid wrongs, particularly when comparing with the civil law countries' institutions, because in the Spanish language, the expression *medidas preventivas* (preventive measures) is used to identify what would be "preliminary or interlocutory injunctions" and not "preventive" injunctions. Thus, in Latin American countries, "preventive measures" (*"medidas cautelares o preventivas"*) are judicial preliminary orders issued to preserve the *status quo* or to restore the factual situation during the development of the

ventive injunctions, it is possible to distinguish the mandatory injunctions,[107] like the writ of mandamus; the prohibitory injunctions,[108] like the writ of prohibition, or the quia-timed injunctions.[109] All these injunctions can be permanent injunctions that affect the legal relationship of the parties until subsequently modified or dissolved.

Second, the structural injunctions, developed by the courts after the *Brown v. Board of Education* case 347 U.S. 483 (1954); 349 U.S. 294 (1955), in which the Supreme Court declared the dual school system discriminatory, using injunction as an instrument of reform, by means of which the courts in certain cases, undertake the supervision over institutional State policies and practices in order to prevent discrimination.[110]

specific trial, similar to the interlocutory injunctions (preliminary injunctions and temporary restraining orders) in the United States.

[107] The mandatory injunction consists in orders issued to the defendant to do an affirmative act or to mandate a specific course of conduct. Regarding the violations of rights made by public authorities, within the mandatory injunction the writ of mandamus must be mentioned, which is issued by a court to compel a government officer to perform certain duties or to execute actions that is obliged to do. See William M. Tabb and Elaine W. Shoben, *Remedies*, Thomson West, 2005, pp. 86 ff.

[108] The prohibitory injunctions are the ones issued in order to forbid or restrain an act. Among these prohibitory remedies the writ of prohibition can also be mentioned, when used as an instrument to correct judicial actions by preventing lower judicial courts from acting in certain ways. *Idem*, pp. 86 ff.

[109] The quia-timed injunction consists of an order granted to prevent an action that has been threatened but has not yet violated the plaintiff rights. *Idem*, pp. 86 ff.

[110] As described by Owen S. Fiss: "Brown gave the injunction a special prominence. School desegregation became one of the prime litigative chores of courts in the period of 1954–1955, and in these cases the typical remedy was the injunction. School desegregation not only gave the injunction a greater currency, it also presented the injunction with new challenges, in terms of both the enormity and the kinds of tasks it was assigned. The injunction was to be used to restructure the educational systems throughout the nation. The impact of Brown on our remedial jurisprudence − giving primacy to the injunction − was not confined to schools desegregation. It also extended to civil rights cases in general, and beyond civil rights to litigation involving electoral reappointments, mental hospitals, prisons, trade practices, and the environment. Having desegregated the schools of Alabama, it was only natural for Judge Johnson to try to reform the mental hospitals and then the prisons of the state in the name of human rights − the right to treatment or to be free from cruel and unusual punishment − and to attempt this Herculean feat through injunction. And he was not alone. The same logic was manifest in actions of other judges, North and South." See Owen M. Fiss, *The Civil Rights Injunctions*, Indiana University Press, 1978, pp. 4–5; and in Owen M. Fiss and Doug Rendelman, *Injunctions*, The Foundation Press, 1984, pp. 33–34. Thus, structural injunctions can be considered a modern constitutional law instrument specifically developed for the protection of human rights, particularly in

Third, the restorative injunctions, also called reparative injunctions, devoted to correct past wrong situations.[111]

And *fourth,* the prophylactic injunctions, issued also to safeguard the plaintiff's rights, preventing future harm, by ordering certain behaviors from the defendant, other than the direct prohibition of future actions.[112]

The most important of all these injunctions, when referred to the protection of rights, are the preventive injunctions (whether mandatory or prohibitory), and the restorative ones; and within this context, the most similar procedural institutions for the protection of constitutional rights to the Latin American amparo actions that exist in the United States, are precisely the equitable remedies, particularly the injunctions.

Yet other than the injunctions for the protection of freedoms and constitutional right, particularly against government actions, the other extraordinary remedy in the United States – following the long British tradition – has been the writ of habeas corpus, the oldest judicial mean for the protection of life and personal integrity, employed to bring a person before a court in order to prove or certify that he is alive and in good health, or to determine that his imprisonment is not illegal.

In conclusion, in the United States, the protection of constitutional rights is assured by the general (ordinary or extraordinary) law and equitable remedies, particularly the injunctions that of course are also used to protect nonconstitutional rights. Consequently, neither the constitution in the United States nor the legal system provides for a specific judicial mean designated for the protection of human rights, contrary to what happens in Latin America with the amparo action.

In Europe, in a similar way to the preventive injunctions in the United States, the protection of human rights is also assured by the general judi-

---

state institutions; an instrument that has been considered to "become an implicit part of the Constitutional guaranty of protecting individual rights from inappropriate government action." See William M. Tabb and Elaine W. Shoben, *Remedies*, pp. 87–88.

[111]In these cases, the court order is devoted to require the defendant to restore the plaintiff to the position it occupied before the defendant committed the wrong. In order to protect a constitutional right, as for instance the right to be elected, the court order can also consist in the repetition of the election process itself. Among these restorative remedies, the writ of error can also be mentioned, which consists in an order for the revision by reasons of unconstitutionality, of a judicial decision of a lower court. See William M. Tabb and Elaine W. Shoben, *Idem,* pp. 86 ff.

[112]These prophylactic injunctions refer to behavior indirectly related to the prohibited conduct, for instance devoted to ask the defendant to develop positive actions in order to minimize the risk of the repetition of the wrong in the future. *Idem*, pp. 86 ff.

cial means, and in particular by the extraordinary preliminary and urgent proceedings established in the Procedural Codes devoted to prevent an irreparable injury from occurring, which can be issued before or during a trial and before the court has the chance to decide the merits on the case. Only in Austria, Germany, Spain and Switzerland can a judicial mean be found that is similar to the Latin American amparo recourse for the protection of fundamental rights.[113] In Spain, in addition to the recourse for amparo filed before the Constitutional Tribunal, the fundamental rights can be immediately protected by ordinary courts by means of the "*amparo juicial.*"[114]

As mentioned, the courts in Europe generally protect rights by means of the ordinary or extraordinary judicial procedures, such as the French *référé*, the Italian extraordinary urgent measures and the precautionary measures ("*medidas cautelares*") regulated in the Civil Procedure Codes, all of them conceived as procedural institutions used for the protection of individual rights, including constitutional rights.

For instance, the *référés*,[115] in general terms, are designated to preserve the status quo in order to prevent irreparable damages before the court

---

[113]See Héctor Fix-Zamudio and Eduardo Ferrer Mac-Gregor, *El derecho de amparo en el mundo*, Edit. Porrúa, México, 2006, pp. 761 ff.; 789 ff., and 835 ff.

[114]See Encarna Carmona Cuenca, "El recurso de amparo constitucional y el recurso de amparo judicial," in *Revista Iberoamericana de Derecho Procesal Constitucional*, Instituto Iberoamericano de Derecho Procesal Constitucional, Editorial Porrúa, n° 5, México, 2006, pp. 3–14.

[115]In France, the Civil Procedural Code (CPC) sets forth the distinction between proceedings regarding the decision of the merits and proceedings refers to decisions that must be taken before deciding on legal grounds ("*avant dire droit*"); these are the writs of *référé*, which are judicial decisions issued in case of urgency, after a party requests, in order that the court adopt the necessary measures to immediately protect a right. There are two types of *référés*: first, the provisional one consisting in orders issued to prevent imminent damages or to order the cessation of an evidently illicit action. They are devoted to protect rights in a preliminary and interlocutory way pending the trial, that is, pending the judicial decision of the merits (Article 809 CPC). Second, the other *référérs* are the ones issued in cases of urgency, based in the existence of an evidently illicit conduct that affects an unquestionable right for its protection. The defendant, of course, must furnish the appropriate proof of the existence of the rights and of the manifest illegality of the defendant actions. These *référés* can also consist in conservatory or restitution measures to prevent imminent damages or to stop illicit actions, and also, orders issued to the plaintiff to accomplish particular duties if the obligations are proved. In this case, the principal procedural element is the need for the court to summon the defendant in order to hear his argument in an oral hearing (Article 811 CPC). See R. Lindon, "Le juge des référés et la presse," *Dalloz 1985*, Chroniques, 61. See the comments by Enrique Paillas, *El recurso de protección ante el derecho comparado,* Santiago de Chile, 1990, pp. 19-26. These *référé* are equivalent to the

decides the substantive merits of a dispute;[116] and also to prevent imminent damages or to stop illicit actions, including orders issued to the plaintiff to accomplish particular duties if the obligations are proved.

Like the injunction in the United States, the *référé* in France is a general procedural mean to seek judicial protection of any kind of rights, and not only constitutional or human rights; but regarding the latter, they have been used successfully to protect them. For instance, regarding the protection of the constitutional right to privacy, and particularly to the individual right of a person to his own image;[117] and regarding the protection to constitutional rights against public official actions, like the

preventive or structural injunctions in the U. S. system, in the sense that they are not only devoted to protect constitutional or human rights but any legal right, and because of their permanent effects. In France they are qualified as "provisional" judicial decisions but only in the sense that they do not produce substantive *res judicata* effects, that is, a definitive judicial decision regarding the merits that could prevent the principal lawsuit that can be brought before the courts. On the contrary, as it happened with the amparo decisions in almost all Latin American countries, the *référé* only produces formal *res judicata* effects in the sense that no other *référé* can be issued in the same matter, and between the same parties. Thus, in the latter case, the *référé* is a judicial decision that is taken independently of the resolution of the controversy on the merits in the principal lawsuit that eventually can be brought before the courts. Consequently, the principal consequence of this "provisional" character of the decision is that if there is no principal lawsuit regarding the substantive merits of the case brought before the courts, the *référé* decisions become permanent.

[116]In the same sense as the injunctions. See William M. Tabb and Elaine W. Shoben, *Remedies*, Thomson West, 2005, p. 4.

[117]This was a case in 1980, of a judicial decision ordering the *Reader's Digest* magazine that published on the front cover of one of its issues, the photo of a doctor showing him practicing medicine, to publish in the following issue, a notice indicating that the affected doctor never gave his consent for the publication of his photograph in the previous issue. See the references in Enrique Paillas, *El recurso de protección ante el derecho comparado*, Santiago de Chile, 1990, pp 22–23. In a similar case in 1981, a photo of a practicing lawyer was published without her consent in the weekly magazine *Le Nouvel Observateur*, showing her wearing professional garb Courts, in order to support an article regarding the legal practice by women. In order to grant the *référé* protection, the same argument of absence of consent of the lawyer to publish her photo in a nonprofessional magazine prevails, considering the courts also, in the case, that the deontological rules of the legal profession allows avoiding any kind of advertisement. The court also considered the right of the lawyer to give of herself the image she wanted to her clients and colleagues. The publication of the photo was also considered an illicit overture of her rights that had to be stopped. Thus the judicial order directed to the weekly magazine to publish in the following issue the notice that the defendant never gave authorization for the publication (*Idem*. pp 23–24).

constitutional right to free enterprise.[118] The *référé* has also been used in France for the protection of property rights, for instance, regarding industrial factories against illegal occupation of its premises by the workers.[119]

In Italy, the judicial mean equivalent to the French *référé* is the urgency procedure set forth in the Civil Procedural Code within the precautionary measures. A party can seek this means if he fears that his rights could be threatened by an imminent and irreparable prejudice during the term taken by an ordinary process to enforce his rights. In such cases, the person may go before the court asking for the necessary urgent decisions that, according to the circumstances, could be suitable in order to provisionally assure the effects of the decision on the merits. This procedure has also been used for the protection of constitutional rights[120] such as the right to protection of health, environmental rights, right to have a name and right to one's own image.

These so-called nonenumerated precautionary judicial powers have also been regulated in the Latin American civil procedural codes, and have been successfully applied in many countries. However, previous to

[118] In a case decided in 1983, such right was protected against the limits imposed by the de facto actions (*voi de fait*) adopted by a city mayor without any previous formal administrative procedure, ordering the mayor to restore the situation of the affected party to what it was before the arbitrary municipal action was taken. See Enrique Paillas, *El recurso de protección ante el derecho comparado,* Santiago de Chile, l990, p. 26.

[119] In such cases, the courts, even though recognizing the workers' constitutional right to strike, in protection of the property rights of the owners of the factory and their rights to have access to their property, considered illegal the de facto occupation of the premises by the workers (*voi de fait illegal*), contrary to the owners' rights, that prevented the continuation of work and impeded the free entrance to the buildings. See Enrique Paillas, *El recurso de protección ante el derecho comparado,* Santiago de Chile, l990, p. 26. In similar situations, an injunction has been issued in the United States, even brought before the courts by the attorney general who asked for the protection of property rights of the United States regarding mail, and the protection of freedom of interstate commerce and of transportation of the mail, against striking workers, members of the American Railway Union, who in l894 had a sit-in at the railroad premises paralyzing the traffic in Chicago. Without challenging the workers' right to quit work and without interfering with the organization of labour, the court considered that the strike interfered with the operation of trains carrying mail and with interstate commerce, and ordered the end of the sit-in. In the well-known *In Re Debs case* 158 U.S. 564, 15 S.ct. 900,39 L. Ed. 1092 (1895), the Supreme Court set forth the basic principles of injunctions, particularly regarding the power the courts have to punish the disobedience of its injunctive rulings by imposing fines and ordering imprisonment for contempt. See Owen M. Fiss and Doug Rendelman, *Injunctions,* The Foundation Press, Mineola, New York, 1984, pp. 13.

[120] See Enrique Paillas, *El recurso de protección ante el derecho comparado*, Santiago de Chile, l990, p. 46.

their development, whether because they were not generally attributed to ordinary judges, or because of the inefficiency of the judiciary to effectively protect constitutional rights, the general trend in almost all of Latin America since the nineteenth century has been the progressive regulation of the amparo action as a special judicial mean exclusively set forth for the protection of constitutional rights.

Finally, the case of Spain muat be mentioned where, in addition to the provision in the 1978 Constitution for a recourse for " amparo" to be filed before the Constitutional Tribunal as a specific judicial mean for the protection of fundamental rights, since the enactment of the Law 62/1978 for the Judicial Protection of Fundamental Rights of persons, the ordinary or judicial amparo (*amparo judicial*) has been established in order to assure the prompt and effective judicial protection of rights by ordinary courts, in the criminal, judicial review of administrative action and civil courts, extended in 1995 to the labor courts.[121]

II. THE SPECIFIC JUDICIAL MEANS FOR THE PROTECTION OF HUMAN RIGHTS

1. *The European amparo actions*

Although the general trend regarding the protection of constitutional rights is achieved in Europe by means of the general ordinary or extraordinary judicial procedures, including the "*amparo judicial*" in Spain, in some countries, individual actions or amparo recourses as specific judicial means for the protection of fundamental rights have been established. This is the case in Austria, Germany, Spain and Switzerland, where a recourse for the protection of some constitutional rights has been regulated, particularly as a consequence of the adoption, under Hans Kelsen's influence, of the concentrated method of judicial review, resulting in the creation of Constitutional Courts or Constitutional Tribunals.[122] These

---

[121]See Encarna Carmona Cuenca, "El recurso de amparo constitucional y el recurso de amparo judicial," in *Revista Iberoamericana de Derecho Procesal Constitucional*, Instituto Iberoamericano de Derecho Procesal Constitucional, Editorial Porrúa, n° 5, México, 2006, pp. 3–14.

[122]The "Austrian method" of judicial review was originated in Europe after the First World War under the influence of the ideas and direct work of Hans Kelsen, particularly regarding the concept of the supremacy of the constitution and the need for a jurisdictional guaranty of that supremacy. See H. Kelsen, "La garantie juridictionnelle de la Constitution (La Justice constitutionnelle)," in *Revue du droit public et de la science politique en France et à l'étranger*, Paris, 1928, pp. 197–257. It was also a direct result of the absence

courts were empowered not only to act as a constitutional judge controlling the constitutionality of statutes, executive regulations and treaties, but also to grant constitutional protection to individuals against the violation of fundamental rights.

The process began in 1920, in Austria, by granting individuals the right to bring before the Constitutional Tribunal, recourses or complaints (*Verfassungsbeschwerde*) against administrative acts when the claimant alleges that they infringe upon rights guaranteed in the constitution (Article 144).[123]

This was the origin of the development of a special judicial mean for the protection of fundamental rights in Europe, although with a concentrated character that establishes the difference with Latin American amparo recourses that, except Costa Rica, El Salvador and Nicaragua, are filed before all the first instance courts.

The Austrian model influenced the establishment of the other concentrated system of judicial review in Europe. It was the case in 1931 of the Spanish Second Republic, where the constitution of that year (December 9, 1931) created a Tribunal of Constitutional Guaranties,[124] which had the exclusive powers to judge upon the constitutionality of statutes, and additionally, to protect fundamental rights by means of a recourse for constitutional protection called "*recurso de amparo*." Some scholars

of a diffuse system of judicial review of the constitutionality of legislation whose exclusion was expressly or indirectly established in the constitution; and of the traditional European distrust regarding the judiciary to control the constitutionality or legislation. Thus, in order to accomplish such a task it was necessary to establish an independent State body. Accordingly, the first constitutional tribunals were established in Czechoslovakia and Austria, in their respective constitutions of February 29 and October 1, 1920. Due to its permanence and its reestablishment in 1945, the Austrian Constitutional Tribunal, created in the 1920 constitution, was to be the leading institution of the "European" concentrated system of judicial review. Hans Kelsen, a member himself of the Constitutional Tribunal until 1929, formulated the original general trends of the institution, very similar to the Czechoslovakian one, later regulated in Articles 137–148 of the Constitution of May 1, 1945. See in I. Méndez de Vigo, "El Verfassungsgerichthof (Tribunal Constitucional Austríaco)," in *Boletín de Jurisprudencia Constitucional*, Cortes Generales, 7, Madrid, 1981, pp. 555–560) and T. Ohlinger, *Legge sulla Corte Costituzionale Austriaca*, Firenze, 1982.

[123]See in general, Norbert Lösing, "El derecho de amparo en Austria," in Héctor Fix-Zamudio and Eduardo Ferrer Mac-Gregor, *El derecho de amparo en el mundo*, Edit. Porrúa, México, 2006, pp. 761–788.

[124]See José Luis Melián Gil, *El Tribunal de Garantías Constitucionales de la Segunda República Española*, Madrid, 1971, pp. 16–17, 53; P. Cruz Villalón, "Dos modos de regulación del control de constitucionalidad: Checoslovaquia (1920–1938) y España (1931–1936), in *Revista española de derecho constitucional*, 5, 1982, p. 118.

have also found some influence of the Mexican amparo[125] on the Spanish one, which disappeared after the Spanish Civil War.

After the Second World War, also following the Austrian model, the 1949 Constitution of Germany created a Federal Constitutional Tribunal (FCT) as the "supreme guardian of the Constitution,"[126] empowered to decide in a concentrated way, not only regarding the abstract and particular control of constitutionality of statutes, but also the constitutional complaints for the protection of a fundamental right. This *Verfassungsbeschwerde,* complaint or recourse can be brought before the Federal Constitutional Tribunal against judicial decisions considered to have violated the rights and freedoms of a person because of the application of a statute that is alleged to be unconstitutional (Article 93, 1, 4,a, FCT Law).[127]

Finally, more recently, the current 1978 Spanish Constitution by recreating the Constitutional Tribunal has also established a concentrated method of judicial review,[128] and in addition to its power to decide the "recourse of unconstitutionality against laws and normative acts with force of law" (Article 161,1,a Constitution), it has also been empowered to decide the *recursos de amparo* for the protection of constitutional rights. These recourses can be directly brought by individuals before the Constitutional Tribunal when they deem their constitutional rights and liberties have been violated by administrative acts, juridical decisions or by simple factual actions from public entities or officials (Article 161,1,b, Constitution; Article 41,2 Organic Law 2/1979),[129] and only when the ordinary judicial means for the protection of fundamental rights have

---

[125]See Eduardo Ferrer Mac-Gregor, *La acción constitucional de amparo en México y España,* Estudio de Derecho Comparado, 2nd Edition, Edit. Porrúa, México, 2000, p. 27; P. Häberle, *La* Verfassungsbeschwerde *nel sistema della giustizia costituzionale tudesca,* Ed. Giuffré, Milan, 2000.

[126]See G. Müller, "El Tribunal Constitucional Federal de la República Federal de Alemania," in *Revista de la Comisión Internacional de Juristas,* Vol VI, Ginebra, 1965, p. 216; F. Sainz Moreno, "Tribunal Constitucional Federal alemán," in *Boletín de Jurisprudencia Constitucional,* Cortes Generales, 8, Madrid, 1981, p. 606.

[127] See in general, Peter Häberle, "El recurso de amparo en el sistema de jurisdicción constitucional de la República Federal Alemana," in Héctor Fix-Zamudio and Eduardo Ferrer Mac-Gregor, *El derecho de amparo en el mundo,* Edit. Porrúa, México, 2006, pp. 695–760.

[128]See P. Bon, F. Moderne and Y. Rodríguez, *La justice constitutionnelle en Espagne,* Paris 1982, p. 41.

[129]This recourse for the protection of fundamental rights can only be exercised against administrative or judicial acts as well as against other acts without force of law produced by the legislative authorities. Article 42, Organic Law 2/1979.

been exhausted (Article 43,1 Organic Law 2/1979). Consequently, the recourse for amparo in general results in a direct action against judicial acts[130] and can only indirectly lead to judicial review of legislation when the particular state act challenged by it is based on a statute considered unconstitutional (Article 55,2 Organic Law 2/1979).[131] The Organic Law of the Constitutional Tribunal was reformed in 2007 (Law 6/2007), imposing the need for the plaintiff to allege and prove the "special constitutional importance" justifying the filing of the recourse and the Constitutional Tribunal decision (Articles 49,2 and 50,1,b).[132]

In Switzerland, a limited diffuse and concentrated system of judicial review was first established in the 1874 constitution, but regarding constitutional rights, the 1999 constitution also established the competence of the Federal Tribunal to decide cases of constitutional complaints that the individuals can file in cases of harms to constitutional rights (Article 189,1,a).[133] This public law recourse before the Swiss Federal Tribunal is essentially of a subsidiary nature, that is it is only admissible when the alleged violation of the right cannot be brought before any other judicial authority through other legal means established either under federal or cantonal law (Article 84,2, Law of Judiciary Organization). Consequently, the action cannot be admitted unless all existing cantonal remedies have been exhausted, except in cases of violation of freedom of establishment, the prohibition of double taxation in fiscal matters, the citizen's right to appear before his "natural" judge, and the right to legal aid (Article 86,2, Law of Judiciary Organization), which can be brought before the Federal Tribunal in a principal way.

A few general trends that can be identified in all these European amparo recourses, in contrast with the Latin American institution: first, it is conceived as a concentrated judicial mean for the protection of funda-

---

[130]See Louis Favoreu, "Actualité et légitimité du Contrôle juridictionnel des lois en Europe occidentale," in *Revue du droit public et de la science politique en France et à l'étranger*, Paris, 1984 (5), pp. 1155–1156.

[131]See in general, Francisco Fernández Segado, "El recurso de amparo en España," in Héctor Fix-Zamudio and Eduardo Ferrer Mac-Gregor, *El derecho de amparo en el mundo*, Edit. Porrúa, México, 2006, pp. 789–834.

[132]See Francisco Fernández Segado, *La reforma del régimen jurídico-procesal del recurso de amparo*, Ed. Dykinson, Madrid, 2008, pp. 86 ff.

[133]See E. Zellweger, "El Tribunal Federal suizo en calidad de Tribunal Constitucional," in *Revista de la Comisión Internacional de Juristas*, Vol. VII (1), 1966, p. 119. See in general, Joaquín Brage Camazano, "La Staatsrechtliche Beschwerde o recurso constitucional de amparo en Suiza," in Héctor Fix-Zamudio and Eduardo Ferrer Mac-Gregor, *Idem*, Edit. Porrúa, México, 2006, pp. 835–857.

mental rights against State actions, by assigning to a single Constitutional Tribunal the power to decide upon them; second, particularly in Germany and Spain, it is established to protect certain constitutional rights listed in the constitutions as "fundamental" rights, more or less equivalent to civil or individual rights; and third, except in Switzerland, it is conceived as an action to be filed only against the State.

In contrast, the Latin American amparo action or recourse, can be exercised before all courts except for in Costa Rica, El Salvador and Nicaragua. In general, and also with some exceptions (Brazil, El Salvador, Mexico, Nicaragua, Panama), it can also be exercised not only against State acts but also against individuals. Additionally, it can be exercised for the protection of all constitutional rights, including social and economic ones, and not only some of them (fundamental rights) except for in Chile and Colombia.

2. The Latin American amparo proceeding

As mentioned before, one important feature of the Latin American regime for the protection of constitutional rights, is that in addition to the common and general judicial guaranties of such rights, the constitutions establish a specific judicial action, recourse or remedy for their guaranty called the *amparo* proceeding, perhaps one of the more Latin American constitutional law institutions.

This proceeding has been named in various ways, always meaning the same, as follows: *Amparo* (Guatemala); *Acción de amparo* (Argentina, Ecuador, Honduras, Paraguay, Uruguay, Venezuela); *Acción de tutela* (Colombia); *Juicio de amparo* (Mexico); *Proceso de amparo* (El Salvador, Peru); *Recurso de amparo* (Bolivia, Costa Rica, Dominican Republic, Nicaragua, Panama); *Recurso de protección* (Chile) or *Mandado de segurança* and *mandado de injunçao* (Brazil).[134] Regardless of the denomination, in all the Latin American countries the amparo is always conceived as a judicial proceeding initiated by means of an action or a recourse filed by a party, which finishes with a judicial order or writ.

This amparo proceeding, to which I will also refer to in the general sense as the amparo action or suit, is expressly regulated in the constitu-

---

[134]See, in general, Allan R. Brewer-Carías, *El amparo a los derechos y garantías constitucionales (una aproximación comparativa)*, Caracas, 1993; Eduardo Ferrer Mac-Gregor, "Breves notas sobre el amparo latinoamericano (desde el derecho procesal constitucional comparado)," in Héctor Fix-Zamudio and Eduardo Ferrer Mac-Gregor, *El derecho de amparo en el mundo*, Edit. Porrúa, México, 2006, pp. 3–39.

tions of Argentina, Bolivia, Brazil, Chile, Colombia, Costa Rica, Ecuador, El Salvador, Guatemala, Honduras, México, Nicaragua, Panamá, Paraguay, Perú and Venezuela. It is established in an indirect way in the Constitution of Uruguay and was admitted without express constitutional provision in the Dominican Republic.[135]

Additionally, the amparo proceeding has been regulated in special Amparo Laws (Argentina, Brazil, Colombia, Dominican Republic, Mexico, Nicaragua, Uruguay, Venezuela), or in general laws specifically referred to the Constitutional Jurisdiction or Constitutional Procedures (Bolivia, Guatemala, Peru, Costa Rica, Ecuador, El Salvador, Honduras). Only in Panama and Paraguay is regulated in the general Procedural Codes. Chile is the only country lacking a statute regulating the recourse for protection, its general procedure rules being established by the Supreme Court.

In the Guatemalan, Mexican and Venezuelan constitutions, the amparo action also includes the protection of personal liberty or freedom (habeas corpus), which contrasts with the constitutional regulations in all other countries where the constitutions have set forth, in addition to the amparo action, a different recourse of habeas corpus for the specific protection of personal freedom and integrity. This is the case of Argentina, Bolivia, Brazil, Colombia, Costa Rica, Chile, the Dominican Republic, Ecuador, El Salvador, Honduras, Nicaragua, Panamá, Paraguay, Peru and Uruguay. Nonetheless, in Guatemala the recourse for personal exhibition has been set forth by statute, as well as the habeas corpus action in Venezuela, conceived as an amparo for the protection of personal freedom.

In recent times, some constitutions have also provided for a recourse called of habeas data (Argentina, Brazil, Ecuador, Paraguay, Peru, Venezuela), by which any person can file a suit in order to ask for information regarding the content of the data referred to himself, contained in public or private registries or data banks, and in case of false, inaccurate or discriminatory information, to seek for its suppression, rectification, confidentiality and updating.

In contrast with all these rich Latin American constitutional regulations, the Constitution of the United States only set forth (Section 9, clause 2) in an indirect way the writ of habeas corpus, when it states that "the privilege of the Writ of Habeas Corpus shall not be suspended,

---

[135]See Allan R. Brewer-Carías, "La admisión jurisprudencial de la acción de amparo, en ausencia de regulación constitucional o legal en la República Dominicana," in *Revista IIDH*, Instituto Interamericano de Derechos Humanos, n° 29, San José, 1999, pp. 95-102; and in *"Iudicium et vita,"* *Jurisprudencia en Derechos Humanos*, n° 7, Edición Especial, Tomo I, Instituto Interamericano de Derechos Humanos, San José, 2000, pp. 334–341.

unless when in cases of rebellion or Invasion the public safety may require it."

3. The writ of amparo in the Philippines

In the Philippines, Section 5,5 of Article VIII of the 1987 Constitution empowers the Supreme Court of Philippines to promulgate rules concerning the protection and enforcement of constitutional rights. Accordingly, on September 25, 2007, the Court adopted Resolution A.M. N° 07-9-12-SC containing The Rule on the Writ of Amparo,[136] seeking for the effective protection of the right to life, to liberty and to security. The Rule was adopted, motivated by the high number of extrajudicial killings and enforced disappearances in the country; and because the inefficacy of the Habeas Corpus regulated since 1901 under Rule 102 of the Rules of the Supreme Court. The writ of amparo, in a certain way, complements the latter writ, which is directed to protect physical liberty by compelling the presentation of the body of a person detained without charges. Now, the writ of amparo grants protection, inspection order and production orders in cases of extralegal killings and enforced disappearances.

The initiative to create the writ of amparo derived from the proposals made in the National Summit on Extrajudicial Killings and Enforced Disappearances convened by the Supreme Court on July 16, 2007, and its purpose was announced by Chief Justice Reynato Puno on September 25, 2007, saying that with the promulgation of the rule, the constitutional right to life, liberty and security will be placed above violation and threats of violation, adding that:

> This rule will provide the victims of extralegal killings and enforced disappearances the protection they need and the promise of vindication for their rights. This rule empowers our courts to issue relieves that may be granted through judicial orders of protection, production, inspection and other relief to safeguard one's life and liberty. The writ of amparo shall hold public authorities, those who took their oath to defend the constitution and enforce our laws, to a high standard of official conduct and hold them accountable to our people. The sovereign Filipino people should be assured that if their right to life and liberty is threatened or violated, they will find vindication in our courts of justice.[137]

---

[136]The Resolution was amended on October 16, and took effect on October 24, 2007.

[137] See the text in *Inquirer.net, News* December 31, 2007

This writ of amparo was created by the Supreme Court following the trends of the Latin American amparo, as a remedy available to any person for the protection of the rights to life, to liberty and to security when violated or threatened with violation by an unlawful act or omission of a public official or employee, and a private individual or entity (Sec. 1). Thus, it is not established for the protection of all constitutional rights, but only the right to life, liberty and security, in a similar sense that it is established in the European amparo and in the amparo regulations of Mexico, Colombia and Chile that establishes the amparo only for the protection of individual guaranties or "fundamental rights."

The petition for the writ of amparo can be filed by the aggrieved party or by any other qualified person or entity, like any member of the immediate family, or collateral relative of the aggrieved party or any concerned citizen, organization, association or institution, if there is no known member of the immediate family or relative of the aggrieved (Sec. 2). The petition can be filed on any day and at any time (Sec. 3) before a variety of courts, namely, the Regional Trial Court of the place where the threat, act or omission was committed or any of its elements occurred, or with the Sandiganbayan, the Court of Appeals, the Supreme Court, or any justice of such courts (Article 3).

According to Section 6 of the Rule, upon the filing of the petition, the court, justice or judge "shall immediately order the issuance of the writ if on its face it ought to issue," fixing date and time for a summary hearing of the petition which shall not be later than 7 days from the date of its issuance. The final judgment of the court must be rendered within 10 days from the time the petition is submitted for decision, and if the allegations in the petition are proven by substantial evidence, the court "shall grant the privilege of the writ and such reliefs as may be proper and appropriate" (Sec. 18).

Immediately after the promulgation of the Rules, various petitions for writ of amparo were filed, particularly referred to cases of disappearances.

PART TWO

THE AMPARO AS A LATIN AMERICAN CONSTITUTIONAL AND INTERNATIONAL LAW INSTITUTION

As aforementioned, the origin of the Latin American amparo as a specific judicial mean for the protection of constitutional rights and guaranties is to be found in Mexico in the 1857 Constitution.[138] So no European or Spanish influence can be found in the Latin American institution.

The initial regulation in Mexico was incorporated in the Constitutional "Reforms Act" of 1848, where a special provision devoted to guaranty the fundamental rights declared in the constitution was included (Article 5), setting forth that in order to assure the rights recognized in the constitution, particularly, freedom, security, property and equality of all inhabitants of the Republic, a statute had to be sanctioned for establishing the means for its enforcement. No statute was sanctioned, but this provision has always been considered as the remote antecedent of the amparo trial or suit.

The *Acta de Reformas* provision was followed by a draft proposal made by one of the members of the Constitutional Commission, the *fórmula Otero* embodied in Article 25 of the 1848 Constitution,[139] which defined

---

[138]See in general, Héctor Fix-Zamudio, *Ensayos sobre el derecho de amparo*, Porrúa, México, 2003; and Héctor Fix-Zamudio and Eduardo Ferrer Mac-Gregor, "El derecho de amparo en México," in Héctor Fix-Zamudio and Eduardo Ferrer Mac-Gregor, (Coord.), *El derecho de amparo en el mundo*, Edit. Porrúa, México, 2006, pp. 461–522.

[139]*Article 25*. The courts of the federation will protect (*ampararán*) any inhabitant of the Republic in the exercise and conservation of the rights granted to him in the constitution and the constitutional statutes, against any offensive action by the Legislative or Executive powers, whether of the Federation or of the states; the said courts being limited to give protection in the particular case to which the process refers, without making any general statement regarding the statute or the act provoking the decision. See the comments on this article in J. Carpizo, *La Constitución Mexicana de 1917*, México, 1979, p. 271; Robert D.

81

jurisdictions developed in almost all civil law countries, following the influence of the French *contentieux-administrative* jurisdiction; and

5) For the protection of peasants' rights derived from the agrarian reform process (called *"amparo agrario"*) equivalent to the agrarian jurisdictions that can be found in almost all Latin American countries.

All these jurisdictions and judicial means, in Mexico function under the same name of amparo or under the same amparo umbrella; which is a unique case in comparative law. No other country in the world follows the Mexican amparo omnicomprehensive trend, which in a certain way has deformed the original amparo judicial mean for the protection of constitutional rights and guaranties, comprising what in almost all civil law countries are separate actions, recourses, procedures or jurisdictions, with very different objectives. In Mexico all are called amparo.

On the other hand, this omnicomprehensive trend of the Mexican amparo resulting from the effort to expand its protection, in the end and paradoxically, in some sense and in some cases has weakened the effective protection of constitutional rights when compared to other regulations.[144]

So from the original Mexican amparo, as we will see, what really spread in almost all the other Latin American countries was basically the name given to the special judicial mean for the protection of constitutional rights (amparo), but not at all its complex content, which as mentioned, is unique to the Mexican system.

In the other Latin American countries, also since the beginning of the nineteenth century, it is also possible to find antecedents of the amparo action or recourse. For instance in Venezuela, the 1811 Declaration of Rights of the People specifically provided the right to petition in order to protect such rights, as follows: "The citizens' freedom of petition before public authorities in order to ask for the protection of his rights, in any way can be impeded or limited" (Article 22). This declaration was followed by the 1830 Constitution declaration regarding the need to a special protective mean of the constitutional rights, in which it was stated, "Every person must find a prompt and safe remedy according to the law

---

[144]See the comments in this regard in Joaquín Brage Camazano, *La Jurisdicción Constitucional de la Libertad Teoría general, Argentina, México, Corte Interamericana de Derechos Humanos*, Editorial Porrúa, Instituto Mexicano de Derecho Procesal Constitucional, México, 2005, p. 156.

regarding the injuries and damages suffered in their persons, properties, honor and esteem" (Article 189).[145]

Leaving aside the remote antecedents, the fact is that after the Mexican amparo was incorporated in the constitution, the action was introduced in the other Latin American countries since the second half of the nineteenth century: El Salvador (1886), Honduras and Nicaragua (1894), and during the twentieth century: Guatemala (1921), Brazil (*mandado de securança* 1934), Panama (1941), Costa Rica (1946), Venezuela (1961), Bolivia, Paraguay, Ecuador (1967), Peru (1979), Chile (*recurso de protección* 1976–1980), Uruguay (1988) and Colombia (*acción de tutela* 1991).[146] In 1994 it was incorporated in the Argentinean Constitution, but since 1957, the amparo action was admitted through court decisions and regulated in positive law in 1966; and since 1999, the Supreme Court has admitted the amparo action in the Dominican Republic, being regulated in 2006 by statute.

So currently, in all Latin American countries, with the exception of Cuba, the habeas corpus and amparo suits, actions or recourses ("*acción de protección*" in Chile, "*acción de tutela*" in Colombia and *mandado de securanca* in Brazil) exist as a specific judicial mean exclusively designed for the protection of constitutional rights.

Also, in all of the Latin American countries, with the exception of the Dominican Republic, the provisions for the action are embodied in the

---

[145] According to this constitutional provision, it was the Organic Statute on the Judiciary of 1850 that attributed to the Superior Courts' powers: "To decide recourses of force, amparo and protection against written and oral orders or prescription, given by authorities of the Republic" (Article 9), using for the first time the word amparo to identify a judicial mean; as well as the person's right to ask for amparo to freedom rights (habeas corpus), as follows: "10. In case in which any public official were forming criminal cause against any person or had issued a detention order, the interested party or anybody acting in his name, can bring before the Superior Court by means of amparo or protection; and the latter, ordering the suspension of the procedure, will ask the files and the presence of the party (en vida), and if it finds the petition according to justice, will level the oppressive order." Nevertheless, and in spite of these provisions, in Venezuela the amparo action was only developed after the enactment of the Constitution of 1961. Yet, in the nineteenth century, in the Venezuelan 1897 Civil Procedure Code, judicial review as a power of all judges to consider null and void legal provisions contrary to the constitution —in the United States' legal tradition— was formally inserted in positive law, allowing judicial protection of constitutional rights.

[146] See Héctor Fix-Zamudio, *Ensayos sobre el derecho de amparo*, Editorial Porrúa, México, 2003, pp. 847 ff; Héctor Fix-Zamudio and Eduardo Ferrer Mac-Gregor (Coord.), *El derecho de amparo en el mundo*, Editorial Porrúa, México, 2006, pp. 16 ff.

bodies,[148] to the superior law of the country, that is, to exercise judicial review of constitutionality of statutes.

In contemporary constitutional law it is possible to distinguish two main systems of judicial review: the diffuse and the concentrated methods, which are not incompatible. Each of them can be established in a given country as the only one existing in it, or they can both be established in a mixed or parallel way, coexisting. The latter is the case of many Latin American countries, where it is possible to identify a mixed system of judicial review, in which the diffuse and concentrated methods of judicial review are combined.[149]

The main criteria for classifying these systems of judicial review of the constitutionality of State acts, particularly of statutes, is referred to the number of courts that must carry out that task of exercising constitutional justice, in the sense that it can be attributed to all the courts of a given country (diffuse method), or only to one single court (concentrated system), whether the Supreme Court or a special Constitutional Court created for such purpose.

In the first case, when all the courts of a given country are empowered to act as constitutional judges and control the constitutionality of statutes, the system has been identified as the "American system," because it was first adopted in the United States particularly after the well-known *Marbury v. Madison* case U.S. (1 Cranch), 137; 2 L. Ed. 60 (1803). Notwithstanding, the system is not only specific to countries with common law systems, because it has also been developed in countries with Roman or civil law traditions, precisely like those in Latin America. This method of judicial review has also been called diffuse or decentralized,[150] because in it, the judicial control belongs to all the courts, from the lowest level up to the Supreme Court of the country, allowing them not to apply a statute in the particular case they have to decide, when they consider it

---

[148]H. Kelsen, "La garantie juridictionnelle de la Constitution (La Justice constitution-nelle)," in *Revue du droit public et de la science politique en France et à l'étranger*, T. XLV, 1928, p.197–257.

[149]See in general M. Cappelletti, *Judicial Review in the Contemporary World*, Indianapolis, 1971, p. 45 and M. Cappelleti and J. C. Adams, "Judicial Review of Legislation: European Antecedents and Adaptations," in *Harvard Law Review*, 79, April 6, 1966, p. 1207.

[150]M. Cappelletti, "El control judicial de la constitucionalidad de las leyes en el derecho comparado," in *Revista de la Facultad de Derecho de México*, n° 61, 1966, p. 28.

unconstitutional and void, thereby giving prevalence to the constitution.[151]

Since the nineteenth century the diffuse method has been applied in almost all Latin American countries, as is the case of Argentina (1860), Brazil (1890), Colombia (1850), Dominican Republic (1844), Mexico (1857), Venezuela (1897), and also since the twentieth century in Ecuador, Guatemala, Nicaragua and Peru.[152] Only in Argentina does the method strictly follow the American model; and in the other countries it exists, but combined with the concentrated method of judicial review.

Following the American model, when applying the diffuse method of judicial review of legislation, the decisions of the courts only have *inter partes* effect, that is, related to a particular case and to the parties in the process. So they do not annul the statute considered unconstitutional, but only declare it void and unconstitutional, and not applicable to the case.

In the second method of judicial review, when the power to control the constitutionality of legislation is given to a single judicial organ of the State, whether it is the Supreme Court or a special constitutional court created for such particular purpose, it has been identified as the "Austrian" system, because in Europe, it was first established in Austria in 1920 due to the influence of Hans Kelsen.[153] It has also been called the "European system" because it was also followed in other European countries after World War II, as is the case of Germany, Italy, France, Portugal and Spain, countries where Constitutional Tribunal or Courts were created. It is a concentrated system of judicial review, as opposed to the diffuse system, because the power to control the constitutionality of statutes is given only to one single Constitutional Court of Tribunal, with powers, in general, to declare the nullity of state acts with general, *erga omnes* effects.

[151]See Allan R. Brewer-Carías, *Judicial Review in Comparative Law,* Cambridge University Press, Cambridge, 1989.

[152]See Allan R. Brewer-Carías, "La jurisdicción constitucional en América Latina," in Domingo García Belaúnde and Francisco Fernández Segado (Coord.), *La jurisdicción constitucional en Iberoamérica,* Dykinson S. L. (Madrid), Editorial Jurídica Venezolana (Caracas), Ediciones Jurídicas (Lima), Editorial Jurídica E. Esteva (Uruguay), Madrid, 1997, pp. 117–161.

[153]See H. Kelsen, "La garantie juridictionnelle de la Constitution (La Justice constitutionnelle), *Revue du droit public et de la science politique en France et à l'étranger,* Paris, 1928, pp. 197–257; Allan R. Brewer-Carías, *Judicial Review in Comparative Law*, Cambridge University Press, Cambridge, 1989.

CHAPTER FOUR

THE AMPARO ACTION IN COUNTRIES THAT APPLY ONLY THE DIFFUSE METHOD OF JUDICIAL REVIEW OF LEGISLATION

The first case refers to the amparo action in countries that only have a diffuse system of judicial review, as is the case of Argentina, which is the only Latin American country where the diffuse method of judicial review remains as being the only one functioning in order to control the constitutionality of legislation, and where the amparo and habeas corpus actions are also conceived as essential adjective tools for such judicial review.

The Constitution of Argentina in an article included in the constitutional reform of 1994 establishes the three specific actions for human rights protection: the amparo, the habeas data and the habeas corpus actions (Article 43). [155]

Regarding the amparo action, the constitution provides that any person may file a prompt and summary proceeding against any act or omission of public authorities or of individuals for the protection of the rights and guaranties recognized by the Constitution, the treaties or the statutes, which can only be brought before a court if there is no other more suitable judicial mean.

The same Article 43 of the constitution also provides for a collective action of amparo that can be filed by the affected party, the people's defendant and nonprofit associations, in order to protect collective rights, like the rights to a proper environment and to free competition, and the

---

[155] See Juan F. Armagnague *et al.*, *Derecho a la información, hábeas data e Internet*, Ediciones La Roca, Buenos Aires, 2002; Miguel Ángel Ekmekdjian *et al.*, *Hábeas Data. El derecho a la intimidad frente a la revolución informática*, Edic. Depalma, Buenos Aires, 1998; Osvaldo Alfredo Gozaíni, *Derecho Procesal Constitucional, Hábeas Data. Protección de datos personales. Ley 25.326 y reglamentación (decreto 1558/2001)*, Rubinzal-Culzoni Editores, Santa Fe, Argentina, 2002.

user and consumer rights, as well as the rights that have general collective impact.

In the case of Argentina, the three specific remedies for the protection of all human rights are regulated in three separate statutes: the amparo Action Statute (*Ley de acción de amparo, Ley 16986/1966*), the Habeas Corpus Statute (*Ley 23098/1984*) and the Personal Data Protection Statute (*Ley 25366/2000*).[156]

Even though the amparo action was regulated for the first time in the 1994 Constitution, in practice it was created five decades before by the Supreme Court in the *Angel Siri* case of December 27, 1957[157] in which the power of ordinary courts to protect fundamental rights of citizens against violation from public authorities' actions was definitively admitted.

At that time, the constitution only provided for the habeas corpus action (Article 18), which was regulated in the provisions of the Criminal Procedural Code (Title IV, Section II, Book IV) established for the protection of physical and personal freedom against illegal or arbitrary detentions.[158] Conversely, regarding other constitutional rights, they were only protected through the ordinary judicial means, so the courts considered that the habeas corpus could not be used for such purpose.

That is why, for instance, in 1950 the Supreme Court of the Nation in the *Bartolo* case[159] rejected the application of the habeas corpus proceeding to obtain judicial protection of constitutional rights other than personal freedom, ruling that "nor in the text, or in its spirit, or in the constitutional tradition of the habeas corpus institution, can be found any basis for its application for the protection of the rights of property or of free-

---

[156]See in general, José Luis Lazzarini, *El Juicio de Amparo*, La Ley, Buenos Aires, 1987; Néstor Pedro Sagües, *Derecho Procesal Constitucional. Acción de Amparo*, Vol 3., Editorial Astrea, Buenos Aires, 1988; and "El derecho de amparo en Argentina," in Héctor Fix-Zamudio and Eduardo Ferrer Mac-Gregor, *El derecho de amparo en el mundo*, Edit. Porrúa, México, 2006, pp. 41–80.

[157]See G. R. Carrio, *Algunos aspectos del recurso de amparo*, Buenos Aires, 1959, p. 9; J. R. Vanossi, *Teoría constitucional*, Vol. II, Supremacía y control de constitucionalidad, Buenos Aires, 1976, p. 277.

[158]See Néstor Pedro Sagües, *Derecho Procesal Constitucional. Hábeas Corpus*, Volume 4, 2nd Edition, Editorial Astrea, Buenos Aires, 1988, p. 116.

[159]See the references to the *Barolo* case in Joaquín Brage Camazano, *La jurisdicción constitucional de la libertad (Teoría general, Argentina, México, Corte Interamericana de Derechos Humanos)*, Editorial Porrúa, Instituto Mexicano de Derecho Procesal Constitucional, México, 2005, p. 66.

claimed protection. So that if they exist, they must be previously exhausted, unless it is proved that they are incapable of redressing the damage and their processing can lead to serious and irreparable harm. This can also be considered as a common trend of the amparo action in Latin America, as an extraordinary remedy, similar to what happens with the injunction procedure in the United States.

As mentioned, the amparo action is filed before the first instance courts and cases can only reach the Supreme Court by means of an extraordinary recourse, which can only be filed when in the judicial decision a matter of judicial review of constitutionality is resolved,[164] in a similar way as constitutional questions can reach the Supreme Court in the United States.

And in fact, the judicial review system in Argentina,[165] of all Latin American countries, is perhaps the one that more closely follows the United States model. It was also founded in the supremacy clause established in the 1860 Constitution that does not expressly confer any judicial review power upon the Supreme Court or the other courts. So in the case of Argentina, judicial review was also a creation of the Supreme Court, based on the same principles of supremacy of the constitution and judicial duty when applying the law.

The first case in which judicial review power was exercised regarding a federal statute was the *Sojo* case (1887), which concerned the unconstitutionality of a statute that tried to extend the original jurisdiction of the Supreme Court[166] as happened in the *Marbury v. Madison* case U.S. (1

---

[164]See Elias Guastavino, *Recurso extraordinario de inconstitucionalidad*, Ed. La Roca, Buenos Aires, Argentina, 1992; Lino Enrique Palacio, *El recurso extraordinario federal. Teoría y Técnica*, Abeledo-Perrot, Buenos Aires, 1992.

[165]See in general Néstor Pedro Sagüés, *Derecho procesal Constitucional*, Ed. Asrea, Buenos Aires, 2002; Ricardo Haro, *El control de constitucionalidad*, Editorial Zavalia, Buenos Aires, Argentina, 2003; Juan Carlos Hitters, "La jurisdicción constitucional en Argentina," in Domingo García Belaunde and Francisco Fernández Segado (Coord.), *La jurisdicción constitucional en Iberoamérica*, Ed. Dykinson, Madrid, España, 1997; Maximiliano Toricelli, *El sistema de control constitucional argentino*, Editorial Lexis Nexis Depalma, Buenos Aires, Argentina, 2002.

[166]See A. E. Ghigliani, *Del control jurisdiccional de constitucionalidad*, Buenos Aires, 1952, p. 5; R. Bielsa, *La protección constitucional y el recurso extraordinario. Jurisdicción de la Corte Suprema*, Buenos Aires, 1958, p. 41, 43, 179 who speaks about a "pretorian creation" of judicial review by the Supreme Court, p. 179. See Jorge Reinaldo Vanossi and P. F. Ubertone, "Control jurisdiccional de constitucionalidad," in *Desafíos del control de constitucionalidad*, Ediciones Ciudad Argentina, Buenos Aires, Argentina, 1996 (also printed as *Instituciones de defensa de la Constitución en la Argentina*, Universidad

Cranch), 137; 2 L. Ed. 60 (1803), in which the constitution was considered as the supreme law of the land and the courts were empowered to maintain its supremacy over the statutes that infringed it.[167]

Therefore, through the work of the courts, in the Argentinean system of judicial review all the courts have the power to declare the unconstitutionality of legislative acts,[168] treaties,[169] executive and administrative acts and judicial decisions, whether at national or provincial levels.

In Argentina, a federal state, the Judiciary is regulated through national and provincial statutes, and the Supreme Court of Justice, the only judicial body created in the constitution, is the "final interpreter" or "the defendant of the Constitution," having also two sorts of jurisdiction: an original and an appellate one.[170] It has been through the appellate jurisdiction and by means of the "extraordinary recourse" in cases decided by the National Chambers of Appeals and by the Superior Courts of the Provinces that the cases can reach the Supreme Court, in particular, when constitutional issues have been resolved.

So in a similar way as the United States (American) system of judicial review, the Argentinean system is also a diffuse one, essentially of an incidental character, in the sense that the question of constitutionality is not the principal matter of a process. The question has to be raised by a party in a particular judicial controversy, case or process, normally

---

Nacional Autónoma de México, Congreso Internacional sobre la Constitución y su defense, México, 1982); H. Quiroga Lavie, *Derecho constitucional*, Buenos Aires, 1978, p. 481. Previously in 1863 the first Supreme Court decisions were adopted in constitutional matters but referred to provincial and executive acts. See A. E. Ghigliani, *Idem*, p. 58.

[167] See. A. E. Ghigliani, *Idem*, p. 58.

[168] See Néstor Pedro Sagüés, *Recurso Extraordinario*, Buenos Aires, 1984, Vol. I, p. 91; Jorge Reinaldo Vanossi and P. F. Ubertone, "Control jurisdiccional de constitucionalidad," in *Desafíos del control de constitucionalidad*, Ediciones Ciudad Argentina, Buenos Aires, Argentina, 1996; J.R. Vanossi, *Teoría constitucional*, Vol. II, Supremacía y control de constitucionalidad, Buenos Aires, 1976, p. 155.

[169] In particular, regarding the unconstitutionality of treaties and the possibility of the Courts to control them, A. E. Ghigliani, *Del control jurisdiccional de constitucionalidad*, Buenos Aires, 1952, p. 62; Jorge Reinaldo Vanossi, *Aspectos del recurso extraordinario de inconstitucionalidad*, Buenos Aires, 1966, p. 91, and *Teoría constitucional*, Vol. II, Supremacía y control de constitucionalidad, Buenos Aires, 1976, p. 277.

[170] See R. Bielsa, *La protección constitucional y el recurso extraordinario. Jurisdicción de la Corte Suprema*, Buenos Aires, 1958, pp. 60–61, 270; J. R. Vanossi and P. F. Ubertone, "Control jurisdiccional de constitucionalidad," in *Desafíos del control de constitucionalidad*, Ediciones Ciudad Argentina, Buenos Aires, 1996.

when the constitutional issue has not been discussed in the lower courts and has not considered it in the decision.[179]

Another aspect that must be highlighted is that in the Argentinean system, the decision on judicial review on constitutional issues is not obligatory for the other courts or for the inferior courts;[180] that is, they do not have *stare decisis* effects.

In the 1949 constitutional reform, an attempt was made to give binding effects on the national and provincial courts to the interpretation adopted by the Supreme Court of Justice regarding articles of the constitution,[181] but this provision was later repealed and the situation today is the absolute power of all courts to render their judgment autonomously with their own constitutional interpretation. Nevertheless, the decisions of the Supreme Court of Justice, as the highest court in the country, have a definitive important influence upon all the inferior courts, particularly when a doctrine has been clearly and frequently established by the Court.

In this Argentinean system of judicial review, of course the amparo action is an important tool to raise constitutional questions. Nonetheless, discussions have been raised regarding the possibility of the applicability of the diffuse method of judicial review by the courts, precisely when deciding actions for amparo.

In the initial development of the amparo, and in spite of the diffuse system of judicial review followed in Argentina, the Supreme Court, in a contradictory way, established the criteria that the judge, when deciding amparo cases, had no power to decide on the constitutionality of legislation, reducing his powers to decide only on acts or facts that could violate fundamental rights. Thus, the amparo could not be granted when the complaint contained the allegation of unconstitutionality of a statute on which the relevant acts or facts were based.[182] This doctrine was incorporated in the Law 16.986 of October 18, 1966, on the recourse for amparo, in which it was expressly established that the "action for amparo will not be admissible when the decision upon the invalidity of the act will re-

---

[179]See R. Bielsa, *Idem*, p. 190, 202–205, 209, 245, 252.

[180]See R. Bielsa, *Idem*, pp. 49, 198, 267; A. E. Ghigliani, *Del control jurisdiccional de constitucionalidad*, Buenos Aires, 1952, pp. 97, 98.

[181]Article 95 of the 1949 Constitution. See C. A. Ayanagaray, *Efectos de la declaración de inconstitucionalidad*, Buenos Aires, 1955, p. 11; R. Bielsa, *Idem*, p. 268.

[182]See the *Aserradero Clipper SRL* case (1961), in J. R. Vanossi, *Teoría constitucional*, Vol. II, Supremacía y control de constitucionalidad, Buenos Aires, 1976, p. 286.

quire.... the declaration of the unconstitutionality of statues, decrees or ordinances" (Article 2,d).

Yet one year later, in 1967, the Supreme Court, without expressly declaring the unconstitutionality of this provision, in the *Outon* case,[183] decided its inapplicability and accepted the criteria that when considering amparo cases, the courts have the power to review the unconstitutionality of legislation.[184]

In spite of Argentina being the only Latin American country that has kept the diffuse method of judicial review as the only one applicable in order to control the constitutionality of legislation, the diffuse method of judicial review is also applied in Brazil, Colombia, Dominican Republic, Ecuador, Guatemala, Mexico, Nicaragua, Peru and Venezuela but with the main difference that it is applied within a mixed system of judicial review (diffuse and concentrated).

---

[183] *Outon* case of March 29, 1967. J.R. Vanossi, *Idem*, p. 288.

[184] See G. J. Bidart Campos, *Régimen legal del amparo*, 1969; G. J. Bidart Campos, "El control de constitucionalidad en el juicio de amparo y la arbitrariedad o ilegalidad del acto lesivo," *Jurisprudencia Argentina*, 23-4-1969; N.P. Sagües, "El juicio de amparo y el planteo de inconstitucionalidad," in *Jurisprudencia Argentina*, 20-7-1973; J. R. Vanossi, *Idem*, pp. 288–292; José Luis Lazzarini, *El juicio de amparo*, La Ley, Buenos Aires, 1987, pp. 80, 86; Alí Joaquín Salgado, *Juicio de amparo y acción de inconstitucionalidad*, Ed. Astrea, Buenos Aires, 1987, p. 58; Joaquín Brage Camazano, *La jurisdicción constitucional de la libertad (Teoría general, Argentina, México, Corte Interamericana de Derechos Humanos)*, Editorial Porrúa, Instituto Mexicano de Derecho Procesal Constitucional, México, 2005, pp. 71, 117.

reestablished in the enjoyment of the rights declared in the Constitution, as well as those fundamental rights set forth in international instruments on human rights applicable in the Republic." The Constitution assigns to the Constitutional Chamber of the Supreme Court the exclusive jurisdiction to decide these actions for protection, which gave birth to a concentrated judicial system of amparo.[188]

In Costa Rica, both the habeas corpus and the amparo recourses are also regulated in a single statute, the Constitutional Judicial Review statute (*Ley de la Jurisdicción Constitucional, Ley n° 7135*) of October 11, 1989.[189]

According to Article 29 of the law, the recourse of amparo can be filed against any provision, decision or resolution and, in general, against any public administration action, omission or material activity that is not founded in an effective administrative act and has violated or threatened to violate the constitutional rights.

As in Argentina, the law excludes the amparo action against statutes or other regulatory provisions. Nonetheless, they can be challenged together with the individual acts applying them, or when containing selfexecuting or automatically applicable provisions, in the sense that their provisions become immediately obligatory simply upon their sanctioning. Yet in such cases, the Chamber must decide the matter of the unconstitutionality of the statute, not in the amparo proceeding, but in a general way following the procedure of the action of unconstitutionality.

The law also excludes the amparo against judicial resolutions and actions of the judiciary, or other authorities' acts when executing judicial decisions, and against the acts or provisions in electoral matters of the Supreme Tribunal of Elections (Article 30).

Regarding individuals, Costa Rica's law as in Argentina, admits the possibility of the amparo actions to be filed against any harming actions or omissions from individuals, but in this case, in a limited way only referred to persons or corporations exercising public functions or powers

---

[188]See, in general, Rubén Hernández Valle, *La tutela de los derechos fundamentales*, Editorial Juricentro, San José, 1990; Rubén Hernández Valle, "El recurso de amparo en Costa Rica," in Héctor Fix-Zamudio and Eduardo Ferrer Mac-Gregor (Coord.), *El derecho de amparo en el mundo*, Universidad Nacional Autónoma de México, Editorial Porrúa, México, 2006, pp. 257–304.

[189]See in general, Rubén Hernández Valle, "El recurso de amparo en Costa Rica," in Héctor Fix-Zamudio and Eduardo Ferrer Mac-Gregor, *Idem,* Edit. Porrúa, México, 2006, pp. 257–304.

that by law or by fact place them in a position of power against which ordinary judicial remedies are clearly insufficient to guaranty the protection of fundamental rights and freedoms (Article 57).

The Constitutional Chamber of the Supreme Court of Costa Rica, before which the amparo recourses are filed, was created by the constitutional reform of 1989, with the exclusive power to exercise the concentrated method of judicial review with powers to declare the unconstitutionality of statutes and other State acts with nullifying effects (Article 10). For this purpose, the Chamber can be reached through various means set forth in the Law on Constitutional Jurisdiction (Article 73).

First, by means of a direct action of unconstitutionality that can be brought before the Chamber against any statute or executive regulation, or international treaty considered contrary to the constitution, and even against constitutional amendments approved in violation of the constitutional procedure.

This principal unconstitutionality action can only be brought before the Constitutional Chamber by the General Comptroller, the Attorney General, the Public Prosecutor and the People's Defendant (Article 75). Nonetheless, the action can also be brought before the Chamber in a similar way to a popular action in cases involving the defense of diffuse or collective interests filed against executive regulation or selfexecuting statutes that do not require additional public actions for its enforcement.[190]

Second, the action can also be exercised in an incidental way before the Constitutional Chamber when a party raises the constitutional question in a particular judicial case, even in cases of habeas corpus and amparo, as a mean for the protection of the rights and interest of the affected parties (Article 75).

In all these cases of actions, the decisions of the Chamber when declaring the unconstitutionality of the challenged statute have nullifying and general *erga omnes* effects.

Third, in addition to the direct or incidental action of unconstitutionality, the other important mean for judicial review is the judicial referrals on constitutional matters that any courts can raise *ex officio* before the Constitutional Chamber when there are doubts regarding the constitutionality of the statute that they must apply for the resolution of the case

---

[190]See Rubén Hernández Valle, *El Control de la Constitucionalidad de las Leyes*, San José, 1990.

actions are regulated in one single statute along with other constitutional procedures, in the Constitutional Tribunal Statute (*Ley n° 1836 del Tribunal Constitucional*) enacted in 1998.[193]

Regarding the amparo, Article 19 of the constitution establishes the action for the protection of all constitutional rights declared in the constitution and in statutes, which can also be filed against any illegal acts or omissions from public officials or private individuals that restrict, suppress or threaten to restrict or withhold personal rights and guaranties recognized by the constitution and the statutes (Article 19). In these cases the action can only be filed when there is no other mean or legal recourse available for the immediate protection of the restricted, suspended or threatened right or guaranty.

Law 1.836 of 1998 of the Constitutional Tribunal provides that the constitutional amparo can be brought before the highest Courts in the Department capitals or before the District Judges in the Provinces (Article 95) and shall be admitted "against any unlawful resolution, act or omission of an authority or official, provided there is no other procedure or recourse available to immediately protect the rights and guaranties," which, as established in Argentina and El Salvador, confirms its extraordinary character. Judicial decisions are excluded from the amparo action when they can be modified or suppressed by means of other recourses (Article 96,3).

The law also admits, like in Argentina, the filing of the amparo action "against any unlawful act or omission of a person or group of private individuals that restricts, suppresses or threatens the rights or guaranties recognized by the Constitution and the Laws" (Article 94).

In Bolivia, according to the constitution (Article 120,7), and the Law of the Constitutional Tribunal (Article 7,8), all the judicial decisions issued on amparo or habeas corpus must be sent to the Constitutional Tribunal in order to be reviewed.

Yet in this case of Bolivia, different to the provisions in Argentina and also in Brazil, Colombia and Venezuela where an extraordinary recourse for revision is provided, the power of the Constitutional Tribunal to review the amparo and habeas corpus decisions is exercised, not because of an extraordinary recourse, but because of an obligatory review duty, for

---

[193]See in general, José A. Rivera Santivañez, *Jurisdicción constitucional. Procesos constitucionales en Bolivia*, Ed. Kipus, Cochabamba, 2004, and "El amparo constitucional en Bolivia," in Héctor Fix-Zamudio and Eduardo Ferrer Mac-Gregor, *Idem*, Edit. Porrúa, México, 2006, pp. 81–122.

which purpose the decisions must automatically be sent by the courts to the Constitutional Tribunal. Through this power, the Tribunal can guaranty the uniformity of the constitutional interpretation.

In Bolivia, the judicial review system has also been configured, since the 1994 constitutional reform, as an exclusively concentrated one,[194] corresponding to the Constitutional Tribunal, the exclusive power to declare the nullity of statutes considered unconstitutional, also with general *erga omnes* effects (Article 58).[195] For such purpose, the question of the unconstitutionality of a statute or general executive acts can be brought before the Tribunal by means of a direct action of abstract character, that can only be filed by the President of the Republic, any senator or representative, the General Prosecutor and the People's Defendant (Article 7,1). It is also possible for the parties in a case or *ex officio* for the judge to raise the question of unconstitutionality of statutes before the Constitutional Tribunal by means of an incidental recourse, when the decision of the case depends upon its constitutionality (Article 59).

So with the exception of the amparo, habeas corpus and habeas data decisions, the ordinary courts cannot rule on constitutional matters, and must refer the control of constitutionality of statutes to the Constitutional Tribunal.

2. *The recourse for protection and of habeas corpus in Chile*

In Chile, Articles 20 and 21 of the constitution, in addition to the habeas corpus recourse and with antecedents in the Constitutional Act n° 3 (Decree-Law 1.552) of 1976, also establishes the amparo recourse called recourse for protection (*recurso de protección*) conceived, as in Colombia, to protect only certain constitutional rights and freedoms, which are

---

[194]See in general José Antonio Rivera Santibañez, "La jurisdicción constitucional en Bolivia. Cinco años en defensa del orden constitucional y democrático," in *Revista Iberoamericana de Derecho Procesal Constitucional,* n° 1, Enero-Junio 2004, Ed. Porrúa, 2004; José Antonio Rivera Santibañez, "El control constitucional en Bolivia," in *Anuario Iberoamericano de Justicia Constitucional.* Centro de Estudios Políticos y Constitucionales n° 3, 1999, pp. 205–237; José Antonio Rivera Santivañez, "Los valores supremos y principios fundamentales en la jurisprudencia constitucional," in *La Justicia Constitucional en Bolivia 1998–2003,* Ed. Tribunal Constitucional-AECI, Bolivia, 2003, pp. 347 ff.; Benjamín Miguel Harb, "La jurisdicción constitucional en Bolivia," in *La Jurisdicción Constitucional en Iberoamérica,* Ed. Dykinson, Madrid, España, 1997, pp. 337 ff.

[195]Jorge Asbún Rojas, "Control constitucional en Bolivia, evolución y perspectivas," in *Jurisdicción Constitucional,* Academia Boliviana de Estudios Constitucionales. Editora El País, Santa Cruz, Bolivia, 2000, p. 86.

eral statute on constitutional proceedings, the Constitutional Judicial Review statute (*Ley sobre la Justicia Constitucional*) of 2004.[200]

Regarding the recourse of amparo, Article 183 of the constitution recognizes the right of any person to file the recourse in order to be restored in the enjoyment of all rights declared or recognized in the Constitution, and in addition, in the treaties, covenants and other international instruments of human rights (Article 183 Constitution, Article 41,1 Law), against public authority actions or facts, comprising statutes, judicial decisions or administrative acts and also omissions or threats of violation (Articles 13 and 41, Law). In this case, and depending on the rank of the injurer's public authority, the action of amparo can be filed before a variety of courts.

Regarding individuals, as in Colombia, Costa Rica and Ecuador, the action can only be filed against their actions when issued exercising delegated public powers, that is, against institutions maintained by public funds and those acting by delegation of a State entity by virtue of a concession, contract or other valid resolution (Article 42).[201]

The Constitution of Honduras also expressly admits the amparo against statutes, establishing the right of any party to file the action for amparo, in order to have a judicial declaration ruling that its provisions do not oblige the plaintiff and are not applicable when they contravene, diminish or distort any of the rights recognized in this Constitution (Article 183,2).

In the case of Honduras, the amparo decisions are subject to an obligatory review by the corresponding superior court, and those issued by the Appellate Courts also subject to review by the Constitutional Chamber of the Supreme Court, but in this case on a discretionary basis, by means of the parties' request (Articles 68, 69, Law). Thus, the Constitutional Chamber can always be the last resort to decide upon the matters of amparo.

---

[200]See in general, Francisco D. Gómez Bueso, "El derecho de amparo en Honduras," in Héctor Fix-Zamudio and Eduardo Ferrer Mac-Gregor, *Idem,* Edit. Porrúa, México, 2006, pp. 409–460; and Allan R. Brewer-Carías, "El sistema de justicia constitucional en Honduras," in *El sistema de justicia constitucional en Honduras (Comentarios a la ley sobre Justicia Constitucional),* Instituto Interamericano de Derechos Humanos, San José 2004, pp, 107–140.

[201]See Francisco Daniel Gómez Bueso, "El derecho de amparo en Honduras," in Héctor Fix-Zamudio and Eduardo Ferrer Mac-Gregor (Coord.), *El derecho de amparo en el mundo,* Universidad Nacional Autónoma de México, Editorial Porrúa, México, 2006, pp. 409–460.

In addition to the amparo and habeas corpus actions, Article 320 of the constitution sets forth the general rule of judicial review consisting that "in cases of incompatibility between a constitutional norm and an ordinary statutory one, the courts must apply the former." In the same sense as it is established in the constitutions of Colombia, Guatemala and Venezuela, this constitutional provision of Honduras establishes the diffuse method of judicial review.[202] Nonetheless, the Law on Constitutional Justice, sanctioned in 2004,[203] failed to regulate such method in the country, and, instead, just established an exclusive concentrated method of judicial review of legislation by attributing to the Constitutional Chamber of the Supreme Court the monopoly to annul statutes on the grounds of their unconstitutionality.

Nonetheless, by means of the amparo action it is possible to consider that in Honduras the diffuse method of judicial review can be applied, in the sense that in a contrary sense to the other Latin American regulations in concentrated systems, the constitution allows the courts to decide that a statute is not to be enforced against the claimant nor is it applicable in a specific case when such statute contravenes, diminishes or distorts a right recognized by this Constitution (183,2 Constitution).

Now, regarding the concentrated method of judicial review, the Constitutional Chamber can declare the unconstitutionality of statutes "on grounds of form or in its contents" (Articles 184; 315,5).

For such purpose, the constitutional questions can reach the Constitutional Chamber also through two means: First, through an action of unconstitutionality that can be brought before the Constitutional Chamber by persons with personal interest against statutes and constitutional amendments when approved contrary to the formalities set forth in the Constitution and against approbatory statutes of international treaties sanctioned without following the constitutional formalities (Article 17). It is also

---

[202]See Allan R. Brewer-Carías, "El sistema de justicia constitucional en Honduras," in *El sistema de Justicia Constitucional en Honduras (Comentarios a la Ley sobre Justicia Constitucional)*, Instituto Interamericano de Derechos Humanos, Corte Suprema de Justicia. República de Honduras, San José, 2004, pp. 27 ff.

[203]See Allan R. Brewer-Carías, "La reforma del sistema de justicia constitucional en Honduras," in *Revista Iberoamericana de Derecho Procesal Constitucional. Proceso y Constitución* (Directores Eduardo Ferrer Mac-Gregor y Aníbal Quiroga León), n° 4, 2005, Editorial Porrúa, México, pp. 57–77; and "El sistema de justicia constitucional en Honduras," in *El sistema de Justicia Constitucional en Honduras (Comentarios a la Ley sobre Justicia Constitucional)*, Instituto Interamericano de Derechos Humanos, Corte Suprema de Justicia. República de Honduras, San José, 2004, pp. 1–148.

admissible against statutes that contravene the provisions of an international treaty or convention in force (Article 76).

Second, the questions of constitutionality can also reach the Constitutional Chamber in an incidental way, as an exception raised by a party in any particular case (Article 82), or by the referral of the case that any court can make before deciding the case, before the Chamber (Article 87).

In both cases, whether through the action of unconstitutionality or by means of the incidental constitutional question, the decision of the Constitutional Chamber regarding the unconstitutionality of statutes also has general *erga omnes* effects (Article 94).

4. The action of amparo and habeas corpus in Panama

Following the general trend of Latin American constitutions, the Constitution of Panama also distinguishes two specific judicial means for the protection of constitutional rights: the habeas corpus and the amparo recourses.

Regarding the recourse of amparo, the Constitution of Panama sets forth the right of any person to have revoked any order to do or to refrain from doing issued by any public servant violating the rights and guaranties set forth in the constitution (Article 50).

Thus, the amparo is also conceived in Panamá for the protection of constitutional rights only against authority actions and is not admitted against individual unconstitutional actions. The action can be filed before the ordinary first instance courts, except in cases of high rank officials, in which cases the Supreme Court is the competent one.[204]

Panama, together with Paraguay, are the only two countries where the statutory regulation regarding habeas corpus and amparo are set forth in the general procedural code, the Judicial Code (*Código Judicial, Libro IV Instituciones de garantía*), Articles 2574–2614 (habeas corpus) and 2615–2632 (*amparo de garantía constitucionales*) of 1987.[205]

---

[204]See Lao Santizo P., *Acotaciones al amparo de garantías constitucionales panameño*, Editorial Jurídica Sanvas, San José, Costa Rica, 1987; Arturo Hoyos, "El proceso de amparo de derechos fundamentales en Panamá," in Héctor Fix-Zamudio and Eduardo Ferrer Mac-Gregor (Coord.), *Idem*, pp. 565–580.

[205]See in general, Arturo Hoyos, "El proceso de amparo de derechos fundamentales en Panamá," in Héctor Fix-Zamudio and Eduardo Ferrer Mac-Gregor, *Idem*, Edit. Porrúa, México, 2006, pp. 565-580.

According to the Code, the "amparo of constitutional guaranties" can be brought before the courts against any acts that harm or injure the fundamental rights and guaranties set forth in the constitution (Article 2615) and also against judicial decisions when all the existing judicial means to challenge them have been exhausted; but it cannot refer to judicial decisions adopted by the Electoral Tribunal or by the Supreme Court of Justice or any of its Chambers.

Regarding the judicial review system of Panama, it is also conceived as a concentrated one, attributing to the Supreme Court of Justice the exclusive power (Article 203,1) to protect the integrity of the constitution and to control the constitutionality of legislation also by means of two different methods: a direct popular action or by means of a question of constitutionality that can be raised by the parties to the case as an incident before a lower court, or *ex officio* by the respective court.

Regarding the action of unconstitutionality, in similar terms as in El Salvador and also in Colombia and Venezuela, it is conceived as a popular action that can be brought before the Supreme Court by anybody in order to denounce the unconstitutionality of statutes, decrees, decisions or acts founded in substantive or formal questions (Article 2556).

In both cases, the Supreme Court's decision is final, definitive, obligatory and with general but nonretroactive effects, and must be published in the *Official Gazette* (Article 2573, Judicial Code).

5. The action for amparo, habeas corpus and habeas data in Paraguay

The Constitution of Paraguay also regulates in a very detailed way the three judicial means for the protection of constitutional rights: the amparo, the habeas corpus (Article 133)[206] and the habeas data recourses (Article 135).

Regarding the petition for amparo, according to Article 134 of the constitution, it can be filed by anyone who considers himself seriously affected in his rights or guaranties by a clearly illegitimate act or omission, either by governmental authorities or individuals, or who may be in imminent danger that his constitutional rights and guaranties may be curtailed, and whom, in light of the urgency of the matter cannot obtain

---

[206]See Evelio Fernández Arévalos, *Habeas Corpus Régimen Constitucional y legal en el Paraguay*, Intercontinental Editora, Asunción, 2000.

adequate remedy through regular legal means. In all such cases, the affected person may file a petition for amparo before a competent judge.[207]

The amparo petition, originally regulated in the 1971 Law n° 341 of Amparo (*Ley 341/71 reglamentaria del amparo*), since 1988 is regulated in a section of the Civil Procedure Code (Articles 565–588), which, as in Argentina and Costa Rica, provides that it is not admissible against judicial decisions and resolutions, nor in the procedure of formation, sanction and promulgation of statutes, or when the matter refers to the individual freedom protected by the recourse of habeas corpus (Article 565,a,b).

According to Article 566 of the Code, the petition for amparo can be filed before any first instance court with jurisdiction in the place where the act or omission could have effect. Nonetheless, regarding electoral questions and matters related to political organization, the competent court will be those of the electoral jurisdiction (Article 134, Constitution).

Except for the resolutions of the amparo action, habeas corpus recourse or habeas data actions, which in general corresponds to all courts of first instance, all other constitutional matters dealing with judicial review of legislation are the exclusive attribution of the Constitutional Chamber of the Supreme Court of Justice, because Paraguay has had a concentrated system of judicial review established since the 1992 Constitution.[208] According to this method, the Supreme Court of Justice has the power to decide actions and exceptions seeking to declare the unconstitutionality and inapplicability of statutes contrary to the constitution. For such purpose, when a judge hearing a particular case considers the applicable statute contrary to the constitution, he must send the files, even *ex officio*, to the Constitutional Chamber of the Supreme Court of Justice, in order for the Court to decide the question of unconstitutionality when evident (Article 582, Code).

The main distinctive feature of the Paraguayan concentrated judicial review system is that contrary to other countries, there is not a direct action of unconstitutionality, so that the constitutional questions regard-

---

[207]See Jorge Seall-Sasiain, "El amparo en Paraguay," in Héctor Fix-Zamudio and Eduardo Ferrer Mac-Gregor (Coord.), *El derecho de amparo en el mundo*, Universidad Nacional Autónoma de México, Editorial Porrúa, México, 2006, pp. 58-591.

[208]See in general, Norbert Lösing, "La justicia constitucional en Paraguay y Uruguay," in *Anuario de Derecho Constitucional Latinoamericano* 2002. Ed. KAS, Montevideo, Uruguay, 2002; Luis Lezcano Claude, *El control de constitucionalidad en el Paraguay*, Ed. La Ley Paraguaya S.A. Asunción, 2000.

ing the unconstitutionality of statutes can only reach the Supreme Court in an incidental way. That is why the Supreme Court decisions only declare in the particular case the inapplicability of the statute provisions, having only *inter partes* effects regarding the particular case (Article 260, Constitution).[209]

6.   The action of amparo and habeas corpus in Uruguay

The Constitution of Uruguay, contrary to all other Latin American constitutions, does not expressly and specifically provide for the action or recourse of amparo, which nonetheless has been deducted from Articles 7,72 and 332 of the 1966 Constitution, when declaring the general right of all inhabitants of the Republic "to be protected in the enjoyment of their life, honor, freedom, safety, work and property." In contrast, the constitution expressly provides for the action of habeas corpus (Article 17) to protect any undue imprisonment.

Nonetheless, the amparo recourse has been regulated in the 1988 *Amparo* Law nº 16.011 (*Ley de amparo*),[210] which establishes that any person, human or artificial, public or private, except in those cases where an action of habeas corpus is admitted, may bring an action of amparo against any act, omission or fact of the public sector authorities, as well as of private individuals that in a illegitimate and evident unlawful way, currently or imminently, impair, restrict, alter or threaten any of the rights and freedoms expressly or implicitly recognized by the constitution (Article 72).

This action of amparo for the protection of all constitutional rights and freedoms may be brought before the judges of first instance in the place where the act, fact or omission under dispute have produced effect (Article 3).[211]

---

[209]L. M. Argaña, "Control de la Constitucionalidad de las Leyes en Paraguay," in *Memoria de la Reunión de Presidentes de Cortes Supremas de Justicia en Iberoamérica, el Caribe, España y Portugal*, Caracas, 1982, pp. 550, 551, 669, 671.

[210]See in general, José R. Saravia Antúnez, Recurso de Amparo. Práctica Constitucional, Fundación Cultura Universitaria, Montevideo, 1993; Héctor Gros Espiell, "El derecho de amparo en Uruguay," in Héctor Fix-Zamudio and Eduardo Ferrer Mac-Gregor, *Idem,* Edit. Porrúa, México, 2006, pp. 633–648.

[211]See in general Luis Alberto Viera *et al.*, *Ley de Amparo. Comentarios, Texto Legal y Antecedentes legislativos a su sanción. Jurisprudencia sobre el amparo*, 2nd Edition, Ediciones IDEA, Montevideo, 1993; Miguel Ángel Semino, "Comentarios sobre la acción de amparo en el Derecha uruguayo," in *Boletín de la Comisión Andina de Jurista*, nº 27,

However, Law N° 16.011, like in Argentina, Costa Rica and Paraguay, excludes all judicial acts issued in judicial controversies from action of amparo. The acts of the Electoral Court, and the statutes and decrees of departmental governments that have force of statute in their jurisdiction (Article 1) are also excluded, as in Costa Rica and Panama.

This action of amparo in the Uruguayan system, as in Argentina, is only admitted when there are no other judicial or administrative means available for obtaining the same result of protection or amparo, or when, if they exist, they are clearly ineffective for protecting the right (Article 2).

In the proceeding of the amparo action, constitutional questions regarding the unconstitutionality of statutes may also arise, but as in Paraguay, the ordinary court cannot resolve them and must refer the matter to the Supreme Court of Justice, which is also a consequence of the concentrated method of judicial review of legislation that exists in Uruguay.[212]

In this regard, Article 256 of the Uruguayan Constitution, since 1934,[213] has assigned the Supreme Court of Justice the exclusive and original power to declare the unconstitutionality of statutes and other State acts with force of statutes, whether founded on formal or substantive reasons as a consequence of an action of unconstitutionality that can be filed before the Court by all those who deem that their personal and legitimate interests have been harmed (Article 258).[214] Thus, regarding

---

Lima, 1986; Héctor Gross Espiel, "El derecho de amparo en el Uruguay," in Héctor Fix-Zamudio and Eduardo Ferrer Mac-Gregor (Coord.), *El derecho de amparo en el mundo*, Universidad Nacional Autónoma de México, Editorial Porrúa, México, 2006, pp. 633–648.

[212] See in general José Korseniak, "La Justicia constitucional en Uruguay," in *La Revista de Derecho*, año III, enero-junio 1989, Facultad de Derecho, Universidad Central, 1989; Héctor Gross Espiell, "La jurisdicción constitucional en el Uruguay," in *La Jurisdicción Constitucional en Iberoamérica*, Ed. Universidad Externado de Colombia, Bogotá Colombia, 1984; Eduardo Esteva G. "La jurisdicción constitucional en Uruguay," in Domingo García Belaunde and Francisco Fernández Segado (Coord.), *La Jurisdicción Constitucional en Iberoamérica*,. Ed. Dykinson, Madrid, 1997; Norbert Lösing, "La justicia constitucional en Paraguay y Uruguay," in *Anuario de Derecho Constitucional Latinoamericano 2002*, Ed. Kas, Montevideo, 2002.

[213] Originally the system was established in 1934, and later in 1951. See H. Gross Espiell, *La Constitución y su Defensa*, Congreso, printed for the International Congress on La Constitución y su Defensa, Universidad Nacional Autónoma de México, México, 1982, pp. 7, 11. The system remained in the 1966 Constitution, in the "Acta Institucional n° 8 de 1977" and in the "Acta Institucional n° 12 de 1981." *Idem*, pp. 16, 20.

[214] Article 258. See H. Gross Espiell, "La Constitución y su Defensa," *Idem*,. 28, 29; J. P. Gatto de Souza, "Control de la Constitucionalidad de los Actos del Poder público en Uru-

the quality to sue (standing), the Uruguayan regulation has similarities with the Honduran one.

The constitutional question can also be submitted to the Supreme Court in an incidental way by a referral made *ex officio* or as a consequence of an exception of unconstitutionality raised by a party in a particular case by an inferior court (Article 258).

In all cases, similar to the Paraguayan solution where the question on the constitutionality of statutes referred only to particular cases, the decisions of the Supreme Court on matters of constitutionality only refer to the particular case in which the question is raised (Article 259)[215] and also has *inter partes* effects.

guay," in *Memoria de la Reunión de Presidentes de Cortes Supremas de Justicia en Ibe-roamérica, el Caribe, España y Portugal,* Caracas, 1982, pp. 661, 662.

[215]This principle is clear regarding the incidental mean of judicial review where the question of constitutionality is raised in a particular case, but originates doubts regarding the action of unconstitutionality. According to the Law n° 13747 of 1969 that regulates the procedures in matters of judicial review, the decision of the Supreme Court impedes the application of the challenged norms declared unconstitutional regarding the plaintiff, and authorizes its use as an exception in all other judicial proceedings, including the judicial review of public administration activities. See H. Gross Espiell, "La Constitución y su Defensa," *Idem,* p. 29.

CHAPTER SIX

THE AMPARO AS A CONSTITUTIONAL RIGHT IN COUNTRIES WITH MIXED SYSTEMS OF JUDICIAL REVIEW OF LEGISLATION

I. THE AMPARO ACTION IN COUNTRIES WITH MIXED SYS-
TEMS (DIFFUSE AND CONCENTRATED) OF JUDICIAL RE-
VIEW

Except in the case of Argentina, which remains the most similar to the
"American model,"[216] the system of judicial review in all the other Latin
American countries applying the same diffuse method of judicial review
has moved from the original, exclusively diffuse one toward a mixed one,
by also adopting the concentrated method. This is the case in Brazil,
Colombia, Dominican Republic, Ecuador, Guatemala, Mexico, Nicaragua,
Peru and Venezuela. That means that in these countries, for the resolution
of particular cases or controversies, all the courts are empowered to decide upon the unconstitutionality of legislation, and not to apply for the
resolution of the case statutes they considered contrary to the constitution, giving preference to the latter; and at the same time, the Supreme
Court or the Constitutional Court or Tribunal is also empowered to decide upon the unconstitutionality of statutes, when requested through a
direct action that can be filed by some high public officials or by the
citizenship, or when deciding incidental referrals on the constitutionality

---

[216]See A. E. Ghigliani, *Del control jurisdiccional de constitucionalidad*, Buenos Aires,
1952, who speaks about "Northamerican filiation" of the judicial control of constitutionality in Argentinian law, p. 6, 55, 115; R. Bielsa, *La protección constitucional y el recurso
extraordinario. Jurisdicción de la Corte Suprema*, Buenos Aires, 1958, p. 116; J.A.C.
Grant, "El control jurisdiccional de la constitucionalidad de las Leyes: una contribución de
las Américas a la ciencia política," in *Revista de la Facultad de Derecho de México*, Universidad Nacional Autónoma de México, T. XII, n° 45, México, 1962, p. 652; C. J. Frie-
drich, *The Impact of American Constitutionalism Abroad*, Boston, 1967, p. 83.

of statutes submitted by lower courts, with powers to annul, with general effects, the challenged statutes.

This has happened even in Mexico, a country that with the peculiarities of its *juicio de amparo* also moved in 1994 from the original diffuse system of judicial review, initially and precisely established with the amparo suit, to the current mixed system of judicial review by attributing to the Supreme Court the power to annul, with general effects, statutes directly challenged by some high officials.

Additionally, in all these countries, the amparo proceeding for the protection of constitutional rights has also been regulated, generally following the diffuse judicial pattern by attributing competence to decide the cases to a variety of courts, mainly the first instance courts, and not to a single one. The only exception is Nicaragua, where the Supreme Court is the only competent court to decide upon amparo matters.

Yet in these countries another distinction can be made regarding the sense of the regulation of the constitutional protection of rights, whether as a substantive constitutional right in itself, or just as a single adjective remedy.

In the first case, when the amparo of constitutional rights and freedoms is also conceived as a constitutional right of the citizens, the main trend of the procedural regulation is that it can be enforced by means of a variety of recourses or actions, including a specific amparo action. In these cases, in addition to a specific judicial amparo action for immediate protection, such means of judicial protection can also be ordinary judicial means.

This first system is followed in Mexico and Venezuela where the amparo has been regulated as a constitutional right (derecho de amparo), originating not just one judicial guaranty (action or recourse) of amparo, but multiple ones, ordinary and specific.

In Mexico all these judicial means to assure the protection of constitutional rights and freedoms have been called *juicio de amparo*; instead, in Venezuela they are conceived as separate and autonomous proceedings all serving the same purpose of protecting constitutional rights.

Because of this feature, it is also in these two countries that no distinction is made between the amparo actions and the habeas corpus actions because the habeas corpus is a sort of amparo when directed to protect personal freedom and safety.

Apart from Mexico and Venezuela, in all the other Latin American countries the amparo is basically conceived just as an adjective instrument, action or recourse, for the protection of constitutional rights.

Consequently, I am going to examine the amparo in all these countries with mixed systems of judicial review of legislation, distinguishing those in which the amparo is conceived as a constitutional right in itself; and those where the amparo is regulated as a specific action or recourse.

The first system where the amparo is conceived as a constitutional right that can be exercised by means of many protective actions or recourses, as mentioned, is followed in Mexico and Venezuela, with the main difference that in the former all are called amparo and in the latter, they remain as being different judicial means.

II. THE MEXICAN SUIT OF AMPARO

In the Mexican Constitution the amparo is conceived as a general proceeding or suit (*juicio de amparo*) that can also be initiated by means of an action brought before the courts of the Federation for the protection of all individual guaranties declared in the Constitution, but only against actions accomplished by authorities, such as statutes, judicial decisions or administrative acts, and not against private individual actions. Since its introduction in the 1847 Acts of Constitutional Reform (Article 25) as the duty of federal courts to provide protection to citizens against State actions, the *juicio de amparo* has allowed the courts to decide, always in particular cases or controversies, without making general declarations concerning the challenged act.

This amparo suit is also set forth to resolve any controversy arising from statutes and authorities' acts that violate individual guaranties; and to resolve any controversy produced by federal statutes or authorities' acts harming or restricting the States' sovereignty, or by States' statutes of authorities' acts invading the sphere or federal authority (Article 1,1 of the Amparo Law).

In all these cases of amparo, the judicial protection is granted by means of a quick and efficient procedure that in the various expressions of the amparo suit, follows the same general procedural trends:[217] the absence of formalisms; the role of the judges as intermediaries between the parties; the inquisitorial character of the procedure that grants the judge a

---

[217]See Héctor Fix-Zamudio, *Ensayos sobre el derecho de amparo*, Universidad Nacional Autónoma de México, Editorial Porrúa, México, 2003; Héctor Fix-Zamudio and Eduardo Ferrer Mac-Gregor, "El derecho de amparo en México," in Héctor Fix-Zamudio and Eduardo Ferrer Mac-Gregor (Coord.), *El derecho de amparo en el mundo*, Universidad Nacional Autónoma de México, Editorial Porrúa, México, 2006, pp. 461– 521.

wide range of powers to conduct and direct it, which can also be exercised *ex officio*; and the concentration of the procedure steps in only one hearing.

Article 107 of the constitution regulates in a very extensive and detailed way the procedural rules for the exercise of the amparo action, and the competent courts to hear the cases. In this basic regulation the traditional Mexican rule is established that in deciding the cases, the courts cannot make any general declaration as to the statute or act on which the complaint is based. The amparo suit has also been regulated in Mexico in a specific amparo statute that develops Articles 103 and 107 of the Constitution *(Ley de amparo reglamentaria de los artículos 103 y 107 de la Constitución Política)* of 1936, which has been amended many times.[218]

However, this trial of amparo, if it is true that it is the only judicial mean that can be used for the judicial protection of constitutional rights and guaranties as well as for judicial review of the constitutionality of legislation, in its substance is a collection of various proceedings assembled in a very complex procedural institution, comprising at least five different judicial processes that in all other countries with a civil law tradition are different ones.

These five different aspects, contents or expressions of the trial for amparo, as systematized by Professor Héctor Fix-Zamudio,[219] are the following:

The first aspect of the *juicio de amparo* is the so-called amparo for the protection of freedom *(amparo de la libertad)*, which is a judicial mean for the protection of fundamental rights established in the constitution.

---

[218]See in general, Hector Fix-Zamudio, *Ensayos sobre el derecho de amparo*, Universidad nacional Autónoma de México, Editorial Porrúa, México, 2003; Ignacio Burgoa, *El juicio de amparo*, Ediorial Porrúa, México, 1991; Eduardo Ferrer Mac-Gregor, *La acción constitucional de amparo en México y España*, Editorial Porrúa, México, 2002; Héctor Fix-Zamudio and Eduardo Ferrer Mac-Gregor, "El derecho de amparo en México," in Héctor Fix-Zamudio and Eduardo Ferrer Mac-Gregor, *Idem,* Edit. Porrúa, México, 2006, pp. 461–521.

[219]See H. Fix-Zamudio, *El juicio de amparo*, México, 1964, p. 243, 377; H. Fix-Zamudio, "Reflexiones sobre la naturaleza procesal del amparo," in *Revista de la Facultad de Derecho de México*, 56, 1964, p. 980; H. Fix-Zamudio, "Lineamientos fundamentales del proceso social agrario en el derecho mexicano," in *Atti della Seconda Assemblea. Istituto di Diritto Agrario Internazionale a Comparato,* Vol. I, Milán, 1964, p. 402; Eduardo Ferrer Mac-Gregor, *La acción constitucional de amparo en México y España, Estudio de Derecho Comparado*, 2nd Edition, Edit. Porrúa, México, 2000; Ignacio Burgoa O., *El juicio de amparo*, Twenty-eighth Edition, Editorial Porrúa S.A., México, 1991.

This trial for amparo is equivalent to the habeas corpus proceeding for the protection of personal liberty, but that in Mexico can also serve for the protection of all other fundamental rights or guaranties established in Articles 1 to 29 when violated by an act of an authority.[220]

The second aspect of the trial for amparo is the amparo against judicial decisions (Article 107, III, V Constitution) called *amparo judicial* or *amparo casación,* filed by a party in a particular case alleging that the judge, when deciding, has incorrectly applied the pertinent legal provision. In this case, the amparo is a recourse to challenge judicial decisions very similar to the recourse of cassation that exists in procedural law in all civil law countries that are filed before the Supreme Courts of Justice to control the legality or constitutionality of judicial decisions.

The institution is elsewhere called *recurso de casación,* according to the French tradition, and is filed before the Court on cassation or before the cassation Chambers of the Supreme Court as an extraordinary judicial means to challenge definitive and final judicial decisions founded on violations of the Constitution, or of statutes or of the judicial procedural formalities. By this judicial means, the Supreme Courts assure the uniformity of judicial interpretation and application of the law. In Mexico this well-known extraordinary judicial recourse is regulated as one of the modalities or expressions of the *juicio de amparo.*

The third aspect of the trial for amparo is the so-called administrative amparo (*amparo administrativo*) through which it is possible to challenge administrative acts that violate the constitution or the statutes (Article 107, IV Constitution), resulting in this case in a judicial means for judicial review of administrative action. These means are equivalent to the *contencioso-administrativo* recourses that, also following the French influence, exists in many of the civil law countries.

These recourses are commonly filed before special courts (*Contencioso administrativo*) specifically established for the purpose to control the legality and constitutionality of Public Administration's actions and, in particular, of administrative acts, seeking their annulment.[221] In Mexico,

---

[220]See Robert D. Baker, *Judicial Review in México. A Study of the Amparo Suit,* University of Texas Press, Austin, 1971, p. 92.

[221]Even in some Latin American countries like Colombia, a Consejo de Estado has been created following the Conseil d'État French model, as the head of a Judicial Review of Administrative Action separate Jurisdiction. In the other countries, the head of the Jurisdiction has been located in the Supreme Court, and the main purpose of it, as mentioned, is to challenge administrative acts seeking their annulment when considered unconstitutional or

on the contrary, the administrative amparo is the judicial means established to control the legality of administrative action and for the protection of individual constitutional rights and guaranties against administrative acts, substituting what in other countries is the *jurisdicción contencioso administrativa.*[222]

The fourth aspect of the trial for amparo is the so-called agrarian amparo *(amparo agrario)*, which is set up for the protection of peasants' rights against acts of public authorities, particularly referring to collective rural property rights (Article 107, II.).

Finally, the fifth aspect of the trial for amparo is the so-called amparo against laws *(amparo contra leyes)*, as a judicial means directed to challenge statutes that violate the constitution, resulting in this case, in a judicial review mean of the constitutionality of legislation. It is exercised in a direct way against statutes without the need for any additional administrative or judicial act of enforcement or of application of the statute considered unconstitutional; which implies that the challenged statute must have a self-executing character.

All five amparo proceedings are developed before a variety of courts, so for instance, when the petition of amparo is filed against federal or local statutes, international treaties, national executive regulations or State's Governors' regulations or any other administrative regulations, it must be filed before the District Courts (Article 114, Amparo Law).[223]

From all these five aspects or expressions of the amparo suit, in Mexico the amparo is not really reduced to one single adjective guaranty (action or recourse) for the protection of constitutional rights, but is rather a varied range of judicial processes and procedures all used for the protection of constitutional guaranties. It is a unique judicial proceeding that with all these procedural peculiarities, cannot be reproduced in any other legal system. It was initially established following the U.S. judicial review model,[224] also as a mean for judicial review of the constitutionality of

---

illegal. The important trend of such jurisdiction is that it is not only devoted to protect human or constitutional rights, but in general, the legality of the administrative actions.

[222] An exception has always been the Tribunal Fiscal de la Federación.

[223] H. Fix-Zamudio, "Algunos problemas que plantea el amparo contra leyes," in *Boletín del Instituto de Derecho Comparado de México,* Universidad Nacional Autónoma de México, México, 1960, pp. 15, 20.

[224] J.A.C. Grant, "El control jurisdiccional de la constitucionalidad de las leyes: una contribución de las Américas a la ciencia política," in *Revista de la Facultad de Derecho de México,* n° 45, México, 1962, p. 657.

statutes following the features of the diffuse method of judicial review of legislation.[225]

In this regard, the amparo suit includes the amparo against statutes, which can only be filed against "public authorities," whether a State body or a public officer, who can be the judge who has issued the judicial decision, the Public Administration authority that has produced the administrative act, or the legislative authorities that have sanctioned the statute.[226]

In this case of the amparo against statutes as a mean for judicial review of the constitutionality of legislation, in Mexico it is sought through an "action of unconstitutionality" that is filed before a federal District Court (Article 107, XII). The defendants in the case are the organs of the State that have intervened in the process of formation of the statute, namely, the Congress of the Union or the state Legislatures that have sanctioned it; the President of the Republic or the Governors of the states that have enacted it, and the Secretaries of State that have countersigned it and ordered its publication.[227] In these cases, it is provided that the federal district courts' decisions are reviewable by the Supreme Court of Justice (Article 107, VIII,a).

The amparo against statutes, therefore, is a direct action filed against a statute when it directly affects the plaintiff's guaranties, without the need of any other intermediate or subsequent administrative or judicial act, that is, a statute that with its sole enactment causes personal and direct prejudice to the plaintiff.[228]

---

[225]H. Fix-Zamudio, "Algunos problemas que plantea el amparo contra leyes," in *Boletín del Instituto de Derecho Comparado de México,* Universidad Nacional Autónoma de México, México, 1960, p. 22, 23.

[226]This aspect, particularly regarding judicial review of statutes, reveals another substantial difference between the Mexican system and the general diffuse system of judicial review, in which the parties in the particular process where a constitutional question is raised, continue to be the same.

[227]H. Fix-Zamudio, "Algunos problemas que plantea el amparo contra leyes," in *Boletín del Instituto de Derecho Comparado de México,* Universidad Nacional Autónoma de México, México, 1960, p. 21.

[228]That is why, in principle, the action seeking the amparo against laws must be brought before the court within thirty days after their enactment, or within fifteen days after the first act of execution of the said statute so as to protect the plaintiff's rights to sue. Article 21, Amparo Law. See H. Fix-Zamudio, *Idem,* pp. 24, 32; Robert D. Baker, *Judicial Review in México. A Study of the Amparo Suit,* University of Texas Press, Austin, 1971, pp. 164, 171, 176.

Regarding the effects of the judicial decision on any of the aspects of the trial for amparo, including the cases of judicial review of constitutionality of legislation, since the initial nineteenth century provision for the trial for amparo, the constitution has expressly emphasized that the courts cannot "make any general declaration as to the law or act on which the complaint is based." Consequently, the judgment can "only affect private individuals" and is limited to protect them in the particular case to which the complaint refers (Article 107,II).[229] Therefore, the decision in a *juicio de amparo* in which judicial review of legislation is accomplished, as it happens in Paraguay and Uruguay, only has *inter partes* effects, and can never consist in general declarations with *erga omnes* effects.

Therefore, the courts, in their amparo decisions regarding the unconstitutionality of a statute, cannot annul or repeal it; and similarly to all legal systems with the diffuse method of judicial review, the statute remains in the books and can be applied by the courts, the only effect of the declaration of its unconstitutionality being directed to the parties in the particular process.

As a consequence, the decisions of the trials for amparo do not have general binding effects, being only obligatory to other courts when a precedent is established by means of *jurisprudencia* (Article 107, XIII, 1 Constitution), which according to that Amparo Law is attained when five consecutive decisions to the same effect, uninterrupted by any incompatible rulings, are rendered by the Supreme Court of Justice or by the Collegiate Circuit Courts.[230] Nonetheless, the *jurisprudencia* can be modified when the respective Court pronounces a contradictory judgment with a qualified majority of votes of its members (Article 139).[231]

---

[229]The principle is named the "Otero formula" due to its inclusion in the 1857 Constitution under the influence of Mariano Otero. See H. Fix-Zamudio, *Idem*, p. 33, 37.

[230]Article 192, 193. See in Robert D. Baker, *Judicial Review in México. A Study of the Amparo Suit*, University of Texas Press, Austin, 1971, pp. 256, 257.

[231]Nevertheless, as *jurisprudencia* can be established by the federal Collegiate Circuit Courts and by the Supreme Court, contradictory interpretations of the constitution can exist, having binding effects upon the lower courts. In order to resolve these conflicts, the constitution establishes the power of the Supreme Court or of the Collegiate Circuit Court to resolve the conflict, when the contradiction is denounced by the Chambers of the Supreme Court or another Collegiate Circuit Court; by the Attorney General or by any of the parties to the cases in which the *jurisprudencia* was established (Article 107, XIII). Any way the resolution of the contradiction between judicial doctrines has the sole purpose of determining one single *jurisprudencia* on the matter, and does not affect particular juridical situations, derived from the contradictory judicial decisions adopted in the respective trials (Article 107, XIII). See the comments in J.A.C. Grant, "El control jurisdiccional de la

It must also be highlighted that according to a constitutional reform passed in 1983, the Supreme Court of Mexico was vested with a discretionary power to review the cases of amparo of constitutional importance (*facultad de atracción*), with some similarities to the writ of certiorari. Nevertheless, Collegiate Circuit Courts' decisions in direct amparo are not reviewable by the Supreme Court if they are based "on a precedent established by the Supreme Court of Justice as to the constitutionality of a statute or the direct interpretation of a provision of the Constitution."

Also, as mentioned, according to another constitutional reform sanctioned in 1988, the Supreme Court was also attributed the power to decide in last instance all cases of amparo where the decision involves the unconstitutionality of a federal statute or establishes a direct interpretation of a provision of the constitution (Article 107,IX).

Both attributions allow the Supreme Court to give final interpretation of the constitution in a uniform way,[232] its decisions limited to resolve upon the actual constitutional questions.

Finally, it must be mentioned regarding judicial review of constitutionality of statutes that with the 1994 constitutional reform, the Mexican system of judicial review, from initially being an exclusively diffuse system by means of the amparo suit, was converted into a mixed system of judicial review by the incorporation of the concentrated method exercised by the Supreme Court by means of an abstract judicial review proceeding of statutes, with the power to decide in these cases with general binding effect.

According to Article 105,II of the constitution, in order for the Supreme Court of the Nation to decide, a judicial action must be filed against federal statutes on the grounds of their unconstitutionality, and the standing to sue is limited to members of Congress in number equivalent to the 33 percent of the members of the Chamber of Representatives or of the Senate; and to the Attorney General of the Republic. In the cases of actions against electoral statutes, the national representatives of the political parties also have standing to sue.

---

constitucionalidad de las leyes: una contribución de las Américas a la ciencia política," in *Revista de la Facultad de Derecho de México*, 45, México, 1962, p. 662.

[232] See Joaquin Brage Camazano, *La jurisdicción constitucional de la libertad (Teoría general, Argentina, México, Corte Interamericana de Derechos Humanos)*, Editorial Porrúa, Instituto Mexicano de Derecho Procesal Constitucional, México, 2005, p. 153–155.

In all these cases, as mentioned, the Supreme Court can declare the invalidity of the statute with general *erga omnes* effects when approved by no less than eight of the eleven votes.[233]

III. THE RIGHT TO AMPARO IN VENEZUELA

The other country with a mixed system of judicial review where the amparo is also conceived as a constitutional right that can be exercised through a variety of actions or recourses is Venezuela,[234] where the mixed system of judicial review, contrary to the recent introduction in Mexico, was established since the nineteenth century.[235]

---

[233]See José Brage Camazano, "El control abstracto de la constitucionalidad de las leyes en México," in Eduardo Ferrer Mac-Gregor (Coordinador), *Derecho Procesal Constitucional,* Editorial Porrúa, México, Vol. I, 2003, pp. 919 ff.

[234]Regarding this constitutional provision, Héctor Fix-Zamudio pointed out in 1970 that Article 49 of the 1961 Constitution, "definitively enshrined the right to amparo as a procedural instrument to protect all the constitutionally enshrined fundamental rights of the human person," in what he described as "one of the most outstanding achievements of the very advanced Magna Carta of 1961. See Héctor Fix-Zamudio, "Algunos aspectos comparativos del derecho de amparo en México y Venezuela," in *Libro Homenaje a la Memoria de Lorenzo Herrera Mendoza,* UCV, Caracas, 1970, Volumen II, pp. 333–390. This trend has been followed in Article 27 of the 1999 Constitution. See Héctor Fix-Zamudio, "La teoría de Allan R. Brewer-Carías sobre el derecho de amparo latinoamericano y el juicio de amparo mexicano," in *El Derecho Público a comienzos del Siglo XXI. Libro Homenaje al profesor Allan R. Brewer-Carías,* Volumen I, Instituto de Derecho Público, Editorial Civitas, Madrid, 2003, pp. 1125 ff.

[235]With respect to this mixed character of the Venezuelan system, the former Supreme Court has analyzed the scope of judicial review of the constitutionality of statutes and has correctly pointed out that this is the responsibility: "not only of the Supreme Tribunal of the Republic, but also of all the judges, whatever their rank and standing may be. It is sufficient that an official is part of the Judiciary for him to be a custodian of the Constitution and, consequently, to apply its ruling preferentially over those of ordinary statutes. Nonetheless, the application of the Constitution by the judges, only has effects in the particular case at issue and, for that very reason, only affects the interested parties in the conflict. In contrast, when constitutional illegitimacy in a law is declared by the Supreme [Tribunal] when exercising its sovereign function, as the interpreter of the Constitution, and in response to the pertinent [popular] action, the effects of the decision extend *erga omnes* and have the force of law. In the first case, the review is incidental and special, and in the second, principal and general. When this happens —that is to say when the recourse is autonomous— the control is either formal or material, depending on whether the nullity has to do with an irregularity relating to the process of drafting the statute, or whether —despite the legislation having been correct from the formalist point of view— the intrinsic content of the statute suffers from substantial defects." See Federal Court (which in 1961 was substituted by the Supreme Court of Justice), decision June 19, 1953, *Gaceta Forense,*

Regarding the diffuse method, it is expressly regulated in Article 334 of the 1999 Constitution, following a legal tradition that can be traced back to the 1897 Civil Procedure Code, by granting all courts, even *ex officio*, the power to declare statutes inapplicable for the resolution of a given case when they consider them unconstitutional and, hence, giving preference to constitutional rules.[236]

On the other hand, Article 336 of the same 1999 Constitution, also following a constitutional tradition that can be traced back to the 1858 Constitution,[237] establishes the concentrated method of judicial review by granting to the Constitutional Chamber of the Supreme Tribunal, as Constitutional Jurisdiction, the power to decide with nullifying effects upon the constitutionality of statutes and other national, state or municipal normative acts and acts of government adopted by the president of the Republic when requested, as is also established in Colombia and Nicaragua, by means of a popular action. This concentrated method of judicial review of the constitutionality of statutes and other similar State acts allows the Supreme Tribunal of Justice to declare them null and void with general *erga omnes* effects when they violate the constitution.

Within this mixed system of judicial review, in addition, as mentioned, the constitution also establishes a "constitutional right for amparo" or to be protected by the courts[238] and not just a particular action or remedy to be filed before a particular court, that everybody have for the protection of all the rights and freedoms enshrined in the constitution and in interna-

---

1, 1953, pp. 77–78. See in general, Allan R. Brewer-Carías, *La Justicia Constitucional (Procesos y Procedimientos Constitucionales)*, Edit. Porrúa, México, 2007.

[236]See in general, Allan R. Brewer-Carías, *El control de la constitucionalidad de los actos estatales,* Caracas, 1977; and also "Algunas consideraciones sobre el control jurisdiccional de la constitucionalidad de los actos estatales en el derecho venezolano," in *Revista de Administración Pública,* n° 76, Madrid, 1975, pp. 419–446.

[237]See J. G. Andueza, *La jurisdicción constitucional en el derecho venezolano*, Caracas, 1955, p. 46.

[238]On the action of amparo in Venezuela, in general, see Gustavo Briceño V., *Comentarios a la Ley de Amparo*, Editorial Kinesis, Caracas, 1991; Rafael J. Chavero Gazdik, *El nuevo régimen del amparo constitucional en Venezuela*, Editorial Sherwood, Caracas, 2001; Gustavo José Linares Benzo, *El Proceso de Amparo*, Universidad Central de Venezuela, Facultad de Ciencias Jurídicas y Políticas, Caracas, 1999; Hildegard Rondón De Sansó, *Amparo Constitucional*, Caracas, 1988; Hildegard Rondón De Sansó, *La acción de amparo contra los poderes públicos*, Editorial Arte, Caracas, 1994; Carlos M. Ayala Corao and Rafael J. Chavero Gazidk, "El amparo constitucional en Venezuela," in Héctor Fix-Zamudio and Eduardo Ferrer Mac-Gregor (Coord.), *El derecho de amparo en el mundo*, Universidad Nacional Autónoma de México, Editorial Porrúa, México, 2006, pp. 649–692.

tional treaties, or which, even if not listed in the text, are inherent to the human person.

As in Guatemala and Mexico, the constitution does not set forth a separate action of habeas corpus for the protection of personal freedom and liberty; instead it establishes that the action for amparo regarding freedom or safety may be exercised by any person in which cases "the detainee shall be immediately transferred to the court, without delay."

Additionally, the Venezuelan Constitution has also set forth the habeas data recourse, guarantying the right to have access to the information and data concerning the claimant contained in official or private registries, as well as to know about the use that has been made of the information and about its purpose, and to petition the competent court for the updating, rectification or destruction of erroneous records and those that unlawfully affect the petitioner's right (Article 28).

The amparo action is regulated in a Statute on Amparo for the protection of constitutional rights and guaranties sanctioned in 1988 (*Ley Orgánica de Amparo sobre derechos y garantías constitucionales*).[239]

This right to amparo can be exercised through an "autonomous action for amparo"[240] that in general is filed before the first instance court[241]

---

[239]See in general, Allan R. Brewer-Carías, *Instituciones políticas y constitucionales, Vol. V, El derecho y la acción de amparo*, Universidad Católica del Táchira, Editorial Jurídica Venezolana, Caracas-San Cristóbal, 1998; Hildegard Rondón de Sansó, *Amparo constitucional*, Caracas, 1988; Gustavo J. Linares Benzo, *El proceso de amparo*, Universidad Central de Venezuela, Caracas, 1999; Rafael J. Chavero Gazdik, *El Nuevo regimen del amparo constitucional en Venezuela*, Editorial Sherwood, Caracas, 2001; Allan R. Brewer-Carías, Carlos Ayala Corao and Rafael J. Chavero G., *Ley Orgánica de Amparo sobre derechos y garantías constitucionales,* Editorial Jurídica Venezolana, Caracas, 2007; Carlos Ayala Corao and Rafael Chavero G., "El amparo constitucional en Venezuela," in Héctor Fix-Zamudio and Eduardo Ferrer Mac-Gregor, *Idem,* Edit. Porrúa, México, 2006, pp. 649–692.

[240]See Allan R. Brewer-Carías, "El derecho de amparo y la acción de amparo," in Revista *de Derecho Público*, n° 22, Editorial Jurídica Venezolana, Caracas, 1985, pp. 51 ff.

[241]According to the constitution, the right to protection may be exercised, according to the law, before "the Courts," and that is why, as it has been said, the organization of the legal and procedural system does not only provide for one single judicial action to guaranty the enjoyment and exercise of constitutional rights to be brought before one single Court. In Venezuela, according to Article 7 of the Organic Law on Amparo, the competent courts to decide amparo actions are the First Instance Courts with jurisdiction on matters related to the constitutional rights or guaranties violated, in the place where the facts, acts or omission have occurred. Regarding amparo of personal freedom and security, the competent courts should be the Criminal First Instance courts (Article 40). Nonetheless, when the facts, acts or omissions harming or threatening to harm the constitutional right or

(Article 7 Amparo Law); or by means of preexisting ordinary or extraordinary legal actions or recourses to which an amparo petition is joined, and the judge is empowered to immediately reestablish the infringed legal situation. In all such cases, it is not that the ordinary means substitute the constitutional right of protection (or diminish it), but that they can serve as the judicial mean for protection because the judge is empowered to protect fundamental rights and immediately reestablish the infringed legal situation.[242]

This last possibility does not presuppose in Venezuela that for the filing of an autonomous amparo action, all other preexisting legal judicial or administrative means have to be exhausted, as is the case for instance, of the recourse for amparo or the "constitutional complaint" developed in Europe, particularly in Germany and in Spain.[243]

---

guaranty occurs in a place where no First Instance court exists, the amparo action may be brought before and any judge of the site, which must decide according to the law, and in a twenty-four hour delay it must send the files for consultation to the competent First Instance court (Article 9). Only in cases in which facts, acts or omissions of the President of the Republic, his Cabinet members, the National Electoral Council, the Prosecutor General, the Attorney General and the General Comptroller of the Republic are involved does the power to decide the amparo actions correspond to the Constitutional Chamber of the Supreme Tribunal of Justice (Article 8).

[242] Allan R. Brewer-Carías, "La reciente evolución jurisprudencial en relación a la admisibilidad del recurso de amparo," in *Revista de derecho público*, n° 19, Caracas, 1984, pp. 207–218.

[243] In these countries, the protective remedy is really an authentic "recourse" that is brought, in principle, against judicial decisions. In Germany, for example, to bring a constitutional complaint for the protection of constitutional rights before the Federal Constitutional Tribunal, the available ordinary judicial means need to be previously exhausted, which definitively entails a recourse against a final judicial decision, even though, in exceptional cases, a direct complaint for protection may be allowed in certain specific cases and with respect to a very limited number of constitutional rights. See K. Schlaich, "Procedures et techniques de protection des droits fondamentaux. Tribunal Constitutionnel Fédéral allemand," in L. Favoreu (ed.), *Cours constitutionnelles européenes et droits fondamentaux,* Paris, 1982, pp. 105–164. In Spain, all legal recourses need to be exhausted in order to bring a "recurso de amparo" of constitutional rights before the Constitutional Tribunal, and, particularly when dealing with protection against administrative activities, the ordinary means for judicial review of administrative decisions must be definitively exhausted. For this reason, the recourse for protection in Spain is eventually a means for judicial review of decisions taken by the Administrative Judicial review courts. See J.L. García Ruíz, *Recurso de amparo en el derecho español,* Madrid, 1980. F. Castedo Álvarez, "El recurso de amparo constitucional," in Instituto de Estudios Fiscales, *El Tribunal Constitucional*, Madrid, 1981, Vol. I, pp. 179-208.

This right for amparo has been regulated in the 1988 Organic Law of Amparo,[244] expressly providing for its exercise, not only by means of an autonomous action for amparo, but also through other preexisting actions or recourses already established in the legal system. This main characteristic of the Venezuelan amparo was summarized in a decision by the former Supreme Court of July 7, 1991 (*Tarjetas Banvenez* case), as follows:

The Amparo Law sets forth two adjective mechanisms: the (autonomous) action for amparo and the joint filing of such action with other actions or recourses, which differs in their nature and legal consequences. Regarding the latter, that is to say, the filing of such action of amparo jointly with other actions or recourses, the Amparo Law distinguishes three mechanisms: a) the action of amparo filed jointly with the popular action of unconstitutionality against statutes and State acts of the same rank and value (Article 3); b) the action of amparo filed jointly with the judicial review of administrative actions recourses against administrative acts or against omissions from Public Administration (Article 5); and c) the amparo action filed jointly with another ordinary judicial actions (Article 6,5).[245]

The same Supreme Court has also ruled that in these latter cases, the action for amparo is not an autonomous action, "but an extraordinary one, ancillary to the action or recourse to which it has been joined, thus subject to its final decision. Being joint actions, the case must be heard by the competent court regarding the principal one."[246]

With these 1991 Supreme Court decisions, it can be said that the intention of the Amparo Law drafters was definitively clarified in the sense of the establishment of this basic distinction between the autonomous action for amparo and the amparo claim as a petition filed jointly with other

---

[244]See Gaceta Oficial n° 33.891 of January 22, 1988. See Allan R. Brewer-Carías, Carlos M. Ayala Corao and Rafael Chavero G., *Ley Orgánica de Amparo sobre Derechos y Garantías Constitucionales*, Caracas, 2007. See also Allan R. Brewer-Carías, *Instituciones Políticas y Constitucionales, Tomo V, El derecho y la acción de amparo*, Editorial Jurídica Venezolana, Caracas, 1998, pp. 163 ff..

[245]See the text in *Revista de Derecho Público*, n° 47, Editorial Jurídica Venezolana, Caracas, 1991, pp. 169–174.

[246]See in *Revista de Derecho Público*, n° 50, Editorial Jurídica Venezolana, Caracas, 1992, pp. 183–184.

existing actions, in which cases, the amparo is a claim dependent on the principal action and has a preliminary protective nature.[247]

Consequently, according to these provisions and to the Supreme Court doctrine, in Venezuela, the right to amparo can be enforced by means of a direct autonomous action for amparo; or by an amparo petition filed conjunctly with another judicial action and proceeding.

Regarding the first mean for protection, as was pointed out by the former Supreme Court of Justice in the already mentioned decision of July 10, 1991, this action for amparo has a re-establishing nature and "is a sufficient judicial mean in itself in order to return the things to the situation they were when the right was violated and to definitively make the offender act or fact disappear." In such cases, the plaintiff must invoke and demonstrate that it is a matter of flagrant, vulgar, direct and immediate constitutional harm, and the courts must decide based on the violation of the constitution and not only on the violation of statutes; adding that:

> On the contrary, it will not be a constitutional action for amparo but rather another type of recourse, for instance, the judicial review action against administrative acts whose annulatory effects do not correspond with the restitutory effects of the amparo; and if such substitution is allowed, the amparo would arrive to substitute not only those actions but all the other procedural means set forth in the legal system and lose its extraordinary character.[248]

That is why, for instance, in order to avoid such substitution and regarding administrative acts, Article 5 of the Organic Amparo Law establishes that:

> The action for amparo can be filed against any administrative act, material actions, factual actions (*vía de hecho*), abstentions or omissions that violate or threaten to violate constitutional rights and guaranties, provided that no other brief, summary and efficient mean exists according to the constitutional protection.

---

[247]See Allan R. Brewer-Carías, "Observaciones críticas al Proyecto de Ley de la Acción de Amparo de los Derechos Fundamentales (1985)"; "Proyecto de Ley Orgánica sobre el Derecho de Amparo (1987)"; and "Propuestas de reforma al Proyecto de Ley Orgánica de Amparo sobre Derechos y Garantías Constitucionales (1987)," in *Estudios de Derecho Público, Tomo III, (Labor en el Senado 1985–1987)*, Ediciones del Congreso de la República, Caracas, 1989, pp. 71–186; 187–204; 205–229.

[248]Decision of July 7, 1991. See the text in *Revista de Derecho Público*, n° 47, Editorial Jurídica Venezolana, Caracas, 1991, pp. 169–174.

The right to amparo can also be enforced by filing an amparo petition conjunctly with other preexisting actions, recourses and proceedings, for which the Amparo Law provides the following possibilities:

First, according to Article 3 of the Amparo Law, it is possible to file an amparo petition against statutes, bringing the petition together or jointly with the popular action of unconstitutionality of statutes exercised before the Constitutional Chamber of the Supreme Tribunal of Justice. In these cases, when the popular action is founded on the violation of a constitutional right or guaranty by the statute, the Organic Law authorizes the Supreme Tribunal to suspend the effects of the disputed statute regarding the specific case and in some cases with general effects, pending the issue of the requested decision on the nullity of the statute. So, because the amparo petition is subordinate to the nullity action against statutes, the amparo decision in the proceeding has a preliminary character of suspending the effects of the challenged statute pending the Court's decision on the merits of the nullity of the statute.

Second, according to Article 5 of the Amparo Law, as already mentioned, it expressly establishes that the petition for amparo against administrative acts and against Public Administration omissions may also be brought before the corresponding courts of the *Jurisdicción contencioso administrativa* jointly with the judicial review of administra-tive actions' recourses.

In such cases, when the motive of the recourse is the violation of a constitutional right by the challenged administrative act, the general admissibility conditions of the *contencioso administrativo* nullity recourse have been made more flexible, in particular referring first to the condition of the need to previously exhaust the exiting administrative procedures, and second, to the term for the filing of the recourse, conditions that have been eliminated when the petition for amparo is filed jointly with the nullity recourse. In such cases, in addition, the courts are allowed to adopt immediate steps for the reduction of procedure terms and also has the power to suspend the effects of the challenged administrative acts while the nullity action is decided (Articles 5, and 6,5). So also in these cases, the amparo protection is reduced to the suspension of the effects of the challenged administrative act pending the court's decision on the nullity of the challenged act.

Third and finally, according to Article 6,6 of the same Amparo Law, it is implicitly recognized that the claim for amparo may also be brought before the courts jointly with any other "ordinary judicial procedures" or with the "preexisting judicial means," through which the "violation or threat of violation of a constitutional right or guaranty may be alleged."

In these cases, for instance, the amparo petition can be filed jointly with the recourse of cassation when the claim against the challenged judicial decision is based on violations of a constitutional right or guaranty. In such cases, the cassation Chambers of the Supreme Tribunal shall follow the procedure and terms established in the Organic Law of Amparo (Article 6,5) and the recourse will anyway have the effect of suspending the challenged decision.

In all these cases of amparo petitions in Venezuela, contrary to the Mexican system, they do not substitute the ordinary or extraordinary judicial means by naming them all as amparo; only providing that the amparo claim can be filed jointly with those other judicial means."[249]

From all these regulations it results that the Venezuelan right for amparo, as it happened with the Mexican system, also has certain peculiarities that distinguish it from the other similar institutions for the protection of the constitutional rights and guaranties established in Latin America.[250] Besides the adjective consequences of the amparo being a constitutional right, it can be characterized by the following trends:

First, the right of amparo can be exercised in Venezuela for the protection of all constitutional rights, not only of civil individual rights. Consequently, the social, economic, cultural, environmental and political rights declared in the constitution and in international treaties are also protected by means of amparo. The habeas corpus is an aspect of the right to constitutional protection, or one of the expressions of the amparo.

Second, the right to amparo seeks to assure protection of constitutional rights and guaranties against any disturbance in their enjoyment and ex-

---

[249] In this regard, the Supreme Court of Justice has clearly set forth the proceeding rules as follows: "The amparo claims filed jointly with another action or recourse have all the inherent adjective character of the actions' joint proceedings, that is: it must be decided by only one court (the one competent regarding the principal action), and both claims (amparo and nullity or other) must be heard in only one proceeding that has two stages: the preliminary one regarding the amparo, and the contradictory one, which must include in its final decision, the preliminary one which ends in such time, as well as the decision on the requested nullity. In other words, if because of the above analyzed characteristics the amparo order [for instance when the amparo is filed conjunctly with other action] is reduced only and exclusively to the preliminary suspension of a challenged act, the decision which resolves the requested nullity leaves without effects the preventive preliminary measure, whether the challenged act is declared null or not." *Idem*, p. 171.

[250] See, in general, H. Fix-Zamudio, *La protección procesal de los derechos humanos ante las jurisdicciones nacionales,* Madrid, 1982, p. 366.

ercise, whether originated by public authorities or by private individuals without distinction.[251]

In addition, in the case of disturbance by public authorities, the amparo is admissible against statutes, against legislative, administrative and judicial acts, and against material or factual courses of action of Public Administration or public officials.

Third, the decision of the judge, as a consequence of the exercise of this right to amparo, whether through the preexisting actions or recourses or by means of the autonomous action for amparo, is not limited to be of a precautionary or preliminary nature, but to reestablish the infringed legal situation by deciding on the merits, that is, the constitutionality of the alleged disturbance of the constitutional right.

Fourth, because the Venezuelan system of judicial review is a mixed one, judicial review of legislation can also be exercised by the courts when deciding action for amparo when, for instance, the alleged violation of the right is based on a statute deemed unconstitutional. In such cases, if the protection requested is granted by the courts, it must previously declare the statute inapplicable on the grounds of it being unconstitutional. Therefore, in such cases, judicial review of the constitutionality of legislation can also be exercised when an action for amparo of fundamental rights is filed.

Finally, in the Venezuelan systems of judicial review and of amparo, according to the 1999 Constitution an extraordinary review recourse can be filed before the Constitutional Chamber of the Supreme Court against judicial final decisions issued in amparo suits, and also against any judicial decision issued when applying the diffuse method of judicial review

---

[251]The constitution makes no distinction in this respect, and thus the action for amparo is perfectly admissible against actions by individuals, the action for amparo has doubtlessly been conceived as a traditional means of protection against actions by the state and its authorities. However, despite this tradition of conceiving the action for protection as a means of protecting rights and guaranties against public actions, in Venezuela, the scope with which this is regulated by Article 27 of the constitution allows the action for amparo to be brought against individual actions, that is to say, when the disruption of the enjoyment and exercise of rights originates from private individuals or organizations. This also differentiates the Venezuelan system from that which exists in other systems such as México or Spain, in which the "action for amparo" is solely conceived against public actions. For this reason, in Spain the recourse of amparo is expressed as a review of decisions by the administrative judicial court when reviewing administrative acts. See J. González Pérez, *Derecho procesal constitucional*, Madrid, 1980, p. 278.

resolving the inapplicability of statutes because they are considered unconstitutional (Article 336,10).

The essential trend of this attribution of the Constitutional Chamber is its discretionary character[252] that allows it to choose the cases to be reviewed. As the same Constitutional Chamber of the Supreme Tribunal pointed out in its decision n° 727 of April 8, 2003, "In the cases of the decisions subject to revision, the Constitution does not provide for the creation of a third instance. What has set forth the constitutional provision is an exceptional and discretional power of the Constitutional Chamber that as such, must be exercised with maximum prudence regarding the admission of recourses for review final judicial decisions."[253]

In absence of the statute regulating the Constitutional Jurisdiction assigned to the Constitutional Chamber, it has been the same Constitutional Chamber that has modeled the framework of this recourse for revision of judicial decisions on constitutional matters. Since the Chamber rulings n° 1, 2, 44 and 714 of 2000, the Supreme Court has established the following conditions that a judicial decision must have in order to be the object of the review recourse as follows:

1°) The decision must have been issued in second instance, by means of an appeal, so that the review cannot be understood as a new instance.

2°) The constitutional revision is only admissible in order to preserve the uniformity of interpretation of constitutional norms and principles, or when it exists a deliberate violation of constitutional prescription, which will be analyzed by the Constitutional Chamber, in a facultative way.

3°) The recourse for revision is not *ipso jure* admissible, because it depends on the party's initiative, and not on the initiative of the courts that issued the decision, unless the Constitutional Chamber *ex officio* decides to accept it bearing always in mind its purpose.[254]

---

[252] As mentioned, in a certain way similar to the *writ of certiorari* in the North American system. See Jesús María Casal, *Constitución y Justicia Constitucional,* Caracas, 2002, p. 92.

[253] See *Revisión de la sentencia dictada por la Sala Electoral en fecha 21 de noviembre de 2002* case, in *Revista de Derecho Público,* n° 93–96, Editorial Jurídica Venezolana, Caracas, 2003.

[254] See decision of November 2, 2000, *Roderick A. Muñoz P.* case, in *Revista de Derecho Público,* n° 84, Editorial Jurídica Venezolana, Caracas, 2000, p. 367.

CHAPTER SEVEN

THE AMPARO AS A CONSTITUTIONAL GUARANTY IN COUNTRIES WITH MIXED SYSTEMS OF JUDICIAL REVIEW OF LEGISLATION

Leaving aside the cases of Mexico and Venezuela, where the amparo has been conceived as a constitutional right enforceable through various actions and proceedings, in the other Latin American countries with a mixed system of judicial review, the amparo is basically conceived as a constitutional guaranty, that is, as a specific adjective institution, claim, petition, recourse, action or proceeding also specifically established together with the habeas corpus and habeas data recourses for the protection of constitutional rights. This is the case in Brazil, Colombia, the Dominican Republic, Ecuador, Guatemala, Nicaragua and Peru.

The only difference between these countries is the fact that in Nicaragua the action for amparo can only be exercised before a single court; and in the other countries, the action is brought before a variety of courts.

I. THE AMPARO AS AN EXCLUSIVE COMPETENCE OF ONE SINGLE TRIBUNAL

The Constitution of Nicaragua provides for a recourse for amparo, as well as the habeas corpus recourse established for the protection of people's freedom, physical integrity and safety (Articles 188 and 189 of the Constitution), both regulated in one general amparo statute (*Ley de amparo*) of 1988.[255]

---

[255] See in general, Iván Escobar Fornos, "El amparo en Nicaragua," in Héctor Fix-Zamudio and Eduardo Ferrer Mac-Gregor, *Idem,* Edit. Porrúa, México, 2006, pp. 523–563.

Regarding the amparo action, the constitution only provides that "the persons whose constitutional rights have been violated or are in peril of being violated, can file the recourse of personal exhibition or the recourse of amparo. No constitutional provision exists regarding the origin of the violation, so that if it is true that the recourse could then be brought against violations provoked by public officials and individuals, the latter case has not been regulated. Like in Costa Rica and El Salvador, Nicaragua has also established a concentrated judicial system of amparo by granting the Supreme Court of Justice the exclusive power to decide the amparo actions (Article 164,3), but with the difference that in those countries, the judicial review system is an exclusively concentrated one, exercised by the Constitutional Chamber of the Supreme Courts. In Nicaragua, the judicial review system is a mixed one.

According to the law, the recourse of amparo in Nicaragua is set forth against any provision, act or resolution, and in general against any action or omission from any official, authority or agent that violates or an attempt to violate the rights declared in the constitution (Article 45), and is not admitted against violations or threats committed by individuals.

Regarding the procedure of the Nicaraguan concentrated amparo, it is also different from the one in Costa Rica and El Salvador, particularly because the recourse for amparo, although being decided by the Supreme Court, is not directly filed before it, but before the Courts of Appeals. So in Nicaragua, the procedure on the amparo suit has two steps: one that must be accomplished, including the possible suspension of the effects of the challenged act, before the Courts of Appeals; and the second that must be accomplished before the Supreme Court where the files must be sent for the final decision. The Courts of Appeals are also empowered to reject the recourses, in which cases the plaintiff can bring the case before the Supreme Court also by means of an action of amparo (Article 25, Law).[256]

However, in contrast with this concentrated judicial power of the Supreme Court to decide the amparo and personal exhibition recourses, as mentioned, the system of judicial review established in Nicaragua is a mixed one, combining the diffuse and the concentrated methods.

According to this mixed system, regarding the diffuse method, the constitution assigns to all courts (Article 182, Constitution) when resolving

---

[256]See Iván Escobar Fornos, "El amparo en Nicaragua," in Héctor Fix-Zamudio and Eduardo Ferrer Mac-Gregor (Coord.), *El derecho de amparo en el mundo*, Universidad Nacional Autónoma de México, Editorial Porrúa, México, 2006, pp. 523–563.

particular cases, the general power to decide upon the unconstitutionality of statutes, of course, with only *inter partes* effects.

On the other hand, the constitution also assigns the Supreme Court of Justice the power to decide upon the unconstitutionality of statutes, decrees or regulations when challenged by means of an action of unconstitutionality which, as in Colombia and Venezuela, is also conceived as a popular action that can be brought directly by any citizen (Article 2 of the Amparo Law). When deciding such popular action, the Supreme Court's decision declaring the unconstitutionality of the challenged statute has general effects, preventing its application by the courts (Articles 18 and 19).

Yet, in the Nicaraguan system, the question of the unconstitutionality of a statute, decree or regulation can also be raised before the Supreme Court by means of recourse of cassation and also, as mentioned, through a recourse of amparo filed by the corresponding party in the procedure of a case. In the former case, the Supreme Court, in addition to the cassation ruling regarding the challenged judicial decision, can also declare its nullity. And in the case of amparo recourses, as mentioned, they can serve as a judicial mean for judicial review of legislation, and the Supreme Court has the exclusive power to decide on the matter. So in these cases, in addition to the constitutional protection granted to the party in accordance to the amparo petition, the Supreme Court can also declare the unconstitutionality of the statute, decree or regulation, also with general effects (Article 18).[257]

The Amparo Law also provides that in any judicial decision other than amparo, issued applying the diffuse method of judicial review with express declaration of the unconstitutionality of a statute, if such decision cannot be challenged by means of a cassation recourse, the respective court must send it to the Supreme Court in order for this Court to ratify the unconstitutionality of the statute, decree or regulation and declare its inapplicability.[258]

According to these means, in order to guaranty the uniformity of jurisprudence in constitutional matters, the Supreme Court in Nicaragua always has the power to review judicial decisions on constitutional matters.

---

[257]Nonetheless, in these cases, the decision does not have retroactive effects in the sense that it cannot affect third-party rights acquired from those statutes or regulations (Articles 20 and 22).

[258]In such cases the decisions also cannot affect-third party rights acquired from those statutes or regulations (Articles 21 and 22).

II. THE ACTION FOR AMPARO EXERCISE BEFORE A VARIETY OF COURTS

1. *Mandado de segurança, mandado de injunção, habeas corpus and habeas data in Brazil*

In Brazil, Article 5 of the constitution establishes four actions for the protection of constitutional rights and guaranties: in addition to the habeas corpus,[259] and habeas data recourses, it provides for the *mandado de segurança* and the *mandado de injunção*, both which are the most similar to the amparo decisions. The *mandado de segurança* is set forth to protect any true and enforceable right not protected by means of habeas corpus or habeas data, against actions from public authorities or corporations exercising public functions; and the *mandado de injunção* can be requested in cases when because of omissions of normative development by statutes or regulations, the exercise of constitutional rights and freedoms and the prerogatives inherent to nationality, sovereignty and citizenship are harmed.

The constitution also provides for a *mandado de segurança coletivo* that can be requested by political parties, labor unions, class entities or associations in defense of the rights of their members or associates.

The procedural rules regarding the *mandado de segurança* are set forth in *Lei* n° 1.533, of December 31, 1951; and *Lei* n° 4.348, of June 26, 1964.[260]

The *mandado de segurança* and the recourse for *habeas corpus* were set forth in the 1934 Constitution;[261] and the *mandado de injuçao* and

---

[259]The habeas corpus can be brought before the courts whenever anyone suffers or feels threatened with suffering violence or duress in his or her freedom of movement because of illegal acts or abuses of power (Article 5, LXVIII, Constitution). The right of movement (*ius ambuland*) is defined as the right of every person to enter, stay and leave national territory with his belongings (Article 5, XV). In principle, the action is brought before the Tribunals of First Criminal Instance, but actions may be heard by the Appeals Tribunals and even by the Supreme Federal Tribunal if action is brought against the Tribunal of First Instance or against the Appeals Tribunal.

[260]See in general, J. Cretella Junior, *Comentários à la Lei do mandado de segurança*, Forense, Rio de Janeiro, 1992; José Afonso da Silva, "El mandamiento de seguridad en Brasil," in Héctor Fix-Zamudio and Eduardo Ferrer Mac-Gregor, *Idem*, pp. 123–157.

[261]Article 113,33 Constitution 1934. See A. Ríos Espinoza, "Presupuestos constitucionales del mandato de seguridad," in *Boletín del Instituto de Derecho Comparado de México*, Universidad Nacional Autónoma de México, n° 46, México, 1963, p. 71. Also published in

142

the recourse of habeas data established in the 1988 Constitution,[262] making Brazil the first Latin American country to have constitutionalized this latter to guaranty the right to have access to official records and the rights to rectify or correct the information they contain (Article 5, LXXII).

The *mandado de segurança* was expressly provided for the protection of fundamental rights, except for personal freedom and the right to free movement, which are protected by the recourse for habeas corpus (Article 153, 21). According to the Law N° 1533 of December 31, 1951, it is only admitted against illegal or abuse of power actions adopted by public authority or corporations when exercising public attributions (Article 5, LXIX). The *mandado de segurança*, as is the case of the amparo action in Argentina, cannot be filed against statutes, even being of auto-applicative or self-executing nature.[263]

The 1988 Constitution also provided for a *mandado de segurança* of a collective nature, conceived as a mean for protecting collective interests that can be brought before the courts by political parties represented in the National Congress, and by trade union and other legally organized entities or associations for the defense of the interests of their members or associates (Article 5, LXX).

This *mandado de segurança* can be brought before a variety of courts, and only if there are no other administrative recourses that can be filed against the challenged act, or if against judicial decisions, when no other recourses are provided in procedural law to obtain for their modification.

The *mandado de injunçao* was established to protect constitutional rights against the omissions of State authorities to regulate their exercise,

---

H. Fix-Zamudio, A. Ríos Espinosa and N. Alcalá Zamora, *Tres estudios sobre el mandato de seguridad brasileño,* México, 1963, pp. 71–96.

[262] See in general. José Afonso da Silva, *Mandado de injunçao e habeas data,* Sao Paulo, 1989; Dimar Ackel Filho, *Writs Constitutionais,* Sao Paulo, 1988; Nagib Slaibi Filho, *Anotaçoes a Constituiçao de 1988,* Río de Janeiro, 1989; Celso Agrícola Barbi, Do *Mandado de Segurança,* 7th Edition de acordo com o Código de Processo Civil de 1973 e legislação posterior, Editora Forense, Río de Janeiro, 1993; J. Cretella Júnior, *Comentários à ley do mandado de segurança (de acordo com a constituição de 5 de outubro de 1988,* 5th Edition, Editora Forense, Río de Janeiro, 1992; José Afonso da Silva, "El mandamiento de seguridad en Brasil," in Héctor Fix-Zamudio and Eduardo Ferrer Mac-Gregor (Co-ord.), *El derecho de amparo en el mundo,* Universidad Nacional Autónoma de México, Editorial Porrúa, México, 2006, pp. 123–157.

[263] See H. Fix-Zamudio, "Mandato de seguridad y juicio de amparo," in *Boletín del Instituto de Derecho Comparado de México,* Universidad Nacional Autónoma de México, N° 46, México, 1963, pp. 11, 17.

particularly referring to constitutional rights related to nationality and citizenship when the lack of legislative or regulatory provisions make them unenforceable (Article 5, LXXI). So the action is filed in order to obtain a court order directed to the legislative or regulatory bodies to produce determined regulatory acts, the absence of which affects or harms the specific right.[264] In these cases, the courts cannot surrogate themselves in the powers of the legislative body, in the sense that they cannot "legislate" by means of this writ of *injunçao*, and are restricted to order or instruct for the protection of the constitutional right when unenforceable because of the lack of regulation.

All these four actions for the protection of constitutional rights established in Brazil within a mixed system of judicial review of the constitutionality of legislation, has been developed since the nineteenth century and combines the diffuse and the concentrated method of judicial review.

The diffuse method, clearly influenced by the U.S. constitutional system,[265] was introduced in the 1891 Federal Constitution by empowering the Supreme Federal Tribunal to review, through an extraordinary recourse, the decisions of the federal courts and of the courts of the States in which the constitutionality of treaties or federal statutes were questioned (Article III, I, 1891 Constitution).

As a consequence of this express constitutional attribution, the Federal Law N° 221 of November 20, 1984, (Article 13,10) expressly assigned to all federal courts the power to judge upon the validity of statutes and executive regulations when they considered them unconstitutional, and to decide upon their inapplicability when deciding a particular case.[266]

According to this diffuse system of judicial review in Brazil, all the courts of first instance have the power to decide not to apply laws (federal, state or municipal) that they deem unconstitutional when a party to

---

[264] If the regulatory omission is attributable to the highest authorities of the Republic, the competent court to decide the *mandado de injunçao* is the Supreme Federal Tribunal. In other cases, the High Courts of Justice are the ones competent to do so.

[265] See O.A. Bandeira de Mello, *A teoria das Constituiçoes rigidas*, Sao Paulo, 1980, p. 157; José Afonso da Silva, *Sistema de defensa da Constituiçao brasileira,* Congreso sobre la Constitución y su Defensa, Universidad Nacional Autónoma de México, México, 1982, p. 29 (mimeo).

[266] Thus, the diffuse system of judicial review of legislation was established in Brazil at the end of the nineteenth century, and was perfected through the subsequent constitutional reforms of 1926, 1934, 1937, 1946 and 1967. See O.A. Bandeira De Mello, *Idem,* pp. 158–237.

the proceeding has raised the question of constitutionality,[267] or when the challenged particular authority act, in cases of *mandado de segurança* or the habeas corpus recourses, is alleged to be issued in execution of a statute deemed unconstitutional. In these cases, the question must be examined before the final decision of the case is adopted in a decision with *inter partes* effects on the case.[268]

The constitutional question can also be decided in the appellate jurisdiction, in which case, if the court of second instance is a collegiate court, the decision upon matters of unconstitutionality of legislation must be adopted by a majority vote.[269]

However, the most distinctive feature of the Brazilian diffuse method of judicial review (Article 119, III,b,c), is that since its constitutional creation in 1894, the power of the Supreme Tribunal to intervene in all proceedings in which constitutional questions are resolved was also established when requested through an extraordinary recourse. In these cases, the Supreme Court's decisions have to be sent to the Federal Senate, which has the power to "suspend the execution of all or part of a statute or decree when declared unconstitutional by the Supreme Federal Tribunal through a definitive decision" (Article 42, VII Federal Constitution) in which case the effects of the Senate's decisions has *erga omnes* and *ex nunc* effects.[270]

This diffuse system of judicial review, initially established in an exclusive way, was transformed into a mixed system in 1934, when in addition, the constitution established the concentrated method of judicial review by empowering the Federal Supreme Tribunal to declare the unconstitutionality of Member States' constitutions or statutes when re-

---

[267] José Afonso da Silva, *Curso de direito constitucional positivo*, Sao Paulo, 1984, p. 18.

[268] José Afonso da Silva, *Sistema de defensa da Constituiçao brasileira,* Congreso sobre la Constitución y su Defensa, Universidad Nacional Autónoma de México, México, 1982, pp. 41, 64.

[269] This qualified vote was first established in the 1934 Constitution (Article 179), and is always required. See O. A. Bandeira De Mello, *A teoria das Constituiçoes rigidas*, Sao Paulo, 1980, p. 159.

[270] Article 119, III b,c, Constitution. See. José Afonso da Silva, *Sistema de defensa da Constituiçao brasileira,* Congreso sobre la Constitución y su Defensa, Universidad Nacional Autónoma de México, México, 1982, pp. 32, 34, 43, 73; José Afonso da Silva, *Curso de direito constitucional positivo*, Sao Paulo, 1984, pp. 17, 18; O.A. Bandeira De Mello, *A teoria das Constituiçoes rigidas*, Sao Paulo, 1980, p. 215; H. Fix-Zamudio and J. Carpizo, "Amerique Latine," in L. Favoreu and J. A. Jolowicz (ed.), *Le contrôle juridictionnel des lois*, Paris, 1986, p. 121.

quested by means of a direct action of unconstitutionality that could be filed directly before the Tribunal by the Attorney General of the Republic (Article 12,2).

This direct action of unconstitutionality, originally established to defend federal constitutional principles against Member States' acts, was extended through subsequent constitutional and statutory reforms (including the 1965 constitutional amendment and the Law n° 2271 of July 22, 1954), in order to allow the constitutional control over Federal and Member States statutes.[271] In these reforms the standing to sue was also extended, so that now, the action of unconstitutionality can be filed by the President of the Republic, by the boards of the Senate and of the Representative Chamber, as well as of the Legislative Assemblies of the States; by the States' governors and by the Attorney General of the Republic. In addition, it can be filed by the Federal Council of the Federal Bar (*Ordem dos advogados de Brasil*), the political parties represented in Congress, and the trade union confederations and class entities (Article 103, Constitution). The decisions of the Supreme Tribunal resolving the actions when declaring the unconstitutionality of statutes have *erga omnes* effects.[272]

Consequently, since 1934 the Brazilian system of judicial review can be considered as a mixed one in which the diffuse method of judicial review operates in combination with a concentrated one.[273]

---

[271] See José Afonso da Silva, *Sistema de defensa da Constituiçao brasileira,* Congreso sobre la Constitución y su Defensa, Universidad Nacional Autónoma de México, México, 1982, p. 31.

[272] See José Carlos Barbosa M, "El control judicial de la constitucionalidad de las leyes en el derecho brasileño: Un bosquejo," in Eduardo Ferrer Mac-Gregor (Coord.), *Derecho Procesal Constitucional,* Tomo III, Editorial Porrúa, México, 2003, Tomo III, p. 1999.

[273] See A. Buzaid, "La accion directa de inconstitucionalidad en el derecho brasileño," in *Revista de la Facultad de Derecho,* UCAB, n° 19–22, Caracas, 1964, p. 55; O. A. Bandeira De Mello, *A teoria das Constituiçoes rigidas,* Sao Paulo, 1980, p. 157. See in general Mantel Goncalves Ferreira Filho, "O sistema constitucional brasileiro e as recentes inovacoes no controle de constitucionalidade," in *Anuario Iberoamericano de Justicia Constitucional,* n° 5, 2001, Centro de Estudios Políticos y Constitucionales, Madrid, España, 2001; José Carlos Barbosa Moreira, "El control judicial de la constitucionalidad de las leyes en el Brasil: un bosquejo," in *Desafios del control de constitucionalidad,* Ediciones Ciudad Argentina, Buenos Aires, Argentina, 1996; Paulo Bonavides, "Jurisdicao constitucional e legitimidade (algumas observacoes sobre o Brasil)," in *Anuario Iberoamericano de Justicia Constitucional* n° 7, Centro de Estudios Políticos y Constitucionales, Madrid, 2003; Enrique Ricardo Lewandowski, "Notas sobre o controle da constitucionalidade no Brasil," in Edgar Corzo Sosa *et al., Justicia Constitucional Comparada,* Ed. Universidad Nacional

However, as mentioned, one of the particular trends of the Brazilian system of judicial review, ever since its establishment in 1891, is the power assigned to the Supreme Tribunal to review lower courts' decisions on matters of constitutionality through an extraordinary recourse that can be brought before the Tribunal against judicial decision issued on matters of constitutionality by the Superior Federal Court or by the Regional Federal Courts, when their decisions are considered to be inconsistent with the constitution; and in cases in which the courts have denied the validity of treaties or federal statutes, or have declared their unconstitutionality; or when a local government law or act has been challenged as unconstitutional for being contrary to a valid federal law (Article 199. III, b,c, Constitution).

2. The action for tutela and habeas corpus in Colombia

In Colombia, also a country with a mixed system of judicial review of legislation, a specific mean for the protection of constitutional rights was also created in the 1991 Constitution named the action for *tutela*, using a word that in Spanish has the same general meaning as amparo and as *protección*.

This action for *tutela* is referred to in Article 86 of the constitution as a preferred and summary proceeding that can be used for the immediate protection of certain constitutional rights which are those listed in the constitution as "fundamental" or that are considered as such because of their connection with them. The constitution refers to the action for *tutela* providing that it can be filed against public officials' violations and also against individuals or corporations whose activities may particularly affect collective interest.

The action can only be filed when the injured party has no other judicial mean for the protection of his rights, unless when the *tutela* action is used as a transitory mean to prevent irreparable damages.

The *tutela* action, created by the 1991 Constitution, was immediately regulated in the decree-law n° 2591 of November 19, 1991, and subsequently developed by decree n° 306 of February 19, 1992, and decree n° 382 of July 12, 2000.[274]

Autónoma de México, México, 1993; Zeno Veloso, *Controle jurisdicional de constitucionalidade*, Ed. Cejup, Belém, Brasil, 1999.

[274]See in general, Manuel José Cepeda, *La Tutela. Materiales y reflexiones sobre su signifycado*, Imprenta nacional, Bogotá, 1992; Juan Carlos Esguerra Portocarrero, *La protec-*

As can be deduced from the drafts discussed in the National Constituent Assembly, the initial intention was to regulate the amparo as a constitutional right,[275] in the same trend as the Mexican and Venezuelan systems of amparo, and not just as a constitutional guaranty.

Nonetheless, in the final version of the constitution, that proposal was abandoned and the action for *tutela* was established with a limited scope as a specific judicial mean for the protection of only some constitutional rights, those qualified in the constitution as "fundamental rights."

In addition to the habeas corpus recourse, which is regulated in the Criminal Code, the constitution also provides for a "popular action" established for the protection of collective rights and interests when related to the protection of public property, public space use, public safety and public health, administrative behavior, the environment, free economic competition and others of the same nature defined by statute.

In particular, regarding the action of *tutela*, its statutory regulation issued by Decree nº 2.591 of 1991,[276] and its very important application by the courts, have molded an effective judicial mean for the protection of

---

ción constitucional del ciudadano, Legis, Bogotá, 2004; Julio César Ortiz Gutierrez, "La acción de tutela en la Carta Politica de 1991. El derecho de amparo y su influencia en el ordenamiento constitucional de Colombia," in Héctor Fix-Zamudio and Eduardo Ferrer Mac-Gregor, *Idem,* Edit. Porrúa, México, 2006, pp. 213–256.

[275]See the draft in Jorge Arenas Salazar, *La tutela. Una acción humaniaria*, Libreria Doctrina y Ley, Bogotá, 1992, pp. 47. See the comments in Allan R. Brewer-Carías, "El amparo a los derechos y libertades constitucionales y la acción de tutela a los derechos fundamentales en Colombia: una aproximación comparativa," in Manuel José Cepeda (editor), *La Carta de Derechos. Su interpretación y sus implicaciones*, Editorial Temis, Bogotá, 1993, pp. 21–81.

[276]See in general, regarding the *tutela* in Colombia, Jorge Arenas Salazar, *La Tutela Una acción humanitaria,* 1st Edition 1992, Ediciones Librería Doctrina y Ley, Bogotá, 1992; Manuel José Cepeda, *La Tutela Materiales y Reflexiones sobre su significado*, Imprenta Nacional, Bogotá, 1992; Oscar José Dueñas Ruiz, *Acción de Tutela, Su esencia en la práctica, 50 respuestas básicas, Corte Suprema, Consejo de Estado, Legislación*, Ediciones Librería del Profesional, Bogotá, 1992; Federico González Campos, *La Tutela: Interpretación doctrinaria y jurisprudencial*, 2nd Edition, Ediciones Jurídicas Gustavo Ibáñez, Bogotá, 1994; Manuel José Cepeda, *Las Carta de Derechos. Su interpretación y sus implicaciones,* Temis, Bogotá, 1993; Juan Manuel Charry U., *La acción de tutela*, Editorial Temis, Bogotá, 1992; Julio César Ortiz Gutierrez, "La acción de tutela en la Carta política de 1991. El derecho de amparo y su influencia en el ordenamiento constituicional de Colombia," in Héctor Fix-Zamudio and Eduardo Ferrer Mac-Gregor (Coord.), *El derecho de amparo en el mundo*, Universidad Nacional Autónoma de México, Editorial Porrúa, México, 2006, pp. 213–256.

fundamental constitutional rights, which can be filed before the courts[277] at all times and in any place for the immediate protection of fundamental constitutional rights, whenever they are harmed by the action or the omission of any public authority or by certain individuals. In the latter case, they must be those rendering a public service, whose conduct can seriously and directly affect collective interests, and regarding which the aggrieved party finds himself in a position of subordination or defenselessness.

The constitution does not exclude any State act from the *tutela* action, so Article 40 of the Decree 2591 expressly provided for the action for *tutela* against judicial decisions. Notwithstanding, the following year this article was annulled by the Constitutional Court by a decision issued on October 1, 1992, considering it unconstitutional[278] because it was contrary to the general principle of *res judicata* effects of the judicial rulings, as an expression of the due process rights. With this Constitutional Court ruling, all arbitrary judicial decisions were left out of specific control. Yet in spite of the annulment of the Article, this situation was amended by the same Constitutional Court through the development of the so-called doctrine of arbitrariness, precisely conceived to allow the admission of the *tutela* actions against judicial decisions when issued as a result of courts arbitrary ruling or *voi de fait*.[279]

According to Article 86 of the constitution, the action for *tutela* can only be admitted when the affected party does not have any other preferred and brief mean for judicial defense (Article 6,2 of the Decree N°

---

[277]The constitution sets forth that the action of *tutela* for the protection of fundamental constitutional rights can be brought "before the judges"; which according to Decree 2.591 of 1991 are those with jurisdiction in the place where the violation or threat of violation have taken place (Article 37). In another Decree n° 1380 of 2000, regarding the courts with jurisdiction to decide the *tutela* actions, it was established that they must be filed before the Districts' Superior Courts when against any national public authority; before the Circuit Courts when against any national or departmental decentralized entity for public services; before the municipal courts when against district or municipal authorities and against individuals; before the Cundinamarca Judicial review of administrative actions when against any general administrative act issued by national authorities; before the respective superior court when against any judicial decision; and before a Corporation in its corresponding Chamber when against the Supreme Court of Justice, the Consejo de Estado or the Superior Council of the Judiciary, or its Disciplinary Chamber.

[278]See the decision n° C-543 of September 24, 1992, in *Derecho Colombiano*, Bogotá, 1992, pp. 471–499; and in Manuel José Cepeda, *Derecho Constitucional Jurisprudencial. Las grandes decisiones de la Corte Constitucional*, Legis, Bogotá 2001, pp. 1009 ff.

[279]See the decision n° T-231 of May 13, 1994, *Idem*, pp. 1022 ff.

2591), and in such cases, when filed "to obtain temporary judicial relief to avoid irreparable harm," being understood as irreparable damage those "that can only be wholly repaired by means of compensation" (Article 6,1). The *Tutela* Law also provides, similar to the Venezuelan amparo regulations, that in these cases "when used as a preliminary protective relief to avoid irreparable harm, the action of *tutela* may be brought conjunctly with the actions for annulment filed against administrative acts before the judicial review of administrative action jurisdiction (*contencioso administrativo*).

In all these cases, the judge may determine that the challenged administrative act "would not be applied to the specific protected situation pending the final decision on the nullity of the challenged act" (Decree n° 2.591, Article 8).

This *tutela* remedy has also been established in Colombia within a mixed system of judicial review of legislation, which in a very similar way to the Venezuelan one, was established since the nineteenth century, mixing the diffuse and concentrated methods of judicial review.[280]

The diffuse method of judicial review was consolidated since the 1910 Constitution, which expressly attributed to all courts the power to declare the inapplicability of statutes deemed contrary to the constitution. As in all cases where the diffuse method is applied, the courts cannot annul the statutes, the declaration of their unconstitutionality only being referred to the particular case, in the sense that the court must limit the ruling to not apply the unconstitutional statute to the case, with *inter partes* effects.

This method was developed in parallel with a concentrated method of judicial review by attributing the former Supreme Court of Justice and now the Constitutional Court, the power to annul statutes with general effects on the grounds of their unconstitutionality, when requested by means of a popular action. It was also in the 1910 Constitution that the role of the Supreme Court as "guardian of the integrity of the Constitution" was

---

[280]See in general Eduardo Cifuentes Muñoz, "La Jurisdicción constitucional en Colombia," in F. Fernández Segado and Domingo García Belaúnde, *La Jurisdicción constitucional en Iberoamérica*, Ed Dykinson, Madrid, 1997; Luis Carlos Sáchica, *La Corte Constitucional y su jurisdicción*, Ed. Temis. Bogotá, 1993. Concerning the mixed character of the system, see J. Vidal Perdomo, *Derecho constitucional general*, Bogotá 1985, p. 42; D. R. Salazar, *Constitución Política de Colombia*, Bogotá, 1982, p. 305; E. Sarria, *Guarda de la Constitución*, Bogotá, p. 78.

consolidated, a role that today is accomplished by the Constitutional Court.[281]

The creation of the Constitutional Court in 1991 as the ultimate guardian of the constitution also originated the attribution to the Court of the power to review all the judicial decisions resolving actions for *tutela*. However, contrary to the Venezuelan or Argentinean regulations on this matter, the competence of the Constitutional Court in Colombia in the case is not the result of the filing of a specific recourse for review, but is an attribution that must be automatically accomplished by the Court, although in a discretionary way (Article 33). For such purpose, in all cases where *tutela* decisions are not appealed, they must always be automatically sent for revision before the Constitutional Court (Article 31). Yet even in cases in which the *tutela* decisions are appealed, the matter must also reach the Constitutional Court because the superior court's decision, whether confirming or revoking the appealed decision, must also be automatically sent for review before the Constitutional Court (Article 32). In all these cases the Constitutional Chamber has discretionary powers to determine which decision of *tutela* will be examined (Article 33).

These Constitutional Court review decisions only produce effects regarding the particular case; thus the first instance court must be immediately notified, and who, in turn, must notify the parties and adopt the necessary decisions in order to conform their own initial ruling to the Constitutional Court decision.

3. *The action of amparo and habeas corpus in the Dominican Republic*

The Constitution of the Dominican Republic only sets forth the judicial guaranties for the protection of personal safety, by means of the action of habeas corpus (Article 8) for the protection of personal freedom, which initially regulated by the 1978 Habeas Corpus statute (*Ley de habeas corpus*), since 2002 has been regulated in the Procedural Criminal Code (Ley 76–02) (Articles 381–392).[282] Based on such regulations, the Su-

---

[281] See Allan R. Brewer-Carías, *El Sistema mixto o integral de control de la constitucionalidad en Colombia y Venezuela*, Universidad Externado de Colombia (Temas de Derecho Público N° 39) y Pontificia Universidad Javeriana (Quaestiones Juridicae N° 5), Bogotá, 1995.

[282] See in general, Juan de la Rosa, *El recurso de amparo*, Edit. Serrales, Santo Domingo, 2001.

preme Court traditionally limited the procedure of habeas corpus for the protection of physical freedom and safety, excluding any possibility of using it in order to protect other constitutional rights. Apart from the Cuban Constitution, it is the only Latin American Constitution that does not expressly regulate the amparo action as a specific judicial mean for the protection of the other constitutional rights.

Nonetheless, this omission did not impede the Supreme Court of Justice from admitting the amparo, applying for that purpose the American Convention on Human Rights. It occured in a decision of February 24, 1999, in the *Productos Avon S.A.* case, when the Supreme Court, based on the American Convention on Human Rights, admitted the amparo recourse for the protection of constitutional rights, in a case involving a judicial decision, assigning the power to decide on amparo matter, to the courts of first instance;[283] and establishing the general procedural rules for the proceeding.

This judicial doctrine regarding the admissibility of the amparo recourse leads to the sanctioning, in 2006, of the Law 437-06 establishing the recourse for amparo (*Ley nº 437-06 que establece el Recurso de Amparo*), "against any act or omission from public authorities of from any individual, which in an actual and imminent way and with manifest arbitrariness and illegality, harms, restrict, alter of threat the rights and guaranties recognized explicit or implicit in the Constitution" (Article 1). Nonetheless, and even though the amparo recourse was admitted by the Supreme Court in 1999 as a public law institution in a case brought before the Court against a judicial decision, the 2006 law expressly has excluded the amparo recourse against "jurisdictional acts issued by any court within the Judicial Power" (Judiciary) (Article 3,a); also providing that no judicial process before any court can be suspended by the exercise of the action for amparo (Article 5).

The courts of first instance are competent on matters of amparo (Article 6), being the recourse an "autonomous action," which imply that in the Dominican Republic, the amparo action is not subjected to the previous

---

[283] Since then, the amparo action was successfully used for the protection of constitutional rights. Among the multiple cases is a very interesting 2002 case in which the Court of First Instance of the National District ordered the National Citizenship Registry to issue the Identification Card to two boys born in the Republic from illegally settled Haitian parents, arguing that the rejection of such documents constituted a violation of the boys' identity and citizenship rights. The matter finally reached the Inter-American Court on Human Rights. See Samuel Arias Arzeno, "El Amparo en la República Dominicana: su Evolución Jurisprudencial," in *Revista Estudios Jurídicos*, Vol. XI, nº 3, Ediciones Capeldom, 2002.

exhaustion of other recourses or judicial means establish to challenge the act or omission (Article 4).

The Dominican Republic also has a mixed system of judicial review that combines the diffuse method of judicial review with the concentrated one. Regarding the former, since 1844, the constitution sets forth that "all statutes, decrees, resolutions, regulations or acts contrary to the Constitution are null and void" (Article 46, 2002, Constitution). It was from this express supremacy clause that the courts developed their general power to declare statutes unconstitutional and not applicable when resolving a particular case.[284]

On the other hand, regarding the concentrated method of judicial review, the Supreme Court of Justice has the exclusive power to hear and decide action of unconstitutionality against statutes that can be filed by the President of the Republic, the Presidents of the National Congress Chambers and also by any interested party (Article 67,1). In such cases, the Supreme Court decisions have *erga omnes* effects.

4. *The action of amparo, habeas corpus and habeas data in Ecuador*

The Constitution of Ecuador also provides for the three fundamental means designed for the protection of human rights: the habeas corpus, habeas data and amparo; but contrary to the general trend of Latin America, not all are set forth as judicial remedies.

This is the case of the habeas corpus recourse, provided in Article 95 of the constitution as a right of "any person who thinks that he has been illegally deprived of his freedom" to file for its protection by an administrative request before the corresponding local government authority or mayor (*alcalde*).

In contrast, regarding the amparo action it is conceived as a judicial remedy, for which, the same Article 95, also sets forth a very extensive regulation providing for a preferred and summary remedy for the protection of any right declared in the constitution or in an international treaty or convention in force, against any illegitimate act or omission from a public authority. In Ecuador, as in Colombia, the amparo action can also be filed if the act or the omission is executed by individuals or corporations rendering public services or that are acting by delegation or concession from a public authority.

---

[284]See M. Berges Chupani, "Informe," in *Memoria de la Reunión de Cortes Superiores de Justicia de Ibero-América, El Caribe, España y Portugal*, Caracas, 1983, p. 380.

In Ecuador, the three remedies, habeas corpus, habeas data and the amparo, are also regulated in one single statute along with other constitutional proceedings: the Constitutional Judicial Review Statute (*Ley de Control Constitucional*, *Ley* n° 000 RO/99) of July 2, 1997.[285]

The purpose of the amparo action, according to Article 95 of the constitution and Article 46 of the law, is to effectively protect the rights enshrined in the Constitution or in international declarations, covenants and instrument, against any threat originated in any public authority illegitimate act or omission that causes imminent, grave and irreparable harm to the plaintiff.[286] The amparo action is also admitted against individuals when their conduct affects in a grave and direct way communal, collective or diffuse rights. It also can be filed against acts or omissions of individuals and corporations, but in this case, as in Colombia, only when they render a public service or act by delegation or concession from a public authority.

The amparo action is not admissible against judicial decisions, and the competent courts to hear the amparo action are the first instance courts (Article 47, Law).

The protective actions of constitutional rights have also been established in Ecuador within a mixed system of judicial review of legislation that combines the diffuse and the concentrated methods. The former is expressly set forth in Article 272 of the constitution, which prescribes not only that "the Constitution prevails over any other legal norm" but that "all the statutes, decrees-law, ordinances, regulations or resolution, must conform to its provisions and in case they enter in contradiction with it or alters their provisions, they will have no value."

As a consequence of this supremacy principle, Article 274 of the constitution reaffirms the diffuse method of judicial review allowing any court whether at the parties' request or, as in Venezuela, raised *ex officio* by the courts, to declare the inapplicability of the provision contrary to the constitution or to international treaties or covenants. According to the

---

[285]See in general, Rafael Oyarte Martínez, *Manual de Amparo Constitucional. Guía de litigio constitucional*, CLD-Konrad Adenauer, Quito, 2003; Hernán Salgado Pesantes, *Manual de Justicia Constitucional Ecuatoriana*, Corporación Editora Nacional, Quito, 2004, and "La garantía de amparo en Ecuador," in Héctor Fix-Zamudio and Eduardo Ferrer Mac-Gregor, *Idem*, Edit. Porrúa, México, 2006, pp. 305–331.

[286]Hernán Salgado Pesantes, "La garantía de amparo en Ecuador," in Héctor Fix-Zamudio and Eduardo Ferrer Mac-Gregor (Coord.), *El derecho de amparo en el mundo*, Universidad Nacional Autónoma de México, Editorial Porrúa, México, 2006, pp. 305–331.

same article, this declaration has obligatory force only in the case in which it is issued, that is to say, only *inter partes* effects.

In all these cases of diffuse judicial review decisions, the court must produce a report on the issue of unconstitutionality of the statute that must be sent to the Constitutional Tribunal in order for it to resolve the matter in a general and obligatory way, that is to say, with *erga omnes* effects.

Thus, in matters of amparo when the constitutional protection is granted by the competent courts applying the diffuse method of judicial review declaring the unconstitutionality of statutes,[287] they must send the report on the question of constitutionality to the Constitutional Tribunal for its confirmation (Article 12,6).

Regarding the concentrated method of judicial review, the 1998 Constitution assigns the Constitutional Tribunal, which was created in substitution of a former Constitutional Guaranties Tribunal,[288] the power to declare the nullity of any statute, decree, regulation or ordinance on the grounds of unconstitutionality with *erga omnes* effects (Article 22). These actions can be brought before the Tribunal by the President of the Republic, the National Congress, the Supreme Court, one thousand citizens or by any person having a previous favorable report from the People's Defendant (Article 18).

Finally, it must be mentioned that for the purpose of unifying the jurisprudence in constitutional matters, all the decisions granting amparo claims must obligatorily be sent to the Constitutional Tribunal in order to be confirmed or repeal. In cases of decisions denying the amparo action (as well as the habeas corpus or habeas data actions), they can be appealed before the same Constitutional Tribunal (Articles 12,3; 31; 52).

---

[287]See Hernán Salgado Pesantes, *Manual de Justicia Constitucional Ecuatoriana*, Corporación Editora Nacional, Quito, 2004, p. 85.

[288]See in general Hernán Salgado Pesantes, "El control de constitucionalidad en la Carta Política del Ecuador," in *Una mirada a los Tribunales Constitucionales. Las experiencias recientes.* Lecturas Constitucionales Andinas n° 4, Ed. Comisión Andina de Juristas, Lima, Perú; Ernesto López Freire, "Evolución del control de constitucionalidad en el Ecuador," in *Derecho Constitucional para fortalecer la democracia ecuatoriana,* Ed. Tribunal Constitucional – Kas, Quito, 1999; Marco Morales Tobar, "Actualidad de la Justicia Constitucional en el Ecuador," in Luis López Guerra, (Coord.), *La Justicia Constitucional en la actualidad*, Corporación Editora Nacional, Quito, pp. 77–165; Oswaldo Cevallos Bueno, "El sistema de control concentrado y el constitucionalismo en el Ecuador," in *Anuario Iberoamericano de Justicia Constitucional*, n° 6, 2002, Madrid, España, 2002.

5.   *The amparo in Guatemala*

In Guatemala, Article 265 of the constitution sets forth the amparo, as a specific judicial mean with the purpose of protecting the people's constitutional rights against the violations or the threats to their rights in order to restore their effectiveness. The constitution emphatically states that "there is no scope that could escape from the amparo as constitutional protection, since it is possible to file the action against acts, resolutions, provisions or statutes which explicitly or implicitly threatens, restricts or violates the rights guaranteed by the Constitution and the statutes" (Article 265).[289]

For such protection, the constitutional provision only refers to actions from public authorities, but this has not prevented the admission of the amparo for the protection of all rights declared in the constitution and also in statutes, as well as against individual actions.

The regulation of the action of amparo in Guatemala is also set forth in a general statute, the 1986 Amparo, Personal Exhibition and Constitutionality Statute (Decree n° 1-86, *Ley de amparo, exhibición personal y de constitucionalidad*).

According to Article 10 of this law, the amparo is established to protect all rights against any situation provoking any risk, threat, restriction or violation, whether from authorities or private entities. Notwithstanding, regarding the latter, Article 9 of the Amparo Laws, restrict the amparo action only against private entities that are supported with public funds or that have been created by statute or by virtue of a concession, or those that act by delegation of the State, by virtue of a contract or a concession. Amparo can also be filed against entities to which certain individuals are legally compelled to be part of them (professional corporations) and other that are recognized by statute, like political parties, associations, societies, trade unions, cooperatives and similar.

Article 10 of the Amparo Law enumerates a few examples according to which everybody has the right to ask for amparo,[290] including the amparo

---

[289] See Jorge Mario García Laguardia, "Las garantías jurisdiccionales para la tutela de los derechos humanos en Guatemala: Hábeas corpus y amparo," in Héctor Fix-Zamudio and Eduardo Ferrer Mac-Gregor (Coord.), *El derecho de amparo en el mundo*, Universidad Nacional Autónoma de México, Editorial Porrúa, México, 2006, pp. 381–408.

[290] Article 10: "Everybody has the right to ask for amparo, among other, in the following cases: a) To ask to be maintained or to be restituted in the enjoyment of the rights and guaranties set forth in the Constitution or any other statute; b) In order to seek a declaration in a particular case, that a statute, regulation, resolution or authority act does not oblige the

against statutes, which is conceived as a mean to obtain in a judicial decision in a particular case, a declaration that a statute, regulation, resolution or act of any authority does not oblige the plaintiff or injured party because it contradicts or restricts any of the rights guaranteed in the Constitution or recognized by any statute (Article 10,b).

Article 263 of the constitution and Article 82 of the Amparo Law also regulate the right to habeas corpus in favor of anyone who is illegally arrested, detained or in any other way prevented from enjoying personal freedom, threatened with losing such freedom, or suffering humiliation, even when their imprisonment or detention is legally founded. In such cases, the affected party has the right to request his immediate personal appearance (habeas corpus) before the court, either for his constitutional guaranty of freedom to be reinstated, for the humiliations to cease, or to terminate the duress to which he was being subjected.

The competent courts to hear and to decide on amparo matters vary regarding the challenged acts,[291] and in all the cases, the amparo decisions are subjected to appeal before the Constitutional Court (Article 60), which can be filed by the parties, the Public Prosecutor and the Human Rights Commissioner (Article 63).

---

plaintiff because it contradicts or restricts any of the rights guarantied in the Constitution or recognized by any other statute; c) In order to seek a declaration in a particular case that a nonlegislative disposition or resolution of Congress is not applicable to the plaintiff because it violates a constitutional right; d) When an authority of any jurisdiction issues a regulation, accord or resolution of any kind that abuses power or exceeds its legal attributions, or when it has no attributions or they are exercised in a way that the harm caused or that can be caused would be irreparable through any other mean of defense. e) When in administrative activities the affected party is compelled to accomplish unreasonable or illegal formalities, task or activities, or when no suppressive mean or recourse exists; f) When the petitions or formalities before administrative authorities are not resolved in the delay fixed by statutes, or in case that no delay exists, in a delay of thirty days once exhausted the procedure, or when the petitions are not admitted; g) In political matters when the rights recognized in the Constitution or statutes are injured by political organizations; h) In judicial and administrative matters, regarding which the statutes set forth procedures and recourses according to due process rules that can serve to adequately resolve them, if after the exhaustion of threat by the interested party, the threat, restriction or violation to the rights recognized in the Constitution and guaranteed by the statute persist."

[291]For instance, according to Articles 11 et seq. of the 1986 Law of Amparo, the Constitutional Court, is competent in the cases of amparo brought against the Congress of the Republic, the Supreme Court of Justice, the President and the Vice-President of the Republic, and the Supreme Court of Justice must decide the cases of amparo brought against the Supreme Electoral Tribunal; Ministers or Vice Ministers of State when acting in the name of their Office.

The Constitutional Court in its decision can confirm, revoke or modify the lower court resolution (Article 67); and can also annul the whole proceeding when it is proved that the formalities had not been observed.

The judicial review system of Guatemala is also a mixed system that combines the diffuse and concentrated methods. The former has been traditionally set forth in Guatemala, derived from the principle of the supremacy of the constitution, expressly provided in Article 115 of the Amparo Law when it declares that all "statutes, governmental dispositions or any order regulating the exercise of rights guarantied in the Constitution shall be null and void if they violate, diminish, restrict or distort them. No statute can contravene the Constitution's disposition. Statutes that violate or distort the constitutional norms are null and void."

On the other hand, the consequence of this principle is the possibility of the parties to raise in any particular case (including cases of amparo and habeas corpus), before any court, at any instance or in cassation, but before the decision on the merits is issued, the question of the unconstitutionality of the statute in order to obtain a declaration of its inapplicability to the particular case (Article 116) In such cases, once the constitutional question is raised before any court, it assumes the character of constitutional tribunal (Article 120).

The question of unconstitutionality can be brought and raised as an action or as an exception or incident in the particular case, before the competent court by the Public Prosecutor or by the parties. The decision that must be issued in three days can be appealed before the Constitutional Courts (Article 121). If the question of unconstitutionality of a statute supporting the claim is raised has an exception or incident, the competent court must also resolve the matter (Article 123); and the decision can also be appealed before the Constitutional Court (Article 130).

The concentrated method of judicial review is exercised by the Constitutional Court, which is empowered to hear actions of unconstitutionality filed against statutes, regulations or general dispositions (Article 133). This action can be brought before the Court by the Public Prosecutor and the Human Rights Commissioner; and also by the board of directors of the Lawyer's (Bar) Association (*Colegio de Abogados*), and by any person with the help of three lawyers who are members of the Bar (Article 134).

The statutes, regulations or general dispositions declared unconstitutional will cease in their effects from the following day after the publication of the Constitutional Court decisions in the *Official Gazette* (Article

140), the decision of the Constitutional Court having general *erga omnes* effects.

6. *The recourse of amparo, habeas corpus and habeas data in Peru*

The Constitution of Peru in its enumeration of the constitutional guaranties also provides for the three actions for constitutional protection: the habeas corpus, the amparo and the habeas data actions (Article 200).[292]

The action of habeas corpus that can be filed against any action or omission by any authority, official or person that impairs or threatens individual freedom, and the action of habeas data can be filed against any act or omission by any authority, official or person that impairs or threatens the rights to request and receive information from any public office, except when they affect personal privacy or were excluded for national security. The action of habeas data can also de filed to assure that public or private information services will not release information that affects personal and familiar privacy (Articles 2, 5 and 6).

All these actions (habeas corpus, amparo and habeas data) have been regulated in the Constitutional Procedural Code sanctioned in 2004 (Ley N° 28.237, *Código Procesal Constitucional*),[293] which provide that in matters of amparo, the competent courts to hear the proceeding are the Civil Courts with jurisdiction on the place where the right is affected, or where the plaintiff or defendant have their residence (Article 51). When the harm is caused by a judicial decision, the competent court is always the Civil Chamber of the respective Superior Court of Justice.

Article 200 of the constitution also establishes the action of amparo to protect all other rights recognized by the constitution that are impaired or threatened by any authority, official or private individuals in order to restore things to the situation they had previous to the violation (Article 1). As in Paraguay, according to the constitution, the action of amparo is not admissible against statutes or against judicial decisions, but with the

---

[292]See in general, Samuel B. Abad Yupanqui, *El proceso constitucional de amparo*, Gaceta Jurídica, Lima, 2004; Domingo García Belaúnde and Gerardo Eto Cruz, "El proceso de amparo en el Perú," in Héctor Fix-Zamudio and Eduardo Ferrer Mac-Gregor, *Idem,* Edit. Porrúa, México, 2006, pp. 593–632.

[293]The Code repealed the previous statutes regulating the amparo and the habeas corpus recourses (Law 23.506 of 1982, and Law 25.398 of 1991). See Samuel B. Abad Yupanqui *et al., Código Procesal Constitucional*, Ed. Palestra, Lima, 2004; Alberto Borea Odria, *Las garantías constitucionales: Habeas Corpus y Amparo,* Libros Perúanos S.A., Lima, 1992; Alberto Borea Odría, *El amparo y el Hábeas Corpus en el Perú de Hoy*, Lima, 1985.

difference that in Peru, the exclusion refers only to judicial decisions issued in a regular proceeding.

According to the same Code, the amparo action shall only be admitted when previous procedures have been exhausted (Articles 5,4; 45); and in any case, when doubts exists over the exhaustion of prior procedures (Article 45).

All judicial decisions denying the habeas corpus, amparo and habeas data can be reviewed by the Constitutional Tribunal, which has the power to hear the cases in last and definitive instance (Article 202,2 Constitution). In addition, all the other decisions can also reach the Constitutional Tribunal of Peru by means of a recourse of constitutional damage (*agravio*) that can be filed against all second instance judicial decision denying the claim (Article 18, Code). If this constitutional damage recourse is denied, the interested party can also file before the Constitutional Tribunal a recourse of complaint (*queja*), in which case, if the Tribunal considered the complaint duly supported, it will proceed to decide the constitutional damage recourse, asking the superior court to send the corresponding files (Article 19).

If the Constitutional Tribunal considers that the challenged judicial decision has been issued as a consequence of a procedural error or vice affecting its sense, it can annul it and order the reposition of the procedure to the situation previous to when the defect happened. In cases in which the vice only affects the challenged decision, the Tribunal must repeal it and issue a substantive ruling (Article 20).

All these protective actions of constitutional rights are established in Peru within a judicial review system of the constitutionality of legislation, also conceived as a mixed one,[294] because it combines the diffuse system of judicial review with the concentrated one attributed to the Constitutional Tribunal.[295] The former is expressly set forth in Article 138 of

---

[294]See Aníbal Quiroga León, "Control difuso y control concentrado en el derecho procesal Perúano," in *Revista Derecho* n° 50, diciembre de 1996, Facultad de Derecho de la Pontificia Universidad Católica del Perú, Lima, 1996, pp. 207 ff.

[295]See in general Domingo García Belaunde, "La jurisdicción constitucional en Perú," in D. García Belaúnde, y F. Fernández Segado (Coord.), *La jurisdicción constitucional en Iberoamérica*, Ed. Dykinson, Madrid, España, 1977; Domingo García Belaunde, "La jurisdicción constitucional y el modelo dual o paralelo," in *La Justicia Constitucional a fines del siglo XX, Revista del Instituto de Ciencias Políticas y Derecho Constitucional,* año VII, n° 6, Palestra editores, Huancayo; Domingo García Belaunde (Coordinador) *La Constitución y su defensa,* Ed Jurídica Grijley, Lima, 2003, p. 96; César Landa, *Teoría del Derecho procesal Constitucional,* Ed. Palestra, Lima, 2004; José Palomino Manchego, José, "Control y magistratura constitucional en el Perú," in Juan Vega Gómez, and Edgar

the 1993 Constitution, which provides that "in any process, if an incompatibility exists between a constitutional provision and a statute, the courts must prefer the former" (Article 138), having of course their decisions, in such cases, only *inter partes* effects.

However, in the case of Peru, the diffuse method of judicial review has a peculiarity in the sense that all the courts' decisions regarding the inapplicability of statutes based on constitutional arguments must obligatorily be sent for revision to the Supreme Court of Justice and not to the Constitutional Tribunal. This provision, sanctioned before the Constitutional Procedures Code was enacted, has remained in force, empowering the Supreme Court, through its Constitutional Law and Social Chamber, to determine if the decision of the ordinary court on constitutional matters was adequate or not (Article 14, Organic Law of the Judiciary).[296]

In addition to the diffuse method of judicial review, a concentrated method is also set forth in the Constitution of Peru, by attributing the Constitutional Tribunal the power to hear in unique instance the actions of unconstitutionality (Article 202,1) that can be filed against statutes, legislative decrees, urgency decrees, treaties approved by Congress, congressional internal regulations, regional norms and municipal ordi-nances (Article 77, Code).

This action can be brought before the Constitutional Tribunal by high public officials, as the President of the Republic, the Prosecutor General, the People's Defendant; by a number equivalent to 25 percent of representatives to the Congress; and also, by five thousand citizens whose signatures must be validated by the National Jury of Elections. When the challenged act is a local government regulation, the action can be filed by one percent of the citizens of the corresponding entity. The Presidents of Regions with the vote of the Regional Councils, or the provincial mayors with the vote of the local Councils can also file actions of unconstitutionality in matter of their jurisdiction; and also the professional associa-

---

Corzo Sosa (Coord.), *Instrumentos de tutela y justicia constitucional, Memoria del VII Congreso Iberoamericano de Derecho Constitucional*, Instituto de Investigaciones Jurídicas, Universidad Nacional Autónoma de México, México; Domingo García Belaúnde and Gerardo Eto Cruz, "El proceso de amparo en el Perú," in Héctor Fix-Zamudio and Eduardo Ferrer Mac-Gregor (Coord.), *El derecho de amparo en el mundo*, Universidad Nacional Autónoma de México, Editorial Porrúa, México, 2006, pp. 593–632.

[296] Aníbal Quiroga León, "El derecho procesal constitucional Perúano," in Juan Vega Gómez and Edgar Corzo Sosa (Coord.) *Instrumentos de tutela y justicia constitucional, Memoria del VII Congreso Iberoamericano de Derecho Constitucional*, Instituto de Investigaciones Jurídicas, Universidad Nacional Autónoma de México, México, pp. 471 ff.

tions (*Colegios*) in matters of their specialty (Article 203; Article 99 Code).

The decision of the Constitutional Tribunal, in all these cases of the concentrated method of judicial review when declaring the unconstitutionality of a statute or normative provision, produces general *erga omnes* effects, from the day of its publication in the *Official Gazette* (Article 204, Constitution; Articles 81,82 Code).

CHAPTER EIGHT

THE AMERICAN CONVENTION ON HUMAN RIGHTS AND THE INTERNATIONALIZATION OF THE AMPARO IN LATIN AMERICA

I. THE INTERNATIONALIZATION OF THE AMPARO PROCEEDING

The inclusion in almost all of the Latin American constitutions of some provisions regarding the constitutional regulations of the amparo action or recourse confirms that the existence of this special judicial mean for the protection of human rights, is one of the most important features of Latin American constitutionalism, in addition to it being of Latin American origin.

Besides its constitutionalization, another feature of this institution in Latin America has been its internationalization, which explains the early incorporation for instance in the 1948 American Declaration of the Rights and Duties of Man of the Organization of American States, the first international declaration on the matter. Article 18 of such Declaration, in fact, when referring to the "right to access to justice," set forth that:

> *Article XVIII.* Every person may resort to the courts to ensure respect for his legal rights. A simple and brief procedure should be available for the courts to protect every person (*que lo ampare*) against acts of authority that, to his prejudice, violate any of the fundamental rights constitutionally enshrined.

A similar regulation was later incorporated in Article 8 of the Universal Declaration of Human Rights adopted by the United Nations in December the same year 1948, in which the right to an effective recourse before the national competent courts is guaranteed to every person for his protection (*que la ampare*) against acts that violate his fundamental rights recognized in the Constitution and in statutes.

163

After these first two International Declarations on Human Rights, in 1950 the European Convention on Human Rights also regulated the "right to an effective recourse" (not necessarily of judicial nature) before a national authority, even when the violation is committed by persons acting in an official capacity (Article 13).[297]

Subsequently, in the 1966 International Covenant on Civil and Political Rights of the United Nations, Article 2,3, the right of any person to an effective remedy (also not necessarily of judicial nature) in case of violations of human rights was also regulated. This right could also be exercised against violations committed by persons acting in their official capacity.

II. THE AMPARO IN THE AMERICAN CONVENTION ON HUMAN RIGHTS

The 1969 American Convention on Human Rights establish "the right to judicial protection," expressly setting forth the amparo recourse, as follows:

Article 25. Right to Judicial Protection

1. Everyone has the right to simple and prompt recourse, or any other effective recourse, before a competent court or tribunal for protection (*que la ampare*) against acts that violate his fundamental rights recognized by the constitution or laws of the state concerned or by this Convention, even though such violation may have been committed by persons acting in the course of their official duties.

In order to guaranty such right, the convention imposes the States Parties the duty:

a. to ensure that any person claiming such remedy shall have his rights determined by the competent authority provided for by the legal system of the state;

b. to develop the possibilities of judicial remedy; and

c. to ensure that the competent authorities shall enforce such remedies when granted.

---

[297] *"Article 13.* Everyone whose rights and freedoms as set forth in this Convention are violated shall have an effective remedy before a national authority notwithstanding that the violation has been committed by persons acting in an official capacity."

This article of the American Convention has been considered by the Inter-American Court on Human Rights as a "general provision that gives expression to the procedural institution known as amparo, which is a simple and prompt remedy designated for the protection of all of the rights recognized in the Constitution and laws of the States parties and by the Convention"; thus, that "can be applied to all rights."[298]

The American Convention, in Article 7 regarding the right to personal liberty and security, also provides for the recourse of habeas corpus as follows:

> 6. Anyone who is deprived of his liberty shall be entitled to recourse to a competent court, in order that the court decides without delay on the lawfulness of his arrest or detention and order his release if the arrest or detention is unlawful...

Examining the habeas corpus and the amparo together, it is possible to conclude, as asserted by the same Inter-American Court on Human Rights, that:

> The amparo comprises a whole series of remedies and that habeas corpus is but one of its components. An examination of the essential aspects of both guarantees, as embodied in the Convention and, in their different forms in the legal systems of the States parties, indicates that in some instances habeas corpus functions as an independent remedy. Here its primary purpose is to protect the personal freedom of those who are being detained or who have been threatened with detention. In other circumstances, however, habeas corpus is viewed either as the amparo of freedom" or as an integral part of amparo.[299]

All these regulations of the American Convention are the result of the process of internationalization of the protection of human rights, in particular regarding the provision for the specific judicial mean for their

---

[298]See *Advisory Opinion OC-8/87 of January 30, 1987, Habeas corpus in emergency situations,* Paragraph 32. "Article 25,1 of the Convention is a disposition of general character which incorporated the institution of amparo, as a simple and prompt procedure for the protection of fundamental rights." See in Sergio García Ramírez (Coord.), *La Jurisprudencia de la Corte Interamericana de Derechos Humanos,* Universidad Nacional Autónoma de México, Corte Interamericana de Derechos Humanos, México, 2001, pp. 1.008 ff.

[299]*Advisory Opinion OC-8//87 of January 30, 1987, Habeas Corpus in Emergency Situations,* Paragraph 34. *Idem.*

protection.[300] As a consequence of this process, therefore, the right to a judicial guaranty of human rights (amparo and habeas corpus) in Latin America, is an international obligation imposed on the Member States to guaranty to their people these effective protective remedies of their human rights. This goes as far as that the lack of internal regulations and of effective functioning of such remedies constitutes a breach of the Convention.

In effect, the most important consequence of the internationalization of the amparo, is that according to Article 1,1 of the Convention, the Member States are obligated not only "*to respect*" the right to amparo recognized in the Constitution, but also "*to ensure* to all persons subject to their jurisdiction the free and full exercise" of such right, without any discrimination. This "implies the duty of States Parties to organize the governmental apparatus and, in general, all the structures through which public power is exercised, so that they are capable of juridically ensuring the free and full enjoyment of human rights."[301]

The actions of the Member State in order to comply with this obligation are not only formal ones, in the sense that as expressed by the Inter-American Court, it is not fulfilled only "by the existence of a legal system designed to make it possible" but that in order to comply with this obligation, it is also required that the government "conduct itself so as to effectively ensure the free and full exercise of human rights."[302] On the contrary, as decided by the Inter-American Court on Human Rights, referring to the amparo as a judicial guaranty of human rights,

> [...] for such a remedy to exist, it is not sufficient that it be provided for by the Constitution or by law or that it be formally recognized, but rather

---

[300] The Inter-American Court of Human Rights, has considered "the writs of habeas corpus and of 'amparo' among those judicial remedies that are essential for the protection of various rights whose derogation is prohibited by Article 27(2) and that serve, moreover, to preserve legality in a democratic society." *Advisory Opinion OC-8/87 of January 30, 1987, Habeas Corpus in Emergency Situation*, paragraph 42; *Advisory Opinion OC-9/87 of October 6, 1987, Judicial Guaranties in Status of Emergency*, Paragraph 33. *Idem*, pp. 1.008 ff., and pp. 1.019 ff.

[301] *Velásquez Rodríguez et al.* case, Decision of July, 29, 1988, Paragraph 166. *Idem*, pp. 58 ff.

[302] *Idem*, Paragraph 167. *Idem*, pp. 58 ff.

it must be truly effective in establishing whether there has been a violation of human rights and in providing redress.[303]

Now, from what is set forth in Article 25 of the American Convention, and referring in particular to the amparo action that has been considered by the Inter-American Court on Human Rights, as "one of the basic pillars not only of the American Convention, but of the rule of Law in a democratic society;"[304] the following elements can be deduced as the ones that must characterize such action in the Inter-American context:

First, the amparo is not only conceived as a specific judicial recourse or action, that is, as a judicial guaranty; but it is also conceived as a fundamental human right in itself, that is to say, the right of citizens to be protected by the Judiciary, as it is reaffirmed in the Mexican and Venezuelan legal systems.

Second, the remedy is conceived to protect human rights recognized not only in the constitutions, but in the statutes and in the Convention, and not only some of them, as it is established in the Colombian and Chilean Constitutions, but all of them.

Third, the recourse to be established in order to seek the judicial protection must be a simple, brief and effective one, as it is regulated in all the Latin American constitutions.

Fourth, the action must be brought before competent courts, which must be independent and autonomous according to the general terms of the judicial guaranty set forth in the Convention, and not only before one single court as in Costa Rica, El Salvador and Nicaragua, which in a certain way limits the access to justice.

Fifth, the protection refers to any kind of violations of human rights, whether produced by acts issued by authorities or by private individuals and corporations, contrary to what is established in Brazil, El Salvador,

---

[303] *Advisory Opinión OC-9/87 of October 6, 1987, Judicial Guaranties in Status of Emergency*, Paragraph 24. See in similar sense, *Comunidad Mayagna (Sumo) Awas Tingni* case, Paragraph 113; *Ivcher Bronstein* case, Paragraph 136; *Cantoral Benavides* case, Paragraph 164; *Durand y Ugarte* case, Paragraph 102. *Idem*, pp. 1.019 ff..; 710 ff.; 768 ff.; 484 ff.

[304] See *Castillo Páez* case, p. 83; *Suárez Rosero* case, p. 65 and *Blake* case, p. 102. See the references in Cecilia Medina Quiroga, *La Convención Americana: teoría y jurisprudencia*, IIDH, San José, 2003, p. 358. See also Sergio García Ramírez (Coord.), *La Jurisprudencia de la Corte Interamericana de Derechos Humanos*, Universidad Nacional Autónoma de México, Corte Interamericana de Derechos Humanos, México, 2001, pp. 273 ff.; 406 ff; 372 ff.

Mexico, Nicaragua and Panama where the amparo can only be filed against authorities or public officials, and not against individuals.

I want to elaborate a little more on the consequences of these elements that characterize the amparo in the American Convention, comparing them with the internal constitutional regulations on the matter,[305] particularly referring to the amparo as a right and as a guaranty, to the rights to be protected by such judicial mean and to the universality of its protection.

III. THE FEATURES OF THE AMPARO AS A RIGHT AND AS JUDICIAL GUARANTY

1. *The amparo as a human right*

First of all, the American Convention conceives the amparo as a human right in itself, when providing that everybody "has the right" to a recourse. This does not mean that people have only a specific adjective law instrument for the protection of other rights, but that everyone has a human and civil right in itself to obtain constitutional protection or amparo regarding all other human rights.

The right the people have is to have at their disposal an effective, simple and prompt judicial mean for the protection of their rights; which additionally, is considered in the Convention as one of the "fundamental" rights that cannot be suspended or restricted in cases of state of emergency (Article 27).

The Inter-American Court on Human Rights, in this regard, has issued two important *Advisory Opinions* considering the suspension of habeas corpus or of amparo in emergency situations as "incompatible with the

---

[305] For that purpose, Article 25 of the Convention provides that everyone has the right to simple and prompt recourse, or any other effective recourse, to a competent court or tribunal for protection (que la ampare) against acts that violate his fundamental rights recognized by the constitution or laws of the state concerned and by the American Convention itself. From this precise provision derives the framework that this action for the protection of fundamental rights should have in internal law and that demands some constitutional changes in many countries where the constitutions establish some restrictions to the exercise of the right to amparo. See Allan R. Brewer-Carías, "El amparo en América Latina: La universalización del régimen de la Convención Americana sobre Derechos Humanos y la necesidad de superar las restricciones nacionales," in *Ética y Jurisprudencia*, 1/2003, Enero-Diciembre, Universidad Valle del Momboy, Facultad de Ciencias Jurídicas y Políticas, Centro de Estudios Jurídicos "Cristóbal Mendoza," Valera, 2004, pp. 9–34.

international obligations imposed on the States by the Convention" and with preserving the "legality in a democratic society."[306]

However, in spite of the American Convention provision considering the amparo as a civil right, in the majority of the internal legislation of Latin American countries, the amparo has just been regulated as a specific adjective institution or remedy. Only in Mexico and in Venezuela can it be said that the amparo is also conceived as a civil right in itself that can be exercised by means of multiple judicial actions or recourses for the protection of other constitutional rights, in addition to the amparo action.

2. *The amparo as a judicial guaranty*

On the other hand, the action or recourse of amparo provided for in the Convention in an article with the title of "Right to judicial protection," above all is a judicial mean for the protection of rights, which differentiates the provisions of the American Convention from those of the International Covenant on Civil and Political Rights (Article 2,3) and of the European Convention on Human Rights, which only provides for an effective recourse, without qualifying it as "judicial."

When regulating this right to judicial protection, the Convention does not establish the need for just one single judicial remedy to exist, so that the protection can also be obtained through other judicial mean ("any other effective recourse") for the protection of human rights. That is why, regarding the amparo action, many Latin American legislations set forth that the amparo action has an extraordinary nature, in the sense that it is admitted only when there are no other effective judicial mean that can protect human rights; in a similar sense to the Anglo-American injunctions.

Being a judicial mean, the Convention prescribes that it can be brought before the "competent courts," being the intention of the Convention to set forth an essential function of the Judiciary, as also happens, for in-

---

[306] *Advisory Opinion OC-8//87 of January 30, 1987, Habeas Corpus in Emergency Situations*, Paragraphs 42, 43. See in Sergio García Ramírez (Coord.), *La Jurisprudencia de la Corte Interamericana de Derechos Humanos*, Universidad Nacional Autónoma de México, Corte Interamericana de Derechos Humanos, México, 2001, pp. 1.008 ff. See also in Florentín Meléndez, *Instrumentos internacionales sobre derechos humanos aplicables a la administración de justicia. Estudio constitucional comparado*, Cámara de Diputados, México, 2004, pp. 104 ff.

stance, under the Anglo-American systems, where the human rights' protection is provided for by means of various writs or injunctions, without it being only one specific judicial mean.

On the other hand, when the American Convention refers to the "competent courts" in order to decide the amparo action, it is not referring to only one specific court, but in principle, to all the Judiciary. That is why, pursuant to the Convention and to the Latin American tradition, competence in amparo matters are in general essentially belonging to the Judiciary, in the sense that such competence shall correspond to "the tribunals," all of them having a judicial duty and not just one of them.

Nonetheless, a reduction of the judicial competence to constitutionally protect constitutional rights through amparo has occurred in some Latin American countries, by assigning to only one single court the exclusive competence to hear the recourse of amparo, as has been the case of the Constitutional Chamber of the Supreme Courts of Costa Rica, El Salvador and Nicaragua, where a concentrated judicial system of amparo has been developed.

3. *The amparo as a simple, prompt and effective judicial guaranty*

The judicial recourse that the Convention guaranties, must be all together "simple, prompt and effective;"[307] concepts that have been elaborated by the Inter-American Court.

Regarding the simplicity, it refers to a procedure that must lack the dilatory procedural formalities of ordinary judicial means, imposed by the need to grant a constitutional – not ordinary – protection; and regarding the prompt character of the recourse, the Inter-American Court has argued for the need for a reasonable delay for the decision, not considering "prompt" recourses, those resolved after "a long time."[308]

The effective character of the recourse refers to the fact that it must be capable to produce the results for which it has been created[309]; in the words of the Inter-American Court on Human Rights,

---

[307]See *Suárez Romero* case, Paragraph 66. See in Sergio García Ramírez (Coord.), *La Jurisprudencia de la Corte Interamericana de Derechos Humanos*, Universidad Nacional Autónoma de México, Corte Interamericana de Derechos Humanos, México, 2001, pp. 406 ff.

[308]See *Ivcher Bronstein* case, Paragraph 140. *Idem,* 768 ff.

[309]See *Velásquez Rodríguez* case, Paragraph 66. *Idem,* 58 ff.

[...] it must be truly effective in establishing whether there has been a violation of human rights and in providing redress. A remedy which proves illusory because of the general conditions prevailing in the country, or even in the particular circumstances of a given case, cannot be considered effective. That could be the case, for example, when practice has shown its ineffectiveness: when the Judicial Power lacks the necessary independence to render impartial decisions or the means to carry out its judgments; or in any other situation that constitutes a denial of justice, as there is an unjustified delay in the decision; or when, for any reason, the alleged victim is denied access to a judicial remedy.[310]

Thus, it is not enough that in order to be effective a recourse be regulated in internal law for the purpose of protecting human rights, the existence of other basic conditions is necessary in order for the recourse to function and to be applied with the expected results.

In this regard, for a judicial recourse to be effective, above all, it is necessary for the Judiciary to be truly independent and autonomous. That is why, for instance, in the *Ivcher Bronstein* case (2000), the Inter-American Court decided that in Peru at the time, the conditions of independence and autonomy of the court were not satisfied in the national proceeding, so the recourses that the plaintiff had, were not effective."[311] The Inter-American Court has also considered that a recourse is not effective when impartiality lacks in the corresponding court.[312]

IV. THE RIGHTS TO BE PROTECTED BY THE AMERICAN CONVENTION AMPARO

1. *The amparo as a judicial guaranty for the protection of everyone's rights and guaranties*

When providing for the amparo, the Convention regulates a right that is guaranteed to "everyone," that is to say, everybody in the very broadest sense, without distinction or discrimination of any kind: individuals,

---

[310] *Advisory Opinion OC-9/87 of October 6, 1987, Judicial Guaranties in Status of Emergency*, Paragraph 24. *Idem,* 1.019 ff.

[311] See *Ivcher Bronstein* case, Paragraph 139. *Idem,* pp. 768 ff.

[312] See *Tribunal Constitucional* case, Paragraph 96. *Idem,* pp. 820 ff.

nationals, foreigners, legally able or not, corporations or entities of public or private law.[313]

The protective tendency regarding the implementation of the amparo has also gradually allowed interested parties to act in representation of diffuse or collective interests when dealing with collective constitutional rights, the violation of which affects the community as a whole, as it has been expressly established in the Argentinean, Brazilian, Colombian and Venezuelan Constitutions.

The American Convention is devoted to declaring human rights in the strict sense of rights belonging to human persons. Nonetheless, in the internal regulations of the countries, another aspect related to the protected persons is the question of whether the private corporations (artificial persons) and public entities can also be plaintiff on matters of amparo. Due to the fact that these entities can also have constitutional rights, such as the right to nondiscrimination, right to due process or right to

---

[313]It is true that Article 1,2 of the Convention sets forth that "for the purposes of this Convention, "person" means every human being." Nonetheless, Article 25 when guarantying the judicial protection right refers to such rights as corresponding to everyone and not to every person, so that regarding internal national law, artificial persons or legal entities have the right to the amparo recourse for the protection of their rights, like for instance, the due process of law and nondiscrimination rights. But setting forth the amparo as a judicial remedy for the protection of any person or entity, that is to say, as a personal remedy, it results in principle, a benefit to the plaintiff, so that the effects of the amparo do not extend to third parties. This feature gives rise, firstly, to the problem of the protection of collective rights, an initiative attributed in some legislation to the Ombudsmen or Defenders of Human Rights. But the fact is that it has been progressively admitted in many internal statutes, the possibility for communities to exercise the action of amparo when collective constitutional rights are being violated. Additionally, as a consequence of reforms tending to increase citizens' access to justice, some statutes have set forth remedies for the protection of diffuse or widespread interests, particularly in regard to third-generation rights, such as the protection of the environment or consumers' rights. In this sense, the standing to bring the action before the courts has being gradually constructed to allow interested parties to act in representation of diffuse or collective interests when dealing with constitutional rights, the violation of which affects the community as a whole. In certain constitutions, such as the Venezuelan Constitution of 1999, there is already no question regarding the possibility of exercising the recourse of amparo to protect collective and diffuse rights, already widely developed by case law. Some statutes have even expressly provided such protection, as occurs with the Organic Statute for the Protection of the Child and the Teenager where a "recourse of protection" is regulated. This recourse may be brought before the Tribunal for the Protection of the Child and the Teenager "against facts, acts or omissions of individuals, public and private entities and institutions that threaten or violate collective or diffuse (widespread) rights of children and teenagers" (Article 177,5 and 318).

own defense, they are also entitled to bring actions, so that the action of amparo must not only be conceived to protect human beings but also all other artificial persons regarding their constitutional rights.

2. *The amparo as a judicial guaranty for the protection of all constitutional rights and guaranties*

Pursuant to the Convention, this right to an effective judicial mean of protection before the courts is established for the protection of all the constitutional rights contained in the Convention, the constitution and statutes or of those that are inherent to the human person. Therefore according to the open clauses of constitutional rights, all rights declared in international instruments are also entitled to protection, as well as all rights inherent to the human person and human dignity. Consequently, according to the American Convention, all rights can be protected by means of amparo actions.[314]

Nonetheless, perhaps because of the influence of the European model of the amparo recourse like the ones regulated in Germany and Spain, in Latin America the Chilean and the Colombian Constitutions have establish a reduced list of rights that can be protected by means of a recourse for *tutela* and for *protección*; a reduction that can be considered incompatible with the international obligations that are imposed on such States by the Convention. The American Convention does not allow the exclusion of determined constitutional rights from the protection by means of the amparo action.

However, it must be highlighted that the courts in Colombia have fortunately been gradually correcting this restriction through constitutional interpretation, in such a way that today, due to the interrelation, universality, indivisibility, connection and interdependence of rights, there are

---

[314] As mentioned, those declared in the texts of the constitutions, of the statutes, of the American Convention, as well as those that are inherent to the human person. As has been stated by the Inter-American Court of Human Rights in its *Advisory Opinion (OC-8/87)* analyzing Article 25,1 of the Convention: "The above text is a general provision that gives expression to the procedural institution known as amparo, which is a simple and prompt remedy designed for the protection of all of the rights recognized by the constitutions and laws of the States Parties and by the Convention." *Advisory Opinion OC-8/87, Habeas Corpus in Emergency Situations*, Paragraph 32. See in Sergio García Ramírez (Coord.), *La Jurisprudencia de la Corte Interamericana de Derechos Humanos*, Universidad Nacional Autónoma de México, Corte Interamericana de Derechos Humanos, México, 2001, pp. 1.008 ff.

almost no constitutional rights that cannot be protected by means of the action of *tutela*.

Anyway, in contrast to such cases of restrictive constitutional provisions regarding the constitutional rights that can be protected by means of a recourse for *tutela* or *protección*, there are other constitutions that expressly set forth as being within the scope of protected rights not only all constitutional rights, but also those that are declared in the international system of protection of human rights as is the case of Argentina, Colombia, Costa Rica and Venezuela. Some constitutions also allow the protection by means of the amparo action of human rights declared in statutes (Argentina, Bolivia, Ecuador, Guatemala and Paraguay).

V. THE UNIVERSAL CHARACTER OF THE PROTECTION IN THE AMERICAN CONVENTION AMPARO

The amparo provided in the American Convention is established for the protection of constitutional rights against any kind of violation, at any moment, even in situations of emergency.

1. *The amparo as a judicial guaranty for the protection of all constitutional rights and guaranties, against any violation or harm from the state or individuals*

The protection that is guarantied in the Convention is against any act, omission, fact or action that violates human rights and, of course, which threatens to violate them without specifying the origin or the author of the harm or threat.

This implies that the recourse of amparo can be brought before the courts against any persons in the sense that it must be admitted not only against the State or public authorities, but also against private individuals and corporations.

In this regard, the action of amparo against individuals in Latin America has been broadly admitted, following a trend that began in Argentina in 1957, when the possibility of exercising a recourse of amparo against individuals was initially admitted.

Nowadays the amparo action against individuals is expressly referred to in the constitutions of Argentina, Bolivia, Paraguay and Peru. In other constitutions it is admitted just regarding certain individuals, such as those who act as agents exercising public functions, or who exercise some kind of prerogative, or who are in a position of control, for example, when rendering public services by means of a concession. This is the case, for example, in Colombia, Ecuador and Honduras. In other countries, it is the legislation or jurisprudence that provide for the amparo against individuals, as is the case of Chile, Costa Rica, Nicaragua, Dominican Republic, Uruguay and Venezuela.

However, some other countries, in a similar way to the European model as is the case of Brazil, El Salvador, Guatemala, Mexico and Panama, no possibility of filing a recourse of amparo against private individuals is admitted; a situation that is distant from the orientation of the American Convention.

But regarding the constitutional protection against actions of the State, another scope of reduction of amparo in many countries that contrasts with the universality deriving from the American Convention refers to the acts of the authorities that may be challenged by means of a recourse of amparo. Pursuant to the American Convention, there cannot exist a single State act that could escape from its scope, as it is declared, for instance in the Guatemalan Constitution. If the amparo is a legal mean for the protection of human rights, it is an action that can be filed against any public conduct or acts that violates them, and therefore it cannot be conceived that certain State acts are excluded from the possibility to be challenged through the amparo action.

Nevertheless, in this regard, a tendency toward exclusion can be identified in Latin America in different aspects.

In some cases, the exclusion refers to actions of certain public authorities, such as the electoral authorities, whose acts are expressly excluded from the recourse of amparo, as it is established in Costa Rica, Mexico, Nicaragua, Panama, Peru and Uruguay.

In other cases, like in Peru, an exclusion from the scope of constitutional protection of the amparo is provided with respect to the acts of the National Council of the Judiciary.

On the other hand, the exclusion from the scope of protection of the recourse of amparo is referred to certain State acts, as happened with regard to the statutes and to judicial decisions. Only a few countries, like Guatemala, Honduras, Mexico and Venezuela, admit the possibility of filing the recourse of amparo against statutes, even though being of a self-executing character. Therefore, contrary to the trend set forth by the American Convention, the exclusion of statutes from the scope of the amparo is the general trend of the Latin American regulations.

In other cases, the restriction of amparo refers to judicial decisions, notwithstanding that when judges decide particular cases, they too can infringe upon constitutional rights. As a matter of principles, no judge is empowered to violate a constitutional right in his decisions; therefore the recourse of amparo must also be admitted against judicial decisions. Nonetheless, only in some countries like Colombia, Honduras, Guatemala, Mexico, Panama and Venezuela the recourse of amparo against judicial decisions is expressly admitted. On the contrary it has been excluded in other countries like Argentina, Uruguay, Costa Rica, Dominican Republic, Panama, El Salvador, Honduras, Nicaragua and Paraguay.

The case of Colombia must be highlighted, because in spite of being the admission for *tutela* against judicial decisions expressly regulated, in 1992, the Constitutional Court considered its admissibility as contrary to the principle of *res judicata*, annulling the respective article of the statute.[315] Nonetheless, in spite of such annulment, all the main courts and the Council of State have progressively admitted the action of *tutela* against judicial decisions when considering arbitrary or the product of a judicial *voi de fait*.[316] It is also the case in Peru where the amparo action against judicial decisions is admitted when it is issued outside a regular procedure.

2. *The amparo as a judicial guaranty that can be filed at any time, including in situations of emergency*

Finally, the amparo recourse as well as the habeas corpus are judicial means for protection that can be filed by the interested party at any time without exception. Particularly, the right cannot be limited because of exceptional situations or states of emergency.[317]

---

[315]See Decision C-543, September 24, 1992, in Manuel José Cepeda, *Derecho Constitucional Jurisprudencial.Las grandes decisiones de la Corte Constitucional*, Legis, Bogotá, 2001, pp. 1.009 ff.

[316]See Decision T-231, May 13, 1994. *Idem,* pp. 1.022 ff.

[317]In particular, it must be mentioned that Article 27,1 of the American Convention allows that in time of war, public danger or other emergency that threatens the independence or security of a State Party, "it may take measures derogating from its obligations under the present Convention to the extent and for the period of time strictly required by the exigencies of the situation, provided that such measures are not inconsistent with its other obligations under international law and do not involve discrimination on the ground of race, color, sex, language, religion, or social origin." Nonetheless, in Article 27,2 it is expressly provided that no suspension at all is allowed regarding the following rights: right to juridi-

These matters have been considered by the Inter-American Court of Human Rights in its *Advisory Opinion* (OC-8/87) of January 30, 1987, on "Habeas Corpus in Emergency Situations" declaring that the habeas corpus and amparo actions must remain in effect even during states of emergency, and even if Article 7 of the American Convention does not list in its provisions that those rights may not be suspended in exceptional circumstances."

The Court has considered that the "writs of habeas corpus and of amparo are among those judicial remedies that are essential for the protection of various rights whose derogation is prohibited by Article 27,2 and which serve to preserve legality in a democratic society." Therefore, the Court ruled that "the constitutions and the legal systems of the States Parties that authorize, expressly or by implication, the suspension of the legal remedies of habeas corpus or of amparo in emergency situations cannot be deemed to be compatible with the international obligations imposed on these States by the Convention."[318]

cal personality (Article 3); right to life (Article 4); right to humane treatment (Article 5); freedom from slavery (Article 6); freedom from ex post facto laws (Article 9); freedom of conscience and religion (Article 12); rights of the family (Article 17); right to a name (Article 18); rights of the child (Article 19); right to nationality (Article 20): and right to participate in Government (Article 23), "or of the judicial guaranties essential for the protection of such rights." Thus, the right to judicial protection of all those rights by means of amparo and habeas corpus cannot be suspended in situations of emergency.

[318] *Advisory Opinion OC-8/87 of January 30, 1987, Habeas corpus in emergency situations*, Paragraphs 37, 42 and 43. Afterwards, the Inter-American Court of Human Rights in its *Advisory Opinion (OC-9/87) of October 6, 1987, Judicial Guaranties in States of Emergency*, emphasizes its ruling, holding that "the judicial guaranties essential for the protection of the human rights not subject to derogation, according to Article 27(2) of the Convention, are those to which the Convention expressly refers in Articles 7(6) and 25(1), considered within the framework and the principles of Article 8, and also those necessary to the preservation of the rule of law, even during the state of exception that results from the suspension of guaranties. See *Advisory Opinion OC-9/87 of October 6, 1987, Judicial Guarantees in States of Emergency*, Paragraph 38. Thus, the final Opinion of the Court was: "1) That the "essential" judicial guaranties which are not subject to derogation, according to Article 27(2) of the Convention, include habeas corpus (Article 7(6)), amparo, and any other effective remedy before judges or competent tribunals (Article 25(1)), which is designed to guaranty the respect of the rights and freedoms whose suspension is not authorized by the Convention. 2) That the "essential" judicial guaranties which are not subject to suspension, include those judicial procedures, inherent to representative democracy as a form of government (Article 29(c)), provided for in the laws of the States Parties as suitable for guarantying the full exercise of the rights referred to in Article 27(2) of the Convention and whose suppression or restriction entails the lack of protection of such rights." Paragraph 41. See in Sergio García Ramírez (Coord.), *La Jurisprudencia de la*

In general terms, these foregoing elements can be considered as the parameter set forth in the American Convention established for the amparo, and this is precisely what should prevail in the internal legal systems, where an additional effort has to be made from the constitutional perspective in order to adapt in some cases, the internal regulations to such international system of protection of human rights.

Corte Interamericana de Derechos Humanos, Universidad Nacional Autónoma de México, Corte Interamericana de Derechos Humanos, México, 2001, pp. 1.008 ff; and in Florentín Meléndez, *Instrumentos internacionales sobre derechos humanos aplicables a la administración de justicia. Estudio constitucional comparado*, Cámara de Diputados, México, 2004, pp. 104 ff.

PART THREE

THE INJURED PARTY AND THE CONSTITU-TIONAL RIGHTS PROTECTED BY MEANS OF THE AMPARO PROCEEDING

One of the most distinguishable principles regarding the amparo proceeding as an extraordinary judicial mean for the protection of constitutional rights is the principle of bilateralism, which implies the need for the existence of a controversy between two or more parties. The main consequence of this principle is that the amparo proceeding can only be initiated at a party's request, which excludes any case of *ex officio* amparo proceeding, except in some countries, on matters of habeas corpus.[319]

Consequently, in order to initiate this proceeding an action, a recourse or a petition must be brought before a court by a plaintiff as the injured party, against the injurer party or parties, who as defendants, must be called to the procedure as having caused the harm or the violation to the constitutional rights of the former.[320] Because of this principle of bilateralism, all the Amparo Laws in Latin America contain specific provisions regarding both parties.

On the other hand, the right violated in order to be protected by means of the amparo proceeding must be a constitutional right declared in the constitution or recognized with constitutional rank.

---

[319]The Amparo Laws in Guatemala (Article 86) and Honduras (Article 20) have empowered the courts to act *ex officio* having the obligation to initiate the habeas corpus proceeding, in cases where they happen to have knowledge of the facts.

[320]The filing of the suit can be through an action or a recourse, the latter being the common way to file the petition, for instance against administrative acts or a judicial decisions, which in some countries are to be challenged only after the exhaustion of the available administrative or judicial recourses. When through an action, the amparo can be brought directly before the courts against facts, acts or omissions, without the need to exhaust previous recourses.

This section of the book is devoted to analyze, separately, the general principles related to the rules of standing, and the justiciable rights by means of the amparo, with particular reference to the question of the justiciability of social rights.

CHAPTER NINE

THE INJURED PARTY: THE PLAINTIFF AND THE RULES OF STANDING

The injured party, that is, the claimant, also called the complainant, the petitioner or the plaintiff, in principle is the person having the constitutional right that has been violated; a situation that gives him a particular interest in bringing the case before a court. That is why the amparo action has been considered as an action *in personam* through which, seeking for the protection of constitutional rights, the plaintiff must be precisely the injured or aggrieved person.

That is why it is generally considered that the Latin American amparo action, in the same sense as the action for injunction in the United States, needs to be personalized, in the sense of being attributed to a particular person that because enjoying the harmed right, has a justiciable interest in the subject matter of the litigation, or a personal interest in the outcome of the controversy.[321]

It is in this sense that the Nicaraguan Amparo Law provides that only the aggrieved party can file the amparo action, defining as such, "any natural or artificial person whose constitutional rights are harmed or that are in a situation of imminent danger of being harmed by any disposition,

---

[321]Regarding injunctions it was ruled in *Parkview Hospital v. Com.*, Dept. of Public Welfare, 56 Pa. Commw. 218, 424 A. 2d 599 (1981) that to bring an action "requires an aggrieved party to show a substantial, direct, and immediate interest is the subject matter of the litigation." See the reference in Kevin Schroder *et al*, "Injunction," *Corpus Juris Secundum*, Thomson West, Volume 43A, 2004, p. 331, note 4. Or as ruled in *Warth v. Seldin*, 422 U.S. 4909, 498-500 (1975): the plaintiff must "allege such a personal stake in the outcome of the controversy" as to justify the exercise of the court's remedial powers on his behalf, because he himself has suffered "some threatened or actual injury resulting from the putatively illegal action." See M. Glenn Abernathy and Barbara A. Perry, *Civil Liberties Under the Constitution*, University of South Carolina Press, 1993, p. 4.

act or resolution, and in general, by any action or omission from any public officer, authority or its agent" (Article 23). [322]

A few questions must be analyzed regarding the injured or aggrieved party, referred to the standing to sue and to the quality of the plaintiff, whether being a physical person or a human being or an artificial person or corporation, including public law entities. Other aspects to be considered are the possibility for the Public Prosecutors or People's Defendants to file the amparo action, as well as the possibility for third parties to intervene in the proceedings on the side of the plaintiff.

I. THE INJURED PERSONS AND THE QUESTION OF STANDING

In the amparo suit, because the action has a personal character, the plaintiff, as the injured party, can only be the titleholder of the violated right;[323] that is, the person whose constitutional rights have been injured or threatened of being harmed.[324] Thus, nobody can file an action for amparo alleging in his own name a right belonging to another.[325]

That is why the amparo action is a personal or "subjective" action, in the sense that it only can be brought before the courts personally by the aggrieved party having a personal, legitimate and direct interest who can act directly *in personam* or through his representative.[326] This is the

---

[322]In this same sense, the Amparo Law of the Dominican Republic set forth that "any natural or artificial person, without distinctions of any kind, have the right to claim for the protection of his individual rights by means of the amparo action" (Article 2).

[323]In this sense, Article 567 of the Paraguayan Civil Procedure Code set forth that "the amparo action can be filed by the titleholder of the harmed right or the right in danger of being harmed."

[324]See decisions of the former Venezuelan Supreme Court of Justice, Politico Administrative Chamber of June 18, 1992, in Revista *de Derecho Público* n° 50, Editorial Jurídica Venezolana, Caracas, 1992, p. 135; and of August 13, 1992, in Revista *de Derecho Público*, n° 51, Editorial Jurídica Venezolana, Caracas, 1992, p. 160.

[325] See decision of the former Venezuelan Supreme Court of Justice, Politico Administrative Chamber, of February 14, 1990, in *Revista de Derecho Público*, n° 41, Editorial Jurídica Venezolana, Caracas, 1990, p. 101.

[326]As it was ruled by the former Supreme Court of Justice of Venezuela regarding the personal character of the amparo suit that imposes for its admissibility: "A qualified interest of who is asking for the restitution or reestablishment of the harmed right or guaranty, that is, that the harm be directed to him and that, eventually, its effects affect directly and indisputably upon him, harming his scope of subjective rights guarantied in the Constitution. It is only the person that is specially and directly injured in his subjective fundamental rights by a specific act, fact or omission the one that can bring an action before the competent courts by mean of a brief and speedy proceeding, in order that the judge decides im-

same principle that applies on matters of standing to seek injunctive relief in the United States, which is only attributed to the person affected,[327] because the injured party is the one that in principle can file the action.[328]

Even though this is the general rule in Latin America, some Amparo Laws authorize other persons different to the injured parties or their representatives to file the amparo suit on their behalf,[329] being then possible to distinguish in this matter, between the *legitimatio* or standing *ad causam* and the *legitimatio* or standing *ad processum.*[330]

The standing *ad causam*, as already mentioned, refers to the person or entity that is the titleholder of the particular constitutional right that has been violated. On the other hand, the standing *ad processum* refers to the particular capacity the persons have in order to act in the procedure (procedural capacity), that is, the ability to appear before the court and to use the appropriate procedures in support of a claim, which can refer to his own rights or to the rights of others.

The standing *ad causam* corresponds in principle to any person whose constitutional rights have been violated or threatened to be violated, and who has the right to seek protection from the courts by means of the action for amparo; whether being a *natural persons* as human beings (with-

mediately the reestablishment of the infringed subjective legal situation." See decision of August 27, 1993 (*Kenet E. Leal* case), in *Revista de Derecho Público*, n° 55-56, Editorial Jurídica Venezolana, Caracas, 1993, p. 322; and decision of the Venezuelan First Court on Judicial review of administrative actions, November 18, 1993, in *Revista de Derecho Público*, n° 55–56, Editorial Jurídica Venezolana, Caracas, 1993, pp. 325–327.

[327]See *Alabama Power Co. v. Allabama Elec. Co-op., Inc.*, 394 F.2d 672 (5th Cir. 1968), in John Bourdeau *et al.*, "Injunctions," in Kevin Schroder, John Glenn and Maureen Placilla (Ed.), *Corpus Juris Secundum*, Vol 43A, West 2004, p. 229.

[328]As is expressly set forth for instance in Ecuador. See Hernán Salgado Pesantes, *Manual de Justicia Constitucional Ecuatoriana*, Corporación Editora Nacional, Quito, 2004, p. 81. In Costa Rica, even though the Amparo Law provides that the action can be filed by anybody (Article 33), the Constitutional Chamber has interpreted that it refers to anybody that has been injured in his constitutional rights (See Decision 93-90. See the reference in Ruben Hernández Valle, *Derecho Procesal Constitucional*, Editorial Juricentro, San José, 2001, p. 234); and in case of an amparo action filed by a person different from the injured party, in order for the proceeding to continue, the latter must approve the filing. Otherwise, there would be lack of standing. See Decision 5086-94, in *Idem*, p. 235.

[329]Article 567, Civil Procedure Code, Paraguay.

[330]See in general, Alí Joaquin Salgado, *Juicio de amparo y acción de inconstitucionalidad*, Astrea, Buenos Aires, 1987, pp. 81 ff; Joaquín Brage Camazano, *La jurisdicción conbstitucional de la libertad*, Editorial Porrúa, México, 2005, pp. 162 ff.

out distinction of being citizens, disabled or foreigners); or an *artificial* persons or entities.[331]

In some cases the standing can also correspond to groups of peoples or collective entities even without formal legal "personality" attributed by law, as has been admitted in Chile regarding the recourse for protection.[332]

1. *Natural persons: Standing ad causam and ad processum*

The general principle in the Latin America Amparo Laws is that all human beings when their constitutional rights are arbitrarily or illegitimately harmed or threatened to be harmed have the necessary standing to file the action for amparo. In the expression "persons" used in such laws, all natural person are essentially comprised without distinctions.

Nonetheless, the expression is not equivalent to "citizens" who are those persons who by birth or naturalization are members of the political community represented by the State. These persons, as citizens, are the only ones having standing for the protection of certain political rights, like the right to vote or to political participation.

On the other hand, on matters of amparo, foreigners in principle have the same general rights as nationals and have the necessary standing to exercise the right to amparo. Only in Mexico can an exception be found regarding the decisions of the President of the Republic, issued according

---

[331]The word "persons" in the Amparo Laws is used in the sense of human beings or entities that are recognized by law as having rights and duties, including corporations or companies: Argentina (Article 5: "any individual or juridical persons"; Dominican Republic (Article 2: "any physical or artificial persons"); Colombia (Article 1: "any person"); Ecuador (Article 48: "natural or juridical persons"); El Salvador (Article 3 and 12: "any person"; Guatemala (Article 8: "persons"), Honduras (Article 41: "any aggrieved person"; Article 44: "any natural or juridical person"), México (Article 39: "affected person"); Panama (Article: 2615: "any person"); Perú (Article 39: "affected" person) Uruguay (Article 1: "any physical or juridical person, public or private"); Venezuela (Article 1: "natural or juridical persons"). In the Philippines Rule the petiton for the writ of amparo is also available to "any person" whose right to life, liberty and security is violated (Sec. 1).

[332]The Chilean Constitution in matter of standing refers to "el que" (who), not mentioning "persons" (Article 20). See Juan Manuel Errazuriz and Jorge Miguel Otero A., *Aspectos procesales del recurso de protección*, Editorial Jurídica de Chile, Santiago, 1989, pp. 15, 50. See the *RP, Federación Chilena de Hockey y Patinaje, C. de Santiago* case, 1984, RDJ, T, LXXXI, n° 3, 2da. P., Secc. 5ta, p. 240. Nonetheless, in other judicial decisions the contrary criteria has been sustained. See the reference in Sergio Lira Herrera, *El recurso de protección. Naturaleza jurídica. Doctrina. Jurisprudencia, Derecho Comparado*, Santiago, 1990, pp. 144–145.

to the constitution, ordering the expulsion of foreigners, who are excluded from the amparo.[333]

Except in this particular case, the general principle in Latin America is to consider that all affected persons have standing *ad causam* to file the amparo suit. For this purpose, the laws have been interpreted in an extensive way, as has happened for instance with the Venezuelan Law of Amparo, which even though providing in its first article that the amparo action can be filed by "all natural persons inhabitants of the Republic,"[334] this expression has been understood as referring to any person, even those not living in the country.[335]

Minors, of course, also have standing *ad causam*, but are only authorized to file amparo actions for the protection of their constitutional rights through their representatives (parents or tutors), who in these cases have standing *ad processum*. Only exceptionally does the Mexican Law allow minors to act personally in cases when their representatives are absent or impaired.[336] In Colombia, when the representative of a minor is in a

---

[333]See Eduardo Ferrer Mac-Gregor, *La acción constitucional de amparo en México y España*, Editorial Porrúa, México, 2002, p. 230.

[334]The main problem with this article resulted from the condition to be "inhabitant of the Republic," that is, to physically be in the territory of the Republic as resident, tourist or in any other situation, which was originally interpreted to deny the right to amparo to persons not living in the country. The former Supreme Court of Justice, progressively widened the interpretation, admitting the amparo action filed by a person not inhabiting the Republic, no matter his nationality or legal condition, provided, according to a decision of August 27, 1993, "that his constitutional rights and guaranties had been directly harmed or threatened by any act, fact or omission carried out, issued or produced in the Republic." See in *Jurisprudencia Ramírez & Garay*, Tomo CXXVI, p. 667. See the references in Allan R. Brewer-Carías, *Instituciones Políticas y Constitucionales*, Vol V, *El derecho y la acciión de Amparo*, Universidad Católica del Táchira, Editorial Jurídica Venezolana, San Cristóbal-Caracas, 1998, p. 319.

[335]The same former Supreme Court, by mean of the exercise of its diffuse judicial review powers, declared unconstitutional the limiting reference of Article 1 of the law when stressing the character of "inhabitants of the Republic," ruling on the contrary, that any person whether or not living in the Republic whose rights are harmed in Venezuela, has enough standing to file an amparo action. See Decision of December 13, 1994, *Jackroo Marine Limited* case. See the reference in Rafael Chavero, *El Nuevo Régimen del Amparo Constitucional en Venezuela*, Caracas, 2001, pp. 98–99.

[336]This is the case of México where the Amparo Law provided that a minor "can ask for amparo without the intervention of his legitimate representative when he is absent or impaired"; adding that "in such case, the court, without being impeded to adopt urgent measures, must appoint a special representative in order to intervene in the suit" (Article 6).

situation of inability to assume his defense, anyone can act on behalf of the injured party (Article 10).[337]

Except in those cases where the representatives of incapacitated natural persons are called to act on their behalf, the general rule of standing *ad processum* regarding natural persons is that they have the possibility to appear before the court as the injured persons for the defense of their own rights. Consequently, as a matter of principle, no other person can judicially act on behalf of the injured person, except when legally appointed representative or acting with power of attorney or letter of authorization (Paraguay, Article 567).

Nonetheless, a general exception to this principle refers to the action of habeas corpus, in which case, because generally the injured person is physically prevented from acting personally because of detention or restrained freedom, the Amparo Law authorizes anybody to file the action on his behalf.[338]

In this same sense, some Amparo Laws, in order to guaranty the constitutional protection, also establish the possibility for other persons to act on behalf of the injured party and file the action in his name. It can be any lawyer or relative as established in Guatemala (Article 23), or it can be anybody, as is set forth in Paraguay (Article 567), Ecuador, Honduras, Uruguay[339] and Colombia, where anyone can act on behalf of the injured

---

[337]What the Legislator wanted to assure in this case, was the possibility for an effective protection of the rights, for instance, in cases of physical violence infringed by parents regarding their children, in which case a neighbor is the person that can intervene filing an action for *tutela*. Otherwise, in such cases, the action for protection could not be filed, particularly because the parents are the legal representatives of their children. See Juan Carlos Esguerra Portocarrero, *La protección constitucional del ciudadano*, Lexis, Bogotá, 2005, p. 122.

[338]Argentina (Article 5: anybody on his behalf); Bolivia (Article 89: anybody in his name); Guatemala (Article 85: any other person); Honduras (Article 19: any person); México (Article 17: any other person in his name); Nicaragua (Article 52: any inhabitant of the Republic); Perú: (Article 26: anybody in his favor); Venezuela (Article 39: anybody acting on his behalf). In México, the law imposes on the injured party the obligation to expressly ratify the filing of the amparo suit, to the point that if the complaint is not ratified it will be considered as not filed (Article 17).

[339]In Ecuador, any spontaneous agent justifying the impossibility of the affected party to do so can file the action in his name, which nonetheless must be ratified within three subsequent days (Article 48). In Honduras the Amparo Law authorizes anyone to act on behalf of the injured party, without needing a power of attorney, in which case Article 44 provides that the criteria of the affected party shall prevail (Article 44). In Uruguay (Article 3) the Amparo Law provides that in cases where the affected party, by himself or through his representative cannot file the action, then anybody can do it on his behalf, the acting per-

party when the latter is in a situation of inability to assume his own defense (Article 10).[340] The same principle is established in the Peruvian Code on Constitutional Procedures.[341]

Also in Philippines, Section 2 of the 2007 Rule on the Writ of Amparo, even though providing that the petition must be filed by the aggrieved person, it allows other "qualified person or entity" to fill the petition in the following order:

1. Any member of the immediate family, namely: the spouse, children and parents of the aggrieved party;

2. Any ascendant, descendant or collateral relative of the aggrieved party within the fourth civil degree of consanguinity or affinity, in default of those mentioned in the preceding paragraph; or

3. Any concerned citizen, organization, association or institution, if there is no known member of the immediate family or relative of the aggrieved.

Another aspect to be pointed out regarding standing is that some Latin American Amparo Laws impose the need for the plaintiff to formally appoint an attorney to assist him, as for instance is set forth in the Panamanian Judicial Code (Article 2261).[342]

---

son being subjected to liability if initiating the amparo with fraud, malice or frivolity (Article 4).

[340]See Carlos Augusto Patiño Beltrán, *Acciones de tutela, cumplimiento, populares y de grupo*, Editorial Leyer, Bogotá, 2000, p. 10; Juan Carlos Esguerra Portocarrero, *La protección constitucional del ciudadano*, Lexis, Bogotá, 2005, p. 122.

[341]Article 41 of the Code establishes; "Any person can appear in court in the name of another person without procedural representation when it is impossible for the latter to file the action on his own behalf, whether because his freedom is being concurrently affected, has a founded fear or threat, there is a situation of imminent danger or any other analogous cause. Once the affected party is in the possibility of acting, he must ratify the claim and the procedural activity followed by the person acting in fact."

[342]In Venezuela, according to what is provided in the Attorneys Law (Ley de Abogados), in all judicial processes the parties must be assisted by lawyers, which was also considered to be applicable to the amparo suit. See for instance decisions of the First Court on Judicial Review of Administrative Action November 18, 1993, *Carlos G. Pérez* case, in *Revista de Derecho Público*, n° 55-56, Editorial Jurídica Venezolana, Caracas, 1993, pp. 353–354. *Cfr.* Decisions of the First Court on Judicial Review of Administrative Actions, September 14, 1989, in Revista *de Derecho Publico* n° 40, Editorial Jurídica Venezolana, Caracas, 1989, p. 105; March 4, 1993, and March 25, 1993, in *Revista de Derecho Público*, n° 53-54, Editorial Jurídica Venezolana, Caracas, 1993, p. 258. Nonetheless, in more recent decisions, the Constitutional Chamber of the Supreme Tribunal, due to the nonformalistic character of the amparo proceeding, has ruled that even though the injured party does not need to be assisted by an attorney when filing the action, it must appoint one in the course

2. Artificial persons: Standing ad causam and ad processum

Besides natural persons, artificial persons also have the right to file amparo actions when their constitutional rights have been violated, so associations, foundations, corporations or companies can also file amparo actions,[343] for instance, for the protection of their rights to nondiscrimination, to due process of law, to defense or to economic and property rights, in which cases, of course, they must act through their directors or representatives according to their by laws (Mexico, Article 8). As decided by the Constitutional Chamber of the Supreme Tribunal of Venezuela, even though the object of the amparo is the reinforced protection of constitutional rights and guaranties enumerated in the Constitution, as well as those set forth in international treaties on human rights ratified by the Republic, and any other inherent to human persons, that "does not imply to restrict the notion of constitutional rights and guaranties only to the rights and guaranties of natural persons, because also artificial persons are holders of fundamental rights."[344]

However, in these cases, a violation of a constitutional right of an artificial person must be caused in order for the Corporation to file the amparo action, because, as argued by the Constitutional Chamber of Costa Rica, "the object and matter of the amparo is not to guaranty in an ab-

of the proceeding or the court must appoint one to act on his behalf. See decision of July 19, 2000 (*Rubén Guerra* case). See the reference and comments in Rafael Chavero, *El nuevo régimen del amparo constitucional en Venezuela*, Caracas, 2001, pp. 129–135.

[343]Also is the case of Colombia where the *tutela* action is established for the protection of immediately applicable "fundamental rights," which includes those of artificial persons like the right to petition (Article 22), due process and defense (Article 29) and review of judicial decisions (Article 31). In Ecuador, the standing of artificial persons to file an amparo action has been denied by Marco Morales Tobar in "La acción de amparo y su procedimiento en el Ecuador," Estudios Constitucionales. *Revista del Centro de Estudios Constitucionales*, Año 1, n° 1, Universidad de Talca, Chile, 2003, pp. 281–282. Even in the Dominican Republic where the amparo suit was admitted by the Supreme Court, even without constitutional or legal provision, precisely in a suit brought before the Court by a commercial company (*Productos Avon S.A.*). See for instance, Juan de la Rosa, *El recurso de amparo, Estudio Comparativo*, Santo Domingo, 2001, p. 69.

[344]See decision n° 1595 of November 2000, *State Merida and other v. Ministry of Finances* case, in *Revista de Derecho Público*, n° 84, Editorial Jurídica Venezolana, Caracas, 2000, pp. 315 ff. The former Supreme Court of Justice, in a previous decision of October 2, 1997, ruled that if "it is undoubted that artificial persons, and consequently, political-territorial entities can be holders of the majority of rights enshrined in the Constitution, as for instance, the rights to defense, nondiscrimination of property." See the reference and comments in Rafael Chavero, *El nuevo régimen del amparo constitucional en Venezuela*, Caracas, 2001, pp. 122–123.

stract way the enforcement of the Constitution, but to protect against the threats and violations of fundamental rights of persons."[345]

In this context of the standing given to artificial persons to file amparo actions, the Paraguayan Civil Procedure Code is particularly enumerative, including: political parties with quality recognized by the electoral authorities; the professional unions and guild; and societies or associations with purposes not contrary to the common good (Article 568).

One important question regarding the standing of artificial persons to file amparo actions refers to the possibility for public entities to file them, that is, the capacity for public entities to file amparo actions.

Historically, the amparo suit, as a specific judicial mean for the protection of constitutional rights, was originally conceived for individuals or private persons to defend themselves against public officers or public entities; that is, a guaranty to seek protection against the State. That is why, initially, it was inconceivable for a public entity to file an amparo action against other public or private entities. Nonetheless, because public entities, as any artificial person, can also be holders of constitutional rights, it is now generally admitted that they can file actions for amparo for the protection of their rights. This is expressly the case of Argentina,[346] Uru-

[345]In the particular case, the ruling referred to an alleged violation of the administrative procedures followed to allow a company the operation of a cellular mobile network, concluding the Chamber that "the violation of Constitutional norms cannot be demanded through an amparo action.," Vote 285-90. See in Ruben Hernández Valle, *Derecho Procesal Constitucional,* Editorial Juricentro, San José, 2001, p. 235.

[346]See José Luis Lazzarini, *El Juicio de Amparo,* Ed. La Ley, Buenos Aires, 1987, p. 238–240; 266. Among the amparo cases decided in Argentina as a consequence of the emergency economic measures adopted by the government in 2001 that froze all deposits in saving and current accounts in all the banks and converted them from U. S. dollars into Argentinean devaluated pesos, one that must be mentioned is the *San Luis* case decided by the Supreme Court on March 5, 2003, in which not only the Court declared the unconstitutionality of the Executive but in the case, "ordered the Central Bank of the Argentinean Nation to reimburse to the Province of San Luis the amounts of North American dollars deposited, or its equivalent in pesos at the value on the day of payments, according to the rate of selling of the free market of exchange." The interesting aspect of the suit was that it was filed by the Province of San Luis against the National State and the Central Bank of the Argentinean Nation, that is, a Federated State (Provincia de San Luis) against the National State for the protection of the constitutional rights to property of the former. See the comments in Antonio María Hernández, *Las emergencias y el orden constitucional,* Universidad Nacional Autónoma de México, Rubinzal-Culsoni Editores, México, 2003, pp. 119 ff.

guay, where it is expressly regulated in the Amparo Law when referring to "public or private artificial persons" (Article 1) and of Venezuela.[347]

Also in Mexico, it is expressly admitted for public corporations to file amparo suits but only regarding their harmed economic interests (*intereses patrimoniales*) (Article 9), which implies that in no other way can a public entity in Mexico, for instance a State, a Municipality or a public corporation, file an amparo suit, because it would otherwise result in a conflict between authorities that cannot be resolved through this judicial action.[348]

It is in this same sense that in Peru, the Code of Constitutional Procedure also expressly declares the inadmissibility of the amparo action when referring to "conflicts between public law internal entities," that is, between the branches of government, or constitutional organs or local or regional governments that must be settled through the constitutional procedures established in the Code (Article 5,9).[349]

This same general discussion regarding the possibility of the exercise of the amparo action between public entities has arisen in other federal

[347]The Constitutional Chamber of the Supreme Court in decision n° 1595 of November 2000, ruled that "the political-territorial entities as the States and the Municipalities, can ... file amparo suits for the protection of the rights and liberties they can be holders of, as the right to due process, or the right to equality or to the retroactivity of the law." See *State Merida and other v. Ministry of Finances* case, in *Revista de Derecho Público*, n° 84, Editorial Jurídica Venezolana, Caracas, 2000, pp 315 ff.

[348]See Eduardo Ferrer Mac-Gregor, *La acción constitucional de amparo en México y España*, Editorial Porrúa, México, 2002, p. 244–245; Richard D. Baker, *Judicial Review in México. A Study of the Amparo Suit*, University Press of Texas, Austin, 1971 pp. 107–109. The Supreme Court has decided that "it is absurd to pretend that a public dependency of the Executive could invoke the violation of individual guaranties seeking protection against acts of other public entities also acting within the Executive branch of government." See "Tesis jurisprudencial 916," *Apéndice al Semanario Judicial de la Federación*, 1917–1988, Segunda Parte, "Salas y Tesis Comunes," p. 1500. See the reference in Eduardo Ferrer Mac-Gregor, *Idem*, p. 245, note 427. In another decision the Supreme Court has ruled that "it is not possible to concede the extraordinary remedy of amparo to organs of the state against acts of the state itself manifested through other of its agencies, since this would establish a conflict of sovereign powers, whereas the amparo suit is concerned only with the complaint of private individual directed against an abuse of power. See *Tesis* 450, III, pp. 868 ff. See the reference in Richard D. Baker, *Idem*, p.108.

[349]The Code substituted the Law 25011 provision that declared inadmissible actions of amparo, but "when filed by the public offices, including public enterprises, against public powers of the State and the organs created in the Constitution, against acts accomplished in the regular exercise of their functions" (Article 5,4, Code). See the comments regarding this provision in the repealed Law 2501,1 in Victor Julio Orcheto Villena, *Jurisdicción y procesos constitucionales*, Editorial Rhodas, Lima, p. 169.

systems, in particular, when directed to protect the constitutional guaranty of political autonomy and self-government. In Germany, for example, it is admitted that a constitutional complaint can be brought before the Federal Constitutional Tribunal by municipalities or groups of municipalities when alleging that their autonomy or self-government rights guaranteed in the constitution (Article 28-2) has been violated by a federal legal provision.[350]

This possibility has been rejected in Mexico where even though Articles 103, III and 107 of the constitution establish that the amparo suit is admissible in cases of controversies arisen when "laws or acts of federal authority infringe or restrict the States sovereignty"; it is understood as only referring to the protection of individual guaranties, and in no way as establishing an action of amparo for the protection of the States' constitutional autonomy regarding the invasions from the federal State.[351]

In Venezuela, also a federal State, the matter has been discussed regarding the protection of the political autonomy rights of the States and Municipalities guaranteed in the constitution, and the possibility of the filing of an amparo action for their protection. An action filed for such purpose, for instance, by Municipalities, was rejected by the former Supreme Court of Justice, arguing that:

> [...] the territorial entities, as artificial persons, can have standing to sue in amparo; but only regarding the protection in a strict sense of constitutional rights and guaranties, thus excluding from the amparo the protection of their prerogatives and powers, as well as to resolve the conflicts

---

[350]In the case of violations by a law of the Lander, such recourse shall be brought before the Constitutional Tribunal of the respective Lander (Article 93,1,4 of the Constitution). A similar situation, albeit debatable, is to be found in Austria with regard to the constitutional recourse. Whatever the case, of course it would not be an amparo for the protection of fundamental rights, but rather of a specific constitutional guaranty of the autonomy of local entities.

[351]The Supreme Court has denied such possibility arguing that "the amparo suit was established in Article 103 of the Constitution not for the protection of all the constitutional text, but for the protection of individual guaranties; and what is established in Section III must be understood in the sense that a federal law can only be challenged in the amparo suit when it invades or restricts the sovereignty of the States, when there is an affected individual which in a concrete case claims against the violation of his constitutional guaranties." See "Tesis jurisprudencial 389," *Apéndice al Semanario Judicial de la Federación*, 1917–1995, Tribunal Pleno, p. 362. See the reference in Eduardo Ferrer Mac-Gregor, *La acción constitucional de amparo en México y España*, Editorial Porrúa, México, 2002, p. 246, note 425.

among those entities between themselves or regarding other Public Power entities.[352]

With similar arguments, the Constitutional Chamber of the Supreme Tribunal of Justice in 2000 also rejected an amparo action filed by a State of the Federation against the Ministry of Finance that, it was alleged, affected their financial autonomy.[353]

---

[352]Decision dated October 2, 1997. In the case, several Municipalities brought an action of unconstitutionality against a national statute limiting the income that higher-level state and municipal officials could have; an action to which the claimants joined an action of amparo for the protection of the constitutional autonomy impaired by the Law. Eventualy the constitutional protection was denied by the then Supreme Court of Justice, in this decision of October 2, 1997, if it is true that the political territorial entities are also "holders of public powers and prerogatives, public functions exclusively directed to obtain constitutional goals" being those prerogatives also guarantied in the constitution, these institutional guaranties cannot be equivalent to the guaranty of constitutional rights; thus not admitting the amparo as a means for protection of such guaranties. Additionally, the Court ruled that since the amparo is an extraordinary action that "can only be filed when no other efficient means for constitutional protection exists," due to the fact that in Venezuela the constitution sets forth a series of recourses directed to impede the misknowledge or invasion of public prerogatives between territorial entities, the amparo cannot be used for those purpose. See the reference and comments in Rafael Chavero, *El nuevo régimen del amparo constitucional en Venezuela,* Caracas, 2001, pp. 122–123.

[353]The Chamber, in decision nº 1595 of November 2000, after accepting that the States and the Municipalities could file amparo suits for the protection of the rights and liberties they can be holders, concluded ruling that "they cannot file an amparo in order to protect the autonomy the Constitution recognized to them or the powers or competencies derived from it." The Constitutional Chamber also ruled as follows: "The autonomy of a public entity only enjoys protection through amparo when the Constitution recognizes it as a concretion of one funded fundamental right, like the universities' autonomy regarding the right to education (Article 109 of the Constitution). In the concrete case, the claimants have not invoked a constitutional right of the States that could have been violated, but the autonomy the Constitution assures, and in particular, "the guaranty of the financial autonomy regulated in Articles 159; 164, section 3; and 167, sections 4 and 6 of the Constitution." Nonetheless, under the concept of constitutional guaranty there cannot be submitted contents completely strange to the range of constitutionally protected public freedoms, as is pretended, due to the fact that the guaranty is closely related with the right. The guaranty can be understood as the constitutional reception of the rights or as the existing mechanisms for its protection. Whether in one or another sense the guaranty is consubstantial to the right, thus it is not adequate to use the concept of guaranty to expand the amparo's scope of protection, including in it any power or competency constitutionally guaranteed. The latter would lead to the denaturalization of the amparo, which would lose its specificity and convert it in a mean for the protection of all the Constitution." See *State Merida and other v. Ministry of Finances* case, in *Revista de Derecho Público,* nº 84, Editorial Jurídica Venezolana, Caracas, 2000, pp. 315 ff.

On the other hand, in systems such as Brazil's, where the *mandado de segurança* can only be brought against the State and not against individuals, it is argued that the State itself or its agencies cannot file the suit.[354]

3. Standing and the protection of collective and diffuse constitutional rights

As mentioned before, the general feature of the amparo proceeding is its personal character, in the sense that it can only be brought before the competent courts by the individual holder of the rights or their representatives, or by one of the affected parties.[355]

Nonetheless, not all constitutional rights are individual, and on the contrary, some are collective by nature, in the sense that they correspond to a more or less defined group of persons, so that their violations affect not only the personal rights of each of the individuals who enjoy them, but also, the whole group of persons or collectivity to which the individuals belongs. In these cases, then, the amparo action can also be filed by the group or the association of persons representing their associates, even if they do not have the formal character of an artificial person.[356]

In some cases, like in Venezuela, the constitution expressly sets forth as part of the constitutional right of everybody to have access to justice, to seek for the enforcement not only of personal rights but also of "col-

---

[354]See Celso Agrícola Barbi, *Do mandado de Seguranca*, Editora Forense, Rio de Janeiro, 1993, pp. 68 ff; José Luis Lazzarini, *El juicio de amparo*, Editorial La Ley, Buenos Aires, 1987, pp. 267–268.

[355]Some legislations like the Brazilian one, regarding the *manado de securança* set forth that in case of rights threatened or violated covering a few persons, any of them can file the action (Article 1,2). In Costa Rica, also, regarding the constitutional right to rectification and response in cases of offenses, the Constitutional Jurisdiction Law provides that when the offended are more than one person, any of them can file the action; and in cases in which the offended could be identified with a group or an organized collectivity, the standing to sue must be exercised by their authorized representative (Article 67).

[356]That is why, for instance, the Civil Procedure Code of Paraguay, when defining standing to sue in matters of amparo, additionally to physical or artificial persons, refers to political parties duly registered, entities with guild or professional identities and societies or associations that without being given the character of artificial persons, according to their by laws their goals are not contrary to public good (bien público) (Article 568). In Argentina, the Amparo Law also provides the standing to file amparo actions by these associations that without being formally artificial persons can justify, according to their by laws that they are not against "public interest" (*bién público*) (Article 5).

lective" and "diffuse" rights (Article 26).[357] Regarding the collective rights, the Constitutional Chamber of the Supreme Tribunal of Justice has considered as such the ones "referring to a determined and identified sector of the population (even though not quantified), when a legal bond exists within a group of persons that unites them"; as for instance, is "the case of damages to professional groups, to groups of neighbors, to labor unions, to the inhabitants of a certain area, etc."[358]

Regarding the diffuse rights, the same Constitutional Chamber has also established that in these cases, what is affected is the population as a whole because they are intended to assure the people, in a general way, an acceptable living standard as basic conditions of existence. That is, when these interests are affected, the living standard of the entire community or society in its different scopes diminishes, and an interest arises in each member of that community and of the other components of society, in preventing that situation to occur, and that it be repaired if that situation already occurred.[359] In this sense, for instance, damages to the

[357]The Constitutional Chamber has referred to the diffuse and collective interests or rights as concepts established for the protection of a number of individuals that can be considered as representing the entire or an important part of a society, which are affected on their constitutional rights and guaranties destined to protect the public welfare by an attack to their quality of life. See decision of the Constitutional Chamber n° 656 of May 6, 2001, *Defensor del Pueblo vs. Comisión Legislativa Nacional* case, as referred in decision n° 379 of February 26, 2003, *Mireya Ripanti et vs. Presidente de Petróleos de Venezuela S.A. (PDVSA)* case, in *Revista de Derecho Público*, n° 93–96, Editorial Jurídica Venezolana, Caracas, 2003, pp. 152 ff.

[358]For example, those not quantifiable or individualized collective rights or interests that correspond to the inhabitants of an urban area affected by an illegal construction that creates problems with the public services in the area. See the same decision of the Constitutional Chamber n° 656 of May 5, 2001, *Defensor del Pueblo vs. Comisión Legislativa Nacional* Case, *Idem*.

[359]Thus, the Constitutional Chamber has ruled, in these cases: "It is a diffuse interest (that originates rights), since it spreads among all the individuals of a society, even though from time to time the damage to the quality of life may be limited to groups that are able to be individualized as sectors that suffer as social entities. It can be the case of the inhabitants of a given sector or people pertaining to a same category, or the member of professional groups, etc. Nevertheless, those affected shall be no specified individual, but a totality or groups of individuals or corporations, since the damaged goods are not susceptible of exclusive appropriation by one subject... Despite the concept that rules the diffuse interest or right as part of the defense of the citizenship, it is aimed at satisfying social or collective needs, before the personal ones. Since the damage is general (to the population or broad parts of it), the diffuse right or interest unites individuals who do not know each other, who individually lack connection or legal relations among them, who at the beginning are undetermined, but united only because of the same situation of damage or danger they are involved in as members of a society and due to the right that arises in everyone to the

environment or to the consumers have expansive effects that harm the inhabitants of large sectors of the population, and respond to the undetermined obligation of protecting the environment or the consumers.[360]

Now, regarding the standing to bring before the courts an action for amparo seeking for the protection of collective and diffuse constitutional rights, the same Constitutional Chamber of the Supreme Court of Venezuela, for instance, has admitted the possibility for "any individual with legal capacity to bring suit, when seeking to impede a damage to the population or parts of it to which he belongs, being entitled to bring to action grounded on diffuse or collective interests."[361]

---

protection of their quality of life, set forth in the Constitution... The common damage to the quality of life, which concerns any component of population or society as such, despite the legal relations they may have with other of these undetermined members, is the content of the diffuse right or interest." See the same decision of the Constitutional Chamber n° 656 of May 6, 2001, *Defensor del Pueblo vs. Comisión Legislativa Nacional* case, as referred in decision n° 379 of February 26, 2003, *Mireya Ripanti et vs. Presidente de Petróleos de Venezuela S.A. (PDVSA)* case, in *Revista de Derecho Público*, n° 93–96, Editorial Jurídica Venezolana, Caracas, 2003, pp. 152 ff.

[360]Thus, according to the doctrine of the Constitutional Chamber, "The diffuse interests are the wider ones, where the damaged good is the most general good, since it concerns the entire population and, contrary to the collective interests or rights, they arise from an obligation of uncertain object; while in the collective ones, the obligation may be concrete, yet not demandable by individualized persons. Consumers are all the inhabitants of the country. The damage to them as such responds to a supra individual or supra personal right, and to an uncertain obligation in favor of them, from those managing goods and services. Their quality of life diminishes, whether they realize it or not, since many massive communicational mechanisms shall annul or alter the conscience of the damage. Their interest, or the one of those affected, for example, due to the damages to the environment, is diffuse and so is the right raised to preventing or impeding the damage. The interest of the neighbors, whose neighborhood is worsened in its public services by a construction, for example, responds as well to a supra personal legal right, yet it can be determined, located in specific groups, and it is the interest that allows a collective action. That is the collective interest. It gives origin to collective rights and may refer to a certain legal object. The truth in both cases (diffuse and collective interest) is that the damage is suffered by the social group equally, even if some members do not consider themselves damaged, since they consent to the damage. This concept differs from the personal damage directed to a personal legal right. This difference does not impede the existence of mixed damages, the same fact damaging a personal legal right and a supra individual one." See the same decision of the Constitutional Chamber n° 656 of May 6, 2001, *Defensor del Pueblo vs. Comisión Legislativa Nacional*.case, *Idem.*

[361]The Venezuelan Constitutional Chamber, regarding the action of amparo for the protection of collective or diffuse interests, has given to Article 26 of the constitution a wide interpretation, by stating that: "Consequently, any individual with legal capacity to bring suit, who is going to impede a damage to the population or parts of it to which he belongs,

This is the case, for instance, of the amparo action filed for the protection of electoral rights, in which case, any citizen, invoking the general

is entitled to bring to suit grounded in diffuse or collective interests, and where he had suffered personal damages, he shall claim for himself (jointly) the compensation of such. This interpretation, grounded in Article 26, extends the standing to companies, corporations, foundations, chambers, unions and other collective entities whose object is the defense of the society, as long as they act within the boundaries of their corporate object, aimed at protecting the interests of their members regarding their object. ... When the damages harm groups of individuals that are legally bound or pertain to the same activity, the action grounded in collective interests, whose purpose is the same as the one of the diffuse interests, shall be brought to suit by the corporations that gather the damaged sectors or groups and even by any member of that sector or group as long as he acts in defense of that social segment ... Due to the foregoing, it is not necessary for whoever brings a suit grounded on diffuse or collective interests, if it is a diffuse one, to have a bond previously established with the offender. It is necessary that he acts as a member of the society, or its general categories (consumers, users, etc.), and invokes his right or interest shared with the citizenship, since he participates with them in the damaged factual situation because of the infringement or detriment of the fundamental rights concerning the collectivity, which generates a common subjective right that despite being indivisible, may be enforced by anyone in the infringed situation, since the legal order acknowledges those rights in Article 26 of the Constitution. ... Even though it is a general right or interest enjoyed by the plaintiff, which allows various plaintiffs, he himself shall be threatened, shall have suffered the damage or shall be suffering it as a part of the citizenship, whereby whoever is not residing in the country, or is not damaged shall lack standing; this situation separates these actions from the popular ones. Whoever brings suit based on collective rights or interests, shall do it in his condition of member of the group or sector damaged, therefore, he suffers the damage jointly with others, whereby he assumes an interest of his own and gives him the right to claim the end of the damage for himself and the others, with whom he shares the right or interest. It shall be a group or sector not individualized, otherwise, it would be a concrete party. In both cases, if the action is admitted, a legal benefit will arise in favor of the plaintiff and his common interest with the society or collectivity of protecting it, maintaining the quality of life. The defense of society's interests is guaranteed. The plaintiff is given the subjective right to react against the damaging act or concrete threat, caused by the offender's violation of the fundamental rights of the society in general. Whoever is entitled to act shall always plea for an actual interest, which does not terminate for the society in one single process. If an individual brings suit grounding his action in diffuse rights or interests, yet the judge considers that it is about them, he shall subpoena the Defender of the People or the entities established by law in particular subjects, and shall notify through an edict all the parties in interest, whether there are processes in which the law excludes and grants representation to other individuals. All these legitimate interested parties shall intervene as third party claimants, if the judge admits them as such taking into consideration the existence of diffuse rights and interests." See decision of the Constitutional Chamber n° 656 of May 6, 2001, *Defensor del Pueblo vs. Comisión Legislativa Nacional* case, *Idem*.

voters' rights, can file the action.[362] In other words, the Constitutional Chamber has admitted that: "Any capable person that tends to impede harm to the population or sectors of it to which he appertains, can file actions in defense of diffuse or collective interest," extending the "standing to the associations, societies, foundations, chambers, trade unions and other collective entities devoted to defend society, provided that they act within the limits of their societal goals referring to the protection of the interests of their members."[363]

In these cases the Constitutional Chamber has determined the general conditions that the action filed must be based "not only on the personal right or interest of the claimant, but also on a common or collective right or interest."[364] Consequently, in these cases, a bond or relation must exist, "even if it is not a legal one, between whoever demands in the general interest of the society or a part of it (social common interest), and the damage or danger caused to the collectivity."[365]

---

[362]In these cases, the Chamber has even granted precautionary measures with *erga omnes* effects "to both individuals and corporations who have brought to suit the constitutional protection, and to all voters as a group." See decision of the Constitutional Chamber n° 483 of May29, 2000, *"Queremos Elegir" y otros* case, in *Revista de Derecho Público*, n° 82, 2000, Editorial Jurídica Venezolana, pp. 489–491. In the same sense, see the decision of the same Chamber n° 714 of July 13, 2000, *APRUM* case, in *Revista de Derecho Público*, n° 83, Editorial Jurídica Venezolana, Caracas, 2000, pp. 319 ff.

[363]The Chamber added that: "Those who file actions regarding the defense of diffuse interest do not need to have any previously established relation with the offender, but has to act as a member of society, or of its general categories (consumers, users, etc.) and has to invoke his right or interest shared with the population's, because he participates with all regarding the harmed factual situation due to the noncompliance of the diminution of fundamental rights of everybody, which gives birth to a communal subjective right, that although indivisible, is actionable by any one place within the infringed situation." Decision of the Constitutional Chamber of June 30, 2000, *Defensoría del Pueblo* case. See also the reference and comments in Rafael Chavero, *El nuevo régimen del amparo constitucional en Venezuela*, Caracas, 2001, pp. 110–114.

[364]That is, the reason of the claim or the action for amparo must be "the general damage to the quality of life of all the inhabitants of the country or parts of it, since the legal situation of all the members of the society or its groups have been damaged when their common quality of life was worsened"; thus the damage "concerns an indivisible right or interest that involves the entire population of the country or a group of it." See decision n° 1948 of February 17, 2000, *William O. Ojeda O. vs. Consejo Nacional Electoral* case.

[365]See decision n° 1948 of February 17, 2000, *William O. Ojeda O. vs. Consejo Nacional Electoral* case. But in spite of all the aforementioned progressive decisions regarding the protection of collective and diffuse rights, like the political ones, in a recent decision dated November 21, 2005, the Venezuelan Constitutional Chamber has reverted its ruling, and in a case originated by a claim filed by the director of a political association named "Un Solo

These "collective" actions for amparo directed to protect diffuse rights[366] particularly on environmental matters have been expressly constitutionalized in Latin America, as is the case for instance in Argentina, where the constitution provides that the amparo suit can be filed by "the affected party, the People's Defendant and the registered associations that tend to those goals" (Article 43):

Against any form of discrimination and regarding the rights for the protection of environment, the free competition, the user and the consumer, as well as the rights of collective general incidence.[367]

Pueblo" against the threat of violations of the political rights of the aforesaid political party and of all the other supporters of the calling of a recall referendum regarding the President of the Republic, the Chamber ruled that: "The action of amparo was filed for the protection of constitutional rights of an undetermined number of persons, whose identity was not indicated in the filing document, in which they are not included as claimants. It is the criteria of this Chamber, those that could result directly affected in their constitutional rights and guaranties by the alleged threat attributed to the Ministry of Defense and the General Commanders of the Army and the National Guard are, precisely, the persons that are members or supporters of "Un solo Pueblo," or those who prove they are part of one of the groups that promoted the recall referendum; in which case they would have standing to bring before the constitutional judge, by themselves or through representatives, seeking the reestablishment of the infringed juridical situation or impeding the realization of the threat, because the *legitimatio ad causam* exists in each one of them, not precisely as constitutionally harmed or aggrieved. Due to the foregoing, the Chamber considers that Mr. William Ojeda, who said he acted as Director of the political association called "Un Sólo Pueblo," a quality that he furthermore has not demonstrated, lacks the necessary standing to seek for constitutional amparo of the constitutional rights set forth in Articles 19, 21 and 68 of the constitution regarding the members, supporters and participants of the mentioned political association as well as the political coalition that proposed the recall referendum of the President of the Republic, and consequently, this Chamber declares the inadmissibility of the amparo action filed. See *Willian Ojeda vs. Ministro de la Defensa y los Comandantes Generales del Ejercito y de la Guardia Nacional* Case, in *Revista de Derecho Público*, n° 104, Editorial Jurídica Venezolana, Caracas, 2005.

[366]In the Dominican Republic, before the sanctioning of the Amparo Law in 2006, once the Supreme Court admitted the amparo action, the courts admitted that any person legally capable and with interest in the general enforcement of collective human rights, such as the right to education, can file an action for amparo if the matter is not only and exclusively a private one. See decision 406-2 of June 21, 2001, First Instance Court of San Pedro Macoris. See the reference in Miguel A. Valera Montero, *Hacia un Nuevo concepto de constitucionalismo*, Santo Domingo, 2006, pp. 388–389.

[367]Four specific collective actions result from this article: amparo against any form of discrimination; amparo for the protection of the environment; and amparo for the protection of free competition, and amparo for the protection of the user and the consumer rights. That is why regarding discrimination, the object of this amparo is not a discrimination

In Peru, Article 40 of the Constitutional Procedure Code also authorizes any person to file the amparo suit "in cases referring to threats or violation of environmental rights or other diffuse rights that enjoy constitutional recognition, as well as the nonlucrative entities whose goals are the defense of such rights."

In a similar sense in Brazil, the constitution established a *mandado de securança* called *colectivo*, devoted to the protection of diffuse or collective rights, to be filed by political parties with representation in National Congress; trade unions, class institutions or associations legally established in defense of the interests of its members and that must have been functioning for at least the previous year (Article 5, LXIII).[368]

In Ecuador, Article 48 of the Amparo Law also authorizes any natural or artificial person to file the amparo action, "when it is a matter of protection of the environment," including the indigenous communities through their representative.[369]

The case of Costa Rica must also be mentioned, where the collective amparo has also been admitted by the Constitutional Chamber of the

---

regarding a particular individual but a group of persons between which a nexus or common trend exists that originates the discrimination. See Joaquín Brage Camazano, *La jurisdicción constitucional de la libertad*, Editorial Porrúa, México, 2005, pp. 94. On the other hand, regarding the protection of the environment, it formalized the trend that began to be consolidated after a 1983 case in which an amparo was filed for the protection of the ecological equilibrium regarding the protection of dolphins. The Supreme Court accepted in that case the possibility for anybody individually or in representation of his family, to file an amparo action when pursuing the maintenance of the ecological equilibrium, due to the right any human being has to protect his habitat. See Alí Joaquin Salgado, *Juicio de amparo y acción de inconstitucionalidad*, Astrea Buenos Aires, 1987, pp. 81–89. Regarding the associations that can file the collective amparo suits, the Supreme Court of Argentina has also considered that they do not require formal registration. See Decisions 320:690, *Asociación Grandes Usuarios* case and Decision 323:1339, *Asociación Benghalensis* case. See the references in Joaquín Brage Camazano, *La jurisdicción constitucional de la libertad*, Editorial Porrúa, México, 2005, pp. 92–93.

[368]In addition, since 1985 a "collective civil action" has been developed in Brazil, with similar trends as the Class Actions of the United States, very widely used for the protection of groups' rights, like consumers though limiting the standing to the public entities (national, state and municipal) and to associations. See Antonio Gidi, "Acciones de grupo y "amparo colectivo" en Brasil. La protección de derechos difusos, colectivos e individuales homogéneos, in Eduardo Ferrer Mac-Gregor (Coordinator), *Derecho Procesal Constitucional*, Colegio de Secretarios de la Suprema Corte de Justicia de la Nación, Editorial Porrúa, Tomo III, México, 2003, pp. 2.538 ff.

[369]Hernán Salgado Pesantes, *Manual de Justicia Constitucional Ecuatoriana*, Corporación Editora Nacional, Quito, 2004, p. 76.

Supreme Court in matters of environment, based on the constitutional provisions establishing the right of everybody "to a healthy and ecologically equilibrated environment" (Article 50); assigning to any person the "standing to denounce the acts infringing such right."[370]

However, contrary to the current tendency expanding the amparo action for the protection of collective rights, in Mexico the amparo proceeding continues to have an essential individual character, based in the personal and direct interest[371] of the plaintiff. The only case in which in a certain way the amparo protects collective interests are those related to the amparo for the protection of peasants and of collective agrarian land owners.[372]

Also in Colombia, the general principle regarding the action for *tutela* is its personal and private character, so it can only be filed by the holder of the fundamental individual right protected in the constitution.[373] Yet this does not mean that the diffuse or collective rights are not protected. If it is true that they are not protected by means of the *tutela* action; not-

---

[370]Even though not expressly referring to the amparo suit, the Constitutional Chamber did refer to a similar norm of the previous constitution (Article 89) that gave standing to anybody "to file amparo actions for the defense of the right to the conservation of the natural resources of the country. Even though a direct and clear suit for the claimant does not exist, as in the concrete case of the State against an individual, all inhabitants, regarding the violations of Article 89 of the Constitution, suffer a prejudice in the same proportion as if it were a direct harm, thus it is accepted that an interest exists in his favor that authorizes him to file an action for the protection of such right to maintain the natural equilibrium of the ecosystem." See Decision 1700-03. See the reference Ruben Hernández Valle, *Derecho Procesal Constitucional*, Editorial Juricentro, San José, 2001, pp. 239–240.

[371]See Eduardo Ferrer Mac-Gregor, *Juicio de amparo e interés legítimo: la tutela de los derechos difusos y colectivos*, Editorial Porrúa, México, 2003, p. 56.

[372]See Eduardo Ferrer Mac-Gregor, *La acción constitucional de amparo en México y España*, Editorial Porrúa, México, 2002, p. 233 ff.

[373]See Juan Carlos Esguerra Portocarrero, *La protección constitucional del ciudadano*, Lexis, Bogotá, 2005, p. 121. That is why, Article 6,3 of the *Tutela* Law expressly provides that the action of *tutela* is inadmissible when the rights seeking to be protected are "collective rights, as the right to peace and others referred to in Article 88 of the Constitution," particularly because for that purpose a special judicial means for protection is established called "popular actions." Article 6,3 of the *Tutela* Law added that the foregoing will not prevent that the holder of rights threatened to be violated or that have been violated can file a *tutela* action in situations compromising collective rights and interest and of his own threatened or violated rights when it is a matter to prevent an irremediable harm.

withstanding they are protected by a specific "popular action" or group action established in the same constitution.[374]

These collective actions have some similarities with the civil rights class actions developed in the United States,[375] where they have been very effective for the protection of civil rights in cases of discrimination.[376]

---

[374]These popular actions are those established in the constitution for the protection of rights and interests related to public property, public space, public security and health, administrative morale, environment, economic free competition and others of similar nature. All these are diffuse rights, and for its protections, the Law 472 of 1998 has regulated these popular actions. This statute also regulates other sorts of actions for the protection of rights in cases of harm suffered by a plural number of persons. Regarding the popular actions, they can be filed by any person, Non Governmental Organizations, the Popular or Civic Organizations, the public entities with control functions, when the harm or threat is not initiated by their activities, the General Prosecutor, the People's Defendant and the District and Municipal prosecutors, and the mayors and public officers that because of their functions they must defend and protect the abovementioned rights (Article 12). Regarding the group actions set forth for the protection of a plurality of persons in cases of suffering harm in their rights in a collective way, the Law 472 of 1998 establishes these actions basically with indemnizatory purposes, and they can only be filed by twenty individuals, all of them acting on their own behalf. Thus, these are not actions directed to protect the whole population or collectivity, but only a plurality of persons that have the same rights, and seek for its protection.

[375]Regulated in the Rule 23 of the Federal Rules of Civil Procedure filed for the protection of civil rights, according to which, in cases of a class of persons whom have questions of law or fact common to the class, but have so many members that joining all of them would be an impracticable task, then the action can be filed by one or more of its members as representative plaintiff parties on behalf of all, provided that the claims of the representative parties are typical of the claims of the class and that such representative parties will fairly and adequately protect the interests of the class (Rule 23, Class Actions, a).

[376]It was the case decided by the Supreme Court in *Zablocki, Milwaukee County Clerk v. Redhail* of January 18, 1978, 434 U.S. 374; 98 S. Ct. 673; 54 L. Ed. 2d 618, as a result of a class action brought before a federal court under 42 U.S.C.S. § 1983, by Wisconsin residents holding that the marriage prohibition set forth in Wisconsin State § 245.10 (1973) violated the equal protection clause, U.S. Constitution, fourteenth amendment. According to that statute, Wisconsin residents were prevented from marrying if they were behind in their child support obligations or if the children to whom they were obligated were likely to become public charges. The Court found that the statute violated equal protection in that it directly and substantially interfered with the fundamental right to marry without being closely tailored to effectuate the state's interests. Another Supreme Court decision, *Lau et al., v. Nichols et al.*, dated January 21, 1974, 414 U.S. 563; 94 S. Ct. 786; 39 L. Ed. 2d 1; 1974 also decided in favor of a class on discrimination violations. In the case, non-English-speaking students of Chinese ancestry brought a class suit in a federal court of California against officials of the San Francisco Unified School District, seeking relief against alleged unequal educational opportunities resulting from the officials' failure to establish a program to rectify the students' language problem. The Supreme Court eventually held that the

II. PUBLIC OFFICIALS WITH STANDING IN THE AMPARO PROCEEDING

Although being of a personal character, even in cases of actions for the protection of collective and diffuse rights, it is generally accepted that some public officers have standing to file amparo actions on behalf of the community or of groups of persons. This traditionally has been the case of the Public Prosecutors and is now the case of the People's Defendant that exists in almost all the Latin American countries.

1. *The People's Defendant's standing to file amparo actions*

In effect, one important aspect of the Latin American system of protection of human rights and particularly regarding the standing to sue for amparo, has been the creation of specific autonomous constitutional entities called the Defendant of the People (People's Defendant) or the Defendant of Human Rights with the particular purpose of protecting and seeking for the protection of constitutional rights, particularly of the diffuse constitutional rights.

In some cases, these institutions follow in general lines the classical Scandinavian Ombudsman model initially conceived as a parliamentary independent institution for the protection of citizens' rights particularly regarding Public Administration, as is the case of Argentina[377] (Defendant of the People), Paraguay (People's Defendant)[378] and Guatemala (Procurator on Human Rights).[379]

---

school district, which received federal financial assistance, violated dispositions that ban discrimination based on race, color, or national origin in any program or activity receiving federal financial assistance, and furthermore violated the implementing regulations of the Department of Health, Education, and Welfare by failing to establish a program to deal with the complaining students' language problem.

[377] In the first group, closer to the European model, the Argentinean Constitution in the chapter referring to the Legislative Power (Article 86) establishes the Defendant of the People for the protection of human rights regarding Public Administration. It is conceived as an independent entity in the scope of the Congress, acting with functional autonomy and without receiving instructions from any authority. Its mission is the defense and protection of human rights guaranteed in the constitutions and statutes against Public Administration facts, acts or omissions, and to control the exercise of administrative functions. The People's Defendant is nominated by the Congress by two-third of the votes of the members present in the voting and can only be removed in the same way.

[378] In the Constitution of Paraguay, the People's Defendant is a parliamentary commissioner for the protection of human rights, for the channeling of popular claims and for the

In other Latin American countries the institution has been conceived with greater autonomy, particularly regarding Parliament and other branches of government, established for the protection of human rights without any specific relation with Public Administration. This is the case of Colombia (People's Defendant),[380] Ecuador (People's Defendant)[381] and El Salvador (Procurator for the Defense of Human Rights)[382] even though in the last two countries it is organized within the Public Prosecutor's Office (*Ministerio Público*). This is also the case of Mexico (Commission on Human Rights),[383] Bolivia (People's Defendant),[384] Peru (Peo-

protection of communitarian interests, without having any judicial or executive functions (Article 276). He is elected by the Chamber of Representatives from a proposal by the Senate with the vote of two-third of its members.

[379]In Guatemala, the constitution establishes a Procurator on Human Rights as a parliamentary commissioner elected by Congress from a proposal made by a Commission on Human Rights integrated by representatives of the political parties in Congress. His mission is to defend human rights and to supervise Public Administration (Article 274). The Law on amparo in Guatemala gives the Public Prosecutor and the Procurator on Human Rights sufficient standing to file amparo actions "for the defense of the interests assigned to them" (Article 25).

[380]In Colombia, the People's Defendant, elected by the representative Chamber of Congress from a proposal formulated by the president of the Republic, is created as part of the Public Prosecutor Office (Article 281) with the specific mission of watching for the promotion, exercise and divulgation of human rights. Within its powers is to invoke the right to habeas corpus and to file actions for *tutela*, without prejudice of the interested party rights. The *Tutela* Law also authorizes the People's Defendant to file these actions on behalf of anyone when asked to do so in cases of the person being in a nonprotective situation (Articles 10 and 46), or regarding Colombians residing outside the country (Article 51). In such cases, the People's Defendant will be considered party in the process together with the injured party (Article 47).

[381]The People's Defendant in Ecuador is a complete independent and autonomous institution regarding the classical branches of government, also elected by the Congress with the vote of the two-third of its members (Article 96). Among its functions are to defend and encourage the respect of the fundamental constitutional rights, to watch for the quality of the public services and to promote and support the habeas corpus and amparo actions at the person's request. The Law regulating the matter in Ecuador also authorizes the People's Defendant to file habeas corpus and amparo actions (Articles 33 and 48).

[382]In El Salvador, the Procurator for the Defense of Human Rights is part of the Public Ministry, together with the Public Prosecutor and the Attorney General of the Republic (Article 191), all elected by the Legislative Assembly by a two-third vote of its members. Within its functions are to watch for the respect and guaranty of human rights and to promote judicial actions for their protection (Article 194).

[383]In México, the constitution has also established that Congress and the state legislatures must create entities for the protection on human rights, and receive grievances regarding administrative acts or omissions of any authority except the judicial power that violates

ple's Defendant Office)[385] and Nicaragua (Procurator for the Defense of Human Rights).[386] Also in Venezuela, the 1999 constitution created the institution known as the People's Defendant, following the tendency to create an independent and autonomous organ of the State for the protection of human rights but in this case, with the extreme situation of formally establishing it as a separate branch of government.[387]

The general trend regarding all these autonomous constitutional institutions for the protection of human rights is the power attributed to such organs to file amparo actions particularly regarding the protection of diffuse constitutional rights, having then the necessary standing to sue,[388]

such rights. At the national level, the entity is named National Commission on Human Rights.

[384] In Bolivia, the constitution also creates the People's Defendant for the purpose of watching for the enforcement and respect of the persons' rights and guaranties regarding administrative activities on all the public sector, as for the defense, promotion and divulgation of human rights (Article 127). The People's Defendant does not receive instructions from the public powers and is elected by Congress (Article 128). Among its functions are to file the actions of amparo and habeas corpus without needing any power of attorney (Article 129).

[385] In Perú, the constitution also creates the People's Defendant Office as an autonomous organ, the head of which is elected by Congress also with two-third vote of its members (Article 162), for the purpose of defending persons and community human and fundamental rights, to supervise for the accomplishment of public administration duties and the rendering of public services to the people. The Constitutional Procedure Code authorizes the People's Defendant, in exercising its competencies, to file amparo actions (Article 40).

[386] In Nicaragua, the constitution only establishes that the National Assembly will appoint the Procurator for the Defense of Human Rights (Article 138,30).

[387] The 1999 Venezuelan Constitution, in this regard, establishes a penta separation of powers, distinguishing five branches of government, separating the Legislative, Executive, Judicial, Electoral and Citizens branches; creating the People's Defendant within the Citizens Power, in addition to the Public Prosecutor Office and the General Comptroller Office (Article 134). The People's Defendant was created for the promotion, defense and supervision of the rights and guaranties set forth in the Constitution and in the international treaties on human rights, as well as for the citizens' legitimate, collective and diffuse interests (Article 281). In particular, according to Article 281 of the constitution, it also has among its functions to watch for the functioning of public services power and to promote and protect the peoples' legitimate, collective and diffuse rights and interests against arbitrariness or deviation of power in the rendering of such services, being authorized to file the necessary actions to ask for the compensation of the damages caused from the malfunctioning of public services. It also has among its functions, the possibility of filing actions of amparo and habeas corpus.

[388] As has been decided by the Constitutional Chamber of the Supreme Tribunal of Venezuela: "As a matter of law, the Defender has standing to bring to suit actions aimed at enforcing the diffuse and collective rights or interests; not being necessary the requirement

for instance, in cases of the protection of indigenous people's rights, the right to the environment and the citizens' right to political participation.[389]

of the acquiescence of the society it acts on behalf of for the exercise of the action. The Defender of the People is given legitimate interest to act in a process defending a right granted to it by the Constitution itself, consisting in protecting the society or groups in it, in the cases of Article 281."

[389]The Constitutional Chamber of the Supreme Tribunal of Venezuela admitted the standing of the Defender of the People to file actions for amparo on behalf of the citizens as a whole, as was the case of the action filed against the Legislative body pretension to appoint the Electoral National Council members without fulfilling the constitutional requirements. In the case, decided on June 6, 2001, the Constitutional Chamber, when analyzing Article 280 of the constitution, pointed out that "the protection of diffuse and collective rights and interests may be raised by the Defender of the People, through the action of amparo," adding the following: "As for the general provision of Article 280 *eiusdem*, regarding the general defense and protection of diffuse and collective interests, this Chamber considers that the Defender of the People is entitled to act to protect those rights and interests, when they correspond in general to the consumers and users (6, Article 281), or to protect the rights of Indian peoples (paragraph 8 of the same Article), since the defense and protection of such categories is one of the faculties granted to said entity by Article 281 of the Constitution in force. It is about a general protection and not a protection of individualities. Within this frame of action, and since the political rights are included in the human rights and guaranties of Title III of the Constitution in force, which have a general projection, among which the ones provided in Article 62 of the Constitution can be found, it must be concluded that the Defender of the People on behalf of the society, legitimated by law, is entitled to bring to suit an action of amparo tending to control the Electoral Power, to the citizen's benefit, in order to enforce Articles 62 and 70 of the Constitution, which were denounced to be breached by the National Legislative Assembly...(right to citizen participation). Due to the difference between diffuse and collective interests, both the Defender of the People, within its attributions, and every individual residing in the country, except for the legal exceptions, are entitled to bring to suit the action (be it of amparo or an specific one) for the protection of the former ones; while the action of the collective interests is given to the Defender of the People and to any member of the group or sector identified as a component of that specific collectivity, and acting defending the collectivity. Both individuals and corporations whose object be the protection of such interests may raise the action, and the standing in all these actions varies according to the nature of the same, that is why law can limit the action in specific individuals or entities. However, in our Constitution, in the provisions of Article 281 the Defender of the People is objectively granted the procedural interest and the capacity to sue." See decision of the Constitutional Chamber n° 656 of May 6, 2001, *Defensor del Pueblo vs. Comisión Legislativa Nacional* case, as referred in Decision n° 379 of February 26, 2003, *Mireya Ripanti et vs. Presidente de Petróleos de Venezuela S.A. (PDVSA)* case, in *Revista de Derecho Público*, N° 93–96, Editorial Jurídica Venezolana, Caracas, 2003, pp. 152 ff.

2. *The question of the standing of other public officers in the amparo suit*

The main consequence of the creation of all these autonomous constitutional institutions for the protection of human rights, with standing to file amparo actions, is the lack of standing that other States' institutions have in order to initiate the amparo proceeding.

Nonetheless, in countries where no specific State institution for the protection of human rights has been created, or where they have a limited scope, other entities like the Public Prosecutors or the Attorney General have been granted the required standing to file actions on behalf of the people for the protection of human rights.

This has been the case in the United States where some public officers and in particular the Attorney General have been considered as having standing to file injunctions for the protection of human rights,[390] which was generalized after the Supreme Court decision in *Brown v. Board of Education of Topeka,* 347 U.S. 483 (1954); 349 U.S. 294 (1955) declaring the dual school system ("separate but equal") unconstitutional.

After that decision, by means of the Civil Rights Act of 1957, the Congress began to authorize the Attorney General to bring injunctive suits for the protection of human rights, particularly to implement the Fifteenth Amendment referring, for instance, to the right to vote in a nondiscriminatory basis.[391]

The consequence of these reforms has been that the Attorney General representing the United States has ceased to participate in civil rights proceedings only as *amicus curia,* and also with other public agencies,

---

[390]The Attorney General, of course, has had the needed standing for the protection of the State's general interest, for instance the control of the mail service, as was admitted in the Supreme Court decision *In Re Debs,* 158 U.S. 565, 15 S.Ct. 900,39 L.Ed. 1092 (1895), being in that case a party against the members of a railway trade union that threatened the functioning of railways. A few years before, the Congress, by means of the Sherman Antitrust Act, granted authority to the Attorney General to commence injunctive proceedings to prevent restraints to trade.

[391]As referred by Owen R. Fiss: "The very next congressional initiative, the Civil Rights Act of 1960, was in large part intended to perfect the Attorney General's injunctive weaponry on behalf of voting rights. In each of the subsequent civil rights acts, those of 1964 and 1968, the pattern was repeated; the Attorney General was authorized to initiate injunctive suits to enforce a wide range of rights —public accommodations (e.g. restaurants), state facilities (e.g. parks), public schools, employments, and housing—." See Owen M. Fiss, *The Civil Rights Injunction,* Indiana University Press, Bloomington & London, 1978, p. 21.

has played a prominent role initiating civil rights proceedings for injunc-tions[392] seeking the protection of some constitutional rights of citizens[393] for instance, referring to public welfare, public safety or public health.[394]

In the Latin American countries, except for the already mentioned case of the standing assigned to the People's Defendant, or in some cases, to the Public prosecutors,[395] no other public officer or agency is entitled to

[392]As mentioned by Fiss: "The civil rights era forced the Attorney General and the courts to re-examine the non-statutory powers of the United States to sue to enforce the constitu-tion." See Owen M. Fiss and Doug Rendleman, *Injunctions*, Second Edition, University Casebook Series, The Foundation Press, Mineola, New York, 1984, p. 35. The standing of the Attorney General was finally generally admitted regarding the protection of human rights in the case *United States v. City of Philadelphia*, 644 F.2d. 187 (3d Cir. 1980), in which the United States authority to sue a city and its officials for an injunction against the violation of the fourteenth Amendment rights of individual because of police brutality was admitted; the United States' was considered as suing as class representative for the city of Philadelphia. The United States Court of Appeals, Third Circuit ruled in the matter, as follows: Article II section 3 of the Constitution charges the Executive to "take care that the Laws be faithfully executed." Independent of any explicit statutory grant of authority, provided Congress has not expressly limited its authority, the Executive has the inherent constitutional power and duty to enforce constitutional and statutory rights by resort to the courts. When Federal courts have upheld executive standing without explicit congressional authority, they have looked to other provisions of the constitution, such as the commerce clause. See, e.g., *Sanitary District of Chicago v. United States*, 266 Us. 405,45 S. Ct. 176, 69 L. Ed. 352 (1925); *In re Debs*, 158 U.S. 564 15 S. Ct. 900, 39 L. Ed. 1092 (1895). In addition, 28 U.S.C. § 518 (b) affords the Attorney General statutory authority to "conduct and argue any case in a court of the United States in which the United States is interested." The Supreme Court has held that this statute confers on the Executive general authority to initiate suits "to safeguard national interests." *United States v. California*, 332 U.S. 19, 27, 67 S. Ct. 1658, 1662, 91 L. Ed. 1889 (1946). Moreover, the Supreme Court has held that the Executive's general constitutional duty to protect the public welfare "is often of itself sufficient to give it standing in court," *In re Debs,* 158 U.S. 564, 584, 15 S. Ct. 900, 906, 39 L. Ed. 1092 (1895). *Idem.*

[393]For example, the standing of the United States and of the Secretary of Education has been recognized to seek an injunction against a university to stop the release of student records in violation of a federal statute (*United States v. Miami University*, 294 F. 3d 797, 166 Ed. Law Rep. 464 2002 FED App. 0213P (6th Cir. 2002). See the reference in John Bourdeau *et al.*, "Injunctions," in Kevin Schroder, John Glenn and Maureen Placilla (Ed.), *Corpus Juris Secundum*, Thomson West, Volume 43A, 2004, p. 252.

[394]That is why, for instance, actions for injunction in cases of the illegal practice of medi-cine and other allied professions had been brought by the Attorney General, a State board of health and a county attorney. See for instance *State ex rel. State Bd. Of Healing Arts v. Beyrle,* 269 Kan. 616, 7 P3d 1194 (2000), *Idem*, p. 276 ff.

[395]In Argentina, the standing of the General Prosecutor to file amparo actions has been accepted. See Nestor Pedro Sagües, "El derecho de amparo en Argentina," in Héctor Fix-Zamudio and Eduardo Ferrer Mac-Gregor, *El derecho de amparo en el Mundo*, Editorial

claim the representation of collective or diffuse rights in order to file an amparo action.

In this sense, it was, for instance, decided in Venezuela by the Constitutional Chamber of the Supreme Tribunal rejecting an amparo action filed by a Governor of one of the federated States, ruling that the States and Municipalities cannot file actions for the protection of diffuse and collective rights and interest except if a statute expressly authorizes them.[396] This doctrine was ratified in another decision issued in 2001 in which the Constitutional Chamber also denied the Governors or Mayors the standing to file collective actions, arguing that "the Venezuelan State, as such, lacks [such standing], since it has mechanisms and other means to cease the damage caused to those rights and interests, specially through administrative procedures"; concluding its ruling affirming that:

> Within the structure of the State... the only one who is able to protect individuals in matters of collective or diffuse interest is the Defender of the People (in any of its scopes: national, state, county or special). The Public Prosecutor, the Mayors, or the Municipal auditors lack both such attribution and the action (unless the law grants them both).[397]

Porrúa, México, 2006, p. 59. In México the Amparo Law authorizes the Federal Public Prosecutor to file action for amparo in criminal and family cases, but not in civil or commercial cases (Article 5, 1,IV).

[396]Decision of November 21, 2000. The Court ruled that the collective and diffuse rights and interests pursue to maintain an acceptable quality of life in all the population or sectors of it in those matters related to the quality of life that must be rendered by the State or by individuals. They are rights and interests that can coincide with individual rights and interests, but that according to Article 26 of the Constitution and unless the statute denies the action, can be claimed by any person invoking a right or interest shared with the people in general or a sector of the population and who fears or has suffered a harm in his quality of life, being part of such collectivity. Now, being for the State to maintain the acceptable quality of life conditions, its bodies or entities cannot ask from it to render an activity; thus, within the structure of the State, the only institution that can file such actions is the People's Defendant, due to the fact that it represents the people and not the State, as well as other public entities when a particular statute gives them such actions. See *Case William Dávila. Gobernación Estado Mérida.* See the comments in Rafael Chavero, *El nuevo régimen del amparo constitucional en Venezuela*, Caracas, 2001, p. 115.

[397]The Constitutional Chamber decided that "actions in general grounded in diffuse or collective rights and interests may be filed by any Venezuelan person or legal entity, or by foreign persons residing in the country who have access to the judicial system through the exercise of this action. The Venezuelan State, as such, lacks standing, since it has mechanisms and other means to cease the damage to those rights and interests, specially through administrative procedures; but the population in general is entitled to bring them in the way

Consequently, the States and Municipal authorities (governors and mayors) have been denied standing to file actions of amparo seekeng the protection of collective constitutional rights, when infringed by nationsl authorities.

III. THE INJURED THIRD PARTY FOR THE PLAINTIFF

In addition to the injured party or to those that have standing to sue on behalf of the injured parties, as in all proceedings, and particularly in matters of amparo for the protection of constitutional rights, it is possible that third parties, not originally connected with the proceeding, could have some personal interest in its development, because the denounced action or omission also affects their constitutional rights, coinciding with the claimant or plaintiff allegations.

Injured third parties, thus, may also be added in the proceedings so that their rights in the subject matter may also be determined and enforced by the corresponding court[398] because they might have a direct interest in the matter that can be affected with the final decision. That is why some

explained in this decision and those can be brought by the Defender of the People, since as stated in Article 280 of the Constitution, the Defendant of the People is in charge of the promotion, defense and guardianship of the legitimate, collective and diffuse interest of the citizens. According to this Chamber, said provision does not exclude or prohibit the citizens the access to the judicial system in defense of the diffuse and collective rights and interests, since Article 26 of the Constitution in force sets forth the access to the judicial system to every person, whereby individuals are entitled to bring to suit as well unless a law denies them the action. Within the structure of the State, since it does not have those attributions granted, the only one who is able to protect individuals in matters of collective or diffuse interest is the Defender of the People (in any of its scopes: national, state, county or special). The Public Prosecutor (except in the case that a law grants it), Mayors, or Municipal auditors lack both such attribution and the action, unless the law grants them both). Decision of the Constitutional Chamber n° 656 of May 6, 2001, *Defensor del Pueblo vs. Comisión Legislativa Nacional* case, as referred in decision n° 379 of February 26, 2003, *Mireya Ripanti et al. vs. Presidente de Petróleos de Venezuela S.A. (PDVSA)* case, in *Revista de Derecho Público*, n° 93–96, Editorial Jurídica Venezolana, Caracas, 2003, pp. 152 ff.

[398] Of course the general rule is the same as in the injunctions proceeding in the United States: persons with a unity of interest in the subject matter of the suit and who are entitled to, and seek the same character of relief may join the plaintiff's claim. See *Jones v. Oklahoma City*, 78 F.2d 860 (C.C.A. 10th Cir. 1935), in John Bourdeau et al., "Injunctions," in Kevin Schroder, John Glenn and Maureen Placilla (Ed.), *Corpus Juris Secundum*, Thomson West, Volume 43A, 2004, p. 332.

Latin American Amparo Laws refer specifically to this intervention of third parties, as is the case of Guatemala,[399] Mexico[400] and Peru.[401]

Finally, it must be mentioned that before the creation of the institution of the People's Defendant, the legal tradition in Latin America, particularly in matters of habeas corpus and amparo, was to consider the Public Prosecutor (*Ministerio Público*) in its character of general guarantor for the protection of constitutional rights, as a *bona fide* third party that was to be summoned to allow its participation in the proceedings, as is provided in the Laws of Argentina,[402] Mexico[403] and Venezuela.[404]

---

[399]In Guatemala, Article 34 of the Law establishes the obligation of "the authority, the person denounced or the claimant, if they arrive to know of any person with direct interest in the subject matter or the suspension of the challenged act, resolution or procedure, whether because they are party in the proceedings or because they have any other legal relation with the exposed situation; to tell the foregoing to the court, indicating name and address and in a brief way, the relation with such interest. In this case the court must hear the referred person, as well as the Public prosecutor, considered as a party."

[400]In México, Article 5 of the Amparo Law, in addition to the aggrieved person or persons and to the challenged authority or authorities, "the affected third party or parties" are also declared as parties in the amparo suit, having the possibility to intervene in such character in the following: a) The counterpart of the injured when the claimed act is issued in a noncriminal trial or controversy, or any of the parties in the same trial when the amparo is filed by a person strange to the procedure: b) The offended or the persons that according to the law have right to have the damage repaired or to demand for civil liability derived from the commitment of the crime in amparo suits filed against criminal judicial decisions, when the latter affects the reparation or the liability; c) The person or persons that have argued in their own favor regarding the challenged act against which the amparo is filed when being acts adopted by authorities other than judicial or labor; or that without arguing in their favor, they have direct interest in the subsistence of the challenged act.

[401]In the case of Perú, the Constitutional Procedural Code following the universal procedural rules, provides that when in the suit for amparo, it appears for the court the need to incorporate third parties not initially summoned, the judge must incorporate them if from the suit or the answer it is evident that the final decision will affect other parties (Article 43). Additionally, Article 54 of the Code provides the right to anybody having legal and relevant interest in the outcome of the trial to be incorporated to the procedure and be declared as a third interested party, being incorporated to the proceedings at the stage as it is.

[402]In this respect, for instance, the Argentinean Habeas Corpus Law regulates the intervention of the Public Prosecutor, for which purpose once the court has received the complaint, they must notify its representatives, which will have in the proceedings the same rights given to all those that intervene in it, without any need to notify them for the accomplishment of any procedural act. The Public Prosecutor can file arguments and make the appeals considered necessary (Article 21).

[403]In México, the Amparo Law guaranties the Public prosecutor its right to intervene in the procedure (Article 5, I, IV).

In a similar sense, regarding this participation of the Public Prosecutor as third party in good faith, in the United States, particularly in matters of judicial protection of civil rights, the Attorney General has also participated as *amicus curiae* in injunctive proceedings, which has also been encouraged by the same courts.[405] It has also been through the exercise of such powers, particularly since the expansion of the injunctive process for the protection of civil rights, which began with school desegregation cases (*Brown v. Board of Education of Topeka* 347 U.S. 483 (1954); 349 U.S. 294 (1955)) that the Attorney General has had a very important role intervening in what has been called "structural injunctions," through which on civil rights massive violation matters, the courts have undertaken to judicially supervise the authorities' institutional policies and practices, in many cases with the active participation of the Attorney General.[406]

---

[404]In a similar sense the Venezuelan Law of Amparo allows the intervention of the Public prosecutors in all amparo suits, but points out that its non-intervention cannot affect the continuity or validity of the procedure (Article 14).

[405] In the Texas prison case *Estelle v. Justice*, 426 U.S. 925; 96 S. Ct. 2637: 49 L. Ed. 2d 380 (1976) the matter was definitively resolved: the trial Judge in the case invited the Attorney general to participate as "litigating amicus," with the same rights normally associated with the party status, for instance to present evidence and to cross-examine witnesses. This participation was challenged by the State but finally was accepted.

[406]As defined by Tabb and Shoben: "Structural injunctions are modern phenomenon born of necessity from development in Constitutional law where the Supreme Court has identified substantive rights whose enforcement requires substantial judicial supervision. These rights concern the treatment of individuals by institutions, such as the right not to suffer inhumane treatment in prisons or public mental hospitals. Enforcement of such rights by injunction has become an implicit part of the Constitutional guaranty of protecting individual liberties from inappropriate government action." See William M. Tabb and Elaine W. Shoben, *Remedies*, Thomson West, 2005, pp. 87–88.

CHAPTER TEN

THE JUSTICIABLE CONSTITUTIONAL RIGHTS BY MEANS OF THE AMPARO AND HABEAS CORPUS ACTIONS

I. CONSTITUTIONAL RIGHTS AND JUSTICIABILITY

As a matter of principle, not all personal rights are justiciables[407] through the habeas corpus or amparo actions,[408] which are only directed to protect those rights enshrined in the Constitution or those that have acquired constitutional rank and value; that is, those that even though also are regulated in statutes, they are out of reach from the Legislator in the sense that they cannot be eliminated, or diminished through statutes.

That is why the constitutional declarations of rights are so important for the Latin American systems of judicial protection of human rights, which have precisely originated the development of the amparo actions as a specific remedy for the protection of such rights in a different way to the United States injunction. In both cases they are extraordinary remedies, but contrary to the amparo that can only be filed for the protection of rights that have constitutional origin or rank, the injunctions are equitable remedies that can be filed for the protection of any kind of personal or property rights, even those of statutory or contractual origin, just provided that they cannot be effectively protected by ordinary common law courts.

---

[407] "Their quality of being suitable to be protected by courts." See Brian A. Garner (Editor in Chief), *Black's Law Dictionary*, West Group, St. Paul, Minn. 2001, p. 391.

[408] As aforementioned, the general trend of the Latin American constitutional provisions regarding constitutional rights and freedoms is that they can all be protected by means of two separate actions: the amparo and the habeas corpus. Nonetheless, in México and Venezuela, because the amparo is considered as a constitutional right in itself, and not exclusively as an adjective mean for protection of human rights, no separate habeas corpus action for the protection of personal freedom exists, as it is just a sort of the amparo action.

In Latin America, on the contrary, rights that are only established in statutes and other lower rank regulations without constitutional foundations or that are not inherent to human beings, cannot be protected by means of amparo and habeas corpus actions, but only through the ordinary judicial remedies.

Yet in the United States, in order to protect rights as fundamental rights by means of the injunctions, in cases in which the courts must decide constitutional questions, for instance, regarding States' legislation, they also need to be declared in the constitution or have been recognized as such by the Supreme Court. Consequently, if the claimed right has no constitutional rank, no constitutional judicial protection can be given against States' legislations, as has happened, for instance, regarding the right to education or the right to dwelling.

In relation to the right to education, which in the United States has not been considered as a fundamental right, the Supreme Court in the case *San Antonio Independent School District et al. v. Rodriguez et al.*, 411 U.S. 1; 93 S. Ct. 1278; 36 L. Ed. 2d 16; (1973), of March 21, 1973, ruled that although education "is one of the most important services performed by the State (as was ruled in *Brown v. Board of Education*), it is not within the limited category of rights recognized by this Court as guaranteed by the Constitution." In this case, the Supreme Court denied to such right the quality of "fundamental right," insisting that "education, notwithstanding its undisputed importance, is not a right afforded explicit or implicit protection by the Constitution."[409]

---

[409]The decision was issued as a result of the challenging of the Texas system of financing public education by Mexican American parents whose children attended the elementary and secondary schools in an urban school district in San Antonio, Texas. They brought a class action on behalf of school children throughout the state who are members of minority groups or who are poor and reside in school districts having a low property tax base. The Court considered that: "[The] financing system did not impinge upon any fundamental right protected by the Constitution, so as to require application of the strict judicial scrutiny test under which a compelling state interest must be shown, since education, notwithstanding its undisputed importance, is not a right afforded explicit or implicit protection by the Constitution; even assuming that some identifiable quantum of education is a constitutionally protected prerequisite to the meaningful exercise of the right of free speech and the right to vote, nevertheless the strict judicial scrutiny rule is not applicable where the state's financing system does not occasion an absolute denial of educational opportunities to any of its children, and where there is no indication or charge that the system fails to provide each child with an opportunity to acquire the basic minimal skills necessary for the enjoyment of the rights of speech and of full participation in the political process."

When resolving the case, the Supreme Court referred to another decision issued in the case *Dandridge v. Williams*, 397 U.S. 471 (1970), where when dealing with matters of public welfare assistance, the Court ruled that:

> It is not the province of this Court to create substantive constitutional rights in the name of guarantying equal protection of the laws. Thus, the key to discovering whether education is "fundamental" is not to be found in comparisons of the relative societal significance of education as opposed to subsistence or housing. Nor is it to be found by weighing whether education is as important as the right to travel. Rather, the answer lies in assessing whether there is a right to education explicitly or implicitly guaranteed by the constitution.

In support of the aforementioned *San Antonio Independent School District et al. v. Rodriguez et al.* case, the Court also referred to another case, *Lindsay v. Normet*, 405 U.S. 56 (1972), issued only one year before, in which the Court firmly reiterated "that social importance is not the critical determinant for subjecting state legislation to strict scrutiny," denying constitutional rank to the right to have dwelling, ruling that without denigrating "the importance of decent, safe, and sanitary housing" the fact is that "the Constitution does not provide judicial remedies for every social and economic ill," being the matter "legislative, not judicial, functions."[410]

Consequently, the key element in order to obtain constitutional justiciability of human rights, also in the United States, is their constitutional rank or recognition as fundamental rights, independently of the possibility for them to be, in addition, regulated in statutes. This is the general situation in Latin America, where, as mentioned, the amparo action is set forth for the pro-

---

[410]The matter referred to the procedural limitations imposed on tenants in suits brought by landlords under Oregon's Forcible Entry and Wrongful Detainer Law. The tenants argued that the statutory limitations implicated "fundamental interests which are particularly important to the poor," such as the "need for decent shelter" and the "right to retain peaceful possession of one's home." The Supreme Court in the reference to the latter case highlighted the following analysis made by Mr. Justice White, in his opinion for the Court, as instructive: "We do not denigrate the importance of decent, safe, and sanitary housing. But the Constitution does not provide judicial remedies for every social and economic ill. We are unable to perceive in that document any constitutional guaranty of access to dwellings of a particular quality or any recognition of the right of a tenant to occupy the real property of his landlord beyond the term of his lease, without the payment of rent . . . Absent constitutional mandate, the assurance of adequate housing and the definition of landlord-tenant relationships are legislative, not judicial, functions." See *San Antonio Independent School District et al. v. Rodriguez et al.* case, the Court also referred to another case, *Lindsay v. Normet*, 405 U.S. 56 (1972).

tection of rights enshrined in the constitutions, independent of if they are additionally regulated in statutes.

That is why, for instance, when the Bolivian Amparo Law establishes that the amparo is set forth for the protection of rights and guaranties "recognized in the Constitution and the laws" (Article 94); the reference to the "laws" (in the sense of statutes) must be interpreted in an accumulative way (Constitution and the laws), and not in an alternative way (Constitution or laws). Consequently, rights that are only established in statutes cannot be protected through amparo actions. In this same sense, Article 1 of the Guatemalan Amparo Law must also be interpreted when referring to "rights inherent to persons protected by the Constitution, the laws and international agreements ratified by Guatemala." In this case, the reference to the laws is also in addition to their declaration in the constitution or to their constitutional rank because of being inherent to human persons.

II. AMPARO FOR THE JUSTICIABILITY OF CONSTITUTIONAL RIGHTS ONLY IN CASES OF CONSTITUTIONAL VIOLATIONS

The consequence of the aforementioned is that because the purpose of the amparo actions is to protect individuals against violations of constitutional rights; it is not possible to file an action for amparo just based in the violation of the statutory provisions that regulate the constitutional right. For instance, as it happens with the right to property, regarding which an amparo action for its protection can be admitted when, for instance, arbitrary administrative acts prevent or impede in absolute terms the use of property; but on the contrary, it is not admitted for the protection of property, for instance, against trespassing, being in these cases, the ordinary civil judicial expedite actions (*interdictos*) the ones that should be filed.[411]

---

[411] Property rights are not only established in the constitutions but are also extensively regulated in the Civil Codes. The latter not only contains substantive regulations regarding the exercise of such rights but they provide for adjective ordinary remedies in case those rights are affected. In particular, the Civil Code and the Civil Procedure Codes establishes some sort of civil injunctions to guaranty immediate protection in cases of trespasses (*interdictos*) for instance of possession rights, which are effective judicial remedies for the protection of land owners or occupant rights. Thus, in cases of property trespass, the *interdicto de amparo* or of new construction are effective judicial means for protection of property rights, not being possible to file an amparo action in such cases. In this regard, the Constitutional Chamber of the Supreme Tribunal of Justice of Venezuela, in a case decided in 2000, argued as follows: "The amparo action protects one aspect of the legal situations

In general terms, this implies the extraordinary character of the amparo action, in the sense that it can only be filed when no other appropriate and effective ordinary judicial means for protection are legally provided or when if provided, they are ineffective.

This condition of admissibility of the amparo actions is very similar to the so-called "inadequacy" condition established in the United States regarding the equitable injunction remedies, in the sense that they are only admissible when there are no adequate remedies in law to assure the protection; or when the law cannot provide an adequate remedy because of the nature of the right involved, as was the case regarding school segregation.[412]

As aforementioned, due to the constitutional nature of the rights that can be protected by means of amparo, this specific action for protection

of persons referred to their fundamental rights, corresponding the defense of subjective rights — different to fundamental rights and public liberties — to the ordinary administrative and judicial recourses and actions. For instance, it is not the same to deny a citizen the condition to have property rights, than to discuss property rights between parties, the protection of which corresponds to a specific ordinary judicial action of recovery (reivindicación). This means that in the amparo proceedings the court judges the actions of public entities or individuals that can harm fundamental rights; but in no case can it review, for instance, the applicability or interpretation or statutes by Public Administration or the courts, unless from them a direct violation of the Constitution can be deduced. The amparo is not a new judicial instance, nor the substitution of ordinary judicial means for the protection of rights and interest; it is an instrument to reaffirm constitutional values, by mean of which the court, hearing an amparo, can decide regarding the contents or the application of constitutional provisions regulating fundamental rights; can review the interpretation made by Public Administration or judicial bodies, or determine if the facts from which constitutional violations are deduced constitute a direct violation of the Constitution." Decision n° 828 of July 27, 2000, *Seguros Corporativos (SEGUCORP), C.A. et al. vs. Superintedencia de Seguros* Case, in *Revista de Derecho Público*, n° 83, Editorial Juridica Venezuelana, Caracas, 2000, pp. 290 ff.

[412]See Owen M. Fiss and Doug Rendleman, *Injunctions,* 2d Ed, The Foundation Press, Mineola, 1984, p. 59. This inadequacy condition, of course, normally results from the factual situations regarding the case or from the nature of the right which in some cases impedes or allows the granting of the protection. In this sense, for instance it was resolved since the well-known case of *Wheelock v. Nooman* (NY 1888); in which case the defendant, having left on the plaintiff's property great boulders beyond the authorization he had, the injunction was granted in order to require such defendant to remove them. The plaintiff in the case could not easily remove the boulders and sued the cost of removal of the trespassing rocks because of their size and weight. On the contrary, in another case, the remedy at law was considered adequate because the litter the defendant left on the property could be removed by the plaintiff paying for someone to remove the trash, in which case he could just sue the defendant for the cost incurred, as was decided in *Connor v. Grosso* (Cal. 1953).

can only be filed when the constitution is directly infringed.[413] Consequently, even if constitutional rights and guaranties are also regulated in statutes, the amparo action cannot be founded only in the violation of such statutory provisions, but need to be founded in the direct violation of the constitution.[414]

This principle has been set forth in many Amparo Laws. For instance, the Colombian Decree n° 306 of February 19, 1992 which regulates Decree 2.591 of 1991 on the *tutela* action, expressly declares that "the action of *tutela* only protects fundamental constitutional rights, and therefore, may not be used to enforce rights that only have legal rank, or to enforce the compliance of laws, decrees, regulations or any other regulation of an inferior level" (Article 2). In a similar sense, the Peruvian Code

---

[413]*Idem.* The Venezuelan First Court on Judicial Review of Administrative Action Jurisdiction, in a decision of December 6, 1989, issued just after the Amparo Law was sanctioned (1988), fixed this doctrine, as follows: "The amparo is admissible only in cases of violations of constitutional rights and guaranties. These rights and guaranties can be regulated in norms of inferior rank, but those are not the norms that can be alleged as violated, and reference must be made to the [constitutional] text that originates them. The extraordinary character of the amparo impedes its use to guaranty the fulfillment of regulations and conditions set forth in statutory norms, which can be discussed by other ordinary judicial means. If it were not conceived like this, the amparo jurisdiction would substitute any other." See in *Revista de Derecho Público*, n° 41, Editorial Jurídica Venezolana, Caracas, 1990, p. 99. This doctrine has been followed in many decisions of the First Court, for instance, Sept. 16, 1992, in *Revista de Derecho Público*, n° 51, Editorial Jurídica Venezolana, Caracas, 1992, p. 151; and December 4, 1992, in *Revista de Derecho Público*, n° 52, Editorial Jurídica Venezolana, Caracas, 1992, p. 165.

[414]As was also ruled by the former Supreme Court of Venezuela in decision of August 14, 1990, the amparo can only be filed because of direct and immediate contraventions of constitutional rights and guaranties; and for that purpose: "It is only necessary to demonstrate the harm to such norms and not to others of infra constitutional character. Thus, the action for amparo is always of constitutional nature, it is justified in the measure that the rights or guaranties harmed or threatened are of such same rank. In conclusion, it is not enough to allege the violation of inferior rank norms, which are not the ones to be protected by amparo but for other means. Even if they develop constitutional provisions, it is indispensable, and also enough, to demonstrate the direct violation of a constitutional provision." See in *Revista de Derecho Público*, n° 44, Editorial Jurídica Venezolana, Caracas, 1990, p. 143. In similar sense, see decisions of the former Supreme Court of Justice, Politico Administrative Chamber, Nov. 8, 1990, in *Revista de Derecho Público*, n° 44, Editorial Jurídica Venezolana, Caracas, 1990, p. 141; April 4, 1990, in *Revista de Derecho Público*, n° 42, Editorial Jurídica Venezolana, Caracas, 1990; p. 112; January 31, 1989, in *Revista de Derecho Público* n° 37, Editorial Jurídica Venezolana, Caracas, 1989, p. 89; August 14, 1989, in *Revista de Derecho Público*, n° 39, Editorial Jurídica Venezolana, Caracas, 1989, p. 144; March 4, 1993, in *Revista de Derecho Público*, n° 53-54, Editorial Jurídica Venezolana, Caracas, 1993, p. 254.

on Constitutional Jurisdiction is precise when establishing the same principle that the "amparo shall not be admitted in defense of a right lacking direct constitutional founding or when it does not directly refer to the protected constitutional aspects of such right" (Articles 5,1 and 38), which confirms the already mentioned principle of the amparo protection only referring to the violation of the constitutional provisions regarding rights.

However, regarding the justiciability of human rights in Latin America, the most important aspect referring to the amparo and habeas corpus actions as means for their protection, refers to the scope of the protection, that is, to determine which justiciable constitutional rights are.

It is possible to say that the general rule is that all constitutional rights must and can be protected, without exception. Yet this rule has its exception, in the cases of Chile, Colombia and Mexico, where the scope of the amparo protection has been reduced to only certain constitutional rights.

In the case of the action for *tutela* in Colombia, it is directed to protect only the constitutional rights that are qualified as "fundamental rights"; and in Chile, the recourse for protection is established only for the protection of a list of rights specifically enumerated in the constitution. In Mexico, the amparo suit is established only for the protection of what are called "individual guaranties," which does not exhaust the constitutional rights.

Thus two general systems can be distinguished in Latin America regarding the protected rights through the amparo action: those in which all constitutional rights and guaranties can be protected through the amparo and habeas corpus actions or recourse; and those where the amparo action is directed to protect only some constitutional rights.

III. AMPARO AND HABEAS CORPUS FOR THE PROTECTION OF ALL CONSTITUTIONAL RIGHTS

According to the first system, which is the general one, the rights protected through the amparo action are the "constitutional rights," expression that comprises, first, the rights expressly declared in the constitution; second, those rights that even not enumerated in the constitutions are inherent to human beings; and third, those rights enumerated in the international instruments on human rights ratified by the State. In the words of the Argentinean (Article 1) and Uruguayan 1988 Amparo Laws (Article 72), the constitutional protection refers to the rights and freedoms "expressly or implicitly recognized by the Constitution."

Consequently, for instance, in the case of Venezuela,[415] all the rights listed in Title III of the constitution, which refers to Human Rights, Guaranties and Duties, are protected though the amparo action. Those rights are the following: citizenship rights, civil (individual) rights, political rights, social and family rights, cultural and educational rights, economic rights, environmental rights and the indigenous people's rights enumerated in Articles 19 to 129. Additionally, all other constitutional rights and guaranties derived from other constitutional provisions can also be protected even if not included in Title III, like for instance, the constitutional guaranty of the independence of the Judiciary, or the constitutional guaranty of the legality of taxation (that taxes can only by set forth by statute).[416]

Regarding the protected rights, through the open clauses of constitutional rights, almost all the Latin American countries have admitted the amparo action for the protection of those other constitutional rights and guaranties not expressly listed in the constitution, but that can be considered inherent to human beings. These open clauses, as have been analyzed, have been extensively applied by the Latin American courts, leaving no loopholes regarding the possibility of the right or guaranty to be constitutionally protected.

These clauses have their direct antecedent in the Ninth Amendment of the U.S. Constitution. In contrast, in the United States, it has only been applied by the Supreme Court in just a few occasions. For instance, in the case *Griswold v. Connecticut* decided on June 7, 1965, 381 U.S. 479; 85 S. Ct. 1678; 14 L. Ed. 2d 510; 1965, in which the Supreme Court declared, even if it was not explicitly mentioned in the constitution, that the right to marital privacy was to be considered as a constitutional right, embraced by the concept of liberty, and constitutionally protected.

---

[415]As it has been expressly set forth in Article 27 of the Constitution of Venezuela, where the action of amparo is conceived as a means for the protection of the enjoyment of absolutely all constitutional rights and guaranties, as well as those inherent to human beings not enumerated in the constitution or in the international instruments on human rights; the expression "instruments" comprising not only treaties, conventions and covenants but also international declarations.

[416]See Allan R. Brewer-Carías, *Instituciones Políticas y Constitucionales*, Vol V, *Derecho y Acción de Amparo,* Caracas, 1998, pp. 209 ff. See decision of the First Court on Judicial Review of Administrative Action, *Fecadove* case, in Rafael Chavero G., *El nuevo régimen del amparo constitucional en Venezuela*, Ed. Sherwood, Caracas, 2001, p. 157.

In this case, Justice Goldberg, delivering the opinion of the Court, held the unconstitutionality of a Connecticut birth-control law because it intruded upon the right of marital privacy, declaring that:

> To hold that a right so basic and fundamental and so deep-rooted in our society as the right of privacy in marriage may be infringed because that right is not guaranteed in so many words by the first eight amendments to the Constitution, is to ignore the Ninth Amendment and to give it no effect whatsoever. Moreover, a judicial construction that this fundamental right is not protected by the Constitution because it is not mentioned in explicit terms by one of the first eight amendments or elsewhere in the Constitution would violate the Ninth Amendment, which specifically states that "the enumeration in the Constitution of certain rights shall not be construed to deny or disparage others retained by the people.[417]

In this regard, the Supreme Court concluded affirming that the right of privacy in marital relation is fundamental and basic, is a personal right 'retained by the people' within the meaning of the Ninth Amendment, thus considering unconstitutional the Connecticut law that prohibits the use of contraceptives.

However, in Latin America, in addition to the rights declared in the constitutions and those derived from the open clauses as inherent to human beings, the rights declared in international treaties can also be protected by means of the amparo action. This is also expressly provided in many countries where the rights declared in international treaties are given a constitutional rank, as is the case of Venezuela (Article 23, Constitution). Also, for instance, in Costa Rica, Article 48 of the constitution is absolutely clear when it guaranties the right of every person to file actions for amparo to maintain or reestablish the enjoyment of all other rights conferred by this constitution as well as those of a fundamental nature established in international instruments on human rights enforce-

---

[417]The Supreme Court also said: "In determining which rights are fundamental, judges are not left at large to decide cases in light of their personal and private notions. Rather, they must look to the "traditions and [collective] conscience of our people" to determine whether a principle is "so rooted [there] ... as to be ranked as fundamental." *Snyder v. Massachusetts*, 291 U.S. 97, 105. The inquiry is whether a right involved "is of such a character that it cannot be denied without violating those 'fundamental principles of liberty and justice which lie at the base of all our civil and political institutions.'" *Powell v. Alabama*, 287 U.S. 45, 67. "Liberty" also "gains content from the emanations of ... specific [constitutional] guaranties" and "from experience with the requirements of a free society." *Poe v. Ullman*, 367 U.S. 497, 517.

able in the Republic. In the same sense it is regulated in the Ecuadorian Law where amparo is established for "the judicial effective protection of all rights enshrined in the Constitution and those contained in the declarations, covenants, conventions and other international instruments in force in Ecuador" (Article 46).

Consequently, the scope of the constitutional amparo protection in Latin America in general is very extensive. This has provoked that in some countries, in order to determine the scope of the constitutional amparo and habeas corpus protection, the special statutes regulating the amparo tend to be exhaustive by listing the rights to be protected, as is the case of Peru, where the Constitutional Procedural Code (Law 28.237 of 2004) expressly lists and identifies which are the rights to be protected by means of amparo and habeas corpus. Regarding the latter, an extensive list is provided in Article 25 of the Law,[418] adding that "habeas corpus shall also be admitted in defense of constitutional rights associated

---

[418]They include: 1. Personal integrity and the right not to be submitted to torture or inhuman or humiliating treatment, nor coerced to obtain declarations. 2. The right not to be forced to render oaths nor be compelled to declare or recognize their own guilt, that of their spouse, or their family members up to the fourth level of consanguinity or second of affinity. 3. The right not to be exiled or banished or confined except by final judicial decision. 4. The right not to be expatriated nor kept away from one's residence except by legal order or by application of the Immigration Law. 5. The right of the foreigner to whom political asylum has been granted, not to be expelled from the country to the country that is persecuting him, or under no circumstance if his freedom or safety is in danger through being expelled. 6. The right of nationals or resident foreigners to enter, transit or leave national territory, except by legal order or application of the Immigration or Health Law. 7. The right not to be detained except by written and justified judicial order, or by the police forces for having committed a flagrant crime; or if he or she has been detained, to be brought before the corresponding Court within twenty-four hours or as soon as possible. 8. The right to voluntarily decide to render military service, pursuant to the law governing such matter. 9. The right not to be arrested for debt. 10. The right not to be deprived of the national identity document, or to obtain a passport or its renewal within the Republic or overseas. 11. The right not to be held incommunicado, except in those cases established under the constitution (Article 2, 24, g). 12. The right to be assisted by a freely chosen defense lawyer at the moment of being summonsed or arrested by the police or other authority, without exception. 13. The right to have removed the surveillance of one's domicile or suspended police trailing, when arbitrary and unjustified. 14. The right of the person on trial or condemned to be released from jail, if his or her freedom has been decided by a judge. 15. The right to have the correct procedure observed in the case of the processing or detention of persons, pursuant to Article 99 of the constitution. 16. The right not to be subject to a forced disappearance. 17. The right of the person under arrest or imprisoned not to be subject to treatment that is unreasonable or disproportional, in respect of the form and conditions in which the order of detention or imprisonment is carried out.

with individual freedom, especially when due process and the inviolability of the home are concerned. Also, regarding the action for amparo, the same Peruvian Code on Constitutional Procedure includes a long list of rights (Article 37) to be protected,[419] including at the end, a reference to all "others recognized in the Constitution," resolving the problems that the practice of listing specific situation in statutes normally have, with the general risk of leaving things out.

The Guatemalan Amparo Law also tends to exhaust the listing of cases in which the amparo action can be filed,[420] adding also in Article 10 that its admission extends to any situation that presents a risk, a threat, a restriction or a violation of the rights recognized by "the Constitution and the laws of the Republic of Guatemala," whether such situation is caused by public or private law entities or individuals.[421]

---

[419] These are: 1. To equality and not to be discriminated because of origin, sex, race, sexual orientation, religion, opinion, economic or social condition, language or any other; 2. To publicly exercise any religious creed; 3. To information, opinion and expression; 4. To contract freely; 5. To the artistic, intellectual and scientific creation; 6. To the inviolability and secrecy of private documents and communications; 7. To assembly; 8. To honor, intimacy, voice, image and to the rectification of incorrect or harmful information; 9. To associate; 10. To work; 11. To unionize, collectively bargain and go on strike; 12. To property and to inherit; 13. To petition before the competent authority; 14. To participate individually and collectively in the political life of the country; 15 To citizenship; 16. To effective judicial protection; 17. To education and the right of the parents to choose the school and participate in the education of their children; 18. To teach according to constitutional principles; 19. To social security 20. To compensation and a pension; 21. To the freedom to lecture; 22. To have access to the media, pursuant to Article 35 of the constitution; 23. To enjoy an environment that is balanced and appropriate for developing one's life; 24. To health; and 25. To others recognized by the constitution.

[420] See Jorge Mario García La Guardia, "La Constitución y su defensa en Guatemala," in *La Constitución y su defensa*, Universidad Nacional Autónoma de México, México, 1984, pp. 717–719; and *La Constitución Guatemalteca de 1985*, México, 1992.

[421] Therefore, as it is listed in Article 10, every person shall have the right to request amparo, in the following cases, among others: a) To be maintained or reinstated in the enjoyment of the rights and guaranties established in the constitution or any other law. b) To seek a decision to declare, in specific cases, that a law, regulation, resolution or act of the authorities shall not be enforced against the plaintiff because it contravenes or restricts a right that is guaranteed by the constitution or any other law. c) To seek a decision to declare in specific cases, that a provision or resolution (not merely legislative) of the Congress of the Republic is not applicable to the plaintiff since it violates a constitutional right. d) When an authority of any jurisdiction issues a regulation, decision or resolution of any kind, abusing its power or exceeding its legal powers, or when such powers are nonexistent or exercised in such a way that the harm caused or likely to be caused cannot be corrected by any other legal means of defense. e) When in administrative proceedings, the affected party is forced to comply with unreasonable or unlawful requirements, procedures or

In all these cases, when enumerating without limiting the constitutional rights to be protected by means of the amparo and habeas corpus actions, if there is no risk of leaving out constitutional rights to be considered as protected, these statutes undoubtedly are important instruments for the judicial enforcement of rights and for the judicial interpretation of the scope of the rights to be protected.

IV. AMPARO AND HABEAS CORPUS FOR THE PROTECTION OF ONLY SOME CONSTITUTIONAL RIGHTS

Yet if it is true that the general principle is that only constitutional rights are to be protected by means of the amparo and habeas corpus, the fact is that not all the Latin American constitutions guaranty that constitutional protection for all the constitutional rights.

As already mentioned, in contrast with the Latin American general protective trend, in the case of Chile and Colombia, the specific action for *tutela* and for protection of constitutional rights and freedoms are only established in the constitution to protect certain rights and guaranties. In these cases, the scope of the amparo action is a restrictive one, which has also characterized the restrictive systems followed in the German and Spanish constitutions regarding the amparo recourses that are established only for the protection of the so-called "fundamental rights."

Also in Mexico, the amparo is only established for the protection of individual guaranties.

activities, or when there is no means or recourse available to suspend their effect. f) When petitions and procedures before administrative authorities are not resolved in the delay established by law, or, in absence of such delay, within thirty days following the exhaustion of the corresponding procedure; and also when petitions are not admitted for processing. g) In political matters, when rights recognized by the law or by the by laws of political organizations are infringed. Nevertheless, in purely electoral matters, the court analysis and examination shall be limited to legal aspects, accepting such questions of fact that are considered proven in the recourse of review. h) In matters of judicial and administrative order, for which procedures and recourses are established by law, and by means of which such matters may be appropriately discussed in accordance with the legal principle of due process, if after the interested party has made use of the recourses established by law, there is still a threat, restriction or violation of the rights guaranteed by the constitution and the law.

1. *The European restrictive scope of the amparo*

In effect, in Germany the protection of constitutional rights is achieved by means of the constitutional complaint (*Verfassungsbeschwerde*) or recourse that can be brought before the Federal Constitutional Tribunal but only for the protection of some basic or fundamental rights directly violated by State acts.

This individual constitutional recourse, originally provided in the 1951 Federal Statute of the Constitutional Tribunal (Article 90, Federal Constitutional Tribunal Law) was constitutionalized in 1969 as a specific judicial mean for the protection of fundamental rights and freedoms against any action of the State organs that violates them, whether legislative, executive or judicial, including statutes. Yet the expression "fundamental rights" is not equivalent to constitutional rights, so according to Article 93, section 1, N° 4a of the Constitution, the rights to be protected only are the basic or fundamental rights established in Articles 1 to 19[422] and those listed in paragraph 4) of Article 20, under Articles 33, 38, 101, 103 or 104,[423] when violated by public authority (Arts. 90–96 FCT Law).[424]

---

[422]These "fundamental rights" (*Grundrechte*) enshrined in Articles 1 to 19 of the constitution are the following: 1. Man's dignity (Article 1); 2. Freedom to develop its own personality (Article 2,1); 3. Right to life and to physical integrity (Article 2,2); 4. Equality (Article 3); 5, Ideological and Religious freedom (Article 4,1); 6. Freedom of cult (Article 4,2); 7. Conscience objection (Article 4,3 y Article 12,a2); 8. Freedom of expression and to inform (Article 5,1); 9. Freedom to teach and to research (Article 5,3); 10. Marital freedom, family protection and nondiscrimination because of extra-matrimonial birth (Article 6); 11. Right to education (Article 7); 12. Freedom of assembly (Article 8); 13. Freedom of association (Article 9); 14. Inviolability of communications secret (Article 10); 15. Freedom of residence and of movement (Article 11); 16. Freedom to freely choose a profession and the place of work (Article 12); 17. Inviolability of domicile (Article 13); 18. Private property rights and to inherit (Article 14); 19. Right to German nationality (Article 16,1); 20. Right to political asylum for aliens (Article 16-2); and 21. Right to petition (Article 17).

[423]It also can be protected by the constitutional complaint, the constitutional rights enshrined in Articles 20-4, 33, 38, 101, 103 and 104 of the same constitution, which are the following: 21. Right to resist against those who act against the constitutional order (Article 20-4); 22. Equal rights and obligations of Germans in all Statutes of the Federation (Article 33,1); 23. Right to have access in equal terms to public positions (Article 33-2); 24. Right to vote and to be elected (Article 38); 25. Prohibition of extraordinary courts and right to "natural judge" (Article 101); 26. Right to be heard by courts (Article 103-1); 27 Right to *non bis in idem* principle (Article 103-3); and 28. Judicial guaranties for deprivation of liberty (Article 104).

[424]See in general Peter Häberle, "El recurso de amparo en el sistema de jurisdicción constitutcional de la República Federal de Alemania," in Héctor Fix-Zamudio y Eduardo

These rights listed as fundamental rights to be protected by the amparo action are almost all civil and political rights, including in such category of fundamental rights, only some social rights, like family rights and the right to education.

This action has a subordinate character, in the sense that it can only be filed before the Federal Constitutional Tribunal once the ordinary judicial means for the protection of the violated fundamental rights have been exhausted (Article 90, 2 Federal Constitutional Tribunal Law).[425] So only if there are no other judicial recourses or actions that can serve for the purpose of protecting fundamental rights, is the constitutional complaint admissible. The only exception is when the Constitutional Tribunal considers the matter as being of general importance, or when it considers that the plaintiff could suffer a grave and irremediable prejudice if the case was sent to the ordinary judicial means for protection (Article 90, 2 Federal Constitutional Tribunal Law).

In all these cases, the constitutional complaint can be exercised directly against a statute or any other normative state act on the grounds that it directly impairs the fundamental rights of the claimant, in which case the proceeding leads directly to the exercise by the Constitutional Tribunal of judicial review powers regarding normative State acts. As a result of this constitutional complaint, if the statute is considered unconstitutional, it must be declared null (Article 95, 3, B FCT Law).[426]

However, regarding the federal form of the German State, it is important to highlight in relation to this constitutional complaint, that Article

---

Ferrer Mac-Gregor (Coord.), *El derecho de amparo en el Mundo*, Universidad Nacional Autónoma de México, Editorial Porrúa, México, 2006, pp. 695–760.

[425] Article 19.4 of the Constitution establishes in general that "Should any person's rights be violated by public authority, resource to the courts shall be open to him. If jurisdiction is not specified, recourse shall be to the ordinary courts."

[426] The basic condition for the admissibility of constitutional complaints against laws is, of course, the fact that the challenged statute or normative State act, must personally affect the claimant's fundamental rights, in a direct and current way, without the need for any further administrative application of the norm. On the contrary, if this further administrative application is needed, he must wait for the administrative execution of the statute to challenge it. This direct prejudice caused by the normative act on the rights of the claimant, as a basic element for the admissibility of the complaint, justifies the delay of one year after its publication established for the filing of the action before the Tribunal (Article 93, 1, B FCT Law). It also explains the power of the Constitutional Tribunal to adopt provisional protective measures regarding the challenged statute, *pendente litis*, in the sense that the Tribunal can even theoretically suspend the application of the challenged law (Article 32, FCT Law).

93, section 1, N° 4b of the Constitution, also empowers the Constitutional Tribunal to decide on complaints of unconstitutionality, "entered by municipalities or associations of municipalities on the ground that their right to self-government under Article 28 has been violated by a statute."

Hence, the direct constitutional complaint against statutes is not only attributed to individuals for the protection of their fundamental rights, but also to the local government entities for the protection of their autonomy and of their self-government guaranties established in the constitution, against federal statutes that could violate them. In these cases, it also results in a direct mean of judicial review of statutes.

Following the features of the German constitutional complaint, the 1978 Spanish Constitution has also established an amparo recourse only to protect some constitutional rights,[427] which are also qualified as "fundamental rights." The recourse in Spain can be brought before the Constitutional Tribunal by any person with direct interest in the matter against State acts but, contrary to the German regulation, it cannot be filed against legislative acts (Article 161,1,b, Constitution; and Article 41,2 Organic Law 2/1979 of the Constitutional Tribunal, modified by Law 6/2007).[428]

This Spanish recourse for amparo is also reduced to protect only certain constitutional rights and freedoms named "fundamental," which are listed in Article 14, in the first section of the Second Chapter (Articles 15–20) and in the second paragraph of Article 30 of the constitution,[429] also

---

[427]See in general Francisco Fernández Segado, " El recurso de amparo en España," in Héctor Fix-Zamudio y Eduardo Ferrer Mac-Gregor (Coord.), *El derecho de amparo en el Mundo*, Universidad Nacional Autónoma de México, Editorial Porrúa, México, 2006, pp. 789–834; Francisco Rubio Llorente, "Derechos fundamentales, Constitución y Tratados," in *Memorias. VI Congreso Iberoamericano de Derecho Constitucional*, Universidad Externado de Colombia, Tomo II, Bogotá 1998, pp. 1.133–1.145.

[428]However, if the recourse for protection is based on the fact that the challenged State act is based on a statute that at the same time infringes fundamental rights or freedoms, the Tribunal must proceed to review its constitutionality through the procedural rules established for the direct action or recourse of unconstitutionality (Article 52,2 Organic Law 2/1979 modified by Law 6/2007).

[429]These are 1. Equality before the law (Article 14); 2. Right to life and physical and moral integrity (Article 15); 3. Ideological, religious and freedoms, and freedom of cult (Article 16); 4. Right to personal freedom and safety (Article 17); 5. Right to honor, personal and familiar intimacy and to one's image (Articles 18,1 and 18,4); 6. Inviolability of domicile (Article 182); 7. Secrecy of communications (Article 18,3); 8. Right to freely choose one's residence, to move within the territory and to freely leave Spain (Article 19); 9. Right to freedom of expression and to freely propagate one's thought (Article 20-1-a);

mainly referring to civil and political rights, including just a few social rights like those referring to education and labor. According to the 2007 reform of the Organic Law, the amparo recourse can only be filed when the plaintiff has justified the special constitutional importance of the recourse, which in a certain way has converted the recourse in an objective judicial mean for the protection of the constitution. [430]

In these two European experiences, the German and the Spanish, notwithstanding the very extensive enumeration of fundamental rights that can be protected by means of the amparo recourse before the constitutional Tribunals, the fact is that other constitutional rights listed in the constitutions are not protected by the constitutional action because they have not been qualified as "fundamental rights." They are, of course, protected by means of the ordinary judicial proceedings and in the case of Spain, also by means of the *amparo judicial* filed before ordinary courts. [431]

This limitative approach to the justiciability of rights by means of amparo is the one exceptionally followed in Latin America, in Chile and Colombia; and in another way, in Mexico.

10. Right to produce and to literary, artistic, scientific and technical creations (Article 20,1,b); 11. Freedom of teaching (chair) (Article 20,1,c); 12. Right to communicate and to receive true information by any mean (Article 20,1,d); 13. Right to meet and to demonstrate (Article 21); 14. Right to association (Article 22); 15. Right to participate in public affairs (Article 23,1); 16 Right to equal access to public functions or positions (Article 23,2); 17. Right to obtain effective protection by courts and judges (Article 24,1); 18. Right to have the ordinary and predetermined judge, to defense and to be assisted by a lawyer, to be informed of the accusation, to a public process without undue delays and with the guaranties of using the pertinent means of evidence for its defense, not to self-incriminate, not to confess culpability and to the presumption of innocence (Article 24-2); 19. Principle of criminal legality (nullum crime sine legge) (Article 25,1); 20. Rights of the detainees to paid work and to the benefits of social security, to have access to culture and to the integral development of one's personality (Article 25,2); 21. Right to education and to the liberty to teach (Article 27,1); 22. Freedom to create teaching centers, within the constitutional principles (Article 27,6); 23. Freedom to freely unionized trade (Article 28,1); 24. Right to strike (Article 28,2); 25. Right to personal and collective petition (Article 29); and 26. Right to conscience objection (Article 30,2).

[430]See Francisco Fernández Segado, *La reforma del regimen jurídico-procesal del recurso de amparo*, Ed. Dykingson, Madrid, 2008, p. 88.

[431]See Encarna Carmona Cuenca, "El recurso de amparo constitucional y el recurso de amparo judicial," in *Revista Iberoamericana de Derecho Procesal Constitucional*, Instituto Iberoamericano de Derecho Procesal Constitucional, Editorial Porrúa, n° 5, México, 2006, pp. 3–14.

2. The Chilean acción de protección for determined rights

In Chile, apart from the action of habeas corpus established to protect any individual against unconstitutional arrests, detention or imprisonment; the recourse for protection is established only to guaranty some constitutional rights, listed in Article 19, numbers 1, 2, 3 (paragraph 4), 4, 5, 6, 9 (final paragraph), 11, 12, 13, 15, 16 of the constitution and in the fourth paragraph and numbers 19, 21, 22, 23, 24 and 25 of the same constitution.[432]

The list also mainly refers to civil or individual rights, also including some social rights, like the right to choose a health care system, the freedom to teach and to work, and to trade union affiliation; some economic freedom and property rights; and the right to have an uncontaminated environment.

Apart from all these constitutional rights and freedoms, the other rights enshrined in the constitution have no specific mean of protection, their protection being in charge of the ordinary courts through the ordinary judicial procedures.

3. The Colombian acción de tutela for the protection of fundamental rights

In the case of Colombia, in addition to the habeas corpus, the constitution also sets forth the action for *tutela* which was established in Article 86 of the constitution for the immediate protection of what are called "fundamental constitutional rights."

In effect, Title II of the constitution is devoted to establish the "the rights, guaranties and duties," listing them in three chapters: Chapter 1 contains the list of "fundamental rights"; Chapter 2 lists the social, eco-

---

[432] These rights are the following: 1. The right to life and to physical and psychological integrity (19,1); 2. Equality before the law (19,2); 3. Right to be judged by one's natural judges (19,3); 4. Right to respect for private and public life and the honor of the individual and his family (19,4); 5. Right to the inviolability of home and all forms of private communication (19,5); 6. Freedom of conscience and of manifestation of all cults (19,6); 7. Right to choose the health system (19,9 fine); 8. Freedom of teaching (19,11); 9. Freedom to express opinions and to disseminate information (19,12); 10. Right to assemble (19,13). 11. Right to associate (19,15); 12. Freedom to work, and the right to free selection and contracting (19,16); 13. Right to affiliate with trade unions (19,19); 14. Economic freedom (19,21); 15. Right to nondiscriminatory treatment (19,22); 16. Freedom to acquire ownership (19,23); 17. Property right (19,24); 18. Right of authorship (19,25); and 19. Right to live in a contamination-free environment (20).

nomic and cultural rights; and Chapter 3 refers to the collective rights and to a safe environment.

From this constitutional declaration of rights, it results that only the so-called "fundamental rights" listed in Chapter 1 (Articles 11 to 41) are those constitutional rights to be protected by means of the *actión de tutela*, and the other constitutional rights are excluded from it, and thus protected only by the ordinary judicial means.

On the other hand, Article 85 of the constitution also indicates that among these "fundamental rights," those of "immediate application," are the ones to be protected by the action of *tutela*.[433]

This list also mainly refers to civil and political rights, and regarding the social rights, it includes the freedom to teach. Other rights enshrined in other articles of the Constitution are also qualified as fundamental rights, like the "fundamental rights" of children listed in Article 44 referring to life, physical integrity, health and social security.

Apart from these constitutional rights expressly declared as "fundamental rights," the other constitutional rights have no constitutional protection by means of the action of *tutela* and are to be protected by means of the ordinary judicial proceeding.

Notwithstanding this limitative regulation, even if a right is not expressly provided in the constitution as being "fundamental," the Colombian Constitutional Court, as the supreme interpreter of the constitution, has recognized such character in other rights, extending the *tutela* protection regarding rights not defined as "fundamental," but considered interdependent with others that have such nature, like the right to life.

---

[433] The rights "of immediate application" and therefore susceptible of constitutional protection through the action of *tutela*, are then the following: 1. Right to life (Article 11). 2. Right to not be disappeared, or be submitted to torture or inhuman or degrading treatment (Article 12). 3. Right to equality (Article 13). 4. Right to personality (Article 14). 5. Right to intimacy (Article 15). 6. Right to the free development of own personality (Article 16). 7. Prohibition of slavery, servitude and human trade (Article 17). 8. Freedom of conscience (Article 18). 9. Freedom of cult (Article 19). 10. Freedom of expression (Article 20). 11. Right to honor (Article 21). 12. Right to petition (Article 23). 13. Freedom of movement (Article 24). 14. Right to exercise one's profession (Article 26). 15. Freedom to teach (Article 27). 16. Personal freedom (Article 28). 17. Right to due process and defense (Article 29). 18. Right to habeas corpus (Article 30). 19. Right to review judicial decisions (Article 31). 20. Right to not testify against oneself (Article 33). 21. Prohibition of deportation, life imprisonment or confiscation penalties (Article 34). 22. Right to assemble (Article 37). 23. Right to political participation and to vote (Article 40).

In this respect, in one of its first decisions (n° T-02 of May 8, 1992) issued in a case regarding educational rights, the Constitutional Court ruled that the principal criteria to identify "fundamental rights," is "to determine if they are or not essential rights to human beings"; a task that must always be accomplished by the *tutela* judge, who must start his ruling by analyzing the first ninety-four articles of the constitution and when necessary, apply the open clause regarding human rights inherent to human persons.

Those articles, interpreted by the Constitutional Court in light of the American Convention on Human Rights, allow the Court to infer what can be considered inalienable, inherent and essential rights of human beings, resulting from this approach that in fact, the list of "fundamental rights" contained in Chapter 1 of Title II of the constitution does not exhaust the "fundamental rights" and does not exclude other rights from being considered fundamental and justiciable by means of *tutela* action.[434]

For the purpose of identifying those fundamental rights, the Constitutional Court has also applied the "connection" principle between the constitutional rights, particularly regarding economic, cultural and social rights, ruling that the acceptance of the *tutela* action regarding these rights is possible in cases in which a violation of a fundamental right has also been produced.

For instance, in the decision n° T-406 of June 5, 1992, the Court admitted a *tutela* action brought in a case of public drainage flooding through which the plaintiff claimed the protection of the right to public health, the right to a healthy environment and to the general population's health. Although the action was rejected by the lower court considering that no fundamental rights were involved in the case, the Constitutional Court admitted it considering that the right to have a sewage system, in circumstances in which it could evidently affect constitutional fundamental rights, such as human dignity, right to life, or rights of the disabled, must be considered justiciable by means of *tutela*.[435]

Through this interpretative principle of the connection with fundamental rights, the fact is that the Colombian courts have protected almost all constitutional rights, even those not listed as fundamental rights.

---

[434]See decision T-02 of May 8, 1992, in Manuel José Cepeda, *Derecho Constitucional Jurisprudencial. Las grandes decisiones de la Corte Constitucional*, Legis, Bogotá, 2001, pp. 49–54.

[435]See decision T-406 of June 5, 1992, in *Idem,* pp. 55–63.

4. *The Mexican amparo for the protection of the "individual guaranties"*

In Mexico, the amparo suit is regulated in the constitution (Article 103,1) only for the protection of the "individual guaranties" declared and enumerated in Section I, Articles 1 to 29 of the constitution, which of course does not exhaust the constitutional right.

In this regard, the *jurisprudencia* or judicial obligatory doctrine of the Supreme Court has traditionally considered that "the amparo suit was established...not to safeguard the entire body of the Constitution but to protect the individual guaranties,"[436] listed in the first twenty-nine articles of the constitution.[437] These articles initially comprised the civil rights and some economic (economic freedom and right to work) and social (education) rights. In successive reforms other social rights have been included in the first articles of the constitution, like the rights of the indigenous peoples (Article 2); the rights of the family to be protected; the right to the protection of health; the rights to an adequate environment; the right to dwelling; and the rights of the minors (Article 4).

Before these reforms, and since the nineteenth century, the restrictive approach regarding the enumeration of constitutional rights provoked discussions and interpretations tending to extend the scope of the amparo protection, and as an example, mention must be made of the opinion of Ignacio L. Vallarta, who served as President of the Supreme Court (1878–1882), who sustained that the individual guaranties cannot be reduced to

---

[436] See Suprema Corte de Justicia, *Jurisprudencia de la Suprema Corte*, Thesis 111, II, 246, in Ignacio Burgoa, *El juicio de amparo*, Editorial Porrúa, México, 1991, p. 250, and Richard D. Baker, *Judicial Review in México. A Study of the Amparo Suit*, University of Texas Press, Austin, 1971, p. 112.

[437] These rights are the following: prohibition of slavery and discrimination (Article 1); rights of the indigenous peoples (Article 2); right to education, and right to educate; (Article 3); right to equal treatment; right to the protection of health; right to an adequate environment; right to dwelling; and minors rights (Article 4); economic and occupation freedom and prohibition to render services without remuneration (Article 5); freedom of expression of ideas (Article 6); freedom of writing and publishing (Article 7); right to petition (Article 8); right to assemble and association (Article 9); right to bear arms (Article 10); right to movement and travel (Article 11); prohibition of nobility title (Article 12); right to natural judge (Article 13); guaranty of nonretroactivity of laws, and due process of law rights (Article 14, 19, 20, 21, 23); rights regarding extradition (Article 15); personal freedom and detention and search guaranties (Article 16, 17, 18, 19, 22); right to justice and access to justice (Article 17, 21); freedom of religion (Article 24); right to privacy of correspondence, mail (Article 25); right to inviolability of home (Article 26); right to property and land ownership (Article 27); prohibition of monopolies (Article 28). Articles 1 and 29 regulate the suspension of guaranties.

those enumerated in the first twenty-nine articles of the constitution, and that rights declared in other articles of the constitution could be protected, provided that they contain an explanation, a regulation, or a limitation or extension regarding the individual guaranties.[438]

According to this doctrine, Vallarta concluded by arguing about the admissibility of the amparo suit not only in the cases defined in Article 103, but also "based on the connection of the guaranties found in Section I of the Constitution with articles not included under that heading."[439] This doctrine that has been the main tool for the extension of the constitutional protection of amparo, particularly regarding social guaranties referred to agrarian and labor matters included in Articles 27 and 123 of the constitution, which are also considered as citizens' guaranties.[440]

Notwithstanding this doctrine, the *jurisprudencia* of the Supreme Court has not been uniform when deciding if the rights not included in the first articles of the constitution can be protected by means of amparo. The Supreme Court has maintained for instance that "the violation of political rights does not give grounds for the admissibility of amparo because

---

[438]Vallarta wrote: "In the case of individual guaranties, it will frequently be necessary to refer to texts other than those that define them in order to decide with certainty whether one of them has been violated. Because of the intimate connection that exists between the articles containing guaranties and others that, although they do not mention them, nonetheless presuppose them, explain them or complement them; because of the undeniable correlation that exists between them, [the guaranty] cannot be considered in isolation without weakening them, without contradicting their spirit, without frequently rendering their application impossible...for instance, in order to know if persons may be deprived of the property guaranteed by Article 27, under the form of taxation, it would be necessary to consider Article 31, which provides that [such] contribution be proportional and equitable; similarly, to determine whether the personal liberty defined in Article 5 is violated by requiring the performance of the public services, it would be necessary to [interpret] it in terms of the same Article 31, which specifies certain limits on that liberty... [or] finally, in order to explain the competence to which Article 16 refers, it is necessary to examine Article 50, which established the constitutional distribution of powers between the three branches of government." See Ignacio L. Vallarta, *Cuestiones constitucionales. Votos del C. Ignacio L. Vallarta, Presidente de la Suprema Corte de Justicia en los negocios más notables*, III, pp. 145–149. See the references in Ignacio Burgoa, *El juicio de amparo*, Editorial Porrúa, México, 1991, p. 253; Richard D. Baker, *Judicial Review in México. A Study of the Amparo Suit*, University of Texas Press, Austin, 1971, p. 113.

[439]*Idem.*

[440]See Ignacio Burgoa, *El juicio de amparo*, Editorial Porrúa, México, 1991, p. 263.

these [rights] are not individual guaranties."[441] Yet in other cases, by means of the "connection" doctrine, the Supreme Court has given protection to political rights, by saying that "even when political rights are in question, if the act complained of may involve the violation of individual guaranties, which cannot be judged *apriori*, the complaint... should be admitted."[442]

So even with the constitutional restriction referring to "individual guaranties," by means of the interpretative "connection" principle between rights, in Mexico, the amparo protection has also covered other constitutional rights.

5. *The writ of amparo in the Philippines for the protection of the right to life, liberty and safety*

In the Philippines, the writ of amparo regulated in the Rule promulgated in September 2007 by the Supreme Court, complementing habeas corpus, has been established as a remedy available to any person for the protection of her right to life, liberty and security when violated or threatened with violation by an unlawful act or omission of a public official or employee, or of a private individual or entity (Sec. 1). Even though the Supreme Court was empowered by Section 5,5 of Article VIII of the 1987 Constitution to promulgate rules concerning the "protection and enforcement of constitutional rights," without any distinction regarding rights to be protected, the The Rule on the Writ of Amparo reduced the scope of the protection by means of such writ only to the right to life, to liberty and to security, adding that "the writ shall cover extralegal killings and enforced disappearances or threats thereof," being its main purpose to grant protection orders, inspection orders and production orders in such cases.

---

[441] See Suprema Corte de la Nación, *Jurisprudencia de la Suprema Corte*, thesis 345, III, 645, in Richard D. Baker, *Judicial Review in México. A Study of the Amparo Suit*, University of Texas Press, Austin, 1971, pp. 130, 156.

[442] See Suprema Corte de la Nación, *Jurisprudencia de la Suprema Corte*, thesis 346, III, 656, in Richard D. Baker, *Idem*, p. 157. The Court has ruled that: "although the Court has established that amparo is inadmissible against the violation of political rights, this jurisprudence refers to cases in which federal protection is sought against authorities exercising political functions and whose acts are directly and exclusively related to the exercise of rights of that nature. It cannot be applied to cases in which amparo is sought against judicial decisions, that although affecting political rights, may also violate individual guaranties." See Suprema Corte de la Nación, Mendoza Eustaquio y otros, 10 S. J. (475) (1922), in Richard D. Baker, *Idem*, pp. 130, 156.

V. THE QUESTION OF THE PROTECTION OF RIGHTS IN SITUA-
TIONS OF EMERGENCY

Another question that must also be mentioned regarding the justiciability of constitutional rights by means of the amparo action is the scope and extension of such constitutional protection and the admissibility of amparo actions in situations of emergency.

For instance, the question was discussed and additionally was regulated in Article 6,7 of the 1988 Venezuelan Amparo Law, which established that the amparo action was inadmissible "in case of suspensions of rights and guaranties" when in cases of interior or exterior conflict, a situation of emergency was declared. This provision was, of course, tacitly repealed, due to the prevalent rank of the American Convention on Human Rights regarding internal law (Article 23 of the 1999 Constitution), which on the contrary provides that even in cases of emergency, the judicial guaranties of constitutional rights cannot be suspended.

In this sense, the prevalent regulation in Latin America is that the actions for amparo and habeas corpus can always be filed even in situations of exception, as for instance it is expressly declared in Article 1 of the Decree regulating the action for *tutela* in Colombia. Regarding the habeas corpus, in a similar sense, Article 62 of the Nicaraguan Law of Amparo sets forth that in case of suspension of the constitutional guaranties of personal freedom, the recourse for personal exhibition will remain in force. The Peruvian Constitutional Procedural Code also establishes the principle that during the emergency regimes, the amparo and habeas corpus, as well as all the other constitutional proceedings, will not be suspended.[443]

In the case of Argentina, regarding the habeas corpus guaranty, the Habeas Corpus Law sets forth that in case of state of siege when personal freedom is restricted, the habeas corpus proceeding is admissible when directed to prove, in the particular case: 1) The legitimacy of the declaration of state of siege; 2) The relation between the freedom-depriving order

---

[443] According to Article 23 of the Code, when the recourses are filed in relation to the suspended rights, the court must examine the reasonability and the proportionality of the restrictive act, following these criteria: 1) If the claim refers to constitutional rights not suspended; 2) If referred to the suspended rights, the founding of the right's restrictive act do not have direct relation with the motives justifying the declaration of state of emergency; 3) If referred to the suspended rights, the right's restrictive act happens to be evidently unnecessary or unjustified bearing in mind the conduct of the aggrieved party or the factual situation briefly evaluated by the judge.

and the situation that originates the declaration of state of siege; and 3) The illegitimate worsening of the detention conditions.

The matter was definitively resolved in October 1986 by the Inter-American Court of Human Rights by means of an Advisory Opinion that was requested by the Inter-American Commission seeking the interpretation of Articles 25,1 and 7,6 of the American Convention on Human Rights, in order to determine if the writ of habeas corpus was one of the judicial guaranties that, pursuant to the last clause of Article 27,2 of that Convention, may not be suspended by a State Party to the Convention.[444]

In its *Advisory Opinion OC-8/87* of January 30, 1987 (Habeas Corpus in Emergency Situations), the Inter-American Court on Human Rights declared that if it is true that "in serious emergency situations it is lawful to temporarily suspend certain rights and freedoms whose free exercise must, under normal circumstances, be respected and guaranteed by the State...it is imperative that "the judicial guaranties essential for (their) protection" remain in force (Article 27,2);"[445] adding that these "judicial remedies that must be considered to be essential within the meaning of Article 27(2) are those that ordinarily will effectively guaranty the full exercise of the rights and freedoms protected by that provision and whose denial or restriction would endanger their full enjoyment."[446]

---

[444] Article 27 of the Convention authorizes States, in time of war, public danger, or other emergency that threatens the independence or security of a State Party, to take measures derogating from its obligations under the Convention; but with the express declaration that such does not authorize any suspension of the following articles: Article 3 (Right to Juridical Personality), Article 4 (Right to Life), Article 5 (Right to Humane Treatment), Article 6 (Freedom from Slavery), Article 9 (Freedom from Ex Post Facto Laws), Article 12 (Freedom of Conscience and Religion), Article 17 (Rights of the Family), Article 18 (Right to a Name), Article 19 (Rights of the Child), Article 20 (Right to Nationality), and Article 23 (Right to Participate in Government), or of the judicial guaranties essential for the protection of such rights.

[445] *Advisory Opinion OC-8/87 of January 30, 1987, Habeas corpus in emergency situations*, Paragraph 27. See in Sergio García Ramírez (Coord.), *La Jurisprudencia de la Corte Interamericana de Derechos Humanos*, Universidad Nacional Autónoma de México, Corte Interamericana de Derechos Humanos, México, 2001, pp. 1.008 ff.

[446] Paragraph 29. The Court also advises that the guaranties must be not only essential but also judicial, an expression that "can only refer to those judicial remedies that are truly capable of protecting these rights" before independent and impartial judicial bodies (Paragraph 30); concluding that: "Paragraph 42. From what has been said before, it follows that writs of habeas corpus and of amparo are among those judicial remedies that are essential for the protection of various rights whose derogation is prohibited by Article 27(2) and that serve, moreover, to preserve legality in a democratic society." Paragraph 43: "The Court must also observe that the constitutions and legal systems of the Member States that

Also in 1986, the Government of Uruguay requested from the Inter-American Court an Advisory Opinion regarding the scope of the prohibition of the suspension of the judicial guaranties essential for the protection of the rights mentioned in Article 27,2 of the American Convention; resulting in the issue of the *Advisory Opinion OC-9/87* of October 6, 1987 (Judicial Guaranties in States of Emergency), in which the Court, following its aforementioned *Advisory Opinion OC-8/97*, empathized that "the declaration of a state of emergency... cannot entail the suppression or ineffectiveness of the judicial guaranties that the Convention requires the Member States to establish for the protection of the rights not subject to derogation or suspension by the state of emergency"; concluding that "therefore, any provision adopted by virtue of a state of emergency which results in the suspension of those guaranties is a violation of the Convention."[447]

The Inter-American Court also indicated that the "essential" judicial guaranties that are not subject to suspension, "include those judicial procedures, inherent to representative democracy as a form of government (Article 29(c)), provided for in the laws of the Member States as suitable for guarantying the full exercise of the rights referred to in Article 27(2) of the Convention and whose suppression or restriction entails the lack of protection of such rights"; and that "the above judicial guaranties should be exercised within the framework and the principles of due process of law, expressed in Article 8 of the Convention."[448]

This doctrine of the Inter-American Court, without doubt, is a very important one regarding the protection of human rights in Latin America, particularly when considering the unfortunate past experiences that some countries have had in situations of emergency or of state of siege, particularly under military dictatorship or internal civil war cases. In such cases, no effective judicial protection was available regarding persons' life and physical integrity; being at some times impossible to prevent their disap-

---

authorize, expressly or by implication, the suspension of the legal remedies of habeas corpus or of amparo in emergency situations cannot be deemed to be compatible with the international obligations imposed on these States by the Convention." *Idem.*

[447] *Advisory Opinion OC-9/87* of October 6, 1987, *Judicial Guaranties in States of Emergency*, Paragraphs 25, 26. The conclusion of the Court then was: 1. That the "essential" judicial guaranties that are not subject to derogation, according to Article 27(2) of the Convention, include habeas corpus (Article 7,6), amparo, and any other effective remedy before judges or competent tribunals (Article 25,1), which is designed to guaranty the respect of the rights and freedoms whose suspension is not authorized by the Convention (Paragraph 41,1). *Idem,* pp. 1.019 ff.

[448] *Idem*, Paragraph 41,2 and 41,3.

pearance or their whereabouts to be kept secret; and being impossible in other times to have effective means to protect persons against torture or other cruel, inhumane, or degrading punishment or treatment.

So after such past experiences, according to the Inter-American Court on Human Rights doctrine following the provisions of the American Convention, it can be said that, in general, in Latin America, exception made of some authoritarian regimes,[449] the discussion that has been held in the United States regarding the possibility to exclude the habeas corpus protection to the so-called "combatant enemies," which were kept for years in custody without any judicial guaranty to protect their rights, could not be held.[450]

---

[449] As has been the case, unfortunately, of Venezuela where for instance, in October 2007, the National Assembly of Venezuela, discussed a constitutional reform draft for the consolidation of a Socialist, Centralized, Militaristic and Police State, as proposed by the President of the Republic, approving the elimination of the prohibition established in Article 337 of the constitution, for the President to suspend, in cases of state of emergency or exception, the peoples' right to be informed and to the process of law guaranties (see in *El Universal*, Caracas, October 11, 2007), which is a regression regarding human rights protection, and a provision contrary to what is established in the American Convention on Human Rights.

[450] The matter was decided by the Supreme Court in *Rasul v. Bush*, 542 U.S. 466; 124 S. Ct. 2686; 159 L. Ed. 2d 548; 2004 in a case referred to aliens captured abroad, from 2002 and onward, by United States authorities during hostilities with the Taliban regime in Afghanistan, and that were held in executive detention at the Guantanamo Bay Naval Base in Cuba. They filed various habeas corpus actions in the United States District Court for the District of Columbia against the United States and some federal and military officials, alleging that they were being held in federal custody in violation of the laws of the United States, that they had been imprisoned without having been charged with any wrongdoing, permitted to consult counsel, or provided access to courts or other tribunals. The District Court's jurisdiction was invoked under the federal habeas corpus provision (28 USCS § 2241(c)(3)) that authorized Federal District Courts to entertain habeas corpus applications by persons claiming to be held in custody "in violation of the Constitution or laws or treaties of the United States." The District Court dismissed the actions for want of jurisdiction, on the asserted ground that aliens detained outside the sovereign territory of the United States could not invoke a habeas corpus petition; and the United States Court of Appeals for the District of Columbia Circuit, in affirming, concluded that the privilege of litigation in United States courts did not extend to aliens in military custody who had no presence in any territory over which the United States was sovereign (355 US App DC 189,321 F3d 1134). On certiorari, the United States Supreme Court reversed and remanded, holding that the District Court had jurisdiction, under 28 USCS § 2241, to review the legality of the plaintiffs' detention. Notwithstanding this Supreme Court decision, the Senate of the United States voted on November 2005 an amendment to a military budget bill, to strip captured "enemy combatants" at Guantánamo Bay of the legal tool given to them by the Supreme Court when it allowed them to challenge their detentions in United States' courts. Next year, in 2006 the Congress rewrote the law limiting the detainees'

As mentioned before, a law banning the habeas corpus action could not be proposed in Latin American countries, due to its regulation in the constitutions and in the American Convention on Human Rights as a right that cannot be suspended even in situations of emergency.

The same occurs, for instance, regarding personal freedom related to the length of administrative detention that in general terms is established in the Latin American constitutions. Thus no legal regulation or amendments can be approved extending police custody length, as for instance has occurred in Europe also due to the war against terrorism.[451] In Latin America, on the contrary, due to the constitutional rank of the regulation, the only way to extend police custody length restriction is through a constitutional amendment or reform; or through *de facto* ways.

However, in these latter cases, unfortunately, even with all the constitutional regulations and restrictions, the problems of the effective protection of constitutional rights remains in Latin America, basically because the absence or restricted independence and autonomy of the Judiciary

avenues of appeal, and in October 2006 the Military Commission Act was signed by the President, which eliminated the federal courts' jurisdiction over habeas corpus challenges by such prisoners ("enemy combatants"). In a decision of February 20, 2007 the United States Court of Appeals for the District of Columbia (*Lakhdar Boumediene v. George W. Bush*, February, 20, 2007, 375 U.S. App. D.C. 48; 476 F.3d 981) found that the new law did not violate the constitutional provision that bars the government from suspending habeas corpus except in "cases of rebellion or invasion," considering that the right of habeas corpus did not extend to foreign citizens detained outside the United States. The Supreme Court in *Boumediene v. Bush*, April 2, 2007, 127 S. Ct. 1478; 167 L. Ed. 2d 578, denied certiorari applying the traditional rules governing the court's decision of constitutional questions and the court's practice, of requiring the exhaustion of administrative remedies as a precondition to accepting jurisdiction over the habeas applications.

[451] In 2006, France extended the period of detention without charge for terror suspects from four to six days; in Italy, the custody was extended from twelve to twenty-four hours and the police were authorized to interrogate detainees in the absence of their lawyers. In 2003, Spain extended the period for which suspected terrorists can be held effectively incommunicado to a maximum of thirteen days; and in 2006, in the United Kindom the period during which a terror suspect can be held in custody without charge was extended to twenty-eight days (in 2001 it was just forty-eight hours). See the report "Europe Takes Harder Line with Terror Suspects," by Katrin Bennhold, *The New York Times*, April 17, 2006. In June 2008, the House of Commons vote a counter-terrorism bill extending the maximum period a terrorist suspect may be detained without charge up to fourty two days. See the report "Detention without charge. Home and dry, just," in *The Economist*, Volume 387, Number 8584, June 14th–20th 2008, pp. 40-41. In Canada, the Supreme Court struck down a law that allows the Canadian government to detain foreign-born terrorism suspects indefinitely using secret evidence and without charges while their deportations are being reviewed. See the report of Ian Austen, "Canadian Court Limits Detention in Terror Cases," *The New York Times*, February 24, 2007.

that many countries still have, whose independence is the essential condition for the enforcement of rights.

CHAPTER ELEVEN

THE QUESTION OF THE JUSTICIABILITY OF SOCIAL CONSTITUTIONAL RIGHTS BY MEANS OF THE AMPARO ACTIONS

I. THE QUESTION OF THE JUSTICIABILITY OF SOCIAL RIGHTS

The most important question regarding the justiciability of constitutional rights in Latin America by means of the amparo action refers to the justiciability of economic, social and cultural rights. In some countries many of those rights are not declared in the constitutions, consequently lacking of constitutional judicial protection because not having constitutional rank. In other countries, as is the case of Colombia and Chile, many of those social rights are not considered as "fundamental rights" that are in general, the only ones that can be protected by means of the *tutela* and protection actions.

Yet even in countries that do not establish any distinction regarding the protected rights, the question of the justiciability of those economic, social and cultural rights continues to be an important issue, particularly because in some cases some sort of additional legislation is required for their full enforcement.

These rights, particularly the social rights, generally imply the obligation for the State to provide or render services or to accomplish activities, for which public expenses must be allocated regarding each service, depending on the political decisions of the government. Consequently, it has been sustained that the provisions establishing such rights can only be enforceable after the sanctioning by Congress of legislation providing the scope of their enjoyment as well as of the State's obligations, and after the adoption of specific public policies by the Executive. Yet such approach has been questioned particularly based in the principle of the connection that exists between social and civil rights, which implies the need to consider new principles deriving from the concept of the Social State and the functioning of the Welfare State.

For instance, in this regard, the Colombian Constitutional Court in its decision N° T-406 of June 5, 1992, established the principle that these rights have their *raison d'étre* in the fact that their minimal satisfaction is an indispensable condition for the enjoyment of the civil and political rights, that "without the respect of human dignity regarding the material conditions of existence, any aspiration of effectively enforcing the classical freedoms and egalitarian rights enshrined in the Constitution, would be just simple and useless formalism." That is why the Constitutional Court considered that "the judicial intervention in cases of economic, social and cultural rights is necessary when it is indispensable in order to assure the respect of other constitutional fundamental rights." Consequently, according to the Constitutional Court, the enforcement of social, economic and cultural rights cannot be confined to the political link existing between the Constituent and the Legislator, in the sense that the constitution's efficiency cannot only be in the hands of the Legislator. On the contrary, "the constitutional provisions would have no value, [if] the Constituent's will is subjected to the Legislator will."[452]

Nonetheless, based on these arguments, the Constitutional Court of Colombia concluded its ruling saying that due to the fact that "the application of social, economic and cultural rights gives rise to the political problem of deciding the allocation of public funds, the admission of *tutela* regarding social, economic and cultural rights can only be accepted in cases where a violation of a fundamental right exists."[453] From this ruling, the principle of the "connection" between social rights and fundamental rights regarding their justiciability, which has been developed in other countries like Mexico (right to life) and the United States (nondiscrimination), has also been applied in Colombia.[454]

---

[452] See decision T-406 of June 5, 1992, in Manuel José Cepeda, *Derecho Constitucional Jurisprudencial. Las grandes decisiones de la Corte Constitucional*, Legis, Bogotá, 2001, p. 61.

[453] *Idem*. p. 61

[454] For instance, the Constitutional Court has protected the right to health of a military servicemen to be treated in a military hospital, even though he was not formally entitled to have such treatment because he had not given his military oath, considering that the right must be protected "when the health service is needed and is indispensable, in order to preserve the right to life, in which cases the State is obligated to render it to needy persons." See Decision T-534 of September 24, 1992, *Idem*, pp. 461 ff.

Consequently, when no such connection between a fundamental right and a social one exists, the latter cannot in itself be protected by means of a *tutela* action, as for instance was the case of the constitutional right to have proper dwelling or housing, regarding which, the same Colombian Constitutional Court ruled that in that case, "as well as regarding other rights of social, economic and cultural contents, no subjective right is given to persons to ask the State in a direct and immediate way in its complete satisfaction."[455]

Those problems, related to the political conditions for the enforcement of some social, economic and cultural rights, have been the basis for the discussion in contemporary constitutional law, not on whether those rights, like education, health, social welfare or housing have or not constitutional rank, but on their justiciability, that is to say, the possibility of their enforcement by means of judicial actions against the State.

II.   THE CASE OF THE RIGHT TO HEALTH AND THE STATE OBLIGATIONS

This discussion has been raised regarding many social rights, and particularly, regarding the right of the people to health, and consequently the obligation of the State in terms of providing public health services.

In almost all the Latin American constitutions, even if the constitutional fundamental character and rank of social, economic and cultural rights has been recognized, the courts have not always granted the amparo protection for their enforcement, particularly when brought against the State. The justiciability of the rights and the scope of the claimed protection, in many cases have been conditioned by the way the right is declared in the constitutions, particularly when the provisions are set forth as "programmatic" ones; an expression that refers to provisions having their contents conceived as a program directed to the Congress in order to legislate and which are not directly enforceable.

On the other hand, regarding for instance the right to health, not all the Latin American constitutions have declared it at all, and when declared, it has not been expressed in the same way. Some constitutions refer to health as a public good, as is the case in El Salvador (Article 65) and Guatemala (Article 95), providing that not only the State but also the individuals have the duty to take care of its preservation and restoration.

[455]See Decision T-251 of June 5, 1995, *Idem*, p. 486.

In contrast, in other constitutions, like those of Bolivia (Article 7,a), Brazil (Articles 6 and 196); Ecuador (Article 46); Nicaragua (Article 59) and Venezuela (Article 84), it is provided for the "right to health" as a constitutional right and even as a "fundamental" constitutional right (Venezuela, Article 83), corresponding in equal terms to everybody, as it is also expressed in the Constitution of Nicaragua (Article 59). This principle of equal treatment is reaffirmed in the Constitution of Guatemala, by providing that "the enjoyment of health is a fundamental right of human beings, without any kind of discrimination" (Article 93).

In other constitutions the right to health derives from the recognition of constitutional rank to the International Covenant on Economic, Social and Cultural rights, as is the case in Argentina (Article 75).

Now, with this constitutional formula of the "right to health," what the constitutions have established is a constitutional right of everybody to have their health protected by the State, which conversely has the obligation, together with all Society, to care for the maintenance and recuperation of people's health.

That is why other Latin American constitutions, instead of providing for the "right to health," set forth in a more precise way for the right of persons "to have their health protected," as it is established in Honduras (Article 145), Chile (Article 19,9), Mexico (Article 4), Peru (Article 7), Cuba (Article 50) and Colombia (Article 49). This implies, in general terms, as it is provided in the Constitution of Panama, that this is a "right to the promotion, protection, maintenance, restitution and rehabilitation of health, and an obligation to maintain it; health understood as the complete physical, mental and social welfare" (Article 105) This right, as it is also declared in the Constitution of Paraguay, implies the obligation of the State "in the interest of community, to protect and promote health as a fundamental right of persons" (Article 68).

Consequently, this right to health, in the sense of a right to be protected by the State, eventually implies a right for all people to have equal access to the public services established for the purpose of taking care of people's health, as it is set forth in the Constitution of Chile, which provides that "the State protects free and equal access to the actions for promotion, protection and recovery of health and of rehabilitation of the individuals" (Article 19,9).

In order to guaranty the access to health services, the Latin American constitutions follow different approaches, from free general access to limited access regarding specific circumstances. Free access is for instance guaranteed in the Cuban Constitution, which sets forth that the

State guaranties the rights of persons to have their health taken care of and protected by means of "rendering free public medical and hospital assistance" (Article 50).

In the case of Chile, a distinction is made between public programs and public services, providing that, on the one hand, "public health programs and actions are free for all"; and on the other, that "public services of medical attention will be free [only] for those who need them" (Article 43), stipulating that "in no case will emergency attention be denied neither in public nor private premises" (Article 43).

In general terms, the principle of free public health care, as a constitutional right is established in the constitutions in benefit of persons lacking financial support and in all cases, where the general public health needs to be protected. In this sense, the Constitution of El Salvador declares that the State must "give free assistance to sick persons lacking resources and in general to all inhabitants, when the treatment is an efficient mean to prevent the dissemination of a transmissible disease" (Article 66).

Regarding the former situation, for instance in Uruguay, the constitution sets forth that "the State must freely provide the means for protection and of assistance only to the needy and to those without enough resources" (Article 44); and in Panama, the constitution establishes that "these health services and medication will be freely rendered to whomever lacks economic resources" (Article 106).

Regarding the latter situation, for instance, the Constitution of Paraguay sets forth that "nobody will be deprived of public assistance in order to prevent or treat diseases, pests or plague, and of help in cases of catastrophes or accidents" (Article 68).

In other cases, the constitutions only express general principles referring to the regulations that must be established by statute. This is the case of the Colombian Constitution (Article 49), which requires the Legislator to "define the terms through which the basic attention for all the inhabitants will be free and obligatory"; and this is also the case of the Mexican Constitution, which indicates that "the rules and conditions for access to health services" must be established by statutes (Article 4).

From all these constitutional regulations, in addition to the general solidarity duties that are imposed on everyone in order to seek for preserving healthy conditions, a series of constitutional duties are also imposed on the State and public entities, which eventually are the ones that determine the scope of their justiciability.

For instance, the Panamanian Constitution provides that "it is an essential function of the State to care for the health of the population" (Article 105); and the Constitution of Guatemala, sets forth as an "obligation of the State" to take "care of the health and social assistance of all inhabitants" and to "develop," through its institutions, "actions for the prevention, promotion, recovery, rehabilitation and coordination in order to seek the most complete physical, mental and social welfare" (Article 94).

The Venezuelan Constitution, after declaring health as a fundamental right, also provides as an obligation of the State, the guaranty of health as part of the right to life (Article 83); and the Honduran Constitution sets forth that "the State must maintain an adequate environment for the protection of people's health" (Article 145).

In this matter of the State's obligations regarding health, other constitutions contain more detailed regulations, as is the case, for instance, of Cuba regarding hospital assistance (Article 50); Panama (Article 106) and Bolivia (Article 158,1) regarding general policies assigned to the State. In this same sense, for instance, the Constitution of Ecuador, establishes that the State guarantees the right to health, and the promotion and protection of health, "by means of the development of the alimentary safety, the provision of drinking water and basic sanitation, the promotion of family, labor and community healthy environment and the possibility to have permanent an uninterrupted access to health services, according the equity, universality, solidarity, quality and efficiency principles" (Article 42). In addition, in Ecuador, the State must promote "the culture for health and life, with emphasis in alimentary and nutrition education of mothers and child and in sexual and reproductive health, by means of societal participation and the social media collaboration" (Article 43). For such purpose, the State must formulate "a national health policy and will watch for its application; will control the functioning of sector entities; will recognize, respect and promote the development of traditional and alternative medicine, the exercise of which will be regulated by statute, and will promote the scientific and technological advancement in health care, subjected to bioethics principles. The State will also adopt programs tending to eradicate alcoholism and other toxic manias" (Article 44).

In a similar sense, the Constitution of Peru provides that "the State must establish the health policy" (Article 9); and the Constitution of El Salvador prescribes that "the State will determine the national health policy and will control and supervise its application" (Article 65). In Nicaragua, the constitution sets forth that the State must establish basic conditions for health promotion, protection, recovery and rehabilitation, and that it must direct and organize health programs, services and actions and promote popular participation in its defense" (Article 59).

In Brazil, the State has the constitutional duty to guaranty health as a right of everyone, "through social and economic policies tending to reduce the risk of sickness and providing a universal and equal access to actions and services for health promotion, protection and recovery" (Article 196).

According to all these expressed constitutional provisions, in some cases vague and in others with very detailed and precise expressions, the protection of health can be considered in general terms as a constitutional obligation of the State, which does not exclude the possibility for individuals to render health care services. So the services for the protection of health can be provided not only by the State, accomplishing an exclusive obligation, as is the case of Cuba, but also by individuals. That is, health services can be public or private; so the Chilean Constitution guaranties the right of "everyone to choose the health care system wanted to be received, whether public or private" (Article 19). This provision also implies the existence of another constitutional right of individuals to render health care services, as an economic right.

This is expressly set forth in the Brazilian Constitution where it is provided that "sanitary assistance is of free private initiative," but subject to express constitutional restrictions, like the possible participation of private institutions in the Unique Health Services (Article 199). Other Latin American constitutions also contain general principles regarding public and private health care services, integrated into a national or unique system (Chile, Article 45; Paraguay, Article 69; Venezuela, Article 84).

Except for the two mentioned cases of the Chilean (Article 19) and Brazilian (Article 197) constitutions, in the other Latin American constitutions references are made to private initiative to render health care services in an indirect way, when attributing to the State the express power to regulate all health care services, as it is provided in the Constitutions of Venezuela (Article 85), Uruguay (Article 44), Honduras (Article 149) and Colombia (Article 49).

The general consequence of all these provisions in the constitutions establishing State obligations to render health care services to satisfy people's constitutional right to be protected, is that such obligations are always materialized in the establishment of public health care services to render care to the people. This is expressly provided in the Colombian Constitution when it declares that "health care and environment sanitation are public services to be rendered by the care of the State" (Article 49); and in the Bolivian Constitution when providing that "social services are State functions," being the norms providing for public health, of "coactive and obligatory character" (Article 164).

In all these cases, the consequence of a constitutional provision establishing the obligation of the State to render a public service to take care of individual's health, is the existence of a constitutional right to use those services, which consequently implies that in principle, they can be judicially claimed and enforced against the State.

III. THE JUSTICIABILITY OF THE RIGHT TO HEALTH

Yet the fact is that the justiciability of the right to health has not had the same solution in all of Latin America.

It is clear, according to all the constitutional regulations that have been mentioned, that a person's constitutional right to health care is generally provided, particularly due to the obligations imposed on the States to render services for the maintenance and recovery of health. However, these provisions and the way they are conceived are, precisely, the ones that raise the question of the justiciability of such right to health, particularly by means of the amparo recourses or actions as specific judicial means for the protection of human rights.

This judicial enforceability of course depends on the way the specific regulations are established in the constitutions and in the statutes on the matter. For example, only in exceptional cases are such judicial protection for the enforceability of the right to health expressly provided for, as is the case in Peru, where the Constitutional Procedure Code expressly sets forth that the amparo recourse can be filed for the defense of the right "to health" (Article 37,24). In the case of Chile, the constitution only refers to the recourse for protection regarding the "right to choose the system of health care" (Article 19,9).

Apart from these two provisions, no other express constitutional or legal regulation exists in Latin America regarding the amparo proceeding for the protection of the right to health, which of course does not exclude such possible judicial protection. On the contrary, the jurisprudence in many countries has shown that as a matter of principle, amparo actions can be brought before the courts for the protection of the people's right to health, although not in a uniform way.

In this regard, from decisions issued by the Constitutional Courts or Constitutional Chambers of Supreme Courts, for instance, in Argentina,

Peru, Colombia, Costa Rica, Chile and Venezuela, or by lower courts in Argentina, it is possible to distinguish at least four general tendencies.

The first tendency can be identified with the protection of health as a collective right, based in collective interest. The second tendency is characterized by granting a wide protection to the right to health in specific cases in connection with the right to life and when a particular legal relationship is established or exists between the plaintiff and the public entity acting as the defendant party, like the one derived from the Social Security programs to which the individual contributes. In this case because of the intimate "connection" with other fundamental rights, like the right to life, the courts have also rejected the "programmatic" character attributed to the right to health. The third tendency is the granting of a limited judicial protection to the right to health, subjected to the existing State policy on the matter, particularly regarding the allocation and availability of public funds. Finally, a fourth tendency can be identified when the protection is denied in cases of abstract claims.

1. *The protection of the right to health as a collective right*

The first tendency of the justiciability of the right to health is based in its consideration as a collective right, as it is established in the International Covenant on Economic, Social and Cultural Rights, where Article 12,1 provides that the States Parties "recognize the right of everyone to the enjoyment of the highest attainable standard of physical and mental health," and consequently, according to Article 12,2,c, it is prescribe that the steps to be taken by the States Parties to achieve the full realization of this right shall include those necessary for "the prevention, treatment and control of epidemic, endemic, occupational and other diseases."

In Argentina, the constitution (Article 75,22) has given constitutional rank to the International Covenant, and as a consequence of this, the collective right to health has been enforced by the courts. It was the case of an amparo action decided by the Federal Administrative Court of Appeals on June 2, 1998 (*Viceconte, Mariela c. Estado Nacional (Ministerio de Salud y Ministerio de Economía de la Nación) s/ Acción de Amparo* case), that was filed as a collective amparo by Mariela Viceconte seeking to force the State to produce the *Candid 1* vaccine, based on her own right to health and that of other few millions of persons exposed to contracting "Argentine Hemorrhagic Fever." The plaintiff specifically alleged a violation of the obligation to prevent, treat and fight epidemic and endemic diseases arising from Article 12.2.c of the International Covenant on Economic, Social and Cultural Rights, and the Court of Appeals concluded that the State's failure to arrange the production of the vaccine was a violation of the right to health under such article of the Covenant. Therefore, the Court ruled that the State had the obligation to manufacture the vaccine and ordered it to comply strictly and without delays with a schedule that had already been designed for such purposes by the Ministry of Health. The Court also asked the National Ombudsman to follow up on the schedule.[456]

2. *The protection of the right to health in connection to the right to life and the social security obligations*

The second tendency regarding the justiciability of the right to health by means of amparo refers to its protection in particular situations, derived from the specific social security obligations regarding specific insured persons.

As an example, the decision of the Constitutional Chamber of the Supreme Tribunal of Justice of Venezuela decision n° 487 of April 6, 2001, (*Glenda López y otros vs. Instituto Venezolano de los Seguros Sociales* case) can be mentioned, through which an HIV/AIDS infected person who filed an action against the Institute for Social Security was protected, compelling the Institute to provide medical attention to the plaintiff. In its decision, the Court pointed out that the right to health or to the protection of health is "an integral part of the right to life, set forth in the Constitution as a fundamental social right (and not simply as an assignment of State purposes) whose satisfaction mainly belongs to the State and its institutions, through activities intended to progressively raise the quality of life of citizens and the collective welfare." This implies, according to the Court's decision that "the right to health is not to be exhausted with the simple physical care of a person, but must be extended to the appropriate treatment in order to safeguard the mental, social, environmental integrity of persons, including the community."

In this particular case decided by the Court, the violation of the right to health and the threats to the right to life was alleged as caused by the Venezuelan Institute for Social Security, which the plaintiff considered

---

[456]See the reference in M. Claudia Caputi, "Reseña jurisprudencial. La tutela judicial de la salud y su reivindicación contra los entes estatales," in *Revista Iberoaméricana de Estudios Autonómicos*, n° 2, Goberna & Derecho, Guayaquil, 2006, pp. 145–164.

was due to "give complete medical care to its affiliates." The Constitutional Chamber ruled that because of the omission of the Institute "to provide to the plaintiffs, in a regular and permanent way, the drugs for the treatment of HIV/AIDS prescribed by the specialist attached to a specific Hospital..., and to practice the specialized medical exams directed to help the efficient treatment of HIV/AIDS"; the right to health and even the right to life of the plaintiff were put in danger.[457]

This connection between the right to health and other fundamental rights, such as the right to life, which can immediately be protected by means of amparo, has also been the tendency followed by the courts in Argentina, Colombia, Costa Rica and Peru.

As aforementioned, in Colombia, the constitution does not include the right to health or to the protection of health within the list of the "fundamental rights," which are the only ones protected by means of the action of *tutela*. Nonetheless, the Constitutional Court, in order to assure its judicial protection, has applied the principle of the connection of the right to health with the right to life. It was the case in decision n° T-484/92 of August 11, 1992, issued when reviewing a lower court's *tutela* decision that was filed against the Institute of Social Security. The plaintiff in the case, also infected with HIV/AIDS, claimed that he was infected while covered by the Social Security program. The claimant had a favorable decision from the first instance Court that ordered the Institute to continue to render the health care services that the plaintiff had been receiving, and the Constitutional Court, when reviewing the case, affirmed that "health is one of those assets that because of its inherent character to the dignified existence of man, is protected, especially regarding persons that because of their economic, physical or mental conditions are in a manifest weakened condition" (Article 13, Constitution). Considering the right to health as being a right that "seeks the assurance of the fundamental right to life" (Article 11, Constitution), the Court ruled that due to its assistance nature, it implies the need for health care to be rendered by public entities, in order for its effective protection."[458]

---

[457]See in *Revista de Derecho Público*, n° 85–88, Editorial Jurídica Venezolana, Caracas, 2001, pp. 139–141.

[458]File n° 2130, *Alonso Muñoz Ceballos* case. See in the same sense, Decision T-534, September 24, 1992, in Manuel José Cepeda, *Derecho Constitucional Jurisprudencial. Las grandes decisiones de la Corte Constitucional*, Legis, Bogotá, 2001, pp. 461 ff.

In addition, the Court developed two sorts of arguments when connecting the right to health with the right to life. First, those that identify the right to health as an immediate condition for the right of life, in which case the harm to a person's health would be equivalent to a threat to his life. Consequently, for instance, actions harming the safe environment (Article 49,1) are to be treated in a concurrent way regarding health problems, resulting in a fundamental right. The second argument tends to connect the right to health to the assistance character of the concept of the Welfare State, in the sense that its recognition in the constitution imposes concrete public actions that must be developed through legislation in order to render public services not only for medical assistance, but also for hospital, pharmaceutical and laboratory rights. The link between the right to health and the right to be assisted, although imprecise and subject to the circumstances of each case (Article 13, Constitution), always allows the Court to construct the existence of the right to health considering "that the right to health is fundamental when related to the protection of life."

Based on these argument, the Court, regarding the particular case of the petitioner infected with HIV/AIDS who received treatment from the health care services of the Institute for Social Security, ratified the lower court's *tutela* decision, bearing in mind that in the particular circumstance, the protection of the right to health, was the condition for the protection of his fundamental right to life.

In a similar case, the Constitutional Chamber of the Supreme Court of Justice of Costa Rica, n° 2003-8377 of August 8, 2003,[459] when deciding an amparo recourse filed by the People's Defendant on behalf of an aggrieved child (*Tania González Valle*) against the Costa Rican Institute for Social Security because of the denial of the requested treatment for a specific disease (known as Gaucher type 1) argued that such denial "harmed the right to life and health of the minor" who required the prescribed drug for "maintaining her life."

The Constitutional Chamber, after referring to the right to life protected in previous decisions that were based on the provision of the constitution (Article 21) establishing the inviolability of human life, concluded by deriving "the right that every citizen has to his health, thus corresponding to the State's responsibility to ensure public health... (n° 5130-94 of 17:33 hrs on 7 September 1994)." The Chamber also referred to "the

---

[459] File. 03-007020-0007-CO, *Tania González Valle* case.

preeminence of life and health as superior values of society [which] must be protected by the State [being] present not only in the Constitution, but also in the various international instruments ratified by the country."[460]

Consequently, due to the responsibilities of the State derived from these provisions, when analyzing the mission and functions of the Costa Rican Institute of Social Security, the Chamber considered, as it was declared in a previous decision (nº 1997-05934 of September 23, 1997), "that the denial by the Costa Rican Institute of Social Security to provide adequate therapy to patients infected with HIV/AIDS harms their fundamental rights." Departing from this assertion, when analyzing the particular case of the child with Gaucher disease, the Chamber found that she was not receiving the prescribed treatment due to the limited financial resources of the Social Security Institute and it concluded that although the cost of the prescribed drugs were undoubtedly onerous, nonetheless, due to the exceptional lethal characteristics of the illness and the impossibility for her parents to cover the costs of the prescriptions, it confirmed the recourse and ordered the Social Security Institute to immediately provide the specific drug in the conditions prescribed by her doctor.[461]

In Peru, the Constitutional Tribunal in a decision of April 20, 2004, also protected the right to health when deciding an extraordinary revision recourse filed against an amparo decision issued by the Superior Court of

---

[460]In particular, the decision made reference to Article 3 of the Universal Declaration on Human Rights, Article 4 of the American Convention on Human Rights; Article 1 of the American Declaration on Rights and Duties of Man; Article 6 of the International Covenant on Civil and Political Rights; Article 12 of the International Covenant on Economic, Social and Cultural Rights; and Articles 14 and 26 of the Convention on Children Rights (Law 7184 of July 18, 1990).

[461]The Court argued as follows: "This Court is conscientious regarding the scattered financial resources of the social security system, nonetheless it considers that the principal challenge the Costa Rican Institution of Social Security faces in this stage of its institutional development, − where Costa Rica has achieved life standards qualities similar to those of developed countries −, is to optimize the management of available resources of the system of health insurance and reduce the administrative costs in order to efficiently invest these resources. The Chamber considers that the prescribed drugs are undoubtedly onerous, nonetheless, due to the exceptional characteristics of the illness suffered, which is lethal, and due to the impossibility for her parents to contribute for the acquisition of the drugs, based on Articles 21 and 173 of the Constitution, and 24 and 26 of the Convention on the Child's Rights, it proceeds to confirm the recourse. The acceptance of the recourse implies that the Costa Rican Institution on Social Security must immediately provide Tania Gonzalez Valle with the drug "*Cerezyme*" (Imuglucerase) in the conditions prescribed by her doctor." File 03-007020-0007-CO, *Tania González Valle* case.

Justice of Lima. The latter had partially granted the amparo protection filed against the Peruvian State (Ministry of Health), ordering to render to the plaintiff, also an HIV/AIDS infected person, "integral health care by means of the constant provision of drugs needed to treat HIV/AIDS, as well as the performance of periodical exams and tests that the doctor orders."[462]

The Constitutional Tribunal, referring to the rights that are protected by means of the action for amparo, although admitting that "the right to health is not among the "fundamental rights" set forth in the Constitution, but is recognized in the Chapter related to social and economic rights[463]; concluded –referring to the Colombian Court doctrine– that in a "similar way as was decided by the Colombian Constitutional Court, when the violation of the right to health compromises other fundamental rights, like the right to life, the right to physical integrity and the right to the free development of one's personality, such right acquires fundamental right characteristics and, therefore, must be protected by means of amparo action (STC n° T- 499 *Corte Constitucional de Colombia*)."[464]

The Peruvian Constitutional Tribunal also ruled that these rights were not to be considered as "programmatic rights" with limited effects, because without dignified education, health and quality of life, it would be difficult to talk about freedom and social equality. This implies that both the Legislator and the Judiciary have to act jointly and interdependently in the recognition of such rights, the satisfaction of which requires a

---

[462]File n° 2945-2003-AA/TC, *Azanca Alhelí Meza García* case.

[463]Since 2004, the right to health is established in the Constitutional Procedure Code, as one of the rights expressly protected by means of the amparo action (Article 37,24).

[464]Considering the nature of the economic and social rights, as is the case of the right to health, which always originates State obligations directed to provide social assistance, the Perúvian Constitutional Tribunal in the same decision argued that the right to health, as all the so-called *"prestacionales"* (which implies to render something), like social security, public health, housing, education and other public services, constitutes "one of the social goals of the State through which individuals can achieve their complete development." Individuals can then "demand" the accomplishment of State duties by "asking the State to adopt adequate measures in order to achieve the social goals." However, the Tribunal recognized that "not in all cases are the social rights legally enforceable by themselves, due to the need of a budget support for its accomplishment." File n° 2945-2003-AA/TC, *Azanca Alhelí Meza García* case.

minimum action from the State, by establishing public services to render health care for all the population.[465]

The Tribunal concluded by affirming that "to judicially file an action claiming the protection of social rights will depend on various factors, such as the seriousness and reasonability of the case, its relation to other rights and the State's budget resources, provided that particular actions for social policies can be accomplished." Regarding the public policies in matters of public health, the Tribunal considered that if it is true that the accomplishment of the State obligations depends on the State's financial resources allocations, "in no way can it justify a prolonged [public] inaction, because it would result in an unconstitutional omission." The conclusion in the case was to grant the claimed protection to a social right as the right to health, due to the fact that in the particular case the conditions justifying it were fulfilled" not only "due to the potential damage to the right to life," but also because of the motives governing the existing legislation, providing the means for maximum protection to the HIV/AIDS infected persons.

---

[465]In this regard, the Tribunal also ruled that for the enforcement of these rights their traditional programmatic conception needed to be surpassed, so that with this criteria "this new vision of the social rights allows to recognize in their essential content, principles like solidarity and human dignity as funding of the Welfare State based on the rule of Law." After analyzing these principles, the Tribunal considered "erroneous the argument of the State defendant that being the national policy of health based on programmatic provisions, it only signifies a plan of action to be followed by the State"; adding that it would be naïve to sustain that the social rights are reduced to be just a matter of political relation between the Constituent and the legislator, which would be "an evident distortion regarding the Constitution's sense and coherence." But insisting on the right to health and its inseparable relation with the right to life, the Tribunal ruled that according to the Constitution "the defense of human beings and the respect of their dignity... presupposes the unrestricted enforcement of the right to life"; because "the exercise of any right, privilege, faculty or power has no sense or results useless in cases of the inexistence of physical life of somebody in favor of which it can be recognized." The Tribunal continued its ruling saying that "28. Health is a fundamental right due to its inseparable relation with the right to life, which is irresoluble, due to the fact that an illness can provoke death or in any case, the deterioration of life conditions. Thus the need to materialize actions tending to take care of life (health care) is evident, oriented to attack the illness signs..." Then, after affirming that the right of people, to "be assigned sanitary and social measures for nourishment, clothing, dwelling and medical assistance, depending on what is allowed by public funds and social solidarity," the Tribunal considered the question of the justiciability of social rights, like the right to health, ruling that "they cannot be requested in the same way in all cases, due to the fact that it is not a matter of specific rendering, because it depends on budget allocations. The contrary, would suppose that each individual could judicially ask at any moment for an employment or for a specific dwelling or for health." *Idem.*

Also in Argentina, the Supreme Court of the Nation in a decision of December 12, 2003 (*Asociación Esclerosis Múltiple de Salta* case), has recognized the amparo action as the most effective judicial mean to exercised in an unavoidable way "in order to safeguard the fundamental right to life and to health."[466]

3. *The limited protection of the right to health and the State's financial resources*

The third tendency regarding the protection of social rights is a restricted or limited one in which the justiciability of the right to health, also regarding HIV/AIDS treatment, has been completely subordinated to the effective disposal of enough financial resources, as was the case of some 2000/2001 Chilean courts' decisions.

In one case, the action for protection was filed against the Ministry of Health for failing to provide medical treatment to a group of HIV/AIDS patients, arguing that it was a violation to the right to life and the right to equal protection. The plaintiff demanded to be treated with the same therapy that was given to other HIV/AIDS patients, which the Ministry denied arguing that it lacked enough economic resources to provide it to all Chilean HIV/AIDS patients. The Court of Appeals of Santiago ruled that the obligation of the Ministry of Health, according to the Law regulating health care provisions (Law n° 2763/1979), was to provide health care in accordance with the resources that were available, and it considered the Ministry's explanation reasonable, that there was a lack of economic resources to provide the best available treatment to the plaintiffs. The decision was later confirmed by the Supreme Court.[467]

In another 2001 case, the same Ministry of Health was sued for the same reasons by HIV patients in more critical conditions, and even though the Court of Appeals of Santiago ruled in favor of the petitioners and ordered the Ministry to immediately provide them with the best

---

[466]See Fallos: 326: 4931. See the reference in M. Claudia Caputi, "Reseña jurisprudencial. La tutela judicial de la salud y su reivindicación contra los entes estatales," in *Revista Iberoamericana de Estudios Autonómicos*, n° 2, Goberna & Derecho, Guayaquil, 2006, pp. 145–164.

[467]See the reference in Javier A. Courso, "Judicialization of Chilean Politics," in Rachel Sieder, Line Schjolden and Alan Angeli (Ed.), *The Judicializacion of Politics in Latin America*, Palgrave Macmillan, New York, 2005, pp. 119–120.

available treatment, the Supreme Court reversed the ruling, arguing that the Ministry had acted in accordance to the law.[468]

4. *The rejection of the amparo protection when argued in an abstract way*

Finally, a forth tendency can be identified related to this limitative tendency to protect the right to health when claimed in an abstract way. In this regard, mention can be made to a 2004 decision of the Venezuelan Constitutional Chamber of the Supreme Tribunal, which ruled that when claimed in an abstract way, the right to health could not be protected by means of amparo actions, but only through political mechanisms of control regarding public policies.

The Chamber, in effect, in decision n° 1002 of May 26, 2004 (*Federación Médica Venezolana* case),[469] rejected an amparo action filed by the Venezuelan Medical Federation "defending diffuse social rights and interests, and in particular those of the physicians" seeking the protection of health against the "omissive" conduct of the Ministry of Health and Social Development and the Venezuelan Institute for Social Security, because failing to "provide efficient services of health to the population in the country, by means of promptly providing the necessary equipment and resources."

The Constitutional Chamber recognized that in the 1999 Venezuelan Constitution, all economic, social and cultural rights are considered "fundamental rights," ruling that this "implies specific consequences, among them, –in principle– the applicability of the protection by means of amparo," particularly "because the Constitution, in contrast to what is established in other legal orders, does not exclude certain rights from that guaranty, nor its immediate applicability, being the constitutional order of an immediate normative value and application, rejecting what are known as programmatic rights." Yet even admitting that because such economic, social and cultural rights have a fundamental character (not just being moral values aspirations) and that "they are undoubtedly judicially protected," nonetheless, the Constitutional Chamber concluded its ruling, constructing the denial of such justiciability regarding social right,

---

[468] *Idem*, p. 120.

[469] See in *Revista de Derecho Público*, n° 97–98, Editorial Jurídica Venezolana, Caracas, 2004, p. 143 ff.

stating that "the point is to determine when one is asking for the enforcement of an economic, social or cultural right, and when one is asking that the Public Administration performs the Welfare State based on the Rule of Law State clause, given that in both cases, the ways to sue or demand differ."[470]

Regarding the particular amparo action, the Constitutional Chamber concluded by affirming that being "of a reestablishing nature, the possibility to judicially control economic, social and cultural policies is not included in this constitutional guaranty." In the claim of the *Federación Médica Venezolana,* the court was asked to order the government to allocate enough funds to the hospitals, and to budget provisions for the acquisition of medical equipment and hospital materials. The claim was rejected by the Chamber considering that those were very evidently political activities and abstract in nature, which made them "impossible to be the object of an amparo action directed to restore particular juridical situations"; concluding that "the enforcement of the Third Generations of rights is not possible, and political control is the only way to verify its accomplishment, that is, to vote to change the government,"[471] thus rejecting the actions brought before the courts by doctors' associations.

In contrast, in a country without the express constitutional provisions regarding the right to health as is the case of Argentina, the courts have

---

[470]The Chamber said: "Policies are, in principle, outside the scope of judicial review, but not for that reason can they escape control; only that this applicable control is the political one also set forth in the Constitution. The State organs act under their own responsibility, which can be challenged in the political level, but it is not possible to challenge their political management before the Judiciary, unless when determining an administrative liability for damages caused by the political activity and putting aside that a fundamental right be affected by the decision, in which case, eventually, the control will not be regarding the political elements of the act and turn to be a control regarding its juridical elements..." The Chamber concluded that " a) The economic, social and cultural rights have, as all rights, judicial protection; b) In order to know if one is facing one of such rights, there must exist a perfectly defined juridical relation where the harm to them derives from a change of the legal sphere of a citizen or of collectivity; c) The State activity directed to satisfy the people's existence needs is an activity with political contents; d) That such activity can manifest itself by acts or through policies; e) That such acts can be the object of judicial control in their juridical elements, not in the political; f) That the policies, in principle, cannot be the object of judicial control but of political control; g) That such judicial impossibility cannot be understood as the rejection of the citizens' right to action." *Idem,* p. 143 ff.

[471]The Court said: "Facing this evident incapacity of Public Administration to efficiently plan its activities, the citizens will withdraw the confidence given to their representatives by means of suffrage, as demonstration of the de-legitimating of the actors." *Idem,* p. 143.

developed a very progressive protective case law, granting amparo protection to the right to health deciding actions filed by various associations of doctors, for instance, ordering public entities to provide economic recourses in order to allow the functioning of hospitals.[472]

[472]See decision of the Appellate Chamber on Judicial Review of Administrative Actions (*Asociación de Médicos Municipales de la C.A.B.A vs. C.A.B.A.* case), of August 2002, regarding the functioning of the histopathology of the General Hospital of Agudos, *Teodoro Alvarez*; and decision of the Second Chamber of the Appellate Criminal Court of August 7, 2002, granting an amparo action filed by the *Doctors Association of the Buenos Aires Province v. IX District*, in order to improve the administration of the public hospital of Mar del Plata. See the reference in M. Claudia Caputi, "Reseña jurisprudencial. La tutela judicial de la salud y su reivindicación contra los entes estatales," in *Revista Iberoaméricana de Estudios Autonómicos*, nº 2, Goberna & Derecho, Guayaquil, 2006, pp. 145–164.

PART FOUR

THE INJURY, THE INJURING PARTY AND THE INJURING ACTS OR OMISSIONS IN THE AMPARO PROCEEDING

The injuries violating constitutional rights, against which the amparo action has been established in Latin America, can consist of harms or threats affecting those rights.

Harms are always damages affecting or destroying the object of the right; and threats are injuries that, without destroying such object, put the enjoyment of the right in a situation of danger or of suffering a decrease.[473]

These injuries –harms or threats– caused to constitutional rights, in order to be protected by means of the amparo proceeding, must fulfill a series of conditions that are commonly established in the Amparo Laws, as conditions for the admissibility of the action.

---

[473]See decision T-412 of the Colombian Constitutional Court, June 17, 1992, in Juan Carlos Esguerra Portocarrero, *La protección constitucional del ciudadano*, Legis, Bogotá, 2005, p. 147; and in Federico González Campos, *La tutela. Interpretación doctrinaria y jurisprudencial,* Ediciones Jurídicas Gustavo Ibáñez, Bogotá, 1994, pp. 46–47. The same Constitutional Court ruled in this regard that: "Harm and threat of fundamental rights are two different concepts clearly distinguishable: the former needs an objective verification that the *tutela* judges must do, by proving its empirical occurrence and their constitutional repercussions; the latter, conversely, adds subjective and objective criteria, conforming itself not by the intention of the public officer or the individual, but by the result the action or omission can have regarding the spirit of the affected person. Thus, in order to determine the constitutional hypothesis of the threat, the confluence of subjective and objective elements are needed: the fear of the plaintiff that feels his fundamental rights are in danger of perishing and the validation of such perception by means of external objective elements, the significance of which is the one offered by the temporal and historical circumstances in which the facts are developing." Decision T-439 of July 2, 1992. *Idem,* p. 148.

In general terms, it is accepted that the injury –whether harms or threats– must be evident, actual and real, that is, it must affect personally and directly the rights of the plaintiff, in a manifestly arbitrary, illegal and illegitimate way, which the plaintiff must not have consented.

Yet in addition to these general conditions, specifically regarding harms, they must have a reparable character; and regarding threats, they must affect the rights in an imminent way. That is why the type of injuries inflicted on constitutional rights, conditions the purpose of the amparo proceeding: if harms, being reparable, the amparo has a restorative effect; and if threats, being imminent, the amparo has a preventive effect.

This section of the book is devoted to analyze, separately, all these general and specific conditions of the injuries, which are at the same time, conditions of admissibility of the amparo action.

CHAPTER TWELVE

THE GENERAL CONDITIONS OF THE INJURY (HARMS AND THREATS)

Regarding the general conditions that the injuries to constitutional rights must comply in order for an amparo actions to be admitted, the following are the ones commonly established in the Latin American Amparo Laws: first, it must have a personal and direct character, in the sense that it must personally affect the plaintiff; second, it must be actual and real; third, it must be manifestly or ostensibly arbitrary, illegal and illegitimate; fourth, it must be evidenced in the case; and fifth, it must not be consented to by the plaintiff.

I. THE PERSONAL AND DIRECT CHARACTER OF THE INJURY

The first condition of the injury inflicted to the plaintiff's constitutional rights, in order for an amparo action to be admitted, is that the plaintiff must have suffered a "direct, personal and present harm or threat in his constitutional rights,"[474] that is, the plaintiff must be personally affected. Consequently, the amparo action cannot be file when the affected rights belong to another person different to the claimant or only affects the plaintiff in an indirect way.[475]

The plaintiff then, must necessarily be the "affected" person as it is called in Argentina (Article 5) and Peru (Article 39); or the "aggrieved"

---

[474] As for example, it has been ruled by the courts in Venezuela: "It is necessary, though, that the denounced actions directly affect the subjective sphere of the claimant, consequently excluding the generic conducts, even if they can affect in a tangential way on the matter." See decision of the First Court on JudIcial Review of Administrative Actions of December 2, 1993, in *Revista de Derecho Público*, n° 55–56, Editorial Jurídica Venezolana, Caracas, 1993, pp. 302–303.

[475] That is why, for instance, the Mexican Constitution, in this regard, expressly refers to the need for the plaintiff to have suffered "a personal and direct" harm (Article 107,I), in the sense that his personal constitutional rights must have been directly affected.

person, as it is called in Nicaragua (Article 23); or the one who "suffers" the harm, as it is referred to in Brazil (Article 1).

If the harm does not affect the constitutional rights of the plaintiff, in a personal and direct way, the action must be considered inadmissible;[476] being also inadmissible when the harm or threat is not attributed to the person identified as the injuring party, that is, when the injury is not personally caused by the defendant.[477]

II. THE ACTUAL AND REAL CHARACTER OF THE INJURY

However, in addition to directly affecting the constitutional rights of the plaintiff, the injury must be "actual," in the sense that by the moment of the filing of the action, the harm or threat must be presently occurring and must not have ceased or concluded. This is, for instance, expressly provided in the Argentinean (Article 1), the Dominican Republic (Article 1) and Uruguayan (Article 1) Amparo Laws.

This same rule is also applied in the United States regarding injunctions, in the sense that for a person to be entitled to injunctive relief, it must establish an actual, substantial and serious injury, or an affirmative prospect of such an injury. Consequently, a petitioner is not entitled to an

---

[476]See Eduardo Ferrer Mac-Gregor, *La acción constitucional de amparo en México y España*, Editorial Porrúa, México, 2002, pp.386–387.

[477]In this sense, for instance, it was decided by the former Venezuelan Supreme Court of Justice in 1999, in an amparo filed against the President of the Republic, denouncing as the injuring acts, possible measures to be adopted by the National Constituent Assembly that the President had convened, once installed. The Court rejected the action considering that "the reasons alleged by the plaintiff were of eventual and hypothetical nature, which contradicts the need of an objective and real harm or threat to constitutional rights or guaranties" in order for the amparo to be admissible. Regarding the alleged defendant in the case, the Court ruled as follow: "This court must say that the action for constitutional amparo serves to give protection against situations that in a direct way could produce harm regarding the plaintiff's constitutional rights or guaranties, seeking the restoration of its infringed juridical situation. In this case, the person identified as plaintiff (President of the Republic) could not be by himself the one to produce the eventual harm which would condition the voting rights of the plaintiff, and the fear that the organization of the constituted branches of government could be modified, would be attributed to the members of those that could be elected to the National Constituent Assembly not yet elected. Thus in the case there does not exist the immediate relation between the plaintiff and the defendants needed in the amparo suit." See decision of April 23, 1999 (*A. Albornoz* case). See the reference in Rafael Chavero, *El nuevo régimen del amparo constitucional en Venezuela*, Ed. Sherwod, Caracas, 2001, p. 240.

injunction where no injury to the petitioner is shown from the action sought to be prevented.[478]

In other words, the injury must be real, in the sense that it must have effectively occurred; a fact that must be clearly demonstrated by the plaintiff in his petition. That is why, as has been ruled by the courts in Venezuela:

> The amparo action can only be directed against a perfectly and deter-mined act or omission, and not against a generic conduct; against an ob-jective and real activity and not against a supposition regarding the inten-tion of the presumed injurer, and against the direct and immediate conse-quences of the activities of the public body or officer.[479]

This actual and real character of the injury regarding the amparo suit implies that it cannot be of a past character, or of a probable future one. In this sense, for instance, the Venezuelan courts have argued that the injury "must be alive, must be present in all its intensity," in the sense of being "referring to the present, not to the past; it does not refer to facts that already had happened, which appertain to the past, but to present situations, which can be prolonged during an indefinite length of time."[480]

---

[478]See *U.S. Boyle v. Landry*, 401 U.S. 77, 91 S. Ct.758, 27 L. Ed. 2d 696 (1971), in John Bourdeau *et al.*, "Injunctions," in Kevin Schroder, John Glenn and Maureen Placilla (Ed.), *Corpus Juris Secundum*, Vol. 43A, Thomson West, 2004, p. 66.

[479]See decision of the Venezuelan former Supreme Court of Justice, Politico Administra-tive Chamber, of December 2, 1993, in which the Court added, "that is why the amparo action is not a popular action for denouncing the illegitimacy of the public entities of control over convenience or opportunity, but a protector remedy of the claimant sphere when it is demonstrated that it has been directly affected," in *Revista de Derecho Público*, n° 55–56, Editorial Jurídica Venezolana, Caracas, 1993, pp. 302–303. In another decision, the same former Supreme Court of Justice ruled about the need that: "The violation of the constitutional rights and guaranties be a direct and immediate consequence of the act, fact or omission, not being possible to attribute or assign to the injurer agent different results to those produced or to be produced. The right's violation must be the product of the harming act." See decision of August, 14, 1992, in *Revista de Derecho Público*, n° 51, Editorial Jurídica Venezolana, Caracas, 1992, p. 145.

[480]See decision of the First Court on Judicial Review of Administrative Actions, May, 7 1987, *Desarrollo 77 C.A.* case, in FUNEDA *15 años de Jurisprudencia de la Corte Prime-ra de lo Contencioso Adminsitrativo 1977–1992*, Caracas, 1994, p. 78. In this sense, Arti-cle 6,1 of the Amparo Law of Venezuela establishes for the admissibility of the amparo action, that the violation "must be actual, recent, alive."

Consequently, as established by the *jurisprudencia* of the Supreme Court of Mexico, the amparo action is inadmissible when referred to "probable future acts"[481]; to acts that have not yet occurred, or to injuries that not only are not present but could never be inflicted.[482]

Based precisely on this condition, the former Supreme Court of Justice of Venezuela rejected the possibility of filing amparo actions against statutes, in cases in which they are not directly applicable, needing additional acts for their execution.[483]

On the other hand, this same condition for the harm or threat to be actual, implies that it must not have ceased or concluded, because on the contrary, as it is expressly provided in Argentina,[484] the claim must be declared inadmissible. Also in the Honduran (Article 46,6) and Nicaraguan (Article 51,3) Amparo Laws it is prescribed that the recourse for amparo is inadmissible when the effects of the challenged act have ceased, in which case the court could *in limine* (*de plano*) reject the claim. The same principle applies in Mexico, where the Amparo Law declares the amparo action inadmissible when the effects of the challenged acts have ceased, or even when subsisting, they cannot produce substantive or legal consequences because they have lost their object or substance (Article 73,XVI). In Peru, the Constitutional Procedure Code

---

[481] *Tesis jurisprudencial* 74, Apéndice al *Semanario Judicial de la Federación*, 1917–1988, Segunda parte, Salas y Tesis Comunes, p. 123. See in Eduardo Ferrer Mac-Gregor, *La acción constitucional de amparo en México y España*, Edit. Porrúa, México, 2002, p. 395.

[482] In this sense, the Supreme Court has ruled that "simple futurity is not in itself a sufficient bar to the suit. If the execution of the act is imminent and certain, although not formally completed or in process, the amparo suit is admissible." *Tesis* 44 and 45. *Jurisprudencia de la Suprema Corte*, pp. 110, 113. See in Richard D. Baker, *Judicial Review in México. A Study of the Amparo Suit*, University of Texas Press, Austin, 1971, p. 96, note 12.

[483] The Court ruled: "When an amparo action is filed against a norm, —that is, when the object of the action is the norm in itself–, the concretion of the possible alleged harm would not be "immediate," due to the fact that it would always be necessary for the competent authority to proceed to the execution or application of the norm, in order to harm the plaintiff. One must conclude that the probable harm caused by a norm will always be mediate and indirect, needing to be applied to the concrete case. Thus, the injury will be caused through and by means of an act applying the disposition that is contrary to the rule of law." See decision of the former Supreme Court of Justice, Politico Administrative Chamber, May 24, 1993, in *Revista de Derecho Público*, n° 55–56, Editorial Jurídica Venezolana, Caracas, 1993, pp. 289–290.

[484] Alí Joaquín Salgado, *Juicio de amparo y acción de inconstitucionalidad*, Astrea, Buenos Aires, 1987, p. 27.

also prescribes the inadmissibility of the amparo action when at the moment of its filing the threat or the violation of the constitutional rights has ceased (Article 5,5).

It is also the case, for instance, when during the course of the procedure the challenged act is repealed.[485] Consequently, in order to grant the amparo protection, the Venezuelan courts have ruled that the harm must not have ceased before the judge's decision is adopted; on the contrary, if the harm has ceased, the judge *in limine litis* must declare the inadmissibility of the action.[486]

For instance, in the case of amparo actions against judicial omissions, if before the filing of the action or during the proceeding the court has issued its decision, the harm can be considered as having ceased[487] and the amparo action must be declared inadmissible.

In a similar sense, the Constitutional Chamber of Costa Rica has ruled as not having jurisdictional interest to examine the circumstances for instance, the suspension of the effects of a challenged act, in cases where the act has been repealed, and when at the moment of filing the recourse, the affected party has already been reestablished in the enjoyment of his rights.[488]

---

[485] In this regard, the First Court on Judicial Review of Administrative Actions of Venezuela resolved the inadmissibility of an action for amparo because, during the proceedings, the challenged act was repealed. Decision of August 14, 1992, in *Revista de Derecho Público,* n° 51, Editorial Jurídica Venezolana, Caracas, 1992, p. 154.

[486] Decision of December 15, 1992, in *Revista de Derecho Público* n° 52, Editorial Jurídica Venezolana, Caracas, 1992, p. 164, See First Court on Judicial Review of Administrative action, decision of December 12, 1992, *Allan R. Brewer-Carías* case, in *Revista de Derecho Público*, n° 49, Editorial Jurídica Venezolana, Caracas, 1992, pp. 131–132; and decision of the former Supreme Court, Politico Administrative Chamber of May 27, 1993, in *Revista de Derecho Público*, n° 53–54, Editorial Jurídica Venezolana, Caracas, 1993, p. 264.

[487] See Rafael Chavero G., *El nuevo régimen del amparo constitucional en Venezuela*, Editorial Sherwood, Caracas, 2001, pp. 237–238.

[488] Decision n° 1051–97, in Rubén Hernández Valle, *Derecho Procesal Constitucional*, Editorial Juricentro, San José 2001, pp. 244–245. But regarding the actual character of the harm, it is possible to consider that when a new fact which was not present at the moment the harm occurred modifies the previous already known and declared situation, the protection formerly rejected can be granted based in the new argument that could result in a different or contradictory outcome. This could occur, for instance, when the amparo judge, who must resolve regarding a specific, actual and determined situation, is asked to determine the existence of a new fact that occurred after the filing of the action, and that could alter or modify that situation, in which case, the action can be admitted and decided protecting the plaintiff, even if it had been beforehand rejected. See the Venezuela Supreme

The same principle applies in the United States regarding the actual character of the harm for granting the injunctive protection because the rule in federal cases is that an actual controversy must exist, not only at the time of the filing of the action, but at all stages of the procedure, even at appellate or certiorari review stages.[489]

Nonetheless, this principle of the actual character of the injury has some exceptions. For instance, in Peru, even though the same general rule is established regarding the inadmissibility of the amparo action "when at the moment of it filing the harm or threat to a constitutional rights has ceased," the Constitutional Procedure Code, has authorized the courts to continue the procedure and also in specific circumstances, to grant the amparo protection,[490] for instance when the purpose of the action is to order the defendant to refrain from performing again the actions or omissions that provoked the filing of the suit.

The same exception applies, for instance in Venezuela, regarding the effects already produced by a challenged act. Because additional suits are necessary in order to establish civil liabilities and compensation, even if

---

Court of Justice, Politico Administrative Chamber decision of August 5, 1992, in *Revista de Derecho Público*, n° 51, Editorial Jurídica Venezolana, Caracas, 1992, p. 145.

[489]Nonetheless, in the important case *Roe v. Wade*, 410 U.S. 113 (1973), the Supreme Court expanded women's right to privacy, striking down states' laws banning abortion. The Court recognized that even if this right of privacy was not explicitly mentioned in the constitution, it was guaranteed as a constitutional right for protecting "a woman's decision whether or not to terminate her pregnancy," even though admitting that the states' legislation could regulate the factors governing the abortion decision at some point in pregnancy based on "safeguarding health, maintaining medical standards and in protecting potential life." But the point in the case was that, pending the procedure, the pregnancy period of the claimant came to term, so the injury claimed lost its present character. Nonetheless, the Supreme Court ruled in the case that "[When], as here, pregnancy is a significant fact in the litigation, the normal 266-day human generation period is so short that pregnancy will come to term before the usual appellate process is complete. If that termination makes a case moot, pregnancy litigation seldom will survive much beyond the trial stage, and appellate review will be effectively denied. Our law should not be that rigid. Pregnancy comes more than once to the same woman, and in the general population, if man is to survive, it will always be with us. Pregnancy provides a classic justification for a conclusion of nonmootness. It truly could be capable of repetition, yet evading review." See M. Glenn Abernathy and Barbara A. Perry, *Civil Liberties under the Constitution*, University of South Carolina Press, 1993, pp. 4–5.

[490]See Luis Sanz Dávalos, "Las innovaciones del Código Procesal constitucional en el proceso constitucional de amparo," in Susana Castañeda *et al*, *Introducción a los procesos constitucionales. Comentarios al Código Procesal Constitucional*, Jurista Editores, Lima 2005, p. 126.

the effects of the challenged act have ceased, the amparo protection can be granted in order for the responsible person to be judicially determined, allowing the subsequent filing of an action just seeking compensation.

III. THE MANIFESTLY ARBITRARY, ILLEGAL AND ILLEGITIMATE INJURY

Yet in order for an amparo action to be admitted, in addition for the injury to be a direct, real and actual one, the harm or threat to the constitutional right must be manifestly arbitrary, illegal or illegitimate.

This is for instance, the general condition expressly established in the Argentinean Amparo Law that provides that for an amparo action to be admissible, the injury, that is, the "harm, the restriction, the alteration or the threat to the constitutional rights and guaranties," must be "manifestly arbitrary or illegal (Article 1)." This admissibility condition is also imposed in the Dominican Republic Amparo Law (Article 1); and in the Uruguayan Amparo Law where it is refers as the need for the challenged act to be "manifestly illegitimate" (Article 1). In this same sense, in the Brazilian Law, regarding the *mandado de segurança*, provides for the need for the violation to be caused illegally or with abuse of power (*ilegalmente ou com abuso do poder*) (Article 1).[491] Also in the 207 Philippines' Rule on the Writ of Amparo, it is provided that the violation must be provoked by "an unlawfull act or omission" (Sec. 1).

Regarding public authorities' acts, this general condition of admissibility of the amparo action derives from the general public law principle of the presumption of validity that benefit the State acts, which implies that in order to overcome such presumption, the plaintiff must demonstrate that the injury caused is manifestly illegal and arbitrary. The same principle applies in the United States precisely imposing on the plaintiff, in civil right injunctions against administrative officials, the burden to prove the alleged violations in order to destroy the presumption of validity of official acts.[492]

---

[491] The principle is also considered to be applicable in Chile and Ecuador. See Juan Manuel Errazuriz G., and Jorge Miguel Otero A., *Aspectos procesales del recurso de protección*, Editorial Jurídica de Chile, Santiago, 1989, pp. 51–55; Hernán Salgado Pesantes, *Manual de Justicia Constitucional Ecuatoriana*, Corporación Editora Nacional, Quito, 2004, p. 79.

[492] As M. Glenn Abernathy and Perry have commented: "The courts do not automatically presume that all restraints on free choice are improper. The burden is thrown on the person

The consequence of this condition is that the challenged act or omission must be manifestly contrary to the legal order, that is, to the rules of law contained in the constitution, the statutes and the executive regulations; must be manifestly illegitimate because lacking of any legal support; and must be manifestly arbitrary, because resulting from an unreasonable or unjust act is an act contrary to justice or to reason.[493]

IV. THE EVIDENT CHARACTER OF THE INJURY

The condition of the injury –harm or threats–, to be manifestly arbitrary, illegal and illegitimate and to affect in a direct and immediate way the plaintiff rights, implies that for the filing of the amparo action, it has to be evident, thus, directly imposing the plaintiff the burden to prove his assertions. That is, the plaintiff has the burden to destroy the presumption of validity, having to build his arguments upon reasonable basis by proving the unreasonable character of the public officer's challenged act or omission, and that it has personally and directly harmed his rights.

Also in this matter, the rule in the amparo proceeding is similar to the rules on matters of injunctions, as they have been resolved by the United States' courts, according to which, "the party seeking an injunction, whether permanent or temporary, must establish some demonstrable injury."[494]

Consequently, in the amparo proceeding, it is for the plaintiff to prove the harm or the threats caused to his rights, and as being caused precisely by the defendant.[495] This implies that when the proof of the harms or

---

attacking acts to prove that they are improper. This is most readily seen in cases involving the claim that an act of the legislature is unconstitutional...Judges also argue that acts of administrative officials should be accorded some presumption of validity. Thus a health officer who destroys food alleged by him to be unfit for consumption is presumed to have good reason for his action. The person whose property is so destroyed must bear the burden of proving bad faith on part of the official, if an action is brought as a consequence." See M. Glenn Abernathy and Barbara A. Perry, *Civil Liberties under the Constitution*, University of South Carolina Press, 1993, p. 5.

[493]See Alí Joaquín Salgado, *Juicio de amparo y acción de inconstitucionalidad,* Astrea, Buenos Aires, 1987, pp. 28–29.

[494]See *Mt. Emmons Min. Co. V. Town of Crested Butte*, 690 P.2d 231 (Colo. 1984), in John Bourdeau *et al.*, "Injunctions," in Kevin Schroder, John Glenn and Maureen Placilla (Editors), *Corpus Juris Secundum*, Vol. 43A, Thomson West, 2004, p. 54.

[495]That is why, the Argentinean courts for instance, have rejected an amparo action against nonproved threats, for instance, when a mother filed a complaint asking for police protection to avoid an order of seizure of a minor, issued by a foreign court, because the

threats can be established by means of written evidence (documents), the Amparo Laws of Argentina (Article 7), Paraguay (Article 569) and Uruguay (Article 5), expressly impose on the claimant the duty to always attach them to the complaint.

The proof of the harm can also be based for instance, on previous acts or behavior of the defendant, or in his past pattern of conduct.[496]

V. THE NON-CONSENTED CHARACTER OF THE INJURY

Finally, the injury to constitutional rights allowing the filing of the amparo action must not only be actual, possible, real and imminent, but must also be an injury that has not been consented by the plaintiff, who, in addition, must not have provoked it.[497] That is, the plaintiff must not have expressly or tacitly consent the challenged act or the harm caused to his right. On the contrary, the amparo action would be considered inadmissible.

---

existence of the order was not proved, nor sufficient elements for judging the case were alleged in order to prove that the local authorities were going to fail to apply the legal dispositions that apply to the execution in the country of foreign judicial decisions, which prescribes enough guaranties for the defense of rights and to protect internal public order. See the references in Nestor Pedro Sagüés, *Derecho Procesal Constitucional*, Vol 3, "Acción de Amparo," Astrea, Buenos Aires, 1988, pp. 117; and in Rafael Chavero, *El nuevo régimen del amparo constitucional en Venezuela*, Ed. Sherwood, Caracas, 2001, pp. 190, 239.

[496] As was the case resolved in the United States, in *Galella v. Onassis* (S.D.N.Y. 1972), in which the wife of J. F. Kennedy, the former President of the United States, filed an injunction against a freelance photographer to restrain him from violating her privacy rights, based on his previous behavior pattern of harassment as a journalist. As it was summarized by Tabb and Shoben: "The evidence showed that the photographer had repeatedly engaged in harassing behavior of the Onassis family in order to obtain pictures, but each time the invasive behavior was different. Based upon the pattern of past conduct, the court concluded that the photographer's behavior would continue indefinitely in the future. The evidence of imminency was very strong because the photographer had even sent an advertisement to customers announcing future anticipated pictures of Onassis. Even though the pattern of behavior was varied in the types of invasive conduct, the overall nature of it was harassing. With sufficient evidence, even an unpredictable pattern can establish imminence." See William M. Tabb and Elaine W. Shoben, *Remedies,* Thompson West, 2005, p. 29.

[497] See Hernán Salgado Pesantes, *Manual de Justicia Constitucional Ecuatoriana*, Corporación Editora Nacional, Quito, 2004, p. 80.

The Amparo Laws in this matter distinguishes two sorts of possible ways of consenting conducts: the express consent and the tacit consent; also with some exceptions.

1. *The express consent*

Regarding the express consent, as established in the Venezuelan Amparo Law, it exists when there are "unequivocal signs of acceptance" (Article 6,4) by the plaintiff, of the acts, facts or omissions causing the injury, in which case the amparo action is inadmissible.

This inadmissibility clause is also expressly regulated in the Amparo Law of México, according to which an express consent regarding the challenged act exists when there is a formal "expression of will of the plaintiff implying such consent" (Article 73,XI). Also in Nicaragua, express consent exists regarding "acts that have been consented by the claimant in an express way" (Article 51,4); and in Costa Rica, "when the action or omission would be legitimately consented by the injured person" (Article 30,ch).

In certain aspects, this inadmissibility clause for the amparo proceeding when an express consent of the plaintiff exists, also has some equivalence in the United States injunctions procedure with the equitable defense called "estopell," referring to actions of the plaintiff prior to the filing of the suit, when being inconsistent with the rights he is asserting in his claim.[498]

2. *The tacit consent*

Apart from the cases of express consent, the other clause of inadmissibility in the amparo proceeding also occurs in cases of tacit consent by the plaintiff regarding the act, fact or omission causing the injury to his rights. This situation is considered as happening when a precise term, legally established to file the complaint, has elapsed without the action being brought before the courts.

---

[498]The classic example of estopell, as referred to by Tabb and Shoben, "is that a plaintiff cannot ask equity for an order to remove a neighbor's fence built over the lot line if the plaintiff stood by and watched the fence construction in full knowledge of the location of the lot line. The plaintiff silence with knowledge of the facts is an action inconsistent with the right asserted in court." See William M. Tabb and Elaine W. Shoben, *Remedies*, Thomson West, 2005, pp. 50–51.

This clause for the inadmissibility of the amparo suit is also equivalent to what in the United States procedure for injunction is called "laches," which seeks to prevent a plaintiff from obtaining equitable relief when he has not acted promptly in bringing the action, which is summarized in the phrase, that "equity aids the vigilant, not those who slumber in their rights."[499]

The difference between the doctrine of "laches" regarding injunctions and the Latin American concept of tacit consent basically lies in the fact that the term to file the amparo action in Latin America is expressly established in the Amparo Laws, so the exhaustion of the term without the filing of the action is what it is considered to produce the tacit consent regarding the act, the fact or the omission causing the injury.

In this regard, and only with the exception of Ecuador[500] and Colombia (where for instance, the *Tutela* Law establishes that the action for *tutela* can be filed at any moment, Article 11), the Amparo Laws in Latin America always set forth specific terms counted in days or months,[501] in order

---

[499]*Idem*, p. 48. As argued in Lake Development Enterprises, *Inc. v. Kojetinsky*, 410 S.W. 2d 361, 367–68 (Mo. App. 1966): "Laches" is the neglect, for an unreasonable and unexplained length of time under circumstances permitting diligence, to do what in law, should have been done. There is no fixed period within which a person must assert his claim or be barred by laches. The length of time depends upon the circumstances of the particular case. Mere delay in asserting a right does not of itself constitute laches; the delay involved must work to the disadvantage and prejudice of the defendant. Laches is a question of fact to be determined from all the evidence and circumstances adduced at trial." See the reference Owen M. Fiss and Doug Rendelman, *Injunctions*, The Foundation Press, Mineola New York, 1984, pp. 102–103.

[500]See Hernán Salgado Pesantes, *Manual de Justicia Constitucional Ecuatoriana*, Corporación Editora Nacional, Quito, 2004, p. 81.

[501]The term in the Latin American Amparo Laws is generally established in a number of days counted from the date of the challenged act or from the day the injured party has known about the violation: Argentina, 15 days (Article 2,e); Brazil, 120 days (Article 18); Dominican Republic, 30 days (Article 3,b); Guatemala, 30 days (Article 20); Honduras, 2 months; México, 15 days as a general rule, but with many other terms to sue with different length of time (Articles 21, 22 and 73,XII); Nicaragua, 30 days (Article 26; 51,4); Paraguay, 60 days (Article 567); Perú, 60 days (Articles 5,10; 44); Uruguay, 30 days (Art 4). In Venezuela, the term is six months (Article 6,4). In the case of Chile, where in the absence of a Statute regulating the action for protection, the term to sue (fifteen days) has been regulated by Supreme Court, discussions have arisen regarding the constitutionality of such norms, due to the criteria that a term to sue of such type must be only established by the Legislator. See Juan Manuel Errazuriz and Jorge Miguel Otero A., *Aspectos procesales del recurso de protección*, Editorial Jurídica de Chile, Santiago, 1989, p. 130. In Costa Rica, the Constitutional Jurisdiction Law establishes that the amparo recourse can be filed at any time while the violation, threat, injury or restriction endures, and up to two months after

to file the action, considering that the plaintiff has tacitly consented to the challenged acts, facts or omissions when the action is not filed within the established term.

The sense of this clause of inadmissibility of the amparo action was summarized by the former Supreme Court of Justice of Venezuela when ruling as follows:

> Since the amparo action is a special, brief, summary and effective judicial remedy for the protection of constitutional rights...it is logical for the Legislator to prescribe a precise length of time between the moment in which the harm is produced and the moment the aggrieved party has to file the action. To let more than 6 months pass from the moment in which the injuring act is issued for the exercise of the action is the demonstration of the acceptance of the harm from the side of the injured party. His indolence must be sanctioned, impeding the use of the judicial remedy that has its justification in the urgent need to reestablish a legal situation.[502]

Of course, as a general rule in this matter, the exhaustion of the term to sue without filing the amparo action, although considered as a tacit consent regarding the injury, as it is expressly regulated in the Costa Rican Law (Article 36),[503] does not prevent the interested party from filing the other possible recourses or actions against the act causing the harm.

3. *Exceptions to the tacit consent rule*

However, regarding this tacit consent effect, a few exceptions have also been constructed.

First of all, there is an exception based on the nature of the constitutional rights to be protected, so an amparo can be filed at any moment regarding the inviolable rights, like the right to life or not to be tortured. In this sense, in the Mexican Amparo Law the exception is established regarding cases of authority acts endangering life, personal freedom,

---

the direct effects regarding the injured party have ceased (Articles 35, 60). This term to sue can also be suspended if the interested party decides to file an administrative recourse against the particular act (Article 31).

[502] See decision of October 24, 1990, in *Revista de Derecho Público*, n° 44, Editorial Jurídica Venezolana, Caracas, 1990, p. 144.

[503] See the comments in Ruben Hernández Valle, *Derecho Procesal Constitucional*, Editorial Juricentro, 2001, pp. 226–229, 243.

deportation, or the forced incorporation to the army (Article 22).[504] In these cases the amparo action can be brought before the courts at any time, as it is also the case of the amparo for the protection of peasants' rights related to communal land (Article 217).

In Costa Rica, Article 20 of the Constitutional Jurisdiction Law also establishes as an exception, the possibility to file an amparo action after the exhaustion of the term, against the risk of an unconstitutional statute or regulation to be applied in a particular case, as well as in cases of manifest possibility of an act to be issued harming the plaintiff's rights.

In a similar sense, the Venezuelan Amparo Law establishes the exception to the tacit consent rule in cases of violations affecting "public order" provisions[505] (Article 6,4), which refers to situations where the application of a statute may concern the general and indispensable legal order for the existence of the community.[506]

This notion of "public order" is important because even when the term to sue has elapsed without the action being filed, the courts can admit the action because of reasons of "public order," not considering applicable in the case the rule of the tacit consent. As was decided by the Venezuelan First Court of Administrative Judicial Review:

> The extinction of the amparo action due to the elapse of the term to sue… is produced in all cases, except when the way through which the harm has been produced is of such gravity that it constitutes an injury to the juridi-

---

[504]Eduardo Ferrer Mac-Gregor, *La acción constitucional de amparo en México y España*, Editorial Porrúa, México, 2002, p. 331.

[505]As ruled by the cassation Chamber of the Supreme Court in Venezuela in a decision of April 3, 1985, "the concept of public order allows the general interest of the Society and of the State to prevail over the individual particular interest, in order to assure the enforcement and purpose of some institutions." See the reference in decisions of the former Supreme Court of Justice, Politico Administrative Chamber, of February 1, 1990, *Tuna Atlántica C.A.,* case and of June 30, 1992, in *Revista de Derecho Público*, n° 60, Editorial Jurídica Venezolana, Caracas, 1992, p. 157. In many cases, it is the Legislator itself that has expressly declared in a particular statute that its provisions are of "public order" character, in the sense that its norms cannot be modified through contracts." See decision of former Supreme Court of Justice, Politico Administrative Chamber, March 22, 1988, in *Revista de Derecho Público*, n° 34, Editorial Jurídica Venezolana, Caracas, 1988, p. 114.

[506]The exception, of course, cannot be applied in cases only concerning the parties in a contractual or private controversy. That is the case for instance, of the Venezuelan 2004 Consumers and Users Protection Law where Article 2 sets forth that its provisions are of public order and may not be renounced by the parties. *Official Gazette*, n° 37.930, May 4, 2004.

cal conscience. It would be the case, for instance, of flagrant violations to individual rights that cannot be denounced by the affected party; deprivation of freedom; submission to physical or psychological torture; maltreatment; harms to human dignity and other extreme cases.[507]

Consequently, in such cases where no tacit consent can be considered as having been produced, the amparo judicial is admitted even though the term to file the action would have been exhausted.

The second general exception to the rule of tacit consent refers to situations where the harms inflicted to the rights are of a continuous nature, that is, when they are continuously occurring. In the same sense, in the United States, it is considered that "laches" cannot be alleged as a defense to challenge a suit for injunction to enjoin a wrong that is continuing in its nature.[508]

For instance, the Venezuelan courts have ruled regarding a defense argument on the inadmissibility of an amparo action because the term of six months to file the action was elapsed, that in the particular case:

> In spite that the facts show that the challenged actions occurred more that six months ago, they have been described revealing a supposed chain of events that, due to their constancy and re-incidence, allows to presume that the plaintiff is presently threatened by those repeated facts. This character of the threat is what the amparo intends to stop. According to what the plaintiff points out, no tacit consent can be produced from his part … Consequently, there are no grounds for the application to any of the inadmissibility clauses set forth in the Amparo Law.[509]

---

[507]See the decisions of First Court on Judicial Review of Administrative Action of October 13, 1988, in *Revista de Derecho Público*, n° 36, Editorial Jurídica Venezolana, Caracas, 1988, p. 95; of the former Supreme Court of Justice, Politico Administrative Chamber, of November 1, 1989, in *Revista de Derecho Público*, n° 40, Editorial Jurídica Venezolana, Caracas, 1989, p. 111; and of the cassation Chamber of the same Supreme Court of Justice, of June 28, 1995, (Exp. n° 94–172). See the reference in Rafael Chavero G., *El nuevo régimen del amparo constitucional en Venezuela*, Editorial Sherwood, Caracas, 2001, p. 188, note 178. See another judicial decision on the matter in pp. 214 and 246.

[508]*Pacific Greyhound Lines v. Sun Valley Bus Lines*, 70 Ariz. 65, 216 P. 2d 404, 1950; Goldstein v. Beal, 317 Mass. 750, 59 N.E. 2d 712, 1945. See in Jhon Bourdeau *et al.*, "Injunctions," in Kevin Schroder, John Glenn and Maureen Placilla (Ed.), *Corpus Juris Secundum*, Vol. 43A, Thomson West, 2004, p. 329.

[509]See decision of October 22, 1990, *María Cambra de Pulgar* case, in *Revista de Derecho Público*, n° 44, Editorial Jurídica Venezolana, Caracas, 1990, pp. 143–144.

Other exceptions to the tacit consent rule refers to cases in which factual situations exist implying the impossibility for the filing of the action. For instance, in Honduras, it is expressly established that the action can be filed after the exhaustion of the term, when the impossibility to bring the action before the court is duly proved (Article 46,3); and in a similar sense, it is also regulated in the Uruguayan Law in cases when the plaintiff has been impeded by "just cause" to file the action (Article 4).

In Mexico, particularly regarding the amparo against laws, the Amparo Law prescribes that the action can be filed not only against the statute, but also after the exhaustion of the term, against the first particular act applying it; so the tacit consent rule applies in this case, only when the latter act is not challenged (Article 73,XII).[510]

In the particular case of Venezuela, the Amparo Law also provides a few exceptions regarding the tacit consent rule, when the amparo action is filed conjointly with another nullity action, in which case the general six-month term established for the filing of the action does not apply. This is the rule in cases of harms or threats that have originated in statutes or regulations, and in administrative acts or public administration omissions, when the amparo action is filed jointly with the popular action for judicial review of unconstitutionality of statutes,[511] or with the judicial review action against administrative actions or omissions.[512]

---

[510]See Eduardo Ferrer Mac-Gregor, *La acción constitucional de amparo en México y España,* Editorial Porrúa, México, 2002, p. 391; Richard D. Baker, *Judicial Review in México. A Study of the Amparo Suit,* University of Austin Press, Austin, 1971, p. 172.

[511]Regarding the judicial review popular action against statutes, it is conceived in the Organic Law of the Supreme Tribunal as an action that can be filed at any time, so if a petition for amparo is filed together with the popular action, no delay is applicable (Article 21,21). See Allan R. Brewer-Carías, *Ley Orgánica del Tribunal Supremo de Justicia,* Editorial Jurídica Venezulana, Caracas, 2006, p. 255. This is why no tacit consent can be understood when the harm is provoked by a statute.

[512]Similarly, the tacit consent rule does not apply either in cases of administrative acts or omissions, when the amparo action is filed together with the judicial review action against administrative acts or omissions, in which case, due to the constitutional complaint, the latter can be filed at any moment, as is expressly provided in the Amparo Law (Article 5).

CHAPTER THIRTEEN

THE REPARABLE CHARACTER OF THE HARMS AND THE RESTORATIVE CHARACTER OF THE AMPARO PROCEEDING

As mentioned, the injury inflicted upon constitutional rights in order to the filing of an amparo action, can be the result of harms or threats, which must fulfill the general conditions aforementioned.

In addition, two other conditions must fulfill the injury, depending on being harms or threats. If it is a harm inflicted on the persons' rights, it has to be a reparable one, the amparo proceeding seeking to restore the enjoyment of the right, having a restorative character; but if the injury is a threat caused upon the right, it must be imminent, the amparo tending to prevent or impede the violation to occur, having a preventive character.

I. THE RESTORATIVE CHARACTER OF THE AMPARO AGAINST HARMS

In effect, in case of harms, the amparo proceeding seeks to restore the enjoyment of the plaintiff's injured right, reestablishing the situation existing when the right was harmed, by eliminating or suspending, if necessary, the detrimental act or fact.

In this regard, the amparo action also has similarities with the reparative injunctions in the United States, which seeks to eliminate the effects of a past wrong or to compel the defendant to engage in a course of action that seeks to correct those effects.[513]

---

[513] As has been explained by Owen M. Fiss: "To see how it works, let us assume that a wrong has occurred (such as an act of discrimination). Then the missions of an injunction —classically conceived as a preventive instrument— would be to prevent the recurrence of the wrongful conduct in the future (stop discriminating and do not discriminate again). But in *United States v. Louisiana* (380 U.S. 145, (1965)), a voting discrimination case, Justice Black identified still another mission for the injunction: the elimination of the effects of the past wrong (the past discrimination). The reparative injunction —long thought by the nineteenth-century textbook writers, such as High (A *Treatise on the Law of Injunction* 3,

However, in some cases, due to the factual nature of the harm that has been inflicted, these restorative effects cannot be obtained, in which cases the amparo decision must tend to place the plaintiff righhts "in the situation closest or more similar to the one that existed before the injury was caused."[514]

II. THE SPECIFIC CONDITION OF THE HARM: ITS REPARABLE CHARACTER

Because of the restorative character of the amparo, the main specific condition the harms must fulfill for an amparo petition to be granted, is that they must have a reparable character. Consequently, as for instance is established in the Venezuelan Amparo Law, the amparo actions are inadmissible, "when the violation of the constitutional rights and guaranties turns out to be an evident irreparable situation, and is impossible to restore." In these cases, the Law defines the irreparable harms as those that by means of the amparo action cannot revert to the status existing before the violation had occurred (Article 6,3).

The main consequence of this reparable character of the harm, and of the restorative effect of the amparo proceeding, is that through the amparo action, it is not possible to create new juridical situations for the plaintiff, nor is it possible to modify the existing legal situations.[515]

1873) to be an analytical impossibility— was thereby legitimated. And in the same vein, election officials have been ordered not only to stop discriminating in the future elections, but also to set aside a past election and to run a new election as a means of removing the taint of discrimination that infected the first one (*Bell v. Southwell*, 376 F.2de 659 (5TH Cir. 1976)). Similarly, public housing officials have been ordered to both cease discriminating on the basis of race in their future choices of sites and to build units in the white areas as a means of eliminating the effects of the past segregative policy (placing public housing projects only in the black areas of the city) (*Hills v. Gautreaux*, 425 U.S. 284 (1976)). Seen Owen M. Fiss, *The Civil Rights Injunction*, Indiana University Press, 1978, pp.7—10.

[514]In this sense, it has been decided by the former Venezuelan Supremo Court of Justice ruling that "one of the principal characteristics of the amparo action is to be a restorative (restablecedor) judicial means, the mission of which is to restore the infringed situation or, what is the same, to put the claimant again in the enjoyment of his infringed constitutional rights." See decision of February 6, 1996, *Asamblea legislativa del Estado Bolívar* case. See in Rafael Chavero, *El nuevo régimen del amparo constitucional en Venezuela*, Ed. Sherwood, Caracas, 2001, pp. 185, 242—243.

[515]See decisions of the Politico Administrative Chamber of the former Supreme Court of Justice, of October 27, 1993, *Ana Drossos* case, and of November 4, 1993, *Partido Con-*

In this sense, for instance, the Venezuelan Constitutional Chamber of the Supreme Tribunal of Justice denied a request formulated by means of an amparo action for the plaintiff to obtain asylum because what it was seeking was to obtain the Venezuelan citizenship without accomplishing the established administrative conditions and procedures. The Court ruled in the case, that "this amparo action has been filed in order to seek a decision from this court, consisting in the legalization of the situation of the claimant, which would consist in the creation of a civil and juridical status that the petitioner did not have before filing the complaint for amparo." Thus in the case, the petition was considered "contrary to the restorative nature of the amparo."[516]

Consequently, regarding harms, the restorative effects of the amparo proceedings, impose the need for the harm to be of a reparable character so the courts can restore things to the status or situation they had at the moment of the injury, disappearing the challenged infringing fact or act. On the contrary, when the violation to a constitutional right turns out to be of an irreparable character, the amparo actions is inadmissible.

This is congruent with the main objective of the amparo proceeding as it is for instance provided in Article 29 of the Venezuelan Constitution and Article 1 of Amparo Law, in the sense that it seeks to "immediately restore the infringed situation or to place the claimant in the situation

---

vergencia case, in *Revista de Derecho Público*, n° 55–56, Editorial Jurídica Venezolana, Caracas, 1993, p. 340.

[516]See decision dated January 20, 2000, *Domingo Ramírez Monja* case, in Rafael Chavero, *El nuevo régimen del amparo constitucional en Venezuela*, Ed. Sherwood, Caracas, 2001, p. 244. In another decision issued on April 21, 1999, *J. C. Marín* case, the former Supreme Court in a similar sense, declared inadmissible an amparo action in a case in which the claimant was asking to be appointed as judge in a specific court or to be put in a juridical situation that he did not have before the challenged act was issued. The Court decided that in the case, it was impossible for such purpose to file an amparo action, declaring it inadmissible, thus ruling as follows: "This Court must highlight that one of the essential characteristics of the amparo action is its reestablishing effects, that is, literally, to put one thing in the situation it had beforehand, which for the claimant means to be put in the situation he had before the production of the claimed violation. The foregoing means that the plaintiff's claim must be directed to seek 'the reestablishment of the infringed juridical situation'; since the amparo actions are inadmissible when the reestablishment of the infringed situation is not possible; when through them the claimant seeks a compensation of damages, because the latter cannot be a substitution of the harmed right; nor when the plaintiff pretends to the court to create a right or a situation that did not exist before the challenged act, fact or omission. All this is the exclusion for the possibility for the amparo to have constitutive effects." *Idem*, pp. 244–245.

more similar to it."[517] In the same sense, the Amparo Laws of Mexico (Article 73,IX) and Honduras (Article 46,5), expressly establish that in cases of harms produced to constitutional rights, the amparo action can only be filed when the injury is a reparable one and the harm is reversible; being inadmissible when the challenged act provoking the harm has already been accomplished or when its effects have already been exhausted or consumed (*consumado*) in an irreparable way. That is, amparo actions cannot be the adequate remedies regarding *fait accompli* or irreparable situations.

The classical example in Mexico regarding this condition of admissibility of the amparo suit is the situation created by an already executed death sentence,[518] in which case it will be wholly irrelevant to file the amparo action. That is why in Mexico, this inadmissibility condition applies to all cases "when it is materially or juridically impossible to return the injured party to the position it had prior to the violation"[519]; or when in general terms the challenged act is in fact irreparable because it is "physically impossible to turn back things to the stage they had before the violation."[520]

This is also a general condition for the admissibility of the injunctions in the United States where the courts have established that because the purpose of an injunction is to restrain actions that have not yet been taken, an injunction cannot be filed to restrain an already completed action at the time the action is brought before the courts since the injury has already been caused.[521]

---

[517]See First Court on Judicial Review of Administrative Action, decision of January 14, 1992, in *Revista de Derecho Público*, n° 49, Editorial Jurídica Venezolana, Caracas, 1992, p. 130; and decision of the former Supreme Court of Justice, Politico Administrative Chamber, of March 4, 1993, in *Revista de Derecho Público*, n° 53-54, Editorial Jurídica Venezolana, Caracas, 1993, p. 260.

[518]*Tesis* 32, II, 90. *Jurisprudencia de la Suprema Corte*. See the reference in Richard D. Baker, *Judicial Review in México. A Study of the Amparo Suit*, University of Austin Press, Austin, 1971, p. 95, note 11.

[519]*Idem*, p.96

[520]*Tesis "Actos consumados de modo irreparable,"* Apéndice al Semanario Judicial de la federación 1917-1988, Segunda Parte, Salas y Tesis Comunes, pp. 106–107. See the reference in Eduardo Ferrer Mac-Gregor, *La acción constitucional de amparo en México y España*, Edit. Porrúa, México, 2002, p. 388, notes 232–233.

[521]"There is no cause for the issuance of an injunction unless the alleged wrong is actually occurring or is actually threatened or apprehended with reasonable probability and a court cannot enjoin an act after it has been completed. An act that has been completed, such that it no longer presents a justiciable controversy, does not give grounds for the

In this same sense, for instance, the former Venezuelan Supreme Court declared inadmissible an amparo action against an illegitimate tax collecting act after the tax was paid, considering that in such case it is not possible to restore the infringed situation.[522] Also regarding women's pregnancy rights, Venezuelan courts have declared inadmissible an amparo action seeking the protection of maternity leave rights when filed after childbirth, ruling that:

> It is impossible for the plaintiff to be restored in her presumed violated rights to enjoy a maternity leave during six month before and after the childbirth, because we are now facing an irremediable situation that cannot be restored, due to the fact that it is impossible to date back the elapsed time.[523]

In other cases, the same former Venezuelan Supreme Court of Justice has considered inadmissible amparo actions when the only way to restore the infringed juridical situation is by declaring the nullity of an administrative act, which the amparo judge cannot do in his decision.[524]

These general trends regarding the reparable character of the harms and the restorative effects of the amparo proceeding can be considered the general ones in the Amparo Laws in Latin America.

As mentioned, there is the case of Mexico, where Article 73,X of the Amparo Law, in addition, prescribes that the amparo is inadmissible against acts adopted in a judicial or administrative proceeding when due to the change of the juridical situation, the violations claimed have oc-

---

issuance of an injunction." See *County of Chesterfield v. Windy Hill, Ltd.*, 263 Va. 197, 559 S.E. 2d 627 (2002); *Kay v. David Douglas School Dist.* n° 40, 303 Or. 574, 738 P 2d 1389, 40 Ed. Law Rep. 1027 (1987); *Exparte Connors*, 855 So. 2d 486 (Ala. 2003); *Patterson v. Council on Probate Judicial Conduct*, 215 Conn. 553, 577 A. 2d 701 (1990), in John Bourdeau *et al*, "Injunctions," in Kevin Schroder, John Glenn, Maureen Placilla (Editors), *Corpus Juris Secundum*, Vol 43A, Thomson West, 2004, p. 73.

[522] See decision of the former Supreme Court of Justice, Politico Administrative Chamber, of March 21, 1988, in *Revista de Derecho Público*, n° 34, Editorial Jurídica Venezolana, Caracas, 1988, p. 114.

[523] See decision of the First Court on Judicial Review of Administrative Actions of September 17, 1989, in *Revista de Derecho Público*, n° 40, Editorial Jurídica Venezolana, Caracas, 1989, p. 111.

[524] See decision of the former Supreme Court of Justice, Politico Administrative Chamber of November 1, 1990, in *Revista de Derecho Publico*, n° 44, Editorial Jurídica Venezolana, Caracas, 1990, pp. 152–153; *Cfr.* First Court on Judicial Review of Administrative Action, decision of September 10, 1992, in *Revista de Derecho Público*, n° 51, Editorial Jurídica Venezolana, Caracas, 1992, p. 155.

curred in an irreparable way. It is also the general trend regarding the *tutela* action in Colombia where the *Tutela* Law provides that the action is inadmissible "when it is evident that the violation originated a completed harm, unless the harming actions or omissions continue" (Article 6,4).

From these regulations it can be sustained, in conclusion, that the amparo proceeding regarding violations are restorative in nature, imposing the need for the illegitimate harm to be possibly stopped or amended, in order for the plaintiff's situation to be restored by a judicial order; or if having continuous effects, for its suspension when not being initiated. Regarding those effects already accomplished, it implies the possibility to set back things to the stage they had before the harm was initiated. Consequently, what the amparo judge cannot do is to create situations that were inexistent at the moment of the action's filing; or to correct the harms infringed on rights when it is too late to do so.[525]

In this regard, for instance, referring to the right to the protection of health, the former Venezuelan Supreme Court of Justice ruled as follows:

> The Court considers that the infringed situation is reparable by means of amparo, due to the fact that the plaintiff can be satisfied in his claims through such judicial mean. From the judicial procedure point of view, for the protection of health it is possible for the judge to order the competent authority to assume precise conduct for the medical treatment of the claimant's conduct. The petitioner's claim is to have a particular and adequate health care, which can be obtained via the amparo action, seeking the reestablishment of a harmed right. In this case, the claimant is not

---

[525] As decided by the First Court on Judicial Review of Administrative Action of Venezuela, regarding a municipal order for the demolition of a building, in the sense that if the demolition was already executed, the amparo judge cannot decide the matter because of the irreparable character of the harm. See the January 1, 1999, decision, *B. Gómez* case, in Rafael Chavero, *El nuevo régimen del amparo constitucional en Venezuela*, Ed. Sherwood, Caracas, 2001, p 242. The First Court also ruled in a case decided in February 4, 1999, *C. Negrín* case, regarding a public university position contest that, "the pretended aggrieved party is seeking to be allowed to be registered himself in the public contest for the Chair of Pharmacology in the School of Medicine José María Vargas, but at the present time, the registration was impossible due to the fact that the delay had elapsed the previous year, and consequently the harm produced must be considered as irreparable, declaring inadmissible the action for amparo." *Idem*, p. 243.

seeking her health to be restored to the stage it had before, but to have a particular health care, which is perfectly valid.[526.]

In Peru, the Constitutional Procedure Code also prescribes that the amparo action, as well as all constitutional proceedings, are inadmissible when at the moment of its filing, the violation of the constitutional rights has become irreparable (Article 5,5).

[526]See decision of March 3, 1990, in *Revista de Derecho Público*, n° 42, Editorial Jurídica Venezolana, Caracas, 1990, p. 107.

CHAPTER FOURTEEN

THE IMMINENT CHARACTER OF THE THREATS AND THE PREVENTIVE CHARACTER OF THE AMPARO PROCEEDING

I. THE PREVENTIVE CHARACTER OF THE AMPARO AGAINST THREATS

However, the amparo proceeding is not only a judicial mean seeking to restore harmed constitutional rights, it is also a judicial mean established for the protection of such rights against illegitimate threats that violate those rights.

It is in these cases that the amparo proceeding has a preventive character in the sense of avoiding harm, similar to the United States preventive civil rights injunctions seeking "to prohibit some act or series of acts from occurring in the future,"[527] and designed "to avoid future harm to a party by prohibiting or mandating certain behavior by another party."[528]

It would be absurd for the affected party, when having complete knowledge of the near occurrence of a harm, to patiently wait for the harming act to be issued with all its consequences in order to file the amparo action. On the contrary, it has the right to file the action to obtain a judicial order prohibiting the action to be accomplished, thus avoiding the harm to occur.

---

[527]See Owen M. Fiss, *The Civil Rights Injunction*, Indiana University Press, 1978, p. 7.

[528]See William M. Tabb and Elaine W. Shoben, *Remedies*, Thompson West, 2005, p. 22. In Spanish the word "preventive" is used in procedural law (medidas preventivas o cautelares) to refer to the "temporary" or "preliminary" orders or restraints that in the United States the judge can issue during the proceeding. So the preventive character of the amparo and of the injunctions cannot be confused with the "medidas preventivas" or temporary or preliminary measures that the courts can issue during the trial for the immediate protection of rights, facing the prospect of an irremediable harm that can be caused.

The main condition for this possibility of filing amparo actions against threats (*amenaza*) to constitutional rights, as it is expressly provided in the Nicaraguan (Articles 51, 57, 79) Peruvian (Article 2) and Venezuelan (Articles 2; 6,2) Amparo Laws, is that they must be real, certain, immediate, imminent, possible and realizable.

On the other hand, there are some constitutional rights that essentially and precisely need to be protected against threats, like the right to life in cases of imminent death threats, because on the contrary, they could lose all sense. In this case, the only way to guaranty the right to life, is to avoid the threats to be materialized, for instance, by providing the person with effective police protection.

II. THE SPECIFIC CONDITION OF THE THREAT: ITS IMMINENT CHARACTER

If the specific main condition for the admissibility of the amparo action against harms to constitutional rights is their reparable character; regarding threats, the specific main condition is that they must be of an imminent character.

This condition is also expressly established in the Amparo Laws, for instance, of the Dominican Republic (Article 1), Nicaragua (Articles 51, 57, 79) Peru (Article 2) and Venezuela (Articles 2; 6,2), which provides that in order to file an amparo action against threats, they must not only be real, certain, possible and realizable, but additionally, they must have an immediate and imminent character, provoking fear to persons, or making persons feel in danger regarding their rights. On the contrary, harm refers to situations in which a fact has already been accomplished, so no threat is possible.[529]

---

[529]Regarding this condition, for instance, the Constitutional Court of Colombia has said: "A threat to a fundamental constitutional right has multiple expressions: it can be referred to the specific circumstances of a person regarding the exercise of the right; to the existence of positive and unequivocal signs regarding the intention of a person capable to execute acts that can violate the right; or be represented in the challenge of someone (attempt), with direct repercussion on the right; also, it can be constituted by non deliberated acts that, according to its characteristics, can lead the amparo court to be convinced that if no order is issued, allowing the conduct to continue, the violation of the right will be produced; also it can correspond to an authority omission whose extension in time allows the risk to appear or to increase; its configuration is also feasible in case of the existence of a norm —authorization or mandate— contrary to the Constitution, the application of which in the concrete case would be in itself an attack or a disregard of the fundamental right." See the reference to decision T-349 of August 27, 1993, in Rafael Chavero, *El nuevo*

Consequently, in order to file an amparo action against a threat, it must consist in a potential harm or violation that must be imminent in the sense that it may occur soon; being this same rule of the imminent character of the threat applied in the United States, as an essential condition for granting preventive injunctions. This means that the courts will order injunctions only when the threat is imminent, prohibiting future conduct; and not when the threat is considered remote, potential or speculative.[530]

In the same sense as the amparo in Latin American countries, the injunctions in the United States cannot be granted "merely to allay the fears and apprehensions or to soothe the anxieties of individuals, since such fears and apprehensions may exist without substantial reasons and be absolutely groundless or speculative."[531] The injunctions, as the amparo, are extraordinary remedies "designed to prevent serious harm, and are not

---

régimen del amparo constitucional en Venezuela, Ed. Sherwood, Caracas, 2001, pp. 238–239. See in the same sense decision of the Venezuelan First Court on Judicial Review of Administrative Action of July 16, 1092, in Revista *de Derecho Público*, n° 51, Editorial Jurídica Venezolana, Caracas, 1992, p. 155.

[530]In *Reserve Mining Co. v. Environmental Protection Agency* 513 F.2d, 492 (8th Cir 1975), the Circuit Court did not grant the requested injunction ordering Reserve Mining Company to cease discharging wastes from its iron ore processing plant in Silver Bay, Minnesota into the ambient air of Silver Bay and the waters of Lake Superior because even though the plaintiff has established that the discharges give rise to a "potential threat to the public health...no harm to the public health has been shown to have occurred to this date and the danger to health is not imminent. The evidence calls for preventive and precautionary steps. No reason exists which requires that Reserve to terminate its operations at once." See the comments in Owen M. Fiss and Doug Rendelman, *Injunctions*, The Foundation Press, Mineola, New York, 1984, pp. 116 ff. In another classically cited case, *Fletcher v. Bealey*, 28 Ch. 688 (1885), which referred to waste deposits in the plaintiff's land by the defendant, the judge ruled that since the action is brought to prevent continuing damages, for a quia-timet action, two ingredients are necessary: "There must, if no actual damage is proved, be proof of imminent danger, and there must also be proof that the apprehended damage will, if it comes, be very substantial. I should almost say it must be proved that it will be irreparable, because, if the danger is not proved to be so imminent that no one can doubt that if the remedy is delayed, the damage will be suffered, I think it must be shown that, if the damage does occur at any time, it will come in such a way and under such circumstances that it will be impossible for the Plaintiff to protect himself against it if relief is denied to him in a *quia timet* action." See the reference in *Idem*, pp. 110–111.

[531]See *Callis, Papa, Jackstadt & Halloran, P.C. v. Norkolk and Western Ry. Co.*, 195 Ill. 2d 356, 254 Ill. Dec. 707, 748 N. E.2d 153 (2001); *Frey v. DeCordova Bend Estates Owners Ass'n*, 647 S.W2d 246 (Tex. 1983); *Ormco Corp. v. Johns*, 19 I.E.R. Cas. (BNA), 1714, 148 Lab. Cas. (CCH), 59741, 2003 WL 2007816 (Ala. 2003), in John Bordeau *et al.*, "Injunctions," in Kevin Schroder, John Glenn and Maureen Placilla (Editors), *Corpus Juris Secundum*, Vol. 43A, Thomson West, 2004, p. 57.

to be used to protect a person from mere inconvenience or speculative and insubstantial injury."[532]

This condition is also generally established in the Latin American Amparo Laws. For instance, in Venezuela, the threats that can be protected by the amparo suits must be imminent (Article 2), so the action for amparo is inadmissible when the threat or violation of a constitutional right has ceased or ended (Article 8,1) or when the threat against a constitutional right or guaranty is not "immediate, possible and feasible (Article 6,2).[533]

In a similar sense, the Constitutional Chamber of the Supreme Court of Costa Rica has ruled that "the amparo against a threat regarding a fundamental right can only be granted if the threat is certain, real, effective and imminent (Article 29, Law); thus, those probable prejudices not capable of being objectively apprehended cannot be protected by amparo."[534]

In the same sense, regarding the imminent character of the threat, the courts in Mexico have ruled that they must be sufficiently proved as almost occurring, because for instance, some previous actions had been taken or it can be considered that some actions will occur as an ineludible consequence of past facts that have also been proved.[535] This distinguishes the imminent actions from those already having occurred or from those that perhaps will occur in the future.

---

[532]See *Kucera v. State, Dept. of Transp.*, 140 Wash. 2d 200, 955 O.2d 63 (200)), *Idem*, pp. 57–58.

[533]See decisions of the former Supreme Court of Justice, Politico Administrative Chamber of June 9, 1988, in *Revista de Derecho Público*, n° 35, Editorial Jurídica Venezolana, Caracas, 1988, p. 114, and of August 14, 1992, in *Revista de Derecho Público*, n° 51, Editorial Jurídica Venezolana, Caracas, 1992, pp. 158–159. See also decision of the First Court on Judicial Review of Administrative Action, decision of June 30, 1988, in *Revista de Derecho Público*, n° 35, Editorial Jurídica Venezolana, Caracas, 1988, p. 115. These general conditions have been considered as being concurrent ones when referring to the constitutional protection against harms that someone will soon be inflicting on the rights of other. See decisions of the former Supreme Court of Justice, Politico Administrative Chamber, of June 24, 1993, in *Revista de Derecho Público*, n° 55–56, Editorial Jurídica Venezolana, Caracas, 1993, p. 289; and of March 22, 1995, *La Reintegradora* case, in Rafael Chavero, *El nuevo régimen del amparo constitucional en Venezuela,* Ed. Sherwood, Caracas, 2001, p. 239.

[534]See Vote 295-93, in Rubén Hernández Valle, *Derecho Procesal constitucional*, Editorial Juricentro, 2001, p. 222.

[535]Joaquin Brage Camazano, *La Jurisdicción Constitucional de la Libertad. Teoría general, Argentina, México,* Corte Interamericana de Derechos Humanos, Ed. Porrúa, México, 2005, pp. 171–173.

The Ecuadorian Constitution also prescribes regarding the "imminent" character of threats for an amparo action to be admitted, that it must be about to occur in the near future, as a true potential injury and not as a mere conjecture. Additionally, the harm must be concrete and real and the claimant must prove how it affects his rights (Article 95).[536]

The imminence of the harm must also be certain, so for example, the Mexican courts have ruled that for instance the sole possibility for the authorities to be able to exercise their powers of investigation and control regarding the plaintiff cannot be sufficient for the filing of an amparo action.[537] In this same sense, in Colombia, the *Tutela* Law refers to the cases in which "there does not exist a threat to a fundamental constitutional right," prescribing that "it will be understood that a fundamental constitutional right cannot be threatened by the sole fact of the opening of an administrative enquiry by the competent authority, subjected to the procedure regulated by law" (Article 3 of Decree 306-92).

In the same sense, the former Supreme Court of Justice of Venezuela ruled in 1989 that:

> The opening of a disciplinary administrative inquiry is not enough to justify the protection of a party by means of the judicial remedy of amparo, moreover when the said proceeding, in which all needed defenses can be exercised, may conclude in a decision discarding the incriminations against the party with the definitive closing of the disciplinary process, without any sanction to the party.[538]

The criteria of the imminent character of the threat to constitutional rights for the admission of the amparo action has also led the former Supreme Court of Justice of Venezuela to reject the amparo proceeding against statutes, arguing that a statute or a legal norm, in itself, cannot

---

[536]See Hernán Salgado Pesantes, *Manual de Justicia Constitucional Ecuatoriana*, Corporación Editora Nacional, Quito, 2004, p. 80.

[537]See *Semanario Judicial de la Federación*, Tomo I, Segunda parte-2, p. 697. See the reference in Joaquin Brage Camazano, *La Jurisdicción Constitucional de la Libertad. Teoría general, Argentina, México, Corte Interamericana de Derechos Humanos*, Ed. Porrúa, México, 2005, p. 173, note 269.

[538]See Decision of the Politico Administrative Chamber of October 26, 1989, *Gisela Parra Mejía* case, in Rafael Chavero, *El nuevo régimen del amparo constitucional en Venezuela*, Ed. Sherwood, Caracas, 2001, pp. 191, 241.

originate a possible, imminent and feasible threat.[539] Nonetheless, the Court has considered that the plaintiff can always file the amparo action against the public officer that must apply the statute, seeking a court prohibition directed to the said public officer, compelling him not to apply the challenged norm."[540]

[539]In a decision of May 24, 1993, the Politico Administrative Chamber of the former Supreme Court ruled: "The same occurs with the third condition set forth in the Law; the threat, that is, the probable and imminent harm, will never be feasible —that is, concreted— by the defendant. If it could be sustained that the amparo could be filed against a disposition the constitutionality of which is challenged, then it would be necessary to accept as defendant the legislative body or the public officer that had sanctioned it, being the latter the one that would act in court defending the act. It can be observed that in case the possible harm would effectively arrive to be materialized, it would not be the legislative body or the state organ which issued it, the one that will execute it, but the public official for whom the application of the norm will be imposing in all the cases in which an individual would be in the factual situation established in the norm. If it is understood that the norm can be the object or an amparo action, the conclusion would be that the defendant (the public entity sanctioning the norm the unconstitutionality of which is alleged) could not be the one entity conducting the threat; but that the harm would be in the end concretized or provoked by a different entity (the one applying to the specific and concrete case the unconstitutional provision)." See in *Revista de Derecho Público*, n° 55-56, Editorial Jurídica Venezolana, Caracas, 1993, pp. 289–290.

[540]In the same decision, the Court ruled as follows: "Nonetheless, this High Court considers necessary to point out that the previous conclusion does not signify the impossibility to prevent the concretion of the harm —objection that could be drawn from the thesis that the amparo can only proceed if the unconstitutional norm is applied—, due to the fact that the imminently aggrieved person must not necessarily wait for the effective execution of the illegal norm, because since he faces the threat having the conditions established in the Law, he could seek for amparo for his constitutional rights. In such case, though, the amparo would not be directed against the norm, but against the public officer that has to apply it. In effect, being imminent the application to an individual of a normative disposition contrary to any of the constitutional rights or guaranties, the potentially affected person could seek from the court a prohibition directed to the said public officer plaintiff, compelling not to apply the challenged norm, once evaluated by the court as being unconstitutional." *Idem*, p. 290.

CHAPTER FIFTEEN

THE INJURING PARTY: THE DEFENDANT
(PUBLIC ENTITIES OR PRIVATE INDIVIDUALS)

I.   THE INJURING PARTY

Because the amparo procedure is governed by the principle of bilateralism, the party that initiates it, that is the plaintiff, whose constitutional rights and guaranties have been injured or threatened, must always file the action against an injuring party, whose actions or omissions are those that have caused the harm or threats.

This means that the action must always be filed against a person or a public entity that must also be individuated as defendant.[541] That is why in the amparo proceeding, as well as the injunctions in the United States, the final result has to be a judicial order "addressed to some clearly identified individual, not just the general citizenry."[542]

Thus, since the beginning of the proceeding when the action is filed, or during the procedure, the bilateral character of the amparo suit implies the need to have a procedural relation that must be established between the injured party and the injuring one who must also participate in the process.[543]

---

[541]The only exception to the principle of bilateralism is the case of Chile, where the offender is not considered a defendant party but only a person whose activity is limited to inform the court and give it the documents it has. That is why in the Regulation set forth by the Supreme Court (*Auto Acordado*) it is said that the affected state organ, person or public officer "can" just appear as party in the process (4). See Juan Manuel Errazuriz G. and Jorge Miguel Otero A., *Aspectos procesales del recurso de protección*, Editorial Jurídica de Chile 1989, p. 27.

[542]See Owen M. Fiss, *The Civil Rights Injunction*, Indiana University Press, 1978, p. 12.

[543]In this regard, the former Supreme Court of Justice of Venezuela in a decision of December 15, 1992, pointed out that: "The amparo action set forth in the Constitution, and regulated in the Organic Amparo law, has among its fundamental characteristic its basic personal or subjective character, which implies that a direct, specific and undutiful relation

1. The question of the individuation of the defendant

This need for the individuation of the defendant also derives from the subjective or personal character of the amparo in the sense that in the complaint, as it is generally provided in all the Latin American Amparo Laws,[544] the plaintiff must clearly identify the authority, public officer, person or entity against whom the action is filed.

According to what is established in some Laws, of course this condition only applies when such individuation is possible.[545] Consequently, as the Paraguayan Civil Procedure Code establishes, when the identification of the defendant is not possible, the judge, in order to guaranty the procedural bilateral relation must provide the necessary means in order to try to determine it (Article 569.b). In this regard, in particular when the injurer party cannot be determined or located, and as it is provided in the Uruguayan Amparo Law, the court must designate a public defendant to represent it in the case.[546]

Nonetheless, in the amparo proceeding, more important than the author of the violation is the inflicted injury to constitutional rights. So when it is impossible for the plaintiff or for the judge to clearly identify the defendant, if the fact or action causing the harm can be clearly determined, even without the identification of the exact author who has produced it, whether an authority, a public officer or an individual, the constitutional complaint can be filed and eventually the protection can be granted.

---

must exist between the person claiming for the protection of his rights, and the person purported to have originated the disturbance, who is to be the one with standing to act as defendant or the person against whom the action is filed. In other words, it is necessary, for granting an amparo, that the person signaled as the injurer be in the end, the one originating the harm." See Supreme Court of Justice, Politico Administrative Chamber, decision dated December 16, 1992, *Haydée Casanova* Caso, in *Revista de Derecho Público*, n° 52, Editorial Jurídica Venezolana, Caracas, 1992, p. 139.

[544] Argentina, Article 6,b; Bolivia, 97,II; Colombia, Article 14; Costa Rica, Article 38; El Salvador, Article 14,2; Guatemala Article 21,d; Honduras, Article 21; 49,4; México 116,III; 166,III; Nicaragua, Article 27,2; Panama, Article 2619,2; Paraguay, Article 568,b; Perú, Article 42,3; Venezuela Article 18,3.

[545] Argentina (Article 6,b); Colombia (Article 14); Nicaragua (Articles 25; 55) and Venezuela (Article 18,3).

[546] In Uruguay, the Amparo Law in this regard, expressly provides the possibility to file the action in urgent cases even without knowing with precision about the person responsible for the harm fact, in which case, the court must publish public notices to identify it, and in case of the responsible party not showing, the court must appoint an ex officio defendant (Article 7).

This main rule has been developed in the Argentinean doctrine that states that "the amparo action tends to focus on the damaging act and only in an accessory way on its author,"[547] so once the injury has been caused and the injuring act has been determined, the fact that its author has not been identified cannot impede the decision to repair the harm, "due to the fact that the amparo action tends more to restore the harmed constitutional rights, than to individualize the author of the injury."[548]

Yet this principle does not mean that the plaintiff can simply get rid of his duty to try to identify the author of the harm inflicted on his rights, so, as was also ruled in Argentina, in cases of absence of individuation of the injuring party, the claim can be rejected when it is determined that what the plaintiff pretended was to force the court to do his job.[549]

---

[547]See Alí Joaquín Salgado, *Juicio de amparo y acción de inconstitucionalidad*, Astrea, Buenos Aires, 1987, p. 92.

[548]See José Luis Lazzarini, *El juicio de amparo*, La Ley, Buenos Aires, 1987, p. 274. That is why, in the Angel Siri Argentinean leading case, in which without statutory regulations the Supreme Court in Argentina admitted the amparo action, the Court protected the owner of a newspaper that was shot down by the government, notwithstanding that in the files there was no clear evidence regarding the authority that closed it, nor the motives of the decision. *Idem*, p. 276.

[549]It was for instance the case decided by the Argentinean Supreme Court rejecting an amparo action that was filed by a former President of the Republic (*Juan D. Perón* case) against dispositions of the government, asking to have the body of his dead wife returned. In that case, the Supreme Court ruled about the need for a "minimal individuation of the author of the act originating the claim," rejecting the amparo action because the lack of minimal individuation of the defendant. The court deduced that what the plaintiff was seeking was to obtain from the courts an order to practice the necessary inquiries regarding the whereabouts of the body. The Supreme Court ruled as follows: "the general principles of procedural law do not suffer any exception due to the exceptional character of the amparo and must be respected in order to eventually assure the exercise of the right to defense, from which the counterpart must not be deprived... This is evident from the text of the suit in which it is affirmed that the act provoking the claim has been executed 'by disposition of the former Provisional Government' without adding any other reference or explanation regarding the pointed public officer or entity. It is evident that the minimal requirements of individuation of the defendant, referred above, have not been accomplished in the case. On the contrary what is revealed in the files of this case, is that in lieu of seeking protection to his constitutional guaranties harmed by an illegal State act, the plaintiff has intended to use the amparo procedure with the purpose of obtaining from the judges the order to practice the necessary inquiries regarding the facts, which are not proved or specified with precision. And it is clear that the performance of the instruction phase cannot be achieved by means of this amparo remedy whose incorporation to Argentinean positive law has purposes different to the one pursued in this case." See Fallos:

However, leaving aside these restricted situations, the general principle regarding the amparo action is the need for the plaintiff to make the necessary individuation of the defendant by means of its identification, whether being a natural person (human being) a corporation, or a public officer or entity, being such person or entity the party causing the harm or threat to the plaintiff's rights.[550]

248–537, referred in José Luis Lazzarini, *El juicio de amparo*, La Ley, Buenos Aires, 1987, p. 275.

[550]That is, as it has been decided by the Venezuelan courts, the aggrieving party must always be directly responsible for the conduct violating the constitutional rights and guaranties of the aggrieved party. See First Court of Judicial Review on Administrative Actions, decision of May 12, 1988, in Revista *de Derecho Público*, n° 34, Editorial Jurídica Venezolana, Caracas, 1988, p. 113. and decision of June 16, 1988, in Revista *de Derecho Público*, n° 35, Editorial Jurídica Venezolana, Caracas, 1988, p. 138. Consequently, if a person is denounced as aggrieving without being so, the amparo action must be rejected. See Supreme Court of Justice, Politico Administrative Chamber, decision dated November 22, 1993, in Revista *de Derecho Público*, n° 55-56, Editorial Jurídica Venezolana, Caracas, 1993, pp. 487–489. As decided by the First Court on Judicial Review of Administrative Action in a decision of July 13, 1993: "Among the basic characteristics of the amparo action is its subjective character, which requires for its admissibility that the threat of violation of a constitutional right be immediate, possible and realizable by the person identified as aggrieving, which means that in the case of a once materialized violation, it must be executed directly by the accused, that is, a direct relation must exist between the person asking for the protection to his rights and the person identified as aggrieving who will be the one with standing, and this being the person against whom the action is filed. This leads to affirm that for the admissibility of the amparo action, it is necessary that the person identified as aggrieving eventually be the one causing the purported harm and the one which would be obliged to follow the amparo order in case of the granting of the protection petition. This essentially personal and subjective character of the amparo action results from the very reading of Article 18,3 of the Amparo Law which imposes on the plaintiff the burden of sufficiently identifying the aggrieving party when possible. It is also evident from Article 32,a, which sets forth the need for the decision to expressly mention "the authority, private body or person against whose acts or resolution the amparo the amparo is conceded; because on the contrary it could happen that processes could be filed against persons different to those that supposedly caused the harm which will be contrary to the spirit, purpose and raison d'être of the Amparo Law. Anyway, the problem of the precise identification of the aggrieving party has been raised regarding amparo actions against Public Administration activities, in order to avoid that the amparo actions be unnecessarily filed against the Republic as a legal person. The necessary identity between the 'aggrieved party and the person accused as being the aggrieving —which must be the one provoking the constitutional harm— has been repeatedly ruled by this Chamber, particularly in order to avoid the filing of amparo processes against the Republic, and to encourage the filing against the specific public officer who produced the purported harm act, fact or omission. In this sense it was decided in ruling n° 391 of August 1, 1991 (*María Pérez* case) where it was said that "the constitutional amparo action, because of its special nature,

In the case of amparo actions filed against artificial persons, public entities or corporations, the petition must also identify them with precision and if possible, also identify their representatives.

In these cases of harms caused by entities or corporations, the action can be filed directly against the natural person acting on his behalf as representative of the entity or corporation, for instance, the public official; or directly against the entity in itself.[551] In this latter case, according to the expression used in civil right injunctions in the United States, the action is filed against "the office rather than [to] the person."[552]

This means, as is the rule in Mexico, that in these cases the amparo is filed against the "responsible authority" expression that is conceived in institutional terms rather than in personal terms, in the sense that the institution involved always remains the responsible author, regardless of the changes of the persons representing it.[553] Consequently, in cases of amparo actions filed against entities or corporations, the natural person representing them can be changed, as it commonly happens regarding public entities, [554] a circumstance that does not affect the bilateral relation between aggrieved and aggrieving parties.

---

is an action directly filed against the administrative authority which harms or threatens to harm the constitutional right." See decision of the former Supreme Tribunal of Justice, Politico Administrative Chamber, December 15, 1992, *Haydée Casanova* case, in *Revista de Derecho Público*, n° 52, Editorial Jurídica Venezolana, Caracas, 1992, p. 139.

[551] This implies that in the filing of the action of amparo in cases of Public Administration activities, "the person acting on behalf of (or representing) the entity who caused the harm or threat to the rights or guaranties must be identified, which is, the signaled person who has the exact and direct knowledge of the facts." See decision of the First Court on Judicial Review of Administrative Actions, dated June 16, 1988, in *Revista de Derecho Público*, n° 35, Editorial Jurídica Venezolana, Caracas, 1988, p. 138.

[552] See Owen M. Fiss, *The Civil Rights Injunction*, Indiana University Press, 1978, p. 15.

[553] See Richard D. Baker, *Judicial Review in México. A Study of the Amparo Suit,* Texas University Press, Austin, 1971, p. 209. In this sense it has been decided by the Supreme Court of México, ruling that the discharge, transfer, promotion, demotion, death, or other removal of the individual who has actually ordered or executed the act object of the complaint, or any transfer of jurisdiction over the matter in contest, is no bar to the suit. See Suprema Corte, *Jurisprudencia de la Suprema Corte, Tesis* 183, II, p. 365; also Suprema Corte, *Montufar Miguel* case, 17 S.J. 798 (1925). See the references in *Idem*, p. 208–109, note 36.

[554] As it has been decided by the Venezuelan First Court on Judicial Review of Administrative Action in a decision of September 28, 1993, regarding an amparo action filed against the dean of a Law Faculty, in which case the person in charge as Dean was changed: "The heading of the position does not change its organic unity. If the dean of the

As aforementioned, the action can also be personally filed against the representative of the entity or corporation himself, for instance the public officer or the director or manager of the entity, particularly when the harm or threat has been personally provoked by him, independently of the artificial person or entity for which he is acting.[555]

In these cases, when for instance the public official responsible for the harm can be identified with precision as the injuring party, it is only him, personally, who must act as defendant in the procedure, in which case no notice is needed to be sent to his superior or to the Attorney General.[556] In such cases, it is the individuated natural person or public officer that must personally act as injuring party.[557]

On the contrary, if the action is filed, for instance, against a Ministerial entity as a Public Administration organ, in this case the Attorney General,

---

Faculty changes, it will always be a subjective figure that substitutes the previous one. That is why in a decision of September 11, 1990, this Court ruled that the circumstance of the head of an organ mentioned as aggrieving being changed does not alter the procedural relation originated with the amparo action. In addition, it must be added that it would have no sense to rule for the procedural relation be continued with the person that doesn't occupy anymore the position, because in case the constitutional amparo is granted, then the ex public official would not be in a position to reestablish the factual infringed situation. As much, the former public officer could be liable for the damages caused, but as it is known, the amparo action has the only purpose of reestablishing the harmed legal situation, and that can only be assured by the current public official." See the First Court on Judicial Review of Administrative Action in a decision of September, 28, 1993, in *Revista de Derecho Público*, n° 55-56, Editorial Jurídica Venezolana, Caracas, 1993, p. 330.

[555]In such cases, when the action is filled against public officers, as it is established in Article 27 of the Venezuelan Amparo Law, the court deciding on the merits must notify its decision to the competent authority "in order for it to decide the disciplinary sanctions against the public official responsible for the violation or the threat against a constitutional right or guaranty."

[556]Venezuelan First Court on Judicial Review of Administrative Action, decision of May 12, 1988, in Revista *de Derecho Público*, n° 34, Editorial Jurídica Venezolana, Caracas, 1988, p. 113; Venezuelan Supreme Court of Justice, Politico Administrative Chamber, decision of March 16, 1989, in *Revista de Derecho Público*, n° 38, Editorial Jurídica Venezolana, Caracas, 1989, p. 110; Venezuelan First Court on Judicial Review of Administrative Action, decision of September 7, 1989, in *Revista de Derecho Público*, n° 40, Editorial Jurídica Venezolana, Caracas, 1989, p. 107.

[557]Former Venezuelan Supreme Court of Justice, Politico Administrative Chamber, March 8, 1990, in *Revista de Derecho Público*, n° 42, Editorial Jurídica Venezolana, Caracas, 1990, p. 114; Venezuelan First Court on Judicial Review of Administrative Action, decision of November 21, 1990, in *Revista de Derecho Público*, n° 44, Editorial Jurídica Venezolana, Caracas, 1990, p. 148.

as representative of the State, is the entity that must act in the process as its judicial representative.[558] In other cases, when the amparo action is exercised against a perfectly identified and individuated organ of a Public Administration and not against the State, the Attorney General, as its judicial representative, does not necessarily have a procedural role to play,[559] and cannot act on its behalf.[560]

2. *The defendant in the amparo suit: authorities and individuals*

The most important aspect in the Latin American amparo proceeding regarding the injuring party, with some exceptions, is that the action for amparo can be filed not only against public authorities but also against individuals. In other words, this specific judicial mean is conceived for the protection of constitutional rights and guaranties against harms or threats regardless of the author, which can be public entities, authorities, individuals or private corporations.

The amparo proceeding was originally created to protect individuals against the State; and that is why some countries like Mexico remain with that traditional trend; but that initial trend has not prevented the possibility in other countries, for the admission of the amparo proceeding for the protection of constitutional rights against other individual's actions.

The current situation is that in the majority of Latin American countries the admission of the amparo action against individuals is accepted, as is the case in Argentina, Bolivia, Chile, the Dominican Republic, Paraguay, Peru, Venezuela and Uruguay, as well as, although in a more restrictive

---

[558]Venezuelan First Court on Judicial Review of Administrative Action, decision of September 7, 1989, in Revista *de Derecho Público*, n° 40, Editorial Jurídica Venezolana, Caracas, 1989, p. 107.

[559]Venezuelan First Court on Judicial Review of Administrative Action, decision of November 21, 1990, in Revista *de Derecho Público*, n° 44, Editorial Jurídica Venezolana, Caracas, 1990, p. 148.

[560]Venezuelan First Court on Judicial Review of Administrative Action, decision of October 10, 1990, in Revista *de Derecho Público*, n° 44, Editorial Jurídica Venezolana, Caracas, 1990, p. 142; Former Supreme Court of Justice, Politico Administrative Chamber, decision of August 1, 1991, in Revista *de Derecho Público*, n° 47, Editorial Jurídica Venezolana, Caracas, 1991, p. 120; Venezuelan First Court on Judicial review of Administrative Action, decision of July 30, 1992, in Revista *de Derecho Público*, n° 51, Editorial Jurídica Venezolana, Caracas, 1992, p. 164; Former Venezuelan Supreme Court of Justice, Politico Administrative Chamber, December 15, 1992, in Revista *de Derecho Público*, n° 52, Editorial Jurídica Venezolana, Caracas, 1992, p. 13.

way, in Colombia, Costa Rica, Ecuador, Guatemala and Honduras. In this sense the writ of amparo is also regulated in the Philippines, which can be filed agaist acts or omission "of a public official or employee, or of a private individual or entity" (Sec. 1). Only a minority of Latin American countries the amparo action remains exclusively as a protective mean against authorities, as happens in Brazil, El Salvador, Panama, Mexico and Nicaragua. This is also the case in the United States where the civil rights injunctions, in matters of constitutional or civil rights or guaranties,[561] can only be admitted against public entities.[562]

A. The amparo against public authorities: public entities an public officers

As mentioned, in Latin America only in Brazil, El Salvador, Panama, Mexico and Nicaragua does the amparo action remain as a protective mean only to be filed against the State, that is, public entities and public officials. In the other countries, in addition to public entities and officials, the amparo action can also be filed against individuals.

The former has been the situation in Mexico since the origin of the amparo suit, when the constitution conceived it to protect individuals against injuries to their constitutional guaranties committed by "authorities" (Article 103). That is why in the Mexican amparo suit, a responsible author-

---

[561] In other matters the injunctions can be filed against any person as "higher public officials or private persons." See M. Glenn Abernathy and Barbara A. Perry, *Civil Liberties under the Constitution*, Sixth Edition, University of South Carolina Press, 1993, p. 8.

[562] As explained by M. Glenn Abernathy and Barbara A. Perry: "Limited remedies for private interference with free choice. Another problem in the citizen's search for freedom from restriction lies in that many types of interference stemming from private persons do not constitute actionable wrongs under the law. Private prejudice and private discrimination do not, in the absence of specific statutory provisions, offer grounds for judicial intervention on behalf of the sufferer. If one is denied admission to membership in a social club, for example, solely on the basis of his race or religion or political affiliation, he may understandably smart under the rejection, but the courts cannot help him (again assuming no statutory provision barring such distinctions). There are, then, many types of restraints on individual freedom of choice which are beyond the authority of courts to remove or ameliorate. It should be noted that the guaranties of rights in the U.S. Constitution only protect against governmental action and do not apply to purely private encroachments, except for the Thirteenth Amendment's prohibition of slavery. Remedies for private invasion must be found in statutes, the common law, or administrative agency regulations and adjudications." *Idem*, p. 6.

ity must always exist;[563] condition that has been developed by the *jurisprudencia* regarding the following aspects:

First, not all public entities can be considered as "authorities," which are only those public entities that are empowered to adopt decisions and to impose or execute them to individuals by use of coactive public power.[564] According to this doctrine, the courts had rejected the amparo suit against public entities that have been considered as not having the power to decide, like those with purely staff or consultative nature.[565] Consequently, for instance, many decentralized public entities like *Petróleos Mexicanos,* the National Commission on Electricity, the Human Rights' Defendant of the UNAM and the Autonomous Universities were initially excluded from the category of "authorities."[566] Nonetheless, the amparo suit has been progressively admitted against some of those entities based on the possible decision powers they have in particular cases.[567]

---

[563] Accordingly, Article 11 of the Amparo Law points out that "the authority responsible is the one who edicts, promulgates, orders, executes or tries to execute the statute or the claimed act." This article has been interpreted in the sense that authorities are not only those superior ones that order the acts, but also those subordinate ones that execute or try to execute them; the amparo being admitted against any of them. See "Autoridades para efectos del juicio de amparo" (*Apéndice al Semanario Judicial de la Federación*, 1917–1988, Segunda parte, Tesis 300, p. 519). See the reference in Eduardo Ferrer Mac-Gregor, *La acción constitucional de amparo en México y España. Estudio de derecho comparado*, Editorial Porrúa, México, 2002, p. 254.

[564] As was defined in the *Campos Otero Julia* case (1935), this term is understood as "an organ of the State legally vested with the powers of decision and command necessary for imposing upon individuals either its own determinations or those that emanate from some other State organs." This definition was expanded to include "all those persons who dispose of public power (fuerza pública) by virtue of either legal or de facto circumstances, and who, consequently find themselves in a position to perform acts of a public character, due to the fact that the power they have is public." See "Autoridades para efectos del juicio de amparo" (*Apéndice al Semanario Judicial de la Federación*, 1917–1988, Segunda parte, Tesis 300, p. 519. See the reference in Eduardo Ferrer Mac-Gregor, *La acción constitucional de amparo en México y España. Estudio de derecho comparado*, Editorial Porrúa, México, 2002, p. 253. Also see Suprema Corte, *Jurisprudencia de la Suprema Corte*, Thesis 179, II, 360. See the reference in Richard D. Baker, *Judicial Review in México. A Study of the Amparo Suit*, Texas University Press, Austin, 1971, p. 94.

[565] *Idem,* p. 95.

[566] See the references to the judicial decisions in Eduardo Ferrer Mac-Gregor, *La acción constitucional de amparo en México y España. Estudio de derecho comparado*, Editorial Porrúa, México, 2002, pp. 255–256.

[567] *Idem,* p. 257.

Second, the *jurisprudencia* has developed the doctrine of the *de facto* public officer, in the sense that even if the offender is not the legitimate holder of the public position, the amparo must be admitted when the harm is caused by someone that pretends to be exercising public power in which case the citizens have the right to legitimate confidence in those who exercise it.

Third, regarding the concept of authority in the amparo action, the plaintiff must identify all those materially involved in the injuring action whom have to be notified by the court; not only those who ordered the challenged activity, but those who have decided it and have executed or applied it.[568]

In contrast with this Mexican approach, in almost all the other Latin American countries, the term "authority" has been interpreted in a wider sense as referring to any public entity or public official, regardless of their powers or functions.

In Argentina, for instance, as established in the Amparo Law, the action can be filed against "any public authority act or omission" (Article 1), the term "public authority" [569] having a wide sense, including all sorts of public entities or officials of all branches of government. Consequently, in spite of some isolated restrictive interpretations,[570] the general trend in

---

[568] As decided by the Supreme Court: if the amparo claim identifies the responsible authority as the one adopting the act or that has ordered it, requesting the suspension of its effects without identifying the authority that has executed the act, the suspension cannot be granted since the execution is considered as being consented to by the plaintiff. On the contrary, if the action only mentions as responsible authorities those who have executed the act, without identifying those ordering it, then if it is true that the suspension can be granted, the case must be discontinued because without identifying the author of the act, the situation must be considered as consented to by the plaintiff. See the Supreme Court jurisprudencia on "Actos Consumados. Suspension improcedente" y "Actos derivados de actos consentidos," in *Apéndice al Semanario Judicial de la Federación,* 1917-1995, Primera Sala, Tesis 1090, p. 756; y Tribunal Pleno, Tesis 17, p. 12. See the references in Eduardo Ferrer Mac-Gregor, *La acción constitucional de amparo en México y España. Estudio de derecho comparado,* Editorial Porrúa, México, 2002, p, 255, notes 450–451.

[569] It must be said that the expression "public authority" in Article 1 of the Amparo Law was incorporated because of the intention of the 1964 legislator to not regulate the amparo against individuals, which nonetheless was already admitted by the Supreme Court and later expressly regulated in the Civil Procedure Code.

[570] In some occasions this expression has also been interpreted in the restrictive way as in México, refering only to public officers with *imperium*, that is, those with power to command and to edict obligatory decisions and to require the use of public force to execute them. See Néstor Pedro Sagüés, "Derecho procesal Constitucional," Vol 3, *Acción de*

Argentina is to understand "authority" in a wide sense, comprising any agent, employee, public official, magistrate of government or any agent acting in such condition, including individuals accomplishing public functions, like the public services concessionaries.[571]

In a similar sense, in Bolivia, Colombia, El Salvador, Peru, Nicaragua, Uruguay and Venezuela, for instance, also in a wide sense, the term "public authorities" has been conceived for the purpose of granting the amparo protection against any public officer or public entity,[572] "no matter its category and functions," as it is provided in the Brazilian statute on the *mandado de segurança* (Article 1). Even some Amparo Laws, in order to dissipate any doubts, are enumerative and include any act from any of the branches of government, including delegated, decentralized or autonomous entities, municipal corporations or those supported with public funds or those acting by delegation from the State by means of a concession, contract or resolution.[573]

In this respect, the only Latin American country where the amparo action regarding authorities is expressly reduced to those conforming to the Executive branch of government is Ecuador, where Article 46 of the Amparo Law only admits the amparo against "public administration authorities" (Article 46).

B. The amparo against individuals or private persons

If it is true that the amparo action, as a specific judicial mean for the protection of constitutional rights and guaranties was originally conceived for the protection of individuals against the State and its public officials, the fact is that it has also progressively been admitted against private

---

amparo, Editorial Astrea, Buenos Aires, 1988, pp. 91–93; Joaquin Brague Camazano, *La Jurisdicción constitucional de la libertad (Teoría general, Argentina, México, Corte Interamericana de Derechos Humanos)*, Editorial Porrúa, México, 2005, p. 97. José Luis Lazzarini, *El juicio de amparo*, Editorial La Ley, Buenos Aires, 1987, pp. 208–209.

[571] In some cases it has even been considered that actions of a Provincial Constituent Assembly violating constitutional rights can be challenged via the amparo action. See Alí Joaquín Salgado, *Juicio de amparo y acción de inconstitucionalidad*, Editorial Astrea, Buenos Aires, 1987, pp. 24–25.

[572] Bolivia (Article 94), Colombia (Article 1), El Salvador (Article 12), Perú (Article 2), Nicaragua (Article 3), Uruguay (Article 2) and Venezuela (Article 2).

[573] Guatemala (Article 9); Honduras (Article 41).

persons, corporations or institutions whose actions can also cause harm or threats regarding constitutional rights of others.

This was admitted for the first time in Argentina, by means of the Supreme Court of the Nation's decision issued in 1958, in the *Samuel Kot* case, in which it ruled that "nothing in the letter and spirit of the Constitution allows for the assertion that the protection of constitutional rights is circumscribed only to attacks from the State," being important not only the origin of the injury on constitutional rights but the rights themselves, thereby accepting the amparo action against individuals.[574]

After this decision, the amparo against individuals was later admitted in many Latin American countries like in Bolivia, Chile, the Dominican Republic, Paraguay, Peru, Uruguay and Venezuela, and also in Colombia, Costa Rica, Ecuador, Guatemala and Honduras, where the amparo action can be filed against individual's acts or omissions causing harm or threats to constitutional rights of other individuals, although not always in the same sense.

In other countries, this possibility of amparo against individuals continues without being admitted, as is the case of Mexico, where the constitutional protection through the amparo suit is established exclusively against authorities.[575] Also in Brazil regarding the *mandado de segurança,* the Constitution provides for its admission only to protect constitutional rights and freedoms "when the party responsible for the illegality or abuse of power is a public authority or an agent of a legal entity exercising attributions of the authorities," thus excluding the recourse of protection against the actions of private individuals.[576] Similar provisions are set forth in the Amparo Law of Panama (Article 50 Constitution; Article

---

[574]See José Luis Lazzarini, *El juicio de amparo,* La Ley, Buenos Aires, 1987, p. 228; Joaquín Brage Camazo, *La jurisdicción constitucional de la libertad (Teoría general, Argentina, México, Corte Interamericana de derechos humanos),* Editorial Porrúa, México, 2005, p. 99; Néstor Pedro Sagüés, "Derecho procesal Constitucional," Vol 3, *Acción de amparo*, Editorial Astrea, Buenos Aires, 1988, pp. 13, 512, 527 ff.

[575]See Eduardo Ferrer Mac-Gregor, *La acción constitucional de amparo en México y España. Estudio de derecho comparado*, Editorial Porrúa, México, 2002, p, 251; Joaquín Brage Camazo, *La jurisdicción constitucional de la libertad (Teoría general, Argentina, México, Corte Interamericana de derechos humanos),* Editorial Porrúa, México, 2005, 184.

[576]See Celso Agrícola Barbi, *Do mandado de segurança*, Editora Forense, Rio de Janeiro, 1993, p. 92.

2608, Judicial Code), El Salvador (Article 12) and Nicaragua (Article 23).

In contrast, as mentioned, the amparo action against individuals is admitted in Argentina, even though the 1966 Law 16.986 only refers to the amparo action against the State, that is "against every act or omission of the authorities" (Article 1); the amparo against individuals being regulated in Articles 321,2 and 498 of the Code of Civil and Commercial Procedure.

In Venezuela, the amparo action is also admitted against acts of individuals. The 1988 Organic Law of Amparo[577] provides that the amparo action "shall be admitted against any fact, act or omission from citizens, legal entities, private groups or organizations that have violated, violates or threaten to violate any of the constitutional guaranties or rights" (Article 2).

In a similar manner, the Uruguayan 1988 Law 16.011 of Amparo admits, in general terms, the action of amparo "against any act, omission or fact of the state or public sector authorities, as well as individuals that currently or imminently, manifestly and unlawfully impair, restrict, alter or threaten any of the rights and freedoms expressly or implicitly recognized by the Constitution" (Article 1).[578] A similar provision is included in the Peruvian Code of Constitutional Procedures (Article 2)[579] and in the Bolivian Constitution (Article 19).

Also in Chile, even without a statute regulating the action for protection, it has been interpreted that the action is established in the Constitution to protect constitutional rights and freedoms against arbitrary or unlawful acts or omissions perturbing or threatening them (Article 20) without any distinction as to their origin, being admitted against acts or omissions from individuals.[580] A similar interpretation was also adopted

---

[577]See Allan R. Brewer-Carías, *Instituciones Políticas y Constitucionales*, Vol V, *Derecho y Acción de Amparo,* Editorial Jurídica Venezolana, Caracas, 1998, pp. 96, 128; Rafael Chavero, *El nuevo régimen del amparo constitucional en Venezuela*, Editorial Sherwood, Caracas, 2001.

[578]See Luis Alberto Viera, *Ley de Amparo*, Ediciones Idea, Montevideo, 1993, pp. 63, 157.

[579]See Samuel B. Abad Yupanqui, *El proceso constitucional de amparo*, Gaceta Jurídica, Lima, 2004, pp. 389 ff.

[580]See Humberto Nogueira Alcalá, "El derecho de amparo o protección de los derechos humanos, fundamentales o esenciales en Chile: evolución y perspectivas," in Humberto Nogueira Alcalá (Editor), *Acciones constitucionales de amparo y protección: realidad y*

by the Supreme Court of the Dominican Republic regarding the admissibility of the amparo against individuals.[581]

Other Latin American countries, such as Guatemala (Article 9), Colombia,[582] Costa Rica,[583] Ecuador[584] and Honduras only admit the amparo

perspectivas en Chile y América Latina, Editorial Universidad de Talca, Talca, 2000, p. 41.

[581]See Eduardo Jorge Prats, *Derecho Constitucional*, Vol. II, Gaceta Judicial, Santo Domingo, 2005, p.390.

[582]In Colombia where the constitution expressly refers to the law for the establishment of "the cases in which the action of *tutela* may be filed against private individuals entrusted with providing a public service or whose conduct may seriously and directly affect the collective interest or in respect of whom the applicant may find himself/herself in a state of subordination or vulnerability" (Article 86). In compliance with this constitutional provision, the Decree 2.591 of 1991 (Article 42) establishes that the action of *tutela* shall be admitted against acts or omissions of private individuals in the following cases: 1.When the person against whom action is brought is in charge of the public service of education in protection of the rights enshrined in Articles 13, 15, 16, 18, 19, 20, 23, 27, 29, 37 and 38 of the Constitution. 2. When the person against whom action is brought is in charge of rendering a public health service, to protect the rights to life, intimacy, equality and autonomy. 3. When the person against whom action is brought is in charge of rendering public services. 4. When the request is directed against a private organization against who effectively controls such organization or is the real beneficiary of the situation that caused the action, provided the claimant is in a position of subordination or defenselessness before such organization. 5. When the person against whom action is brought violates or threatens to violate Article 17 of the Constitution. 6. When the private entity is the one against which the request for habeas data would have been brought, pursuant to Article 15 of the Constitution. 7. When requesting the rectification of incorrect or erroneous information. In this case it is necessary to attach the transcription of the information or copy of the publication and of the rectification requested that was not published in such a way that its effectiveness be assured. 8. When the individual acts or should act in exercise of his or her public functions, in which case the same regime that regulates public authorities shall be applied. When the request is for the *tutela* of the life or safety of the person who is in a position of subordination or defenselessness with respect to the matter against which action was brought. The minor who brings an action of *tutela* shall be presumed defenseless.

[583]In this regard, the Costa Rican Law of Constitutional Jurisdiction restricts the amparo against individual. See Ruben Hernández Valle, *Derecho Procesal Constitucional,* Editorial Juricentro, San José, 2001, pp. 275, 281 ff. Article 57 establishes: "The recourse of amparo shall also be admitted against actions or omissions of individual subjects of the law when they act or should act in exercise of public functions or authority, or are by right or in fact in a position of power before which ordinary jurisdictional remedies are clearly insufficient or belated for guarantying the rights and freedoms referred to in Article 2,a of this Law."

[584] In Ecuador, the amparo actions is admitted against entities that although not being public authorities, render public services by delegation or concession and in general terms against individuals but only when their actions or omissions cause harm or threats to con-

action against individuals in a restricted way, in the sense that it can only be filed against individuals or corporations that are in a position of superiority regarding citizens or that in some way, exercise public functions or activities, or are rendering public services or public utilities.[585]

In this regard, for instance, amparo actions can also be filed against political parties or their officials when their conduct violates the rights of citizens, as it has also been admitted in the United States.[586]

II. THE PARTICIPATION OF THIRD PARTIES FOR THE DEFEN-DANT IN THE AMPARO PROCEEDING

In the amparo proceeding the injuring or damaging parties are those authorities, public officials, private persons, entities or corporations duly individuated whose actions or omissions are those causing the harm or threats to the constitutional rights and guaranties of the plaintiff.

Nonetheless, in the amparo procedure, third parties can also act in the process, defending the injurer party position, like for instance, the beneficiaries of the challenged authority acts. That is why the Mexican Amparo Law provides that besides the injured and the injuring parties, the persons that have obtained the challenged act or those that could have direct interest in its effects also are considered parties in the amparo suit (Article 5, III, c).[587] In a similar sense in the United States procedure on injunctions, all persons whose interest will necessarily be affected by the decree in a suit for injunction can properly join as defendants.[588]

---

stitutional rights and affect in a grave and direct way common, collective or diffuse interests (Article 95,3).

[585] In a similar way to the injunctions admitted in the United States against public services corporations. See for instance *Wiemer v. Louisville Water Co.*, 130 F. 251 (C.C.W.D. Ky. 1903), in John Bourdeau *et al*, "Injunctions," in Kevin Schroder, John Glenn and Maureen Placilla, *Corpus Juris Secundum*, Volume 43A, Thompson West, 2004, p. 182 ff.

[586] *Maxey v. Washington State Democratic Committee*, 319 F. Supp. 673 (W.D. Wash. 1970), *Idem*, p. 240.

[587] See Eduardo Ferrer Mac-Gregor, *La acción constitucional de amparo en México y España. Estudio de derecho comparado*, Editorial Porrúa, México, 2002, pp. 249–250.

[588] Silva V. Romney, 473 F. 2d 287 (1st Cir. 1973); *Greenhouse v. Greco*, 368 F. Supp. 736 (W.D. La. 1973). See the reference in John Bourdeau *et al.*, "Injunctions," in Kevin Schroder, John Glenn and Maureen Placilla, *Corpus Juris Secundum*, Volume 43A, Thompson West, 2004, pp. 332–333.

Due to the general bilateral procedural rule, the principle of the third parties participation applies in all Latin American countries, including Chile, where, as mentioned, the bilateralism of the procedure is not always admitted.[589] In some cases the participation of third parties for the defendant is necessary, as is the case in Venezuela on the amparo actions against judicial decisions, in which case the party beneficiary of the challenged ruling must obligatorily be notified to participate in the procedure as defendant of the challenged decision.[590]

[589]The *Auto Acordado* establishing the rules of the recourse for protection allows any affected person or authority to be party in the procedure (4). See Juan Manuel Errazuriz G. and Jorge Miguel Otero A., *Aspectos procesales del recurso de protección*, Editorial Jurídica de Chile, 1989, p. 149.

[590]See Rafael Chavero, *El nuevo régimen del amparo constitucional en Venezuela*, Editorial Sherwood, Caracas, 2001, pp. 489.

CHAPTER SIXTEEN

THE INJURING PUBLIC ACTIONS AND OMISSIONS OF PUBLIC AUTHORITIES CAUSING THE HARMS OR THE THREATS

Being the amparo action originally established to defend constitutional rights from State and authorities violations, the most common and important injuring parties in the amparo proceedings regulations in Latin America are, of course, the public authorities or public officials when their acts or omissions, whether of legislative, executive or judicial nature, cause the harm or threats.

The general principle in this matter, with some exceptions, is that any authority can be questioned through amparo actions, and that any act, fact or omission of any public authority or entity or public officials causing an injury to constitutional rights can be challenged by means of such actions. It is in this sense that the Guatemalan Amparo Law sets forth the principle that "no sphere shall be excluded from amparo," being admitted against "any act, resolution, disposition and statute of authority which could imply a threat, a restriction or a violation of the rights guarantied in the Constitution and in statutes" (Article 8).

This is the same wording used in the Amparo Law of Venezuela, providing that the action can be filed against "any fact, act or omission of any of the National, State, or Municipal branches of government" (*Poderes Públicos*) (Article 2); which mean that the constitutional protection can be filed against any public action, that is, any formal state act, any substantive or any factual activity (*vía de hecho*) (Article 5); as well as against any omission from public entities. That is also why the courts in Venezuela have decided that "there is no State act that can be excluded from revision by means of amparo, the purpose of which is not to annul State acts but to protect public freedoms and restore its enjoyment when violated or harmed," thereby admitting that the constitutional amparo action can be filed even against acts excluded from judicial review, when a harm or violation of constitutional rights or guaranties has been alleged.[591]

[591]See the former Supreme Court of Justice decision dated January 31, 1991, *Anselmo Natale* case, in *Revista de Derecho Público*, n° 45, Editorial Jurídica Venezolana, Caracas, 1991, p. 118. See also the decision of the First Court on Judicial Review of Administrative Action of June 18, 1992, in *Revista de Derecho Público*, n° 46, Editorial Jurídica Venezolana, Caracas, 1991, p. 125. This universality character of the amparo regarding public authorities acts or omissions, according to the Venezuelan courts, implies that: "From what Article 2 of the Amparo law sets forth, it results that no type of conduct, regardless of its nature or character or their authors, can per se be excluded from the amparo judge revision in order to determine if it harms or doesn't harm constitutional rights or guaranties." See decision of the First Court on Judicial Review of Administrative Action of November 11, 1993, *Aura Loreto Rangel* case, in *Revista de Derecho Público*, n° 55–56, Editorial Jurídica Venezolana, Caracas, 1993, p. 284. The same criterion was adopted by the Political Administrative Chamber of the former Supreme Court of Justice in a decision of May 24, 1993, as follows: "The terms on which the amparo action is regulated in Article 49 of the Constitution (now Article 27) are very extensive. If the extended scope of the rights and guaranties that can be protected and restored through this judicial mean is undoubted; the harm cannot be limited to those produced only by some acts. So, in equal terms it must be permitted that any harming act —whether an act, a fact or an omission— with respect to any constitutional right and guaranty, can be challenged by means of this action, due to the fact that the amparo action is the protection of any norm regulating the so-called subjective rights of constitutional rank, it cannot be sustained that such protection is only available in cases in which the injuring act has some precise characteristics, whether from a material or organic point of view. The jurisprudencia of this Court has been constant regarding both principles. In a decision n° 22, dated January 31, 1991, *Anselmo Natale* case, it was decided that 'there is no State act that could not be reviewed by amparo, the latter understood not as a mean for judicial review of constitutionality of State acts in order to annul them, but as a protective remedy regarding public freedoms whose purpose is to reestablish its enjoyment and exercise, when a natural or artificial person, or group or private organization, threatens to harm them or effectively harm them. See, regarding the extended scope of the protected rights, decision of December 4, 1990, *Mariela Morales de Jimenez* case, n° 661, in *Revista de Derecho Público*, n° 55-56, Editorial Jurídica Venezolana, Caracas, 1993, pp. 284–285. In another decision dated February 13, 1992, the First Court ruled: "This Court observes that the essential characteristic of the amparo regime, in its constitutional regulation as well as in its statutory development, is its universality.., so the protection it assures is extended to all subjects (physical or artificial persons), as well as regarding all constitutionally guaranteed rights, including those that without being expressly regulated in the Constitution are inherent to human beings. This is the departing point in order to understand the scope of the constitutional amparo. Regarding Public Administration, the amparo against it is so extended that it can be filed against all acts, omissions and factual actions, without any kind of exclusion regarding some matters that are always related to the public order and social interest." See in *Revista de Derecho Público*, n° 49, Editorial Jurídica Venezolana, Caracas, 1992, pp. 120–121.

Notwithstanding this general principle of the universality of the amparo, a series of exceptions can be identified in many Latin American Amparo Laws, regarding some particular and specific State acts or activities that are expressly excluded from the amparo proceedings, whether of legislative, executive, administrative or judicial nature.

I. AMPARO AGAINST LEGISLATIVE ACTIONS

The first question on this matter refers to the possibility to file amparo actions against legislative actions or omissions, when they cause harms on constitutional rights of individuals. The violation in these cases can be caused by statutes or by other decisions adopted, for instance, by parliamentary commissions.

1. *Amparo against parliamentary bodies' and their commissions' decisions*

Regarding Congress and parliamentary commissions' acts, including regional or municipal legislative councils, when they harm constitutional rights and guaranties, in principle, it is possible to challenge them through amparo actions before the competent courts.[592] This has been expressly admitted, for instance, in Argentina,[593] Costa Rica[594] and Venezuela.[595]

---

[592] In the United States, municipal council acts can be challenged through injunctions. See *Stuab v. City of Baxley*, 355 U.S. 313 (1958). See the comments in M. Glenn Abernathy and Barbara A. Perry, *Civil Liberties under the Constitution*, University of South Carolina Press, 1993, pp. 12–13.

[593] In Argentina, it was the case of the parliamentary enquiries developed in 1984 regarding the facts occurred during the previous de facto government, in which a parliamentary commission ordered a breakin into a Law Firm office and the seizure of documents. In the Supreme Court decisions in the *Klein* case in 1984, without questioning the powers of the parliamentary commissions to make inquiries, it was ruled that they cannot, without formal statutory provisions, validly restrict individual rights, in particular, to break into the personal domicile of people and to seize their personal documents. In the case, it was thus decided that the order could only be adopted based on a statutory provision, and not by the sole decision of the commissions, and eventually based in a judicial order. See the comments on the First Instance decision of 1984 (1ª. InstCrimCorrFed, Juzg n° 3, 10-9-84, ED 110-653), in Néstor Pedro Sagüés, *Derecho procesal Constitucional*, Vol 3, *Acción de amparo*, Editorial Astrea Buenos Aires, 1988, pp. 95–97; Joaquin Brague Camazano, *La Jurisdicción constitucional de la libertad (Teoría general, Argentina, México, Corte Interamericana de Derechos Humanos)*, Editorial Porrúa, México, 2005, p. 98; José Luis Lazzarini, *El juicio de amparo*, Editorial La Ley, Buenos Aires, 1987, pp. 216–216.

In contrast, in Mexico, Article 73,VIII of the Amparo Law expressly excludes from the amparo suit, the resolutions and declarations of the Federal Congress and its Chambers, as well as of the State Legislative bodies and their Commissions, regarding the election, suspension or dismissal of public officers in cases where the corresponding constitutions confer them the power to resolve the matter in a sovereign or discretionary way.[596] The decisions adopted by the Representative Chamber of the Senate in cases of impeachments, which are declared as nonchallenging ones[597] (Article 110 of the constitution) are also excluded from the amparo suit.

In similar sense, in the United States, the general rule is that injunctions may not be directed against Congress; so injunctions have been rejected for instance when seeking to suspend a congressional subpoena, regarding which the plaintiff had an adequate remedy to protect his rights.[598]

[594] See Rubén Hernández Valle, *Derecho Procesal Constitucional*, Editorial Juricentro, San José, 2001, pp. 211–214.

[595] In Venezuela, in a similar sense, the Supreme Court, even recognizing the existence of exclusive attributions of legislative bodies, which according to the 1961 Constitution (Article 159) were not subjected to judicial review, admitted the amparo protection against them for the immediate restoration of the plaintiff's harmed constitutional rights; and it admitted the amparo action against legislative acts, in a decision dated January 31, 1991 (Caso: *Anselmo Natale*), ruling as follows: "The exclusion of judicial review regarding certain parliamentary acts —except in cases of extra limitation of powers— set forth in Article 159 of the Constitution, as a way to prevent, due to the rules of separation of powers, that the executive and judicial branches could invade or interfere in the orbit of the legislative body which is the trustee of the popular sovereignty, is restricted to determine the intrinsic regularity of such acts regarding the Constitution, in order to annul them, but it does not apply when it is a matter of obtaining the immediate reestablishment of the enjoyment and exercise of harmed rights and guaranties set forth in the Constitution." See in *Revista de Derecho Público*, n° 45, Editorial Jurídica Venezolana, Caracas, 1991, p. 118.

[596] See Richard D. Baker, *Judicial Review in México. A Study of the Amparo Suit*, Texas University Press, Austin, 1971, p. 98.

[597] See Eduardo Ferrer Mac-Gregor, *La acción constitucional de amparo en México y España. Estudio de derecho comparado*, Editorial Porrúa, México, 2002, p. 378.

[598] See *U.S.-Mins et al. v. McCarty*, 209 F. 2d 307 (D.C. Cir. 1953), in John Bourdeau *et al.,* "Injunctions," in Kevin Schroder, John Glenn and Maureen Placilla, *Corpus Juris Secundum*, Volume 43A, Thompson West, 2004, p. 230.

2. *Amparo against laws (statutes)*

Yet apart from legislative body actions, one of the most important aspects of the Latin American amparo proceeding refers to the possibility of filing the amparo action against statutes.

If it is true that in some countries it is expressly accepted as is the case of Guatemala, Honduras, Mexico and Venezuela; in the majority of the Latin American countries it is expressly excluded, as is the case in Argentina, Bolivia, Brazil, Colombia, Chile,[599] Costa Rica, the Dominican Republic, Ecuador, El Salvador,[600] Panama, Peru, Paraguay, Nicaragua and Uruguay (Article 1,c Amparo Law).

Regarding the countries where the amparo action is accepted against statutes, in Mexico and Venezuela the filing of the action is limited only regarding self-executing statutes that can harm the constitutional rights without the need for any other State act executing or applying them, or only regarding the acts applying the particular statute. Only in Guatemala and Honduras, the amparo action is admitted directly against statutes.

In effect, in Mexico, Article 1,I of the Amparo Law establishes that the amparo can be filed against self-executing or self-applicable statutes (laws) when causing a direct harm to the constitutional guaranties of the plaintiff without any need for an administrative or judicial act of its application.[601] In such cases, the amparo action can be filed directly against the statute giving rise to a judicial mean for judicial review of the constitutionality of the statutes. In these cases, the action can be filed directly against the statute.

---

[599]Humberto Nogueira Alcalá, "El derecho de amparo o protección de los derechos humanos, fundamentales o esenciales en Chile: evolución y perspectivas," in Humberto Nogueira Alcalá (Editor), *Acciones constitucionales de amparo y protección: realidad y perspectivas en Chile y América Latina*, Editorial Universidad de Talca, Talca, 2000, p. 45.

[600]See Edmundo Orellana, *La Justicia Constitucional en Honduras*, Universidad Nacional Autónoma de Honduras, Editorial Universitaria, Tegucigalpa, 1993, p. 102, note 26.

[601]See *Garza Flores Hnos., Sucs.* case, 28 S.J. 1208 (1930). See the reference in Richard D. Baker, *Judicial Review in México. A Study of the Amparo Suit*, Texas University Press, Austin, 1971, p. 167. In these cases, the action has to be filed within thirty days following their enforcement. In such cases, the defendants are the supreme institutions of the State that had intervened in the drafting of the statute, that is, the Congress of the Union or the legislatures of the States that passed the statute, the President of the Republic or State Governors that ordered its execution and the Executive Secretariats that approved it and ordered its enactment.

Consequently, the amparo against laws in Mexico is considered a judicial mean for the direct control of the constitutionality of statutes, even though the action is not filed in an abstract manner, due to the fact that the claimant must have been directly harmed, without the need for another state act for its application. On the contrary, when the statute in itself does not cause direct and personal harm to the claimant, because not being self-executing, the amparo action is inadmissible unless it is filed against the State acts that apply it to a specific person.[602]

The Mexican solution referring to self-executing statutes is similar to the United States exceptions to the doctrine of non-interference, according to which, injunctions, if they are not admitted in principle against legislative acts, are admitted against municipal ordinances and regulations, when by its mere passage they immediately produce some irreparable loss or injury to the plaintiff.[603]

In Venezuela, due to the universality character of the system for constitutional protection, which eventually was consolidated in the 1999 Constitution, one of the most distinguishable innovations of the 1988 Amparo Law was to establish the amparo action against statutes and other normative acts, complementing the general mixed system of judicial review.[604]

---

[602] As it is expressly set forth in Article 73,VI, the amparo suit is inadmissible "against statutes, treaties or regulations that, by its sole passing, do not cause harm to the plaintiff, but need a subsequent act of its application in order for the prejudice to initiate." In these cases of statutes that are not self-executing, the amparo action must be filed within fifteen days following the issuing of the first act of its execution or application. See Eduardo Ferrer Mac-Gregor, *La acción constitucional de amparo en México y España. Estudio de derecho comparado*, Editorial Porrúa, México, 2002, p, 387. The main aspect to be stressed on the matter, of course, is the distinction between the self-executing and not self executing laws. Following the doctrine established in the case of Villera de Orellana María de los Angeles *et al.*, the former are those immediately obligatory, in which provisions the persons to whom are applicable are clearly and unmistakably identified, being *ipso jure* subjected to an obligation that implies the accomplishment of acts not previously required, resulting in a prejudicial modification of the person's rights. Suprema Corte de Justicia, 123 S.J. 783 (1955). See the comments in Richard D. Baker, *Judicial Review in México. A Study of the Amparo Suit*, Texas University Press, Austin, 1971, p. 168–173.

[603] See *Larkins v. City of Denison*, 683 S.W. 2d 754 (Tex. App. Dallas 1984). See in John Bourdeau *et al.*, "Injunctions," in Kevin Schroder, John Glenn and Maureen Placilla, *Corpus Juris Secundum*, Volume 43A, Thompson West, 2004, pp. 257–260.

[604] According to Article 3 of the Amparo Law, two ways are established through which an amparo pretension can be filed before the competent court: in an autonomous way, or exercised together with the popular action of unconstitutionality of statutes. In the latter case, the amparo pretension is subordinated to the principal action for judicial review, producing only the possibility for the court to suspend the application of the statute pending the unconstitutionality suit. See Allan R. Brewer-Carías, *Instituciones Políticas y*

When filed directly against statutes, the purpose of the Law provision was to secure the inapplicability of the statute to the particular case, with *inter partes* effects.[605] Yet in spite of the Amparo Law provisions, the jurisprudence of the Supreme Tribunal rejected such actions, imposing the need to file them only against the State acts issued to apply the statutes and not directly against them.[606] The Court, in its decisions, even though admitting the distinction between the self-executing and not self-executing statutes,[607] concluded its ruling declaring the impossibility for a real normative act to directly and by itself, harms the constitutional rights of an individual. The Court also considered that a statute cannot be a threat to constitutional rights, because for an amparo to be filed, a threat must be "imminent, possible and realizable," considering that in the case of statutes such conditions are not fulfilled.[608]

Constitucionales, Vol V, *Derecho y Acción de Amparo*, Editorial Jurídica Venezolana, Caracas, 1998, pp. 227 ff. In this case, the situation is similar to the one of the popular action of unconstitutionality in the Dominican Republic when the amparo pretension is filed together with it. See Eduardo Jorge Prats, *Derecho Constitucional*, Vol. II, Gaceta Judicial, Santo Domingo, 2005, p. 399.

[605] See Allan R. Brewer-Carías, *Instituciones Políticas y Constitucionales*, Vol V, *Derecho y Acción de Amparo*, Editorial Jurídica Venezolana, Caracas, 1998, pp. 224 ff; Rafael Chavero, *El nuevo régimen del amparo constitucional en Venezuela*, Editorial Sherwood, Caracas, 2001, pp. 553 ff.

[606] In a decision dated May 24, 1993, the Politico Administrative Chamber of the former Supreme Court issued a decision that has been the leading case on the matter, ruling that: "thus, it seem that there is no doubt that Article 3 of the Amparo law does not set forth the possibility of filing an amparo action directly against a normative act, but against the act, fact or omission that has its origin in a normative provision which is considered by the claimant as contrary to the Constitution and for which, due to the presumption of legitimacy and constitutionality of the former, the court must previously resolve its inapplicability to the concrete case argued. It is obvious, thus, that such article of the Amparo law does not allow the possibility of filing this action for constitutional protection against a statute or other normative act, but against the act which applies or executes it, which is definitively the one that in the concrete case can cause a particular harm to the constitutional rights and guaranties of a precise person." See in *Revista de Derecho Público*, n° 55-56, Editorial Jurídica Venezolana, Caracas, 1993, pp. 287–288.

[607] Ruling that the self-executing statutes imposes an immediate obligation for the persons to whom it is issued, with its promulgation; and on the contrary, those statutes not self-executing requires an act for its execution, in which case its sole promulgation cannot produce a constitutional violation. See in *Revista de Derecho. Público*, n° 55-56, Editorial Jurídica Venezolana, Caracas, 1993, p. 285

[608] The Court, in the same decision, rejected the possibility of a threat caused by a statute, with the following argument: "In case of an amparo action against a norm, the concretion of the possible harm would not be 'immediate', because it will always be the need for a

In contrast with the Mexican and Venezuelan regulations, in Guatemala the amparo against laws is established in a direct way, the Constitutional Courts being empowered to "declare in specific cases that a statute, a regulation, resolution or act of the authorities does not oblige the claimant, since it contravenes or restricts any of the rights guaranteed by the constitution or recognized by any Law (Article 10,b Guatemala Law). This same judicial power, but only regarding executive regulations, is established in Honduras (Article 41,b Law). In both cases, the judicial decisions on the amparo proceeding has the effect of suspending the application of the statute or the executive regulation regarding the claimant, and if applicable, the re-establishment of the juridical situation affected or the cessation of the measure (Article 49,a Guatemala).[609]

However, with the exception of Mexico, Venezuela, Guatemala and Honduras, as aforementioned, in the other Latin American countries the amparo against statutes is expressly excluded.

In effect, in Argentina, even with its longstanding tradition on judicial review of legislation by means of the diffuse method of judicial review,

---

competent authority to execute or apply it in order for the statute to effectively harm the claimant. It must be concluded that the probable harm produced by the norm will always be a mediate and indirect one, due to the need for the statute to be applied to the particular case. So that the harm will be caused by mean of the act applying the illegal norm. The same occurs with the third condition, in the sense that the probable and imminent threat will never be made by the possible defendant. If it would be possible to sustain that the amparo could be admissible against a statute whose constitutionality is challenged, it would be necessary to accept as aggrieved party the legislative body issuing it, being the party to participate in the process as defendant. But it must be highlighted that in the case in which the possible harm could be realized, it would not be the legislative body the one called to execute it, but rather the public officer that must apply the norm in all the cases in which an individual is located in the situation it regulates. If it is understood that the object of the amparo action is the statute, then the conclusion would be that the possible defendant (the public entity enacting the norm whose unconstitutionality is alleged) could not be the one that could make the threat. The concrete harm would be definitively made by a different entity or person (the one applying the unconstitutional norm to a specific and concrete case). See in *Revista de Derecho Público*, n° 55-56, Editorial Jurídica Venezolana, Caracas, 1993, pp. 288 a 290. From the abovementioned, the Venezuelan Supreme Court concluded rejecting the amparo action against statutes and normative acts, not only because it considered that the Amparo Laws do not set forth such possibility —bypassing its text–, but because even being possible to bring the extraordinary action against a normative act, it would not comply with the imminent, possible and realizable conditions of the threats set forth in Article 6,2 of the Amparo Law.

[609]See Edmundo Orellana, *La justicia constitucional en Honduras*, Universidad Nacional Autónoma de Honduras, Tegucigalpa, 1993, p. 102, note 26.

the amparo against statutes is not admitted.[610] Nonetheless, if in an amparo action against State acts, the statute in which the challenged act is based is considered unconstitutional, the amparo judge, by means of the diffuse method of judicial review can decide upon the inapplicability of the statute in the case.[611]

In Brazil, the *mandado de segurança* is also excluded against laws or legal provisions when they have not yet been applied through administrative acts.[612]

In Uruguay, in a similar sense, although being a country with a concentrated system of judicial review, the amparo against statutes is also excluded regarding statutes and State acts of similar rank (Article 1,c, Law 16011). The only mean to challenge the constitutionality of a statute, when a judicial action is filed before the Supreme Court is to obtain a declaration of its unconstitutionality in a particular case. In such cases, the amparo pretension can only have a suppressive effect regarding the application of the statute to the plaintiff pending the Supreme Court's decision on the unconstitutionality of the statute.[613] The Amparo Law in Paraguay also provides that when for the decision of an amparo proceeding, the constitutionality or unconstitutionality of a statute must be determined, the court must send the files to the Constitutional Chamber of the Supreme Court in order to decide upon its unconstitutionality. This incident would not suspend the procedure before the lower court, which must continue it up to the stage before its decision (Article 582).

In Costa Rica, the Law on Constitutional Jurisdiction also provides that the amparo action against statutes and other regulatory provisions is not admissible, but with the exception when challenged together with the acts

---

[610]See José Luis Lazzarini, *El juicio de amparo*, Editorial La Ley, Buenos Aires, 1987, p. 214; Néstor Pedro Sagüés, *Derecho procesal Constitucional*, Vol 3, "Acción de amparo," Editorial Astrea, Buenos Aires, 1988, p. 97.

[611]In this regard, Article 2,d of the Amparo Law set forth that the amparo action is not admissible "when for the purpose of determining the invalidity of the challenged act, the declaration of the unconstitutionality of the statute is required. This has been considered as not being in force because it contradicts Article 31 of the constitution (supremacy clause). Néstor Pedro Sagüés, *Derecho procesal Constitucional*, Vol 3, *Acción de amparo*, Editorial Astrea Buenos Aires, 1988, p. 243–258. Additionally, Article 43 of the 1994 Constitution, now regulating the amparo action, has expressly solved the discussion by setting forth that "In the case, the judge can declare the unconstitutionality of the norm in which the act or omission is based."

[612]See José Luis Lazzarini, *El juicio de amparo*, La Ley, Buenos Aires, 1987, pp. 213–214.

[613] See Luis Alberto Viera, *Ley de Amparo*, Ediciones Idea, Montevideo, 1993, pp. 23.

individually applying it, or when dealing with automatically enforced regulations, in such a way that their prescriptions become automatically enforceable simply by their enactment, without the need for other regulations or acts that develop them or render them applicable to the claimant (Article 30,a Costa Rica Law). Nonetheless, in these cases, the amparo against the self-executing statute is not directly decided by the Constitutional Chamber, instead, it must be converted into a direct action on judicial review of the constitutionality of the challenged statute.[614] In such cases, the President of the Constitutional Chamber must suspend the amparo procedure and give the plaintiff fifteen days in order for him to formalize a direct action on judicial review of constitutionality against the statute (Article 48, Costa Rica Law). So, only after the statute is annulled by the Constitutional Chamber, the amparo action will be decided.

In Peru, in a similar sense to the Argentinean solution, and after discussions held under previous legislation,[615] the Constitutional Procedure Code established that: "When it is argued that the acts causing threats or violation are based in the application of a norm not compatible with the Constitution, the decision declaring the claim founded must additionally decide on the inapplicability of such norm" (Article 43). In this case, also, in order to decide, the court must use its judicial review powers through the diffuse method.

Also in Colombia, the *tutela* action is excluded regarding all "acts of a general, impersonal and abstract nature" (Article 6,5); and in Nicaragua, the amparo action is not admissible "against the process of drafting the statute, its promulgation or publication or any other legislative act or resolution" (Article 51, Law).

II. AMPARO AGAINST EXECUTIVE AND ADMINISTRATIVE ACTS AND ACTIONS

1. *Amparo and executive acts*

Regarding executive authorities, the general principle is that the action is admitted against acts, facts or omissions from public entities or bodies

---

[614]See Rubén Hernandez, *Derecho Procesal Constitucional*, Editorial Juricentro, San José 2001, pp. 45, 208–209, 245, 223.

[615]Particularly, regarding amparo actions against self-executing statutes, see Samuel B. Abad Yupanqui, *El proceso constitucional de amparo*, Gaceta Jurídica, Lima, 2004, pp. 352-374.

conforming to the Public Administration at all its levels (national, state, municipal), including decentralized, autonomous, independent or deconcentrated bodies and including acts issued by the Head of the Executive, that is, the President of the Republic. This last aspect, for instance, is contrary to the rule regarding injunctions in the United States where the principle is that such coercive remedy cannot be directed against the President.[616]

Yet regarding Executive and administrative acts, some specific restrictions have been established in Latin America, for instance, in Mexico where the specific presidential act of expulsion of foreigners from the territory (Article 33)[617] cannot be challenged through an amparo action, and in Uruguay, against executive regulations.[618]

Regarding administrative acts, as mentioned, all Latin American countries admit the filing of amparo actions against them, and even in some countries, such as Venezuela, the Amparo Law (Article 5) provides for possibility of exercising the amparo action in two ways: in an autonomous way or conjunctly with a nullity recourse for judicial review of the act.[619]

---

[616]See *Sloan v. Nixon*, 60 F.R.D. 228 (S.D.N.Y. 1973), aff'd, 93 F.2d 1398 (2d Cir. 1974), judgment aff'd, 419 U.S. 958, 95 S. Ct. 218, 42 L. Ed. 2d 174 (1974), in John Bourdeau *et al.*, "Injunctions," in Kevin Schroder, John Glenn and Maureen Placilla, *Corpus Juris Secundum*, Volume 43A, Thompson West, 2004, p. 229.

[617]See Eduardo Ferrer Mac-Gregor, *La acción constitucional de amparo en México y España. Estudio de derecho comparado*, Editorial Porrúa, México, 2002, p. 377.

[618] See Luis Alberto Viera, *Ley de Amparo*, Ediciones Idea, Montevideo, 1993, p. 99.

[619]Regarding the latter, the former Supreme Court of Justice in the decision of July 10, 1991 (*Tarjetas Banvenez* case), clarified that in such case, the action is not a principal one, but subordinated and ancillary regarding the principal recourse to which it has been attached, and subjected to the final nullifying decision that has to be issued in it. See the text in *Revista de Derecho Público*, nº 47, Editorial Jurídica Venezolana, Caracas, 1991, pp. 169–174, and comments in *Revista de Derecho Público*, nº 50, Editorial Jurídica Venezolana, Caracas, 1992, pp. 183–184. That is why, in such cases, the amparo pretension that must be founded in a grave presumption of the violation of the constitutional right, has a preventive and temporal character, pending the final decision of the nullity suit, consisting in the suspension of the effects of the challenged administrative act. This provisional character of the amparo protection pending the suit is thus subjected to the final decision to be issued in the nullity judicial review procedure against the challenged administrative act. See in *Revista de Derecho Público*, nº 47, Editorial Jurídica Venezolana, Caracas, 1991, pp. 170–171.

The main distinction between both means[620] lies, first, in the character of the allegation: in the first case, the alleged and proved constitutional right violation must be a direct, immediate and flagrant one; in the second case, what has to be proved is the existence of a grave presumption of the constitutional right violation. And second, in the general purpose of the proceeding: in the first case, the judicial decision issued is a definitive constitutional protection one, of restorative character; in the second case, it has only preliminary character of suspension of the effects of the challenged act pending the decision of the principal judicial review process.[621]

In a similar way to the Venezuelan solution, Article 8 of the Colombian *Tutela* Law establishes the possibility to file a "*tutela* as a transitory mean" against administrative acts conjunctly with the judicial review nullity action exercised before the Judicial review of administrative action Jurisdiction (*Jurisdicción contencioso-administrativa*).[622]

---

[620]The main difference between both procedures according to the Supreme Court doctrine is that: in the first case of the autonomous amparo action against administrative acts, the plaintiff must allege a direct, immediate and flagrant violation to the constitutional right, which in its own demonstrates the need for the amparo order as a definitive means to restore the harmed juridical situation. In the second case, given the suspensive nature of the amparo order which only tends to provisionally stop the effects of the injuring act until the judicial review of administrative action confirming or nullifying it is decided, the alleged unconstitutional violations of constitutional provisions can be formulated together with violations of legal or statutory provisions developing the constitutional ones, because it is a judicial review action against administrative acts, seeking their nullity, they can also be founded on legal texts. What the court cannot do in these cases of filing together the actions, in order to suspend the effects of the challenged administrative act, is to found its decision only in the legal violations alleged, because that would mean to anticipate the final decision on the principal nullity judicial review recourse. *Idem*, pp. 171–172.

[621]*Idem*, p. 172. See also regarding the nullity of Article 22 of the Organic Amparo Law the former Supreme Court decision dated May 21, 1996, in Allan R. Brewer-Carías, *Instituciones Políticas y Constitucionales, Vol. V, Derecho y Acción de Amparo*, Editorial Jurídica Venezolana, Caracas, 1996, pp. 392 ff.

[622]The article, in effect, establishes that even in case the injured party would have another judicial means of protection, the action for *tutela* will be admitted when used as a transitory means in order to prevent an irreparable damage. In such cases, the court will expressly rule in its decision that the protection [order] will be in force only during the term the competent judicial court will use in order to decide on the merits of the action brought by the injured party. In any case, the affected party must file such action in the maximum delay of four months from the *tutela* decision. In case that the action is not filed, the *tutela* decision will cease in its effects. In cases in which the *tutela* is used as a transitory means in order to prevent an irreparable injury, the action for *tutela* can also be filed together with the nullifying action before the judicial review of administrative action (*contencioso*

2. *Amparo and the political questions*

An important question related to executive acts and their justiciability by means of amparo is related to the so-called political questions, which nonetheless in Latin America is only applicable in Argentina and Peru.

According to this judicial doctrine, which was originated in the United States regarding judicial review of the constitutionality, the questions related to the principle of "separation of powers" and to "the relationship between the judiciary and the co-ordinate branches of the Federal Government"[623] are considered as nonjusticiables. In these cases, it is considered that the preemptive political nature of the questions imply that their solution corresponds to the political branches of government rather than to the courts, which are considered excluded, not only from judicial review, but also from the injunction proceedings.

The main question considered as political and thus as nonjusticiable by the United States Supreme Court is related to foreign affairs involving, "considerations of policy, considerations of extreme magnitude, and certainly entirely incompetent to the examination and decision of a Court of Justice."[624] In all these cases, of course, even though a list of "political questions" considered as nonjustifiable can be elaborated, the ultimate responsibility in determining them appertains to the Supreme Court.[625]

---

administrativo) jurisdiction. In these cases, if the court deems it justified, it could order, pending the process, the non-application of the particular act regarding the concrete juridical situation whose protection is being demanded.

[623] *Baker v. Carr,* 369 U.S. 186 (1962). See in M. Glenn Abernathy and Barbara A. Perry, *Civil Liberties under the Constitution,* Sixth Edition, University of South Carolina Press, 1993, pp. 6–7.

[624] *Ware v. Hylton,* 3 Dallas, 199 (1796). Decisions concerning foreign relations therefore, as stated by Justice Jackson in *Chicago and Southern Air Lines v. Waterman Steamship Co.* (1948): "Are wholly confined by our constitution to the political departments of the government. ... They are decisions of a kind for which the Judiciary has neither aptitude, facilities nor responsibility and which has long been held to belong in the domain of political power not subject to judicial intrusion or inquiry." *Chicago and Southern Air Lines v. Waterman Steamship Co.,* 333 US 103 (1948), p. 111. Even though developed mainly on matters of foreign affairs, the Supreme Court has also considered as political questions certain matters relating to the government of internal affairs, which are thus nonjusticiable; like for instance the decision as to whether a state must have a republican form of government, which in *Luther v. Borden* (1849) was considered a "decision binding on every other department of the government, and could not be questioned in a judicial tribunal." *Luther v. Borden* 48 U.S. (7 Howard), 1, (1849). *Idem,* pp. 6–7.

[625] As the Court said in *Baker v. Carr* 369 U.S. 186 (1962): "Deciding whether a matter has in any measure been committed by the constitution to another branch of government,

Following this doctrine, and also without any constitutional provision, the Supreme Court of Justice in Argentina and the Constitutional Tribunal in Peru[626] have developed the same exception for judicial review and for amparo action on matters concerning political questions.

The Argentinean exception refers mainly to what has been called "acts of government" or "political acts," referring for instance to the declaration of war, of state of siege; of federal intervention in the provinces; of "public convenience" for means of expropriation; or of emergency to approve certain direct tax contributions; to acts concerning foreign relations, like the recognition of new foreign states or new foreign governments; or to the expulsion of aliens.[627]

All these acts are considered as political questions in Argentina, being powers exercised by the political bodies according to powers attributed exclusively and directly to them in the constitution and are excluded from the amparo action.

Regarding the nonjusticiability of some Executive and administrative acts and actions, mention must also be made to the restriction, also established in the Argentinean Amparo Law, declaring the inadmissibility of the amparo action against acts issued in express application of the Law of National Defense (Article 2,b Law 16.970).[628]

3. Amparo proceedings and the functioning of public services

Finally, regarding administrative acts, also in Argentina, the Amparo Law sets forth the inadmissibility of the amparo action in cases in which

or whether the action of that branch exceeds whatever authority has been committed, — said the Court is itself a delicate exercise in constitutional interpretation, and is a responsibility of this Court as ultimate interpreter of the constitution." *Idem,* p. 6-7.

[626]See Samuel B. Abad Yupanqui, *El proceso constitucional de amparo*, Gaceta Jurídica, Lima, 2004, pp. 128 ff.

[627]For this exception to be applied, it has been considered that the challenged act must in a clear and exact way rely on the provisions of such law. See José Luis Lazzarini, *El juicio de amparo*, La Ley, Buenos Aires, 1987, p. 190 ff.; Néstor Pedro Sagüés, *Derecho procesal Constitucional*, Vol 3, "Acción de amparo," Editorial Astrea, Buenos Aires, 1988, pp. 270 ff.; Alí Joaquín Salgado, *Juicio de amparo y acción de inconstitucionalidad*, Astrea, Buenos Aires, 1987, p. 23.

[628]See *Diario El Mundo c/ Gobierno nacional* case, CNFed, Sala 1 ContAdm, April, 30, 1974, JA, 23-1974-195. See the comments in Néstor Pedro Sagüés, *Derecho procesal Constitucional,* Vol 3, *Acción de amparo*, Editorial Astrea, Buenos Aires, 1988, pp. 212–214.

"the judicial intervention could directly or indirectly impair or affect the regularity, continuity and efficacy of public service related to the essential activities of the State" (Article 2,c). The same provision is established regarding the amparo action in the Civil Procedure Code of Paraguay (Article 565,c).

Due to the elusive expressions used in these texts (compromising, directly, indirectly, regularity, continuity, efficacy, rendering, public service), and due to the fact that any administrative activity of the State can always be related to a public service,[629] this provision has been highly criticized in Argentina, considering that with its application, "it would be difficult for an amparo against the State to be granted."[630]

In any case, the final decision corresponds to the court, and if it is true that in practice the exception has hardly been used,[631] in some important matters it has been alleged.[632]

---

[629] *Idem*, pp. 226 ff.

[630] José Luis Lazzarini, *El juicio de amparo*, La Ley, Buenos Aires, 1987, p. 231.

[631] *Idem*, p. 233; Néstor Pedro Sagüés, *Derecho procesal Constitucional*, Vol 3, *Acción de amparo*, Editorial Astrea, Buenos Aires, 1988, p. 228.

[632] It happened for instance in the amparo actions filed in 1985 against the Central Bank of the Republic decision suspending for a few months the delay of the payments of the deposits in foreign currency. Even though some courts rejected amparo actions in the matter (see CFed *BBlanca* case, August 13, 1985, ED, 116-116, in Alí Joaquín Salgado, *Juicio de amparo y acción de inconstitucionalidad*, Editorial Astrea 1987, p. 51, note 59), in the *Peso* case the Federal National Chamber on judicial review of administrative actions of Buenos Aires decided to reject the arguments asking for the rejection of the amparo action based in the consideration of the matter as related to a "public service," considering that the Central bank activities have not the elements to be considered as a public service in the sense of public utility. See CNFedConAdm, Sala IV, June 13, 1985, ED, 114-231in Alí Joaquín Salgado, *Juicio de amparo y acción de inconstitucionalidad*, Editorial Astrea 1987, p. 50, note 56. A few years later, regarding a similar decision of the Central Bank on the nonpayments of deposit in foreign currencies, in the cases referred to as the *Corralito*, there was no allegation whatsoever considering those Central Bank decisions, which were adopted on situation of state of economic emergency, as public service activities. In such cases, the amparo actions were admitted and granted, but with multiple judicial incidents. See for instance the *Smith* and the *San Luis* cases, 2002, in Antonio María Hernández, *Las emergencias y el orden constitucional*, Universidad Nacional Autónoma de México, México, 2003, pp. 71 ff., 119 ff. In such cases, the Laws and Decrees of Economic Emergency were declared unconstitutional.

III. AMPARO AGAINST JUDICIAL ACTS AND DECISIONS

1. The admission of amparo actions against judicial decisions

In contrast with the general Latin American acceptance of the amparo action against executive and administrative acts, including those administrative acts issued by courts and tribunals, the same cannot be said regarding judicial decisions issued on jurisdictional matters.

That means that if it is true that in some countries the amparo action is admitted against judicial acts, in the majority of Latin American countries, the amparo actions against judicial decisions has been expressly excluded and considered inadmissible, specifically when the judicial decisions are issued applying jurisdictional power.[633]

Regarding the countries admitting the amparo action for the protection of constitutional rights against judicial decisions, this has been the tradition in Mexico, where the direct amparo suit finds its broadest application (amparo cassation),[634] and is also the case in Guatemala (Article 10,h), Honduras (Articles 9,3 and,10,2,a), Panama (Article 2615),[635] Peru and Venezuela.

The general principle in these cases, as set forth in the Peruvian Code on Constitutional Procedures, is that the amparo is admitted against definitive judicial resolutions when "they had manifestly impaired the effective procedural protection, affecting the rights to access to justice and to due process" (Article 4).[636] In the case of Venezuela, in a similar way to what was established in the Peruvian legislation prior to the sanctioning of the Code, Article 4 of the Amparo Law provides that in the cases of judicial decisions "the action for amparo shall also be admitted when a court, acting outside its competence, issues a resolution or decision, or orders an action that impairs a constitutional right." Because no court has any power to unlawfully cause harm to constitutional rights or guaranties,

---

[633]Consequently, administrative acts issued by courts can be challenged by means of amparo. See for example, regarding Argentina, Néstor Pedro Sagüés, *Derecho procesal Constitucional*, Vol 3, *Acción de amparo*, Editorial Astrea, Buenos Aires, 1988, pp. 197 ff.

[634]See Richard D. Baker, *Judicial Review in México. A Study of the Amparo Suit*, Texas University Press, Austin, 1971, p. 98.

[635]In this case, with no suspensive effects. See Boris Barrios González, *Derecho Procesal Constitucional*, Editorial Portobelo, Panama, 2002, p. 159.

[636]See Samuel B. Abad Yupanqui, *El proceso constitucional de amparo*, Gaceta Jurídica, Lima, 2004, p. 326.

the amparo against judicial decisions is extensively admitted when a court decision directly harms the constitutional rights of the plaintiff, normally related to the due process of law rights.[637]

The case of Colombia must also be specially mentioned due to the fact that Article 40 of the Decree Nº 2.591 of 1991 admitted the *tutela* action against judicial decisions, a possibility that was not excluded in the constitution. Consequently, the Decree expressly established the possibility of filing action for *tutela* against judicial acts when they inflict direct injuries to fundamental rights. In those cases, the *tutela* has to "be brought together with the appropriate recourse," that is, the recourse of appeal. Notwithstanding this statutory admissibility of *tutela* against judicial decisions, in 1992, the Constitutional Court declared its unconstitutionality, annulling the provision because it was considered contrary to the principle of the intangibility of the *res judicata* effects.[638]

Consequently, the *tutela* action against judicial decisions was eliminated, but not for long. Just one year later, and after numerous judicial decisions on the matter, the same Constitutional Court readmitted the *tutela* action against judicial decisions when they constitute a *vía de hecho* (*voi de fait*) or factual action,[639] that is, when issued as a consequence of an arbitrary exercise of the judicial function, violating the constitutional rights of the plaintiff.[640] Consequently, according to this

---

[637]As was decided by the cassation Chamber of the former Supreme Court of Justice in a decision of December 5, 1990, the amparo against judicial decisions is admitted "when the decision in itself injures the juridical conscience, when harming in a flagrant way individual rights that cannot be renounced or when the decision violates the principle of juridical security (judicial stability), deciding against *res judicata*, or when issued in a process where the plaintiff's right to defense has not been guaranteed, or in any way the due process guaranty has been violated." Case *José Díaz Aquino*, also referred to in decision dated December 14, 1994, of the same cassation Chamber. See the reference in Allan R. Brewer-Carías, *Instituciones Políticas y Constitucionales, Vol V, Derecho y Acción de Amparo*, Universidad católica del Táchira, Editorial Jurídica Venezolana, Caracas, 1998, pp. 261 ff; Rafael Chavero, *El nuevo régimen del amparo constitucional en Venezuela*, Editorial Sherwood, Caracas, 2001, pp. 483 ff.

[638]See decision C-543 of October 1, 1992, in Manuel José Cepeda Espinosa, *Derecho Constitucional jurisprudencial. Las grandes decisiones de la Corte Constitucional*, Legis, Bogotá, 2001, pp. 1009 ff.

[639]See decision S-231 dated May 13, 1994, *Idem*, pp. 1022 ff.

[640]The Constitutional Court has ruled: "The ostensible and grave violation of the rules governing the process in which the challenged decision was issued, up to the point that because the flagrant disregard of the due process and other constitutional rights, the plaintiff's constitutional rights had been directly violated by the challenged act. This means that the via de hecho is in fact the arbitrary exercise of the judicial function, in such terms that

doctrine, which is applicable to almost all cases in which the amparo action is filed against judicial decisions, these, in order to be challenged through a *tutela* action, must have been issued in a grave and flagrant violation of the due process of law guaranties, constituting an unlawful or arbitrary decision, without legal support whatsoever.

In a certain way regarding injunctions on judicial matters, it can also be said that in the United States, injunction can also be granted when for instance, it clearly appears that the prosecution of law actions are the result of fraud, gross wrong or oppression, in which cases justice clearly requires equitable interference.[641]

Besides the general established condition of the need for the previous exhaustion of the available ordinary judicial recourses against the challenged decision, in the Latin American countries where the amparo action against judicial decisions is admitted, some restrictions have been established regarding the decisions of the Supreme Courts (Mexico, Panama, Article 2.615; Venezuela, Article 6,6) or the Constitutional Tribunal (Peru), which cannot be challenged by means of the amparo actions.

In other cases, in particular, it is expressly provided that the judicial decision already issued in amparo proceedings cannot be the object of another amparo action, as is established in Honduras (Article 45,2) and Mexico (Article 73,II).[642] This exception is similar to the one established in

the deciding court has decided not according to law —which thus has been violated— but only according to its personal will." See SU-1218 decision of November 21, 2001. See in Juan Carlos Esguerra, *La protección constitucional del ciudadano,* Legis, Bogotá, 2004, p. 164. See Eduardo Cifuentes Muñoz, "Tutela contra sentencias (El caso colombiano)," in Humberto Nogueira Alcalá (Ed.), *Acciones constitucionales de amparo y protección: realidad y perspectivas en Chile y América Latina,* Editorial Universidad de Talca, Talca, 2000, pp. 307 ff.

[641] As has been decided by the courts: "The power of a court of equity to interfere with the general right of a person to sue and to restrain the person from prosecuting the action will be exercised only where it appears clearly that the prosecution of the law action will result in a fraud, gross wrong, or aggression and that conscience and justice clearly require equitable interference. Accordingly, an action at law may be restrained under these restrictive rules where a person is attempting to, or would, through the instrumentality of an action at law, obtain an unconscionable advantage of another." See *Miles v. Illinois Cent.* R. Co. 315 U.S. 698, 62 S. Ct. 827, 86 L. Ed. 1129, 146 A.L.R 1104 (1942); *Langenau Mfg. Co. v. City of Cleveland,* 159 Ohio St. 525, 50 Ohio Op. 435, 112 N.E. 2d 658 (1953); *Kardy v. Shook,* 237 Md. 524, 207 A2d 83 (1965), in John Bourdeau *et al.,* "Injunctions," in Kevin Schroder, John Glenn and Maureen Placilla, *Corpus Juris Secundum,* Volume 43A, Thompson West, 2004, pp. 114–115.

[642] See Eduardo Ferrer Mac-Gregor, *La acción constitucional de amparo en México y España. Estudio de derecho comparado,* Editorial Porrúa, México, 2002, p. 379.

the United States regarding an injunction against another injunction, sometimes referred to as a "counter injunction," which cannot be admitted.[643]

In other countries, on the contrary, the amparo actions are admitted even against previous amparo judicial decisions as is the case of Colombia,[644] Peru[645] and Venezuela,[646] considering that those decisions can also, by themselves, violate constitutional rights of the plaintiff or of the defendant, different to those claimed in the initial amparo action.

2. *The exclusion of the amparo actions against judicial decisions*

However, as mentioned, the fact is that the majority of Latin American countries rejects the amparo action against judicial decisions, as is the case in Argentina (Article 2,b),[647] Bolivia (Article 96,3), Brazil (Article 5,II), Costa Rica (Article 30,b),[648] Chile,[649] the Dominican Republic (Ar-

---

[643]See *Sellers v. Valenzuela*, 249 Ala. 620, 32 So. 2d 520 (1947), in John Bourdeau *et al.*, "Injunctions," in Kevin Schroder, John Glenn and Maureen Placilla, *Corpus Juris Secundum*, Volume 43A, Thompson West, 2004, pp. 87.

[644]See Juan Carlos Esguerra, *La protección constitucional del ciudadano*, Legis, Bogotá, 2004, p. 164.

[645]See Samuel B. Abad Yupanqui, *El proceso constitucional de amparo*, Gaceta Jurídica, Lima, 2004, pp. 327, 330.

[646]See Allan R. Brewer-Carías, *Instituciones Políticas y Constitucionales,* Vol V, *Derecho y Acción de Amparo*, Editorial Jurídica Venezolana, Caracas, 1998, pp. 263 ff.

[647]See Joaquin Brague Camazano, *La Jurisdicción constitucional de la libertad (Teoría general, Argentina, México, Corte Interamericana de Derechos Humanos)*, Editorial Porrúa, México, 2005, p. 98. José Luis Lazzarini, *El juicio de amparo*, Editorial La Ley, Buenos Aires, 1987, pp. 218–223; Alí Joaquín Salgado, *Juicio de amparo y acción de inconstitucionalidad*, Astrea, Buenos Aires, 1987, p. 46.

[648]See Rubén Hernández Valle, *Derecho Procesal Constitucional*, Editorial Juricentro, San José, 2001, pp. 45, 206, 223, 226.

[649]See Juan Manuel Errazuriz G. and Jorge Miguel Otero A., *Aspectos procesales del recurso de protección*, Editorial Jurídica de Chile, Santiago, 1989, p. 103. Nonetheless, some authors consider that the recourse for protection is admissible against judicial decisions when issued in an arbitrary way and in violation of due process rights. See Humberto Nogueira Alcalá, "El derecho de amparo o protección de los derechos humanos, fundamentales o esenciales en Chile: evolución y perspectivas," in Humberto Nogueira Alcalá (Editor), *Acciones constitucionales de amparo y protección: realidad y perspectivas en Chile y América Latina*, Editorial Universidad de Talca, Talca, 2000, p. 45.

ticle 3,a),[650] Ecuador,[651] Nicaragua (Article 51,b) Paraguay (Article 2,a) and Uruguay (Article 2,a).[652]

In El Salvador and Honduras the exclusion is limited to judicial acts issued "in purely civil, commercial or labor-related judicial matters, and in respect to definitive decisions in criminal matters" (El Salvador, Article 13; Honduras, Article 45,6). Also, in Brazil the *mandado de segurança* is excluded against judicial decisions when according to the procedural regulations a judicial recourse against them exists, or when such decisions can be modified by other means (Article 5,II).

IV. AMPARO AGAINST ACTS OF OTHER CONSTITUTIONAL ENTITIES AND AGAINST PUBLIC OMISSIONS

1. *Acts of other constitutional entities*

However, beside the legislative, executive and judicial branches of government, in contemporary Latin American constitutional law, the separation of powers principle has given origin to other State organs independent from the three classical branches. This is the case, for instance of the Electoral bodies in charge of governing the electoral processes, of the People's Defendant or Human Rights Defendants Offices, of the Public Prosecutor Offices, of the General Audit entities (*Contraloría General*) and of the Council of the Judiciary established for the government and administration of courts and tribunals.

Because those entities are State organs, in principle their acts, facts and omissions can also be challenged by means of amparo actions when violating constitutional rights. Nonetheless, some exceptions also have been established denying the justicability of their actions by means of amparo actions, as is the case regarding the Electoral bodies of Costa Rica (Article 30,d),[653] Mexico (Article 73,VII),[654] Nicaragua (Article 51,5), Pa-

---

[650]See Eduardo Jorge Prats, *Derecho Constitucional*, Vol. II, Gaceta Judicial, Santo Domingo 2005, p. 391.

[651]Hernán Salgado Pesantes, *Manual de Justicia Constitucional Ecuatoriana*, Corporación Editora Nacional, Quito, 2004, p. 84.

[652]See Luis Alberto Viera, *Ley de Amparo*, Ediciones Idea, Montevideo, 1993, pp. 50, 97.

[653] See Rubén Hernández Valle, *Derecho Procesal Constitucional*, Editorial Juricentro, San José, 2001, pp. 228–229. Other matters decided by the Tribunal Supremo de Elecciones like citizenship, personal capacity or personal status matters are justiciables by means of amparo. See José Miguel Villalobos, "El recurso de amparo en Costa Rica," in Humberto Nogueira Alcalá (Editor), *Acciones constitucionales de amparo y protección:*

nama (Article 2.615),[655] Peru (Article 5,8)[656] and Uruguay (Article 1,b). In a similar sense, injunctions are excluded in the United States regarding actions of the electoral officers in the performance of their duties.[657]

In Peru, the Code on Constitutional procedure also excludes from the amparo action the acts of the Council of the Judiciary (*Consejo de la Magistratura*), when issued in cases of dismissal or ratification of judges (Article 5,7) in a duly motivated way and when the interested party has been heard.[658]

2. Public entities omissions

Apart from the positive acts or actions from public officers, authorities or from individuals, that amparo action can also be filed against the omissions of authorities when the corresponding entities or public officials fail to comply with their general obligations, thereby causing harm of threat to constitutional rights.

In the cases of public officers' omissions, the amparo action in Latin America is generally filed in order to obtain from the court an order directed against the public officer compelling him to act in a matter with respect to which he has the authority or jurisdiction. In these cases, the effects of the amparo decision regarding omissions is similar to the United States mandamus or mandatory injunction,[659] which consists in "a

---

realidad y perspectivas en Chile y América Latina, Editorial Universidad de Talca, Talca, 2000, pp. 222–223.

[654] See Eduardo Ferrer Mac-Gregor, *La acción constitucional de amparo en México y España. Estudio de derecho comparado*, Editorial Porrúa, México, 2002, p. 378; See Richard D. Baker, *Judicial Review in México. A Study of the Amparo Suit*, Texas University Press, Austin, 1971, pp. 98, 152.

[655] See Boris Barrios González, *Derecho Procesal Constitucional*, Editorial Portobelo, Panamá, 2002, p. 161.

[656] Nonetheless, the amparo action can be admitted if the decision of the *Jurado Nacional de Elecciones* does not have jurisdictional nature or if having jurisdictional nature, it violates the effective judicial protection (due process). See Samuel B. Abad Yupanqui, *El proceso constitucional de amparo*, Gaceta Jurídica, Lima, 2004, pp. 128, 421, 447.

[657] See *Boyd v. Story*, 350 Ark. 56, 84 S.W.3d 444 (2002), in John Bourdeau *et al.*, "Injunctions," in Kevin Schroder, John Glenn and Maureen Placilla, *Corpus Juris Secundum*, Volume 43A, Thompson West, 2004, pp. 238–239.

[658] See Samuel B. Abad Yupanqui, *El proceso constitucional de amparo*, Gaceta Jurídica, Lima, 2004, p. 126.

[659] In the United States, it has been considered that while as a general rule courts will not compel by injunction the performance by public officers of their official duties (*Bellamy v.*

writ commanding a public officer to perform some duty which the laws require him to do but he refuses or neglects to perform."[660]

In any case, for an omission to be the object of an amparo action, it must also inflict a direct harm to the constitutional right of the plaintiff, so if the violation is only referring to a right of legal rank, in some countries like Venezuela, the amparo action is inadmissible and the affected party is obliged to use the ordinary judicial remedies, like the judicial review of administrative omission action to be filed before the special courts of the matter (*contencioso-administrativo*).[661] In order to determine when it is possible to file an amparo action against public officers' omissions, the key element established by the Venezuelan courts refers to

---

Gates, 214 Va. 314, 200 S.E. 2d 533, (1973)), a court may compel public officers or boards to act in a matter with respect to which they have jurisdiction or authority (*Erie v. State By and Through State Highway Commission*, 154 Mont. 150, 461 P 2d 207 (1969)). See in John Bourdeau *et al.*, "Injunctions," in Kevin Schroder, John Glenn and Maureen Placilla, *Corpus Juris Secundum*, Volume 43A, Thompson West, 2004, pp. 221, 222, 244.

[660]The consequence of this rule is that mandamus cannot be used if the public officer has any discretion in the matter; "but if the law is clear in requiring the performance of some ministerial (nondiscretionary) function, then mandamus may properly be sought to nudge the reluctant or negligent official along in the performance of his or her duties." As it was decided by the Supreme Court in *Wilbur v. United States*, 281 U.S. 206, 218 (1930): "Where the duty in a particular situation is so plainly prescribed as to be free from doubt and equivalent to a positive command, it is regarded as being so far ministerial that its performance may be compelled by mandamus, unless there be provision or implication to the contrary, but where the duty is not thus plainly prescribed but depends upon a statute, the construction or application of which is not free from doubt, it is regarded as involving the character of judgment or discretion which cannot be controlled by mandamus." See the references in M. Glenn Abernathy and Barbara A. Perry, *Civil Liberties under the Constitution*, Sixth Edition, University of South Carolina Press, 1993, p. 8.

[661]According to the judicial doctrine established by the former Supreme Court of Justice of Venezuela, the amparo action against omissive conducts of Public Administration, must comply with the following two conditions: "a) That the alleged omissive conduct be absolute, which means that Public Administration has not accomplished in any moment the due function; and b) that the omission be regarding a generic duty, that is, the duty a public officer has to act in compliance with the powers attributed to him, which is different to the specific duty that is the condition for the judicial review of administrative omissive action. Thus, only when it is a matter of a generic duty, of procedure, of providing in a matter which is inherent to the public officer position, he incurs in the omissive conduct regarding which the amparo action is admissible." See the decisions of the former Supreme Court of Justice, Politico Administrative Chamber, dated November 5, 1992, *Jorge E. Alvarado* case, in *Revista de Derecho Público*, n° 52, Editorial Jurídica Venezolana, Caracas, 1992, p. 187; and November 18, 1993, in *Revista de Derecho Público*, n° 55-56, Editorial Jurídica Venezolana, Caracas, 1993, p. 295.

the nature of the public officers' duties because the amparo action is only admissible when the matters refer to a generic constitutional duty and not to specific legal ones.[662]

Because the judicial order of mandamus in the amparo decision regarding public authorities' omissions is a command directed to the public officer to perform the duty the constitution requires him to do, which he has refused or neglected to perform,[663] the general rule is that the court order cannot substitute the public officer's power to decide.[664] Only in cases when a specific statute provides what it is called a "positive silence" (the presumption that after the exhaustion of a particular term, it is considered that Public Administration has tacitly decided accordingly to what has been asked in the particular petition) the judicial order is considered as implicitly giving positive effects to the official abstention or omission.[665]

---

[662]As defined by the same Supreme Court in a decision dated February 11, 1992: "In cases of Public Administration abstentions or omissions, a distinction can be observed regarding the constitutional provisions violated when they provide for generic or specific duties. In the first case, when a public entity does not comply with its generic obligation to answer [a petition] filed by an individual, it violates the constitutional right to obtain prompt answer [to his petition] as set forth in Article 67 of the Constitution; whereas when the inactivity is produced regarding a specific duty imposed by a statute in a concrete and ineludible way, no direct constitutional violation occurs, in which case the Court has imposed the filing of the judicial review of administrative omissions recourse..." The Court continued: "From the aforementioned reasons the Court deems conclusive that the inactivity of Public Administration to accomplish a specific legal duty precisely infringes in a direct and immediate way the legal (statutory) text regulating the matter, in which case the Constitution is only violated in a mediate and indirect way. For the amparo judge, in order to detect if an abstention of the aggrieved entity effectively harms a constitutional right or guaranty, it must first, rely himself on the supposedly unaccomplished statute in order to verify if the abstention is regarding a specific obligation; in which case it must deny the amparo action, having the plaintiff the possibility to file another remedy, like the judicial review action against Public Administration omissions." See in *Revista de Derecho Público*, n° 53-54, Editorial Jurídica Venezolana, Caracas, 1993, pp. 272–273.

[663]For instance, to promptly issue the corresponding decision accordingly to the formal petition filed before the authority (Article 51, Constitution). See the former Venezuelan Supreme Court decision dated August 26, 1993, *Klanki* case, in *Revista de Derecho Público*, n° 55-56, Editorial Jurídica Venezolana, Caracas, 1993, p. 294.

[664]See for instance in Argentina, Néstor Pedro Sagüés, *Derecho procesal Constitucional*, Vol 3, "Acción de amparo," Editorial Astrea, Buenos Aires, 1988, pp. 73 ff.

[665]See the Venezuelan former Supreme Court decision dated December 20, 1991, *BHO, C.A.* case, in *Revista de Derecho Público*, n° 48, Editorial Jurídica Venezolana, Caracas, 1991, pp. 141–143.

PART FIVE

THE EXTRAORDINARY CHARACTER OF THE AMPARO PROCEEDING

Being a judicial means specifically established for the protection of constitutional rights, the amparo action is conceived of in Latin America as an extraordinary instrument that, consequently, does not substitute for all the other ordinary judicial remedies established for the protection of personal rights and interest. This implies that the amparo action, as a matter of principle, only can be filed when no other adequate judicial mean exists and is available in order to obtain the immediate protection of the violated constitutional rights.

The main consequence of this extraordinary character of the amparo proceeding has been the development of a series of specific procedure rules imposed by the need to grant immediate protection to constitutional rights, that in many cases are different from the general rules that govern the ordinary judicial procedures, particularly when that protection cannot be obtained through the ordinary judicial means.

The first group of these procedural rules, as mentioned, refers to the admissibility of the action, established in order to determine the existence or inexistence of other adequate judicial mean for the immediate protection of the rights, which justifies or not the use of the extraordinary action. The second group of the rules refers to the main principles that govern the amparo proceeding as an extraordinary one, giving it its adjective specificity. The third group of the rules refers to the specific configuration of the basic phases of the procedure in the amparo action, originated, precisely, because of the same extraordinary character of the proceeding. The fourth group of rules refers to the preliminary amparo measures that can be issued pending the development of the trial. The fifth group of rules refers to the definitive judicial adjudication in the amparo proceeding and to its effects; and the sixth group of rules refers to the revision of the amparo decisions by the Constitutional or Supreme Courts.

This section of the book is devoted to analyze, separately, all these general groups of procedural rules that are specific to the amparo proceeding, with particular reference to the conditions of admissibility of the amparo action, and to the characteristics of the preliminary and definitive judicial adjudication in the amparo suit.

CHAPTER SEVENTEEN

THE QUESTION OF THE ADMISSIBILITY OF THE AMPARO ACTION AND ITS RELATION WITH THE ORDINARY JUDICIAL MEANS

The first question refers to the adjective rules of the admissibility of the amparo action derived from the relation that exists between the amparo action as an extraordinary judicial mean and the other ordinary judicial means.

In this context, the general rule of admissibility refers to two aspects: first, that the amparo action can only be admissible when there are no other judicial means for granting the constitutional protection; and second, that when the legal order provides for these other judicial means for protection of the right, they are inadequate in order to obtain the immediate protection of the harmed or threatened constitutional rights. In a contrary sense, the amparo action is inadmissible for the protection of a constitutional right if the legal order provides for other actions or proceedings that are adequate for such purpose, guarantying immediate protection to the right.

This rule of admissibility of the amparo action is similar to the general rule existing in the United States regarding the injunctions and all other equitable remedies, like the mandamus and prohibitions, all reserved for extraordinary cases,[666] in the sense that they are available only "after the applicant shows that the legal remedies are inadequate."[667]

---

[666] *Ex-parte Collet*, 337 U.S. 55, 69 S. Ct 944, 93 L. Ed. 1207, 10 A.L.R. 2D 921 (1949). See in John Bourdeau *et al.*, "Injunctions," in Kevin Schroder, John Glenn and Maureen Placilla, *Corpus Juris Secundum*, Volume 43A, Thomson West, 2004, p. 20. This main characteristic of the injunction as an extraordinary remedy has been established since the nineteenth century in *In re Debs* 158 U.S. 564, 15 S.Ct 900, 39 L. Ed. 1092 (1895), in which case, in the words of Justice Brewer, who delivered the opinion of the court, it was decided that: "As a rule, injunctions are denied to those who have adequate remedy at law. Where the choice is between the ordinary and the extraordinary processes of law, and the

This rule always imposes the need for the plaintiff and for the court to determine in each case, not only the existence and availability of ordinary judicial means for obtaining the constitutional protection, but also the adequacy of such existing and available recourses for granting the immediate constitutional protection to the constitutional right.

Nonetheless, in some countries, the admissibility condition only refers to the first question of the existence and availability, but not regarding the adequacy of the ordinary means, imposing on the plaintiff the need to obligatory exhaust the existing ordinary judicial means, even if they are inadequate.

So, three questions must be analyzed related to this matter of admissibility of the amparo action based on the relation that exists between the amparo action and the other ordinary judicial means: first, the main question of the need to determine the existence or availability of adequate means for protection; second, in some cases, the question of the subordinate character of the action that exists in some countries due to the need for the previous exhaustion of the existing ordinary means; and third, the question of the adjective consequences resulting from the plaintiff's previous election of other remedies for the claimed protection filed before the amparo action.

I. THE CONDITION OF THE NON-AVAILABILITY OF OTHER ADEQUATE JUDICIAL MEANS FOR THE PROTECTION OF CONSTITUTIONAL RIGHTS

As mentioned, the general rule for the admissibility of the amparo action in the Latin American countries derives from the need to determine the existence and availability of other judicial means, and in some cases, also, of administrative means, for the protection of the harmed right; and the adequacy or inadequacy of such existing judicial means for the immediate protection that is needed regarding the constitutional right.

As mentioned, this general principle of the admissibility of the amparo action is very similar to the one referred to the admission of the injunction remedies in the United States' system, where the traditional and fundamental principle for granting an injunction is the condition of the inadequacy of the existing legal remedies (*Beacon Theatres, Inc. v. West-*

former are sufficient, the rule will not permit the use of the latter." See in Owen M. Fiss and Doug Rendleman, *Injunctions*, The Foundation Press, Mineola, 1984, p. 8.

[667] *Idem,* p. 59.

over, 359 U.S. 500, 79 S.Ct. 948, 3L.Ed. 2d 988, 2 Fed. R. Serv. 2d 650 (1959)).[668]

This condition of the "availability" or of the "sufficiency"[669] has also been referred to as the rule of the "irreparable injury," meaning that the injunction is only admissible when the harm "cannot be adequately repaired by the remedies available in the common law courts." That is, if the threatened rights are rectified by a legal remedy, then the judge will refuse to grant the injunction.[670]

This same general principle of the existence and availability, and of the adequacy of other means, although without any relation to the distinction between law and equitable remedies but only to the distinction between ordinary and extraordinary judicial means, is also applied in many Latin American Amparo laws like, for example, those of Argentina, Chile, Uruguay and Venezuela. In these countries, in general terms, because the

---

[668] See in John Bourdeau *et al.*, "Injunctions," in Kevin Schroder, John Glenn and Maureen Placilla, *Corpus Juris Secundum*, Volume 43A, Thomson West, 2004, p. 89. The judicial doctrine on the matter has been summarized as follows: "An injunction, like any other equitable remedy, will only be issued where there is no adequate remedy at law. Accordingly, except where the rule is changed by statute, an injunction ordinarily will not be granted where there is an adequate remedy at law for the injury complained of, which is full and complete. Conversely, a court of equitable jurisdiction may grant an injunction where an adequate and complete remedy cannot be had in the courts of law, despite the petitioner's efforts. Moreover, a court will not deny access to injunctive relief when procedures cannot effectively, conveniently and directly determine whether the petitioner is entitled to the relief claimed." See in *Idem*, pp. 89–90; 119 ff.; 224 ff.

[669] *Idem*, pp. 119 ff.

[670] See Owen M. Fiss and Doug Rendleman, *Injunctions*, The Foundation Press, Mineola New York, 1984, p. 59. This situation, as pointed out by Owen M. Fiss "makes the issuance of an injunction conditional upon a showing that the plaintiff has no alternative remedy that will adequately repair the injury. Operationally this means that as general proposition the plaintiff is remitted to some remedy other than an injunction unless he can show that his noninjunctive remedies are inadequate." See Owen Fiss, *The Civil Rights Injunction*, Indiana University Press, 1978, p. 38. This term "inadequacy," according to Tabb and Shoben, "has a specific meaning in the law of equity because it is a shorthand expression for the policy that equitable remedies are subordinate to legal ones. They are subordinate in the sense that the damage remedy is preferred in any individual case if it is adequate." See William M. Tabb and Elaine W. Shoben, *Remedies*, Thomson West, 2005, p. 15. But in particular, regarding constitutional claims involving constitutional rights such as those for school desegregation, it has been considered that their protection precisely requires the extraordinary remedy that can be obtained by equitable intervention, as was decided by the Supreme Court regarding school desegregation in its second opinion in *Brown v. Board of Education* (S. Ct. 1955) and regarding the unconstitutional cruel and unusual punishment in the prison system in *Hutto v. Finney* (S.Ct. 1978). *Idem,* pp. 25–26.

amparo action is considered as an extraordinary and residual judicial mean for protection,[671] the general rule is that it is inadmissible if another adequate judicial mean for the immediate protection of the constitutional right exists.

In the Dominican Republic this was also the general principle established before the sanctioning of the Amparo Law in 2006,[672] which now even though it does not provide on the matter of admissibility, establishes the principle that the amparo action is an autonomous one that is not subordinate to the exhaustion of other recourses or means established in statutes to challenge the act of omission considered as harming a fundamental right (Article 4).

In the case of Argentina, the adequacy rule is provided in the constitution setting forth that the amparo action is admissible "as long as no other more adequate judicial mean exist" (Article 43). The condition is also established in the Amparo Law, which provides for the inadmissibility of the amparo action "when other juridical or administrative recourses or remedies exists allowing to obtain the protection of the constitutional right or guaranty" (Article 2,a). This rule of the adequacy is established also regarding the administrative remedies[673] and not only the judicial

---

[671]This is the rule in Argentina, where the amparo action has been considered by the courts as an extraordinary and residual judicial remedy reserved for the "delicate and extreme situations in which, because of the lack of other legal means, the safeguard of fundamental rights is in danger." CSJN, March 7, 1985, LL, 1985-C-140; *id., Fallos*, 303–422; 306; 1253. See in Néstor Pedro Sagüés, *Derecho procesal Constitucional,* Vol 3, *Acción de amparo*, Editorial Astrea, Buenos Aires, 1988, p. 166. These same expressions regarding the "extraordinary or residual" character of the amparo action are used by the Uruguayan courts. J.L. Cont. Adm. 2° S. 194, Sept. 9, 1992; TAC 7° S. 171, Sept. 25, 1992; TAC 7° S. 27 de Feb. 28, 1990; J.L. Cont. Adm, 2° res., Oct. 10, 1991. See in Luis Alberto Viera, *Ley de Amparo*, Ediciones Idea, Montevideo, 1993, pp. 145, 148, 149.

[672] In the Dominican Republic the Supreme Court has ruled as follows: "According to the Dominican legal doctrine, as well as to the international doctrine and jurisprudence, the amparo action has a subordinate character, which implies that it can only be filed when the interested person does not have any other mean to claim for the protection of the harmed or threatened right; the principle supposes that the amparo action cannot be filed when other procedures exists in parallel, in which the injured party has the possibility to claim for the protection of the same fundamental rights." See in Manuel A. Valera Montero, *Hacia un nuevo concepto de Constitución. Selección y clasificación de decisiones de la Suprema Corte de Justicia de la República Dominicana en materia constitucional 1910-2004*, Santo Domingo, 2006, pp. 374–375.

[673]Because in Argentina the amparo action is not admitted against judicial decisions, this article is applicable to the amparo against administrative acts, referring, first, to the availability of judicial and administrative means for the protection; and second, to the adequacy

means, so that if such administrative means for the defense of the plaintiff rights are available, the amparo action is considered inadmissible.

Nonetheless, regarding this condition of admissibility, an exception is established in Argentina in the sense that even when other remedies exist, the amparo action is admissible when their use can cause grave and irreparable harm or when they cannot grant the adequate and immediate protection required regarding the harmed or threatened constitutional right.[674]

As mentioned, the same principle of the adequacy is applied in Uruguay where the Amparo Law also sets forth that the action can "only be admissible when no other judicial or administrative means exist" to guaranty the protection of the constitutional rights or when if existing, because of the circumstances they are ineffective for such purpose.[675] In Chile, lacking of a Statute regulating the action for protection, some authors consider that the same rule applies;[676] and in Venezuela without an

of those means, in the sense that they must be adequate, sufficient and effective in order to protect the plaintiff.

[674] See José Luis Lazzarini, *El juicio de amparo*, Ed. La Ley, Buenos Aires, 1987, p. 94–95, 122 ff., 139; Alí Joaquín Salgado, *Juicio de amparo y acción de inconstitucionalidad*, Editorial Astrea, Buenos Aires, 1987, pp. 31 ff. Being a condition of admissibility, it is for the plaintiff to allege and prove that there are no other adequate means for the protection of his rights. See Néstor Pedro Sagüés, *Derecho Procesal Constitucional*, Vol 3, *Acción de Amparo*, Editorial Astrea, Buenos Aires, 1988, p. 170. As was decided by the Supreme Court: "It is indispensable for the admission of the exceptional remedy of amparo that those claiming judicial protection prove, in due form, the inexistence of other legal means for the protection of the harmed right or that the use of the existing could provoke an ulterior irreparable harm." Case *Carlos Alfredo Villar v. Banco de la República Argentina*. See the reference in Samuel B. Abad Yupanqui, *El proceso constitucional de amparo*, Gaceta Jurídica, Lima, 2004, pp. 223–224.

[675] Articles 2 and 9,B of the Amparo Law. It is also this admissibility condition that gives the amparo action in Uruguay its "extraordinary, exceptional, residual character, in the sense that it is admissible when the normal means for protections will be powerless." See Luis Alberto Viera, *Ley de Amparo*, Ediciones Idea, Montevideo, 1993, p. 20. See the comments on the court's decisions regarding the "residual" rule in pp. 57, 131 ff; 154 ff.; and 158 ff.

[676] See Humberto Nogueira Alcalá, "El derecho de amparo o protección de los derechos humanos, fundamentales o esenciales en Chile: evolución y perspectivas," in Humberto Nogueira Alcalá (Editor), *Acciones constitucionales de amparo y protección: realidad y perspectivas en Chile y América Latina*, Editorial Universidad de Talca, Talca, 2000, p. 27. Nonetheless, in contrary sense, see Emilio Pfeffer Urquiaga, "Naturaleza, características y fines del recurso de protección," in Humberto Nogueira Alcalá (Editor), *Acciones constitucionales de amparo y protección: realidad y perspectivas en Chile y América Latina*, Editorial Universidad de Talca, Talca, 2000, p. 153.

express provision in the Amparo Law, the Supreme Court has ruled that "the amparo is admissible even in cases where, although ordinary means exist for the protection of the infringed juridical situation, they would not be suitable, adequate or effective for the immediate restoration of the said situation."[677]

Of course, this question of the availability and of the adequacy of the existing judicial means for the admissibility or inadmissibility of the amparo action eventually is a matter of judicial interpretation and adjudication, which must always be decided in the particular case decision, when evaluating the adequacy question.[678]

---

[677]See decision of the former Supreme Court of Justice of Venezuela of March 8, 1990, in *Revista de Derecho Público*, n° 42, Editorial Jurídica Venezolana, Caracas, 1990, pp. 107–108. In a similar sense, the Supreme Court in a decision dated December 11, 1990, ruled that: "The criteria of this High Court as well as the authors' opinions has been reiterative in the sense that the amparo action is an extraordinary or special judicial remedy that is only admissible when the other procedural means that could repair the harm are exhausted, do not exist or would be inoperative. Additionally, Article 5 of the Amparo Law provides that the amparo action is only admissible when no brief, summary and effective procedural means exist in accordance with the constitutional protection." This objective procedural condition for the admissibility of the action turns the amparo into a judicial mean that can only be admissible by the court once it has verified that the other ordinary means are not effective or adequate in order to restore the infringed juridical situation. If other means exist, the court must not admit the proposed amparo action." See in *Revista de Derecho Público*, n° 45, Editorial Jurídica Venezolana, Caracas, 1991, p. 112. The Supreme Court in another decision dated June 12, 1990, decided that the amparo action is admissible: "when there are no other means for the adequate and effective reestablishment of the infringed juridical situation. Consequently, one of the conditions for the admissibility of the amparo action is the nonexistence of other more effective means for the reestablishment of the harmed rights. If such means are adequate to resolve the situation, there is no need to file the special amparo action. But even if such means exists, if they are inadequate for the immediate reestablishment of the constitutional guaranty, it is also justifiable to use the constitutional protection mean of amparo." See the decision of the Politico Administrative Chamber of the Supreme Court of Justice of June 12, 1990, in *Revista de Derecho Público* n° 43, Editorial Jurídica Venezolana, Caracas, 1990, p. 78. See also in *Revista de Derecho Público*, n° 55-56, Editorial Jurídica Venezolana, Caracas, 1993, pp. 311–313.

[678]For instance, in a decision of the First Court on administrative jurisdiction dated May 20, 1994 (*Federación Venezolana de Deportes Equestres* case), it was ruled that the judicial review of administrative acts actions were not adequate for the protection requested in the case, seeking the participation of the Venezuelan Federation of Equestrian Sports in an international competition, being the opinion of the courts "that when the action was brought before it, the only mean that the claimant had in order to obtain the reestablishment of the infringed juridical situation was the amparo action, due to the fact that by means of the judicial review of administrative acts recourse seeking its nullity, they could never be able to obtain the said reestablishment of the infringed juridical situation that was

In Venezuela, particularly regarding the amparo action against administrative acts, the prevalent doctrine on the matter for many years, established by the former Supreme Court of Justice, was to admit the amparo action in spite of the existence of the specific recourse before the Judicial Review of Administrative Action Jurisdiction. Yet this wide protective doctrine has been unfortunately abandoned in recent years by the Supreme Tribunal of Justice, applying a restrictive interpretation regarding the adequacy of the judicial review action for the annulment of administrative acts, and rejecting the amparo action when filed directly against them.[679]

to assist to the 1990 international contest." See the reference in Rafael Chavero G. *El nuevo amparo constitucional en Venezuela*, Ed. Sherwood, Caracas, 2001, p. 354.

[679]This can be realized from the decision taken in a recent and polemic case referring to the expropriation of some premises of a corn agro-industry complex, which developed as follows: In August 2005, officers from the Ministry of Agriculture and Land and military officers and soldiers from the Army and the National Guard surrounded the installation of the company *Refinadora de Maíz Venezolana, C.A. (Remavenca)*, and announcments were publicly made regarding the appointment of an Administrator Commission that would be taking over the industry. These actions were challenged by the company as a *de facto* action alleging the violation of the company's rights to equality, due process and defense, economic freedom, property rights and to the nonconfiscation guaranty of property. A few days later, the Governor of the State of Barinas, where the industry was located, issued a Decree ordering the expropriation of the premises, and consequently the Supreme Tribunal declared the inadmissibility of the amparo action that was filed, basing its ruling on the following arguments: "The criteria established up to now by this Tribunal, by which it has concluded on the inadmissibility of the autonomous amparo action against administrative acts has been that the judicial review of administrative act actions –among which the recourse for nullity, the actions against the administrative abstentions and recourse filed by public servants– are the adequate means, that is, the brief, prompt and efficient means in order to obtain the reestablishment of the infringed juridical situation, in addition to the wide powers that are attributed to the administrative jurisdiction courts in Article 29 of the Constitution. Accordingly, the recourse for nullity or the expropriation suit are the adequate means to resolve the claims referring to supposed controversies in the expropriation procedure; those are the preexisting judicial means in order to judicially decide conflicts in which previous legality studies are required, and which the constitutional judge cannot consider. Thus, the Chamber considers that the claimants, if they think that the alleged claim persists, can obtain the reestablishment of their allegedly infringed juridical situation, by means of the ordinary actions and to obtain satisfaction to their claims. So because of the existing adequate means for the resolution of the controversy argued by the plaintiff, it is compulsory for the Chamber to declare the inadmissibility of the amparo action, according to what is set forth in Article 6,5 of the Organic Law." See decision of the Constitutional Chamber of the Supreme Tribunal of Justice n° 3375 of November 4, 2005, *Refinadora de Maíz Venezolana, C.A. (Remavenca), y Procesadora Venezolana de Cereales, S.A. (Provencesa) vs. Ministro de Agricultura y Tierras y efectivos de los componentes Ejército*

337

II. THE CONDITION OF THE PREVIOUS EXHAUSTION OF OR- DINARY JUDICIAL MEANS

As mentioned, the general rule of the availability and adequacy regarding other judicial means for the admissibility of the amparo action has an exception in countries where the only rule that is applied is the availability rule but not the adequacy one.

That is, in some countries, the condition for the admissibility only re- fers to the question of the existence or availability of other judicial ordi- nary means without consideration of their adequacy for the immediate constitutional protection, imposing to the plaintiff the previous exhaus- tion of the existing ordinary judicial or administrative means in order to file an amparo action. This is the case in Brazil, Colombia, Guatemala, Mexico and Peru, where the need to previously exhaust the existing ordi- nary judicial and in some cases the administrative means, is imposed as a condition for the filing of the amparo action, independently of any con- sideration about their inadequacy. In these countries the amparo action has a subordinate (*subsidiario*) character,[680] although also with the same exceptions related to the irreparable harms that could provoke the said exhaustion.

Something similar happens in the United States regarding injunctions against administrative acts, in which cases, the rule of the inadequacy is abandoned, and another rule prevails in such cases, that the injunction can only be filed after the available administrative remedies have been exhausted (*Zipp v. Geske & Sons, Inc*, 103 F. 3d 1379 (7th Cir. 1997)). However, even in these cases, the rule is not applicable when the exhaus- tion of the remedy can cause imminent and irreparable harm to the plain-

---

y Guardia Nacional de la Fuerza Armada Nacional Case. See in *Revista de Derecho Público*, n° 104, Editorial Jurídica Venezolana, Caracas, 2005, pp. 239 ff.

[680] In a similar sense in Spain the general principle is that since the protection of constitu- tional rights and liberties is a task attributed to all the courts, the filing of an amparo action before the Constitutional Tribunal can only be admitted when the ordinary judicial means have been exhausted, so that an amparo action can only be brought before the Constitu- tional Tribunal when filed against a final judicial decision on the particular case. That is why the amparo action in Spain is considered as a *subsidiaria* action in the sense that it can only be filed after the prior exhaustion of the ordinary legal remedies once their judgment has been issued. See Eduardo Ferrer Mac-Gregor, *La acción constitucional de amparo en México y España. Estudio de derecho comparado*, Editorial Porrúa, México, 2002, pp. 292 ff.

tiff (*State ex rel. Sheehan v. District Court of Minn. In and For Hennepin County*, 253 Minn. 462, 93 N.W.2d 1 (1958)).[681]

In Mexico, this condition responds to the principle of the need for the challenged act to have a "definitive character" (*definitividad*), which exists when the act cannot be challenged by any other judicial mean,[682] implying that only those acts can be the object of amparo actions. Nonetheless, some exceptions are also established regarding this condition when the challenged act implies a danger to the plaintiff's life, or of deportation from the country, or a violation of the due process of law rights provided in Article 20 of the constitution. So in those cases, even when other remedies exist, the amparo action can be filed.

The general consequences of this principle of the "definitive" character of the challenged act are not only the necessary previous filing of the existing recourses and means of defense against the act that can modify or repeal it, but that the stages of those judicial means must be exhausted. Consequently, it is not only sufficient for them to be filed, but they must be pursued up to the final stage of the procedure concluding with the definitive decision from the corresponding authority.[683]

A similar principle is established by the Guatemalan Amparo Law, but which extends the availability condition not only regarding judicial means but also regarding administrative recourses.[684]

---

[681]See the reference in John Bourdeau *et al.*, "Injunctions," in Kevin Schroder, John Glenn and Maureen Placilla, *Corpus Juris Secundum*, Volume 43A, Thomson West, 2004, p. 225.

[682] In this sense, Article 103 of the Constitution and Article 73 of the Amparo Law provides that when the amparo action is directed against a judicial act, it can only be filed against the definitive and final judicial rulings, regarding which there is no other judicial remedy available to obtain its modification or repeal (Article 73, XIII). The same principle applies regarding administrative acts, in which case, the amparo action is only admissible when they cannot be challenged by another recourse, suit or any other means of defense, allowing the suspension of its effects provided that they have no additional conditions to those set forth in the Amparo Law (Article 73, XV).

[683]See Eduardo Ferrer Mac-Gregor, *La acción constitucional de amparo en México y España. Estudio de derecho comparado*, Editorial Porrúa, México, 2002, pp. 315, 392 ff.; Richard D. Baker, *Judicial Review in México. A Study of the Amparo Suit*, University of Texas Press, Austin, 1971, p. 100.

[684]The Law sets forth that "in order to file an amparo, it is necessary to exhaust the ordinary judicial and administrative recourses by means of which the matter can be adequately resolved according to the due process principles (Article 19). See the courts' decision in this sense in Jorge Mario García Laguardia, *Jurisprudencia constitucional, Guatemala, Honduras, México, Una Muestra*, Guatemala, 1986, pp. 43, 45. In this case, the exhaustion

It is also the principle applied in Colombia, where Article 86 of the constitution provides that the *tutela* action can only be filed when the affected party does not have another judicial mean available for the protection of his right,[685] because the judge is the one to determine if there are other judicial means for protection.[686]

Yet this case of the residual character (*subsidiario*) of the Colombian *tutela* only refers to the existence of other judicial means, and not to administrative means or recourses that are considered in Colombia as optional for the plaintiff (Article 9, *Tutela* Law).[687]

The only exception in Colombia to the rule that imposes the need to file other judicial existing means for protection before filing a *tutela* action, is the possibility to use the *tutela* as a transitory protective mean also in order to avoid harms considered irreparable (Article 8), [688] in which case

rule refers not only to judicial recourses but also to administrative ones. In Honduras, for instance, regarding the habeas data action, Article 40 of the Amparo Law sets forth that it can only be filed when the corresponding administrative procedures are exhausted.

[685] The same condition is set forth in Article 6,1 of the *Tutela* Law prescribing that the amparo action is inadmissible "when other judicial recourses or means of defense exist," being nonetheless possible to file the *tutela* action as a transitory mechanism to prevent irreparable harms. In this later case, the question of the efficacy of the existing judicial means must be appreciated in particular, according to the circumstances of the plaintiff (Article 6, 1). The other judicial means for protection in Colombia, that instead of the *tutela* action are considered as serving for the effective protection of fundamental rights, are the public action of unconstitutionality, the exception of unconstitutionality, the habeas corpus action, the action for compliance, the popular actions, the judicial review of administrative acts actions, the exception of illegality and the provisional suspension of the effects of administrative acts. See Juan Carlos Esguerra Portocarrero, *La protección constitucional del ciudadano*, Legis, Bogotá, 2004, p. 125.

[686] As was ruled by the Constitutional Court when deciding that: "When the *tutela* judge finds that other judicial defense mechanisms exists are applicable to the case, he must evaluate it according to the facts expressed in the claim and the scope of the harmed or threatened fundamental right, the available remedies include all the relevant aspects for the immediate, complete and efficient protection of the violated rights, in matters of proof and of the alternate defense decision mechanism." See decision 100/94, March 9, 1994. See the reference in Samuel B. Abad Yupanqui, *El proceso constitucional de amparo*, Gaceta Jurídica, Lima, 2004, p. 229.

[687] Also in Costa Rica, it is expressly stated in the Amparo Law that it is not necessary to file any administrative recourse prior to the filing of the amparo action (Article 31). See Rubén Hernández, *Derecho Procesal Constitucional*, Editorial Juricentro, San José, 2001, p. 242.

[688] See Juan Carlos Esguerra Portocarrero, *La protección constitucional del ciudadano*, Legis, Bogotá, 2004 p. 127.

their imminence and gravity impose the need for the immediate adoption of protection.

In Peru, the Constitutional Procedures Code also requires for the admissibility of the amparo action the need for the previous exhaustion of the existing "previous means" (Articles 5 and 45); in this case referring to the administrative recourses that can be filed against administrative acts before the organs of the Public Administration, like the hierarchical recourse seeking to obtain a decision issued by the head of the Administrative organization.[689]

Nonetheless, the Peruvian Code also establishes the same exceptions to the rule (Article 45) when the exhaustion of the administrative recourse can turn the injury into an irreparable one, in the sense of impeding the harmed right to be restored to the situation existing before the harm was caused.[690] Other exceptions refer to cases when the challenged decision has been already enforced;[691] when the previous means are not regulated or have been unnecessarily initiated by the injured party; and when the filed administrative recourse has not been promptly resolved. The amparo action must also be admitted if the previous mean is not resolved within

---

[689] As was justified by the Constitutional Tribunal, "the need for the exhaustion of such [administrative] means before filing the amparo, is founded in the need to give the Public Administration the possibility to review its own acts in order to allow the possibility for the Administration to resolve the case, without the need to appear before the judicial organs." See Exp 1042-AA-TC, decision of December 6, 2002, F.J. n° 2. See the reference in Samuel B. Abad Yupanqui, *El proceso constitucional de amparo*, Gaceta Jurídica, Lima, 2004, p. 234. This condition for the admissibility of the amparo action, also established in general for judicial review of administrative actions, has been considered as a Public Administration "privilege" that could harm the general constitutional right to access to justice.

[690] Consequently, the amparo action must be admitted in cases when the exhaustion of the previous mean provoked the aggression to become irreparable. For instance, when a local government decision orders the demolition of a building, executed during the exhaustion of the administrative recourse. See the Constitutional Tribunal decision of September 9, 2002, Exp. n° 1266-2001-AA/TC, in *El Peruano. Garantías Constitucionales,* April 4, 2003, p. 6081. See the reference in Samuel B. Abad Yupanqui, *El proceso constitucional de amparo*, Gaceta Jurídica, Lima, 2004, pp. 251–255.

[691] It is the case when an administrative act, even not being the last that can be issued in the administrative procedure, has been executed before the exhaustion of the term established in order to be considered as consented by the plaintiff. Regarding this exception, the Constitutional Tribunal has considered that the amparo action is admissible in all cases in which the challenged resolution has been immediately executed by the Public Administration before any possibility for the affected party to challenge it in the administrative procedure. See Samuel B. Abad Yupanqui, *El proceso constitucional de amparo*, Gaceta Jurídica, Lima, 2004, pp. 246–250.

the terms fixed for its resolution, which is established in order to avoid the perpetuation of undefined situations provoked by the lack of decision regarding administrative petitions[692]

Regarding the amparo actions against judicial decisions, even though it is not expressly regulated, the Peruvian Constitutional Tribunal also imposes the need for the previous exhaustion of the ordinary judicial means in order to bring the amparo action before the competent court;[693] when the due process rights are being clearly and ostensibly harmed; and always bearing in mind their adequacy for the constitutional protection.[694]

It must also be mentioned the case of Brazil, where Article 5,1 of the *Mandado de Segurança* Law sets forth that the action will not be admissible against administrative acts regarding which administrative recourses with suppressive effects can be filed, independently of bail. Consequently, also in this case, the condition for the admissibility of the *mandado* imposes the need to exhaust those recourses, previously to the filing of the petition.

III. THE QUESTION DERIVED FROM THE PREVIOUS FILING OF OTHER REMEDIES THAT ARE PENDING DECISION, INCLUDING AMPARO SUITS

The other question related to the admissibility of the amparo action is related to the question of the existence of a pending action or recourse already filed or brought before a court for the same purpose of protecting a constitutional right.

This question regarding the admissibility of the amparo action has also some similarities with what in the United States' injunctions procedure regarding defenses is called the "doctrine of the election of remedies," which is applied when an injured party having two available but inconsis-

---

[692] See Samuel B. Abad Yupanqui, *El proceso constitucional de amparo*, Gaceta Jurídica, Lima 2004, pp. 258–260.

[693] Exp. n° 1821-98, decisión, June 25, 1999, *El Perúano, Jurisprudencia*, November 7, 2001, p. 4501. See the reference in Samuel B. Abad Yupanqui, *El proceso constitucional de amparo*, Gaceta Jurídica, Lima, 2004, p. 242.

[694] See Luis R. Sáenz Dávalos, "Las innovaciones del Código Procesal Constitucional en el recurso constitucional de amparo," in Susana Castañeda *et al.*, *Introducción a los procesos constitucionales. Comentarios al Código Procesal Constitucional*, Jurista Editores, Lima, 2005, p. 135.

tent remedies to redress a harm, chooses one, such act being considered as constituting a binding election that forecloses the other.[695]

In a similar sense this is the general rule in Latin America, as it is, for instance, established in Chile,[696] Peru, Mexico, Argentina and in Venezuela.

Consequently as established in Peru, the action is inadmissible "when the aggrieved party has previously chosen other judicial processes seeking protection of his constitutional right."[697] Also in Mexico, the action is inadmissible when the plaintiff has already filed before a court any recourse or action against the harming act seeking protection;[698] and the same rule is applied in Venezuela, where the amparo action is inadmissible "when the injured party has chosen other ordinary judicial mean or has used other preexisting judicial means,"[699] and particularly when the suspension of the effects of the injuring act has been requested before a court.[700]

---

[695]See William M. Tabb and Elaine W. Shoben, *Remedies,* Thomson West, 2005, p. 56.

[696]See Juan Manuel Errazuriz G. and Jorge Miguel Otero A., *Aspectos procesales del recurso de protección*, Editorial Jurídica de Chile, Santiago, 1989, p. 114.

[697]Article 5, 3, Code on Constitutional Procedures.

[698]Article 73, XIV of the Mexican Amparo Law is that the amparo suit is inadmissible "when the claimant has already brought before an ordinary court any recourse or legal defense seeking to modify, repeal or nullify the challenged act." So pending the decision on such judicial process in which the claimant has asked the same protective remedies, the amparo suit cannot be admissible. See Eduardo Ferrer Mac-Gregor, *La acción constitucional de amparo en México y España. Estudio de derecho comparado*, Editorial Porrúa, México, 2002, pp. 393; Richard D. Baker, *Judicial Review in México. A Study of the Amparo Suit*, University of Texas Press, Austin, 1971, p. 100.

[699]Article 6,5, Amparo. In such cases, when the violation or threat of constitutional rights and guaranties has been alleged, the court must follow the procedure set forth in the Amparo Law (Articles 23, 24 and 25), in order to provisionally suspend the effects of the challenged act. This inadmissibility clause is only applicable when in the other judicial action or recourse the constitutional violation has been alleged; so that the constitutional protection can be obtained. Thus, in such cases, it is possible to obtain in an immediate way the effective protection of the constitutional rights, justifying the inadmissibility of the amparo action.

[700]This inadmissibility clause, in particular, has been applied in cases of exercise of judicial review actions against administrative acts, when a petition for the protection of constitutional rights has been conjunctly requested, seeking the suspension of the effects of the challenged injuring administrative acts, in which cases the amparo action has been considered inadmissible. In these cases, the First Court on Administrative Jurisdiction in a decision dated May 11, 1992 (*Venalum* case), ruled as follows: "It has been the criteria of this court that Article 6,5 of the Amparo law imposes the inadmissibility of the amparo action

It must also be highlighted that in Venezuela this inadmissibility rule only applies when the plaintiff has filed other judicial mean for protection; not being applied if only administrative recourses have been filed before the Public Administration organs.[701] On the contrary, in Argentina, the rule of the inadmissibility when a previous recourse has been chosen also applies in cases of administrative recourses.[702]

Nonetheless, in order to assure the effective protection of rights, the courts in Argentina also have developed an exception to the rule, establishing that even in cases in which the interested party has chosen to use

when the aggrieved party has chosen the ordinary judicial means or has used the preexistent judicial means. The court has considered in previous cases that when the plaintiff is asking for the suspension of the challenged administrative act according to Article 136 of the Supreme Court Organic Law, that means the use of a parallel mean for protection that turns the amparo action inadmissible, because such petition for a provisional remedy requested conjunctly with the nullity action, is in itself a cause of inadmissibility." See in *Revista de Derecho Público*, n° 50, Editorial Jurídica Venezolana, Caracas, 1992, pp. 187–188. See also the decisions of the First Court of February 21, 1991, in Revista *de Derecho Público*, n° 45, Editorial Jurídica Venezolana, Caracas, p. 146; December 5, 1991, and April 1, 1993, in *Revista de Derecho Público*, n° 53-54, Editorial Jurídica Venezolana, Caracas, 1994, p. 263. See also the decision of the Politico Administrative Chamber of the Supreme Court of July 13, 1992 (*Municipio Almirante Padilla* case), in Revista *de Derecho Público*, n° 51, Editorial Jurídica Venezolana; Caracas, 1992, pp. 215–216; and the decision of November 11, 1993, Caso *UNET*, in *Revista de Derecho Público*, n° 55–56, Editorial Jurídica Venezolana, Caracas, 1993, p. 489.

[701] In this case, the inadmissible clause is not applied, because the administrative recourses are not judicial ordinary means that can prevent the filing of the amparo action. See the decision of the First Court on administrative jurisdiction, which decided on a decision dated March 8, 1993, *Federico Domingo* case, in *Revista de Derecho Público*, n° 53-54, Editorial Jurídica Venezolana, Caracas, 1994, p. 261. See also the decision dated May 6, 1994, *Universidad Occidental Lisandro Alvarado* case, in *Revista de Derecho Público*, n° 57-58, Editorial Jurídica Venezolana, Caracas, 1994. See Rafael Chavero G. *El nuevo amparo constitucional en Venezuela*, Ed. Sherwood, Caracas, 2001, pp. 250 ff.

[702] As was decided in the *Hughes Tool Company S. A.* case, "the sole fact that the plaintiff has chosen to file a petition or recourse before the Administration, provokes the inadmissibility of the amparo action, because a claim of this nature cannot be used to take the case from the authority intervening in the case because so asked by the same plaintiff." See in Alí Joaquín Salgado, *Juicio de amparo y acción de inconstitucionalidad*, Editorial Astrea, Buenos Aires, 1987, pp. 33. In other cases, the decision has been that "it is not legal nor logic for a plaintiff in parallel and simultaneously to use two means of different procedural nature, one ordinary and the other extraordinary, because it would be incompatible and it would place the claimant in a position of privileged or advantage contrary to the principle of equality in the exercise of procedural rules." See ST La Rioja, January 27, 1971, J.A., 10-1971-782. See the reference in Néstor Pedro Sagüés, *Derecho procesal Constitucional*, Vol 3, Acción de amparo, Editorial Astrea, Buenos Aires, 1988, p. 187.

other mean for the protection of the harmed constitutional rights, the amparo action can be admissible when there is an excessive delay in the resolution of the previous pending procedure; a delay that can provoke a grave and irreparable harm that can justify the filing of the amparo action in order to obtain the immediate protection needed.[703]

This condition of inadmissibility of the amparo action when the plaintiff has chosen to file another action has been regulated in some Latin American countries, in particular regarding the case of the previous filing of another amparo action that is pending to be decided. In this regard, the inadmissibility of the new amparo action is expressly established in the legislation of Bolivia,[704] Ecuador,[705] Mexico[706] and Venezuela,[707] in cases in which a previous amparo action has been filed regarding the same violation, the same action and the same persons.

In Philippines, the condition of admissibility of the petition for the writ on amparo when pending other judicial petitions has been established only regarding criminal actions, by providing that "when a criminal action has been commenced, no separate petition for the writ shall be filed" but "the reliefs under the writ shall be available by motion in the criminal case" (Sec. 1).

---

[703]See Alí Joaquín Salgado, *Juicio de amparo y acción de inconstitucionalidad*, Editorial Astrea, Buenos Aires, 1987, p. 34; José Luis lazzarini, *El juicio de amparo*, Ed. La Ley, Buenos Aires, 1987, p. 143.

[704]In Bolivia the Amparo Law provides that the amparo action is inadmissible when a previous constitutional amparo action has been filed with identity on the person, the object and the cause (Article 96, 2)

[705]In Ecuador, the Amparo Law forbids the filing of more than one amparo action regarding the same matter and with the same object before more than one court. That is why persons filing an amparo action must declare under oath in a written request that they have not filed another amparo action before other courts with the same matter and object (Article 57).

[706]In México, Article 73,III of the Amparo Law also provides the inadmissibility of the amparo action against statutes and acts that have been the object of another previous amparo suit pending resolution, filed by the same aggrieved party, against the same authorities and regarding the same challenged act, even if the constitutional violations are different.

[707]Also in Venezuela, Article 6,8 of the Amparo Law provides the inadmissibility of the action for amparo when a decision regarding another amparo suit has been brought before the courts regarding the same facts and is pending decision. See for instance the decision of the Politico Administrative Chamber of the Supreme Court of Justice of October 13, 1993, in *Revista de Derecho Público*, n° 55-56, Editorial Jurídica Venezolana, Caracas, 1993, pp. 348–349.

CHAPTER EIGHTEEN

THE MAIN PRINCIPLES OF THE PROCEDURE IN THE AMPARO PROCEEDING

The second aspect specifically conditioned by the extraordinary character of the amparo proceeding refers to the general rules governing the procedure, which in general terms are related to its bilateral character; to the brief and preferred character of the procedure; to the role of the courts directing the procedure and to the need for the substantial law to prevail regarding formalities.

I. THE BILATERAL CHARACTER OF THE PROCEDURE

One of the fundamental principles regarding the amparo proceeding is that although being of an extraordinary nature, the bilateral character of the proceeding must always be guarantied. This implies that the amparo proceeding must always be initiated by a party or parties (the injured or offended party), so no *ex officio* amparo proceeding is admissible.[708] Consequently, the amparo proceeding must always be initiated by means of an action or a recourse brought before the competent court by a party against another party (the injurer or offender party) whose actions or omissions have violated or have caused harm to his constitutional rights. This party, as defendant, must always be brought to the procedure in order to guaranty his rights to defense and due process.

The final outcome of the amparo proceeding is always a judicial order, as also happens in the United States with the writs of injunction, mandamus or error, which are directed to the injuring party ordering to do or to abstain from doing something, or to suspend the effects, or annul the

---

[708] Only in cases of habeas corpus actions do some Amparo Laws provide for the power of the courts to initiate the proceeding *ex officio*: Guatemala (Article 86), Honduras (Article 20).

damaging act.[709] However, in Latin America, the amparo statutes not only refer to the amparo as a remedy or as the final court written order (writ) commanding the defendant to do or refrain from doing some specific act, but in addition, it is regulated as a complete proceeding that is specifically designed to protect constitutional rights following an adversary procedure according to the "cases or controversy" condition. All the phases or stages of the procedure are regulated; the procedure ending with a judicial decision or judicial order directed to protect the constitutional rights of the injured party.

Consequently, the general rule in the amparo proceeding is that although being brief and speedy, the procedural adversary principle or the principle of bilateralism,[710] must be preserved, assuring the presence of both parties and the respect of the due process constitutional guaranties, particularly the rights to defense.[711] That is why, for instance, the Para-

---

[709]The amparo suit has similarities with the civil suit for an injunction that an injured party can bring before a court to seek for the enforcement or restoration of his violated rights or for the prevention of its violation. It also can be identified with a "suit for mandamus" brought by an injured party before a court against a public officer whose omission has caused harm to the plaintiff, in order to seek for a writ ordering the former to perform a duty that the law requires him to do but he refuses or neglects to perform. Also, the suit for amparo has similarities with a "suit for writ of error" brought before the competent superior court by an injured party whose constitutional rights have been violated by a judicial decision, seeking the annulment or the correction of the judicial wrong or error.

[710] José Luis Lazzarini, *El Juicio de Amparo*, Editorial La Ley, Buenos Aires, 1987, pp. 270 ff. In the proceeding, the interested third parties that can be harmed or benefited by the action and its results, as well as the Public Prosecutor (Attorney General) or the People's Defendant are also considered as parties.

[711]Thus, a judicial guaranty of constitutional rights as is the amparo suit can in no way transform itself in a proceeding violating the other constitutional guaranties like the right to defense. Except regarding preliminary judicial orders, the principle of *audi alteram partem* (hear the other party or listen to both sides) must then always be respected. That is why, for instance, the Supreme Court of Justice of Venezuela in a 1996 judicial review procedure annulled Article 22 of the 1988 Amparo Law, which allowed the courts to adopt final decisions on amparo matters in cases of grave violations of constitutional rights, reestablishing the constitutional harmed right without any formal or summary inquiry and without hearing the plaintiff or potential injurer. Even if the article could have been constitutionally interpreted as only directed to allow the adoption of *inaudita partem* preliminary decisions or injunctions in the proceeding, the Supreme Court considered its contents as a vulgar and flagrant violation of the constitutional right to self-defense, and annulled it. See Decision of the Supreme Court of Justice of May 21, 1996, in *Gaceta Oficial Extra*. n° 5071 of May 29, 1996. See the comments in Allan R. Brewer-Carías, *Instituciones Políticas y Constitucio-nales*, Vol V, *Derecho y Acción de Amparo*, Universidad Católica del Táchira, Editorial Jurídica Venezolana, Caracas, 1998, pp. 389 ff.; and in Rafael Chavero, *El Nuevo*

guayan Procedural Code regarding the amparo proceeding expressly states that the amparo judge must always assure within the summary nature of the procedure, the adversary principle (contradiction) (Article 586).

The only exception in this regard can be found in Chile where in the absence of a statutory regulated action for protection, it has been considered that the procedure of the recourse for protection is not based on a controversy between parties, but on a request raised by a party before a court, being the procedural relation the one established between a complainant and a court, and not between two parties, an injured and an injurer party.[712] Nonetheless, as aforementioned, any affected person can be a party in the procedure.

Except in this case of Chile, the bilateral character of the amparo procedure imposes the respect of the due process of law guaranties tending to assure the right of the defendants and other interested parties to defend themselves.

That is why no definitive amparo adjudication can be issued without the participation of the defendant or at least without his knowledge about the filing of the action; the exception to this rule being very rare, as is the case of Colombia, where the *Tutela* Law admits the possibility for the court to grant the constitutional protection (tutela) *in limene litis*, that is, "without any formal consideration and without previous enquiry, if the decision is founded in an evidence that shows the grave and imminent violation of harm to the right" (Article 18).

This Colombian provision undoubtedly was inspired by the Venezuelan Amparo Law that also provided for the possibility for the amparo judge "to immediately restore the infringed juridical situation, without considerations of mere form and without any kind of brief enquiry," requiring in such cases, that "the amparo protection be founded in an evidence consti-

---

Régimen del Amparo Constitucional en Venezuela, Caracas, 2001, pp. 212, 266 ff. and 410 ff.

[712] See for example Sergio Lira Herrera, *El recurso de protección. Naturaleza jurídica, doctrina, jurisprudencial, derecho comparado*, Santiago de Chile, 1990, pp. 157 ff.; Juan Manuel Errazuziz G. y Jorge Miguel Otero A, *Aspectos procesales del recurso de protección,* Editorial Jurídica de Chile, Santiago, 1989, pp. 39, 40 y 157. In a contrary sense, see Enrique Paillas who considers that in the recourse for protection, the principle of bilateralism applies. See Enrique Paillas, *El recurso de protección ante el derecho comparado*, Editorial Jurídica de Chile, Santiago, 1990, pp. 105.

tuting a grave presumption of the violation of harm of violation" (Article 22).

Nonetheless, in Venezuela this article was annulled by the former Supreme Court, which refused to interpret it as only providing for preliminary decisions and as not intending to establish the possibility of a definitive amparo decision that could be issued *inaudita parte* because it would be unconstitutional. In particular, in the popular action process followed before the former Supreme Court of Justice based on the alleged unconstitutionality of such provision, it was requested to the Court to interpret it according to the constitution (*secundum constitucione*), in the sense that what was intended was to establish a legal authorization for the courts to just adopt in an immediate way preliminary protective measures, pending the resolution of the case, but not definitive amparo decisions. Nonetheless, the court rejected this interpretation, and eventually annulled the article of the Amparo Law,[713] considering that it violated in a flagrant way the constitutional right to defense. The adjective consequence was that failing to interpret the norm according to the constitution, no legal support could be identified in the special Amparo Law empowering the courts to adopt provisional or preliminary relief,[714] which were then adopted applying the general provisions of the Procedural Civil Code.

II. THE BRIEF AND PROMPT CHARACTER OF THE PROCESS

Because the amparo suit is an extraordinary remedy for the immediate protection of constitutional rights, its main feature is the brief and prompt character of the procedure, which is justified because the purpose of the action is to immediately protect persons in cases of irreparable injuries or threats to constitutional rights.

This irreparable character of the harm or threat and the immediate need for protection have been the key elements that have molded the procedural rules not only of the amparo proceeding, but also of the injunctions

---

[713]Decision dated May 21, 1996. See in *Gaceta Oficial Extra* n° 5071 May 29, 1996. See the comments in Allan R. Brewer-Carías, *Instituciones Políticas y Constitucionales*, Vol. V, *Derecho y Acción de Amparo,* Editorial Jurídica Venezolana, Caracas, 1998, pp. 388–396; Rafael Chavero Gazdik, *El nuevo régimen del amparo constitucional en Venezuela,* Edit. Sherwood, Caracas, 2001, pp. 212, 266 ff., 410 ff.

[714]See the comments in Allan R. Brewer-Carías, *Instituciones Políticas y Constitucionales*, Vol V, *Derecho y Acción de Amparo*, Universidad Católica del Táchira, Editorial Jurídica Venezolana, Caracas, 1998, pp. 398.

in the United States, where the judicial doctrine on the matter is also that "an injunction is granted only when required to avoid immediate and irreparable damage to legally recognized rights, such as property rights, constitutional rights or contractual rights." [715]

The same principles also apply to the amparo proceeding, originating the configuration of a brief and preferred procedure, precisely justified because of the protective purpose of the action and the immediate protection required because of the violations of constitutional rights.

For these purposes, many Latin American Amparo Laws expressly provide for some general guidelines containing general principles that must govern the procedure. For instance, in Colombia, the *Tutela* Law refers to "the principles of publicity, prevalence of substantial law, economy, promptness and efficacy" (Article 3). In Ecuador, the Law refers to "the principles of procedural promptness and immediate [response]" (*inmediatez*) (Article 59); in Honduras, mention is made to the "principles of independence, morality of the debate, informality, publicity, prevalence of substantial law, free, promptness, procedural economy, effectiveness, and due process" (Article 45); and in Peru, the Code refers to "the principles of judicial direction of the process: free regarding the plaintiff's acts, procedural economy, immediate and socialization" (Article III).

---

[715]Consequently, "There must be some vital necessity for the injunction so that one of the parties will not be damaged and left without adequate remedy," *Treadwell v. Investment Franchises, In*c., 273 Ga. 517,543 S.E.2d 729 (2001). In other words, "to warrant an injunction it ordinarily must be clearly shown that some act has been done, or is threatened, which will produce irreparable injury to the party asking for the injunction," *U.S. v. American Friends Service Committee*, 419 U.S. 7, 95 S.Ct. 13, 42 L. Ed. 2d 7 (1974). In the same sense it has been established that: "The very function of an injunction is to furnish preventive relief against irreparable mischief or injury, and the remedy will not be awarded where it appears to the satisfaction of the court that the injury complained of is not of such a character," *State Com'n on Human Relations v. Talbot County Detention Center*, 370 Md. 115, 803 A.2d 527 (2002). More specifically, a permanent, mandatory injunction, a preliminary, interlocutory or temporary injunction, a preliminary mandatory injunction, or a preliminary, interlocutory or temporary restraining order, "will not, as a general rule, be granted where it is not shown that an irreparable injury is immediately impending and will be inflicted on the petitioner before the case can be brought to a final hearing, no matter how likely it may be that the moving party will prevail on the merits," *Packaging Industries Group, Inc. v. Cheney*, 380 Mass. 609, 405 N.E.2d. 106 (1980). See the reference to the corresponding cases in John Bourdeau *et al.*, "Injunctions," in Kevin Schroder, John Glenn and Maureen Placilla, *Corpus Juris Secundum*, Volume 43A, Thomson West, 2004, pp. 76–78.

It is in this regard that Article 27 of the Venezuelan Constitution also expressly provides that the procedure of the constitutional amparo action must be oral, public, brief, free and not subject to formality.[716]

III. THE PREFERRED CHARACTER OF THE PROCEDURE AND THE ROLE OF THE COURTS

One of the consequences of the brief and prompt character of the procedure in the amparo proceeding is its preferred character that imposes, as it is provided in the Venezuelan Constitution, that "any time will be workable time, and the courts will give preference to the amparo regarding any other matter" (Article 27), principles that are set forth in almost all the Amparo Laws in Latin America by expressly providing that the amparo action can be filed at any time,[717] even on holidays and out of labor hours.[718]

This preferred character of the procedure also implies that the procedure must be followed with preference, so when an amparo action is

---

[716]Regarding some of these principles, the Venezuelan First Court on Judicial Review of Administrative Actions, even before the sanctioning of the Amparo Law in 1988, ruled that because of the brief character of the procedure, it must be understood as having "the condition of being urgent, thus it must be followed promptly and decided in the shortest possible time"; and additionally it must be summary, in the sense that "the procedure must be simple, uncomplicated, without incidences and complex formalities." In this sense, the procedure must not be converted in a complex and confused procedural situation." See decision of January 17, 1985, in *Revista de Derecho Público*, n° 21, Editorial Jurídica Venezolana, Caracas, 1985, p. 140. According to these principles, the 1988 Venezuelan Amparo Law provided for the brief, prompt and summary procedure that governed the amparo proceeding up to the enactment of the 1999 Constitution, when the Constitutional Chamber of the Supreme Tribunal of Justice interpreted the provisions of the Law, according to the new Constitution, in some way re-writing its regulations through constitutional interpretation. See the decision of the Constitutional Chamber of the Supreme Tribunal of Justice n° 7 dated February 1, 2000 (Case *José Amando Mejía*), in *Revista de Derecho Público*, n° 81, Editorial Jurídica Venezolana, Caracas, 2000, pp. 245 ff. See the comments in Allan R. Brewer-Carías, *El sistema de justicia constitucional en la Constitución de 1999. Comentarios sobre su desarrollo jurisprudencial y su explicación, a veces errada, en la Exposición de Motivos*, Editorial Jurídica Venezolana, Caracas, 2000; and in Rafael Chavero Gazdik, *El nuevo régimen del amparo constitucional en Venezuela*, Edit. Sherwood, Caracas, 2001, pp. 203 ff.

[717]See Colombia, Articles 1 and 15; Honduras, Article 16; Guatemala, Article 5.

[718]See Costa Rica, Article 5; Ecuador, Article 47; El Salvador, Article 79; Paraguay, Article 585.

filed, the courts must postpone all other matters of different nature.[719] The exception to this rule is on matters of habeas corpus, in which the preeminence of personal liberty over other rights impose the need to continue with the procedure.[720]

In the amparo procedure, as a general rule, due to its brief character, the procedural terms cannot be extended, nor suspended, nor interrupted, except in cases expressly set forth in the statute;[721] any delay in the procedure being the responsibility of the courts.[722] In this regard, for instance, the Philippines 2007 Rule on the Writ of Amparo enumerated in an extended way the different pleading and motions that are prohibited on matters of the amparo procedure: "Motion to dismiss; 2. Motion for extension of time to file return, opposition, affidavit, position paper and other pleadings; 3. Dilatory motion for postponement; 4. Motion for a bill of particulars; 5. Counterclaim or cross-claim; 6. Third-party complaint; 7. Reply; 8. Motion to declare respondent in default; 9. Intervention; 10. Memorandum; 11. Motion for reconsideration of interlocutory orders or interim relief orders; and 12. Petition for certiorari, mandamus or prohibition against any interlocutory order" (Sec. 11).

In this same regard, in the amparo proceeding, no procedural incidents are allowed.[723] In addition, in some cases no recuse or motion to recuse the judges are admitted or they are restricted,[724] and some Amparo Laws provides for specific and prompt procedural rules regarding the cases of impeding situations of the competent judges to resolve the case.[725]

---

[719]See Guatemala, Article 5; Honduras, Article 4,3; Perú; Venezuela, Article 13. On the contrary, the Amparo Law of the Dominican Republic establishes that the exercise of the amparo action will not suspend any judicial process in course (Article 5).

[720]See Colombia, Article 15; Brazil, Article 17; Costa Rica, Article 39; Honduras, Article 51.

[721]See Costa Rica, Articles 8 and 39; El Salvador, Article 5; Honduras 4; Perú, Articles 33,8.

[722]See Costa Rica, Article 8; Honduras, Article 4,8; Perú, Article 13.

[723]See Honduras, Article 70; Uruguay, Article 12; Panama, Article 2610; Paraguay, Article 586; Uruguay, Article 12.

[724]See Argentina, Article 16; Colombia, Article 39; Ecuador, Article 47, and 59; Honduras, Article 18; Panama, Article 2610; Paraguay, Article 586; Perú, Article 33, 1 and 2; Venezuela, Article 11.

[725]See Costa Rica, Article 6; Guatemala, Articles 17, 111; México, Article 66; Panama, Article 2610; Perú, Article 52; Venezuela, Article 11; Dominican Republic, Article 8.

Additionally, it is provided that the notifications made by the court can be done by any means including technical or electronic ones.[726]

IV. THE ACTIVE ROLE OF THE COURTS

Another general trend to be found in the amparo proceeding in Latin America is the active role that the Amparo Laws assigns to the courts in directing the procedure, empowering them, in some cases, even to act *ex officio*[727] also in matters of evidence[728]; the inertia of the parties not being valid to justify any delay.[729]

V. THE PREVALENCE OF SUBSTANTIVE LAW

Another principle governing the procedural rules in matters of amparo, in order to guaranty the brief and prompt character of the procedure, is the principle of the prevalence of substantive law over formal provisions, which for instance is referred to in the Honduran Amparo Law, by stating that "the merits on the matter must prevail," so that the "formal defects must not prevent the prompt development" of the procedure. Eventually, it is the principle of the prevalence of "substantive justice" over "formal justice."

Consequently, it is provided that "the parties can correct their own mistakes, if remediable" and the courts are also authorized to *ex officio* correct them.[730] That is why, for instance, the Peruvian Code specifies that "the judge and the Constitutional Tribunal must adjust the formalities set forth in the Code, to achieve the purposes of the constitutional processes" (Article III), which is the immediate protection of constitutional rights.

---

[726]See El Salvador, Article 79.

[727]See El Salvador, Article 5; Guatemala, Article 6; Honduras, Article 4,4; Perú, Article III; Dominican Republic, Article 17.

[728]See Dominican Republic, Article 5.

[729]See Costa Rica, Article 8; El Salvador, Article 5.

[730]See Honduras, Article 4,5; Guatemala, Article 6; Paraguay, Article 586; and El Salvador, Article 80.

CHAPTER NINETEEN

THE CONFIGURATION OF THE MAIN PHASES OF THE AMPARO PROCEEDING

The third aspect to be analyzed regarding the procedure in the amparo proceeding refers to the specific configuration of the main phases or steps of the proceeding, in particular, those related to the filing of the petition, the court decision on the admissibility of the action, the evidence activity, the defendant pleading, and the hearing of the case. Regarding all these phases, the Amparo Laws in Latin America provide some specific rules.

I. GENERAL PROVISIONS REGARDING THE FILING OF THE PETITION

The first specific trend to be highlighted regarding the judicial procedure of the amparo proceeding refers to the formalities of the petitions that are to be brought before the courts.

The general principle established in this matter in all the Latin American Amparo Laws, as is also the case regarding the injunctions in the United States,[731] is that the petition must be filed in writing. Nonetheless, some exceptions have been established allowing the oral presentation of the amparo in cases of urgency as established in Venezuela, Colombia, Honduras and Peru;[732] or in cases of danger to life, of deprivation of liberty without judicial process, of deportation or exile as it is established

---

[731]See *Vasquez v. Bannworths, Inc.*, 707 S.W.2d 886 (Tex. 1986); *Hall v. Hanford*, 64 So. 2d 303 (Fla. 1953), in John Bourdeau *et al.*, "Injunctions," in Kevin Schroder, John Glenn and Maureen Placilla, *Corpus Juris Secundum*, Volume 43A, Thomson West, 2004, pp. 346 ff.

[732]See Venezuela, Articles 16, 18; Colombia, Article 14; Honduras, Article 16; Perú, Article 27.

in Mexico;[733] or in cases where the plaintiff lacks economic means, as it is provided in Guatemala.[734] Nonetheless, in such cases of oral filing, the petitions must be subsequently ratified in writing.

In other cases, when the plaintiff is incapable of writing the petition, he is allowed to use the services of the Secretariat of the court to file the petition.[735] In other cases, the claimant is authorized to bring the petition before the court through telegrams or radiograms[736] and even through electronic means.[737]

In any case, in the written text of the action, the petitioner must always express in a clear and precise manner all the necessary elements regarding the alleged right to be protected and the arguments for the admissibility of the action. That is why the Amparo Laws in Latin America, and also the Rule on the Writ of Amparo in Philippines (Sec. 5), normally establish, in general terms, the minimal content of the petition or complaint, which in particular must refer to the following aspects.

First, the complete identification and information regarding the plaintiff,[738] and if someone is acting on behalf of the plaintiff, his identification is also required. If the plaintiff is an artificial person, its registration as well as the representative's complete identification is also required.[739]

Second, the petition must establish the individuation of the injurer party.[740] When the action is filed against public entities, the harming public authority must be identified.[741]

---

[733]See México, Article 117.

[734]See Guatemala, Article 26; Honduras, Article 22 (habeas corpus).

[735]Dominican Republic, Article 12.

[736]Brazil, Article 4; Costa Rica, Article 38.

[737]Perú, Article 27.

[738]See Argentina, Article 6,a; Bolivia, Article 97,I; Colombia, Article 14; El Salvador, Article 14; México, Articles 116,1 and 166,1; Nicaragua, Article 27,1; Perú, Article 42,2; Paraguay, Article 569,a; Venezuela, Article 18, 1 and 2; Dominican Republic, Article 11,b; Philippines, Sec. 5,1.

[739]See El Salvador, Article 14,1; Guatemala Article 21,b and c; Honduras, Article 49,2; Dominican Republic, Article 11,b.

[740]See Argentina, Article 6,b; Bolivia, Article 97, II; Honduras, Article 49,2; Paraguay, Article 569,b; Venezuela, Article 18,2; Dominican Republic, Article 11,c; Philippines, Sec. 5,2.

[741]See Colombia, Article 14; Costa Rica, Article 38; El Salvador, Article 14; Guatemala, Article 21,d; Panama, Article 2619,2; México, Articles 116,III and 166,III; Nicaragua, Articles 27,2 and 55.

When possible, the organ provoking the harm or threat must also be identified.

Third, the detailed narration of the circumstances in which the harm or the threat has been caused.[742] In particular, the petition must identify the act, action, omission or fact causing the harm or threat.[743]

Fourth, the written text of the petition must indicate the constitutional right or guaranty that has been violated, harmed or threatened,[744] with precise reference to the articles of the constitution or the international treaties containing the rights or guaranties denounced as violated or harmed.[745] Nonetheless, for example, the Colombian *Tutela* Law exempts the need of identifying the article of the constitution provided that the harmed or threatened right is identified with precision (Article 14). A similar provision is set forth in the Costa Rican Constitutional Jurisdiction Law (Article 38).

Fifth, the plaintiff must specify the particular protective request asked from the court as well as the judicial order to be issued in protection of his rights that is requested from the court.[746]

And, finally, the plaintiff must argue about the fulfillment of the conditions for the admissibility of the action, in particular, regarding the inadequacy of other possible judicial remedies and the irreparable injury the plaintiff will suffer without the amparo suit protection.[747]

---

[742] See Argentina, Article, 6,c; Bolivia, Article 97,III; Colombia, Article 14; Costa Rica, Article 38; El Salvador, Article 14,5; Guatemala, Article 21,e; Panama, Article 2619,3; Paraguay, Article 569,d; Honduras, Article 49,5; Nicaragua, Article 55; Perú, Article 42,4; Venezuela, Article 18,5; Dominican Republic, Article 11,d; Philippines, Sec. 5,3.

[743] See El Salvador, Article 14,3; Honduras, Article 49,3; Nicaragua, Article 27,3; Paraguay, Article 569,d; Perú, Article 42,5; México Arts. 116, IV and 166,IV18,5; Dominican Republic, Article 11,d.

[744] See Bolivia, Article 97,IV; Colombia, Article 14; El Salvador, Article 14,4; Panama, Article 2619,V; Honduras, Article 49,6; Venezuela, Article 18,418,5; Dominican Republic, Article 11,c; Philippines, Sec. 5,3.

[745] See Guatemala, Article 21,f; México, Articles 116,V and 166,VI; Nicaragua, Article 27,4.

[746] See Argentina, Article 6,d; Bolivia, Article 97,VI; Honduras, Article 49,7; Perú. Article 42,6; Paraguay, Art 569,d; Philippines, Sec. 5,6.

[747] In a similar way as in the injunction petition in the United States." See *International Westminster Bank Ltd. V. Federal Deposit Ins. Corp.*, 509 F2d 641 (9th Cir. 1975); *Thomas v. Morton*, 408 F. Supp. 1361 (D. Ariz. 1976), judgment aff'd, 552 F. 2d 871 (9th Cir. 1977), in John Bourdeau *et al.*, "Injunctions," in Kevin Schroder, John Glenn and Maureen Placilla, *Corpus Juris Secundum*, Volume 43A, Thomson West, 2004, pp. 346, 352.

In order to soften the consequences of not mentioning correctly all the above-mentioned requirements that have to be contained within the written text of the petition, almost all the Latin American Amparo Laws, in protection of the injured party's right to sue, provide that the courts are obliged to return to the plaintiff the petition that does not conform with those requirements in order for the plaintiff to make the necessary corrections.

Consequently, in these cases, the petition will not be considered inadmissible because of formal inadequacies regarding the noncompliance with the petition's requirements set forth in the statutes, and in order to have them corrected or mended the court must return it to the petitioner for him to correct it in a brief amount of time. Only if the petitioner does not make the corrections will the complaint be rejected.[748]

II. THE DECISION REGARDING THE ADMISSIBILITY OF THE PETITION

Another important phase of the procedure in the amparo proceeding is the power of the competent courts at the beginning of the procedure to decide upon the admission of the petition when all the admissibility conditions set forth in the Amparo Laws are satisfied.

Consequently, the courts are also empowered to decide *in limine litis* about the inadmissibility of the action when the petition does not accomplish in a manifest way the conditions determined in the statute;[749] for instance, when the term to file the action is evidently exhausted; when the challenged act is one of those excluded from the amparo protection; when there are ordinary means for the protection of the rights that must be previously filed or that gives adequate protection; or when ordinary judicial means that can adequately guaranty the claimed rights have already been filed.

The main effect of the admission decision of the action is for the court to notify the interested parties of the initiation of the process; to request from the defendant a report on the violations; and to adopt, if necessary, preliminary amparo decisions for the immediate protection of the harmed

[748]See Colombia, Article 17; Costa Rica, Article 42; El Salvador, Article 18; Guatemala, Article 22; Honduras, Article 50; México, Article 146; Nicaragua, Article 28; Perú, Article 48; Paraguay, Article 7; Venezuela, Article 19.

[749]See Argentina, Article 3; Bolivia, Article 98; Costa Rica, Article 9; México, Article 145; Paraguay, Article 570; Perú, Article 47; Uruguay, Article 2.

or threatened constitutional rights, pending the development of the process.

III. GENERAL PRINCIPLES REGARDING EVIDENCE AND BURDEN OF PROOF

The third phase in the procedure of the amparo proceeding refers to the evidence activity and the burden of proof.

As has been mentioned, the amparo suit is a specific judicial mean regulated in Latin America in order to obtain the immediate protection of constitutional rights and guaranties when the aggrieved or injured parties have no other adequate judicial means for such purpose. That is why this situation must be alleged and proven by the claimant.

This implies that in order to file an amparo action and to obtain the immediate judicial protection, the violation of the constitutional right must be a flagrant, vulgar, direct and immediate one, caused by a perfectly determined act or omission. Regarding the harm or injury caused to the constitutional rights, it must be manifestly arbitrary, illegal or illegitimate, a consequence of a violation of the constitution. All these aspects for obtaining the immediate judicial protection must be clear and ostensible, the plaintiff being obliged to argue them in his petition and support it with the needed evidence.

Consequently, as it is also established in the United States regarding the injunctions,[750] in the amparo proceeding, the plaintiff has the burden to prove the existence of the right, the alleged violations of threat, and the illegitimate character of the action causing it, with clear and convincing evidence.

That is why, for instance, the Amparo Laws in Latin America require that all the circumstances of the case must be explained in the text of the petition, attaching all the evidence supporting it. In particular, some statutes impose the need for the petition to be filed with all the documentary evidence,[751] and specifying all the other evidence to be presented.[752] In

---

[750]See *U.S. School Dist. 151 of Cook County*, Ill., 404 F. 2d 1125 (7th Cir. 1968); *Dickey v. Williams*, 1940 OK 28, 186 Okla. 376, 98 P. 2d 604 (1940), in John Bourdeau *et al..*, in "Injunctions," in Kevin Schroder, John Glenn and Maureen Placilla (Editors), *Corpus Juris Secundum*, Vol. 43A, Thomson West, 2004, p 54.

[751]See Argentina, Article 7; Bolivia, Article 97,V; Guatemala, Article 21,g; Panama, Article 2619; Paraguay, Article 569, in fine; Uruguay, Article 5.

[752]See Argentina, Article 7; Uruguay, Article 5.

Mexico for instance, the evidence must be shown in the hearing, except the documentary evidence that can be filed before (Article 151).

The consequence of the aforementioned is that in matters of amparo, due to the brief and prompt character of the procedure, the immediate protection of constitutional rights that can be granted needs to be based on existing sufficient evidence. That is why the amparo process cannot be involved in complex evidence activity. For instance, the Argentinean Amparo Law provides for the inadmissibility of the amparo action, in cases "where in order to determine the invalidity of the [challenged] act, a major scope of debate or proof is required." (Article, 2d)

Accordingly, the courts have rejected amparo actions in complex cases where a major debate is needed, and in cases in which proof is difficult to provide,[753] which is considered incompatible with the brief and prompt character of the amparo suit that requires that the alleged violation be "manifestly" illegitimate and harming. Even without clear provisions on the matter, as the one established in the Argentinean Law, this same principle has been considered as applicable regarding the *mandado de segurança* in Brazil, and the amparo in Uruguay[754] and Venezuela.[755]

On the other hand, regarding the "evidence phase" of the amparo procedure, although some Laws specifically regulate it,[756] some legislation, as is the case of Peru, discards its existence, providing that the evidence must be shown with the petition, and is to be accepted if it does not require further procedural developments (Article 9).

In this matter of constitutional protection, some Amparo laws give the courts among their *ex officio* powers, the competence to obtain evidence;[757] provided that it does not cause an irreparable prejudice to the parties;[758] or that it does not affect the term of the procedure, not requir-

---

[753]See José Luis Lazzarini, *El juicio de amparo*, Ed. La Ley, Buenos Aires, 1987, p. 94–95, 173 ff.; Alí Joaquín Salgado, *Juicio de amparo y acción de inconstitucionalidad*, Editorial Astrea, Buenos Aires, 1987, pp. 52; Néstor Pedro Sagüés, *Derecho procesal Constitucional*, Vol 3, Acción de amparo, Editorial Astrea, Buenos Aires, 1988, pp. 231–239.

[754]See Luis Alberto Viera, *Ley de Amparo*, Ediciones Idea, Montevideo, 1993, p. 17.

[755]See Rafael Chavero G., *El nuevo amparo constitucional en Venezuela*, Ed. Sherwood, Caracas, 2001, p. 340.

[756]See El Salvador, Article 29; Guatemala, Article 35.

[757]See Costa Rica, Article 47; Guatemala, Article 36; Dominican Republic, Articles 17 and 21.

[758]See Venezuela, Article 17; Dominican Republic, Article 17.

ing the formal and previous notice to the parties.[759] Nonetheless, the piece of evidence obtained by the courts must be shown to the parties.[760]

On the other hand, the general principle in the amparo procedure is that all kind of evidence is admitted, so the court can base its decision to grant or not the required protection in any evidence.[761] Nonetheless, some legislation forbids some kind of evidence in the amparo suit, as is the case of confession, particularly regarding public officials,[762] and those considered contrary to morality or good behavior.[763]

IV. THE DEFENDANT'S (THE INJURER OR AGGRIEVING PARTY) PLEADING OR ANSWER

Another phase of an amparo proceeding expressly regulated in almost all the Latin American Amparo Laws is the need for the court to notify the aggrieving party in order to request from it a formal written answer or report regarding the alleged violations of constitutional rights of the plaintiff.

Due to the bilateral and adversary character of the procedure, as also happens in the injunctive relief procedure in the United States, an amparo ruling must not be issued until the defendant has been asked to file its plea.[764] In the cases of Bolivia and Ecuador, the Amparo Laws do not require the filing of a formal report or answer, which nonetheless can be presented before the court in the hearing of the case.[765]

Thus, in general terms, after admitting the claim, the first procedural step the court must take is to request from the defendant a formal answer, return or report to the petition filed by the injured party,[766] to which, in

---

[759] See Perú, Article 9.

[760] See Dominican Republic, Article 17.

[761] See Colombia, Article 21.

[762] See Argentina, Article 7; El Salvador, Article 29; México, Article 150; Paraguay, Article 12. In Venezuela it is established in the Judicial Review of Administrative Action Jurisdiction regulations.

[763] See México, Article 150.

[764] See *Conseco Finance Servicing Corp. v. Missouri Dept. of Revenue*, 98 S.W. 3d 540 (Mo. 2003), in John Bourdeau *et al.*, "Injunctions," in Kevin Schroder, John Glenn and Maureen Placilla, *Corpus Juris Secundum*, Volume 43A, Thomson West, 2004, pp. 357 ff.

[765] See Bolivia, Article 100; Ecuador, Article 49.

[766] In the same sense in Philippines, Sec. 6.

addition, the defendant can put forward his counter evidence, before the hearing on it.[767]

This defendant's answer or plea regarding the harm or threat alleged by the plaintiff must be sent to the court within a very brief term,[768] which is generally established in terms of hours[769] or of days, for instance, three days,[770] five days[771] or ten days.[772] In the Philippines Rule on the Writ of Amparo, the burden of proof is specifically regulated regarding the respondent (Sec. 17).

In Argentina, the Amparo Law expressly provides that the omission by the court to request the defendant's answer produces the nullity of the process (Article 8), which is a general rule in all the countries guarantying due process of law rules.

The omission of the defendant to send his report or plea in answer to the court, in many countries implies that the facts and acts causing the harm or threat alleged by the injured party must be considered as certain.[773] In other countries, like Honduras, it implies that the constitutional right or guaranty that is alleged to be violated must be considered as effectively violated.[774] And also in other countries, like Venezuela, it implies that the plaintiff's alleged facts must be considered as accepted by the defendant.[775] In Philippines, the Rule provides that the defenses that are not raised in the return or answer "shall be deemed waived" (Sec. 10).

In many Amparo Laws it is provided that the consequence of the omission by the defendant to send his answer to the court is that the amparo

---

[767]This is what was established in the Venezuelan Amparo Law (Article 24); which nonetheless has been eliminated by the Constitutional Chamber in its decision n° 7 of February 1, 2000, *José A. Mejía et al.* ccse, interpreting the Amparo Law according to the new 1999 Constitution, and reshaping the amparo suit procedure. See in *Revista de Derecho Público*, n° 81, Editorial Jurídica Venezolana, Caracas, 2000, pp. 349 ff. See Rafael Chavero G., *El nuevo amparo constitucional en Venezuela*, Ed. Sherwood, Caracas, 2001, pp. 264 ff.

[768]See Argentina, Article 8; Bolivia, Article 100; Panama, Article 2591.

[769]Twenty-four hours: El Salvador, Article 21; forty-eight hours: Venezuela, Article 23.

[770]See Colombia, Article 19; Costa Rica, Artsicle.19, 43, 61; Paraguay, Article 572.

[771]See Honduras, Articles 26, 52; México, Articles 147, 149; Perú, Article 53; Philippines, Sec. 9.

[772]See Nicaragua, Article 37.

[773]See Colombia, Article 19; Costa Rica, Article 45; El Salvador, Article 22; Honduras (habeas corpus), Article 26; México, Article 149; Nicaragua, Article 39.

[774]See Honduras, Article 53.

[775]See Venezuela, Article 23.

should be granted,[776] although in some cases, the effect of such omission is just to grant a preliminary relief, suspending the effects of the challenged act.[777] In Philippines, Section 12 of the Rule on the Writ of Amparo establishes that "in case the respondent fails to file a return, the court, justice or judge shall proceed to hear the petition ex parte."

Notwithstanding, in many countries the Amparo Laws provide that in case of omission, the court can insist on requesting the remittance of the answer by the defendant.[778]

V. THE PUBLIC HEARING IN THE AMPARO SUIT

Finally, in all the Latin American Amparo Laws, one of the most important steps in the procedure is the hearing that the court must convene, also in a very prompt period of time, seeking the participation of the parties before adopting its decision on the case.[779] This hearing in principle must always take place and must not be suspended.

In general terms, as established in the Dominican Republic Amparo Law, this hearing in the amparo proceeding must always be oral, public and contradictory (Article 15).

The absence of the defendant's participation in the hearing, in general terms, does not produce its suspension,[780] in which case, the evidence presented by the plaintiff will be accepted and the court must then proceed to decide.[781] Regarding the plaintiff, according to some Amparo Laws, his absence from the hearing is understood as his abandonment of the action, being liable for the payment of the costs.[782]

---

[776]See Argentina, Article 20; Costa Rica, Article 45; Honduras, Article 53.

[777]See Guatemala, Article 33.

[778]See Argentina, Articles 20, 21; Colombia, Article 21; Costa Rica, Article 45; Perú, Article 53.

[779]See Argentina, Article 9; Bolivia, Article 100; Ecuador, Article 49; Uruguay, Article 6; Paraguay, Article 575; Venezuela, Article 26; Dominican Republic, Article 13; Philippines, Sec. 6, 13.

[780]See Bolivia, Article 100; Ecuador, Article 5; Dominican Republic, Article 18,I.

[781] See Ecuador, Article 10; Paraguay, Article 575.

[782]See Argentina, Article 10; Ecuador, Article 50; Paraguay, Article 575.

The final decision of the amparo proceeding must be adopted after the hearing has taken place, although some Latin American Laws set forth that the court must make its decision in the same hearing or trial.[783]

---

[783]See Bolivia, Article 100; Uruguay, Article 6. In Venezuela, the Amparo Law established that the decision ought to be issued in the following days (Article 24) after the hearing. Nonetheless, the Constitutional Chamber in decision n° 7 of February 1, 2000 (*José A. Mejía et al.* case), has modified this provision, providing that the decision must be issued at the end of the hearing. See in *Revista de Derecho Público*, n° 81, Editorial Jurídica Venezolana, Caracas, 2000, pp. 349 ff.

CHAPTER TWENTY

THE ADJUDICATION IN THE AMPARO PROCEEDING AND THE PRELIMINARY PROTECTIVE MEASURES

The purpose of the amparo proceeding eventually is for the plaintiff to obtain a judicial adjudication from the competent court, providing for the immediate protection of his harmed or threatened constitutional rights, for instance, through a judicial decision restraining some actions, preserving the status quo, or commanding or prohibiting actions.[784]

Amparo and injunctions are both extraordinary remedies having the same purpose, the main difference between them being the rights to be protected. In the United States, injunctions are equity remedies that can

---

[784] In a very similar way to the injunctive decisions that the United States' courts can adopt for the immediate protection of rights, which can consist of restrain action or interference of some kind (*Putnam v. Fortenberry*, 256 Neb. 266, 589 N.W.2d 838, 1999; *Anderson v. Granite School Dist.*, 17 Utah 2d 405, 413 P2d 597, 1996); to furnish preventive relief against irreparable mischief or injury; or to preserve the *status quo* (*Jenkins v. Pedersen*, 212 N.W.2d 415 Iowa 1973; *Snyer v. Sullivan*, 705 P.2d 510, Colo 1985). It is a remedy designed to prevent irreparable injury by prohibiting or commanding certain acts (*National Comprsed Steel Cor. V. Unified Government of Wyandotte County/Kansas City*, 272 Kan. 1239, 38 P.3d 723, 2002). The function of injunctive relief is to restrain motion and to enforce inaction (*State ex rel. Great Lakes College, Inc. v Medical Bd.*, 29 Ohio St. 2d 198, 58 Ohio Op. 2d 406, 280 N.E 2dd 900, 1972). An injunction is designed to prevent harm, not redress harm; it is not compensatory (*Klinicki v. Lundgren*, 298 Or. 662, 695 P.2d 906, 1985; *Simenstad v. Hagen*, 22 Wis. 2d 653, 126 N.W.2d 529, 1964). The remedy grants prospective, as opposed to retrospective, relief (*Jefferson v. Big Horn County*, 2000 MT 163, 300 Mont. 284, 4 P3d 26, 2000); it is preventive, protective or restorative (*Hunsaker v. Kersh*, 1999 UT, 106, 991 P2d 67, Utah 1999; *Colendrea v. Wilde Lake Community Ass'n, Inc.*, 361, Md. 371, 761 A.2d 899, 2003; *Stoetzel & Sons, Inc. v. City of Hatings*, 265 Neb. 637, 658 N.W.2d 636, 2003; *U.S. v. White County Bridge Commission*, 275 F.2d 529, 7th Cir. 1960), but not addressed to past wrongs (*Snyder v. Sullivan*, 705 P.2d 510, Colo. 1985). See in John Bourdeau *et al.*, "Injunctions," in Kevin Schroder, John Glenn and Maureen Placilla, *Corpus Juris Secundum*, Volume 43A, Thomson West, 2004, p. 20.

be used for the protection of any kind of personal or property rights, but in Latin America, the amparo proceeding is conceived only for the protection of constitutional rights, which explains its regulations in the constitutions, and not for the protection of rights established in statutes.[785]

In this matter of the amparo proceeding, as well as in matters of injunctions, two general sorts of judicial adjudications can be issued by the courts for the protection of constitutional rights: preliminary measures that can be ordered from the beginning of the procedure, with effects subject to the final court ruling; and definitive decisions preventing the violation or restoring the enjoyment of the threatened or harmed rights.

---

[785] In this sense, in Venezuela the courts have ruled that the harm caused must always be the result of a violation of a constitutional right that must be "flagrant, vulgar, direct and immediate, which does not mean that the right or guaranty is not due to be regulated in statutes, but it is not necessary for the court to base its decision in the latter to determine if the violation of the constitutional right has effectively occurred." See Supreme Court of Justice, *Tarjetas Banvenez* case, July 10, 1991, in *Revista de Derecho Público*, n° 47, Editorial Jurídica Venezolana, Caracas, 1991, pp. 169–170. See also decision of May 20, 1994, First Court on Judicial Review of Administrative Actions, *Federación Venezolana de Deportes Ecuestres* Case, in *Revista de Derecho Público*, n° 57-58, Editorial Jurídica Venezolana, Caracas, 1994. In other words, only direct and evident constitutional violations can be protected by means of amparo; thus, for instance, as ruled in 1991 by the Venezuelan courts, the internal electoral regime of political parties or of professional associations could not be the object of an amparo action founded in the right to vote set forth in the constitution, "which only applies to the national electoral process [not being applied] to the internal electoral process of the political parties," concluding that the amparo only protects constitutional rights and guaranties and not legal (statutory) ones, and much less the ones contained in association's by laws." See decision of August 8, 1991, in *Revista de Derecho Público*, n° 47, Editorial Jurídica Venezolana, Caracas, 1991, p. 129. In other decisions, the courts declared inadmissible amparo actions for the protection of rights when the allegations were only founded "in legal (statutory) considerations," as the right to work commonly conditioned by statutes regarding dismissals. Thus, the amparo is not the judicial mean for the protection of such right if the violation is only referring to the labor law provisions. See decision of October 8, 1990, in *Revista de Derecho Público*, n° 44, Editorial Jurídica Venezolana, Caracas, 1990, pp. 139–140. In a similar sense, the violation of the right to self-defense because a party's right to cross-examine a witness was denied according to Article 349 of the Civil Procedural Code cannot be founded in Article 68 of the Constitution because it implies the need to analyze norms of legal rank and not of constitutional rank. In this regard it was decided by the former Supreme Court of Justice, Politico Administrative Chamber, decision of November 8, 1990, in *Revista de Derecho Público*, n° 44, Editorial Jurídica Venezolana, Caracas, 1990, pp. 140–141.

I. THE PRELIMINARY AMPARO MEASURES

In Latin America, according to the regulations established in the Civil Procedure Codes, all courts are empowered to adopt, during the course of a procedure, what are called "*medidas preventivas*" or "*medidas cautelares*," that is, interlocutory and temporal judicial measures that are also applied to the amparo proceeding. The expression refers to interlocutory or preliminary measures; so in this sense, a "*medida preventiva*" is not equivalent to the English expression "preventive measure," which is used in the sense of to prevent or to avoid harm, which can be decided both in a definitive or a preliminary injunction.[786]

That is, both the definitive and preliminary judicial amparo decisions can have "preventive" effects in the sense of preventing harms or preserving the status quo, the preliminary ones having only a temporary basis, pending the termination of the procedure.[787]

Consequently, in order to avoid confusion, I will use the expression "preliminary" measures to identify what in the Latin American procedural law are called "*medidas preventivas o cautelares*," as interlocutory, preliminary and temporal judicial protective measures that can be issued pending the procedure, similar to the United States "preliminary injunctions" also issued as interlocutory and temporal relief pending the trial.[788]

---

[786] In other words, as explained by Tabb and Shoben: "The classic form of injunctions in private litigation is the preventive injunction. By definition, a preventive injunction is a court order designed to avoid future harm to a party by prohibiting or mandating certain behavior by another party. The injunction is "preventive" in the sense of avoiding harm. The wording may be either prohibitory ("Do not trespass") or mandatory ("Remove the obstruction")." See William M. Tabb and Elaine W. Shoben, *Remedies*, Thomson West, 2005, p. 22.

[787] As the same authors Tabb and Shoben have said: "Upon a compelling showing by the plaintiff, the court may issue a coercive order even before full trial on the merits. A preliminary injunction gives the plaintiff temporary relief pending trial on the merit. A temporary restraining order affords immediate relief pending the hearing on the preliminary injunction. Both of these types of interlocutory relief are designed to preserve the status quo to prevent irreparable harm before a court can decide the substantive merits of the dispute. Such orders are available only upon a strong showing of the necessity for such relief and may be conditioned upon the claimant posting a bond or sufficient security to protect the interests of the defendant in the event that the injunction is later determined to have been wrongfully issued." *Idem*, p. 4.

[788] In both cases, the preliminary measures are different to the final judicial protective (permanent injunction) decisions which can have preventive or restorative effects. See *Bayer v. Associated Underwriters, Inc.*, 402 S.W.2d 11 (Mo. Ct. App. 1966), in John

Based on this distinction between preliminary measures (*cautelares*) and definitive adjudications or decisions, the amparo proceedings in Latin America is not just of a *"cautelar"* or preliminary nature, and on the contrary, it seeks to protect in a definitive way the constitutional right alleged as harmed or threatened. The precision is important because in some countries a distinction has been made in procedural law between *"cautelar"* measures and *"cautelar"* actions, causing some terminological confusion when giving to the amparo the character of a *"cautelar"* action. In such cases, the expression is used, not in the sense of just having a "preliminary" nature, but in the sense of being confined just to decide the immediate protection of a constitutional right without resolving any other matters or merits of the controversy.[789]

However, putting aside these terminological differences, in the amparo procedure, preliminary measures can be adopted by the courts pending the final adjudication and with effects during the development of the procedure, in order to preserve the status quo, avoiding harms or restoring the plaintiff's situation to the original one it had before the harm was inflicted.

These preliminary measures are generally regulated in statutes (Amparo Laws or Civil Procedure Codes) in two ways: first, by enumerating them in a restrictive way, called *medidas cautelares nominadas*, like, for instance, in matter of amparo, the suspension of the effects of the chal-

---

Bourdeau *et al.*, "Injunctions," in Kevin Schroder, John Glenn and Maureen Placilla, *Corpus Juris Secundum*, Volume 43A, Thomson West, 2004, pp. 24 ff.

[789]In this sense, in Ecuador and Chile, the amparo proceeding has been considered to have "cautelar" nature, but in a sense not equivalent to a "preliminary" nature. The Constitutional Court of Ecuador, for instance, has decided as followed: "That the amparo action set forth in Article 95 of the Constitution is in essence *cautelar* regarding the constitutional rights, not allowing [the court] to decide on the merits or to substitute the proceedings set forth in the legal order for the resolution of a controversy, but only to suspend the effects of an authority act which harms those rights; and the decisions issued in the amparo suit do not produce *res judicata*, so the authority, once having corrected the incurred defects, may go back to the matter and issue a new act, providing it is adjusted to the constitutional and legal provisions." See the text and comments in Hernán Salgado Pesantes, *Manual de Justicia Constitucional Ecuatoriana,* Corporación Editora Nacional, Quito, 2004, p. 78. In a similar way, in Chile the action for protection has been considered to have a *"cautelar"* nature, not in the sense of "preliminary" measures, but as tending to obtain a definitive protective adjudication regarding constitutional rights. See Eduardo Soto Kloss, *El recurso de protección. Orígenes, doctrina y jurisprudencia*, Editorial Jurídica de Chile, Santiago, 1982, p. 248; Juan Manuel Errazuriz and Jorge Miguel Otero A., *Aspectos procesales del recurso de protección*, Editorial Jurídica de Chile, Santiago, 1989, pp. 34–38.

lenged act; and second, without any particular enumeration of the measures that can be adopted (*medidas cautelares innominadas*), giving in this case, extended power to the courts to adopt any measure needed for the protection of the injured right.

In the Philippines Rule on the Writ of Amparo, these preliminary measures are established as "interim reliefs," that can be granted upon filling of the petition or at any time before the final judgments, for instance, consisting on a Temporary Protection Order, which can also be issued *ex officio*, for " the petitioner or the aggrieved party and any member of the immediate family be protected in a government agency or by an accredited person or private institution capable of keeping and securing their safety" (Sec. 14,1). The interim relief can also consist on Inspection, Production, or Witness Protection Orders (Sec. 14).

II. THE SUSPENSION OF THE EFFECTS OF THE CHALLENGED ACT AND OTHER PRELIMINARY MEASURES

The most common preliminary judicial measure provided in the Amparo Laws when the action is filed against acts, particularly administrative acts, is the power given to the courts to suspend their effects during the course of the procedure and pending the final decision of the proceeding.

It is the most traditional preliminary measure on the amparo proceeding, derived from the initial conception of the amparo as a judicial mean for the protection of constitutional rights, in particular, against State acts. Its main purpose, as for instance is established in the Argentinean Amparo Law (Article 15), is to maintain the status quo, paralyzing the effects of the challenged act that, notwithstanding the filing of the action, can continue to affect the harmed right, and could prevent the possibility to obtain a final integral repairing of such right. These measures of suspension of the effects of the challenged act, as all preliminary judicial measures, tend to assure the effectiveness of the definitive decision, in the sense of having the same efficacy as if it had been issued at the moment of the filing of the action.[790]

In the Latin American Amparo laws the suspension of the effects of the challenged act can be produced in two ways: as an automatic result of the

---

[790]See José Luis Lazzarini, *El juicio de amparo*, Ed. La Ley, Buenos Aires, 1987, pp. 314–315; Alí Joaquín Salgado, *Juicio de amparo y acción de inconstitucionalidad,* Editorial Astrea, Buenos Aires, 1987, pp. 109; Néstor Pedro Sagüés, *Derecho procesal Constitucional,* Vol 3, "Acción de amparo," Editorial Astrea, Buenos Aires, 1988, p. 460.

filing of the action before the court without a party request; or as the result of an express court decision adopted at the plaintiff's request.

In the specific case of Costa Rica, for instance, the suspension of the effect of the challenged act is an automatic preliminary effect derived from the filing of the amparo action, when filed against administrative acts (not regarding statutes or other normative State act) (Article 41, Constitutional Jurisdiction Law). Yet in addition, at the parties' request, the Constitutional Chamber can also adopt any other adequate conservatory or security measure in order to protect the right, prevent material risks or avoid the production of other harming consequence that could eventually turn illusory the final resolution granting the amparo protection (Article 41).

Regarding the automatic suspension of the challenged act as a consequence of the filing of the amparo action, the only possibility for the challenged act to produce its effects are when, in serious exceptional cases and at the express request of the Public Administration representative, the court orders its execution, after establishing the necessary balance between the personal interest of the plaintiff in his action and the general interest derived from the effects of the challenged act.

This possible decision preventing the suspension of the effects of the challenged act can also be adopted *ex officio* by the court, in cases when the suspension of the effects of the act may cause or threaten to cause effective and imminent damages and prejudices to the public interest, bigger than those that the challenged act can cause to the injured party (Article 41).[791]

Except in this case of the Costa Rican Law regarding the automatic suspension of the effects of the challenged acts, in all the other Latin American Amparo Laws their suspension is established as a preliminary protective measure that the court must expressly adopt at the request of the affected party, and in some cases, *ex officio*.

The initial regulations on the matter began with the Amparo Law in Mexico where the suspension of the challenged act is the classic preliminary measure that must be decided by the courts, whether *ex officio* or at the request of the party (Article 122).

In the former case, the decision can be adopted in specific cases when the execution of the challenged act could imply the danger of deprivation

---

[791]See Rubén Hernández Valle, *Derecho Procesal Constitucional*, Editorial Juricentro, San José, 2001, pp. 248–254.

of life, deportation, or expulsion, or when its execution could turn physically impossible for the plaintiff to enjoy the claimed individual guaranty.

This *ex officio* suspension power can consist, not only in stopping the execution of those acts, but also in ordering things to be maintained in the situation they had, the court also having the power to adopt the adequate measures in order to avoid the consummation of the harm caused by the challenged acts (Article 123).

In all other cases, the suspension can only be decided at the request of the party when the harm caused to the plaintiff could turn to be difficult to repair if the act is executed; or when because of the suspension, no prejudice is provoked to the social interest, or no public order norms are contravened. The latter situation is understood to be caused when the suspension of the effects of the challenged act, for instance, could allow the continuation of vicious or criminal activities or of activities related to drug production or trafficking, to alcoholism, or could prevent the adoption of the adequate measures needed for controlling grave diseases (Articles 124, 130).[792]

These general provisions of the Mexican Amparo Law regarding the suspension of the effects of the challenged acts, as a preliminary protective measure, can also be found in many other Latin American Amparo Laws, like those of Nicaragua (Article 31 ff), Guatemala, where it is called "provisional amparo" (Article 23 ff), Honduras (Articles 57 ff), El Salvador (Article 20), Brazil (Article 7,2), Colombia (Article 7), Paraguay (Article 8) and Venezuela (Article 5).

One example of a clear regulation on this preliminary measure of suspending the effects of the challenged act can be found in the Nicaraguan Amparo Law, as follows:

1) Three days after the filing of the petition, the court *ex officio* or at the party's request can suspend the effects of the challenged act (Article 31).

2) The suspension can be decided *ex officio* when the challenged act, if executed, would make it physically impossible to restore the enjoyment of his right to the plaintiff, or when it appears there exists a notorious

---

[792]See Richard D. Baker, *Judicial Review in México. A Study of the Amparo Suit,* University of Texas Press, Austin, 1971, p. 233 ff.; Joaquín Brage Camazano, *La jurisdicción constitucional de la libertad (Teoría general, Argentina, México, Corte Interamericana de derechos humanos)*, Editorial Porrúa, México, 2005, p. 197.

lack of jurisdiction of the authority, or when the public officer author of the challenged act has no authority to execute it (Article 32).

3)   If the suspension is requested by the party, it will be granted when the following circumstances concur: a) that the suspension causes no harm to the general interests nor it be contrary to public order provisions; b) that the damages and prejudices that could be caused to the injured party with the execution of the act, the court considers difficult to repair; c) that the petitioner post sufficient bond or guaranty in order to repair the damages or to compensate the prejudices that the suspension could cause to third parties, in case the amparo action is rejected (Article 33).

4)   Once the suspension order is issued, the court must establish the situation according to which things must remain, and adopt the adequate measures for the conservation of the situation protected, up to the end of the procedure (Article 34).

5)   The suspension will lose its effects if an interested third party gives sufficient bond in order to restore things to the stage they had before the challenged act was issued and pays for the damages and prejudices that could be inflicted to the plaintiff if the amparo is granted (Article 35).

The Colombian *Tutela* Law also summarizes the general trends on the matter, establishing not only the suspension of the effects of the challenged act but also the possible adoption by the courts of other "provisional measures for the protection of a right."[793]

Another important provision is contained in the El Salvador Amparo Law, where in addition to the general possibility for the court to decide "the immediate provisional suspension of the challenged act when its execution could cause irreparable harm or damages of difficult reparation by the definitive ruling" (Article 20), it is expressly established that the provisional suspension must only refer to acts with positive effects (Article 19). That is, no suspension is admitted regarding acts with negative ef-

---

[793]In this regard, the *Tutela* Law provides: Article 7. "From the filing of the petition, when the court considers it expressly necessary and urgent for the protection of a right, it will suspend the application of the particular act that threatens or harms it. Nonetheless, at the party request or *ex officio*, the execution or the continuation of the execution of the act can be decided in order to avoid certain and imminent prejudices to public interest. In any case, the court must order what it considers necessary to protect the rights and to prevent that the effects of an eventual decision in favor of the plaintiff become illusory. The court, *ex officio* and at the request of a party, according to the circumstances of the case, can also issue any conservatory or security measure tending to protect the right or to avoid further damages produced by the facts."

fects, like those denying a petition, because if suspended that would be equivalent to a provisional granting of the original petition, creating new juridical situations that cannot be obtained with the amparo proceeding.

Also in Brazil, in the *mandado de segurança* regulations, it is set forth as a provisional measure the possibility for the court to suspend the effects of the challenged act if from the evidence filed with the petition, it is clear that if the suspension is not decided, the definitive decision that could eventually be granted, would be ineffective (Article 7,2).[794]

In the case of Venezuela, in addition to the provision establishing the courts' possible decision to suspend the effects of the challenged acts, in the case of the filing of the amparo petition conjunctly with other actions seeking judicial review of statutes or administrative acts, the amparo essentially has suspensive effects.[795]

Yet apart of the suspension of the effects of the challenged act, many Latin American Amparo Laws empower the courts to also adopt other preliminary measures to protect the injured rights, as it is provided for instance in Colombia (Article 7), Costa Rica (Article 21),[796] Paraguay (Article 8), in Uruguay (Article 7)[797] and in Bolivia (Article 99) in order to avoid the completion of the threat caused to constitutional rights or guaranties, or to prevent the configuration of an irreparable situation that could make the amparo relief futile (Article 99).

---

[794]See José Luis Lazzarini, *El juicio de amparo*, Ed. La Ley, Buenos Aires, 1987, p. 319.

[795]When the amparo action is filed jointly with the judicial review popular action for nullity against statutes or with the judicial review of administrative actions recourse, the amparo petition has always this preliminary (*cautelar*) character, in the sense that the decision granting the amparo pending the principal nullity suit is always of a preliminary character of suspension of the effects of the challenged act. Thus, in case of statutes, the Constitutional Chamber the competent court decides to suspend its effects, in such cases, even with *erga omnes* effects. See Rafael Chavero G. *El nuevo amparo constitucional en Venezuela,* Ed. Sherwood, Caracas, 2001, pp. 468 ff. 327 ff.; Allan R. Brewer-Carías, *Instituciones Políticas y Constitucionales,* Vol V, *Derecho y Acción de Amparo,* Editorial Jurídica Venezolana, Caracas, 1998, pp. 277 ff.; and regarding administrative acts, the courts of the Administrative Jurisdiction are the ones that can decide the matter of the suspension of the effects of the administrative challenged act, pending the judicial review proceeding final decision. *Idem*, pp. 281 ff.

[796]See Rubén Hernández, *Derecho Procesal Constitucional,* Editorial Juricentro, San José, 2001, pp. 248, 252.

[797]See Luis Alberto Viera, *Ley de Amparo,* Ediciones Idea, Montevideo, 1993, pp. 41, 206.

III. THE CONDITIONS FOR THE ISSUING OF PRELIMINARY PRO-
TECTIVE MEASURES

In order to adopt all these preliminary measures, a few conditions must be fulfilled that have been summarized in the already mentioned Nicaraguan Amparo Law (Article 33) and in the Peruvian Code on Constitutional Procedures, establishing that in order to issue them, the courts must consider, first, "the apparent existence of a "good right" (*buen derecho*); second, the existence of a "situation of danger caused by the delay" to decide; and third, "the adequacy of the petition to guaranty the efficacy of the claim." These measures can be issued without the knowledge of the other party and the appeal is only granted without suspensive effects.[798]

In many other countries, the same conditions have been established but through *jurisprudencia*, identifying as follows:

First, the need for "the appearance of the existence of a good right" (*fumus boni juris*), that is, the need for the petitioner to prove the existence of his constitutional right or guaranty as being violated or threatened.

Second, the "danger because of the delay" (*periculum in mora*), that is, the need to prove that the delay in granting the preliminary protection will make the harm irreparable.

Third, the "danger of the harm" (*periculum in dammi*"), that is the need to prove the imminence of the harm that can be caused.

And a fourth condition can be mentioned in order for the courts to issue preliminary measures, which is the need to balance the collective and particular interest involved in the case.[799]

As was ruled by the Supreme Tribunal of Justice of Venezuela, in a decision nº 488 dated March 3, 2000:

In order for an anticipated protective measure to be granted, due to its preliminary content it is necessary to examine the existence of three es-

---

[798]See Samuel B. Abad Yupanqui, *El proceso constitucional de amparo*, Gaceta Jurídica, Lima, 2004, pp. 491, 422 ff. 501 ff.

[799]As for instance has been decided by the Venezuelan First Court on Administrative Jurisdiction, *Video & Juegos Costa Verde, C.A. vs. Prefecto del Municipio Maracaibo del Estado Zulia* case, in *Revista de Derecho Público*, nº 85-98, Editorial Jurídica Venezolana, Caracas, 2001, p. 291.

sential elements, always balancing the collective or individual interest; such conditions are:

1. *Fumus Boni Iuris*, that is, the reasonable appearance of the existence of a "good right" in the hands of the petitioner alleging its violation, an appearance that must derive from the written evidences (documents) attached to the petition.

2. *Periculum in mora*, that is, the danger that the definitive ruling could be illusory, due to the delay in resolving the incident of the suspension.

3. *Periculum in Damni*, that is, the imminence of the harm caused by the presumptive violation of the fundamental rights of the petitioner and its irreparability. These elements are those that basically allow one to seek the necessary anticipatory protection of the constitutional rights and guaranties.[800]

All these general conditions for the issuance of the preliminary protective measures in the Latin American amparo proceeding are very similar to those prerequisites needed to be tested by the United States' courts when issuing the preliminary injunctions, which are: 1) a probability of prevailing on the merits; 2) an irreparable injury if the relief is delayed; 3) a balance of hardship favoring the plaintiff; 4) and a showing that the injunction would not be adverse to the public interest; all of which must be proven by the plaintiff.[801]

IV. THE *INAUDITA PARS* ISSUING OF THE PRELIMINARY PROTECTIVE MEASURE

Due to the extraordinary character of the amparo action, the preliminary protective measures requested by the plaintiff, if the above-mentioned conditions are fulfilled, can be decided and issued by the court in an immediate way, even without a previous hearing of the potential defendants, that is, *inadi alteram parte* or *inaudita pars*, as it is expressly provided in the Peruvian Constitutional Procedures Code (Article 15).[802] This is also the general rule on the matter in Latin America, where in addition some

---

[800]See the Politico Administrative Chamber decision in the *Constructora Pedeca, C.A. vs. Gobernación del Estado Anzoátegui* case, in *Revista de Derecho Público*, n° 81, Editorial Jurídica Venezolana, Caracas, 2000, p. 459.

[801]See William M. Tabb and Elaine W. Shoben, *Remedies*, Thomson West, 2005, p. 63.

[802]See Samuel B. Abad Yupanqui, *El proceso constitucional de amparo*, Gaceta Jurídica, Lima, 2004, pp. 508.

Amparo Laws, like those of Colombia (Article 7); Mexico (Article 123,II); El Salvador (Article 24) and Honduras (Article 60), provide for the need of an immediate notice to the corresponding authority when a preliminary protective measure suspending the effects of the challenged act is adopted.

In a similar sense, the courts in the United States, in cases of great urgency and when an immediate threat of irreparable injury exists, can issue preliminary injunctions or restraining orders without giving reasonable notice to the plaintiff, but always balancing the harm sought to be preserved with the rights of notice and hearing.[803]

Due to this character of being decided without previously hearing the defendant, as it is expressly provided in the Honduras Law (Article 58), the preliminary decision is always adopted at the responsibility and risk of the plaintiff. For this reason, as it is also provided in other Amparo Laws like in Mexico (Article 124 ff.); Honduras (Article 58) and Paraguay (Article 8), the courts are empowered to ask for the posting of a bond in order to guaranty the damages that can be caused by the measure, particularly regarding third parties.

V. THE MODIFIABILITY OF THE PRELIMINARY MEASURES

Finally, regarding the effects of the preliminary measures, the general rule is that in the amparo proceeding, as it is established in Colombia (Article 7); Honduras (Article 61) and Guatemala (Article 30), and as it is also the rule regarding the injunctions in the United States,[804] they are essentially modifiable or revocable by the court, particularly at the request of the defendant or of third parties.

In Mexico, even third parties can place a bond requesting the repealing of the preliminary measure of suspension of the challenged acts effects, in order to restore things to how they were before the guaranty was vio-

---

[803]See for instance *Carroll v. President and Com'rs of Princess Anne*, 393 U.S. 175, 89 S. Ct. 347, 21 L. Ed.2d 325, 1968; *Board of Ed. of Community Unit School Dist. No 101 v. Parlor*, 85 Ill. 2d 397, 54 Ill. Dec 249, 424 N.E 2d 1152, 1981; in John Bourdeau *et al.*, "Injunctions," in Kevin Schroder, John Glenn and Maureen Placilla, *Corpus Juris Secundum*, Volume 43A, Thomson West, 2004, pp. 339 ff.

[804]See for instance *García-Marroquin v. Nueces County Bail Bond Bd.*, 1 S.W.3d 366 (Tex. App. Corpus Christi 1999), in John Bourdeau *et al.*, "Injunctions," in Kevin Schroder, John Glenn and Maureen Placilla, *Corpus Juris Secundum*, Volume 43A, Thomson West, 2004, pp. 421.

lated and in case the amparo is granted, to pay the damages and prejudices that could be caused to the petitioner (Article 126).

On the other hand, as mentioned, the preliminary measures have effects during the course of the procedure, finishing with the definitive decision granting or rejecting the amparo. In this regard, for instance, the Peruvian Code is one of the few that expressly regulates the *res judicata* effects regarding the preliminary orders or measures issued during the procedure, providing that they will be automatically extinguished with the final decision. Nonetheless, if the final decision grants the amparo, the effects of the preliminary measures will be kept and be converted if definitive (Article 16).

CHAPTER TWENTY-ONE

THE DEFINITIVE JUDICIAL ADJUDICATION IN THE AMPARO SUIT

I. THE GENERAL CONDITIONS OF THE DECISION

Regarding the definitive judicial decisions in the amparo proceedings, their purpose for the injured party (the plaintiff) is to obtain the requested judicial protection (*amparo, tutela, protección*) of his constitutional rights when illegitimately harmed or threatened by an injuring party (the defendant).

Consequently, the final result of the process, characterized by its bilateral nature that imposes the need for the defendants to have the right to participate and to be heard,[805] is a formal judicial decision or order issued by the court for the protection of the threatened rights or to restore the enjoyment of the harmed one, which can consist, for instance, in a decision commanding or preventing an action, or commanding someone to do, not to do or to undo some action.[806] This is to say, the amparo, as the injunction,[807] is a writ framed according to the circumstances of the case

---

[805]Similarly, regarding definitive injunctions, they only can be granted if process issues and service is made on the defendant. See for instance *U.S. v. Crusco*, 464 F.2d 1060, #d Cir. 1972; *Murphy v. Washington American League Baseball Club, Inc.*, 324 F2d. 394, D.C. Cir. 1963, in John Bourdeau *et al.*, "Injunctions," in Kevin Schroder, John Glenn and Maureen Placilla, *Corpus Juris Secundum*, Volume 43A, Thomson West, 2004, p. 339.

[806]In the United States' injunction, the order can be commanding or preventing virtually any type of action (*Dawkins v. Walker*, 794 So. 2d 333, Ala. 2001; *Levin v. Barish*, 505 Pa. 514, 481 A.2d 1183, 1984), or commanding someone to undo some wrong or injury (*State Game and Fish Com'n v. Sledge*, 344 Ark. 505, 42 S.W.3d 427, 2001). It is a judicial order requiring a person to do or refrain from doing certain acts (*Skolnick v. Altheimer & Gray*, 191 Ill 2d 214, 246 Ill. Dec. 324, 730 N.E.2d 4, 2000), for any period of time, no matter its purpose (*Sheridan County Elec. Co-op v. Ferguson*, 124 Mont. 543, 227 P.2d 597, 1951). *Idem*, p. 19.

[807]See *Nussbaum v. Hetzer*, 1, N.J. 171, 62 A. 2d 399 (1948). *Idem*, p. 19.

commanding an act that the court regards as essential in justice, or restraining an act that it deems contrary to equity and good conscience.

Consequently, the function of the amparo court's decision is, on the one hand, to prevent the defendant from inflicting further injury on the plaintiff, that can be of a prohibitory or mandatory character; or on the other hand, to correct the present by undoing the effects of a past wrong.[808]

That is why the amparo judicial order in Latin America, even without the distinction between equitable remedies and extraordinary law remedies, is very similar in its purposes and effects not only to the United States' injunction, but also to the other equitable and nonequitable extraordinary remedies, like the mandamus, prohibition and declaratory legal remedies. Accordingly, for instance, the amparo order can be first, of a prohibitory character, similar to the prohibitory injunctions, issued to restrain an action, to forbid certain acts or to command a person to refrain from doing specific acts. Second, it can also be of a mandatory character, that is, like the mandatory injunction requiring the undoing of an act, or the restoring of the status quo; and like the writ of mandamus, issued to compel an action or the execution of some act, or to command a person to do a specific act. Third, the amparo order can also be similar to the writ of prohibition or to the writ of error when the order is directed to a court,[809] which normally happens in the cases of amparo actions filed against judicial decisions. And fourth, it can also be similar to the declaratory legal remedy through which courts are called to declare the constitutional right of the plaintiff regarding the other parties.

Consequently, in the amparo proceeding, the Latin American courts have very extensive powers to provide for remedies in order to effectively protect constitutional rights, issuing orders to do, to refrain from doing, to undo or to prohibit.[810] The problems lie in the effectiveness of

---

[808]Similar to the "preventive injunction" and to the "restorative or reparative injunction," in the United States. See William M. Tabb and Elaine W. Shoben, *Remedies*, Thomson West, 2005, pp. 86–89; John Bourdeau *et al.*, "Injunctions," in Kevin Schroder, John Glenn and Maureen Placilla, *Corpus Juris Secundum*, Volume 43A, Thomson West, 2004, pp. 28 ff.

[809]See William M. Tabb and Elaine W. Shoben, *Remedies*, Thomson West, 2005, pp. 86 ff. 246 ff.; and in John Bourdeau *et al.*, "Injunctions," in Kevin Schroder, John Glenn and Maureen Placilla, *Corpus Juris Secundum*, Volume 43A, Thompson West, 2004, pp. 21 ff.; 28 ff.

[810]See Allan R. Brewer-Carías, *Instituciones Políticas y Constitucionales, Vol V, Derecho y Acción de Amparo,* Editorial Jurídica Venezolana, Caracas, 1998, pp. 143 ff.

the judicial functions and on the autonomy and independence of the courts. [811]

The contents of the final adjudication have been regulated in the Amparo Laws and can consist, as is set forth in Article 86 of the Colombian Constitution, in an order directed to the person or persons "against whom the *tutela* is filed, in order to act or to refrain from acting." In the *Tutela* Law it is set forth in a more generic way that the decision must establish "the conduct to be accomplished in order to make effective the *tutela*" (Article 29,4).[812] In a similar sense, in Argentina (Article 12,b);[813] the Dominican Republic (Articles 24,c; 26); Honduras (Article 63,3),[814] Mexico (Article 77,III); Nicaragua (Article 45); Paraguay (Article 578,b); Peru (Article 17,5); Uruguay (Article 9,b);[815] and Venezuela (Article 32,b),[816] the Amparo Laws establish that the final definitive amparo decision must "determine the conduct to be accomplished," bearing in mind, as it is established in the Honduran Law, that the purpose of the courts' decisions, is "to guaranty the injured party the complete enjoyment of his fundamental rights and to return things, when possible, to the status they had previous to the violation" (Article 63).

In Philippines, Section 18 of the Rule on the Writ of Amparo establishes that "if the allegations in the petition are proven by substantial evidence, the court shall grant the privilege of the writ and such reliefs as may be proper and appropriate."

---

[811]Contrary to what happens in the United States and Britain. See F. H. Lawson, *Remedies of English Law,* Londres, 1980, p. 175; B. Schwartz y H. W. R. Wade, *Legal control of government,* Oxford, 1978, p. 205.

[812]Juan Carlos Esguerra Portocarrero, *La protección constitucional del ciudadano*, Legis, Bogotá, 2004, p. 153.

[813]See Néstor Pedro Sagüés, *Derecho procesal Constitucional,* Vol 3, "Acción de amparo," Editorial Astrea, Buenos Aires, 1988, p. 434; Alí Joaquín Salgado, *Juicio de amparo y acción de inconstitucionalidad*, Editorial Astrea, Buenos Aires, 1987, p. 100; José Luis lazzarini, *El juicio de amparo*, Ed. La Ley, Buenos Aires, 1987, pp. 345, 359.

[814]Edmundo Orellana, *La justicia constitucional en Honduras*, Universidad Nacional Autónoma de Honduras, Tegucigalpa, 1993, pp. 181, 208, 216.

[815]See Luis Alberto Viera, *Ley de Amparo*, Ediciones Idea, Montevideo, 1993, p. 52, 207 ff.

[816]Rafael Chavero G. *El nuevo amparo constitucional en Venezuela*, Ed. Sherwood, Caracas, 2001, p. 185 ff., 327 ff.; Allan R. Brewer-Carías, *Instituciones Políticas y Constitucionales,* Vol V, *Derecho y Acción de Amparo,* Editorial Jurídica Venezolana, Caracas, 1998, pp. 399 ff.

II. THE PREVENTIVE AND RESTORATIVE NATURE OF THE AMPARO

The judicial amparo order can be of a restorative or of a preventive nature. In the first case, it may consist in an order seeking for the reestablishment of the juridical situation of the plaintiff to the stage it had before the violation or to the most similar one; and in the second case, when of a preventive nature, it can consist in compelling the defendant to do or to refrain from doing certain acts in order to maintain the enjoyment of the plaintiff's rights.

As it is expressly provided in Article 80 of the Mexican Amparo Law regarding the positive or negative effects of the challenged act:

> *Article 80*. When the claimed act is of a positive character, the decision granting the amparo will have the purpose of restoring the complete enjoyment of the harmed constitutional guaranty to the aggrieved party, reestablishing things to the stage they had before the violation. When the claimed act is of negative character, the effect of the amparo will be to compel the responsible authority to act in the sense to respect the guaranty and to accomplish what the same guaranty implies.[817]

A similar provision is set forth in Article 49 of the Costa Rican Constitutional Jurisdiction Law; as well as in Article 46 of the Nicaraguan Amparo Law.

Accordingly, it can be said that one of the main characteristics of the amparo proceeding in all Latin American countries, when directed against harms caused by positive actions, is its restorative or reestablishing purpose. As it is provided, for example, in the Colombian *Tutela* Law: "when the claim is directed against an authority action, the *tutela* decision has the purpose of guarantying the complete enjoyment of his

---

[817] As it has been explained by Baker: "When the act complained of is of a positive character, the writ of amparo has the form of a prohibitory injunction plus whatever additional elements that may be necessary to repair damages already inflicted. The latter is to be accomplished by reproducing the situation that existed before the Constitution was violated. When the act is negative in character, the writ takes the form of an order directing the responsible authority to actively comply with the provisions of the violated constitutional guaranty. In both cases, the purpose of the judgment is to restore to the complaint the full and unimpaired enjoyment of his constitutional rights. Consistent with this purpose, monetary damages are not appropriate remedies in amparo." See Richard D. Baker, *Judicial Review in México. A Study of the Amparo Suit,* University of Texas Press, Austin, 1971, p. 238.

right to the injured party and when possible, to return the situation to the stage existing previous to the violation" (Article 23). A similar provision is established in El Salvador (Article 35), Costa Rica (Article 49) and in Peru (Article 1), where in addition, Article 55,3 of the Constitutional Procedures Code provides as one of the contents of the amparo decision "the restitution or reestablishment of the aggrieved party in the complete enjoyment of his constitutional rights ordering that things will revert to the stage they had before the violation," as well as the order for the conduct to be accomplished for the effective compliance with the decision (Article 55,4).

Regarding these effects of the amparo decision in Guatemala, the Amparo Law provides that regarding the claimant, the court will suspend the application of the challenged statute, regulation, resolution or act, and when needed, the reestablishment of the affected juridical situation or the ending of the measure" (Article 49,a). A similar regulation is established in Ecuador (Article 51), and Honduras (Constitutional Justice Law, Article 63,2). In Colombia, according to Article 29,6 of the *Tutela* Law, "when the violation or threat of harming derives from the application of a norm incompatible with the fundamental rights, the resulting judicial decision resolving the action must also order the inapplicability of the challenged norm in the concrete case."

However, the amparo decision can also have a protective character when issued against omissions or negative actions from a public authority, in which cases, as it is provided in the Colombian *Tutela* Law, "the decision will order the issuance of the act or the accomplishment of the corresponding actions, establishing a prompt term" (Article 23). A similar provision is established in the Amparo Laws of El Salvador (Article 35), Ecuador (Article 51), Guatemala (Article 49,b) and Costa Rica (Article 49). In this latter country, in addition it is provided that in cases in which the amparo action is filed against omissions of authorities, for instance, to issue a regulation regarding a statute, in its decision the Constitutional Chamber must determine the basic elements to be applied in the case according to the general principles of law (Article 49,c), establishing a term of two months for the authority to sanction the regulation (Article 49).

Yet regarding threats, the amparo decision can also have a preventive nature, as is also provided, for instance, in the Costa Rican Constitutional Jurisdiction Law (Article 49) and in the Colombian *Tutela* Law (Article 23), establishing that the *tutela* decision can "order the immediate ending of the threat, as well as the necessary measures to prevent any new violation or threat, disturbance or restriction."

Also, in cases where if at the moment when the *tutela* protection is granted, the challenged act has ceased in its effects or has already produced them, making it impossible to restore the enjoyment of his rights to the plaintiff, the court can warn the public authority not to cause again in any way the actions or omissions that originated the *tutela* suit (Colombia, Article 24). In a similar way it is provided for in the Peruvian Constitutional Procedures Code (Article 1).

III. THE QUESTION OF THE ANNULLING CONTENT OF THE AMPARO

Although being of a restorative character, in general terms, when the amparo action is filed against acts, particularly authorities' acts causing the harms or threats to constitutional rights, the immediate effect of the decision is to suspend the effects of the challenged act regarding the plaintiff, the amparo proceeding not having in general terms the purposes of annulling those State acts. In principle, it is for the Constitutional Jurisdiction and for the Administrative Jurisdictions' courts and not for the amparo judges to adopt decisions annulling statutes or administrative acts.

In particular, regarding statutes and specifically self-executing ones, when an amparo action is filed directly against them, as it is provided in the Amparo laws of Mexico,[818] Guatemala,[819] Honduras[820] and Venezuela,[821] the amparo judge when granting the amparo has no power to annul them, and in order to protect the harmed or threatened right what he can do is to declare their inapplicability to the plaintiff in the particular case.

---

[818] See Eduardo Ferrer Mac-Gregor, *La acción constitucional de amparo en México y España. Estudio de derecho comparado*, Editorial Porrúa, México, 2002, pp. 262–263; Richard D. Baker, *Judicial Review in México. A Study of the Amparo Suit*, University of Texas Press, Austin, 1971, p. 270.

[819] See in Jorge Mario García Laguardia, *Jurisprudencia constitucional. Guatemala, Honduras, México. Una Muestra*, Guatemala, 1986, pp. 23, 24, 92, 93.

[820] See Edmundo Orellana, *La justicia constitucional en Honduras*, Universidad Nacional Autónoma de Honduras, Tegucigalpa, 1993, pp. 208, 221.

[821] Rafael Chavero G. *El nuevo amparo constitucional en Venezuela*, Ed. Sherwood, Caracas, 2001, pp. 468 ff.; Allan R. Brewer-Carías, *Instituciones Políticas y Constitucionales*, Vol V, *Derecho y Acción de Amparo*, Editorial Jurídica Venezolana, Caracas, 1998, pp. 399 ff.

In particular, regarding statutes, in countries where the concentrated method of judicial review is applied, as is the case of all the Latin American countries except in Argentina, the annulment of statutes is a judicial power reserved to the Constitutional Jurisdictions (Supreme Courts or Constitutional Courts or Tribunal), and it is not possible for the amparo judges to annul statutes. On the other hand, in countries where the diffuse method of judicial review is applied, the ordinary courts have no judicial power to annul statutes, being empowered just to declare their unconstitutionality regarding the particular case, and to decide their inapplicability in the case.

Even in Costa Rica, where an absolute concentrated judicial review system exists assigning to the Constitutional Chamber of the Supreme Court the power to decide both, the amparo actions as well as of the actions seeking to declare the nullity of unconstitutional statutes; the Constitutional Jurisdiction Law provides that when the amparo is filed against a statute or when the Constitutional Chambers determines that the challenged acts are founded in a statute, it cannot annul the statute in the amparo proceeding, which it must suspend, requesting the plaintiff to file a separate petition for judicial review of the unconstitutionality of the statute that must be filed before the same Chamber in a term of fifteen days (Article 48).

In Venezuela, regarding the power of all the Chambers of the Supreme Tribunal to decide cases applying the diffuse method of judicial review of the constitutionality of statutes when deciding a particular case, including cases of amparo, the Law regulating the Tribunal provides that they must notify the Constitutional Chamber for it to proceed to examine the constitutionality of the statute in an abstract way, and eventually declare its nullity (Articles 5, 1,22; and 5,5).[822]

Regarding administrative acts, the general rule is also that the amparo decision cannot annul the challenged administrative act, being the amparo judge only empowered to suspend its effects and application to the plaintiff. In general terms, in these cases, the power to annul administrative acts is also exclusively a power attributed to the Administrative Jurisdiction courts, as is the case in Venezuela.[823]

---

[822]See Allan R. Brewer-Carías, *Ley Orgánica del Tribunal Supremo de Justicia*, Editorial Jurídica Venezolana, Caracas, 2004, p. 40.

[823]See Rafael Chavero G. *El nuevo amparo constitucional en Venezuela,* Ed. Sherwood, Caracas, 2001, pp. 358 ff.; Allan R. Brewer-Carías, *Instituciones Políticas y Constitucio-*

Nonetheless, some exceptions can be identified regarding this general trend in this matter of amparo against administrative acts, and some countries in case of amparo actions against administrative acts, admit the annulment powers of the amparo judges.

In the case of Mexico, where due to the fact that one of the modalities of the amparo suit is the amparo against administrative acts, in a similar way as the *contencioso-administrativo* proceedings in other countries, the amparo decision in such cases has annulling effects.

On the other hand, the Constitutional Procedures Code in Peru expressly provides that the amparo decision must contain "the declaration of the nullity of the decision, act or resolution that has impeded the complete exercise of the constitutional rights protected with the ruling, and in the case, the extension of its effects" (Article 55).[824] Also in Costa Rica, according to Article 49 of the Constitutional Jurisdiction Law, in case of amparo actions against administrative acts, the granting of the amparo implies the annulling effects of the challenged act.

Regarding the amparo actions filed against judicial decisionsthe effects of the ruling granting the amparo protection also consists in the annulment of the challenged judicial act or decision, as is the case in Venezuela.[825]

IV. THE NON-COMPENSATORY CHARACTER OF THE AMPARO DECISION

Another aspect that must be mentioned regarding amparo decisions in Latin America is that in general terms they have not compensatory character[826] because it is the function of the courts in these proceedings only

---

nales, Vol V, *Derecho y Acción de Amparo,* Editorial Jurídica Venezolana, Caracas, 1998, pp. 144; 400.

[824] See Samuel B. Abad Yupanqui, *El proceso constitucional de amparo*, Gaceta Jurídica, Lima, 2004, p. 186.

[825] See Rafael Chavero G. *El nuevo amparo constitucional en Venezuela,* Ed. Sherwood, Caracas, 2001, p. 511; Allan R. Brewer-Carías, "Derecho y Acción de Amparo, Vol V, *Instituciones Políticas y Constitucionales* Editorial Jurídica Venezolana, Caracas, 1998, p. 297; Allan R. Brewer-Carías, "El problema del amparo contra sentencias o de cómo la Sala de Casación Civil remedia arbitrariedades judiciales," in *Revista de Derecho Público*, N° 34, Editorial Jurídica Venezolana, Caracas, abril-junio 1988, pp. 157–171.

[826] In a similar way to the United States injunctions. See *Simenstad v. Hagen,* 22 Wis. 2d 653, 126 N.W.2d 529, 1964, in John Bourdeau *et al.,* "Injunctions," in Kevin Schroder,

to protect the plaintiff's rights and not to condemn the defendant to pay the plaintiff any sort of compensation for damages caused by the injury.[827] That is, the amparo proceeding is, in general terms, a preventive and restorative process, but not a compensatory one,[828] the courts being empowered to prevent harms or to restore the enjoyment of a right, for instance by suspending the effects of the injuring act, but not to condemn the defendant to the payment of a compensation.

However, this general trend also has some exceptions in a few Latin American Amparo Laws that give compensatory character to the amparo proceeding. This is the case of Bolivia[829] and Guatemala[830] where the amparo courts must determine the existence of civil and criminal liability, establishing the amount of the damages and prejudices to be paid to the plaintiff.

In other legislations, such as the Colombia and Costa Rica Laws, the compensatory effects of the amparo decision are admitted, but only in an abstract way. For such purpose in Costa Rica, Article 51 of the Constitutional Jurisdiction Law provides that "always when an amparo is granted, the court, in abstract, will condemn for the compensation of damages and prejudices," the settlement of them belonging to the stage of the execution of the decision.[831]

John Glenn and Maureen Placilla, *Corpus Juris Secundum*, Volume 43A, Thomson West, 2004, p. 20.

[827] For instance in the case of an illegitimate administrative order issued by a municipal authority demolishing a building, if executed, even if it violates the constitutional right to property, the amparo action has not the purpose to compensate, being in this case inadmissible, particularly due to the irreparable character of the harm.

[828] See José Luis Lazzarini, *El juicio de amparo*, Ed. La Ley, Buenos Aires, 1987, pp. 346–347; Néstor Pedro Sagüés, *Derecho procesal Constitucional,* Vol 3, *Acción de amparo*, Editorial Astrea Buenos Aires, 1988, p. 437; Rafael Chavero G. *El nuevo amparo constitucional en Venezuela*, Ed. Sherwood, Caracas, 2001, pp. 185, 242, 262, 326, 328; Allan R. Brewer-Carías, *Instituciones Políticas y Constitucionales,* Vol V, *Derecho y Acción de Amparo,* Editorial Jurídica Venezolana, Caracas, 1998, p. 143.

[829] In Bolivia, Article 102,II of the Law, regarding the content of the amparo decision, states that when granting the amparo the court will determine the existence of civil and criminal liability, fixing the amount of the damages and prejudices to be paid.

[830] Also, in Guatemala, Article 59 of the Law refers to the damages and prejudices, stating that when the court in its decision condemns to the payment of damages and prejudices, it must fix its amount or at least establish the basis for its determination (Article 59).

[831] Article 52 of the Constitutional Jurisdiction Law establishes that when the amparo action is filed against authorities, the condemnation will be issued against the State or against the entity where the defendant works, and jointly with the latter if he has acted with

Also in Colombia, Article 25 of the *Tutela* Law provides that when the affected party has no other means, and the violation of his rights is manifest, clear and an indisputable consequence of an arbitrariness, the court, *ex officio*, in the decision granting the *tutela*, can order in an abstract way the compensation of the damages caused, provided its necessity in order to assure the effective enjoyment for the right. Also, similarly to what is provided in the Costa Rican Law, Article 23 of the Colombian Law establishes that the condemn will be issued against the entity where the defendant works, and jointly with the latter if he has acted with dolus or guilt, without excluding all other administrative, civil or criminal liabilities. The settlement of the compensation corresponds to the Administrative Jurisdiction courts in an incidental procedure that must take place within the following six months.[832]

Except for these cases of Bolivia, Guatemala, Colombia and Costa Rica, in all the other Latin American countries, the judicial actions tending to seek for compensation from the defendant, because of its liability as a consequence of the injury inflicted to the constitutional right of the plaintiff, must be filed by means of a separate ordinary judicial remedy established for such purpose before the civil or administrative judicial jurisdiction. This is provided in the Amparo Laws of El Salvador (Article 35); Panama (Article 2627) and Venezuela.[833]

---

dolus or guilt, without excluding all other administrative, civil or criminal liabilities. Also, in cases when the amparo process is pending and the challenged State act is revoked, stopped or suspended, the amparo will be granted only to the effects of the corresponding decision awarding compensation (Article 52). In these cases the settlement will be made by the Administrative Jurisdiction courts. In cases where the amparo action is filed against individuals, Article 53 of the same Law provides that when granting the amparo, the court must also condemn the person or responsible entity to compensate for the damages and prejudices, the settlement of which will be made in the civil judicial execution of the decision. See Rubén Hernández, *Derecho Procesal Constitucional*, Editorial Juricentro, San José, 2001, p. 268; José Luis Villalobos, "El recurso de amparo en Costa Rica," in Humberto Nogueira Alcalá (Editor), *Acciones constitucionales de amparo y protección: realidad y perspectivas en Chile y América Latina*, Editorial Universidad de Talca, Talca, 2000, p. 229.

[832] See Juan Carlos Esguerra Portocarrero, *La protección constitucional del ciudadano*, Legis, Bogotá, 2004, p. 155. Also, in cases where the *tutela* process is pending and the challenged State act is revoked, stopped or suspended, the *tutela* will be granted only to the effects of the corresponding decision awarding the compensation (Article 26).

[833] Article 27 of the Venezuelan Amparo Law also expressly provides that in cases of granting an amparo, the court must send copy of the decision to the competent authority where the public officer causing the harm works, in order to impose the corresponding disciplinary measures.

V. THE PAYMENT OF THE COSTS OF THE PROCEDURE

Finally, regarding the economic consequences of the amparo suit, in general terms in the Latin American Laws, as it is provided in Argentina (Article 14); Bolivia (Article 102,III); Colombia (Article 25); Costa Rica (Articles 51, 53); El Salvador (Article 35); Guatemala (Articles 44, 45, 100); Honduras (Article 105); Paraguay (Article 587) and Peru (Article 56), the party against whom the decision is directed is due to pay the costs of the process.

Only in Venezuela is the order to pay the costs established in a restrictive way, only regarding the amparo proceedings filed against individuals and not against public authorities (Article 33).

VI. THE EFFECTS OF THE DEFINITIVE JUDICIAL DECISION ON THE AMPARO SUIT

Another important aspect of the amparo definitive decisions is related to their effects, first, regarding their scope, whether *inter partes* or general effects; second, regarding the *res judicata* effects of the decision; and third, regarding the consequences of the obligatory character of the ruling.

1. *The* inter partes *effect and its exceptions*

The general rule regarding the amparo judicial decisions, effects is that they only have *inter partes* effects, that is, between the parties that have been involved in the suit (the plaintiff, the defendant and the third parties) and those that have participated in the process. This is expressly established in the Mexican[834] and in the Nicaraguan (Article 44) Amparo Laws.

So in a similar way to the injunctive decisions in the United States,[835] the amparo decisions in Latin America only have binding effects regard-

---

[834] Article 76 of the Amparo Law establishes that "the decisions in the amparo suits only refers to the individuals or corporations, private or public which filed the actions, limiting their scope to protect them in the case, without making general declarations regarding the statute or act causing the suit."

[835] See for instance *ESP Fidelity Corp. v. Department of Housing & Urban Development*, 512 F.2d 887, (9th Cir. 1975), in John Bourdeau *et al.*, "Injunctions," in Kevin Schroder, John Glenn and Maureen Placilla, *Corpus Juris Secundum*, Volume 43A, Thomson West, 2004, pp. 414.

ing the parties to the suit, and only regarding the controversy; this being the most important consequence of the personal character of the amparo, as an action mainly devoted for the protection of personal constitutional rights or guaranties.[836]

The only exception to this principle in the United States refers to the effects of the ruling when constitutional questions are decided by the Supreme Court, in which cases, due to the doctrine of precedent (*stare decisis*), all courts are obliged to apply the same constitutional rule in cases with similar controversies.[837] The same rule exists in some Latin American countries, for instance when a *jurisprudencia* is established by the Supreme Court of Mexico, or in cases regarding constitutional inter-pretations when decided by the Supreme Courts or by the Constitutional Courts, the ruling of which have been entrusted with obligatory general effects. This is the case in Venezuela, regarding the Constitutional Chamber rulings (Article 336 of the Constitution) and the case in Peru, regarding the Constitutional Tribunal decisions (Article VII, Code on Constitutional Procedures).

Yet with this exception, the general principle regarding the particular rulings in the amparo proceedings is that the decisions have only binding effects regarding the parties to the process, including third parties. Those are the beneficiaries and the obliged parties.

Nonetheless, this general principle also has its exceptions due to the progressive development of the collective nature of some constitutional rights, as for instance, is the case of violation of environmental rights, indigenous People's rights and other diffuse rights,[838] in which cases,[839] the definitive ruling can benefit other persons different to those that have actively participated in the procedure as plaintiff.

---

[836] The Venezuelan regulations can be highlighted in this regard. In principle, the court decisions have been constant in granting the action of *amparo* a personal character where the standing belongs firstly to "the individual directly affected by the infringement of constitutional rights and guaranties." See for example, decision of the Constitutional Chamber of March 15, 2000, in *Revista de Derecho Público*, n° 81, Editorial Jurídica Venezolana, 2000, pp. 322–323.

[837] See M. Glenn Abernathy and Barbara A. Perry, *Civil Liberties under the Constitution*, University of South Carolina Press, 1993, p. 5.

[838] See Rafael Chavero G. *El nuevo amparo constitucional en Venezuela,* Ed. Sherwood, Caracas, 2001, pp. 333 ff.

[839] As also happens regarding the Class Actions in the United States. See M. Glenn Aber-nathy and Barbara A. Perry, *Civil Liberties under the Constitution*, University of South Carolina Press, 1993, p. 6.

This is the case of the amparo decisions regarding collective rights, like environmental rights in Argentina and Brazil. In Venezuela, due to the constitutional provision regarding the protection of diffuse or collective interests, the Constitutional Chamber of the Supreme Tribunal has admitted action for amparo seeking for the protection and enforcement of those collective interests, including for instance, voting rights. In such cases, the Chamber has even granted *erga omnes* effects to the precautionary measures adopted "for both the individuals and entities that have filed the action for constitutional protection and to all the voters as a group.[840]

In addition, the Office of the People's Defendant has the authority to promote, defend, and guard constitutional rights and guaranties "as well as the legitimate, collective or diffuse interests of the citizens" (Articles 280 and 281,2 of the Constitution); being consequently his standing admitted to file actions for amparo on behalf of the citizens as a whole.[841] In all these cases, consequently, the judicial ruling benefits all the persons enjoying the collective rights or interest involved.

---

[840]See decision of the Constitutional Chamber n° 483 of May 29, 2000, *"Queremos Elegir"* y *otros* case, in *Revista de Derecho Público*, n° 82, Editorial Jurídica Venezolana, 2000, pp. 489–491. In the same sense, decision of the same Chamber n° 714 of July 13, 2000, *APRUM* Case, in *Revista de Derecho Público*, n° 83, 2000, Editorial Jurídica Venezolana, pp. 319 ff. The Constitutional Chamber has decided that "any individual is entitled to bring suit based on diffuse or collective interests" and has extended "standing to companies, corporations, foundations, chambers, unions and other collective entities, whose object is the defense of society, as long as they act within the boundaries of their corporate objects, aimed at protecting the interests of their members regarding those objects. See decision of the Constitutional Chamber n° 656 of May 6, 2001, *Defensor del Pueblo vs.Comisión Legislativa Nacional* Case, as referred in decision n° 379 of February 26, 2003, *Mireya Ripanti et vs. Presidente de Petróleos de Venezuela S.A. (PDVSA)* case, in *Revista de Derecho Público*, n° 93-96, Editorial Jurídica Venezolana, Caracas, 2003, pp. 152 ff.

[841]In one case the Defender of the People acted against a threat by the 2000 National Legislative Commission to appoint the Electoral National Council members without fulfilling constitutional requirements. In that case, the Constitutional Chamber decided that "the Defender has standing to bring actions aimed at enforcing diffuse and collective rights or interests" without requiring the acquiescence of the society on whose behalf he acts, but this provision does not exclude or prevent citizens' access to the judicial system in defense of diffuse and collective rights and interests (Article 26). Decision of the Constitutional Chamber n° 656 of May 6, 2001, *Defensor del Pueblo vs. Comisión Legislativa Nacional* case, *Idem.*

2. The question of the scope of the res judicata effects

On the other hand, as all definitive judicial decisions, the amparo decisions in Latin America also have *res judicata* effects, providing stability to the ruling. That means that the courts' decisions are binding not only for the parties in the process or its beneficiaries, but also regarding the court itself, which cannot modify its ruling (immutability).

Res judicata implies then, the impossibility for a new suit to take place regarding the same matter already adopted, or that a decision is issued in a different sense than the one already decided in a previous process.[842]

Although the *res judicata* effects are the general principles in Latin America regarding the amparo decisions, discussions have been held in many countries regarding the scope of those effects, based in a traditional distinction that has been established in procedural law, between the so-called "substantive" (*material*) and "formal" *res judicata* effects, in order to determine which one applies to the amparo ruling.

In general terms, the concept of "formal *res judicata*" effects applies to judicial decisions that even when enforced do not impede the development of a new process between the same parties, provided that the matter has not been decided in the amparo proceeding on the merits of the case and its defense. On the other hand, the concept of "substantive *res judicata*" effects applies when the judicial decision has decided on the merits, not allowing for other processes to develop regarding the same matter.

The matter decided in the amparo proceeding, that is the merits of the case, is related to the manifest illegitimate and arbitrary harm or threat caused by an identified injuring party to the constitutional right or guaranties of the plaintiff; a matter that is to be resolved in a brief and prompt procedure. Thus, the merits on the matters in the amparo proceeding are reduced to determining the existence of such illegitimate and manifest

---

[842]In contrast, these *res judicata* effects, as a general rule, are not applicable to the injunction orders in the United States which can be modified by the court. As it has been summarized regarding the judicial doctrine on the matter: "Injunctions are different from other judgments in the context of *res judicata* because the parties are often subject to the court's continuing jurisdiction, and the court must strike a balance between the policies of *res judicata* and the right of the court to apply modified measures to changed circumstances." See *Town of Durham v. Cutter*, 121 N.H. 243, 428 A. 2d 904 (1981), in John Bourdeau *et al.*, "Injunctions," in Kevin Schroder, John Glenn and Maureen Placilla, *Corpus Juris Secundum*, Volume 43A, Thomson West, 2004, p. 416. See also Owen M. Fiss and Doug Rendleman, *Injunctions*, The Foundation Press, 1984, pp. 497–498, 526.

violation of the right, regardless of the other possible matters that can or may be resolved by the parties in other processes.

In this regard, for instance, the Argentina Amparo Law establishes the following:

> *Article 13.* The definitive decision declaring the existence or nonexistence of an arbitrary or manifestly illegal harm, restriction, alteration or threat regarding a constitutional right and guaranty, produces *res judicata* regarding the amparo, and does not prevent the exercise of the actions or recourses that could correspond to the parties.[843]

A similar provision is set forth in the Paraguayan (Article 579) and Uruguayan (Article 11)[844] Amparo Law.

The Venezuelan Amparo Law, in a similar way to the Argentinean provision, and with the same different approach regarding the substantive or formal *res judicata* effects[845] provides:

> *Article 36.* The definitive amparo decision will produce legal effects regarding the right or guaranty that has been the object of the process, with-

---

[843]This provision, regarding the effects of the *res judicata*, has been interpreted in two ways: On the one hand, Lazzarini has considered it to establish the "substantive *res judicata*" effects regarding the protective amparo decision, arguing that the allusion the article makes regarding other actions or recourses, are referring to criminal actions tending to punish the offenses causing the harm, or to civil actions tending to obtain compensation, but not to other actions in which the amparo could be again reargued. See José Luis Lazzarini, *El juicio de Amparo,* Ed. La Ley, Buenos Aires, 1987, pp. 356 ff. On the other hand, Sagües has considered that even though the amparo suit is a bilateral process, due to its brief and prompt character with the consequent restrictions regarding proofs and formalities, there cannot be a decision on the merits of the matter, so no substantive *res judicata* can be produced, but only a formal one, being possible for the merits to be resolved through the ordinary judicial means, only if the parties allege a violation to their due process rights occurred (for instance, regarding evidences) in the amparo process. See Néstor Pedro Sagües, *Derecho procesal Constitucional,* Vol 3*, Acción de amparo,* Editorial Astrea, Buenos Aires, 1988, pp. 449 ff.

[844]See Luis Alberto Viera, *Ley de Amparo,* Ediciones Idea, Montevideo, 1993, p. 40.

[845]In this regard, the First Court on Administrative Jurisdiction, in a decision dated October 16, 1986, *Pedro J. Montilva* case, decided that if in a case "the action of amparo is filed with the same object, denouncing the same violations, based on the same motives and with identical object as the previous one and directed against the same person, then it is evident that in such case, the res judicata force applies in order to avoid the rearguing of the case, due to the fact that the controversy to be resolved has the same subjective and objective identity than the one already decided." See Rafael Chavero G. *El nuevo amparo constitucional en Venezuela,* Ed. Sherwood, Caracas, 2001, pp. 338 ff.; Gustavo Linares Benzo, *El proceso de amparo en Venezuela,* Caracas, 1999, p. 121 f.

out prejudice of the actions or recourses that legally correspond to the parties.

According to this provision, the *res judicata* in the amparo suit only refers to what has been argued and decided in the case regarding the violation or injury inflicted to a constitutional right or guaranty,[846] Thus, in general terms, the amparo decision does not resolve all the other possible matters that could be raised, but only the aspect of the violation or injury to the constitutional rights or guaranties, this being the only aspect regarding which the decision can produce *res judicata* effects. For example, if an amparo decision is issued regarding an administrative act because it causes harm to constitutional rights, it only has restorative or reestablishing effects suspending the application of the challenged act, but it does not have annulling effects.[847] Consequently, the amparo decision in such cases does not have *res judicata* effects regarding the judicial review action that can be filed against the administrative act before the Administrative Jurisdiction courts in order to have its nullity declared.[848]

In these cases, after the amparo decision has been issued, other legal questions can remain pending to be resolved in other processes, and that is why the amparo decision in these cases is issued "without prejudice of the actions or recourses that could legally correspond to the parties." In this case, as has been said, the amparo decision has formal *res judicata* effects.[849] In this sense, also, the Philippines Rule on the Writ of Amparo

---

[846]See in *Revista de Derecho Público,* n° 28, Editorial Jurídica Venezolana, Caracas, 1986, p. 106.

[847]Due to this fact, by means of the amparo suit, as it has been ruled by the Supreme Court of Venezuela, "none of the three types of judicial declarative, constitutive or to condemn decision can be obtained, nor, of course, the interpretative decision." See decision of the Politico Administrative Chamber of July 15, 1992, in *Revista de Derecho Público,* n° 51, Editorial Jurídica Venezolana, Caracas, 1992, p. 171.

[848]See Allan R. Brewer-Carías, *Instituciones Políticas y Constitucionales,* Vol V, *Derecho y Acción de Amparo,* Editorial Jurídica Venezolana, Caracas, 1998, pp. 346 ff.

[849]See in this respect, Juan Manuel Errazuriz and Jorge Miguel Otero A., *Aspectos procesales del recurso de protección,* Editorial Jurídica de Chile, Santiago, 1989, pp. 195 ff, 202. These effects of the amparo decision also exist regarding the amparo suit against individuals, and a case can illustrate the matter: in 1987 a controversy arose in a Venezuelan private Caracas, University (*Santa María*), regarding the position for the Head of the institution (Rector), a position that was disputed by two professors arguing they had been appointed by the University bodies. The First Court on Administrative Jurisdiction in a decision dated December 17, 1987, issued an amparo decision on the matter filed by one of the *Rectores* in order to assure legal security to the University community, due to the fact

set forth that "this Rule shall not preclude the filing of separate criminal, civil or administrative actions" (Sec. 21)

In many other cases, of course, the amparo decision regarding the violation of the right by the illegitimate action of omissions, resolves the matter leaving no room to discuss any other legal matter through any other subsequent process, in which cases, the amparo ruling has substantive *res judicata* effects.

These different approaches to the *res judicata* effects regarding amparo decisions have been expressly referred, for instance, in the El Salvador Amparo Law, which prescribes the following:

> *Article 81.* The definitive amparo decision produces *res judicata* effects against any person or public officer, having intervened or not in the process, only regarding the matter of the challenged act being unconstitutional or contrary to the constitutional provisions. The content of the decision does not constitute in itself a declaration, recognition or constitution of private rights of individuals or of the state; consequently the decision can not be opposed as a *res judicata* defense regarding any action that could be filed afterward before the courts of the Republic.

The Honduran (Article 72), and Guatemalan Amparo Laws also provide in similar terms that "the decisions issued in the amparo suits have declarative effects and do not originate the *res judicata* defense, without prejudice of the provisions derived from the *jurisprudencia* on the matter" (Article 190).

Finally, in Peru, the Code of Constitutional Procedures does not resolve the discussion, just declaring that "in the constitutional processes, only the final rulings deciding the merits acquire the *res judicata* authority" (Article 6).[850]

---

that the matter regarding who was the Head of the University could not remain indefinitely unresolved. It ruled considering legitimate the designation of one of the *Rectores,* "until the controversy regarding the legitimacy of the bodies that resolved the appointments by the judicial competent court." See in *El Universal,* Caracas, December 27, 1987, p. 2–5. According to this decision, a further civil action was needed to be resolved in order to resolve the merits.

[850]See Samuel B. Abad Yupanqui, *El proceso constitucional de amparo*, Gaceta Jurídica, Lima, 2004, pp. 194 ff.

VII. THE OBLIGATORY CHARACTER OF THE AMPARO RULINGS AND THE SANCTION FOR CONTEMPT POWER

One last aspect that must be highlighted regarding the effects of the amparo decision referred to its obligatory character. As all judicial decisions, the amparo ruling is obligatory not only for the parties to the process but regarding all other persons or public officers that must apply them. The defendant, for instance, is compelled to immediately obey it, as it is expressly set forth in the Amparo Laws of Bolivia (Article 102); Colombia (Articles 27, 30); Costa Rica (Article 53); Ecuador (Article 58); Honduras (Article 65); Nicaragua (Article 48); Paraguay (Article 583); Peru (Articles 22, 24) and Venezuela (Articles 29, 30).

In order to execute the decision, the courts, *ex officio* or at the party's request, can adopt all the measures directed to its accomplishment, being empowered, for instance in the Guatemalan Law, to issue orders and mandamus to the authorities and public officers of Public Administration or obligated persons (Article 55). The amparo courts, as it is provided in the Amparo Laws of Guatemala (Article 105); Ecuador (Article 61); El Salvador (Article 61) and Nicaragua (Article 77), are also empowered to use public enforcement means to assure the accomplishment of its decisions.

Yet the amparo judges in Latin America do not have direct power to punish by imposing criminal sanctions for disobedience of their rulings. In other words, they do not have criminal contempt power, which in contrast is one of the most important features of the injunctive relief system in the United States.[851] These contempt powers are precisely what gave

---

[851] This is particularly important regarding criminal contempt, which was established since the *In Re Debs* case (158 U.S. 564, 15 S.Ct. 900, 39 L.Ed. 1092 (1895)), where according to Justice Brewer who delivered the court's opinion, it was ruled: "But the power of a court to make an order carries with it the equal power to punish for a disobedience of that order, and the inquiry as to the question of disobedience has been, from time immemorial, the special function of the court. And this is no technical rule. In order that a court may compel obedience to its order it must have the right to inquire whether there has been any disobedience thereof. To submit the question of disobedience to another tribunal, be it a jury or another court, would operate to deprive the proceedings of half its efficiency." In *Watson v. Williams,* 36 Miss. 331, 341, it was said: "The power to fine and imprison for contempt, from the earliest history of jurisprudence, has been regarded as the necessary incident and attribute of a court, without which it could no more exist than without a judge. It is a power inherent in all courts of record, and coexisting with them by the wise provisions of the common law. A court without the power effectually to protect itself against the assaults of the lawless, or to enforce its orders, judgments, or decrees against the recusant parties before it, would be a disgrace to the legislation, and a stigma

the injunction in the United States its effectiveness regarding any disobedience, being the same court empowered to vindicate its own power by imposing criminal or economic sanctions by means of imprisonment and fines.[852] The Latin American courts, in contrast, do not have such powers, or they are very weak.

In effect, even though the disobedience of the amparo ruling is punishable in the Latin American Amparo Laws, it is not for the same amparo court to apply sanctions personally affecting the disobedient. These sanctioning powers are attributed or to Public Administration or to different criminal court. So, for instance, in case of disobedience, the amparo court must seek for the initiation of an administrative disciplinary procedure against the disobedient public officer that must be decided by the corresponding superior organ in Public Administration, as is established in Colombia (Article 27); Peru (Article 59); and Nicaragua (Article 48).

Regarding the application of criminal sanctions to the disobedient party, the amparo courts or the interested party must seek for the initiation of a judicial criminal procedure against the disobedient to be brought before the competent criminal courts, as it is the general rule established in Bolivia (Article 104); Colombia (Articles 27, 52, 53); Costa Rica (Article 71); Ecuador (Article 58); El Salvador (Articles 37, 61); Guatemala (Articles 32, 54, 92); Honduras (Article 62); Mexico (Articles 202, 209); Nicaragua (Article 77); Panama (Article 2632); Paraguay (Article 584) and Venezuela (Article 31). In some exceptional cases, as in Colombia (Article 27), the *tutela* judge can only impose administrative detentions on the disobedient party.

Therefore, the amparo judges in Latin America do not have the power to directly impose disciplinary or criminal sanctions to those that disobey their orders, and only in some countries do they have powers to directly impose fines (*astreintes*) to the disobeying parties in a continuous way, up to the accomplishment of the order. This is the case in Colombia (Ar-

---

upon the age which invented it." See Owen M. Fiss and Doug Rendleman, *Injunctions*, The Foundation Press, 1984, p. 13. See also William M. Tabb and Elaine W. Shoben, *Remedies*, Thomson West, 2005, pp. 72 ff.

[852] In Philippines, the Rule on the Writ of Amparo empowers the competent court to "order the respondent who refuses to make a return, or who makes a false return, or any person who otherwise disobeys or resists a lawful process or order of the court to be punished for contempt. The contemnor may be imprisoned or imposed a fine."

ticle 27); the Dominican Republic (Article 28); Guatemala (Article 53); Nicaragua, (Article 66); and Peru (Article 22).[853]

---

[853] See Samuel B. Abad Yupanqui, *El proceso constitucional de amparo*, Gaceta Jurídica, Lima, 2004, p. 136.

CHAPTER TWENTY-TWO

THE REVISION OF THE AMPARO DECISIONS BY THE CONSTITUTIONAL COURT OR THE SUPREME COURT

Due to the general by-instance procedural principle, the amparo decisions and also the judicial decisions issued applying the diffuse method for judicial review can be appealed before the superior courts according to the general rules established in the procedural codes. This general principle, of course, does not apply when the only competent court in amparo matters is the highest court in the country, as happens in Costa Rica, Nicaragua and El Salvador (Constitutional Chamber of the Supreme Court of Justice); or regarding decisions on judicial review of the constitutionality of legislation when the countries follow only a concentrated system.

Consequently, except in these cases, the amparo decisions cannot normally arrive for their revision before the Supreme Court or the Constitutional Court, except when deciding on appellate jurisdiction or when an extraordinary mean for revision is established, in some cases similar to the writ for certiorari in the United States.

In effect, particularly when constitutional issues are involved, the United States Supreme Court, when considering a petition for a writ of certiorari, is authorized to review all the decisions of the federal courts of appeals, and of the specialized federal courts, and all the decisions of the supreme courts of the states involving issues of federal law, but on a discretionary basis. In all such cases where there is no right of appeal and no mandatory appellate jurisdiction of the Supreme Court established, the cases can reach the Supreme Court as petitions for certiorari, when a litigant who has lost in a lower court petitions a review in the Supreme Court, setting out the reasons why review should be granted.[854] This

---

[854] See L. Baum, *The Supreme Court*, Washington, 1981, p. 81.

method of seeking review by the Supreme Court is expressly established in the cases set forth in the 28 U. S. Code, and according to Rule n° 10 of the Rules of the Supreme Court adopted in 2005, where it is established as not being "a matter of right, but of judicial discretion," granted only "for compelling reasons," that is, when there are special and important reasons.

According to this rule, consequently, in order to promote uniformity and consistency in federal law, the following factors might prompt the Supreme Court to grant certiorari: 1. Important questions of federal law on which the court has not previously ruled; 2. Conflicting interpretations of federal law by lower courts; 3. Lower courts' decisions that conflict with previous Supreme Court decisions; and 4. Lower courts' departures from the accepted and usual course of judicial proceedings.[855]

Of course, review may be granted on the basis of other factors, or denied even if one or more of the above-mentioned factors is present. The discretion of the Supreme Court is not limited, and it is the importance of the issue and the public interest considered by the Court in a particular case that leads the Court to grant certiorari and to review some cases.

Although in different ways, in the Latin American systems of judicial review and amparo proceedings, a general trend can be identified by the assignment to the Supreme Court of Justice or the Constitutional Tribunals, with some judicial powers to review lower courts' decisions on constitutional matters, whether issued in amparo proceedings or applying the diffuse method of judicial review. The concern for having some instrument to assure the uniformity of constitutional interpretation and constitutional rights' enforcement has provoked the incorporation in the constitutions and in the Laws regulating constitutional proceedings, of judicial means through which the highest courts eventually have the last word on constitutional matters.

The question, of course, has been resolved in countries where the concentrated method of judicial review is established as the only one to assure judicial review of statutes, and where, in addition, a concentrated judicial amparo system is also established, as is the case of Costa Rica and El Salvador where the Supreme Court through its Constitutional Chamber is the only court in the country with the exclusive power to decide amparo actions and to control the constitutionality of statutes.

---

[855] See regarding the previous Rule n° 17,1: R. A. Rossum and G. A. Tarr, *American Constitutional Law*, New York, 1983, p. 28.

In other countries, where judicial review of statutes is assigned in a diffuse way to all courts, and where amparo actions are also filed before a variety of lower courts, various adjective procedures have been established in order for the constitutional questions or the amparo decisions to reach the Supreme Court or the Constitutional Court.

This has happened, for instance, in Argentina, which has the diffuse method of judicial review as the only existing one, by means of the extraordinary recourse.

In other countries where a concentrated method of judicial review has been established in an exclusive way, as is the case of Bolivia, Costa Rica, Chile, El Salvador, Honduras, Panama, Paraguay and Uruguay, the Supreme Courts of Justice or the Constitutional Tribunals have the monopoly to decide on judicial review of constitutionality of legislation, assuring in that way the uniformity of the *jurisprudencia* in constitutional matters. Yet in all those countries, the amparo proceeding is not a concentrated one, and on the contrary corresponds to a variety of lower courts, so also in these matters procedural correctives have been established, for instance in Bolivia and Honduras, in order to allow the Supreme or Constitutional Tribunal to give the final interpretation on amparo matters.

On the other hand, in Brazil, Colombia, Ecuador, Guatemala, Mexico, Peru and Venezuela where the diffuse method is combined with the concentrated one, even though the constitutional doctrine can be set by a variety of lower courts (by means of judicial review or through amparo decisions), also specific adjective or procedural correctives have also been established in order to allow the Supreme Courts or the Constitutional Tribunals to seek for the uniformity of the jurisprudence on constitutional and amparo matters. Only in Nicaragua is there a specific case in which within a mixed system of judicial review of legislation, the amparo judicial system has been concentrated in the Supreme Court.

The purpose of this Part is to analyze all these judicial means by which, in matters of judicial review decisions and in amparo rulings when issued by a variety of lower courts, the matters can reach the Supreme Courts or the Constitutional Tribunals, in order to give the last interpretation of the constitution. For such purpose, the general classification according to the judicial review method that the countries applied, will be the following: countries with only the diffuse method; countries with only the concentrated method, and countries having a mixed system of judicial review.

I. THE EXTRAORDINARY RECOURSE IN ARGENTINA AND THE MANDATORY JURISDICTION OF THE SUPREME COURT

The first group refers to those countries having only the diffuse method of judicial review, where the Supreme Court of the Nation has powers to review lower courts' decisions in constitutional matters. It is the case of Argentina, being the only Latin American country that remains as having the diffuse method of judicial review as the only one applied to control the constitutionality of statutes by lower courts, in particular first instance courts, which also are the ones called to decide amparo actions.

In both cases, the courts' decisions on constitutional questions can only reach the Supreme Court of the Nation by means of an extraordinary recourse that can only be filed against the second instance superior courts' decisions when the validity of a treaty or of a statute has been questioned, or in general terms a matter of judicial review of constitutionality of statutes is resolved in the judicial decision.[856] This is, undoubtedly, the judicial mean through which the Supreme Court normally decides upon the final interpretation of the constitution when reviewing the constitutionality of state acts, and consequently it is the most important mean for judicial review.

According to this power, the Supreme Court is vested in the Argentinean system with two sorts of appellate jurisdiction, an ordinary appellate jurisdiction and "extraordinary appellate jurisdiction," the latter being the one that can be exercised by the Supreme Court through this so-called "extraordinary recourse" through which the Court can assure the uniformity of constitutional interpretation.

However, different to the United States system of the petition for writ of certiorari, where the parties have not appeal rights and the Supreme Court has discretional power to grant the order, the Supreme Court of Argentina exercises a mandatory jurisdiction, as a consequence of a right the parties have to file the recourse, but having discretionary power to reject the petition.[857]

---

[856]See Ley n° 48, Article 14. See Elias Guastavino, *Recurso extraordinario de inconstitucionalidad,* Ed. La Roca, Buenos Aires, 1992; Lino Enrique Palacio, *El recurso extraordinario federal. Teoría y práctica,* Abeledo-Perrot, Buenos Aires, 1992, p. 14.

[857]See Lino Enrique Palacio, *El recurso extraordinario federal. Teoría y práctica,* Abeledo-Perrot, Buenos Aires, 1992, p. 26.

Of course, when deciding these extraordinary recourse, the Supreme Court does not act as a third instance court because its power of review is only referred to matters regarding constitutional questions.

The Supreme Court's decisions on judicial review on constitutional issues are not formally obligatory for the other courts or for the inferior courts[858]; but because they are issued by the highest court in the country, they have a definitive important influence upon all the inferior courts' particularly when a doctrine has been clearly and frequently established by the Court.

Finally, it must be mentioned that although without any statutory foundations, in 1990, through a series of judicial decisions, the Supreme Court admitted what has been called the *per saltum* extraordinary recourse, that is, an extraordinary recourse filed before the Supreme Court against first instance judicial decision (not against Superior courts' decisions) in extraordinary circumstances of grave institutional interest.[859] In these cases, in a very exceptional way, the Supreme Court has intervened in judicial processes after the first instance court has surpassing the appeal before the superior court, in cases of great institutional or State importance.

II. THE CONSTITUTIONAL JURISDICTION REVIEW POWERS IN COUNTRIES HAVING ONLY A CONCENTRATED METHOD OF JUDICIAL REVIEW

The second group refers to countries where the only method of judicial review of constitutionality of statutes that is applied is the concentrated one. In these cases, the question of the Constitutional Jurisdiction court power, whether being the Supreme Court or a Constitutional Court, to decide matters on constitutional questions, varies according to the extension of the concentration method. In this regard, two group of countries can be distinguished: one, referred to countries with an absolute concentrated judicial system on constitutional matters attributed to the Constitu-

---

[858]See. R. Bielsa, *La protección constitucional y el recurso extraordinario. Jurisdicción de la Corte Suprema*, Buenos Aires, 1958, pp. 49, 198, 267; A. E. Ghigliani, *Del control jurisdiccional de constitucionalidad*, Buenos Aires, 1952, pp. 97, 98.

[859]See Ricardo Haro, "El *per saltum* en la justicia federal Argentina," in his book, *El Control de Constitucionalidad*, Editorial Zavalía, Buenos Aires, 2003, pp. 87–122; Lino Enrique Palacio, *El recurso extraordinario federal. Teoría y práctica,* Buenos Aires, 1992, pp. 111–118.

tional Jurisdiction; and second, referred to countries that, although only applying the concentrated method of judicial review, in matters of amparo the powers to resolve the proceedings are attributed to a variety of lower courts and not only to the Constitutional Jurisdiction court.

The first group is composed by Costa Rica and El Salvador; and the second group, by Bolivia, Chile, Honduras, Panama, Paraguay and Uruguay, where only in Bolivia and Honduras a review power of lower courts amparo decisions has been granted to the Constitutional Jurisdiction courts.

1. *The exclusive power of the Constitutional Chambers of the Supreme Courts in Costa Rica and El Salvador in constitutional matters*

As mentioned, only two countries in Latin America have adopted what can be considered an absolute concentrated system of judicial review and of amparo proceeding, organizing a Constitutional Jurisdiction by assigning the Supreme Court of Justice of the country with the exclusive power to decide on all matters of judicial review of legislation and on all matters of amparo proceedings. These two countries are Costa Rica and El Salvador, where consequently, the uniformity of the jurisprudence on constitutional matters is automatically assured.

In Costa Rica, according to the 1989 Constitutional Jurisdiction Law, the recourse of amparo and habeas corpus can only be brought before the Constitutional Chamber of the Supreme Court of Justice; this Chamber also being the Constitutional Jurisdiction court with the exclusive power to exercise the concentrated method of judicial review regarding the unconstitutionality of statutes and other State acts, through decisions with *erga omnes* nullifying effects (Article 10).

Also in El Salvador, an absolute and concentrated judicial review system is established, empowering the Constitutional Chamber of the Supreme Court of Justice with the exclusive attribution to declare the unconstitutionality of statutes, decrees and regulations when challenged by means of a direct and popular action, with the power to annull them with general, *erga omnes* effects (Articles 2 and 10, Law). In addition, in a similar way to the Costa Rican regulations, also in El Salvador, the Constitutional Chamber of the Supreme Court of Justice is the only judicial body with the exclusive power to decide recourses of amparo and habeas corpus for the protection of the rights declared in the constitution (Article 247).

The only exception to this rule in El Salvador exists in matters of habeas corpus when the injury to the constitutional rights takes place outside the capital, San Salvador. In such cases, it is possible to file the recourse before the Chambers of Second Instance (Article 42), and if the judicial decision denies the liberty of the aggrieved party, the case can be reviewed by the Constitutional Chamber.

2. *The Constitutional Jurisdiction Courts review powers in constitutional matters in Bolivia and Honduras*

The other Latin American countries with an exclusive concentrated method of judicial review of statutes are Bolivia, Chile, Honduras, Panama, Paraguay and Uruguay. In all these countries, although the Constitutional Jurisdiction court has the exclusive power of judicial review of statutes, the power to decide amparo actions is also attributed to a variety of lower courts.

Regarding judicial review of legislation, the uniformity of the constitutional interpretation is assured because one single Supeme Court or Constitutional Court is the only one called to decide on the matter, generarlly by two means: when deciding direct actions of unconstitutionality of statutes that are filed before the Supreme or Constitutional Court, or when deciding constitutional questions raised before the Supreme or Constitutional Court by a lower courts, when in a particular case the constitutionality of a statute has been challenged.

However, as mentioned, in these countries with an exclusive concentrated system of judicial review, the amparo judicial power has been attributed to a variety of lower courts, in many cases by means of a by-instance judicial system. In these cases of amparo, in order to seek for the uniformity of constitutional interpretation, only in Bolivia and Honduras, the Constitutional Jurisdiction courts have the power to review the lower courts amparo decisions, although in a different way.

In the other countries with concentrated system of judicial review and diffuse judicial amparo system, as is the case of Chile, Panama, Paraguay and Uruguay, no particular regulations have been established to assure the reviewing by the Supreme or Constitutional Court of the amparo decisions.

A. The automatic and mandatory review jurisdiction of the Constitutional Tribunal in Bolivia

In Bolivia, according to the Constitution (Article 120,7) and the Law of the Constitutional Tribunal (Article 7,8), the Constitutional Tribunal not only is the only court with exclusive competence to decide on matters of judicial review of legislation, by means of a direct action and through an incidental request, but additionally, has the power to review all decisions issued by the lower courts in matters of amparo or habeas corpus (Article 120,7, Constitution Articles 7,8; 93; 102,V, Law). In this case, different to the provisions in Argentina, no extraordinary recourse for revision is provided, so the power of the Constitutional Tribunal to review the amparo and habeas corpus decisions is exercised automatically as a mandatory review duty.

For such purpose the judicial decisions on the matter must be sent by the courts to the Constitutional Tribunal, so it can guaranty the uniformity of the constitutional interpretation.

B. The appellate and discretionary review jurisdiction of the Constitutional Chamber in Honduras

In Honduras, the Constitutional Chamber of the Supreme Court of Justice also has the exclusive power to control the constitutionality of statutes, whether by means of a direct action or through a referral of the constitutional question by a lower court. The only exception regarding this concentration refers to the cases when judicial review of legislation is requested in an amparo action, that is, in matters of amparo actions filed against statutes. In these cases, the courts can decide not to apply a statute in a particular case regarding the interested party, when it is considered contrary to constitutional rights.

In all the amparo cases, the lower courts decisions are subjected to an automatic review by the corresponding superior court, and the decision issued by the Appellate Courts can also be subjected to review by the Constitutional Chamber of the Supreme Court, by means of the parties' request, but in this case on a discretionary basis (Articles 68, 69, Law), having the Constitutional Chamber the possibility to be the last resort to decide on amparo matters.

III. THE CONSTITUTIONAL JURISDICTION REVIEW POWERS IN COUNTRIES HAVING A MIXED SYSTEM OF JUDICIAL REVIEW

The third group of Latin American countries refers to those combining the diffuse method of judicial review with the concentrated one, in a mixed system of judicial review of legislation, composed by Brazil, Colombia, Ecuador, Guatemala, Mexico, Nicaragua, Peru and Venezuela. In all these countries, the amparo proceedings are also developed before a variety of lower courts, with the only exception of Nicaragua, where the competence for amparo has been concentrated in the Supreme Court.

Regarding the application by lower courts of both the diffuse method of judicial review and the amparo decisions, in order to seek for the uniformity of the constitutional interpretation, various mechanisms have been established in order for the cases to reach the Supreme Court or Constitutional Court.

1. The Supreme Court of Nicaragua and its review powers in matters of judicial review through the cassation recourse

As mentioned, on matters of judicial review, the Nicaraguan constitutional system applies a mixed system of judicial review of legislation, combining the concentrated judicial review powers of the Supreme Court, with the general power of all courts to decide on matters of the constitutionality of statutes when deciding particular cases and with limited *inter partes* effects.

In these latter cases, in order to assure the uniformity of the constitutional interpretation, the courts' decisions on matters of unconstitutionality of statues, decrees or regulations can reach the Supreme Court by means of a recourse of cassation or through a recourse of amparo filed before the Supreme Court by the corresponding party in the proceeding of a case. Only when such decision cannot be challenged by means of cassation recourse, the Amparo Law prescribes that the respective court must send it to the Supreme Court in order for this Court to ratify the unconstitutionality of the statute, decree or regulation and to declare its inapplicability. In such cases, the decisions, although declaring the nullity of the statute, cannot affect third-party rights acquired from those statutes or regulations (Articles 21 and 22).

Yet regarding amparo and habeas corpus actions, in Nicaragua, a concentrated judicial system has been established by assigning the Supreme Court of Justice the exclusive power to decide the amparo and personal exhibition recourses. Consequently, in this matter, the uniformity of constitutional interpretation regarding the protection of constitutional rights is automatically assured.

2. *The Constitutional Jurisdiction review powers on constitutional matters in Brazil, Colombia, Ecuador, Guatemala, Mexico, Peru and Venezuela*

In all the other Latin American countries with a mixed system of judicial review, the judicial competence on matters of amparo actions are attributed to a variety of lower courts. This is the case of Brazil, Colombia, the Dominican Republic, Ecuador, Guatemala, Mexico, Peru and Venezuela.

Also in all these countries, except the Dominican Republic, adjective mechanisms have been established in order to allow the Supreme Court or the Constitutional Court to review the lower courts' decisions both in matters of amparo and on judicial review of statutes, allowing the Constitutional Jurisdiction to seek for the uniformity of constitutional interpretation. In this regard, two review means can be distinguished: the automatic review jurisdiction assigned to the Constitutional Tribunals and the appelate review jurisdiction assigned to the Constitutional Jurisdiction courts.

A. The automatic review jurisdiction of the Constitutional Tribunals in Ecuador and Colombia

In two Latin American countries, Ecuador and Colombia, their Constitutional Tribunals are empowered to automatically review the judicial decisions on matters of amparo, with the difference that in Ecuador the Constitutional Tribunal has a mandatory jurisdiction, and in Colombia, the Constitutional Court has a discretionary jurisdiction.

a. The mandatory revision in matters of amparo and the obligatory constitutional report in matters of judicial review in Ecuador

In Ecuador, which also has a mixed system of judicial review, all the courts can adopt decisions applying the diffuse system of judicial review of statutes, and in parallel, the Constitutional Tribunal is empowered to declare the nullity of statutes on the grounds of their unconstitutionality (Article 22), when an action is brought before it by the corresponding high officers or State bodies.[860]

For the purpose of unifying the jurisprudence in constitutional matters, the decisions issued by the lower courts applying the diffuse method of judicial review and also regarding amparo decisions, the cases can reach the Constitutional Tribunal through various means.

Regarding amparo decisions, the Amparo Law provides that all decisions granting amparo adopted by the first instance courts must automatically be sent to the Constitutional Tribunal in order to be confirmed or revoked. In the case of decisions denying amparo actions (as well as the habeas corpus or habeas data actions), they can be appealed before the same Constitutional Tribunal (Articles 12, 3; 31; 52).

On the other hand, regarding judicial decisions issued applying the diffuse method of judicial review, the courts must write a report on the issue of unconstitutionality of the statute that must be sent to the Constitutional Tribunal in order for it to resolve the matter in a general and obligatory way, that is to say, with *erga omnes* effects. Also when in matters of amparo, the competent judges applying the diffuse method of judicial review declares the unconstitutionality of statutes and grants constitutional protection,[861] they must send the report on the question of constitutionality to the Constitutional Tribunal for its confirmation or revocation (Article 12,6).

---

[860]See in general Hernán Salgado Pesantes, *Manual de Justicia Constitucional Ecuatoriana*, Corporación Editora Nacional, Quito, Ecuador, 2004; Hernán Salgado Pesantes, "El control de constitucionalidad en la Carta Política del Ecuador," in *Una mirada a los Tribunales Constitucionales. Las experiencias recientes*. Lecturas Constitucionales Andinas n° 4, Ed. Comisión Andina de Juristas, Lima, Perú; Ernesto López Freire, "Evolución del control de constitucionalidad en el Ecuador," in *Derecho Constitucional para fortalecer la democracia ecuatoriana*, Ed. Tribunal Constitucional - Kas, Quito, Ecuador, 1999; Marco Morales Tobar, "Actualidad de la Justicia Constitucional en el Ecuador," in Luis López Guerra (Coord.), *La Justicia Constitucional en la actualidad*, Corporación Editora Nacional, Quito, Ecuador, pp. 77–165; Oswaldo Cevallos Bueno, "El sistema de control concentrado y el constitucionalismo en el Ecuador," in *Anuario Iberoamericano de Justicia Constitucional*, n° 6, Madrid, España, 2002.

[861]See Hernán Salgado Pesantes, *Manual de Justicia Constitucional Ecuatoriana*, Corporación Editora Nacional, Quito, Ecuador, 2004, p. 85.

b. The discretionary review jurisdiction of the *tutela* decisions in Colombia

In Colombia, a Constitutional Court was also created in 1991, as the ultimate guardian of the constitution, empowered to annul statutes by means of a popular action, with general effects on the grounds of their unconstitutionality.[862] This concentrated method of judicial review is established in parallel with the diffuse method of judicial review applied by all courts; and by the attribution to a variety of lower courts to decide on matters of *tutela*. Regarding the latter, the Constitutional Court has the power to review all the lower courts *tutela* decisions.

However, in this case, contrary to the Argentinean solution, and similar to the Ecuadorian one, there is not a specific extraordinary recourse for review, being the remission of the files obligatory for the courts, having the Constitutional Courts discretionary review powers.

For such purpose, the *Tutela* Law establishes that in cases when a *tutela* decision is not appealed, it must always be automatically sent for revision to the Constitutional Court (Article 31); and when the decisions are appealed, the corresponding Superior Court's decision, whether confir-ming or revoking it, must also be automatically sent to the Constitutional Court for its revision (Article 32). In all these cases the Constitutional Chamber has discretional powers to determine which decision of *tutela* will be examined (Article 33).[863]

According to the *Tutela* Law, all the Constitutional Court's reviewing decisions modifying or revoking *tutela* decision, unifying the constitutional judicial doctrine (*jurisprudencia*) or clarifying the scope of constitutional provisions must be motivated; and all the others, must be justified (Article 35).

---

[862]See J. Vidal Perdomo, *Derecho constitucional general*, Bogotá 1985, p. 42; D.R. Salazar, Constitución Política de Colombia, Bogotá, 1982, p. 305; E. Sarria, *Guarda de la Constitución*, Bogotá, p. 78.

[863]For that purpose,) the Constitutional Court must appoint two of its magistrates in order to select, without express motivation and according to their criteria, the *tutela* decisions that are to be reviewed. Nonetheless, any of the Magistrates of the Court and the People's Defendant can request the revision of the excluded decision when they deem that the review can clarify the scope of a right or avoid a grave prejudice. Also, according to Decree 262 of February 2000, the General Attorney of the Nation can ask for the revision of *tutela* decisions when he deems necessary to defend the legal order, the public patrimony and the fundamental rights and guaranties (Article 7, 12).

On the other hand, the Constitutional Court's review decisions only produce effects regarding the particular case; thus the first instance court must immediately be notified, which in turn must notify the parties, and adopt the necessary decisions in order to adequate its own decision to the Constitutional Court's ruling.

No extraordinary revision has been established on matters of judicial review of legislation by the lower courts according to the diffuse method of judicial review that also exists in Colombia.

B. The appellate review jurisdiction of the Constitutional Jurisdictions in Brazil, Guatemala, Mexico, Peru and Venezuela

In matters of amparo decisions, in the other countries with a mixed system of judicial review, an appellate review jurisdiction of the Supreme Courts or of the Constitutional Courts has been established in order to review the amparo decisions. In the case of Brazil, Guatemala and Peru, where the appellate jurisdiction is a mandatory one; and of Mexico and Venezuela, where the appellate jurisdiction is a discretional one.

a. The mandatory jurisdiction of the Constitutional Jurisdictions in Brazil, Guatemala and Peru

The Brazilian system of judicial review, since 1934, was transformed into a mixed one, in which the diffuse method of judicial review established since the nineteenth century operates in combination with a concentrated one, exercised by the Federal Superior Tribunal.

Regarding the diffuse method of judicial review, in order to allow the Supreme Tribunal to decide in last resort on matters of judicial review of statutes, since its establishment in 1891, a power was assigned to the Supreme Tribunal to review lower courts' decisions on matters of constitutionality through an extraordinary recourse. This recourse can be filed against judicial decision issued on matters of protection of constitutional rights by the Superior Federal Court or by the Regional Federal Courts when it is considered that the courts have made the decisions in a way inconsistent with the constitution, or in cases in which the courts have denied the validity of a treaty or federal statute, or when the decisions have declared the unconstitutionality of a treaty or of a Federal Law; or when they deem local government laws or acts as unconstitutional or contrary to a valid federal law (Article 199,III,b and c, Constitution).

In Guatemala, a mixed system of judicial review also exists, allowing all courts to resolve the unconstitutionality of statutes by means of the diffuse method of judicial review, in parallel to the concentrated method assigned to the Constitutional Court that can declare the nullity of statutes when requested by means of an action of unconstitutionality. Additionally, the amparo proceeding has also been attributed to a variety of lower courts.

In order to assure the final intervention of the Constitutional Court on these constitutional matters regarding amparo decisions, the latter are subjected to appeal before the Constitutional Court (Article 60), which can be filed by the parties, the Public Prosecutor and the Human Rights Commissioner (Article 63).

The Constitutional Court's decision can confirm, revoke or modify the lower court's resolution (Article 67) and can also annul the whole proceeding when it is proven that the legal prescription had not been observed in the proceedings.

Yet as mentioned, the question of unconstitutionality of a statute can be raised as an action or as an exception or incident in the particular case, brought or raised before the competent court by the Public Prosecutor or by the parties. In these cases, the decision of the court applying the diffuse method of judicial review can also be appealed before the Constitutional Courts (Article 121).

If the question of unconstitutionality of a statute supporting the claim is raised, the competent court must also resolve the matter (Article 123); and the decision can also be appealed before the Constitutional Court (Article 130).

The Constitutional Tribunal of Peru, as the Constitutional Jurisdiction Court, also exercises the concentrated method of judicial review, basically by means of deciding actions of unconstitutionality of statutes (Article 202,1, Constitution; Article 77, Code), within a mixed system of judicial review, which empowers all courts to apply the diffuse method of judicial review. The amparo actions are also filed before a variety of lower courts.

For the purpose of seeking uniformity of constitutional interpretation, also in Peru some adjective instruments have been implemented, although not in a uniform way.

In matters of habeas corpus, amparo and habeas data, Article 202,2 of the constitution attributed to the Constitutional Tribunal the power to review in last and definitive instance, all judicial decisions denying them;

which can reach the Constitutional Tribunal of Peru, by means of a recourse of constitutional damage (*agravio*) that can be filed against the second instance judicial decision denying the claim (Article 18, Code).

If this constitutional damage recourse is denied, the interested party can also file before the Constitutional Tribunal recourse of complaint (*queja*), in which case, if the Tribunal considers the complaint duly supported, it will proceed to decide the constitutional damage recourse, asking the superior court to send the corresponding files (Article 19).

If the Constitutional Tribunal considers that the challenged judicial decision is affected by a defect or vice in the procedure, it can annul it and order the reposition of the procedure to the situation existing previous to the defect. In cases in which the vice only affects the challenged decision, the Tribunal must repeal it and issue a substantive ruling (Article 20).

On the other hand, on matters of judicial decisions issued by lower courts applying the diffuse method of judicial review, when the ordinary judges decide the inapplicability of statutes based on constitutional arguments, according to Article 14 of the Organic Law of the Judiciary, they must obligatorily send their decisions for review to the Supreme Court of Justice. It must be highlighted that in this case, this remission is not made to the Constitutional Tribunal, but to the Supreme Court, through its Constitutional Law and Social Chamber, in order for it to determine if the decision of the ordinary court on constitutional matters was adequate or not, validating the non-applicability of the statute to the particular case.[864]

b.   The discretionary jurisdiction of the Constitutional
      Jurisdiction in Mexico and Venezuela

In other countries with a mixed system of judicial review, as is the case in Mexico and Venezuela, the appellate jurisdiction of the Supreme Court as Constitutional Jurisdictions in order to review lower courts' decisions on constitutional matters, is also established but in a discretionary basis.

One of the most important instruments for judicial review in Mexico is the amparo against laws or statutes, through which the courts can exercise

---

[864]See Aníbal Quiroga León, "El derecho procesal constitucional Perúano," in Juan Vega Gómez and Edgar Corzo Sosa, (Coord.) *Instrumentos de tutela y justicia constitucional, Memoria del VII Congreso Iberoamericano de Derecho Constitucional,* Instituto de Investigaciones Jurídicas, Universidad Nacional Autónoma de México, México, pp. 471 ff.

judicial review of the constitutionality of legislation when deciding an "action of unconstitutionality" that can be filed before a federal district court (Article 107, XII). In these cases of amparo against laws, as well as regarding the amparo decisions when the unconstitutionality of a statute is decided, the federal district courts' decisions are reviewable by the Supreme Court of Justice (Article 107,VIII,a), which has the final power to decide on the matter, when deciding review recourses that can be filed by the parties.

In particular, according to a constitutional reform sanctioned in 1988, the Supreme Court was attributed the power to decide in last instance all cases of amparo where the decision involves the unconstitutionality of a law or establishes a direct interpretation of a provision of the constitution (Article 107, IX). For such purpose, the recourse for revision was regulated by the Supreme Court regulation N° 5/1999 of June 21, 1999,[865] and is for the Supreme Court to determine if the matter of constitutionality involved in the lower court decision has the needed importance as to be reviewed by the Court. According to this regulation, the matter considered as having importance are those where the arguments are exceptional, that is, of special interest, and those of transcendental character, when the resolution of the case could have outstanding effects on constitutional matters (Article I).

This attribution allows the Supreme Court to give final interpretation of the Constitution in a uniform way,[866] its decisions limited to resolve upon the actual constitutional questions.

In Venezuela, the system of judicial review is also a mixed one, the diffuse method functioning in parallel with the concentrated one assigned to the Constitutional Chamber of the Supreme Tribunal of Justice, with powers to annul statutes when requested through a popular action.

In these systems of judicial review, and regarding the decisions issued by the lower courts applying the diffuse method and also the decisions issued on amparo proceedings, the 1999 Constitution established an extraordinary recourse for review, which allows the Constitutional Chamber

---

[865]See *Diario Oficial de la Federación* June 22, 1999. See the text in Eduardo Ferrer Mac Gregor, *La acción constitucional de amparo en México y España. Estudio de derecho comparado*, Editorial Porrúa, México, 2002, pp. 403 ff.

[866]See Joaquín Brage Camazano, *La jurisdicción constitucional de la libertad (Teoría general, Argentina, México, Corte Interamericana de Derechos Humanos)*, Editorial Porrúa, Instituto Mexicano de Derecho Procesal Constitucional, México, 2005, pp. 153–155.

of the Supreme Court to issue final judgments in all cases of constitutional importance.

This extraordinary review recourse can be filed, as mentioned, against judicial final decisions issued in amparo proceedings and also, against any judicial decision in which constitutional questions regarding the inapplicability of statutes are involved because considered unconstitutional (Article 336,10).

This appellate extraordinary jurisdiction of the Constitutional Chamber is also conceived in Venezuela as a discretionary one,[867] through which the Constitutional Chamber can give uniformity to the judicial constitu-tional interpretation and enforcement of human rights made by ordinary courts, having power to give to its interpretation of the constitution general binding effects, similar to the *stare decisis* (Article 335) effects.

3. *The* ex officio *discretional review jurisdiction of the Constitutional Jurisdictions in constitutional matters*

In addition to the automatic or appellate review jurisdiction of the Constitutional Jurisdiction regarding judicial decisions issued by lower courts on constitutional matters and when deciding amparo actions, in some Latin American countries the Constitutional Jurisdiction has been granted *ex officio* powers in order to review such decisions when important constitutional matters are involved.

In the case of Mexico, where according to the constitutional reform passed in 1983, the Supreme Court of Mexico has been vested with a discretionary power to select the cases of amparo of constitutional importance to be reviewed, when requested by the Circuit courts, *ex officio* or at the request of the General Procurator of the Republic. The main characteristic of this "power to attract" (*facultad de atracción*) is that no party request is possible.

In Venezuela, it has been the Constitutional Chamber of the Supreme Court, as Constitutional Jurisdiction, the one that has developed *ex officio* powers for reviewing lower courts' decisions on constitutional matters, without any constitutional or statutory support. Based in the aforementioned power of the Constitutional Chamber to review in a discretionary way, judicial lower courts' decisions on constitutional matters because

---

[867]In a similar way to the writ of certiorari in the United States. See Jesús María Casal, *Constitución y Justicia Constitucional,* Caracas, 2002, p. 92.

their constitutional importance, the Constitutional Chamber distorting its review powers, extended it far beyond the precise cases of decisions adopted on judicial review and on amparo proceedings established in the constitution. Through obligatory judicial doctrine, the Chamber extended its review power regarding any other judicial decision issued in any matters when it considers it contrary to the constitution, a power that the Chamber considered authorized to exercise although without any constitutional provision, even *ex officio*. These review powers have also been developed in cases of particular judicial decision when considered contrary to a Constitutional Chamber interpretation of the constitution, or when considered that is affected by a grotesque error regarding constitutional interpretation.[868]

On the other hand, since 2004, the new Organic Law of the Supreme Tribunal, following such doctrine established by the same Tribunal, gave general powers to all the Chambers of the Tribunal, to take away cases (*avocamiento*) from the jurisdiction of lower courts, also *ex officio* or through a party petition, when considered convenient, and to decide them (Articles 5,1,48; and 18,11).[869]

This power, which has been highly criticized because it breaks the due process rights, and particularly, the right to trial in a by-instance basis by the courts, has allowed the Constitutional Chamber to intervene in any kind of processes, including cases being trialed by the other Chambers of the Supreme Tribunal, with very negative effects. For instance, the Constitutional Chamber power was used in order to annul a decision issued by the Electoral Chamber of the Supreme Tribunal[870] seeking to protect the citizens' right to political participation, in which the latter suspended

---

[868]See decision n° 93 of February 6, 2001, *Olimpia Tours and Travel vs. Corporación de Turismo de Venezuela* Case, in *Revista de Derecho Público*, N° 85-88, Editorial Jurídica Venezolana, Caracas, 2001, pp. 414–415. See Allan R. Brewer-Carías, "*Quis Custodiet ipsos Custodes*: De la interpretación constitucional a la inconstitucionalidad de la interpretación," in *VIII Congreso Nacional de Derecho Constitucional, Perú, September 2005,* Fondo Editorial, Colegio de Abogados de Arequipa, Arequipa, 2005, pp. 463–489.

[869]See Allan R. Brewer-Carías, *Crónica de la "In"justicia consituticonal. La Sala Constitucional y el autoritarismo en Venezuela,* Editorial Jurídica Venezolana, Caracas 2007, p. 91 ff.

[870]See Decisions n° 24 of March 15, 2004, (Exp. AA70-E 2004-000021; Exp. x-04-00006); and n° 27 of March 29, (*Julio Borges, César Pérez Vivas, Henry Ramos Allup, Jorge Sucre Castillo, Ramón José Medina y Gerardo Blyde vs. Consejo Nacional Electoral* case (Exp. AA70-E-2004-000021- AA70-V-2004-000006). See in *Revista de Derecho Público,* n° 97-98, Editorial Jurídica Venezolana, Caracas, 2004, pp. 373 ff.

the effects of a decision of the National Electoral Council (Resolution n°
040302-131 of March 2, 2004), objecting the presidential repeal referendum petition of 2004.

The Constitutional Chamber, in this way, by means of a decision n° 566
of April 12, 2004, interrupted the process that was normally developing
before the Electoral Chamber of the Supreme Tribunal, took away the
case from such Chamber, and annulling its decision, decided in contrary
sense, according to what was the will of the Executive, restricting the
people's right to participate through petitioning referendums.[871]

---

[871]See in Allan R. Brewer-Carías, *La Sala Constitucional versus el Estado Democrático
de Derecho. El secuestro del poder electoral y de la Sala Electoral del Tribunal Supremo y
la confiscación del derecho a la participación política*, Los Libros de El Nacional, Colec-
ción Ares, Caracas, 2004.

CONCLUSION

The almost two centuries of Latin American constitutional tradition of inserting very extensive declarations on human rights in the constitutions, has proven that in order for human rights to be effectively protected, independently of such formal declarations, the most important and necessary tool is to have not only effective judicial remedies for the immediate protections of rights but an independent and autonomous Judiciary.

Due to the traditional inefficacy of the ordinary and extraordinary judicial remedies that in other countries have proven to be effective for the protection of rights, in Latin America, since the nineteenth century, the constitutions have incorporated express provision regarding the judicial guaranty of constitutional rights, establishing a specific judicial remedy for its protection, called the amparo action, recourse, suit or proceeding, having different procedural rules when compared with the general judicial remedies the legal systems provides for the protection of personal or property rights. As it has been analyzed, this constitutional feature is one of the most important of Latin America constitutional law, particularly when contrasted with the constitutional system of the United States or of the United Kingdom, where the protection of human rights is effectively carried on through the general judicial actions and equitable remedies, that are also used to protect any kind of personal or property rights or interests.

This amparo remedy has been a very effective mean for the protection of constitutional rights, particularly in democratic regimes where the Judiciary has been preserved as an independent branch of government. Consequently, even providing in the constitution for this specific remedy of amparo to assure the immediate protection of constitutional rights, the very essence of its effectiveness is the existence of an independent and autonomous Judiciary that could effectively protect human rights. Unfortunately, in the Latin American countries, the judiciary has not always accomplished its fundamental duty, so that in spite of the constitutional declarations and provisions for amparo, many countries have faced, and others are still facing, a rather dismal situation regarding the effectiveness of the Judiciary as a whole, as an efficient and just protector of fundamental rights.

That is why, in spite of the extensive constitutional declarations of rights, in order to achieve the aims of the State of Justice, the most elemental institutional condition needed in any country, is the existence of a really autonomous and independent Judiciary, out of the reach and control from the other branches of government, empowered to interpret and apply the law in an impartial way and protect citizens, particularly when referring to the enforcement of rights against the State. Such Judiciary has to be built upon the principle of separation of powers. If this principle is not implemented and the Government controls the courts and judges, no effective guaranty can exist regarding constitutional rights, particularly when the offending party is a governmental agency. In this case, and in spite of all constitutional declarations, it is impossible to speak of rule of law, as happens in many Latin American countries.

This is important, precisely on matters of amparo, particularly when the petition is filed against a government or authority act, in which case, no judicial protection can be given if the government controls the Judiciary. Just one example can highlight this situation, in a case developed in Venezuela in 2003, where as a consequence of an amparo decision, the Judicial Review of Administrative Action Jurisdiction (*Jurisdicción contencioso-administrativa*) was intervened by the government, after being for three decades a very important autonomous and independent jurisdiction in order to control the legality of Public Administration activities.

Based on the democratic tradition the country had since 1958 in matters of control and review of Public Administration actions, on July 17, 2003, the Venezuelan National Federation of Doctors brought before the aforementioned Judicial Review of Administrative Actions highest Court in Caracas (First Court), a nullity claim against the Mayor of Caracas and the Ministry of Health and the Caracas Metropolitan Board of Doctors (*Colegio de Médicos*) acts deciding to hire Cuban doctors for an important popular governmental health program in the Caracas slums, but without complying with the legal conditions established for foreign doctors to practice the medical profession in the country. The National Federation of Doctors considered that the program was discriminatory and against the rights of Venezuelan doctors to exercise their medical profession, allowing foreign doctors to exercise it without complying with the Medical Profession Statute regulations. The consequence was the filing an amparo petition against both public authorities, seeking the collective protection of the Venezuelan doctors' constitutional rights.[872]

One month later, in August 21, 2003, the First Court issued a preliminary protective amparo measure, considering that there were sufficient elements to deem that the equality before the law constitutional guaranty was violated in the case. The Court ordered in a preliminary way the suspension of the Cuban doctors' hiring program and ordered the Metropolitan Board of doctors to substitute the Cuban doctors already hired, by Venezuelan ones or foreign Doctors who had fulfilled the legal regulations in order to exercise the medical profession in the country.[873]

The governmental response to that preliminary judicial amparo decision, which had touched a much publicized governmental program, was the public announcement by the Minister of Health, by the Mayor of Caracas, and even by the President of the Republic himself, expressing that the preliminary amparo judicial decision issued was not going to be respected nor executed.[874]

These announcements were followed by a few governmental decisions: The government-controlled Constitutional Chamber of the Supreme Tribunal adopted a decision without mediating any appeal, taking the case and annulling the First Court preliminary amparo; a group of Secret Service police officials seized the lower First Court's premises, after detaining a clerk on futile motives; the President of the Republic, among other expressions he used, publicly called the President of the First Court that issued the ruling, a bandit[875]; and a few weeks later, a Special Commission for the Intervention of the Judiciary that in spite of being unconstitutional, continued to exist, dismissed all five of the judges of the intervened Court.[876] In spite of the protest of all the Bar Associations of the

[872]See Claudia Nikken, "El caso "Barrio Adentro": La Corte Primera de lo Contencioso Administrativo ante la Sala Constitucional del Tribunal Supremo de Justicia o el avocamiento como medio de amparo de derechos e intereses colectivos y difusos," in *Revista de Derecho Público*, n° 93-96, Editorial Jurídica Venezolana, Caracas, 2003, pp. 5 ff.

[873]See Decision of August, 21 2003, in *Idem*, pp. 445 ff.

[874]The President of the Republic said: "*Váyanse con su decisión no sé para donde, la cumplirán ustedes en su casa si quieren...*" (You can go with your decision, I don't know where; you will enforce it in your house, if you want...) Talk in the TV program *Aló Presidente*, n° 161, August 24, 2004.

[875]Public speech, September 20, 2003.

[876]See the information in *El Nacional*, Caracas, November 5, 2003, p. A2. In the same page, the dismissed President of the First Court said: "*La justicia venezolana vive un momento tenebroso, pues el tribunal que constituye un último resquicio de esperanza ha*

country and also of the International Commission of Jurists;[877] the fact was that the First Court remained suspended without judges, and its premises remained closed for more than ten months,[878] during which simply no judicial review of administrative action could be sought in the country.

This was the governmental response to an amparo judicial preliminary decision that affected a very sensitive governmental social program; a response that was expressed and executed through the government-controlled judiciary.[879] The result was that the subsequent newly appointed judges replacing those dismissed, began to "understand" how they needed to behave in the future. That same Commission for the Intervention of the Judiciary, as mentioned, was the one that massively dismissed without due disciplinary process almost all judges of the country, substituting them with provisionally appointed judges, thus dependent on the ruling power, who in 2006 were granted permanent status without complying with the constitutional provisions.[880]

---

sido clausurado" ("Venezuenal judiciary lives a tenebrous moment, because the court that was our last hope has been shot down"). The case was denounced by the former judges of the First Court before the Inter-American Commission of Human Rights for violations of their constitutional rights. After the Commission filed the complaint before the Inter-American Court of Human Rights, the process concluded on August 5th, 2008, with a decision in the *Apitz Barbera y otros ("Corte Primera de lo Contencioso Administrativo")* vs. *Venezuela* Case, in which the Court ruled that the Venezuelan State had violated in the case the judicial guaranties of the dismissed judges established in the American Convention of Human Rights, comdemning the State to pay them due compensation, to reinstate them to a similar position in the Judiciary, and to publish part of the decision in Venezuelan newspapers.

[877]See in *El Nacional*, Caracas, October 12, 2003, p. A-5; and *El Nacional*, Caracas, November 18,2004, p. A-6.

[878]See in *El Nacional*, Caracas, October 24, 2003, p. A-2; and *El Nacional*, Caracas, July 16, 2004, p. A-6.

[879]See Allan R. Brewer-Carías, "La progresiva y sistemática demolición institucional de la autonomía e independencia del Poder Judicial en Venezuela 1999–2004," in *XXX Jornadas J.M Domínguez Escovar, Estado de derecho, Administración de justicia y derechos humanos,* Instituto de Estudios Jurídicos del Estado Lara, Barquisimeto, 2005, pp. 33–174; "La justicia sometida al poder (La ausencia de independencia y autonomía de los jueces en Venezuela por la interminable emergencia del Poder Judicial (1999-2006))," in *Cuestiones Internacionales. Anuario Jurídico Villanueva 2007,* Centro Universitario Villanueva, Marcial Pons, Madrid, 2007, pp. 25–57.

[880]In this regard, the Venezuelan 1999 Constitution established, in general terms, the regime for entering the judicial career and promotion only "through public competition that assures suitability and excellence," guarantying "citizen's participation in the procedure of

This emblematic case, contrast with the very progressive constitution in force in Venezuela (1999), which contains one of the most extensive declaration of constitutional rights in all Latin America, including the provision for the amparo action, even considering it as a constitutional right; shows that the judicial guaranty of constitutional rights always requires an independent and autonomous Judiciary, conducted out of the reach of the government. On the contrary, with a Judiciary controlled by the Executive, as the aforementioned case illustrates, the declarations of constitutional rights will be death letter. That is why the first and main problem of the Rule of Law in Latin America, even in democratic regimes, continues to be the functioning of the judicial systems.

selection and appointment of the judges." The consequence is that they may not be removed or suspended from their positions except through a legal proceeding before a disciplinary jurisdiction (Article 255). This, again, unfortunately is just a theoretical aim, because all contests for judge's appointment have been suspended since 2002. Almost all judges are being provisionally appointed without citizen participation, and there is no disciplinary jurisdiction for their dismissal. Furthermore, the suspension and dismissal of all judges corresponds to a Commission for the intervention of the Judiciary that is not regulated in the constitution. See Inter-American Commission on Human Rights, *Informe sobre la Situación de los Derechos Humanos en Venezuela*, OEA/Ser.L/V/II.118, d.C. 4 rev. 2, December 29, 2003, Paragraph 11, p. 3.

LIST OF LATIN AMERICAN CONSTITUTIONS

1. **ARGENTINA.** Constitución Nacional de la República Argentina, 1994.

2. **BOLIVIA.** Constitución Política de la República de Bolivia, 1967 (Last reform, 2005).

3. **BRAZIL.** Constituçåo da República Federativa do Brasil, 1988 (Last reform, 2005).

4. **COLOMBIA.** Constitución Política de la República de Colombia, 1991 (Last reform, 2005).

5. **COSTA RICA.** Constitución Política de la República de Costa Rica, 1949 (Last reform, 2003).

6. **CUBA.** Constitución Política de la República de Cuba, 1976 (Last reform, 2002).

7. **CHILE.** Constitución Política de la República de Chile, 1980 (Last reform, 2005).

8. **ECUADOR.** Constitución Política de la República de Ecuador, 1998.

9. **EL SALVADOR.** Constitución de la República de El Salvador, 1983 (Last reform, 2003).

10. **GUATEMALA.** Constitución Política de la República de Guatemala, 1989 (Last reform, 1993).

11. **HONDURAS.** Constitución Política de la República de Honduras, 1982 (Last reform, 2005).

12. **MÉXICO.** Constitución Política de los Estados Unidos Mexicanos, 1917 (Last reform, 2007).

13. **NICARAGUA.** Constitución Política de la República de Nicaragua, 1987 (Last reform, 2005).

14. **PANAMA.** Constitución Política de la República de Panamá, 1972 (Last reform, 1994).

15. **PARAGUAY.** Constitución Política de la República de Paraguay, 1992.

16. **PERÚ.** Constitución Política del Peru, 1993 (Last reform, 2005).

17. **REPÚBLICA DOMINICANA.** Constitución Política de la República Dominicana, 2002.

18. **URUGUAY.** Constitución Política de la República Oriental del Uruguay, 1967 (Last reform, 2004).

19. **VENEZUELA.** Constitución de la República Bolivariana de Venezuela, 1999.

LIST OF LATIN AMERICAN AMPARO LAWS
(Statutes)

1. **ARGENTINA.** Ley N° 16.986. Acción de Amparo, 1966.

2. **BOLIVIA.** Ley N° 1836. Ley del Tribunal Constitucional, 1998.

3. **BRAZIL.** Lei N° 1.533. Mandado de Segurança, 1951.

4. **COLOMBIA.** Decretos Ley N° 2591, 306 y 1382. Acción de *Tutela*, 2000.

5. **COSTA RICA.** Ley N° 7135. Ley de la Jurisdicción Constitucional, 1989.

6. **ECUADOR.** Ley N° 000. RO/99. Ley de Control Constitucional, 1997.

7. **EL SALVADOR.** Ley de Procedimientos Constitucionales, 1960.

8. **GUATEMALA.** Decreto N° 1-86. Ley de Amparo. Exhibición personal y Constitucionalidad, 1986.

9. **HONDURAS.** Ley sobre Justicia Constitucional, 2004.

10. **MÉXICO.** Ley de Amparo, reglamentaria de los artículos 103 y 107 de la Constitución Política, 1936 (Last reform, 2006).

11. **NICARAGUA.** Ley N° 49. Amparo, 1988.

12. **PANAMA.** Código Judicial, Libro Cuarto: Instituciones de Garantía, 1999.

13. **PARAGUAY.** Ley N° 1.337/88. Código Procesal Civil, Titulo II. El Juicio de Amparo, 1988.

14. **PERÚ.** Ley N° 28.237. Código Procesal Constitucional, 2005.

15. **REPÚBLICA DOMINICANA.** Ley N° 437-06 que establece el Recurso de Amparo, 2006.

16. URUGUAY. Ley N° 16.011. Acción de Amparo, 1988.

17. VENEZUELA. Ley Orgánica de Amparo sobre Derechos y Garantías Constitucionales, 1988.

INDEX